Human-Computer Interaction Series

T0134816

Human-Computer Interaction is a multidisciplinary field focused on human aspects of the development of computer technology. As computer-based technology becomes increasingly pervasive – not just in developed countries, but worldwide – the need to take a human-centered approach in the design and development of this technology becomes ever more important. For roughly 30 years now, researchers and practitioners in computational and behavioral sciences have worked to identify theory and practice that influences the direction of these technologies, and this diverse work makes up the field of human-computer interaction. Broadly speaking it includes the study of what technology might be able to do for people and how people might interact with the technology.

In this series we present work which advances the science and technology of developing systems which are both effective and satisfying for people in a wide variety of contexts. The human-computer interaction series will focus on theoretical perspectives (such as formal approaches drawn from a variety of behavioral sciences), practical approaches (such as the techniques for effectively integrating user needs in system development), and social issues (such as the determinants of utility, usability and acceptability).

Authoring guidelines: Springer.com/Our services for Authors/Author Guidelines

Also in this series

Rossi, G., Pastor, O., Schwabe, D., Olsina, L. (Eds.)
Web Engineering – Modelling and Implementing Web Applications
ISBN 978-1-84628-922-4

Lieberman, H., Paternò, F., Wulf, V. (Eds.)
End User Development
Vol. 9, ISBN 978-1-4020-4220-1, 2006

Lieberman, H., Paternò, F., Wulf, V. (Eds.)
End User Development
Vol. 9, ISBN 978-1-4020-5309-2, 2006
(softcover)

Seffah, A., Gulliksen, J., Desmarais, M.C. (Eds.)
Human-Centred Software Engineering –
Integrating Usability in the Software Development Lifecycle
Vol. 8, ISBN 978-1-4020-4027-6, 2005

Ruttkay, Z., Pelachaud, C., (Eds.)
From Brows to Trust – Evaluating Embodied
Conservational Agents
Vol. 7, ISBN 978-1-4020-2729-1, 2004

Ardissono, L., Kobsa, A., Maybury, M.T. (Eds.)
Personalized Digital Television – Targeting Programs to Individual Viewers
Vol. 6, ISBN 978-1-4020-2147-3, 2004

Karat, C.-M., Blom, J.O., Karat, J. (Eds.)
Designing Personalized User Experiences in eCommerce
Vol. 5, ISBN 978-1-4020-2147-3, 2004

Ivory, M.Y.
Automating Web Site Evaluation – Researchers' and Practitioners' Perspectives
Vol. 4, ISBN 978-1-4020-1672-1, 2004

Blythe, M.A., Overbeeke, K., Monk, A.F., (et al.) (Eds.)
Funology – From Usability to Enjoyment
Vol. 3, ISBN 978-1-4020-2966-0, 2004
(softcover)

Blythe, M.A., Overbeeke, K., Monk, A.F., (et al.) (Eds.)
Funology – From Usability to Enjoyment
Vol. 3, ISBN 978-1-4020-1252-5, 2003

Schreck, J.
Security and Privacy in User Modeling
Vol. 2, ISBN 978-1-4020-1130-6, 2003

Chi, E.H.
A Framework for Visualizing Information
Vol 1, ISBN 978-1-4020-0589-2, 2002

Effie Lai-Chong Law · Ebba Thora Hvannberg
Gilbert Cockton
Editors

Maturing Usability

Quality in Software, Interaction and Value

Foreword by Robin Jeffries and Dennis Wixon

 Springer

Effie Lai-Chong Law, PhD
Institut TIK
ETH Zürich
Switzerland

Ebba Thora Hvannberg, PhD
Computer Science Department
University of Iceland
Iceland

Gilbert Cockton, MA, PGCE,
PhD, CITP, FBCS, FRSA
University of Sunderland
UK

British Library Cataloguing in Publication Data
A catalogue record for this book is available from the British Library

Human-Computer Interaction Series ISSN 1571-5035
ISBN: 978-1-84996-681-8   e-ISBN: 978-1-84628-941-5

Printed on acid-free paper

9 8 7 6 5 4 3 2 1

Springer Science+Business Media
springer.com

In Memory of David Carr

Acknowledgements

The idea of this book was conceived when the First COST294-MAUSE International Workshop on User Interface Quality Models (UIQM'05; Vanderdonckt, Law & Hvannberg, 2005) was being prepared and implemented. Interesting and inspiring discussions took place in the workshop. Specifically, Gilbert Cockton (one of the three editors of this book) observed that maturing usability manifests in terms of quality in *software*, quality in *interaction*, and quality in *value*. This proposal then became the skeleton for this book. Calls for chapter proposals were distributed. Each submitted proposal was peer-reviewed for quality, fit, and feedback. Accepted proposals were extended to full chapters, each of which was also peer-reviewed (sometimes twice) to ensure high quality. The book then had flesh on its bones.

In the early phase of this project, David Carr, who was an experienced HCI researcher and an active member of COST294-MAUSE, passed away. His untimely death was a great loss to the HCI community, as well as to our project. It is really unfortunate that he could not see the publication of this book, which we sincerely dedicate to him.

Thanks are also due to all the authors and peer reviewers who have made this book possible (Table A-1):

Table A-1 List of peer reviewers.

Name	Affiliation
Aline Chevalier	University of Paris 10, France
Andy Brooks	University of Akureyri, Iceland
Ann Blandford	University College London Interaction Centre, UK
Arnold Vermeeren	TU Delft, the Netherlands
Dominic Furniss	University College London Interaction Centre, UK
Ebba T. Hvannberg	University of Iceland, Iceland
Effie L.-C. Law	ETH Zürich, Switzerland
Erik Frøkjær	University of Copenhagen, Denmark
Fabio Paternò	HIIS Lab., ISTI – C.N.R, Pisa, Italy
Gilbert Cockton	University of Sunderland, UK
Inger Boivie	Guide Redina AB, Sweden
Jan Gulliksen	Uppsala University, Sweden
Jan Stage	Aalborg University, Denmark
Joseph Dumas	Bentley College, USA

(Continued)

Table A-1 (*Continued*)

Name	Affiliation
Kasper Hornbæk	University of Copenhagen, Denmark
Luis Olsina	University of La Pampa, Argentina
Manfred Tscheligi	ICT&S/ Universität Salzburg, Austria
Marta Kristín Lárusdóttir	Reykjavik University, Iceland
Michael Harrison	Newcastle University, UK
Oddur Benediktsson	University of Iceland, Iceland
Panos Markopoulos	TU Eindhoven, the Netherlands
Paul Curzon	Queen Mary, University of London, UK
Philippe Palanque	LIIHS-IRIT Université Paul Sabatier, France
Silvia Abrahão	Universidad Politécnica de Valencia, Spain
Sissel Guttormsen Schär	Universität Bern, Switzerland
Timo Jokela	University of Oulu, Finland
Witold Suryn	École de Technologie Supérieure – ETS, Canada

We would also like to express gratitude to our sponsor–European Cooperation in the field of Scientific and Technical Research (COST); www.cost.esf.org. COST is an intergovernmental European framework for international cooperation between nationally funded research activities. COST creates scientific networks and enables scientists to collaborate in a wide spectrum of activities in research and technology. COST activities are administered by the COST Office. COST Action 294 (*http://www.cost294.org*), which is also known as MAUSE, was officially launched in January 2005. The ultimate goal of COST294-MAUSE is to bring more science to bear on Usability Evaluation Methods (UEM) development, evaluation, and comparison—aiming for results that can be transferred to industry and educators, thus leading to the increased competitiveness of European industry and benefit to the public.

Last but not least, we are also grateful to Beverley Ford and Helen Desmond (London Springer) for their professional advice on the editing of the book and their kind patience.

Effie Lai-Chong Law
Ebba Thora Hvannberg
Gilbert Cockton

References

Vanderdonckt, J., Law, E. L-C., & Hvannberg, E. T. (2005). *Proceedings of the First COST294-MAUSE International Workshop on User Interface Quality Models* (UIQM'05) in conjunction with INTERACT 2005, 12–13 September 2005, Rome, Italy.

Foreword: Making the Future Real

Robin Jeffries[1] and Dennis Wixon[2]

[1] Google, e-mail: robin.jeffries@gmail.com
[2] Microsoft Games Studio

When we first read the chapters that make up this book, we were both struck by the ways they exemplify the evolution of the usability field over the last quarter century. Both of us began our careers before usability was recognized as an important characteristic of systems, and are pleased to have this opportunity to reflect on the ways the field has matured. Even in the early days, some companies realized that as the cost of computing dropped, their success would depend on their ability to expand the market for computing. Expanding the market required applications that were both useful (did things that people wanted done) and were usable (could be learned and used without extensive training). As the market has evolved, the definition of usability has been extended to include desirability (products people want to own). Usability has evolved into user experience—the factors that impact the totality of one's experience with a product, from initial awareness to upgrading to the next version.

One of the challenges in front of the community of usability practitioners and researchers has been to establish a set of methods that facilitate the creation of superior user experiences—i.e., products that are useful, usable, and desirable. We've come a long way. The field now has a broad collection of methods that can be replicated from lab to lab, and there is common agreement as to when particular methods are useful. Usability is integrated into companies' standard development processes, with expectations of scheduled deliverables going both ways—prototypes delivered for evaluation, and usability findings delivered to development. User experience professionals collaborate with other functions across the company—product management, user assistance, engineering, and marketing. Hundreds of products and millions of users have benefited from the work of the usability community. None of these statements would have been true even ten years ago. Some of the chapters in this book describe in detail the maturation of these aspects, and lay out visions for ways that the field can further mature.

However, the main theme that ties these chapters together, is not how far we have come, but what lies ahead. The chapters talk of new methods or approaches that will enhance the field of usability. We can think of these new approaches as impacting products at one of three levels: 1) new methods that will enable us to evaluate products in contexts that we couldn't serve well before; 2) new contexts, where usability is applied in different development environments, and 3) real-world impacts, where the authors look at the broader milieu in which usability lives, and at its impact outside the development organization. We cluster the chapters according to this framework below. In addition, for a number of chapters we suggest the next steps that should bring the concepts and tools described in the chapter into wider use and closer to their full potential.

New Methods

In the area of new methods, Abrahão, Iborra, and Vanderdonckt (Chapter 1) consider the task of evaluating model-generated user interfaces. These model-generated user interfaces hold the promise of producing platform-independent systems and making development more efficient. In their case study, the automatic generation tools produced systems that could be used by experienced users but had numerous problems (e.g., convoluted task flows, unlabeled fields, meaningless error messages) that were identified in both usability tests and heuristic evaluations. This represents progress, but there is clearly more to be done.

Harrison, Campos, Doherty, and Loer (Chapter 3) cover the evaluation of ambient mobile systems, where it is very costly and risky to evaluate them in their true context. The authors argue for the development of formal models reviewed by domain experts. This approach could insure that the systems support experts and reduce the risk of catastrophic errors. It seems that the next step to realizing the promise of such an approach would be to apply it to a real-world problem.

Bernhaupt, Navarre, Palanque, and Winckler (Chapter 5) describe the evaluation of multi-modal safety critical systems, and (like Harrison et al.) they adopt a model-based approach. The models provide both an overview of the paths through their system and an evaluation of components. The approach addresses one of the major challenges of usability work in practice—providing sufficient coverage of a complex system in limited time. A next step would be to determine where tests are needed to refine the interface.

A very thorough review of remote usability evaluation methods is offered by Paternò and Santoro (Chapter 9). They then extend the state of the art of remote evaluation into multiple sources of information, including a tool to extract converging evidence from these multiple information streams. Validating the tool with real evaluators working on real products would be a desirable next step.

Lindgaard and Parush (Chapter 10) encourage us to extend our thinking to emotional and aesthetic responses and to social and cultural context. They cover recent research on aesthetics and emotion and apply it to an understanding of what makes an effective emotional user experience. Similarly, they review work on collaboration and social computing with an eye to convincing practitioners to include such aspects in their evaluations. An obvious next step is to establish evaluation methods that cover both the emotional and social aspects of product user interfaces.

New Contexts

The set of development contexts is particularly broad. At one end, Suryn (Chapter 2) and Jokela (Chapter 8) take a historical view of how usability methods fit into new software development paradigms based on capability/maturity models encompassing ISO standards and framing ISO standards in terms of UCD. Suryn points out that quality metrics are sometimes irrelevant to success/failure when products are deployed in the real world and offers some recommendations to minimize the likelihood of such a serious disconnect between what is needed by customers and what is built. Jokela proposes a new, more systematic version of ISO standard 13407 (human-centered design processes for interactive systems) that can be used to educate organizations about UCD and to plan and evaluate UCD processes. Most practitioners will find the most valuable takeaways to be Fig. 8.3, which is a very nice visualization of UCD activities and their relationship—and Appendix 8.3, which is a high level rewrite of the standard and may be a useful document to introduce the user-centered process to managers and teams that are not yet familiar with its scope.

Looking at a completely different development process, Ambler (Chapter 4) focuses on agile software development and appeals to the community of agile developers and usability practitioners to collaborate. He provides an excellent starting point for the usability practitioner to learn about agile methods. He also points out some natural linkages between agile software development and usability methods. Usability practitioners have traditionally advocated the early development of a working system (Gould and Lewis, 1985). Gould and Lewis also emphasized iterative evaluation, and more recent developments—Rapid Iterative Testing and Evaluation (RITE) (Medlock, et al. 2005) – take rapid iteration to its logical conclusion. Similarly, agile methods stress the need for developing working components early and incorporate an iterative approach.

Savioja and Norros (Chapter 6) couch usability in an activity theoretic perspective, showing us how the goals of evaluation change in response to dramatic shifts in context (e.g., the goals of the system and the interaction pattern of the users change dramatically when an emergency occurs in a nuclear power plant or in an aircraft in flight). Based on the evolution of ever more capable, embedded, and ubiquitous systems, they make a persuasive argument for activity as the focus for HCI in the future.

Furniss, Blandford, and Curzon (Chapter 7) provide a refreshing study of the practice of usability work in website design. They take a grounded theory approach and interview practitioners with respect to their experience working with teams. Their findings lead them to focus on the relationship between usability practitioners and the design/development teams they work with. Their study strongly supports Redish's conclusion (Redish et al. 2002) that the most important factor in getting recommendations incorporated into products is the long-term relationship between the practitioner and the development team. That consideration should be a pivotal factor in the adoption of any method.

Hornbæk (Chapter 12) attempts to move us from conceptualizing usability evaluation as defect identification to thinking of it as a way to generate ideas that will produce a superior product. He argues that this approach will unify design and evaluation by having the output of evaluation be design proposals that are significantly more novel and inventive. The chapter proposes a novel evaluation method that is based on existing ideational fluency models.

Real World Impacts

In the area of real-world impact, Cajander, Boivie, and Gulliksen (Chapter 11) cover the impact of poor usability on work stress and, indirectly, on health. They describe a large case study where there was a significant disconnect between those who created the IT systems and their (in-house) users. The systems focused on efficiency, surveillance, control, and routinization of complex work, which led to significant increases in worker stress. Their research is a reminder to all of us that usability can have a much larger impact than is visible from the narrow window we often have into users' interactions with the technology.

In a similar vein, economic aspects of the user experience of online services are the focus of Sikorski's chapter (Chapter 14). He defines the user experience as the totality of interactions a user has with the service, including such things as return policies and instore experiences. This leads to the notion of value-centered design, which is focused on turning user experiences into relationships which generate customer loyalty and value.

Cockton (Chapter 13) extends the idea of value-centered design to the notion of worth maps, based on a hierarchical cascading of values (both positive and negative) of a user experience from the perspectives of different stakeholders (e.g., customers and management). Such maps lead evaluators to new insights of how usability fits into product goals and of ways to enhance value through focusing on the usability aspects that will have the largest impact on the worth of the system.

The book ends with two very useful summative chapters. Rosenbaum (Chapter 15) looks back at the history of usability through the special lens of a consultant who has seen the role of usability, its position in the organization, and its impact on products and product development change over the years. She uses that to forecast forward to where we can expect to see the usability field move over the next decade. The book's editors (Law, Hvannberg, and Cockton, Chapter 16) sum up the contributions of all the chapters by placing them in the broader context of the value that usability work can contribute. Their analysis is deeper and more provocative than our Foreword here, and will help readers make valuable connections among the various papers in this volume.

The history of usability methods has been one of creativity and adaptation. It is easy to forget that 25 years ago we had no systematic and documented approaches for providing user data to improve products. Now we have a multitude of methods and more are being created every day. The successful methods have been adapted to fit the business and development environment of companies, and they have been widely adopted. The methods here show great promise. They have been created to address the challenges of new technologies, new environments, new classes of users, and new user tasks. Some promise to address age-old problems or provide new efficiencies. The challenge for most of the authors is to step into the real world and try these methods on real-world sized problems. That is the best way that they can demonstrate their true potential, adapt them to a business/development environment, and gain the widespread adoption that they deserve.

References

Gould, J. & Lewis, C. (1985). Designing for usability: Key principles and what designers think. *Communications of the ACM,. 28*(3), 300–311.

Medlock, M., Wixon, D., McGee, M., & Welsh, D. (2005). The rapid iterative testing and evaluation method: Better products in less time. In R. Bias & D. Mayhew (Eds.), *Cost Justifying Usability: An Update for the Internet Age*. Morgan Kaufman.

Redish, J., Bias, R., Bailey, R., Molich, R., Dumas, J., & Spool, J.M. (2002). Usability in practice: formative usability evaluations – evolution and revolution. In *CHI'02 Extended Abstracts on Human Factors in Computing Systems* (pp. 885–890), Minneapolis, Minnesota, USA.

References

...

Biography[1]

Silvia Abrahão is a tenure-track assistant professor in computer science at the Valencia University of Technology (Spain), and was a visiting professor at the Louvain School of Management of Université Catholique de Louvain (Belgium) during 2006–2007. She received a PhD in computer science from the Valencia University of Technology in 2004. She is currently working in the fields of usability engineering, software metrics, web engineering, and empirical software engineering. She is a member of the management committee of the COST Action 294 "Towards the Maturity of IT Usability Evaluation" (MAUSE-*www.cost294.org*).

Scott W. Ambler is the practice leader of agile development in IBM Rational's methods group, a contributor to the OpenUP software process, and a senior contributing editor with *Dr. Dobb's Journal*. He is the founder of agile modeling (AM), agile data (AD), agile unified process (AUP), and enterprise unified process (EUP) methodologies. Scott is also the (co)author of several books, including *Refactoring Databases*, *Agile Modeling*, *Agile Database Techniques*, *The Object Primer 3rd Edition*, and *The Enterprise Unified Process*. His personal home page is www-306.ibm.com/software/rational/bios/ambler.html.

Regina Bernhaupt is currently working as an assistant professor at the HCI Unit of the ICT&S Center, working on her habilitation in the area of usability evaluation methods. She holds a Masters degree in psychology and in computer science from the Salzburg University. In 2002, she finished her technical dissertation in computer science in the field of intelligent systems (time coded artificial neural networks). She teaches programming courses, user interface techniques and design, and human-computer interaction at Salzburg University and the applied university of Salzburg. She is leading several projects in the area of home entertainment (interactive TV, games, new ways of entertainment) and is responsible for new forms of usability and user experience evaluation in various contexts such as mobile interfaces and ambient technologies.

Ann Blandford is a professor of human-computer interaction and director of the UCL Interaction Centre. There, she leads a team of twenty academics and

---

[1] The list is sorted according to the last name of the contributors.

researchers studying various aspects of HCI. Her research focuses on seeking a better understanding of interactive systems from a user perspective, and using that understanding to support the design and evaluation of systems. Her research activities include the development and testing of theories and methods for evaluating interactive systems, and the use of evaluation methods in practice.

Inger Boivie has a Ph.D. in human-computer interaction and her research focused on UCSD and usability and the relations between the systems development process and health issues in computer-supported work. Inger has also extensive practical experience from more than ten years as a practitioner and consultant in UCSD and usability in bespoke systems development. After her Ph.D., Inger returned to the IT industry, and now works as a usability designer in an IT consulting company.

Åsa Cajander is a Ph.D. student in human-computer interaction (HCI) from Uppsala University, Sweden. Her research interests include usability and user-centered design with a special focus on occupational health. She has also several years of industrial expertise as an IT consultant.

José Creissac Campos is an assistant professor at the Department of Computer Science of the University of Minho (Portugal). He holds a *licentiate* degree in computer science and systems engineering and a Master's degree in computer science (both from the University of Minho), and a doctorate in applying automated deduction approaches to usability reasoning from the University of York (UK). His current research interests include applying formal and software engineering approaches to interactive systems design, and user interfaces for mobile and ubiquitous systems. He is particularly interested in the analysis of interactive systems' behavior using model checking.

Gilbert Cockton is Research Professor in HCI and Chair of the Interactive Digital Media subarea in the School of Computing and Technology at the University of Sunderland. Since his appointment in 1997, he has secured funding exceeding €9M for research, consultancy, knowledge transfer projects, and infrastructure. He recently served as vice-chair of IFIP TC13 (2004–2005), and chaired the British HCI Group (2001–2004) and the ACM CHI conference (2003). A member of COST Action 294 (MAUSE) on usability evaluation, his work on value-centered design is currently supported by a UK NESTA fellowship (until 2008). He has been active in several research areas since 1984, with over 200 publications and invited presentations on formal design notations, software architecture, design for usage contexts, usability evaluation, accessibility, affective HCI, and value-centered development.

Paul Curzon is a reader in computer science at Queen Mary, University of London. His main research interests include formal user modeling and the verification of interactive systems. He also has a wider interest in both usability evaluation methods and the use of machine-assisted proof for hardware and software verification, as well as the verification of the verification systems themselves.

Gavin Doherty has been a lecturer at the Department of Computer Science, Trinity College Dublin since 2001. He holds a doctorate obtained at the HCI group in the University of York, where his work focused on reasoning about interactive systems using specifications. His current research interests include display design, the design of mobile applications, and design methods for complex work environments, with applications in the manufacturing and healthcare sectors. He is also active in research on technology interventions in talk-based mental health care.

Dominic Furniss is a PhD research student at UCL Interaction Centre (UCLIC), London, UK, under the supervision of Professor Ann Blandford and Dr. Paul Curzon. He is looking at system-level features of usability practice (e.g., expertise, methods, people, relationships, and processes) and comparing website design with safety-critical system development. This perspective is emerging from talking with practitioners directly, while using grounded theory as the method for analysis. His previous work includes operationalizing distributed cognition for team working environments.

Jan Gulliksen is a professor in HCI from Uppsala University. He has a Master of science in engineering physics and a PhD in systems analysis. Jan is the chairman of IFIP WG 13.2 on "Methodologies for User-Centered Systems Design," and a member of ISO standardization in software ergonomics and human computer dialogues and human-centered design processes for interactive systems. Jan runs a research group on usability and user-centered systems design that does applied research in cooperation with several industries and public authorities. Jan has recently co-edited *Human-Centered Software Engineering*, published by Springer in 2005.

Michael Harrison has been a professor of informatics within the School of Computing Science, and director of the Informatics Research Institute at the University of Newcastle upon Tyne since July 2004. He is a computer scientist by background (doctorate in the semantics of programming languages) but has worked on the connection between formal specifications of computer systems and HCI for a number of years. His current research interests include the analysis of the dependability of interactive systems using model-checking techniques and making the interface to model checkers more accessible to system designers. He is particularly interested in modelling and analyzing human interface properties of ambient and mobile systems.

Kasper Hornbæk is an associate professor at the Department of Computer Science, University of Copenhagen. He earned a PhD in computer science from University of Copenhagen in 2002. His research interests include HCI, usability engineering, interfaces for information access, eye-tracking, and information visualization. He is a member of the editorial board of the Journal of Usability Studies, and is involved in national and European research projects on usability. He has published more than 30 papers in journals and conferences, including ACM Conference on Computer-Human Interaction, International Journal of Human-Computer Studies, and Transaction on Computer Human-Interaction.

Ebba Thora Hvannberg is a professor in the computer science department, University of Iceland. Dr. Hvannberg has a B.S. in computer science from the University of Iceland, and an M.S. and Ph.D. from Rensselaer Polytechnic Institute, New York. Her research areas include HCI, software science, distributed systems, multimedia, and formal methods. She has participated in a number of international and Icelandic research projects. She has been an active member of the research community by publishing papers, and reviewing proposals and papers. Dr. Hvannberg has several administrative duties, including being a board member of three companies, as well as research and educational programs.

Emilio Iborra is a practitioner with over 20 years of experience in high performance systems development and IT-related consultancy. In 1999, he joined CARE Technologies to pioneer new techniques in conceptual modeling techniques and model execution. His main areas of interest are Ambiental Intelligence and HCI. Currently, he is co-founder of Ami2 – a Research and Development company in ambiental Intelligence and user interaction.

Robin Jeffries is currently User Experience Lead at Google, where she works to better understand the broad spectrum of Google users and to adapt usability techniques to new application paradigms. Prior to that, she was a distinguished engineer at Sun Microsystems, where she worked in the CTOs office bringing attention to users and user experience across the company. She has been a researcher at Hewlett-Packard Laboratories, Carnegie-Mellon University, and the University of Colorado. Her research has focused on comparing usability methods as used by practitioners and improving various aspects of usability methodologies.

Timo Jokela, PhD, is an acting professor in usability at the University of Oulu, Finland. Earlier in 1990's he pioneered usability at Nokia, getting hands-on experience on the challenges of integrating usability engineering into product development. Timo's research interests are processes, methods, and organizational issues of designing usability. He is involved in ISO standardization of user-centered design issues.

Effie Lai-Chong Law is a research fellow at ETH Zürich (Switzerland) and at the University of Leicester (UK). She obtained her Masters in Psychology from the University of Hong Kong, and her PhD in Psychology from the University of Munich (LMU), Germany. Her research interests include HCI, technology-enhanced learning, cognitive theories, and creativity. Her research activities are highly interdisciplinary, synergizing ideas from psychology, technology, and education. She has presented and published a number of papers in international conferences, books, and journals. Currently, she is chairing and participating actively in several international and national research projects on usability and CSCW.

Gitte Lindgaard, PhD, is the Director of the Human Oriented Technology Lab (HOTLab) and a full professor in the Department of Psychology, Carleton University, Ottawa, Canada. Previously, she was principal scientist and Head of the

Human Factors Team at Telstra Research Laboratories, Australia. She was chair of CHISIG of the Ergonomics Society of Australia (ESA) for many years, where she founded the OZCHI conference. She is a fellow of the HF&ESA, Associate Editor, *International Journal of Human Computer Studies*, and deputy editor of *Interacting with Computers*. Her research interests include multimedia/multimodal and mobile technologies, aesthetics and emotion in computing, and human decision-making in medicine.

Karsten Loer is senior project engineer and subproject manager in the Strategic Research Department at Germanischer Lloyd AG Headquarters in Hamburg, Germany. He works on industrial design and research projects with a focus on R&D projects in system safety assessments, demonstration of safety equivalency, and human factors analyses. He is a risk assessment trainer and certified FMEA facilitator. In 2003, he received a doctorate degree in computer science from the University of York, UK. His work focused on the application of model-checking in the analysis of dependable interactive systems. Dr Loer received a diploma in computer science from University of Bielefeld, Germany in 1998, where he was involved in the development and application of formal incident and accident analysis techniques.

David Navarre is a lecturer in computer science at University of Social Sciences, Toulouse, France. He has been working since 1998 on notations and tools for the specification, prototyping, validation, and implementation of Safety Critical Interactive Systems. He has contributed to the improvement of the formal description technique called Interactive Cooperative Objects by making it able to address the modelling of post-WIMP safety-critical interactive systems. By working on several large projects (industrial or not), he applied the approach to several application domains, including air traffic control, military and civil aircraft cockpits, as well as several real-time command and control systems.

Leena Norros is a research professor and psychologist working on human factors issues in complex industrial systems at VTT (Technical Research Centre of Finland), where she is leading a human factors research team. She first studied at University of Helsinki, and later worked on her doctoral degree both at the Technical University of Dresden, Germany and at the Helsinki University in Finland. She has developed an original research approach to human action, labeled the Core-Task Analysis. Her current interests are to implement this method to design and evaluate ICT artifacts from a holistic, systems usability perspective. She is the Finnish delegate at the OECD/NEA Working Group for Human and Organizational Factors (WGHOF) and has been actively associated with the European Association of Cognitive Ergonomics, the North American naturalistic decision-making community, and the International Ergonomics Association. She has about 130 scientific publications in international journals, books, and conference proceedings.

Philippe Palanque is a professor in computer science at University Paul Sabatier, Toulouse, France, and has been the head of Logiciels Interactifs et Interaction

Homme-Système (*http://liihs.irit.fr/LIIHS*) research group for the last eight years. He has been working for about 15 years on notations and tools for the specification, prototyping, validation, and implementation of Safety-Critical Interactive Systems. He has been involved in the design of a notation called Interactive Cooperative Objects, and in the implementation of the supporting case tool called PetShop, applying the approach to several application domains including air traffic control, military and civil aircraft cockpits as well as several real-time command and control systems. He is currently chairing the IFIP 13.5 working group on Human Error, Safety and Systems Development and is an adjunct chair for specialized conferences for the ACM SIGCHI.

Avi Parush has a professional career in human factors engineering (HFE), usability engineering, and HCI spanning over 20 years. He has been involved in the design and testing of user interfaces in a large variety of domains and projects. Avi Parush is the founder and editor-in-chief of the *Journal of Usability Studies*. His academic background is in cognitive-experimental psychology and he is presently a professor of psychology and a member of the Human Oriented Technology lab at Carleton University, Ottawa.

Fabio Paternò is Research Director and Head of the laboratory on Human Interfaces in Information Systems at ISTI-CNR, Pisa, Italy. He has been the scientific coordinator of four EU projects and one of the main investigators in several others. He has published over 150 papers in international conferences or journals. He has been a member of the Programme Committee of the main international HCI conferences including Paper Co-Chair at ACM CHI2000 and Co-Chair of IFIP INTERACT 2005. His current research interests include methods and tools for multimodal user interface design and evaluation, accessibility, user interfaces for ubiquitous environments, model-based design of interactive systems, and end-user development.

Stephanie Rosenbaum is founder and president of Tec-Ed, Inc.—a 15-person consultancy specializing in usability research and user-centered design, with offices in Michigan, California, and New York. Tec-Ed clients include eBay, Cisco Systems, Google, Microsoft, Yahoo!, and many smaller firms. A charter member of the Usability Professionals' Association, Stephanie has presented sessions at every ACM SIGCHI conference since 1990; she co-chaired the Usability Community for the CHI 2006 Conference. She is a past vice-chair of ACM SIGDOC and was awarded an IEEE Millennium Medal in 2000. Stephanie's publications include a chapter on "Making User Research Usable" in *Software Design and Usability*. She co-authored a chapter in the second edition of *Cost-Justifying Usability*. Her research background includes anthropology studies at Columbia University and experimental psychology research for the University of California at Berkeley.

Carmen Santoro graduated in Computer Science at from the University of Pisa (Italy) and received a PhD in computer science from the University of Toulouse 1 (France). During the last ten years, she has been working as a researcher in the HIIS Lab of ISTI/CNR in Pisa. She has published papers in international conferences and journals on HCI; she has been member of the program committees of international conferences like INTERACT and MobileHCI, and reviewer for several international HCI conferences, journals, and books. She was the Organizational Overviews Co-Chair of INTERACT 2005 Conference, and Workshop and Tutorial Chair of MobileHCI 2002. She is currently Workshop Co-Chair for CHI 2008 Conference. Her current research interests include methods and tools for the analysis, design and development of multimodal and multiplatform interactive applications.

Paula Savioja is a research scientist at VTT, technical research center of Finland. She has a Master of Science degree in engineering from Helsinki University of Technology and she is currently working on her PhD dissertation on the usability of complex work systems. She has carried out research related to quality of work tools in several domains that can be characterized as dynamic, uncertain, and complex–for example, nuclear power operation, vessel traffic services, and steel casting. She has published her work in international scientific conferences related to ergonomics, automation, and the nuclear industry.

Marcin Sikorski is an associate professor and the head of the Ergonomics Department in the Faculty of Management and Economics, Gdansk University of Technology (Poland). He teaches courses on the ergonomics of interactive systems, HCI design, and information visualization. His research areas cover HCI, user-centered design (UCD), and usability evaluation methods. Economical aspects of usability engineering and organizational aspects of intranet development are his latest research interests. He is author of more than 40 publications, conference papers, and keynote presentations. In addition to teaching and research, Marcin has extensive experience in usability consulting for commercial clients, especially in the areas of web applications and intranet design.

Witold Suryn is a professor at the École de technologie supérieure, Montreal, Canada (engineering school of the Université du Québec network of institutions) where he teaches graduate and undergraduate software engineering courses and conducts research in the domain of software quality engineering, software engineering body of knowledge, and software engineering fundamental principles. Dr. Suryn is also the principal researcher and the director of GELOG: IQUAL, the Software Quality Engineering Research Group at École de technologie supérieure. Dr. Suryn also holds the position of ISO expert and International Secretary of ISO/IEC Subcommittee SC7–System and Software Engineering.

Jean Vanderdonckt is a professor of computer science at the Louvain School of Management of Université catholique de Louvain (Belgium) where he leads the Belgian Laboratory of Computer-Human Interaction (BCHI-*www.isys.ucl.ac.be/bchi*). This laboratory is conducting research, development, and consulting services in the domain of user interface engineering. This domain is located at the crossroads of software engineering, HCI, and usability engineering. Current topics of interest include user interface forward and reverse engineering, context-aware computing, multimodal interaction, mixed reality systems, and user interface adaptation.

Marco Winckler graduated with a B.S. in computer science in 1996 from UPF (Passo Fundo, Brazil) and received a Master's degree in computer science at the UFRGS (Porto Alegre, Brazil) in 1999. He obtained his PhD degree in 2004 from University of Toulouse 1 (Toulouse, France). His current research is focused on model-based approaches for the design and evaluation of Web-based interactive systems. Other topics of interest include automation of guidelines inspection, navigation, and dialog modeling through formal description techniques, and task models and diagrams for supporting the design of interactive systems (*http://liihs.irit.fr/winckler/*).

Dennis Wixon is the user research manager for Microsoft Games studios, where he manages a group of 21 usability engineers supporting over 40 games. Dennis previously worked at Digital Equipment Corporation, where a number of important usability methods such as usability engineering and contextual inquiry were developed. Dennis has been an active member of the human factors community for many years and is currently vice president for conferences for ACM SIGGCHI. Dennis has authored numerous articles on HCI methods and co-edited the *Field Methods Case Book for Software Design*. Dennis has a PhD in social Psychology from Clark University.

Contents

Part I
Quality in Software

Chapter 1
Usability Evaluation of User Interfaces Generated with a Model-Driven Architecture Tool

Silvia Abrahão[1], Emilio Iborra[2] and Jean Vanderdonckt[3]

[1] Department of Information Systems and Computation,
   Valencia University of Technology, Spain, e-mail: sabrahao@dsic.upv.es
[2] Ami2 – Ambiental Intelligence & Interaction, Spain
[3] Belgian Lab. of Computer-Human Interaction (BCHI),
   Université Catholique de Louvain, Belgium

Abstract Model-driven architecture (MDA) has recently attracted the interest of both the research community and industry corporations. It specifies an automated process for developing interactive applications from high-level models to code generation. This approach can play a key role in the fields of software engineering (SE) and human-computer interaction (HCI). Although there are some MDA-compliant methods for developing user interfaces, none of them explicitly integrates usability engineering with user interface engineering. This chapter addresses this issue by showing how the usability of user interfaces that are generated automatically by an industrial MDA-compliant CASE tool can be assessed. The goal is to investigate whether MDA-compliant methods improve software usability through model transformations. To accomplish this, two usability evaluations were conducted in the code model (final user interface). Results showed that the usability problems identified at this level provide valuable feedback on the improvement of platform-independent models (PIM) and platform-specific models (PSM) supporting the notion of *usability produced by construction*.

1.1 Introduction

The object management group (OMG) launched an initiative called model-driven architecture (MDA) to support the development of large, complex, interactive software applications providing a standardized architecture with the following features (MDA 2005):

- Interactive applications can easily evolve to address constantly evolving user requirements
- Old, current, and new technologies can be harmonized
- Business logic can be maintained constantly or can evolve independently of technological changes, or of the rest of the interactive application
- Legacy systems can be integrated and unified with new systems

E. Law et al. (eds.), *Maturing Usability.*
© Springer-Verlag London Limited 2008

In this approach, models are applied in all the steps of development up to a target computing platform. This provides a complete software production process where model transformation at different levels of abstraction becomes the basic strategy for obtaining a software application from models.

An MDA development process basically transforms a PIM into one or more PSMs, which then are transformed into code (code model–CM). The CM is just the actual code generated from PSMs through transformation. Here, the goal is to decouple the way in which interactive applications are currently defined, which is dependent on the technology they use. The purpose of this decoupling is to ensure that the investments made in building systems can be preserved even when the underlying technological platforms change. MDA has been applied to many kinds of business problems and integrated with a wide range of other common computing technologies, including user interfaces (UIs). It makes sense, therefore, to assess the usability of UIs in an interactive application resulting from a MDA process.

The MDA paradigm is a recent manifestation of the old tradition of model-based interface design environments (MB-IDEs) (Puerta 1997), which are aimed at generating the UI of an interactive application as automatically as possible from a conceptual model. Technicians have long observed that the usability of such an automatically generated UI is not known and should be compared with respect to the usability of a manually produced UI. The goal of this chapter, therefore, is to show how to assess the usability of UIs that are automatically generated by a MDA-compliant CASE tool. We also show how the usability evaluation process provides feedback to improve the models that are obtained in an MDA process.

The research question addressed by this study is the following: *Can MDA-compliant methods improve software usability through model transformations?* Specifically, our motivations are the following:

- Information systems (online or offline) probably represent a very significant portion of the total portfolio of today's interactive applications and are used by the widest and mostly diversified population of users. Therefore, it is important to assess the usability of this type of system.
- Because MDA is a modern method for developing information systems, and because it represents a family of development methods that is largely applied in the field of SE, we will focus on this family of methods by selecting a representative member of this family.
- Some works have been conducted in the field of SE (OMG 2006), as well as in HCI (Jespersen and Linvald 2003), to show how MDA can effectively be applied. However, we are not aware of any existing usability assessment of an UI obtained by a MDA-compliant method.
- We select a representative MDA-compliant CASE tool to support the complete development life cycle of the systems we are considering. This CASE tool enables us to automatically generate a completely running interactive application from conceptual models.
- If the usability of an automatically generated UI could be assessed, we would be able for the first time to predict (to some extent) the usability of any future UI produced by this CASE tool. In other words, we will talk about a UI that is (to some extent) *usable by construction*, at least.

We structure the remainder of this chapter as follows: the next section summarizes a literature review used to identify MDA-compliant methods and tools for developing interactive applications. The presentation of our strategy to integrate usability into MDA processes follows. Next, we describe an experimental study to evaluate the usability of a UI generated by a MDA-compliant CASE tool at its code model. The following section presents a comparative analysis of results. We also analyze the identified usability problems and their implications for the PIM and PSM. We then answer the stated research question. Finally, the chapter provides some conclusions and a discussion on future trends in the last section.

1.2 Related Work

According to OMG, there are today around 40 commercial or open source tools (OMG 2006) that follow the MDA paradigm (e.g., Rational Software Architect, ArcStyler, Together Architect, AndroMDA, REP ++ Studio, and OlivaNova). They normally use a UML (OMG 2003) class diagram to capture the system structure and a process model for its functionalities.

These tools support one or more features of MDA, such as UML modeling support, transformation rules, model integration, and code generation. Interaction modeling, however, is not a key issue when requirements and conceptual modeling are represented in a software production process. An exception to this is the OlivaNova tool (CARE 2005). This tool allows the representation of user interaction through a pattern-based approach. A presentation model that is built upon a UML-like class diagram represents user interaction, and other models represent user behavior. All these models, which act as a PIM, automatically transform into code for different target platforms.

Akhter and Tariq (2005) present a comparison of nine selected MDA-based tools (i.e., Optimal J, Arcstyler, Together Architect, MDE Studio, XMF-Mosaic, Ameos, Objecteeing, Constructor, and Codagen Architect). The comparison is done on the basis of identified evaluation criteria organized into three sections: UML and modeling support, a *core models* (PIM, PSM, and CM) approach, and a *transformation* approach. Results show that these tools are not fully compliant with the MDA specification. Most of them provide good support for modeling with UML but need to improve their transformation capabilities.

In the HCI field, many techniques exist in MB-IDEs to automatically generate the UI code: model transformation (Vanderdonckt 2005), static analysis (Eisenstein, Vanderdonckt, and Puerta 2001), skeleton or template-based programming (Janssen, Weisbecker, and Ziegler 1993; Vanderdonckt and Bodart 1993), generative programming, hierarchy construction (Lonczewski and Schreiber 1996), and pattern-based design (Molina, Meliá, and Pastor 2002), to name a few. Although we could identify the differences between these techniques in terms of strengths and weaknesses, it is still impossible to know today which technique is the most efficient.

In Silva's survey (2001), most of the MB-IDEs are reviewed, distinguishing two generations of tools. The goal of the first generation was to provide a runtime environment for UI models—for example, HUMANOÏD (Szekely 1996). The goal of the second generation was to provide more support for interface modeling at a high level of abstraction. Examples of these environments are FUSE (Lonczewski and Schreiber 1996), GENIUS (Janssen, Weisbecker, and Ziegler 1993), TRIDENT (Bodart et al. 1995), MASTERMIND (Szekely et al. 1996), and MECANO (Puerta, 1996). Most environments of this second generation rely on a domain model. This model is often a description of the domain entities and relationships among them, which are represented as a declarative data model (as in MECANO), an entity-relationship data model (as in GENIUS and TRIDENT), or an object-oriented data model (as in FUSE). Some proposals like FUSE, TRIDENT, and TEALLACH (Griffiths et al. 2001) add task models as a primary way for abstracting the user interaction, from which the abstract interface models (or their equivalent dialog models) are later derived.

Other proposals appear with the advent of the MDA initiative. Jespersen and Linvald (2003) proposed a model-based approach to UI engineering that generates domain-specific J2EE applications from a declarative application description. More recently, Mori et al. (2004) proposed a method and the associated tool (TERESA) to support the development of multiplatform user interfaces from conceptual models and transformations between them. Mori's work also briefly reports on the usability evaluation of the user interfaces generated by TERESA done at Motorola.

Vanderdonckt (2005) proposed a UI engineering methodology that adheres to the principles of MDA. It is structured on three axes: models and their specification language, method, and the tools that support the method based on the underlying models. Relevant aspects are stored in UsiXML (www.usixml.org) files to generate different types of UIs (e.g., graphical, vocal, multimodal, and virtual) on different types of computing platforms.

Even though the industry has launched many attempts to establish a comprehensive model-based approach for developing UIs, no consensus has been reached and no method has really emerged from these initiatives—perhaps because the resulting usability remains uncharacterized. In addition, only a few of these environments are MDA-compliant in a genuine way.

Although the need for generating more than merely the UI has been raised (Balzert et al. 1995), the MB-IDEs proposed in the HCI field also do not allow obtaining an entire software system (only its UI).

While experts in the fields of SE and HCI have conducted several works to see how MDA could effectively and efficiently be applied, we are not aware of any existing work that actually performs any explicit usability evaluation of the UI obtained by such a model-based software production method. There are some methods to develop a UI according to a MDA-compliant method, but none of them explicitly integrates usability engineering with UI engineering. This is particularly important because the code portion devoted to the UI could be very important in terms of lines of code: Myers and Rosson (1992) observed that the UI could range from 20 percent for almost non-interactive applications to 85 percent for highly-interactive applications, with a mean of 50 percent.

1.3 Integrating Usability into a MDA Process

The usability of an interactive application obtained from a transformation process can be evaluated at several stages of a MDA process: i) in the CIM, by evaluating the requirements models (i.e., use cases), task models or domain models which represent the user requirements and tasks; ii) in the PIM, by evaluating the models that represent the abstract user interface such as presentation models or dialog models; iii) in the PSM, by evaluating the concrete interface models (if they exist); and iv) in the CM, by evaluating the final user interface.

Figure 1.1 shows the correspondence between the models obtained in a generic MDA process and the usability evaluation activities.

It should be noted that the entire MDA process is driven by the PIM, which is automatically transformed into a PSM, and from there to code; therefore, modeling becomes, in fact, programming on a higher level of abstraction, where the PIM specifies the code that needs to be produced. The aim of a usability evaluation done at the PIM[1] (e.g., presentation models, dialog models) is to produce a *platform-independent usability report*. This report provides feedback to improve the PIM (1A in Figure 1.1) and the PSM (1B in Figure 1.1).

By means of model transformations and the explicit traceability between models, the changes performed in the PIM directly reflect into the PSM, avoiding usability problems in the interactive application (CM) obtained as part of the transformation process. The evaluation at the PIM or PSM should be done in an iterative way until these models have the required level of usability. The UEMs that can be applied in this stage include heuristic evaluation, standards inspection, and action analysis.

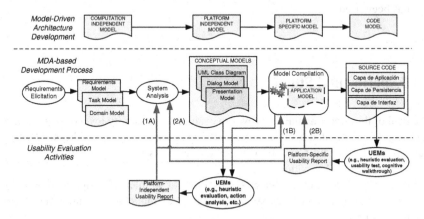

Fig. 1.1 Correspondence between the activities in a MDA process and the usability evaluation activities

---

[1] Although the evaluation can also be done at the CIM (e.g., requirement and task models), we focus on the transformations between the PIM-PSM-CM models.

On the other hand, other usability factors (i.e., efficiency, satisfaction) can only be evaluated on a specific platform and taking into account the concrete interface components that constitute the resulting user interface (CM). At this stage, we can apply usability inspection methods (e.g., heuristic evaluation) or other empirical methods that include the active participation of users (e.g., user testing, cognitive walkthrough). As a result, we obtain a *platform-specific usability report*.

Note that instead of relating a given usability problem with changes in the interface tier (code model level), as is usual in other approaches, we relate it to the conceptual primitives of the PIM that are affected by it (2A in Figure 1.1). Another benefit, which has no precedents in the MDA literature, is the opportunity to provide feedback to the transformation rules (2B in Figure 1.1). This allows improving of the model compilers and guaranteeing that the generated user interfaces will be usable to some extent.

We believe that construction can estimate the usability of an interactive application resulting from a MDA process. This means that each generated user interface satisfies a certain level of usability resulting from the application of the transformations. Each transformation may improve or diminish the whole usability depending on how they produce their output. This level of usability is no longer resulting from a manual programming process, but from the automated application of transformations. In the domain of theorem-proving, experts say that a program could be proven correct by construction by proving that the different instructions of this program correctly transform an initial precondition into a final valid postcondition. The principle is similar here for usability produced by construction: if we estimate the usability of a user interface produced by any transformation, then we can predict the usability of the final user interface produced by the whole set of transformations that has been used.

1.4 Experimental Study

The goal of the experimental study was to evaluate the usability level of UIs that are automatically generated using a MDA tool. The research question addressed by this study is the following: Can MDA-compliant methods improve software usability through model transformations?

To accomplish this, we evaluated the usability of an interactive application without users and with users using two UEMs at its code model level (implementation) as shown in Figure 1.1.

The methods chosen were action analysis (Olson and Olson 1990) and user testing (Dumas and Redish, 1999). These two UEMs were chosen because of their complementary character. An evaluation without users can catch usability problems (UPs) that an evaluation with only a few users may not reveal. Action analysis allows us to predict the time to complete tasks and the time to learn the interface. Testing with end users provides information about how people use the application and their problems with a specific user interface. We produced a list of usability problems from the two evaluations. These problems were addressed by changing the PIM, the model transformation strategy (PSM), or both.

1.4.1 Context of the Experiment

Instead of considering any MDA-compliant method, we relied on the process adopted by the OlivaNova – The Programming Machine tool (CARE 2005). We selected this CASE tool for the following reasons:

- It adheres to MDA principles
- It automatically generates an entire information system (including its user interface) based on conceptual models
- It is one of the tools available in the industry that is referenced on the OMG website

Figure 1.2 shows the methodological process followed by OlivaNova. In the following section, we describe in more detail the set of models and the transformation strategy on which the OlivaNova tool is based.

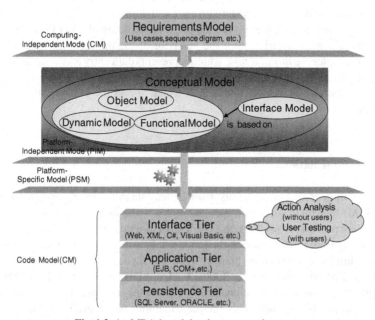

Fig. 1.2 An MDA-based development environment

Models

After specifying the requirements model, a PIM called a conceptual model represents the system data and behavior issues. It consists of the following: an *object model* to represent the structure of the interactive application in terms of classes and their relationships; a *dynamic model* to model the behavior of the system in terms of valid object lives and interaction between objects; and a *functional model* to represent the semantics associated with the state changes of the objects.

To support the conceptual modeling of user interfaces, the conceptual model has been enriched with a *presentation model*. It is composed with a pattern language called Just-UI (Molina, et al. 2002), which decomposes the user interaction in three main levels:

- *Level 1: Hierarchy of Actions Tree (HAT)*—organizes the semantic functions that will be presented to the different users who access the system. The HAT is a tree where intermediate nodes are labels for organizing the functionality and leaf nodes containing the functionality with links to the corresponding *interaction units*.
- *Level 2: Interaction Units (IUs)*—represents abstract interface units (Vanderdonckt and Bodart 1993) with which the users will interact to carry out their tasks. There are four types of interaction units: the Service IU, the Instance IU, the Population IU, and the Master/Detail IU. A *Service IU* models a dialog whose objective is to help the user executing a service. An *Instance IU* models the data presentation of a class instance. A *Population IU* models the presentation of a set of instances of a class. Finally, a *Master/Detail IU* models a complex user interaction that deals with master/slave presentations.
- *Level 3: Elementary Patterns*—are the primitive building blocks of the user interface and allow the restriction of the behavior of the different interaction units. Some examples are *introduction*, which represents data entry and validation in the system; *filter*, which defines selection criteria and obtains the instances that fulfill the constraint expressed; and *action*, which allows the user to execute object services.

Model Transformations

A model compiler that implements a set of mappings between conceptual primitives (PIM) and their software representations in the code model automates the development process. Nowadays, the OlivaNova tool provides model compilers that automatically transform the conceptual model into a full interactive application for the following target computing platforms: Visual Basic, C #, ASP and NET, Cold Fusion and JSP using SQL Server 2000, Oracle, or DB2 as a repository. The resulting application consists of three-layers that include the interface tier, the application tier, and the persistence tier. This unique capability of generating code for multiple targets is the cornerstone of model-based approaches for multi-platform UIs

(Eisenstein, Vanderdonckt, and Puerta 2001) as they represent instances relevant for various technological spaces whose variety is recognized (Lyytinen and Yoo 2002).

1.4.2 Experimental Object

The chosen application is the information management system of Aguas del Bullent S.A., a water supply service company located in Oliva, Spain. The Aguas del Bullent information management software (AdB) supports management for clients, orders, invoices, etc. It is important to note that AdB is a Microsoft-certified application and that it was completely generated from the conceptual model without any manual-based activity. From this application, we selected two representative tasks for conducting the UEMs. These tasks were selected through a questionnaire for the AdB application users to identify the most commonly used and representative tasks. This questionnaire resulted in the following two tasks: *create a subscriber*, and *create a product in stock*. The next section describes both tasks in different levels according to the MDA approach.

1.4.2.1 Task Description in the Computation Independent Model

At this level, we describe the user tasks to be carried out and the domain-oriented concepts that use the ConcurTaskTrees notation (CTT, http://giove. cnuce.cnr.it/ConcurTaskTrees.html). This is done in the Requirements Model step of the process shown in Figure 1.2.

The task model representing the end user's viewpoint of the *create a subscriber* task is shown in Figure 1.3. This is a complex domain-dependent task. As a water supply service company, AdB handles a strongly regulated set of concepts. The local administration controls the physical unit called a *water meter*. It is installed in homes and buildings, and is referred to as a *subscriber*. When the same *client* has more than one water meter installed (for example, if the same person owns

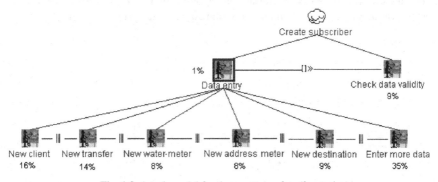

Fig. 1.3 A task model for the *create a subscriber* task

two apartments), each meter may be a different size, may be used for a different purpose (private or industrial use, etc.) or may be in a different area. In this case, we will use the concept of *subscriber* for each unit, and the service is invoiced separately.

When new areas need to be supplied with water, AdB is notified in advance by municipal administrations. There are no streets (nor streets names), but there are maps that are divided into lots. These lots are known as *destinations* and are introduced in the application when the infrastructure is done. It then creates and names streets. Some contractors ask AdB to install all the water meters before selling the properties. This is when most *subscribers* and *water meter addresses* are created. The property is later sold, and a new *client* is created and the corresponding subscriber updated to be linked to the new client.

This task is decomposed into the following subtasks: create a *new client*, create a *new transfer,* create a *new water meter*, create a *new address meter*, create a *new destination, enter more data*, and *check the validity* of the entered data. Given the complexity of the task, we assigned a percentage of task completeness for each subtask to indicate how much of task has been properly achieved. This could be improved in the future by assigning a weight that is a function of the amount of the subtask, but also of the importance of the subtasks.

Similarly, the task model representing the end user's viewpoint of the *create a product in stock* task is shown in Figure 1.4. This is a moderately complex domain-independent task that allows the introduction of a certain number of products in a warehouse. It is carried out in the following sub-tasks: create a *new product, select warehouse*, and *introduce number of products in stock*. As in Task 1, we assigned a percentage of completeness for each subtask.

1.4.2.2 Task Description in the Platform-Independent Model

At this level, the tasks to be performed are described as abstract user interfaces using the Presentation model. This corresponds to the last step of building the system conceptual model, as shown in Figure 1.2. An abstract user interface is a canonical expression of the rendering of the domain concepts and tasks in a way that is independent from any modality of interaction (Vanderdonckt 2005). It is considered an abstraction of a concrete user interface with respect to interaction modality.

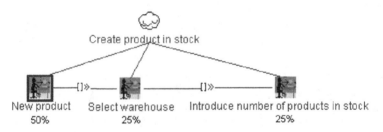

Fig. 1.4 A task model for the *create a product in stock* task

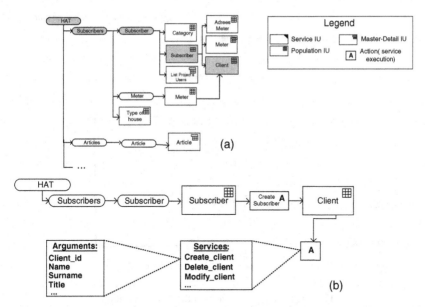

Fig. 1.5 Excerpt of the Presentation model for the AdB application

Figure 1.5 shows a piece of the Presentation model for the AdB application using the Just-UI patterns (Molina, et al. 2002)—(a) shows the HAT of the application, including the intermediate nodes (the menu/submenu options) and the *interaction units* that the users will interact with; and (b) shows all the *actions* (class services) accessible from the Client Population IU, accessed by following the path highlighted in (a) and the arguments of the *create_client* service.

1.4.2.3 Task Description in the Code Model

The model compilation shown in the process shown in Figure 1.2 defines an application model that is equivalent to the Platform-Specific model in MDA. However, as this model is implicit in ONME, there is no need to describe the tasks at this level. Consequently, the last level is the Code model. It corresponds to the final user interface that allows the tasks to be described by explaining the navigation between windows and the expected interaction between the user and the system.

Figure 1.6 shows part of the final UI for the AdB application running in the .NET platform (CARE 2006b), generated from the Presentation model shown in Figure 1.6. In the figure, (a) shows a form obtained for a *Service IU* (NewSubscriber). Once the data is entered, the user can launch the service or cancel it. Also in the figure, (b) shows a form obtained for the *Client Population IU* that is accessed by selecting the first lens icon in the NewSubscriber Service IU. This form is delimited by three zones—the central zone shows the client instances, the upper zone is used to perform searches using filters, and the right side zone is a toolbar to access the

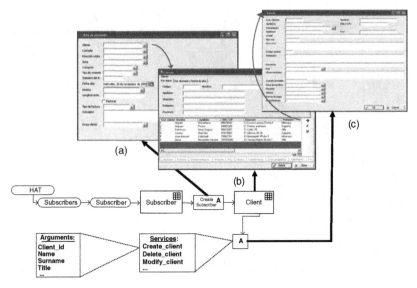

Fig. 1.6 Final user interfaces of the AdB application

create_client, *modify_client* and *delete_client* actions. In the figure, (c) shows a form obtained for the *NewClient Service IU* that is accessed by selecting the *create_client* action in the Client Population IU.

1.4.3 Usability Evaluation without Users

In this section, we describe how to conduct the usability evaluation of the AdB application without users using the two selected tasks. This kind of evaluation is useful for identifying usability problems and improving the usability of an interface by checking it against a standard. In this study, the results of applying the *action analysis* method (Olson and Olson 1990), based on the recommendations of Holzinger (2005), are used as standard. It is divided into *formal* and *back-of-the-envelope* action analysis. We used the formal approach that is often called *keystroke-level* analysis. It allows more accurate predictions of the time it takes a skilled user to complete the tasks. In addition, this prediction is done within a 20 percent margin of error, as reported by Lewis and Rieman (1993).

The keystroke-level analysis requires close inspection of the action sequences that a user performs to complete a task. It has two phases: the first phase determines the physical and mental steps a user performs to complete one or more tasks with the interface to predict the time that the user needs to do the task; and the second phase analyzes these steps, looking for problems. Some UPs that the analysis might reveal are that it takes too many steps to perform a simple task, or that it takes too long to perform the task, or that there is too much to learn about the interface, etc.

1.4.3.1 Keystroke-Level Analysis

We decomposed the two selected tasks into a sequence of actions that the user must perform to complete each task in order to predict the tasks' performance times. To do this, a time is associated with each one of these actions or sequence of operators (physical or mental), and they are then totaled. The time is calculated by using the average time that it takes a skilled user to complete the action, as suggested by Lewis and Rieman (1993). For example, one keystroke on a standard keyboard is considered a physical movement that takes 0.28 seconds, whereas learning a single *step* in a procedure is considered a mental movement that takes 0.25 seconds. Below, we describe some of the low-level physical and mental actions required to perform the *create a subscriber* task.

Subtask 1: Data Entry

1.1.	Recognize the menu entry "Create subscriber"	(0.34 s)
	This is a combination of moving the eyes, reading the name of the label, and performing the mental step of matching.	
1.2.	Move the mouse to the option "Create subscriber" and click it	(1.5 s)
	This is a standard mouse movement time. We know from the selection rule that the hand is already on the mouse.	
1.3.	See the action result. The screen is similar to Figure 1.6 (a)	(0.23 s)

Subtask 2: New Client

2.1	Recognize the client label	(0.34 s)
2.2	Move the mouse to the client lens icon and click it	(1.5 s)
2.3	See the action result. The screen is similar to Figure 1.6 (b)	(0.23 s)
2.4	Recognize the add client label	(0.34 s)
2.5	Click on "add client"	(1.5 s)
2.6	See the action result. The screen is similar to Figure 1.6 (c)	(0.23 s)
2.7	Recognize the client code label	(0.23 s)
2.8	Remember the client code	(1.2 s)
	This is just recalling an item from long-term memory	
2.9	Write the client code	0.84 s (0.28 * 3)
2.10	Recognize the client name label	(0.34 s)
2.11	Remember the client name	(1.2 s)
2.12	Write the client name	2.52 s (0.28 * 9)
...		
2.19	Recognize the *title* label	(0.34 s)
2.20	Move the mouse to the title lens icon and click it	(1.5 s)
2.21	See the action result	(0.23 s)
2.22	Remember the desired title	(1.2 s)
2.23	Find the desired title	12.58 s (0.34 * 37)
2.24	Move the mouse to click the desired title	(1.5 s)
2.25	Return the focus to add client screen	(0.23 s)
...		

Table 1.1 shows the time prediction for the eight subtasks (ST) of the *create a subscriber* task. It means that on average, a skilled user will take about 467.34 seconds (7.79 min.) to complete the task.

Table 1.1 Time prediction for Task 1

ST 1	ST 2	ST 3	ST 4	ST 5	ST 6	ST 7	ST 8	Total
40.65 s	157.9 s	77.05 s	28.48 s	30,25 s	40,51 s	67.19 s	25.34 s	467.34 s

Similarly, the keystroke-level predictions for the performance times of the *create a product in stock* task are as follows:

Subtask 1: New Product

1.1.	Recognize the "Articles" menu entry	(0.34 s)
1.2.	Move the mouse to the "Articles" menu	(1.5 s)
1.3.	See the action result	(0.23 s)
1.4.	Recognize the "Article" menu entry inside "Articles"	(0.34 s)
1.5.	Move the Mouse to the submenu entry called "Article"	(1.5 s)
1.6.	See the action result	(0.23 s)
1.7.	Recognize the add article with supplier label	1.02 s (0.34 * 3)
1.8.	Click on "add article" with supplier	(1.5 s)
1.9.	See the action result	(0.23 s)
1.10.	Recognize the *family* label	(0.34 s)
1.11.	Move the mouse to the family lens icon and click it	(1.5 s)
1.12.	See the action result	(0.23 s)
1.13.	Remember the desired family	(1.2 s)
1.14.	Find the desired family	4.08 s (0.34 * 12)
1.15.	Move the mouse to click the desired family	(1.5 s)
1.16.	Return the focus to add article with supplier	(0.23 s)
…		

Table 1.2 shows the time prediction for *create a new product in stock* (Task 2). The three subtasks (ST) are the following: *new product*, *select warehouse*, and *introduce number of products in stock*. The total time is 152.76 seconds (7.55 min.).

1.4.3.2 Analysis and Interpretation of Results

Even though the action analysis method is mainly used to predict task time, it can also highlight other UPs. One issue revealed by the analysis was that Task 1 might take too long because it is a complex task composed of several subtasks and steps. Specifically, Subtask 2, *New client*, is the subtask that takes the longest.

One of the causes of this problem is the use of the lens icon. For instance, the first field of the window shown in Figure 1.6(a) is dealt with by executing Steps 2.1 to 2.12. Similarly, the other eight lens icons must also be dealt with. This means executing 96 steps to accomplish Task 1. Note that the same interaction pattern

Table 1.2 Time prediction for Task 2

ST 1	ST 2	ST 3	Total
78.75 s	32.62 s	41.39 s	152.76 s

occurs during the execution of Task 2 (Steps 1.10 to 1.16). A possible solution for making Task 1 easier is to split it into smaller tasks, in contrast with Task 2, which is already well divided into subtasks (the subtasks have similar times).

Another question that the analysis highlights is the user workload. The higher the workload is, the higher the probability of making errors will be. During the interaction, the user needs to select the lens icon to enter the information in another window. For instance, in the third field of the window shown in Figure 1.6(c), a lens icon is provided to help the user enter the client title (e.g., Mr. or Mrs.). To do this, Steps 2.19 to 2.25 must be executed. This requires navigation to a new window, in which the user must select a title that already exists or create a new title.

The analysis also calls into question the large number of steps needed to do this fairly simple subtask. It is widely accepted that the shorter the required actions are, the faster the interactions will be. It can be noted that this potential problem is recurrent, because the other six lens icons (i.e., country, geography zone, and currency) must be dealt with in the same way. This means executing 36 additional steps. Of course, because any analysis at this level produces a *large* number of steps, it must first be determined whether or not there is a problem by comparing the task to other tasks of similar complexity.

Therefore, the workload must be reduced to increase the dialog efficiency. To do this, some of the lens icons should be changed into a list box or a combo box. This requires some further thought, because the data selection technique used should be consistent as well as quick. Another feature that could be included is the option to write and recognize the data entry. Also during data entry, the application should display default values in their appropriate data fields.

A related issue is the long-term memory requirements of the task. The analysis makes it clear that the user must recall several pieces of data during the task execution. This can be observed in Step 2.8 and Step 2.11 of Task 1. To avoid this, the application should not require data entry by the user when the data can be derived. We also noticed that, in some contexts, no feedback for user selection (i.e., color change) was provided. The problems found in the analysis facilitated the drafting of design usability requirements.

1.4.4 Usability Evaluation with Users

In December 2005, a user test was conducted in CARE Technologies. The goal was to evaluate how well or poorly the AdB application and its user interface performed, and how satisfied the users were in completing the two selected tasks. Specifically, we measured user *effectiveness*, *efficiency*, and *satisfaction* (ISO 1998). Effectiveness relates the goals of using the product to the accuracy and completeness with which these goals are achieved. It was measured using the following measures proposed in the Common Industry Format (CIF) for usability tests: the completion rate and the frequency of assists. The *completion rate* is the percentage of participants who completed each task correctly. We distinguished between two types of rates: i) *unassisted completion rate,* which is the rate achieved without intervention from the testers, and the ii) *assisted completion rate,* which is the rate achieved with tester intervention. The *frequency of assists* is the number of times that the experimenter assisted the user. Efficiency relates the level of effectiveness achieved to the quantity of resources expended. It was measured in terms of *goal achievement* divided by *task time.* Finally, satisfaction was measured as Questionnaire for User Interaction Satisfaction (QUIS) scores (see http://lap.umd.edu/QUIS).

1.4.4.1 Subjects

The test involved eight[2] expert and inexperienced end-users. They were internal employees of Aguas del Bullent and CARE Technologies. Five of them were male and three were female. Their expertise in the application domain and technology was considered as an independent variable.

Table 1.3 shows the distribution of users into four groups: novice in domain experience (DE) and technology experience (TE) (Group 1), novice in DE and expert in TE (Group 2), expert in DE and novice in TE (Group 3), and expert in DE and TE (Group 4). The decomposition of the user population into two dimensions (i.e., DE and TE) results from characterizing a user population along the two dimensions of syntactical knowledge and semantic knowledge, as recommended in (Jarke and Vassiliou 1985). The syntactic knowledge refers to the user's ability to interact technically with an interactive system through its devices, and is independent of any domain. The semantic knowledge refers to the user's knowledge in a particular domain of human activity. These two dimensions are independent.

1.4.4.2 Procedure and Instrumentation

We set up a usability laboratory in CARE Technologies to conduct the test. The interaction between the user and the AdB application was video-recorded and logged. An instructor and one independent observer participated in the study. The

Table 1.3 Distribution of subjects

Individual Testers (N = 8)		Domain Experience (DE)	
		Novices	Experts
Technology Experience (TE)	Novices	User7	User5
		User8	User6
	Experts	User3	User1
		User4	User2

---

[2] Prior research has shown that using four subjects in a usability test maximizes the ratio of the number of UPs found to the effort involved in running the test (Nielsen and Landauer 1993).

instructor interacted with the user while the observer took a record of observations and assists during the user test. Users were informed that the usability of the AdB application was going to be tested to check whether the system met their needs. No pretask training was scheduled. The design of the test followed a logical sequence of events for each user and across tests. The testing procedure was as follows:

- Users were given information about the goals and objectives of the test. They were told that it was not a test of their abilities. They were also informed that their interaction would be recorded.
- Users were asked to fill in a *demographic questionnaire* prior to the testing. It was used to confirm their job description, time in their job (years), education level, and age. They also scored their attitude towards technology in general, the use of computers, the use of the AdB application, and their experience with the OlivaNova technology (on a scale of 1 to 5).
- Users were then given a series of clear *instructions* that were specific for the test. They were advised to try to accomplish the tasks without any assistance, and that they should only ask for help if they felt unable to complete the task on their own.
- Users were asked to complete the two tasks. To avoid a possible ceiling effect, there was no time limit to complete the tasks.
- Users were then asked to complete a *QUIS* after completing the last task. This questionnaire is arranged in a hierarchical format and contains: 1) a demographic questionnaire, 2) six scales that measure overall reaction ratings of the system, and 3) four measures of specific interface factors—screen factors, terminology and system feedback, learning factors, and system capabilities. Each of the four specific interface factors has a main component question followed by related subcomponent questions. Each item is rated on a scale from one to seven with positive statements on the right side and negative statements on the left side. In addition, *not applicable* is listed as a choice. Additional space that allows the users to make comments is also included in the questionnaire. The comment space is headed by a statement that prompts the user to comment on each of the specific interface factors. Users are tracked by a number.
- Users were given a small reward for their participation.

After the experimental session, a we conducted a debriefing to collect information about how to improve the application.

1.4.4.3 Operation and Data Collection

We also followed a strict protocol for the usability testing to ensure consistency of the data collected. The test user was expected to accomplish the two tasks without being assisted. In any case, if the user got stuck on one task and felt unable to continue, he/she could ask for help—the instructions given to the users clearly stated that they should only ask for assistance as a last resort. When a user asked for assistance, the task was marked as *assisted*. Therefore, that instance of the task was computed in the assisted completion rate variable and not in the unassisted completion rate variable.

We recorded the data times using the Allnetic Time Tracking software (www.allnetic.com). Times were collected for each user, task, and subtask. We also included remarks about the type of help or assistance given to the user. The instructor was aware of any point where the user got stuck, because he/she was following the users' actions on a screen and checking the actions made by the user in a follow-up list based on the user manual. When the user asked for help, the instructor explained the next step that the user needed to take. The user performed the next step in the presence of the instructor. The assistance given was documented by annotating the step where the user got confused or lost.

1.4.4.4 Analysis and Interpretation of Results

In this section, we discuss the results and findings of the usability study. Table 1.4 shows the characteristics and capabilities of the users.

The demographic data for subjects revealed that 62 percent of the subjects were male; 62 percent of them ranged in age from 20–39 years; and 25 percent of the subjects had experience with the application they were evaluating.

Table 1.5 shows the participants' effectiveness and efficiency in executing Task 1. It illustrates that, on average, the users took 14 minutes to complete the task. The *new client*, *new water meter*, and *new address meter* subtasks took longer to perform. The data also shows that three out of eight users successfully completed the task without assistance and that three out of eight users completed the task with assistance.

In terms of frequency of assists, Subtasks 4 and 6 are the ones for which the users required more assistance (three assists), followed by Subtask 5 with two assists, and Subtask 7 (*enter more data*) and 8 (*check the validity of the data entered*) with one assist each. User 3 was the only user that required assistance on Subtasks 3 to 8. However, even with these assists, this user was not able to complete the task. This indicates that the most difficult or problematic subtasks are *new water meter* (Subtask 4) and *new address meter* (Subtask 5).

Looking at the videotapes, we could verify that the users got confused and lost in these subtasks. In Subtask 4, the reason was that, when the users selected the action to create the new water meter, a meaningless error message appeared: *"There is an open DataReader that corresponds to this connection. You must close it."* In Subtask 5, the user must select a *subscriber* that has not yet been created because the creation of an address meter is part of the creation of the subscriber. This is because the application does not maintain the reference of the new subscriber that is being created. In terms of efficiency, Users 4, 5, and 8 performed better than the others. These users completed the tasks without any assistance. This suggests that the efficiency is independent of the domain and technology experiences as they pertain to different categories. Indeed, Users 4 and 8 were considered novices in domain experience.

Table 1.6 shows the effectiveness and efficiency of the users executing Task 2. As can be observed, the users took an average of eight minutes to complete the task. The *new product* subtask took longer than the others. In terms of effectiveness,

Table 1.4 Characteristics of users

	Gender	Age	Education level	Job	Time in Job (Years)	Computer Usage Freq. (Windows / Others)	Attitude Towards Technology	AdB App. Usage Frequency	Expertise Level in Water Supply	OlivaNova Tech. Experience (End User / Analyst)
1	M	35	B	A	13	5/0	2	4	2	5/0
2	M	33	C	A	10	5/0	2	5	2	5/0
3	M	62	D	M	11	5/0	1	0	4	0/0
4	M	45	D	M	6	4/0	2	0	3	1/1
5	F	29	D	AN	6	5/0	2	0	2	4/5
6	F	32	D	S	6	5/0	1	0	1	5/3
7	F	26	C	R	0,25	5/1	2	0	1	0/3
8	M	43	C	P	–	5/0	2	0	1	0/0

Education level: A = school-leaving certificate, B = secondary graduate, C = qualified / technical engineer, D = graduate / engineer

Job: A = administration staff, M = management, AN = analyst, S = support, R = research, P = programming

Table 1.5 Task 1: Effectiveness and efficiency measures

User #	Unassisted Task Completion Rate[a] (%)	Assisted Task Completion Rate (%)	Task Time[b] (min)	Completion Rate / Task Time	Assists
1	39%	8%	21.0	1.86%	1
2	31%	17%	10.0	3.10%	2
3	31%	69%	41.0	0.76%	5
4	100%	0%	17.0	5.88%	0
5	100%	0%	09.0	11.11%	0
6	47%	9%	16.0	2.94%	1
7	31%	8%	9.0	3.44%	1
8	100%	0%	20.0	5.00%	0
Mean	64%	6%	14.57	4.76%	1.25
Std. Error	12.8%	2.4%	1.96	1.17	0.59
Std Dev.	34.1%	6.4%	5.1	3.10	1.66
Min	31%	0%	9.0	1.86%	0
Max	100%	17%	21.0	11.11%	5

[a] Rate of subtasks achieved without testers' intervention

[b] Period of time that the user executes the task without assistance (until the first time s/he asks for assistance). Summary data are given for the seven participants who completed the task.

four out of eight users successfully completed the task without assistance, two users completed the task with assistance, and the other two could not complete the task. In terms of assistance, two assists were given in each subtask. Again, User 3 was the user that required the most assistance and was not able to complete the task.

With respect to efficiency, Users 4, 5 and 6 performed better than the others. This shows that users who are domain experts but technology novices do not experience significant trouble in finding their way in the system generated by OlivaNova.

Descriptive statistics for overall user reaction ratings of the AdB application, the four measures of specific interface factors, and the general user satisfaction are

Table 1.6 Task 2: Effectiveness and efficiency measures

User #	Unassisted Task Completion Rate (%)	Assisted Task Completion Rate (%)	Task Time (min)	Completion Rate / Task Time	Assists
1	50%	25%	7.0	7.14%	1
2	75%	25%	9.0	8.33%	1
3	0%	100%	12.0	0%	3
4	100%	0%	7.0	14.29%	0
5	100%	0%	4.0	25%	0
6	100%	0%	6.0	16.67%	0
7	100%	0%	15.0	6.67	0
8	0%	50%	0	0%	1
Mean	87.5%	8.33%	8.0	13.01%	0.33
Std. Error	8.5	5.2%	1.5	2.91%	0.21
Std. Dev.	20.9	12.9%	3.7	7.14%	0.51
Min	50%	0%	4.0	6.67%	0
Max	100%	25%	15.0	25%	1

Summary data are given for the six participants who completed the task.

Table 1.7 Descriptive statistics for perception-based variables

	Minimum	Maximum	Mean	Median	Std. Deviation
Overall User Reactions	2.00	5.33	3.97	4.33	1.145
Screen Factors	2.25	6.75	4.00	3.75	1.42
Terminology and System Feedback	1.83	5.83	4.27	4.1	1.31
Learning Factors	1.83	6.40	4.57	4.80	1.39
System Capabilities	4.60	6.0	5.35	5.40	.57
Satisfaction	2.35	5.59	4.36	4.75	1.07

presented in Table 1.7. A participant's score for a perception-based variable was calculated as the mean of the scores assigned to the different items of that variable. Higher scores indicated greater user satisfaction with the use of the application. With the exception of the overall user reactions' measurement, the mean scores for all the other measures were higher than the middle score (i.e., a score of 4) on the Likert scale. The mean question scores varied from 3.97 to 5.35, with standard deviations ranging between 0.57 and 1.42. Novice users in the domain and technology (first-time users) judged the application more satisfactory than other types of users.

For these measures to be considered valid, however, an analysis of the construct validity and reliability of the QUIS are needed. The construct validity was carried out through an *inter-item correlation analysis* of the questionnaire. To do this, we used the concepts of convergent and discriminant validity, as proposed by Campbell and Fiske (1988).

An item is considered valid if its convergent validity (CV) is higher than its discriminant validity (DV). We assumed that all items associated with a particular construct have equal weights. As a result, Items Q4, Q15, and Q16, as well as the system capability items, were invalid (the DV for these items was higher than their CV). For this reason, these items were excluded from the analysis. With the exclusion of these items, the results of the validity analysis improved. The mean correlations between each main item and a general satisfaction scale ranged between 0.64 and 0.94. This suggests that there is a strong correlation between the items of the QUIS and general user satisfaction.

We also conducted a reliability analysis on the items used to measure the perception-based variables. Reliability of an instrument describes the consistency (or repeatability) that the instrument gives in measuring the same phenomenon over time or by different people. For this reliability analysis, items Q4, Q15, and Q16, as well as the system capability construct, were excluded. The results obtained for each construct using Cronbach alpha are: overall user reactions = 0.842; screen factors = 0.814; terminology and system feedback = 0.922; and learning factors = 0.805. These values are all 0.7 or above as required for constructs to be deemed reliable, as suggested by Nunally (1978). In addition, the general Cronbach alpha obtained for the instrument was 0.8. As a result, we conclude that the items on the survey (except the excluded items) are reliable and valid measures of the underlying perception-based constructs.

1.5 Correlation between Results

We performed a Spearman's rank order correlation analysis to assess the relationships that exist among usability measures. The results in Table 1.8 show that the unassisted task completion rate (UTCR) and task time are significantly negatively correlated ($r = 0.910$). This indicates (as expected) that when task time decreases, UTCR increases. Similarly, UTCRs are significantly negatively correlated with assists ($r = 0.877$). There is also a significant positive correlation between task time and assists ($r = 0.898$). As the assists increase, the task time also increases. Exceptions are the perception-based variables where most of the correlations are not significant at the 95 percent confidence level. The exception are screen factors that have a positive correlation with task time ($r = 0.548$). These results are in accordance with other studies that reveal that the aforementioned aspects of usability are not well understood for complex tasks (Frøkjær et al. 2000). Frøkjær's study also suggests that a weak correlation between usability measures is to be expected, and that efficiency, effectiveness, and satisfaction should be considered independent aspects of usability.

On the other hand, one of the reasons for conducting user testing was to get a baseline for the evaluation of the AdB application by comparing the users' performances with the prediction obtained with the action analysis. Because the action analysis provides quantitative estimates of task execution time, it can properly be considered as a benchmark. Table 1.9 shows a comparison between the predicted and measured time spent for the users to perform the two selected tasks. In this analysis, we included only the users that successfully completed the task without assistance. As noted, the efficiency of the users performing the tasks did not match the task time predictions. On average, the time it took users to complete the two tasks were 96.4 percent and 389 percent, respectively. This can be explained by the fact that the keystroke-level analysis model does not take into account individual differences among users. In addition, the accuracy of a model of this kind is highly dependent on the estimates of the operator time values for a specific user. As the prediction is made for expert users who do not make any errors, the novices who need to learn the application are not considered.

Table 1.8 Spearman's correlation between user performance and perceptions

		UTCR	Task Time	Assists	Learning Factors	Terminology and System Feedback	Screen Factors
UTCR	$p < 0.0001$	1.000	−0.910[a]	−0.877[a]	,205	−0.084	−0.359
	Sig. 1-tailed		0.001	0.002	0.313	0.422	0.191
Task	$p < 0.0001$	−.910[a]	1.000	0.687[b]	−0.335	0.143	0.548
Time	Sig. 1-tailed	0.001	.	0.030	0.208	0.368	0.080
Assists	$p < 0.0001$	−.877[a]	0.898	1.000	−, 111	−0.184	0.172
	Sig. 1-tailed	0.002		.	0.397	0.331	0.342

[a] Correlation is significant at 0.01
[b] Correlation is significant at 0.05

Table 1.9 Comparison between measured and predicted performance times

User	$T1_{pred.}$ [sec]	$T1_{mes.}$ [sec]	Diff. [%]	$T2_{pred.}$ [sec]	$T2_{mes.}$ [sec]	Diff. [%]
4	467.34	1020	118%	152.76	420	274%
5	467.34	540	15%	152.76	240	157%
6	467.34	–	–	152.76	360	235%
7	467.34	–	–	152.76	1020	667%
8	467.34	1200	156%	152.76	–	–

1.6 Usability Problems and their Implications for PIM and PSM

This section discusses how the identified usability problems relate to the models obtained in a MDA process. We also show how the two different evaluation methods produce problems originated in different models.

Section 1.4.3 discusses some of the most common usability problems identified in the evaluation without users. They are mainly related to long tasks that require long-term memory requirements and cause user workload problems. In addition, it was detected that the application does not provide feedback for user selection in some specific contexts.

In contrast, the evaluation with users revealed a set of usability problems that were mainly identified through the videotapes and observation records. Some of these problems were: lack of descriptive labels, difficult navigation (cyclic and unnecessary steps), inflexible/invalid search capabilities, inconsistent menu items and window labels, no feedback for user selection, lack of descriptive labels in some fields, and meaningless error messages. We also verified that some of the identified problems during the user test were further supported by the comments made by the subjects in the post-task questionnaire. Some answers for the question "List the three things that you least liked in the application" included:

1. The organization of the window in frame: the functionality of one of them appears hidden. [#2]
2. The navigation through lens icons: I lost the source window.
3. The data that was just entered does not appear: it is needed to search it manually when the application could provide it. [#3]
4. Error messages lack clarity and understanding. [#2]

On the other hand, some answers for the question "List the three things that you most liked in the application" included:

1. The application structure and menu are very intuitive and clear. I have no prior knowledge in the use of the application.
2. The possibility to find the information from different places of the application. [# 2]
3. The interface is simple (visually)
4. The application is very fast in searches and in all the actions that I executed. [#4]

Table 1.10 Usability problems by usability evaluation method

Usability Problem	Action Analysis	User Testing		Source
		Videotape	QUIS	
Inconsistent menu item and window labels		√		PIM
User workload (unnecessary searching)	√		√	PIM/PSM
Lack of descriptive labels		√	√	PIM
Difficult navigation	√	√	√	PIM
Inflexible/invalid search capabilities		√	√	PSM
No feedback for user selection	√	√	√	PIM/PSM
Invalid filters		√	√	PIM
Meaningless error messages		√	√	PIM/PSM
Long-term memory requirements	√		√	PIM

Table 1.10 shows a classification of UPs by evaluation method. As can be observed, the problems identified with the action analysis are related to procedural issues of usability (i.e., too many steps to complete the task, difficult navigation) as this method only represents the procedural aspects of a task. In contrast, the problems identified in the user test are more concerned with perceptual (i.e., meaningless error messages) and conceptual issues than verifying whether the user has an appropriate *mental model*. Another important issue is determining the source of the identified UPs (model level, pattern level, code transformation level, or platform level). This information will be used to create a plan for design recommendations, modifications, and improvements in the AdB conceptual model or transformation engines.

The issue of meaningless messages is related to the quality of error messages. An error message that appeared when one of the users finished Task 1 was the following: *"Maximum cardinality for Subscriber is not satisfied. At most 1 instances of subscriber are allowed."* Although the message includes prompting about the way to correct the error, the indications are not meaningful to end-users. The source of this problem is in the model level (Presentation model). It was the property *validation message* of the *Introduction* pattern of a Service UI (see Section 1.4.1). This pattern captures the main features of data types that the user introduces into the system. It includes the definition of edition masks, value by default, rank of values, help messages, and validation messages.

The source for the lack of descriptive labels and the inconsistent page problems is also in the model/pattern level. The former is related to the lack of *supplementary information* patterns, which is used to define additional information that will be shown when a user selects an object (i.e., field). The latter problem is related to consistency. This happened because the analyst gave a different name to a leaf node of the HAT (i.e., menu item of the application) and the title of the interaction unit (window) associated with it (see Section 1.4.1).

We also observed other UPs in the code transformation level. They were related to the implementations of the OlivaNova transformation engines. A frequent problem in Task 2 was that the user could not find the action to create an article (Subtask 1).

This occurred because the *action* icon was hidden, even if the window was maximized. Other problems in this level were the following: the help reference was not linked to the generated application and the F1 functionality on controls was not implemented, and the data of a display set (e.g., grid) was not refreshed when a service (i.e., create new client) was executed. A possible solution was to refresh data after a service execution.

1.7 Answering our Research Question

Thanks to the model transformations that implement the relationships between abstract UI, concrete UI, and the final UI, the usability of an application can be produced by construction. Depending on the transformation rules that are applied, the abstract presentation patterns (abstract interaction objects, AIOs) are instantiated in the corresponding software components in the target platform architecture (concrete interaction objects, CIO) (Vanderdonckt and Bodart 1993). This strategy is called reification (Vanderdonckt 2005). In this way, the changes made to fix usability problems will be always preserved during transformation.

The duality between COIs and AOIs has allowed us to abstract usability attributes and other relevant properties from the user interface elements. We have verified that some usability attributes are dealt with during the reification process. For instance, the following user guidance attributes related to visual feedback are directly ensured—visual feedback in menus or dialog boxes where choices can be selected or where the cursor is pointing, visual feedback where options are already selected for multiple options, and visual feedback when objects are selected. In addition, other attributes related to the legibility of the UI are also ensured—prompts and error messages always appear in the same place(s), and error messages displayed in pop-up windows indicate the field(s) where the error has occurred, etc.

The results of this study not only provide feedback to improve the AdB conceptual model, but also provide feedback to improve the .NET model compiler (CARE 2006b). For instance, one usability problem revealed by the action analysis was that Task 1 might take too long. A possible cause is the use of *lens icons*, which imply additional navigation. This occurs because the object-valued service arguments of a Service UI (Table 1.11) are implemented using generic control selectors that are, in turn, translated into the fields using an associated *lens icon* (one-to-one mapping). To address this problem, the code generator should be changed to allow different implementations for the same generic control selector (concrete object interface).

All these results provide evidence that the usability of an interactive application can be produced by construction. It is our belief that model-driven development provides the basis for tight integration of usability evaluation in the MDA development process, allowing usability issues to be addressed as an integrated part

Table 1.11 Correspondences between the presentation model, the transformation engine component, and the final user interface

Presentation Model (PIM)	.NET Code Generator (PSM)	Final Interface (CM)
Hierarchical action tree (HAT)	Application menu	File Changes Others Window
Service IU	MDI child form with entry controls	The whole window
Service throw and Cancellation	"accept" and 'cancel' buttons and code to validate, invoice and close the service	OK Cancel
Simple type service argument	Entry control	Identifier:
Object-valued service argument	Generic control OIDSelector	Employee:
Introduction pattern for a date field	Generic control OIDSelector	Code for validating date format

of the system design and not just as an ad-hoc solution after most of the development has been completed. It also provides the basis for platform-independent usability assessment, where the generic part of a system is assessed at the platform level, and not from scratch, for each platform-specific technology. This is a promising result and supported our research question. We are aware, however, that these are only the first results in this direction and that more experimentation is needed.

1.8 Conclusion and Perspectives

We have presented an empirical study to evaluate the usability of user interfaces that were automatically generated by a MDA-compliant tool. The generated application was evaluated without users and with users using two UEMs at its Code model level. The results were collected using both quantitative and qualitative data, ranging from manually capturing user behavior to measuring user satisfaction using a post-test questionnaire.

The evaluation without users revealed UPs that are more procedurally oriented, while the evaluation with users revealed problems that are more perceptual and cognitively oriented. It is encouraging, however, that the kinds of UPs identified with different methods are quite similar, which suggests convergent validity. Although the evaluations were conducted in the Code model (final user interface), they provided valuable feedback on the improvement of the Platform-Independent model and the Platform-Specific model, as well as the Code model, as a consequence of the model transformation process. Our study also provides some empirical evidence of the intrinsic quality of the user interfaces generated by a tool, and to the notion of *usability proven by construction*. Usability by construction is analogous to the concept of *correctness by construction* (Hall and Chapman 2002) introduced to guarantee the quality of a safety-critical system. In this development method, the authors argue that to obtain software with almost no defect (0.04% per KLOC), each step in the development method should be assessed with respect to correctness. Figure 1.7 depicts when defects are introduced and then removed in a development method that does not rely on correctness. For instance, 38 defects were introduced during the Specification step and removed later on during the Code step. If we can maintain proof of the correctness of a software from its inception until its delivery, it would mean that we can prove that it is correct by construction. Similarly, if we can maintain proof of the usability of a user interface from its specifications until the final code, it would mean that we can prove that it is usable by construction.

Of course, in the experiment conducted here, we can only show that each applied pattern reaches a certain level of usability. Therefore, we may predict the global usability of an entire interface by estimating the relative usability levels of the patterns and transformations involved in the development method. We cannot prove that a UI is entirely usable, but we can prove that it is usable at a certain level.

As a consequence, the evaluation of the UIs obtained by such an MDA tool poses new challenges. For example, the usability problems discussed here could be used to define design guidelines or antipatterns for analysts (e.g., van Welie et al. 2000). The explicit operationalization of these guidelines will help to obtain usable interactive applications from conceptual models. This could be done by using these guidelines or anti-patterns as the driving force for model transformation, supporting the concept of usability-driven model transformation.

The conclusions regarding the applicability of usability evaluation methods drawn from this experiment should, therefore, be generalized to a wide range of MDA-based tools. To address this issue, we plan to compare the usability of the UIs obtained with the OlivaNova tool with those obtained with other MDA-compliant tools, such as VisualWade (http://www.visual wade.com). Other future work includes the execution of several experiments to compare a UI designed

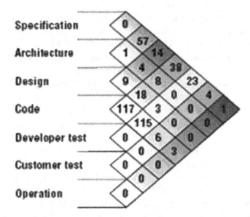

Fig. 1.7 Life-cycle phases where defects were introduced and then removed. (Source: Hall & Chapman, 2002)

by several experienced designers, and a UI generated by a MDA tool for the same interactive application starting from the same models. This would enable us to identify the differences between a manually produced UI and an automatically generated UI.

Acknowledgment The authors would like to thank Sergio España, Ignacio Panach, and Inés Pederiva for their full support while conducting this experiment. We would also like to thank the users who evaluated the system for their time and efforts. This work was partially supported by the COST Action n°294 (www.cost294.org), by the SIMILAR network of excellence (www.similar.cc). Jean Vanderdonckt would also like to thank Valencia University of Technology for its support.

References

Balzert, H., Hofmann, F., Kruschinski, V., & Niemann, Ch. (1995). The JANUS application development environment – Generating more than the user interface. In Vanderdonckt, J. (Ed.), *Computer-Aided Design of User Interfaces, Proc. of 2nd Int. Workshop on Computer-Aided Design of User Interfaces CADUI'96* (pp 183–208). Presses Universitaires de Namur, Namur.

Bodart, F., Hennebert, A.M., Leheureux, J.M., Vanderdonckt, J. (1995). A model-based approach to presentation: A continuum from task analysis to prototype. In *Focus on Computer Graphics Series* (pp. 77–94). Springer-Verlag.

Campbell, D.T., & Fiske, D.W. (1959). Convergent and discriminant validation by the multitrait-multimethod matrix. *Psychological Bulletin, 56*, 81–105

Care Technologies (2005) http://www.care-t.com/products/index.html. Last access: Nov. 2005.

Care Technologies (2006a) http://www.care-t.com/downloads, *OlivaNova Modeller User Manual.* Last update: Jan. 2006.

Care Technologies (2006b) http://www.care-t.com/downloads, *OlivaNova .NET Business Logic for Scalable Transactional Architecture Manual.* Last update: Feb. 2006.

Dumas, J.S., & Redish, J.C. (1999). *A practical guide to usability testing.* Intellect Ltd (UK).

Eisenstein, J., Vanderdonckt, J., & Puerta, A.R. (2001). Model-based user-interface development techniques for mobile computing. In *Proc. of 5th ACM Int. Conf. on Intelligent User Interfaces IUI'01* (pp. 69–76). New York: ACM Press.

Frøkjær, E., Hertzum, M., & Hornbæk, K. (2000). Measuring usability: Are effectiveness, efficiency, and satisfaction really correlated? In *Proc. of the ACM Conference on Human Factors in Computing Systems CHI'00* (pp. 345–352). New York: ACM Press.

Griffiths, T., Barclay, P.J., Paton, N.W., McKirdy, J., Kennedy, J.B., Gray, P.D., Cooper, R., Goble, C.A., & Silva, P.P. (2001). Teallach: A Model-based user interface development environment for object databases. *Interacting with Computers, 14(1),* 31–68

Hall, A., & Chapman, R. (2002). Correctness by construction: Developing a commercial secure system. *IEEE Software, 19*(1), 18–25

Holzinger, A. (2005) Usability engineering methods for software developers. *Communications of the ACM, 48(1),* 71–74

ISO 9241-11 (1998). *Ergonomic requirements for office work with visual display terminals (VDTs) Part 11: Guidance on usability.*

Janssen, C., Weisbecker, A., & Ziegler, J. (1993). Generating user interfaces from data models and dialogue net specifications. In *Proc. of the ACM Conference on Human Aspects in Computing Systems CHI'93* (pp. 418–423), Amsterdam. New York: ACM Press

Jarke, M., & Vassiliou, Y. (1985). A framework for choosing a database query language. *ACM Computing Surveys, 17(3),* 313–370

Jespersen, J.W., Linvald, J. (2003). Investigating user interface engineering in the model driven architecture. In M.B. Harning & J. Vanderdonckt (Eds.), *Closing the gap: Software engineering* *and human-computer interaction, Proc. of the 2nd IFIP TC 13 WG2.7/13.4 Workshop on Integrating Software Engineering and Human-Computer Interaction, IFIP* (pp. 63–66). Accessible at http://www.se-hci.org/bridging/interact/proceedings.htm

Lewis, J., & Rieman, J. (1993). *Task-centered user interface design: A practical introduction.* Accessible at ftp.cs.colorado.edu in /pub/cs/distribs/clewis/HCI-Design-Book). <*>document</*>

Lonczewski, F., & Schreiber, S. (1996). The FUSE-system: an integrated user interface design environment. In J. Vanderdonckt (Ed.), *Computer-aided design of user interfaces, Proc. of 2nd Int. Workshop on Computer-Aided Design of User Interfaces CADUI'96* (pp. pp 37–56). Namur: Presses Universitaires de Namur.

Lyytinen, K., & Yoo, Y. (2002). Issues and challenges in ubiquitous computing. *Communications of the ACM, 45*(12), 62–65

MDA: http://www.omg.org/mda. Last access: Dec. 2005

Molina, P.J., Meliá, S., & Pastor, O. (2002). JUST-UI: A user interface specification model. In Ch. Kolski & J. Vanderdonckt (Eds.), *Proc. of 4th Int. Conf. on Computer Aided Design of User Interfaces CADUI'02* (pp. 63–74). Dordrecht: Kluwer Academics Publishers.

Mori, G., Paternò, F., & Santoro, C. (2004). Design and development of multi-device user interfaces through multiple logical descriptions. *IEEE Transactions on Software Engineering, 30*(8), 507–520

Myers, B.A., Hudson, S.E., & Pausch, R.F. (2000). Past, present, and future of user interface software tools. *ACM Transactions on Computer-Human Interaction, 7(1)*, 3–28.

Myers, B.A., & Rosson, M.B. (1992). Survey on user interface programming. In *Proc. of ACM Conference on Human Factors in Computing Systems CHI'92*, Monterey (pp. 195–202). New York: ACM Press.

Nielsen, J., & Landauer, T.K. (1993). A mathematical model of the finding of usability problems. In *Proc. of Conf. on Human Factors in Computing Systems INTERCHI'93* (pp. 206–213), Amsterdam. New York: ACM Press.

Nunally, J. (1978). *Psychometric Theory*(2nd *ed.*) New York: McGraw-Hill

Olson, J.R., & Olson, G.M. (1990). The growth of cognitive modeling in human-computer interaction since GOMS. *Human-Computer Interaction, 5*, 221–265.

OMG (2006). *Committed companies and their products.* Accessible at http://www.omg.org/mda/committed-products.htm

OMG (2003) *Unified Modeling Language v1.5.* http://www.omg.org/cgi-bin/doc? formal/03-03-01. Last access: Feb. 17, 2005.

Pastor, O., Gómez, J., & Insfran, E., & Pelechano, V. (2001). The OO-method approach for information systems modelling: from object-oriented conceptual modeling to automated programming. *Information Systems, 26(7):* 507–534

Puerta, A.R. (1996). The mecano project: Comprehensive and integrated support for model-based interface development. In J. Vanderdonckt (Ed.), *Computer-aided design of user interfaces, Proc. of 2nd Int. Workshop on Computer-Aided Design of User Interfaces CADUI'96* (pp 19–36). Namur: Presses Universitaires de Namur.

Puerta, A.R. (1997). A model-based interface development environment. *IEEE Software, 14(4)*, 41–47.

Silva, P.P. (2000). User interface declarative models and development environments: A survey. In *Proc. of 7th Int. Workshop on Design, Specification, and Verification of Interactive Systems DSV-IS'00, Lecture Notes in Computer Science 1946* (pp. 207–226). Berlin: Springer-Verlag.

Szekely, P.A. (1996). Retrospective and challenges for model-based interface development. In F. Bodart & J. Vanderdonckt (Eds.), *Proc. of the 3rd Int. Eurographics Workshop on Design, Specification, and Verification of Interactive Systems DSV-IS'96* (pp. 1–27), Namur. Berlin: Springer-Verlag.

Szekely, P.A., Sukaviriya, P., Castells, P., Muthukumarasamy, J., & Salcher, E. (1996). Declarative interface models for user interface construction tools: the MASTERMIND approach. In L.J. Bass & C. Unger (Eds.), *Engineering for human-computer interaction, Proc. of the IFIP TC2/WG2.7 Working Conf. on Engineering for HCI EHCI'95* (pp. 120–150), Yellowstone Park.

Tariq, N.A., & Akhter, N. (2005). *Comparison of model driven architecture (MDA) based tools.* Master Thesis, Royal institute of Technology (KTH), Stockholm, Sweden, URL: http://dis.dsv.su.se/~emis-nat/CMDA/MainPage.htm

Vanderdonckt, J. (2005). A MDA-compliant environment for developing user interfaces of information systems. In O. Pastor & J. Cunha (Eds.), *Proc. of 17th Int. Conference on Advanced Information Systems Engineering CAiSE'05*, Porto. Lecture Notes in Computer Science n°3520 (pp. 16–31). Berlin: Springer-Verlag.

Vanderdonckt, J., & Bodart, F. (1993) Encapsulating knowledge for intelligent automatic interaction objects selection. In *Proc. of the ACM Conf. on Human Factors in Computing Systems INTERCHI'93* (pp. 424–429), Amsterdam. New York: ACM Press.

van Welie, M., van der Veer, G.C., & Eliëns, A. (2000). Patterns as tools for user interface design. In *Proc. of the Int. Workshop on Tools for Working with Guidelines* (pp. 313–324). London: Springer.

Chapter 2
Software Quality Engineering:
The Leverage for Gaining Maturity

Witold Suryn

École de Technologie Supérieure – ETS, Montréal, Québec, Canada,
e-mail: wsuryn@ele.etsmtl.ca

Abstract For users, a software product frequently corresponds to a black box that must effectively support their business processes. Consequently, what a stakeholder seeks is a software product that possesses *both* required functionality and required quality. Young, immature companies usually can only afford developing functionalities, while mature organizations can develop quality, as well. In this sense, the level of quality observed in a software product is an indicator of the level of maturity of its developer. One may even say that because functionalities are always in a product and quality only sometimes, quality is a more restrictive indicator. Having this in mind, in this chapter we present software quality engineering from both implementation and managerial perspectives, discuss aspects of functionality-quality conflict in the economic and business dimensions, and finally give a few practical observations and recommendations that might find merit in the real, software development lifecycle.

2.1 Quality of a Software Product as the Indicator of Maturity

For users, a software product frequently corresponds to a black box that must effectively support their business processes. In consequence, what a stakeholder seeks is a software product that possesses *both* required functionality and required quality. Young, immature companies usually can only afford developing functionalities, while mature organizations can develop quality too. In this sense the level of quality observed in a software product is an indicator of the level of maturity of its developer. In the following chapter we will discuss software quality engineering methods, processes and models as the leverage for gaining such maturity.

2.1.1 Quality and a Customer

What exactly constitutes the quality of a product is often the subject of a hot debate. For some it is "[the] degree to which a set of inherent characteristics fulfills requirements" (ISO/IEC, 2000), while for others it can be synonymous with *customer value*, or even *defect levels* (Highsmith, 2002). One of the most renowned classifications of quality is a multi-perspective view proposed by Kitchenham and Pfleeger (Kitchenham, 1996):

- The transcendental perspective deals with the metaphysical aspect of quality
- The user perspective is concerned with the appropriateness of the product for a given context of use
- The manufacturing perspective represents quality as conformance to requirements
- The product perspective implies that quality can be appreciated by measuring the inherent characteristics of the product
- The value-based perspective recognizes different importance (or value) of quality to various stakeholders

A quite natural trend that is observed nowadays among IT customers is the desire to be properly served without the need to become proficient in information technology. A customer just wants to buy, learn how to use, and then simply use a software product to his satisfaction, just like with a car or a TV. This boils down to an extended responsibility on the part of a software supplier, who now has to be mature enough to know what the customer is able to express, as well as what the customer does not know that he knows. And then, when all questions are asked and answered, the supplier must continue on his way until the quality product is built and delivered to the satisfaction of the customer.

2.1.2 Quality and CMM/CMMI

The Capability Maturity Model (CMM) emerged in 1990 as a result of the research effort conducted by specialists from Software Engineering Institute (SEI) of Carnegie Mellon University (CMMI, 2002). Its next version, Capability Maturity Model Integration (CMMI^{SM}), known in the industry as a best practices model, is mostly used to "provide guidance for an organization to improve its processes and ability to manage development, acquisition, and maintenance of products and services."

What, then, is the link between the maturity of an organization's processes and quality of its products? First and foremost, it is *non-automatic*. The organization may have all best processes in place and be continuously certified ISO 9000 and still manufacture products that will not survive a day. If the level of maturity could be compared to the knowledge of a battlefield–the deeper that knowledge is, the higher the chances of victory are. But they are still only chances, not certainties.

2.1.3 Quality and SPICE

Software Process Improvement and Capability dEtermination (SPICE) is an international initiative to support the development of an International Standard for Software

Process Assessment (El Emam, et al. 1997). In 1998, the document was published as ISO/IEC TR 15504:1998–Software Process Assessment, which now has five parts (ISO/IEC, 2006):

- Part 1 – Concepts and vocabulary
- Part 2 – Performing an assessment
- Part 3 – Guidance on performing an assessment
- Part 4 – Guidance on use for process improvement and process capability determination
- Part 5 – An exemplar Process Assessment Model

SPICE or the ISO/IEC 15504 series of standards provides a framework for the assessment of processes. This framework can be used by organizations involved in planning, managing, monitoring, controlling, and improving the acquisition, supply, development, operation, evolution, and support of products/services. Process assessment examines the processes used by an organization to determine whether it is effective in achieving its goals. The results may be used to drive process improvement activities or process capability determination.

Through this, the organization is expected to become a capable organization that maximizes its responsiveness to customer and market requirements, minimizes the full life-cycle costs of its products, and, as a result, maximizes end-user satisfaction.

2.1.4 Quality and SWEBOK

The purpose of the Guide to Software Engineering Body of Knowledge (SWEBOK 2004) is "to provide a consensually-validated characterization of the bounds of the software engineering discipline and to provide a topical access to the Body of Knowledge supporting that discipline." The Body of Knowledge is subdivided into ten knowledge areas (KA), among which a KA dedicated to software quality has its distinctive place. In SWEBOK, the software quality subject is decomposed in individual topics (15) grouped in four sections:

- Software Quality Concepts (SQC)
- Purpose and Planning of SQA and V&V (P&P)
- Activities and techniques for SQA and V&V (A&T)
- Other SQA and V&V Testing (OT)

In *Software Quality Concepts*, the Guide discusses the issues of identification and management of costs related to quality, modeling of quality, and the existence of quality perspectives other than these "classical" ones. *Purpose and Planning of SQA and V&V* analyzes the planning and objectives of software quality assurance (SQA) and verification and validation (V&V) processes in the context of what should be achieved, when it should be achieved, and how it should be achieved. *Activities and techniques for SQA and V&V* tackle the practicalities of SQA and V&V execution, presenting (among others) static and dynamic techniques recommended for these processes. *Measurement applied to SQA and V&V*

presents basic notions of measurement theory and practice in the context of software and software qualitymeasurement.

SWEBOK discusses software quality in a comprehensive way, yet still leaves room for additional perspectives. One of them is the *engineering* perspective of making the real quality happen (hands-on engineering interventions). This hypothesis lay at the foundations of the research program conducted in 2005 by Suryn et al (Suryn et al. 2006), with the objective of evaluating each KA constituting SWEBOK to verify the level of software quality engineering in its content. The results published in (Suryn et al. 2006) can be summarized as follows:

- Quality as *engineering process* is addressed in a limited form
- The basic, quality engineering activities, like quality requirements specification or modelling, are not addressed
- Quality testing is discussed mainly with reference to V&V processes, while, in fact, real evaluation of software product happens all along the life cycle
- Practical aspects of engineering quality in a software product are omitted, while their treatment would be helpful at least in the Software Constriction KA

2.2 Basic Concepts in Software Quality Engineering

2.2.1 An Engineering Process

An engineering process can basically be expressed in terms of a problem and its resolution. In other words, an *engineer* is a knowledgeable person who, through his or her education supported by experience, is able to understand (i.e., investigate, identify, and decompose) a problem and deliver a solution that resolves it.

The best known definition of *engineering* is the one proposed and published by The Accreditation Board for Engineering and Technology (ABET). It states:

Engineering is the profession in which a knowledge of the mathematical and natural sciences, gained by study, experience, and practice, is applied with judgment to develop ways to utilize, economically, the materials and forces of nature for the benefit of mankind

On a smaller scale, but still in a similar way, the following definition of software engineering has been proposed by IEEE CS in its standard IEEE 610.12 (IEEE, 1990):

1. The application of a systematic, disciplined, quantifiable approach to the development, operation, and maintenance of software; that is, the application of engineering to software.
2. The study of approaches as in (1).

Finally, the definition of software quality engineering that complements the one from IEEE 610.12 has been developed and proposed by Suryn in 2003 (Suryn 2003):

1. The application of a continuous, systematic, disciplined, quantifiable approach to the development and maintenance of quality throughout the whole life cycle of software products and systems; that is, the application of engineering to quality of software.
2. The study of approaches as in (1).

What should be noted in this definition of software quality engineering is the notion of its applicability within the life cycle of the software (product or system). This idea translates into a practical approach that is of fundamental value to building software of quality, the approach that is *known* but often neglected within software development industry: *building quality into software is an engineering effort that must be active throughout the whole life cycle of software to bring required results.*

2.2.2 Quality Models

Quality models present an approach to tie together different quality attributes with basic objectives to:

- Help understand how the several facets of quality contribute to the whole
- Emphasize clearly that software quality is more than simply faults and failures
- Help to navigate through the map of quality characteristics, sub-characteristics and appropriate measures (measurement formulas and scales)
- Help to define our evaluation profile (what precisely we want to evaluate)

There are several quality models known to industry and academia, like the ones of McCall (McCall, et al. 1977), Boehm (Boehm, et al. 1978) or Dromey (1995), but only one gained broader, international acceptance—the model developed by the International Organization for Standardization (ISO) published in the standard ISO/IEC 9126 (1991): Software product evaluation, Quality characteristics and guidelines for their use.

This standard aimed to define a quality model for software product and a set of guidelines for measuring the characteristics associated with it. In further revisions of the standard, ISO/IEC JTC1 committee SC7 created its new, four-part version:

- ISO/IEC 9126-1 (ISO/IEC 2001) defines an updated quality model
- ISO/IEC 9126-2 (ISO/IEC 2003a) defines a set of external measures
- ISO/IEC 9126-3 (ISO/IEC 2003b) defines a set of internal measures
- ISO/IEC 9126-4 (ISO/IEC 2004) defines a set of quality in use measures

The new quality model defined in ISO/IEC 9126-1 recognizes three aspects of software quality and defines them as follows:

- Quality in use:. "Quality in use is the user's view of the quality of the software product when it is used in a specific environment and a specific context of use. It measures the extent to which users can achieve their goals in a particular environment, rather than measuring the properties of the software itself" (ISO/IEC 2004)

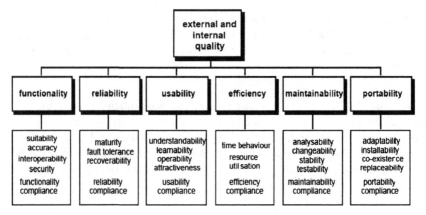

Fig. 2.1 Three-layer model for internal and external quality (© ISO/IEC, 2001)

- External quality: "External quality is the totality of characteristics of the software product from an external view. It is the quality when the software is executed, which is typically measured and evaluated while testing in a simulated environment with simulated data using external metrics" (ISO/IEC 2003a)
- Internal quality: "Internal quality is the totality of attributes of a product that determine its ability to satisfy stated and implied needs when used under specified conditions. Details of software product quality can be improved during code implementation, reviewing and testing, but the fundamental nature of the software product quality represented by the internal quality remains unchanged unless redesigned" (ISO/IEC 2003b)

ISO/IEC 9126 internal and external quality model (Figure 2.1) is a three-layer model composed of quality characteristics and subcharacteristics with more than 200 associated measures. The *quality in use* model (Figure 2.2) is a two-layer model composed of characteristics and quality measures.

Theoretically, internal quality, external quality, and quality in use are linked together in a predictive relationship stating that once the requirements are established and software construction is underway, the quality model can be used to predict the overall quality. In reality, no model may claim to follow this prediction mechanism perfectly. In the case of ISO/IEC 9126, the links between internal

Fig. 2.2 Quality in use model (© ISO/IEC, 2004)

and external quality seem rather obvious because the models are essentially the same, but caution must be exercised as to the links between external quality and quality in use.

2.2.3 Quality Measurement

Measurement requires both particular knowledge and commitment, because measurement activities are too often considered in software engineering as non-productive, or worse, disturbing the already nervous rhythm of development. So, the very fundamental question is: *why measure*? What are the benefits of measuring in software engineering? Some responses are:

- Effective and precise communication
- Means to control and supervise projects
- Quick identification of problems and their eventual resolutions
- Taking complex decisions based on data not on guesses
- Rational justification of decisions

While the above approach is mainly of an organizational nature, it requires some particular, technical knowledge in its execution. To render valid and usable results, the measurement process should be executed in a professional and scientifically sound manner. The generic measurement model (Figure 2.3), developed by ISO/IEC SC7, helps to transit from the point of identification of measurable attributes, through measurement methods and analysis activities to finally reach the phase of *information product*. This last result is the most important outcome of the whole process, because it is used *to make a decision*.

In software quality engineering, measurement is a pivotal concept. In other words, quality cannot be effectively engineered without measurement because measurement gives us the objective means to verify the presence of quality in a developed software product.

The most important issue arises, however, when a software quality engineer attempts to really measure the quality. His or her primary concerns usually are:

- What to measure
- How to measure
- Where to seek for support (practical or scientific)

One of ways to address these concerns would be to use the standard offered in ISO/IEC 9126 as a practical support. The standard proposes three distinctive perspectives on the analysis of the quality of a software product (internal quality, external quality, and quality in use), associates a large amount of measures to choose from with each of these perspectives, and gives some recommendations on how to interpret the obtained results. It also positions, as is shown in Figure 2.4, quality perspectives and their measures against each other, both in requirements definition and implementation phases.

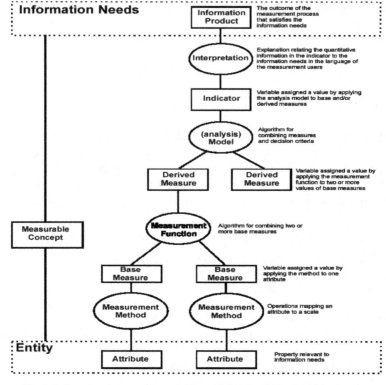

Fig. 2.3 Generic measurement model from ISO/IEC 15939 (© ISO/IEC 2002)

2.2.4 Quality Evaluation

The evaluation of software product quality is important to both the acquisition and development of software. The essential parts of the software quality evaluation process are:

- The quality model
- The method of evaluation
- Software measurement
- Supporting tools

For anyone attempting to execute a software quality evaluation, it is important to remember that an evaluation must be coupled with measurement and must be designed and tailored precisely to the purposes of the evaluation. It is also important to realize that an evaluation is a complex task that should follow a well-defined process and plan (Figure 2.5).

The ultimate purpose of an evaluation is to obtain reliable information, allowing us to make a wise and justified decision in an actual situation (or stage) of the development process.

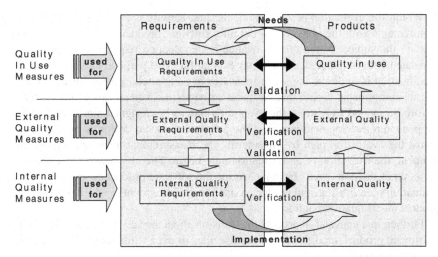

Fig. 2.4 Software product quality lifecycle and related measures (© ISO/IEC 2006)

In software quality, the *actual situation* often refers to the type of intermediate or final software product to be evaluated, which, in turn, points to the stage in the life cycle and the purpose of the evaluation. For a software product in its context of use, quality in use should be evaluated; for a software product as a part of a system in operation, external quality should be evaluated and, finally, static artifacts of a software product in development require an evaluation of internal quality.

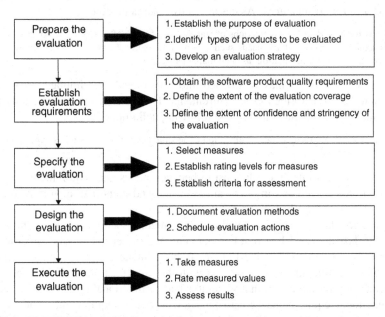

Fig. 2.5 ISO/IEC 25000 SQuaRE model for a generic software quality evaluation process (© ISO/IEC 2005)

Within the evaluation process itself, the first activity is establishing evaluation requirements with the objective of defining software product quality requirements that are the subject of the quality evaluation. Evaluation requirements are further translated into the specification of an evaluation. The purpose of the evaluation specification is to define the set of measures to be applied to the software product and its components during measurement activities, as well as assessment criteria. Before the actual execution, the evaluation has to be designed similarly to what happens in a development process. The purpose of such a design is principally to adjust the evaluation plan by considering the measurement to be applied. In this moment, the execution of an evaluation may begin. The objective of this phase is to obtain evaluation results from measuring the software product as specified in the evaluation specification, and produce a statement of the extent to which the software product meets quality requirements.

Further, in a managerial process the decision about the acceptance or rejection of a software product, modification of release plan, or even withdrawing from production may be made.

2.3 Defining Quality Requirements

2.3.1 What are Quality Requirements?

Before discussing software quality requirements, it is important to define a *requirement* as different from a *need*. As described by Azuma in (Azuma, 2001):

> "Needs for a product are expectations of stakeholders for the effects of the product when it is actually operated, which means such actions to the software product as development, distribution, release, installation, use and maintenance."

Going further, needs may be divided into stated needs and implied needs, and both should be transformed into requirements. The difference between needs and requirements may be illustrated by the following definition:

> "Requirements are the external specification of specific needs that a product is expected to satisfy."

Figure 2.6 illustrates the relationship between needs and requirements. Stakeholders' needs (stated and implied) are collected and identified, then transformed into functional and quality requirements.

The establishing of software quality requirements emerged as a separate activity in the last decade when requirements engineering encountered difficulties in capturing all of their types (like functional, performance, organizational, or quality). First, the difficulty was associated with the non-functional requirements and supplementary requirements that were attached to functional requirements. Later, non-functional requirements were associated with quality requirements, where more research concentrated on their modeling and representation and on negotiation of conflicts between different categories of requirements.

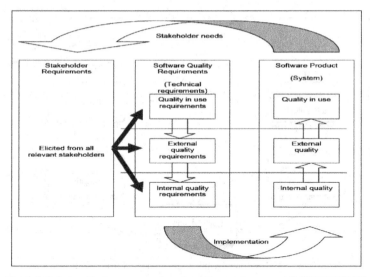

Fig. 2.6 Relationship between needs and quality requirements (© ISO/IEC 2005)

As a result, *"identifying quality requirements that can be elicited, formalized and further evaluated in each phase of full software product lifecycle became a crucial task in the process of building a high quality software product."* (Suryn & Abran, 2003).

2.3.2 Interception and Identification of Quality Requirements

Quality requirements may possess distinctive features that differentiate them from other categories of requirements, but there is one important tool that all of them usually share: the identification/formalization process. This process tool (Robertson, 1999), as shown in the example in Figure 2.7, identifies all phases or actions necessary to produce a valid and reliable list of requirements, despite their nature.

Before the interception and identification of quality requirements occur, however, it is necessary to know the perspectives (or categories) of quality in which these requirements will be sought and placed when they are found. What immediately comes to mind is the application of a quality model, treated in this situation as a *menu*, helping to set up the research area. There is, of course, a freedom of choice from different existing models; however the practical decision must take into account the existence of verification mechanisms associated with the model of choice and the existence of measures that will allow for verification of the realization of identified quality requirements. From this perspective, the model from ISO/IEC 9126 seems to be one of the better choices, and as such will be further used in this chapter.

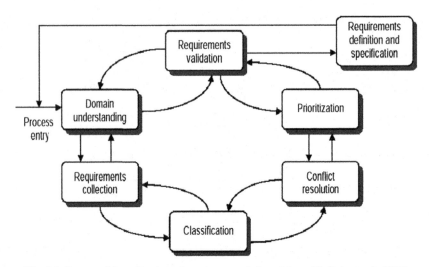

Fig. 2.7 Process of formalization of requirements (adopted from (© Robertson), 1999)

It is perhaps worthwhile to position quality requirements (based on our choice of ISO/IEC 9126 quality model) within the overall structure of software requirements. In most cases, the requirements definition phase begins with *high level of abstraction* discussions, sometimes called *business vision*, where stakeholders express their requirements in business-, service- and (quite often) usability-related terms. It is then the responsibility of an analyst to *translate* such nontechnical information into a technical representation useful in development projects. As presented in Figure 2.8, this translation may produce three immediate categories of requirements: functional, nonfunctional (quality excluded), and quality requirements. It should be stressed that the traditional categorization of quality requirements (usually only a

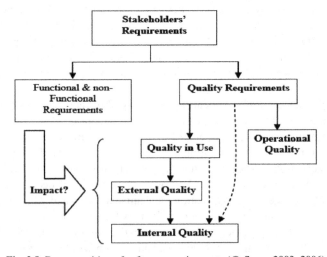

Fig. 2.8 Decomposition of software requirements (© Suryn 2003–2006)

few, arbitrarily chosen) as *nonfunctional* is replaced here by a separate, distinctive category of *quality requirements*. The latter may be further decomposed, according to ISO/IEC 9126, into quality in use, external, and internal quality requirements. In the case of a massive deployment of a software product, it may be worthwhile to consider the fourth category of quality requirements–*operational quality requirements*. This category, based on definitions published by QuEST Forum in TL 9000 standards (TL9000 2001), identifies quality attributes associated with statistical parameters of software usage.

One of the important questions a software engineer may ask could be: *why quality requirements should be treated separately and what makes them different from all other types of requirements?*

The simple answer is: while (ideally speaking) functional and nonfunctional requirements could be complete and *frozen* before any development actually starts (Figure 2.9), the quality requirements are in fact partial.

Let us examine the categories of quality requirements that can be identified when discussing a *business vision* with a stakeholder:

2.3.2.1 Operational Quality Requirements

If the software product to be developed is planned for a large population of users, this category is valid, and the analyst may seek more details to identify related requirements. If developed software is personalized, singular, or will be deployed in small quantity, this category is void because no statistically valid data will be available.

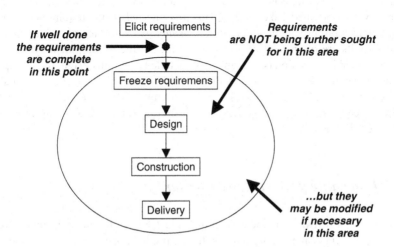

Fig. 2.9 Ideal execution of functional requirement definition

2.3.2.2 Quality in Use Requirements

Because this category represents purely application context-oriented quality requirements, the *business vision* is a good and usually rich source of information. Most
quality in use requirements could and should be identified in this phase.

2.3.2.3 External Quality Requirements

This perspective of quality refers to a software product that is complete and operational but observed from a technical perspective (like that of a technical support or
maintenance team). Because the software product does not physically exist yet, and
a business vision-oriented stakeholder is usually not able to give enough information to immediately identify external quality requirements, these requirements must
be sought either through *deduction* from quality in use requirements (results are
always partial) or further in the development cycle when more technical information is available (like high- and mid-level architectural design, for example). There
is, however, one very interesting exception—usability. This quality characteristic is
classified in ISO/IEC 9126 as *external*, but in several facets it represents end-user
concerns and can be clearly expressed by a stakeholder in the business vision phase.
As stated originally in the standard, for example, "an external learnability [metric]
should be able to assess how long users take to learn how to use particular functions,
and the effectiveness of help systems and documentation," which can be expressed
very early in the requirements definition phase.

2.3.2.4 Internal Quality Requirements

This perspective of quality applies to static artifacts like code, low-level design, and
documentation, and there is little chance to gather any useful information from a
business vision-oriented stakeholder. To identify internal quality requirements, these
requirements must be sought either through *deduction* from external quality requirements (results are often relatively rich) or further in the development cycle when
more technical information is available (like detailed program design, for example).

The above analysis (presented in Figure 2.10) signals that the software quality
requirements engineering processes may considerably differ from those associated
with classical software development, by illustrating the rather specific nature of
quality requirements.

2.3.3 From a Requirement to a Measure

When asking a software engineer from the industry what the most difficult task is
when *engineering* some quality into a software product, one may receive responses
like these (as quoted from the author's experience):

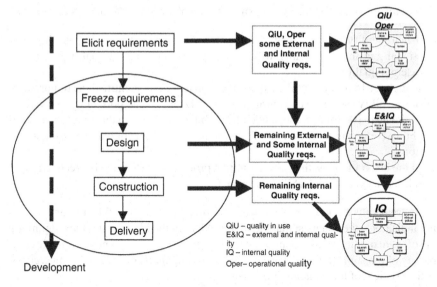

Fig. 2.10 Simplified software quality requirements identification/definition process

- Identification and further definition of quality requirements
- Translating requirements into something tangible and verifiable (let us call it *measures*)
- Making it happen, which translates into methods, processes, and sometimes even banal recipes for developing software systems that actually *have* the quality in them
- Verifying that required quality is in fact there (let us call it *evaluation*)

The fact that the definition of quality requirements is on this list of answers raises another question: *Is it really so difficult to squeeze the information required to at least start defining quality requirements from a business story?*

To answer this question, we will use the results of an experiment repeated continuously for last four years, in which software engineering master students participating in the software quality engineering course at École de technologie supérieure (Montreal, Canada) are asked to identify as many quality requirements as possible in 30-minutes from a simple business vision story presented by a window manufacturer. The windows manufacturer presented his business vision by identifying services that are required from his new IT system:

A. Control manufacturing process operational 24 hours per day
B. Allow for ERP-type production supervision (ERP – Enterprise Resource Planning)
C. Control and manage export of ready products, including adding new offices in other countries
D. Offer an online ordering service
E. Offer an online follow-up service for active orders (note indentation change– proof reader)

The results obtained during the experiment were very similar in all four sessions:

- When identifying applicable quality categories, the students ruled out the operational and internal quality without exception, focusing on quality in use and external quality
- In the first 15 minutes of the experiment, most of them identified the requirement of reliability (Service A), security (Services D and E) and portability (Service C)
- In the next 10 minutes, they added learnability, understandability, and maintainability (referring to customer's IT ignorance and international expansion ambitions)
- In the last 5 minutes, they also identified productivity (Service B), recoverability (all services) and adaptability (Service C)

These results are neither exhaustive nor complete, but they still carry an interesting indicator—they suggest that the real problem in the identification and definition of software quality requirements may not be due entirely to the unquestionable complexity of the subject. It may partially lie in missing *quality engineering awareness*, still so typical of the contemporary IT industry.

The next step is the identification of quality attributes and corresponding measures that should be applied and later measured in course of the development project.

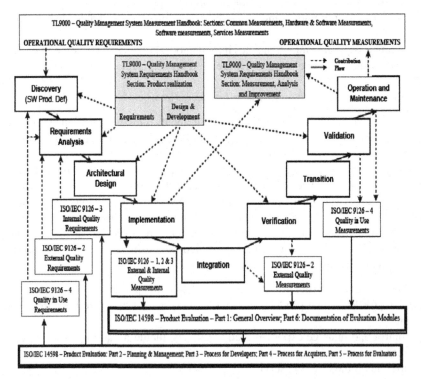

Fig. 2.11 Suryn and Abran's Consolidated Quality Lifecycle model. (© Suryn and Abran 2004–2005)

It has to be stated clearly that there is no recipe for choosing the measures, but the challenge is smaller when requirements are known.

To help a software quality engineer identify and apply the normative and/or scientific support relative to the phase of the system life cycle in which his project actually is, Suryn and Abran (Suryn 2005) created the 2004/2005 Consolidate Quality Lifecycle model (Figure 2.11). As a result, the software quality engineer may be able to identify and define quality requirements and then, using the recommended references, identify measures that best serve his professional purposes.

2.4 Software Quality – Making it Happen

2.4.1 Software Quality Implementation Model (SQIM)

In practical terms, the quality to be attained cannot be *made* here and there—a little bit today and some more tomorrow. As a matter of fact, a good, recommended practice is to start engineering the quality the moment the development project has been opened. This approach, however, requires a tool—a method that will rule and control quality engineering activities in concert with those of software development. Such a tool, called the Software Quality Implementation Model (SQIM), is presented in Figure 2.12. Four basic hypotheses lie at foundations of developing SQIM:

1. Engineering quality into a software product is an effort that should be conducted throughout the whole life cycle of software development.
2. Because the process of quality engineering is similar in many ways to a development process, it seems appropriate that it follows similar rules and applies similar structures.
3. Because several software development process models exist, SQIM adheres to the most widely recognized and accepted, which is the generic model published in ISO/IEC 15288 Information Technology – Life Cycle Management – System Life Cycle Processes.
4. The quality model that SQIM adheres to is the one that is widely accepted and recognized—the quality model from ISO/IEC 9126.

SQIM (Suryn 2003) is organized in phases that correspond to phases of the generic development process, indicating activities that are required from a software quality engineer to attain quality in each of the phases. It can be noted that the subject of complexity of software quality requirements definition is clearly addressed in SQIM, offering guidance on what could and should be identified and defined (and when) to the user.

Each phase of SQIM has its own set of activities and subprocesses that should be observed by a quality engineer in his or her daily practice. For details, interested readers may refer to Suryn and Gil (2005). The engineers who seek a practical complement to SQIM can refer to the Consolidated Quality Lifecycle model (CQL) presented earlier.

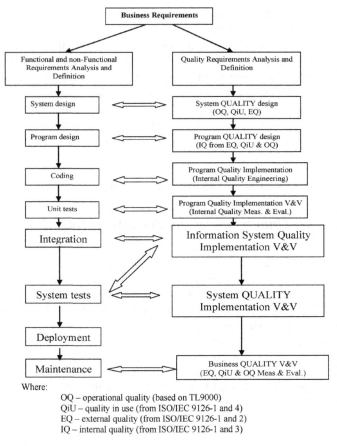

Fig. 2.12 Software Quality Implementation Model SQIM. (© Suryn 2003–2006)

2.4.2 Managing the Process of Software Quality Engineering

When undertaking the challenge of managing software quality engineering, one could take into consideration a few basic facts from life:

- Everything in software engineering boils down to user satisfaction
- Satisfaction is conditional on the overall behavior of the system, with the software product in first place
- The behavior of any software product is perceived through *features* and *quality*
- The features and quality of the software product are expressed through requirements
- Any behavior-related requirement for a software product may only be realized through code

With the above in mind, let us consider the following statement:

In most development projects, functionality and quality are natural enemies.

Fig. 2.13 Functionality-
quality battlefield. (© Suryn
2003–2006)

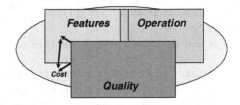

Is it really true? Unfortunately for all IT users, it is true. There are, in fact, very rare situations where the project budget is open. In all other cases, the budget defines the battlefield where functionality and quality fight for the upper hand.

It is rather easy to imagine why quality and functionality are enemies in projects with a *predefined* budget. It is even easier to identify the winner. As shown below, function-quality-cost (FQC) economic perspectives are merciless: implementation of functionalities and quality is expensive, so for a constant budget (C), more functions (af) mean less quality (bq) (© Suryn 2003–2006). And the converse is also true, but this is much more rare than the former situation. From what can be observed in the market of software products, functionalities constantly win, even if such victories quite often prove short-sighted. The first positive impressions based on functional richness quickly turn into disappointment or rage when the software starts producing *blue screens*.

Economic perspective

$$\text{Cost} = a \sum \text{features} + b \sum \text{quality aspects}$$

or

$$C = af + bq$$

Where:

a, b – proportions of investment

So, is a software quality engineer in a lost position by default? Well, the position surely is not an easy or comfortable one, but it is still manageable and capable of success, as long as some of the recommendations below are taken into consideration:

- From the very beginning, negotiate functional requirements with quality requirements in mind. Later may be too late
- Evaluate the list of *features* against the budget as soon as possible. This will be your first indication about a possible level of quality, and your first argument in renegotiating the FQC proportions
- Any functionality has its quality counterpart. FIND IT!
- The quality counterpart may require *development* or other forms of *expenditures*. Take it into account when evaluating the project
- Analyze the existing FQC well. If the Q (quality) part is considerably too low, the project may quickly run into a high-risk scenario

- A new functionality may kill the overall quality of the product, so negotiate carefully
- A new quality requirement rarely or never harms the product

Apart from the common duties of planning and managing a project, managing software quality engineering also presents the considerable and difficult duty of change and conflict management. The higher than usual level of difficulty of this task comes from heavy interdependence between development and quality engineering processes and their final results (Suryn 2003).

2.4.3 Direct and Cross-Traceability – Model CTM

There is a very important rule in software engineering that states: *Any software/system component that cannot be traced to at least one requirement has been developed for nothing and the resources used to develop it must be booked as a loss* (rephrased after Pfleeger, 2005).

This is also very true in software quality engineering, but the situation is a bit more complex. The classic traceability approach presented in the lower part of Figure 2.14 documents the links between all generic phases of the development process and their related by-products to the requirements. Jointly applying SQIM, ISO/IEC 9126, and CQL allowed for creating a complementary model dedicated to quality traceability (QTM, upper part of Figure 2.14), with every link from lowest level quality measure traceable to quality requirements. Merging the two models and adding an intermediate influence layer between the two parts gives a

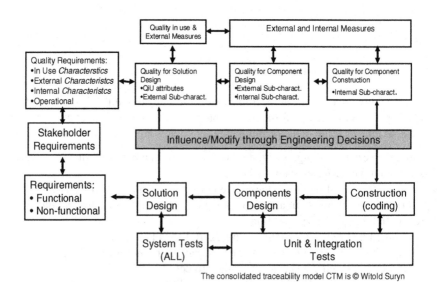

The consolidated traceability model CTM is © Witold Suryn

Fig. 2.14 Consolidated traceability model for software quality engineering. (© Suryn 2003–2006)

consolidated traceability model (CTM) allowing for building complete functionality/quality traceability matrix (Figure 2.14).

The model incorporates both technological and procedural structures that help to identify the correspondence between the stages of development, related by-products, associated quality elements (by-products or attributes), and requirements of all types. The engineer can thus monitor the relationships among all of them and then trace them back to their relevant requirements.

2.4.4 Synchronizing Quality and Software Engineering

How could the synchronization of quality engineering and software development processes be attained? There is no one good answer to this question. A large, mature, and professional organization could steer in the direction of a specialized group, with members being *continuously* involved in development team work, while a start-up company might prefer the *discreet involvement* of a part-time quality specialist. It all depends on available resources and the goals to be reached. When comparing both methods, the first impression may be that the discreet approach is rarely recommendable. If the developed software is created for the first time (and so has some R&D taste) this impression has its merit, but when the system is being continuously manufactured and sold for several years, all the *secrets* are most likely known by the development team, and quality engineering may be quite effective even if applied in a discrete form. Continuous synchronization between quality engineering and software development processes, while being much more resource-consuming, offers an incomparably higher level of controllability and effectiveness at the same time.

Whatever the method and phase of the project, a software quality engineer brings a unique expertise to the team, allowing the *nonquality* specialists to develop software that can demonstrate high quality and help maintain the budget and schedule.

2.4.5 Applying SQIM in Most Popular Development Models

In the case of the V-model, the mapping to SQIM is straightforward, because the V-model itself is very closely linked to the model proposed in ISO/IEC 15288, which lies at the foundations of SQIM. For a basic spiral model, because its third quadrant (*develop, verify next-level product*) contains most of the engineering activities, mapping SQIM to it requires some repositioning of its phases in order to build the applicative links.

In the prototyping model, the application of SQIM requires that one take into consideration the repetitive nature of each phase of this model. Each phase of SQIM associated with its counterpart in the prototyping model will have to run through the same loops of verifying and validating before the obtained status will allow you to move to the next phase.

Last but not least, mapping SQIM to the incremental model can be reduced to a choice from the three options discussed above. The very nature of the incremental model describes the way in which a software product is being *delivered* more than the way in which it is really developed.

2.5 Conclusions

While evaluating the maturity of a software development organization, one can apply sophisticated methods and models like CCMI, SPICE, or ISO9000, and still arrive at a conclusion that may not entirely reflect reality. All best processes will not replace the tangible indicators of the real maturity—functionalities and quality of the product. One may even say that because functionalities are always in a product, but quality is only sometimes, quality is a more restrictive indicator. Having this in mind, we presented software quality engineering from both implementation and managerial perspectives, and discussed aspects of functionality-quality conflict in the economic and business dimensions to finally give a few practical observations and recommendations that might establish their merit in the real, software development lifecycle.

References

ABET. www.abet.org.

Azuma, M. (2001). *SQuaRE -Software product quality requirements and evaluation*. Revision of WG6 N474 based on discussion at the C7/WG6 Prague Meeting ISO/IEC JTC1/SC7/WG6.

Boehm, B. W., Brown, J. R., Kaspar, J. R., Lipow, M. L. & MacCleod, G. (1978). *Characteristics of software quality*. New York: American Elsevier.

Bourque, P., Dupuis, R., Abran, A., Moore, J.W., Tripp, L., & Wolff, S. (2002). Fundamental principles of software engineering – A Journey. *Journal of Systems and Software, 62*(1), 59–70.

Capability Maturity Model Integration (CMMI) (2002).Version 1.1. Software Engineering Institute. Pittsburgh, PA: Carnegie Mellon University.

Dromey, R. G. (1995). A model for software product quality. *IEEE Transactions on Software Engineering, 21*, 146–162.

El Emam, K., Drouin, J-N., & Melo, W. (1997). *Spice: The Theory and Practice of Software Process Improvement and Capability Determination*. Wiley-IEEE Computer Society Press.

Highsmith, J. (2002). *Agile software development ecosystems*. Addison-Wesley Professional.

ISO/IEC 12207 (1995). *Information technology – Software life cycle processes*. Geneva, Switzerland: International Organization for Standardization.

ISO/IEC 15504 Parts 1–5 (1998–2006). *Information technology – software process assessment* (in development). Geneva, Switzerland: International Organization for Standardization.

ISO/IEC 15939 (2002). *Information technology – software engineering – software measurement process*. Geneva, Switzerland: International Organization for Standardization.

ISO/IEC 9000(2000). *Quality management systems -Fundamentals and vocabulary*. Geneva, Switzerland: International Organization for Standardization.

ISO/IEC 9126-1 (2001): *Software engineering-software product quality-Part 1: Quality model*. Geneva, Switzerland: International Organization for Standardization.

ISO/IEC DTR 9126-4 (2001). *Software engineering-Software product quality-Part 4: Quality in use metrics*. Geneva, Switzerland: International Organization for Standardization.

ISO/IEC TR 9126-2 (2003a). *Software engineering-software product quality-Part 2 : External metrics*. Geneva, Switzerland: International Organization for Standardization.

ISO/IEC TR 9126-3 (2003b): *Software engineering-Software product quality-Part 3: Internal metrics*. Geneva, Switzerland: International Organization for Standardization.

Kitchenham, B., & Pfleeger, S.L. (1996). Software quality: The elusive target. *IEEE Software, 13*(1), 12–21.

McCall, J. A., Richards, P. K., & Walters, G. F. (1977). *Factors in software quality*. Griffiths Air Force Base, N.Y.: Rome Air Development Center Air Force Systems Command.

Pfleeger S. L. (2005). *Software engineering – theory and practice* (3rd ed.) Prentice-Hall.

Robertson, S., & Robertson, J. (1999). *Mastering the requirements process*. Addison-Wesley.

Suryn ,W., & Abran, A. (2003). ISO/IEC SQuaRE. The 2nd generation of standard for quality of software product. *Proceedings of 7th IASTED International Conference on Software Engineering and Applications* (pp. 807–814), SEA 2003, November 3–5, 2003, Marina del Rey, CA, USA.

Suryn, W. (2003). *Ingénierie de la qualité logicielle"*. *École de Technologie Supérieure*, Montréal, Canada. 2003–2006.

Suryn, W., & Gil, B. (2005). ISO/IEC9126–3 internal quality measures: are they still useful? *Proceedings of 11th International Conference on Human-Computer Interaction*, Volume 8, CD-ROM, 22–27 July 2005, Las Vegas, USA.

Suryn, W., & Girard, D. (2005). Consolidated Quality Lifecycle (CQL) Model – the Applicative Evolution. *Proceedings of 8th International Conference on Business Information Systems (BIS 2005)*. Poznan, Poland, 20–22 April 2005. Pages 126–146.

Suryn W., Kahlaoui A., Georgiadou E. (2005). Quality engineering process for the Program Design Phase of a generic software life cycle. *Proceedings of 13th International Software Quality Management & INSPIRE Conference 2005* (pp. 253–266), Gloucestershire, Cheltenham, UK 21–23 March 2005.

Suryn, W., Stambollian, A., Dormeux, J-C.,& Bégnoche, L. (2006). Software quality engineering – where to find it in Software Engineering Body of Knowledge (SWEBOK). *Proceedings of 14th International Software Quality Management & INSPIRE Conference 2006* (pp. 97–110), Southampton, Hampshire, UK 10–12 April 2006.

SWEBOK (2004). *Guide to the Software Engineering Body of Knowledge*, Version 2004, SWEBOK®. A project of the IEEE Computer Society Professional Practices Committee, http://www.swebok.org.

TL9000 (2001). Quality Management System Requirements Handbook, Release 3.0. *QuEST Forum* 2001.

Chapter 3
Connecting Rigorous System Analysis to Experience-Centered Design

Michael Harrison[1], José Creissac Campos[2], Gavin Doherty[3] and Karsten Loer[4]

[1] Informatics Research Institute, Newcastle University, UK,
  e-mail: Michael.Harrison@newcastle.ac.uk
[2] Department of Informatics/CCTC, University of Minho, Portugal
[3] Department of Computer Science, Trinity College Dublin, Ireland
[4] Division Strategic Research and Development, Germanischer Lloyd AG, Germany

Abstract This chapter explores the role that formal modelling may play in aiding the visualization and implementation of usability, with a particular emphasis on experience requirements in an ambient and mobile system. Mechanisms for requirements elicitation and evaluation are discussed, as well as the role of scenarios and their limitations in capturing experience requirements. The chapter then discusses the role of formal modelling by revisiting an analysis based on an exploration of traditional usability requirements before moving on to consider requirements more appropriate to a built environment. The role of modelling within the development process is re-examined by looking at how models may incorporate knowledge relating to user experience, and how the results of the analysis of such models may be exploited by human factors and domain experts in their consideration of user experience issues.

3.1 Introduction

Ambient and mobile systems are often used to bring information and services to the users of physical environments that are technology rich. Examples include leisure complexes, hospitals, airports, and museums. Such systems are always on in the background, and they deploy information to the user according to their context and location. Their success depends on how users *experience* the space in which they are situated, as well as more conventional issues of usability. What experiencing a system in a particular way might mean is difficult to express and implement in a system. Examples of experience are the experience of *place* as opposed to a forbidding sterile space within a built environment, or anxiety (or lack of anxiety) when traveling in an unfamiliar world. This chapter is concerned with whether systems will satisfy experience requirements and how this framework for reasoning might be integrated with more traditional analyses of interaction with the devices and displays involved. The chapter is speculative about the set of tools and techniques required to achieve experience-centered design. Its purpose is also to explore issues relating

E. Law et al. (eds.), *Maturing Usability.*

to the maturity of more formal usability analysis tools, and to broaden an understanding of usability. In this respect, it explores a combination of formal techniques and prototyping in assessing these further qualities of experience in the design of an interactive system.

A focus on experience in ambient and mobile systems provides an opportunity for a fresh look at evaluation in interactive systems. Traditional notions of usability need reconsideration. Ambient and mobile systems have distinctive characteristics that lead to a requirement for special treatment:

- The impact of the environment as the major contributor in understanding how the system should work—its texture and complexity
- The use of location and other features of context to infer implicit or incidental user action—how natural and transparent this inference is

A distinction is made here between the *physical* environment (the walls, windows, notices, and position of the public displays and passengers within this environment) and the software model of context (what the system knows about the physical environment and the user). Context is updated by interaction with the environment and by tracking user characteristics—what they do and what they like. Physical environment is crucial to an understanding of how the system is experienced. For this reason, it is difficult to envisage how a system can be evaluated during early design stages before the full system has been configured in its proposed target environment. The chapter explores how experience requirements can be related to more rigorous methods of software development, as a means of capturing important characteristics of the design even at the early stages.

Although the chapter is mainly concerned with how experience requirements can be gathered and applied in ambient and mobile systems, the techniques described are also relevant to more traditional usability requirements. For this reason, the first example focuses on how a method of analysis can be applied to more traditional usability properties. Section 3.2 discusses methods for eliciting experience requirements and explores the limitations of scenarios and personae. Section 3.3 explores methods of assessing and evaluating a proposed design against such requirements. The ingredients and requirements for a tool that combines the analysis of usability requirements with experience requirements are developed. Two examples are discussed. The first focuses on usability requirements for a mobile device that supports process control (Section 3.4). The second focuses on experience requirements by considering how information flows (Section 3.5) within an airport system. Finally, the chapter sketches a future agenda for completing a toolset to support the established objectives.

3.2 Eliciting and Making Sense of User Experience Requirements

It is difficult to assess whether particular usability requirements are implemented in ambient and mobile systems without observing systems in their target contexts. This creates a problem, because it is usually infeasible to explore the role of a prototype system in this way, particularly when failure of the system might have safety or commercial consequences. For example, a prototype running in a busy airport will certainly have consequences for passenger satisfaction and, therefore, commercial consequences if it fails, and may have consequences if crucial safety information is not provided in a timely way. Methods are needed to enable the implementation of usability and experience requirements and to explore whether they are satisfied in the implemented system. Here it is envisaged that implementation of requirements means that a typical user's experience is consistent with the requirements. Ideally, this kind of assessment should be realistically possible before expensive decisions are made.

Two mobile and ambient systems are examined. The first example is used to focus the analysis on more conventional usability requirements. It relates to the design of a mobile device to control a chemical process. The second focuses on how a system might capture experience requirements. It concerns a system designed to provide information to passengers in an airport. Two brief scenarios illustrate the second example. This example provides the chapter's main illustration of experience requirements.

> **Scenario One**: Upon entry to the departures hall, a sensor recognizes the electronic ticket and subscribes the passenger to the appropriate flight, while updating the passenger's context to include current position in the departures hall. The flight service publishes information about the status and identity of queues for check-in. A message directing the passenger to the optimal queue is received by the passenger's hand-held device, because the passenger's context filter contained in the device permits its arrival. This information is displayed on a public display in the departures hall. When the passenger enters the queue, a sensor detects entry and adds the queue identifier to the passenger information. As a result, different messages about the flight are received by the passenger—this might include information about seating so that the passenger can choose a seat while waiting to check in baggage. This process continues as the passenger progresses through the various stages of embarkation.

> **Scenario Two**: The passenger enters the main hall. The passenger is now additionally subscribed to a retail service. Information about available facilities is received by the passenger according to preferences and flight status.

Eliciting usability requirements, including experience requirements, for an envisaged ambient and mobile system can be carried out using a combination of techniques. Some of these techniques have been developed to deal with the broader class of usability requirements of a system.

First, stories can be gathered about the current system, capturing a variety of issues relating to usability and experience—both normal and extreme. Different types of user or persona (see Grudin & Pruitt [2002] for a discussion of the role of personae) can be used to explore the particular requirements of user types. The results of this story-gathering process are a collection of scenarios that can be used to explore how the new design would behave. They can be used to evaluate the design (see, for example, Rosson & Carroll 2002), perhaps using a specification of the design or using a rapidly developed prototype.

In addition to scenario-orientated techniques for elicitation, other techniques are valuable. Techniques such as cultural probes (Gaver et al. 1999) can be used to elicit *snapshot experiences*. The elicitation process here involves subjects collecting material—photographs, notes, sound recordings—to capture important features of their environment. While these snippets may make sense as part of a story, they may equally well be aspects of the current system that are common across a range of experiences or stories.

A further process of probing is described by Buchenau & Suri (2002). Their approach (*experience-centered design*) involves the construction of prototypes— sometimes very inexpensive and approximate prototypes—which can be used to imagine the experience that users would have with the design. The quality and detail tends to vary, from *mocking up* (using prototypes that simply look like the proposed device but have no function), to more detailed prototypes that are closer to the final system. In the earliest stages, this technique can be used for requirements elicitation, while in the later stages more refined prototypes may be evaluated. To explore and to visualize the proposed design effectively, it is important that systems can be developed with agility, trying out ideas and disposing of prototypes that are not effective and using a context that is close to the proposed target environment. They help envision the role of the *to-be-developed* artefact within the user's activity. Prototypes can be used to *probe*—that is, explore how valid and representative the scenarios are and thereby generate a discussion about alternative or additional scenarios. Testing the prototypes appropriately can help develop an understanding of the experience of the system in its proposed setting.

In the settings illustrated in this chapter, there are a combination of ambient displays, kiosks, and mobile services for hand-held devices. Facilities and information provided by services are distributed through the built environment by means of hand-held devices and public displays, making use of context information to infer parameters to supply to the services. They combine to provide an environment in which passengers can obtain the information they need, in a form that they can use it, to experience the place. Information about the environment relevant to an understanding of this experience might be captured using a combination of cultural probes and scenario analysis. For example, in the case of cultural probes, passengers might be asked to identify those elements in the space that relate strongly to their experience of the airport, perhaps by taking photographs or making audio-video recordings and then annotating these snapshots. In addition, they might be asked to tell stories about situations where they did or did not experience place. The following examples might derive from such elicitation:

- Photographs of the main display board with comments such as, "I like to be in a seat in which I can see this display board"; "I wish that the display board would tell me something about my flight—it disturbs me when it simply says wait in lounge"
- Photographs of signposts pointing to where the gate is annotated with "I wish I had better information about how far it was and whether there were likely to be any delays on the way"
- Tape recordings of helpful announcements and unhelpful announcements, with annotations such as "These announcements do not happen often enough and announcements for other flights distract me"

- Stories about where the airport helped the customer feel aware of what was happening, for example: "There has been an incident at Paris airport which means that one of the runways has been closed"
- Stories of long and complicated situations that may have caused problems. For example, a narrative describing how the airline provided new tickets for a different airline for the passenger to fly to Los Angeles via London, managed the retrieval of baggage and organized checking in again, or simply caused the passenger to have to move from location to location to collect the bags, get the new ticket and check in

In this way, an idea can be obtained about how the system works. Further elicitation gathers information about noncentral features of the system, capturing stories that deal with other subsets of the facilities and functionality—for example, relating to food services, dealing with extreme situations, or where there are reasons for delay. Another story might relate to whether there is enough time to get a meal and whether the meal is vegetarian. Throughout this process, in the spirit of an agile approach to development, more than one prototype would be developed to explore the different stories, producing segmented functionality—for example, a prototype dealing with flights and flight schedules and a prototype dealing with retail services. Prototypes might be explored, running in-situ using the user stories as the means of testing, exploring the prototype in a simulation of the situation, and assessing whether an experience of place is being contributed to. This means that the whole system might be built using partial prototypes, thereby reducing the need to wait until a complete system is available. These prototypes can be explored both from the perspective of user experience and from the perspective of usability.

A limited set of scenarios cannot capture all aspects of the experience of place in the airport. The value of cultural probes is that they provide an orthogonal viewpoint. To achieve an experience of place, the familiar things—for example, the constant presence of the notice board—must be captured across scenarios. Further exploration may be required to assess and probe how well these static elements of the environment (such as the continually present notice board) are represented across a wider set of design behaviors. It is also necessary to investigate the unforeseen consequences of the proposed design—for example, a passenger walking close to another passenger whose flight is closing might miss important information about a gate change because of the urgent messages displayed for the late passenger. The complexity and interaction between the different components of the system may result in unexpected, emergent properties of behaviors. As a system design evolves, so will the experience associated with using the system. This can contribute to producing a more consistent overall experience, even though the design of the system has emerged in piecemeal fashion.

The physical characteristics of alternative platforms may be important in contributing to the experience of sense of place—frequent flyers may use smart phones, large plasma screens may be placed in the space in a number of different ways. The advantage of using walkthrough techniques is that early exploration may be carried out before the platform is decided, and may assist an understanding of whether a particular combination of system components is appropriate.

Given some means of eliciting the significant requirements, the next question is to assess whether a design or implementation will satisfy them.

3.3 Analysis and Evaluation

McCarthy and Wright (2004) have argued that while the emphasis within the GUI paradigm has been on technology as tools, the new paradigms require thought about the technology we live with (see also Bannon 2005). Elsewhere, this has been characterized as a shift from understanding the use of artifacts to understanding their presence in people's lives (Halnass & Redstrom 2002). While user-centered design helps understand the practices and routines into which technologies are expected to fit, it is not helpful in accounting for feelings of resistance, engagement, identification, disorientation, and dislocation. Prototypes can be explored from a variety of perspectives—from a spectrum of usability-engineering evaluation techniques to *experiencing* explorations through active engagement with prototypes (see Buchenau & Suri 2000). The techniques that are used should be formative. Therefore, prototypes developed within the simulated scene may be used to stimulate communication and the exploration of design ideas as a dialogical process between user, designer and software engineer. A number of techniques may be used to identify the experience characteristics of a design.

3.3.1 Scenario Analysis

Scenario analysis (Rosson & Carroll, 2002) can be used at a number of levels to explore the role that the system might play, and to evaluate usability and experience issues. Scenarios can be used to capture important characteristics of the environment, either typical uses of the system or *critical incidents* where current arrangements have failed users. They can be analyzed by usability engineers to explore how the system would work—what information would be displayed at specific times within the scenario, what actions the user would have to take to obtain further information, and so on. Techniques such as cognitive walkthrough (Lewis et al. 1990) and THEA (Pocock et al. 2001) are designed to be used at the action level by usability engineers who have enough knowledge of the environment. Both approaches involve consideration of a sufficiently detailed scenario to be able to visualize the design. While reservations are appropriate in terms of their objectivity (Gray & Salzmann 1998), they are nevertheless of value as a formative mechanism in the hands of designers because they provide feedback that can be used constructively to improve the design.

Scenarios can also be *visualized* by users. In other words, they are encouraged to re-experience the scenario in their imaginations in the context of the new design. This might involve the user adopting a persona (Grudin & Pruitt 2002)—for example, a frequent flyer who is also an anxious flyer. This would not create a detailed account of how the technology works, but would provide an impression of aspects that require further analysis. There are, of course, problems with this approach. Ideally, assessing how an artifact contributes to the experience requires observation or an assessment of the artifact embedded in the proposed situation. Although experience prototypes can be constructed, an important issue is how to provide a simulation of the envisaged environment. The aim is that there are sufficiently realistic scenarios that a *passenger-to-be* might visualize the effect that the proposed technology would have and how it would feel to use it. Consider, for example, a system developed to help passengers experience a sense of place at check-in, security screening, passport control, and while waiting in the main body of the airport, encouraging passengers to make use of the many facilities available to them.

3.3.2 Alternatives to Scenario Analysis

Scenario analysis inevitably restricts consideration of the system to particular situations as captured by a limited number of narratives. Issues of coverage, therefore, become important. In practice, requirements that relate to experience lead to properties that hold true whatever the circumstances, and cannot, therefore, be captured in a limited set of scenarios. Experience-level requirements that can be captured specifically for the application in question can be used as probes of a design representation in the same way as usability heuristics (Nielsen 1992), perhaps using the expertise of a multidisciplinary team.

Campos and Harrison (2001), as well as Loer and Harrison (2006), explore the synergistic role that modelling and scenario-based evaluation can play. In these papers, properties that capture formal expressions of usability heuristics are used to generate traces. Traces are sequences of states or actions in the model that serve to demonstrate a situation where the property does not hold. Domain experts can use a bare sequence of actions to create a plausible narrative to form the basis for a scenario. This scenario can then be subjected to an analysis such as a cognitive walkthrough to explore potential problems with the design interface. Alternative perspectives can be explored using representative personae. Consider an example of mode confusion—a system is checked for some formal representation of mode confusion and a trace is generated that indicates a circumstance where confusion might occur. This forms the basis for a scenario that is investigated.

It is quite possible that, although formally there is mode confusion, the interface signals the mode clearly. While a persona representing a newly trained operator will perceive the mode change, an experienced operator who has seen and ignored the signal many times is more likely to fail to notice it. This kind of analysis can also be carried out for properties that result from an exploration of the experience requirements of the design. Suppose that a passenger reports that she wants to be able to access up-to-date flight information wherever she is. An appropriate model might be used to explore possible physical paths in the environment that passengers might take to reach the flight gate, and whether up-to-date flight information is always available. This approach is analogous to that taken in Loer and Harrison

(2005), where a system is explored that controls a process either using a central control room or a hand-held PDA. This will be explored in more detail in the next section.

3.3.3 Modelling and Prototyping

Formal modelling techniques and agile software development may together make contributions to experience-centered design, as well as in the assessment of more conventional usability. As discussed above, the modelling approach provides the basis for exploring paths—that is, sequences of states of the system. These paths can be used by domain experts or usability experts to create narratives that can then be used to explore how the system would be experienced through an appropriate evaluation technique. The modelling challenge is to develop a model at an appropriate level of detail to provide a basis for expressing properties, and thereby generating appropriate sequences. The prototyping issue is to be able to produce systems quickly enough to explore the role that the system will play. Here, modelling and analysis based on model-checking provides a more rigorous analysis of unforeseen consequences. Once scenarios have been described, they can be visualized through a variety of means, as discussed in the previous section.

For example, a team-based analysis approach might make use of model animation following a sequence, using tools supported by systems such as uppaal (Behrmann, et al. 2004). Alternatively, the model may be used as a basis for the construction of a *throw-away* prototype. The prototype can then be used to explore an elicited scenario in some more realistic situation with potential users. An envisaged design process is depicted in Figure 3.1.

By this means, agile techniques (Agile 2004) are combined with formal techniques. The complementary nature of the approaches is enhanced if the software

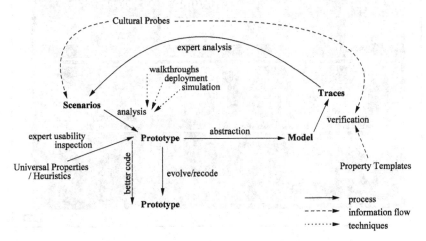

Fig. 3.1 The formal process of experience requirements exploration

framework with which the prototype is developed has a semantic underpinning that will assure the designer that the prototype is consistent with the properties of the model.

The two examples already introduced illustrate a range of properties, capturing features of two types of ambient and mobile systems. In the first example, the focus of the exploration is the interface with a mobile device, where the behavior of the device is affected by its location within a processing plant. The analysis compares a proposed new interface to the handheld device with the existing control room interface. The focus of the specification in this example is the device design in the context of a controlled process model and its location. In the second example, the focus is the model of the broader system in the built environment, concerned with location sensors, passenger devices, and public displays, and the means by which information is distributed through the environment.

3.4 Properties of Interactive Devices

The system involves the operator interface to a process control system from a centralized control room (see Figure 3.2), as well as an alternative hand-held device (see Figure 3.3) (Nilsson et al. 2000). A limited subset of information and controls for these components is *stored* in the hand-held device to ease access to them in the future—analogous to putting them on the desktop. These desktop spaces are called *buckets* in Nilsson et al. (2000).

The operator can view and control the current state of the components when in their immediate vicinity. Context is used in identifying the position of an operator,

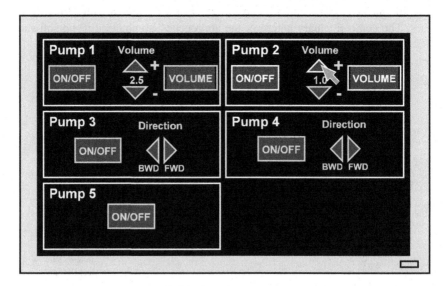

Fig. 3.2 Control screen layout

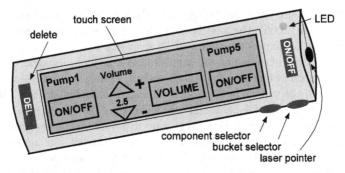

Fig. 3.3 A hand-held control device (modified version of the *Pucketizer* in Nilsson, et al. (2000))

checking the validity of a given action, inferring an operator's intention, and checking action against an operator's schedule, while assessing and indicating the urgency of these actions.

In this type of system, context confusions can be avoided through design by changing the action structure (for example, using interlocks) so that these ambiguities are avoided, or by clearly marking the differences to users. There are a variety of other properties that could be considered here, including experience requirements—for example, a requirement of the system is that it should provide an experience that enhances the safe operation of the system. Requirements associated with such experience criteria might include a requirement that the operator maintains overall situation awareness about the plant, or ready access to current data trends to provide confidence that the system is running smoothly. The analysis takes the exploratory approach described in the previous section to scrutinize *interesting* traces. Questions or properties are articulated in linear temporal logic (LTL) via a number of templates designed to make the formulation of properties in LTL easier for human factors engineers. The properties are used to check models using the SMV model checker (McMillan, 1993). Details of the specifications and of the mechanism for formulating properties using templates, and the link with SMV is described in Loer and Harrison (2006). They are omitted here because the emphasis is on the process of analysis rather than the detailed specification.

The hand-held device, the control room, and the plant were modelled using Statecharts (Harel 1987). A possible set of top-level requirements that might plausibly have been elicited is that the interactive system

- Should inform the operator about progress
- Should allow the operator to intervene appropriately to control the process
- Should alert the operator to alarming conditions in the plant
- Should enable recovery from these conditions

The plant involves tanks, pipes, valves, and pumps that feed material between tanks. The tanks are designed to be used for more than one process, and to change processes a tank must be evacuated before material can be pumped into it. To achieve this, some of the pumps are bidirectional. The functioning of the plant—the flows and evacuations—can be expressed as a simple discrete model so the significant features of the environment can be explored. This is discussed in more detail in Loer and Harrison (2006). The model of the plant captures the characteristics of the plant in the simplest terms consistent with its relevance to the actions and displays provided in the control room and the handheld device. Hence the state of the tank is simply described as one element of the set {full, empty, holding}—there is no notion of quantity or volume in the model. This is a minimal model that will allow analysis to take account of the physical consequences of the system.

The control room, with its central panel, aims to provide the plant operator with a comprehensive overview of the status of all devices in the plant. Situation awareness is considered to be critical to the operator's work in the system and can be seen to be contributing to the operator's experience so that they know what is going on. Availability and visibility of action are therefore seen to be primary concerns. For this reason, a model of the interface is chosen that focuses on these aspects of the design. Other models can also be considered to focus on other facets—for example, alarms or recoverability. The control panel is implemented by a mouse-controlled screen (see Figure 3.2). Screen icons are both displays and controls at the same time—clicking on an icon will have an effect. These features of the design are all modelled, showing when icons are illuminated and when actions trigger corresponding actions in the underlying process.

The hand-held device uses individual controls that are identical to the central control panel. However, there is only a limited amount of space available for them. As a controller walks past a pump, she may *save* controls onto the display. While the controls continue to be visible on the display, the pumps relating to the controls can be manipulated from anywhere in the system. The hand-held control device (Figure 3.3) knows its position within the spatial organization of the plant. An area that merits further consideration is the visibility of these displays and the status of saved controls.

By being in the vicinity of a plant component and pressing the component selector button, the status information for that component and its controls are transferred into the currently selected bucket. Components can be removed from a bucket by pressing the Delete button. The user can cycle through buckets using the Bucket Selector button. The specification of the hand-held device describes both the physical buttons that are accessible continuously, and other control elements like pump control icons that are available temporarily and depend on the position of the device. When the operator approaches a pump, its controls are automatically displayed on the screen (it only requires an explicit component selection if the controls and status information are to be saved in a bucket). Controls for plant devices in locations other than the current one can be accessed remotely if they have been previously stored in a bucket. When a plant component is available in a bucket, and the bucket is selected, the hand-held device can transmit commands to the processing plant, using the pump control icons.

In the case of the hand-held control device, the interface to be explored is the device in the context of its environment. The environment in this case is a composition of the tank content model and the device position model. The model presumes that the appliance should always know its location. An alternative approach would allow the designer to explore interaction issues when there is a dissonance between the states of the device and its location. The effect of the type of software architecture used to implement these types of system is to mask the possibility of discrepancy from the implementer.

To explore the effect of the difference between the control room and the hand-held device, and to generate traces that may be of interest, a reachability property is formulated for a user-level system goal. The goal chosen here for illustration is Produce substance C. This is a primary purpose of the system. The analysis proceeds by making a comparison between traces generated by the alternative models, using domain knowledge and user experience to generate appropriate scenarios. The checker is used to generate traces. An iterative process can be used to generate an interesting trace, successively refining the property being checked to include further assumptions about the requirements of the interaction.

Such analysis can also incorporate assumptions about user tasks (see Fields 2001). In Fields' thesis, the model checker is used to explore the defined task—a particular way in which the goal is designed to be achieved. This chapter takes the alternative perspective that any behaviors required to achieve a goal may be of interest. Fields (2001) acknowledges the possibility that a user might not perform tasks in the ways that were originally envisaged.

The sequences in Figure 3.4 represent the traces obtained by checking for different models, including representing different devices and adding constraints to capture some characteristics of users. In each case, the sequence gives one example of how the plant can deliver Substance C to the outside world. The property asserts that Pump 5 will eventually be turned on with Tank 1 holding Substance C. The target state in this case is openP5 (see Figure 3.4). These sequences provide the basis for the scenarios that the domain expert or human factors expert will use to assess the interaction. A narrative based around the sequence could be used by a potential operator to visualize the experience that they would have using the designed system. This process of visualization may be aided by a process of stepping through the specification using path exploration tools, as provided by several model checkers. Alternatively, the generated scenario may be used as the basis for exploring a prototype of all or part of the system. The first sequence in Figure 3.4 has been constructed by checking the property against the control room interface, while the other sequences were checked against the hand-held device model. While the first two sequences assume a serial use of pumps, the third and fourth sequences achieve the same goal with a concurrent use of pumps. Simple comparison of these sequences yields information about the additional steps that have to be performed to achieve the same goal.

As a result of this process—and, in particular, the comparison—it is observed that the repetitive process of saving controls may cause slips or mistakes—a direct effect of location on the actions of the hand-held device. While these slips or mistakes may not be dangerous, it may be concluded that the frustration of continual delays due to omitting actions may be significant. A further assumption can be used to constrain the property, namely that an operator might forget certain steps.

If it is assumed that controls for the pumps are not saved and the original property is checked, the sixth sequence in Figure 3.4 is obtained. This sequence highlights the likelihood of context confusions as well as user frustrations, and therefore the

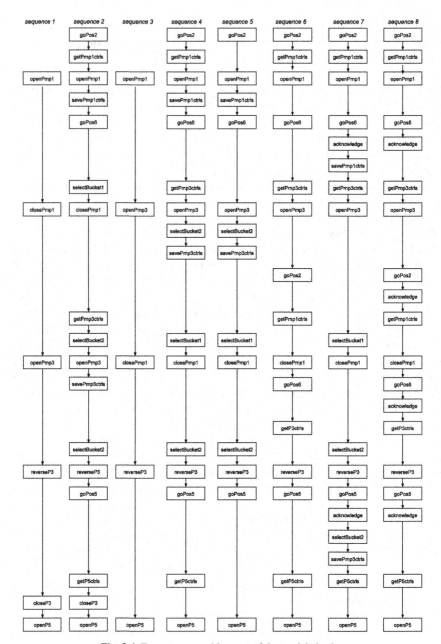

Fig. 3.4 Traces generated by runs of the model checker

need for the redesign of the device. In this case, identical subsequences of actions at Positions 2 and 6 have different effects. An interlock mechanism could be introduced to reduce the frustration caused by forgetfulness. The proposed redesign warns the user and asks for acknowledgement that the currently displayed control elements are about to disappear. The warning is issued whenever a device position is left and the device's control elements are neither on screen nor stored in a bucket. It is straightforward to adjust the model of the interface to the hand-held device to capture this idea, and this specification is given in Loer and Harrison (2004). The design, however, does not prevent the user from acknowledging and then doing nothing about the problem. Checking the same properties and adding assumptions about the forgetful user produces Sequences 7 and 8 in Figure 3.4. Throughout the example, the central control panel is used to identify the key actions necessary to achieve the goal because the additional actions introduced by the hand-held device are concerned exclusively with the limitations that the new platform introduces— dealing with physical location, uploading, and storing controls of the visited devices, as appropriate.

The analysis highlights these additional steps to allow the analyst to judge if they are likely to be problematic from a human factors perspective. The reasons why a given sequence of actions might be problematic may not be evident from the trace, but it provides an important representation that allows a human factors or domain analyst to consider these issues. For example, some actions might involve a lengthy walk through the plant, while some actions may be performed instantaneously, and some might depend on additional contextual factors like network quality. The current approach leaves the judgement of the severity of such scenarios to the human factors expert or the domain expert. It makes it possible for these experts to draw important considerations to the designer's attention.

In summary, from the perspective of the process diagram (Figure 3.1), a property template (reachability of a goal) has been used to generate traces from a system model (the right side of the diagram). Through expert analysis, scenarios were identified based on these traces and, as a result, alternative options were identified both in terms of user behavior and by developing alternative models. The piece of the figure that is not dealt with in this example is the rapid development of prototypes based on the consistent software framework.

3.5 Information Arrival

The second case study is concerned with information flow throughout a built environment, therefore location and message arrival are important issues. This case study is more directly focused on requirements that relate to experience. Consider a system development where requirements elicitation has yielded a number of such experience related requirements.

A number of different modelling frameworks would be appropriate for capturing different properties of the model, and for carrying out verification. Indeed, it is envisaged that a toolset for this process would include patterns and guidance about different features of the system and how they should be modelled, and templates representing classes of property that relate to experience requirements. It is envisaged that generic models of ambient and mobile systems will be developed similar to Garlan, et al. (2003) and Baresi, et al. (2005). Both are concerned with generic models of publish-subscribe systems.

Many characteristics of systems associated with timeliness or likelihood of occurrence contribute to the experience that we have with them. Such properties require models that incorporate notions of time (the message relating to the flight will be received within a fixed time span) and stochastic models (with a given probability). Loer et al. (2004) have used uppaal (Behrmann et al., 2004) models to analyze human scheduling behavior in relation to process control systems. Uppaal has been used by Harrison & Loer (2006) to describe the features of an airport system. Doherty, et al. (2001) have explored stochastic properties of interactive systems and ten Beek, et al. (2006) have used both timed model checking and stochastic model checking to analyze a groupware system. Properties that are relevant here relate to the dispatching of messages. For example,

- The message is the next message
- The message is most likely to be the next message (deNicola, et al. 2005)
- The message will arrive within 30 seconds (Loer, et al. 2004)

Rather than focusing on the modelling and analysis aspects of this example, the chapter focuses on the properties that would be checked of such a system that are relevant from an experience perspective. The following concrete properties all have characteristics that would improve the experience of the passenger while they are within the built environment. While these properties are not usability properties as conventionally understood, they nevertheless capture important features of the users' acceptability of a system:

- When the passenger enters a new location, the sensor detects the passenger's presence and the next message received concerns flight information and updates the passenger's hand-held device with information relevant to the passenger's position and stage in the embarkation process
- When the passenger moves into a new location and is the first from that flight to enter, public displays in the location are updated to include this flight information
- When the last passenger on a particular flight in the location leaves it, the public display is updated to remove this flight information
- As soon as a queue sensor receives information about a passenger entering a queue, queue information on the public display will be updated

The system's failure to adhere to all of these properties does not mean that the system does not perform correctly. Although the correct information might be passed around the environment, the system could fail to generate the information in the right place at the right time. As a result, the user's experience of knowing what to do and where to go in the environment would be compromised. Returning to the process described in Figure 3.1, checking these properties of the model will detect traces that require expert analysis and will thereby generate scenarios. These scenarios may then be used, perhaps simply as written narratives, to help the user visualize how different personae would experience them. These scenarios might also be prototyped using a software framework to provide a richer environment for understanding the passenger's experience of the new system.

Further experience properties of the airport system would be more difficult to evaluate through prototypes using sample passengers. For example,

- No matter how many services a user is subscribed to, the flight information service will be dispatched both to the user's device and to the local display within a defined time interval
- Any service that is offered to a subscriber will only be offered if there is a high probability that there is enough time to do something about the service
- When the passenger moves into the location, flight status information is presented to the passenger's hand-held device within 30 seconds
- Information on public displays should reflect the current state of the system within a time granularity of 30 seconds
- If the passenger enters a location, the passenger's trail will be updated with the action that should occur at that stage (for example screening hand baggage) within an appropriate time (two minutes). If not, a reminder of the current activity will be delivered to the user's hand-held device
- Information relating to the best queue to join for a specific flight will be designed to avoid jitter. It will be updated frequently enough to improve the experience of passengers but not so frequently that it will annoy passengers

Properties such as these will be particularly appropriate to meet passenger uncertainties about flight status, avoid the frustration of jittering information about queues, and offering services that cannot be received through lack of time.

3.6 Conclusions

While the primary focus of this chapter has been experience requirements, the two examples have illustrated how a range of properties might be explored through a combination of modelling and prototyping techniques. Ambient and mobile systems provide a rich context for the process of requirements elicitation. They challenge our presumptions about how to analyze interactive systems. Two ambient and mobile systems have been considered here. The first was concerned with the use of a hand-held mobile controller in a process plant. This involved reconsidering an analysis that was performed with a more traditional usability perspective. The second example illustrated a type of system aimed at providing occupants of a built environment with a sense of the space—to support a feeling of place and provide access to the services that are offered within the environment.

This example was derived from the specific concerns of an ambient and mobile system in an airport environment. The evaluation of the effectiveness of these systems requires the full richness of the target environment. In reality, it is not possible to explore these systems in a live environment for a variety of reasons. The possibility that these systems can be explored through a process that involves the use of formal methods has been discussed.

Formal techniques can be used to capture abstractly the important features of the prototype currently being developed. They can also be used as a means of simulation or exhaustive path checking to enable an assessment of the kinds of situations that a person might find her self in. But in themselves they do not provide a rich contextual account. We argue, however, that sequences generated by model checking can be enriched through the intervention of domain and human factors experts. The model can be developed at the same time as the prototype. Using the model, further properties may be appropriate and may be within the scope of the kind of system we describe. For example, it would be feasible to capture the knowledge that users in the environment might have (Fagin, et al. 2004) or the resources for action that are required by users (Campos & Doherty 2006).

The development of prototypes that support a subset of functions may be accompanied by simple models and simulations in which these prototypes can be explored. So, for example, separate models can be developed to explore the features pertaining to movement through space, and the actions that the user may perform explicitly using the system. Analysis by simulation or model-checking can lead to the discovery and exploration of paths that were not envisaged in the original set of scenarios. With the help of domain experts, situations can be envisaged in which the design fails to provide the passenger with the information they need to experience place.

Two important issues underpin our agenda for future research. The first concerns the mapping between models and prototypes. It concerns how to maintain an agile approach to the development of prototypes, while at the same time providing the means to explore early versions of the system using formal models. Our concern is to produce generic models that reflect the software architecture used for rapid development and to maintain synchrony between prototype and model. The second concerns the class of models required to analyze the range of requirements that would be relevant to ambient and mobile systems—how to ensure practical consistency between them and to avoid bias and inappropriate focus as a result of modelling simplifications.

Acknowledgment Michael Harrison and Karsten Loer acknowledge support of the Dependability Interdisciplinary Research Collaboration (DIRC), funded by the UK Engineering and Physical Sciences Research Council (EPSRC). José Campos was supported by the IVY Project, funded by the Portuguese Science and Technology Foundation (FCT) and the European Regional Development Fund (FEDER) under contract POSC/EIA/56646/2004.

References

Agile working group (2004). The agile manifesto. http://agilemanifesto.org.

Bannon, L. (2005). A human-centred perspective on interaction design. In A. Pirhonen, H. Isomäki, C. Roast, P. Saariluoma (Eds.), *Future Interaction Design* (pp. 31–52). Springer-Verlag

Baresi, L., Ghezzi, C., & Zanolin, L. (2005). Modeling and validation of publish / subscribe architectures. In S. Beydeda & V. Gruhn (Eds.), *Testing Commercial-off-the-shelf Components and Systems* (pp. 273–292). Springer-Verlag.

Behrmann, G., David, A., & Larsen, K. (2004). A tutorial on uppaal. In M. Bernardo & F. Corradini, F. (Eds.), *Formal methods for the design of real-time systems*. Springer Lecture Notes in Computer Science n° 3185 (pp. 200–236). Springer-Verlag.

Buchenau, M., & Suri, J. (2000). Experience prototyping. In *Proceedings Designing Interactive Systems (DIS'00)* (pp. 424–433). New York: ACM Press.

Campos, J. & Doherty, G. (2006). Supporting resource-based analysis of task information needs. In M. Harrison & S. Gilroy (Eds.), *Proceedings 12th International Workshop on the Design, Specification and Verification of Interactive Systems*. Springer Lecture Notes in Computer Science n° 3941 (pp. 188–200). Springer-Verlag.

Campos, J. & Harrison, M. (2001). Model checking interactor specifications. *Automated Software Engineering, 8*, 275–310.

De Nicola, R., Latella, D., & Massink, M. (2005). Formal modelling and quantitative analysis of KLAIM-based mobile systems. In H. Haddad, L. Liebrock, A. Omicini, R. Wainwright, M. Palakal, M. Wilds, H. Clausen (Eds.), *Applied Computing 2005: Proceedings of the 20th Annual ACM Symposium on Applied Computing* (pp. 428–435).

Doherty, G., Massink, M., & Faconti, G. (2001). Using hybrid automata to support human factors analysis in a critical system. *Journal of Formal Methods in System Design, 19(2)*, 143–164.

Fagin, R., Halpern, J., Moses, Y., & Vardi, M. (2004). *Reasoning about knowledge*. MIT Press.

Fields, R. (2001). *Analysis of erroneous actions in the design of critical systems*. PhD thesis, Department of Computer Science, University of York, Heslington, York, YO10 5DD.

Garlan, D., Khersonsky, S., & Kim, J. (2003). Model checking publish-subscribe systems. In *Proceedings of the 10th International SPIN Workshop on Model Checking of Software (SPIN 03)*, Portland, Oregon.

Gaver, W., Dunne, T., Pacenti, E. (1999). Design: cultural probes. *ACM Interactions, 6(1)*, 21–29.

Gray, W., & Salzman, M. (1998). Damaged merchandise? a review of experiments that compare usability evaluation methods. *Human Computer Interaction 13(3)*, 203–261.

Grudin, J. & Pruitt, J. (2002). Personas, participatory design and product development: an infrastructure for engagement. In *Proceedings PDC 2002* (pp. 144–161).

Halnass, L. & Redstrom, J. (2002). From use to presence: on the expressions and aesthetics of everyday computational things. *ACM Transactions on Computer-Human Interaction, 9(2)*, 106–124.

Harel, D. (1987). Statecharts: A visual formalism for complex systems. *Science of Computer Programming, 8*, 231–274.

Harrison, M., & Loer, K. (2006). *Time as a dimension in the design and analysis of interactive systems*. Technical Report CS-TR-980, School of Computing Science, University of Newcastle.

Lewis, C., Polson, P., Wharton, C., & Rieman, J. (1990). Testing a walkthrough methodology for theory based design of walk-up-and-use interfaces. In: J. Chew & J. Whiteside (Eds.), *ACM-CHI 90* (pp. 235–242). Addison-Wesley.

Loer, K., & Harrison, M. (2004). *Analysing and modelling context in mobile systems to support design*. Technical Report CS-TR-876, School of Computing Science, University of Newcastle upon Tyne.

Loer, K., & Harrison, M. (2005). Analysing user confusion in context aware mobile applications. In M. Constabile M & F. Paternò (Eds.), *Proceedings INTERACT 2005*, Springer Lecture Notes in Computer Science n° 3585 (pp. 184–197). Springer-Verlag.

Loer, K., & Harrison, M. (2006). An integrated framework for the analysis of dependable interactive systems (IFADIS): its tool support and evaluation. *Automated Software Engineering, 13(4)*, 469–496.

Loer K, Hildebrandt, M., & Harrison, M. (2004). Analysing dynamic function scheduling decisions. In C. Johnson & P. Palanque (Eds.), *Human Error, Safety and Systems Development* (pp. 45–60). Kluwer Academic.

McCarthy, J., & Wright, P. (2004). *Technology as experience*. MIT Press.

McMillan, K. (1993) *Symbolic model checking*. Kluwer.

Nielsen, J. (1992). Finding usability problems through heuristic evaluation. In *Proc. of ACM CHI'92 Conference on Human Factors in Computing Systems* (pp. 249–256). New York: ACM.

Nilsson, J., Sokoler, T., Binder, T., & Wetcke, N. (2000). Beyond the control room: mobile devices for spatially distributed interaction on industrial process plants. In P.Thomas & H. W. Gellersen (Eds.), *Handheld and Ubiquitous Computing, HUC'2000*, Springer Lecture Notes in Computer Science n° 1927 (pp. 30–45). Springer-Verlag.

Pocock, S., Harrison, M., Wright, P., & Johnson, P. (2001). THEA: A technique for human error assessment early in design. In M. Hirose (Ed.), *Human-Computer Interaction INTERACT'01 IFIP TC.13 International Conference on human computer interaction* (pp. 247–254). IOS Press.

Rosson, M., & Carroll, J. (2002). *Usability Engineering: scenario-based development of human computer interaction*. Morgan Kaufman.

ten Beek, M., Massink, M., & Latella, D. (2006). Towards model checking stochastic aspects of the thinkteam user interface. In M. Harrison & S. Gilroy (Eds.), *Proceedings 12th International Workshop on the Design, Specification and Verification of Interactive Systems*. Springer Lecture Notes in Computer Science n° 3941(pp. 39–50). Springer-Verlag.

Chapter 4
Tailoring Usability into Agile Software Development Projects

Scott W. Ambler

Practice Leader Agile Development, IBM Rational, e-mail: scott-ambler@ca.ibm.com

Abstract Usability, user interface, and interaction design are among the group of vital, yet mostly overlooked, skills that all software developers require, yet few seem to have. This is just as true of agile developers as it is of traditional developers. This chapter examines both user experience (UEX) and agile software development (ASD) approaches, comparing and contrasting the underlying philosophies and practices of each. Using agile model-driven development (AMDD) as the foundation, it then describes strategies for tailoring UEX into agile methods. It is possible to address UEX concerns on agile projects, but it requires flexibility and a willingness to work together on the part of both UEX and ASD practitioners.

4.1 Laying the Groundwork

In *The Inmates Are Running The Asylum*, Alan Cooper (2004) indicates that many of today's software-based products suffer from usability challenges. He believes that the key to solving the problem is performing what he calls interaction design before the programming effort to design the way that software behaves before it is built. Cooper believes programmers consciously design the code inside programs but only inadvertently design the interaction with humans. Although programmers work hard to make their software easy to use, their frame of reference is themselves—as a result, they make it easy for other software engineers, not normal human beings. He argues that programmers have too much influence over the design of the human interface and, due to a lack of skills in this area, do a poor job of it. In other words, the programming inmates are running the software development asylum.

My experience is similar to Cooper's. There is a need for improved interaction design skills within the programming community, although I don't agree with his proposed solution. Reading between the lines of both *The Inmates Are Running the Asylum* and a discussion between Kent Beck and Cooper (Nelson 2002), it seems to me that most of Cooper's experiences are with traditional development teams but not agile teams. Although I believe that his observations about the interaction design skill levels of developers apply to both the traditional and agile software development (ASD) communities, I fear that his advice is difficult for traditionalists to implement and all but impossible for agilists.

E. Law et al. (eds.), *Maturing Usability.*
© Springer-Verlag London Limited 2008

The goal of this chapter is to show how to make the advice of the user experience community palatable—or perhaps *usable* is a better term—to the ASD community. First, I begin by reviewing both ASD and UEX concepts and terminology to get everyone on the same level. Second, I explore the differences between the two approaches—in particular, the philosophical underpinnings of the two. Luckily, there is great similarity between the two. Third, I explore the ASD lifecycle in a bit more detail so we can identify potential opportunities to address UE issues. Fourth, I present a call to action to both communities and finish with an overview of the potential challenges that we will still face when following this strategy.

4.1.1 Agile Software Development (ASD)

To address the challenges faced by software developers, an initial group of 17 methodologists formed the Agile Software Development Alliance (www.agilealliance.com), often referred to simply as the Agile Alliance, in February of 2001. An interesting thing about this group is that they all came from different backgrounds, yet were able to come to an agreement on issues that methodologists typically don't agree upon. This group of people defined a manifesto (Agile Alliance 2001; Ambler 2006d) for encouraging better ways of developing software, and this manifesto defines the criteria for ASD processes. The manifesto defines four values and twelve principles that form the foundation of the agile movement.

The important thing to understand about the four value statements is that while you should value the concepts on the right hand side, you should value the things on the left-hand side (presented in italics) even more. The manifesto defines preferences, not alternatives, encouraging a focus on certain areas but not eliminating others. The four agile values are

- *Individuals and interactions* **over processes and tools**—teams of people build software systems, and to do that they need to work together effectively, including but not limited to programmers, testers, project managers, modelers, and your customers
- *Working software* **over comprehensive documentation**—documentation has its place. Written properly, it is a valuable guide for people's understanding of how and why a system is built and how to work with the system. However, never forget that the primary goal of software development is to create software, not documents—otherwise it would be called documentation development wouldn't it?
- *Customer collaboration* **over contract negotiation**—only your customer can tell you what they want. Successful developers work closely with their customers, they invest the effort to discover what their customers need, and they educate their customers along the way
- *Responding to change* **over following a plan**—as work progresses on your system, your project stakeholder's understanding of the problem domain and of what you are building changes. Your project plan must be malleable. There must be room to change it as your situation changes, otherwise your plan quickly becomes irrelevant

To help people gain a better understanding of what agile software development is all about, the members of the Agile Alliance refined the philosophies captured in their manifesto into a collection of twelve principles. These principles are

1. Our highest priority is to satisfy the customer through early and continuous delivery of valuable software.
2. Welcome changing requirements, even late in development. Agile processes harness change for the customer's competitive advantage.
3. Deliver working software frequently, from a couple of weeks to a couple of months, with a preference for the shorter time scale.
4. Business people and developers must work together daily throughout the project.
5. Build projects around motivated individuals. Give them the environment and support they need, and trust them to get the job done.
6. The most efficient and effective method of conveying information to and within a development team is face-to-face conversation.
7. Working software is the primary measure of progress.
8. Agile processes promote sustainable development. The sponsors, developers, and users should be able to maintain a constant pace indefinitely.
9. Continuous attention to technical excellence and good design enhances agility.
10. Simplicity—the art of maximizing the amount of work not done—is essential.
11. The best architectures, requirements, and designs emerge from self-organizing teams.
12. At regular intervals, the team reflects on how to become more effective, then tunes and adjusts its behavior accordingly.

Just as the Software Engineering Institute's (1995) Capability Maturity Model (CMM) defines the requirements for a heavy-weight software development process, the agile manifesto defines the requirements for an agile software process. Full-fledged ASD processes that reflect these requirements include

- **Microsoft Solutions Framework (MSF) for Agile**—the MSF for Agile (Microsoft 2004), among the newest of the agile processes, has arguably been the most influenced by UEX practices. It is often adopted by Microsoft customers who wish to follow a well-defined, yet streamlined, software development process. The main development artifacts are personas, usage scenarios, domain-specific models (DSMs), tests, and source code
- **Agile Unified Process (AUP)**—the AUP (Ambler 2005) is a highly collaborative, streamlined version of the Unified Process (Jacobson, Booch, & Rumbaugh 1999). It is often adopted by organizations that want a well-defined yet agile software process, particularly those that like the Rational Unified Process (RUP) (Kruchten 2004) but find it too heavy for their environment. The main development artifacts of AUP are use cases, UML sequence and class diagrams, acceptance tests, unit tests, physical data models (PDMs), and source code
- **Dynamic System Development Method (DSDM)**—DSDM (Stapleton 2003) is an agile process introduced in the mid-1990s that is typically used to develop UI-intensive applications. The main development artifacts of DSDM projects are UI prototypes, design models, tests, and source code

- **Extreme Programming (XP)**—XP (Beck 2000) is likely the best-known agile process, due in part to its name, but mostly due to the fact that it works incredibly well. XP is defined as a collection of practices—such as pair programming (Williams & Kessler 2002), refactoring (Fowler 1999), test-first design (TFD), and onsite customer—which require great discipline on the part of developers. XP is very successful for teams of less than ten people, although when combined with Scrum has been shown to work well on teams that are much larger. The main development artifacts of XP are user stories, acceptance tests, unit tests, and source code
- **Feature Driven Development (FDD)**—FDD (Palmer & Felsing 2002; Anderson 2001) is an agile process for development of object technology-based systems. It is based on the concept that you should do some initial domain object modeling and feature identification early in the project, and then incrementally flesh out the domain model throughout the project. The main development artifacts of FDD projects are features, object models, tests, and source code
- **Rational Unified Process (RUP)**—although RUP is often instantiated as a *heavy-weight* software process, Kroll and MacIsaac (2006) show this does not necessarily have to be the case. The RUP can, in fact, be instantiated as a very agile process if you choose to do so (Ambler 2004b). The main development artifacts of the RUP are the same as those of the AUP described above

There are also several common *partial* agile processes which focus on an aspect of software development. These processes are

- **Agile Data (AD)**—the AD method (Ambler 2003c) is defined as a collection of six philosophies and four roles which can be tailored into other agile methods to define how data professionals may be effective members of an agile team. The AD method is supported by evolutionary database development techniques such as agile data modeling, database regression testing, configuration management of data-oriented work products, and database refactoring (Ambler & Sadalage 2006)
- **Agile Modeling (AM)**—the AM method (Ambler 2002) defines a collection of principles and practices for effective modeling and documentation efforts. AM is tailored into other agile methods to make modeling and documentation explicit, and into methods such as the RUP to help streamline it
- **Scrum**—*Scrum* (Beedle and Schwaber 2001) is a project and requirements management methodology which is often tailored into other agile methods, in particular XP. Scrum sets out simple rules for authority and responsibility—if you are on the team, you are a *pig* that has the responsibility and authority to get the job done. If you are not on the team, you are a *chicken* who provides information when requested but otherwise get out of the way
- **Usage-Centered Design (UCD)**—UCD (Constantine & Lockwood 1999) is a systematic, model-driven approach to improving product usability, where the focus is on the usage of the product. The main artifacts are user role, task, and interface content definitions. UCD can be tailored into both agile and nonagile development process to guide the user interface design toward a better fit with the real needs of users

4.1.2 User Experience (UEX)

Because this is a usability book, I will only briefly define the usability-related terminology. Other chapters describe these concepts much more thoroughly. Within this chapter, usability is a quality attribute of a system that encompasses learnability, efficiency, memorability, error recovery, and end-user satisfaction (Neilson 1994). User-centered design (also known as UCD, although I will use that abbreviation for *usage-centered design* described above) is a highly structured, product-development process where the focus is on understanding the needs and goals of the user of the product. Interaction design (ID) is a methodology described by Alan Cooper (2004) where the goal is to provide end-users with functions that are both desirable and useful. In ID, interaction designers focus on what is desirable, while engineers focus on what they're capable of building, and business stakeholders focus on what is viable. I use the term *user experience* (UEX) to encompass all of these concepts. Although there is good reason to distinguish between the various ideas, that is not relevant to my current discussion.

An important question to ask is why should ASD practitioners consider UEX important? Patton (2004) believes that UEX addresses several issues that are critical to the success of ASD teams. First, UEX places emphasis on the usage necessary for roles to meet their goals. Second, UEX helps meet the goal of identifying the behavior the software should have. Third, UEX practices can be applied with varying degrees of formality, thereby making them compatible with agile methodologies.

Other important terminology that I use in this chapter includes

- **System**—the product, which often includes software, under development
- **User**—also known as an end-user, a user is a person who will actually work with the system/product being built
- **Developer**—an IT professional involved with the creation of the system
- **Stakeholder**—a stakeholder is anyone who has a stake in the creation or operation of the system. This includes people who are direct users, indirect users, managers of users, senior managers, developers, operations staff members, support (help desk) staff members, developers working on other systems that integrate or interact with the one under development, or maintenance professionals potentially affected by the development and/or deployment of a software project. Some agile methodologies, XP in particular, uses the term *customer*
- **Acceptance testing**—a testing technique, the goal of which is to determine whether a system satisfies its acceptance criteria, and to enable the stakeholder(s) to determine whether to accept the system
- **Usability testing**—a method by which users of a system are asked to perform certain tasks in an effort to measure the system's ease-of-use, task time, and the user's perception of the experience. Usability testing can be both formal and informal, using dedicated rooms and equipment to simply using physical mock ups of the system
- **User testing**—testing activities, including both acceptance and usability testing, where stakeholders are actively involved

Why distinguish between users, developers, and stakeholders? Fundamentally, they have different levels of responsibility and involvement with a software development project. Developers are responsible for building the system and working closely with their stakeholders to do so. Stakeholders are active participants on agile projects (more on this later) who make decisions and provide information in a timely manner, and better yet are actively involved with the modeling and testing efforts. End users should be involved throughout the project to validate the work that the developers have done and to ensure that the stakeholders accurately represent the user community at large. Constantine (2001) points out that users outnumber stakeholders and are a critical source of information for user interface design, and are the key people required for usability testing.

4.2 Current State of the Art

First I will share the good news. I believe that there is a growing recognition within both the ASD and UEX communities that they can benefit by working closely with the other. Within the ASD community, Larry Constantine's UCD work is well-respected and the UEX community seems intrigued by the promises of ASD. There is an active Agile Usability mailing list (http://groups.yahoo.com/group/agile-usability/) where ASD and UEX practitioners interact regularly. There are also agile usability tutorials at conferences, including UPA 2005 (www.upassoc.org/conferences_and_events/upa_conference/2005/), Agile 2005 (www.agile2005.org/track/tutorials), and Agile 2006 (www.agile2006.com). There seems to be a will to bring the two communities together.

Now I will share the bad news. There are several challenges that need to be overcome if we are to work together effectively, and just the fact that we talk about two different communities indicates that we have a problem. These challenges include

- **Different goals**—Lee (2006) points out that "software engineers focus on the design, implementation, and maintenance of software systems, but often marginalize the design of the human-computer interfaces through which those systems are used. On the other hand, usability engineers focus on developing systems so end-users can use them effectively but do not account for the underlying system design, implementation or market-driven forces that guide much of software engineering." I believe that these goals are complementary, and show in this chapter that it is fairly straightforward to achieve both
- **Different approaches**—similarly, Desilets (2005) argues that UEX methodologies are centered on the user, whereas agile methodologies take a broader view and focus on the stakeholder. With UEX methods, one tries to get a holistic view of user needs and come up with an overall plan for the user interface before starting implementation. Agile methods favor little up-front design and focus instead on delivering working software early

- **Organizational challenges**—the ASD community follows a highly collaborative and fluid organizational strategy where teams are self organizing. This doesn't appear to always be the case with the UEX groups within some organizations. Hodgetts (2005) believes that when a separate UEX group exists, including UEX practitioners on an agile project team can be problematic. This is particularly true in organizations with a strong management hierarchy, because the resulting *command-and-control* mindset hampers an agile team's ability to self organize. While a center for UEX is important to provide the needed practices, tools, and standards, a strong organizational and management hierarchy can be problematic. We need to find a way to keep the good aspects yet discard the bad

- **Process impedance mismatch**—the ASD community forgoes detailed modeling up early in the project, something they refer to as Big Design Up Front (BDUF). Many within the UEX community prefer more comprehensive modeling early in the project to design the user interaction properly before construction begins. A C.C. Pace (2003) whitepaper points out that once an application reaches a certain level of complexity without an up-front vision, the result is awkward or unnecessarily complicated user interfaces designed around back-end functionality instead of a user's end goals. As I show below, what we need to do is some initial modeling up front to think through the big issues, at a very broad but shallow level, but that we don't need the comprehensive modeling that some within the UEX community expect. In short, we need to find the sweet spot in the middle.

- **UEX practitioners struggle to be heard**—although this is true within traditional teams as well, my experience is that this is not as problematic with ASD teams for the simple reason that ASD practitioners favor high levels of collaboration. I believe that the fundamental problem is that UEX practitioners are not integrated well into the teams, and will argue that they need to expand their skill sets so that they can do more than just UEX if they are to be effective on agile teams. Jokela and Abrahamsson (2004) believe that UEX practitioners often complain that the results of their work are not considered in the design decisions. They also point out that no UEX practitioners were invited to participate in the formation of the Agile Alliance (www.agilealliance.com), which may be why there has been insufficient UEX influence to date within the ASD community. As I indicated earlier, I believe the two communities are coming together.

- **Our thought leaders may be a bit too extreme**—Elden Nelson (2002) facilitated a discussion between Kent Beck, the founder of Extreme Programming (XP), and Alan Cooper, the founder of Interaction Design (ID). Many interesting points came out of the discussion pertaining to the differences between ASD and UEX philosophies, as summarized in Table 4.1. Unfortunately, both Beck and Cooper seem to be at the extreme end of the discussion, and you can see in Nelson's interview that there were bones of contention that were not resolved. I posit that we need to find something in between, and that although the Beck/Cooper discussion was effective at identifying issues, it wasn't good at identifying the requisite *sweet spot* between the extremes (although, to be fair, Beck did seem more flexible than Cooper).

Table 4.1 Comparing the Agile and UEX philosophies

Agile Philosophies	UEX Philosophies
• Asks "How can what we have now be improved this iteration?" • You should work closely with your stake-holders/customers to identify their exact needs. • Details behind requirements can be identified on a just-in-time (JIT) basis during development. • Detailed, up-front modeling is a risky endeavor at best. • Interaction design has a role to play from the beginning of a project, as a way to come up with the metaphors for the project.	• Asks "What is the ideal system?" • Defining the behavior of software-based products and services is very difficult and has to be done from the point of view of understanding and visualizing the *behavior* of complex systems, not the *construction* of complex systems. • All behavioral issues need to be addressed before construction begins.

4.3 Clearing Up A Few Misconceptions

To help promote effective collaboration between the two communities, we need to clear up a few misconceptions that each community may have with the other. There are several that UEX practitioners may have about the ASD community:

- **Agilists do not model**—Constantine (2001) points out that one misconception is that agilists "don't waste time in analysis or design, [they] just start cutting code." The actual fact is that ASD practitioners do in fact model, it is just that they discourage extensive up-front design work (McInerney & Maurer 2005) in favor of more agile approaches to modeling (Ambler 2002; Ambler 2004a). A quick perusal of the original XP book (Beck 2000) reveals diagrams throughout, and if you were to read it you would see significant discussions about user stories, acceptance tests, and class responsibility collaborator (CRC) modeling. This may not be *traditional* modeling, but modeling it is
- **Agilists are continually deploying software into production**—although some teams do this, it is not the norm. What is common is to deliver working software on a regular basis, perhaps every few weeks, into an internal environment for system and user testing. Deployment into production may occur every six-to-twelve months, if not longer, based on need and the ability of our end-users to accept new releases
- **XP is the only game in town**—this is a serious misunderstanding, because UEX practitioners who believe this miss agile methods such as Scrum, Agile Modeling, Agile MSF, and DSDM, which are arguably more attuned to their philosophies
- **There is a single "agile way" of doing things**—as I describe above, there are many agile software processes, each of which have their own way of working. For example, a UEX practitioner will interact with an RUP team in a slightly different manner than they will interact with an FDD team. On a RUP team,

everyone works from use cases as the primary requirements artifact, while on an FDD team they work from features.

- **There is no role for UEX practitioners**—many agile methods forgo the concept of specific roles in favor of more generic roles such as developer/programmer, coach/leader, and customer/stakeholder. McInerney and Maurer (2005) point out that the agile literature does not identify a distinct UEX role, and therefore the onus remains on UEX practitioners to justify their involvement on the team. I believe that Constantine and Lockwood's (1999) UCD work, and my own agile modeling methodology, clearly provide paths for UEX practitioners to do exactly this. More on this can be found next
- **Agilists are not specialists**—this statement is partly true. McInerney and Maurer (2005) point out that ASD methodologies prefer generalists, but what is truly preferred are people who are *generalizing specialists*, who have one or more specialties, a general knowledge of software development, and better yet at least a general knowledge of the domain that they are working in (Ambler 2003b)
- **User interfaces shouldn't be refactored**—user interfaces should not be refactored because changing the UI architecture is unavoidably disruptive for end-users. This ignores the facts that the UI platform changes over time—notice the differences between Windows 95, 98, 2000, and Windows XP for example—and that every new release of your system is very likely to have new UI functionality. The reality is that UI refactoring results in the slow, but safe, evolution of the UI, thereby improving its design. Yes, the UI changes, hopefully for the better, but the only people affected by the changes on a continual basis are those actively involved in user testing. And when you stop to think about it, shouldn't developers act on the findings of usability testing efforts and thereby improve the UI?

The ASD community equally suffers from debilitating misperceptions about the UEX community:

- **All you need is a good set of UI guidelines**—that is a good start, but there is a fair bit more to UEX than creating consistent UIs
- **Working closely with stakeholders is good enough**—that is also a good start, but Jokela and Abrahamsson (2004) found that even a close and frequent cooperation between developers and stakeholders does not ensure good usability at all. They believe that, without explicit UEX practices added to agile methods, good usability of the software would be more or less a coincidence resulting from the intuition of the customer and/or the intuition of the developers
- **UEX is just about UI design**—UI design is clearly a part of UEX, but so is understanding how your users will work with your system and what their goals for using the system are so that you can build something that is usable by them. This requires significant modeling and collaboration skills to accomplish
- **UEX relies on comprehensive up-front modeling**—although some people in the UEX community want you to believe that, many others believe different

4.4 Examining Agile Software Development

To understand how UEX techniques can be applied on ASD projects, we must first understand how these projects work. The vast majority of ASD projects are teams of less than ten people, are colocated, have direct access to stakeholders, have access to inclusive modeling tools such as whiteboards and corkboards, have their own development machines, and have access to the development tools that they require, including testing tools. Having said that, some agile teams are very large (upwards to several hundred people), some are dispersed geographically, and some do not always have easy access to stakeholders (Eckstein 2004). Although most agile teams take a test-driven development (TDD) approach (Astels 2003; Beck 2003), where they write a unit test before writing just enough production code to fulfill that unit test, they typically do not have access to UI testing tools. Furthermore, they rarely have access to a usability lab, so in this respect, ASD is little different than traditional development.

Of course, there is a bit more to ASD than being colocated and following the values and principles of the Agile Alliance. To identify how UEX practices would fit into ASD, you must also understand

- The agile software development lifecycle
- Modeling on an agile project
- User testing on an agile project

4.4.1 The Agile Software Development Lifecycle (SDLC)

Figure 4.1 depicts my rendition of a generic agile SDLC (Ambler 2006a), which is comprised of four phases: Iteration 0, Development, End Game, and Production. Although many agile developers may balk at the idea of phases, the fact is that it has been recognized that processes such as XP, AUP, and MSF for Agile (which calls phases *tracks* instead) do, in fact, have phases.

Let us consider each phase in turn:

- **Iteration 0**—the first week or so of an agile project is often referred to as *Iteration 0*. The goal during this period is to initiate the project by garnering initial support and funding for the project, actively working with stakeholders to initially model the scope of the system at a high-level, starting to build the team, modeling an initial architecture for the system, and setting up the environment
- **Development phase**—during development iterations, agilists incrementally deliver high-quality working software that meets the changing needs of stakeholders. During a development iteration, ASD practitioners collaborate closely with both stakeholders and other developers; implement functionality in the priority order defined by stakeholders; analyze the requirements and design them through model-storming on a just-in-time (JIT) basis; take a TDD approach to development, which is effectively JIT-detailed design; ensure quality by

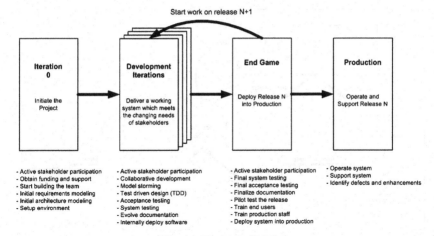

Fig. 4.1 The Agile SDLC

following guidance, such as coding conventions and modeling-style guidelines; ensure quality by refactoring application code and/or database schema as required to ensure that they have the best design possible; and regularly deliver working software (minimally, at the end of each development cycle/iteration there should be a partial, working system to show people, and better yet to deploy into a pre-production testing/QA sandbox for user and system testing). These development activities are overviewed in Figure 4.2

- **End Game phase**—during the End Game iterations(s) agile practitioners transition the system into production. They do this by doing final testing of the system (including both user and system testing); rework, because there is no value testing the system if you do not plan to act on the defects that you find; finalization of any system and user documentation; training of end-users, operations staff, and support staff; and deployment of the system into production

- **Production**—the goal of this phase is to keep systems useful and productive after they have been deployed in the user community. The fundamental goal is to keep the system running and help users to use it

On the surface, the agile SDLC of Figure 4.1 looks very much like a traditional SDLC, but when you dive deeper you quickly discover that this is not the case. Because the agile SDLC is highly collaborative, iterative, and incremental, the roles that people take are much more robust than on traditional projects. In the traditional world, a business analyst created a requirements model that is handed off to an architect, who creates design models that are handed off to a coder, who writes programs that are handed off to a tester, and so on. On an agile project, developers work closely with their stakeholders to understand their needs, they pair together to implement and test their solution, and the solution is shown to the stakeholder for quick feedback. Instead of specialists handing artifacts to one another, and thereby injecting defects at every step along the way, agile developers are generalizing specialists with full lifecycle skills. More importantly, from an UEX point of view, they take a very different approach to modeling and testing than do traditionalists.

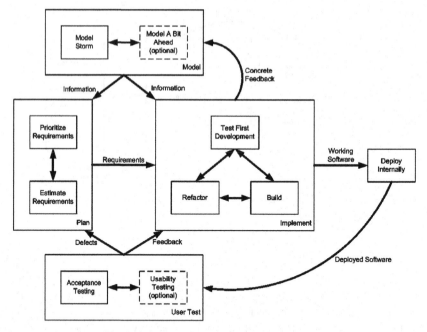

Fig. 4.2 Activities during a development iteration

4.4.2 Modeling on an Agile Project

ASD practitioners are very pragmatic when it comes to modeling. The AM methodology (Ambler 2002) describes in detail how agilists approach both modeling and documentation. Figure 4.3 overviews the lifecycle of an AMDD approach to ASD—an approach that originally grew out of the XP community but seems to capture the essence of the modeling approach on agile projects in general. Each box in the diagram represents a development activity. The initial modeling activity during Iteration 0 includes two main subactivities—initial requirements modeling and initial architecture modeling, which are done iteratively in parallel. The model-storming and implementation activities potentially occur during any iteration, including Iteration 0 (yes, the rumors are true—ASD practitioners will often implement working software the very first week of a project). The time indicated in each box represents the length of an average session. During development, for example, you'll often model-storm for a few minutes with a stakeholder to explore a requirement and then code for several hours.

The initial modeling effort is typically performed during the first week of a project. For short projects (perhaps several weeks in length), you may do this work in the first few hours; and for long projects (perhaps on the order of twelve or more months), you may decide to invest up to two weeks in this effort. There are two aspects to the initial modeling effort:

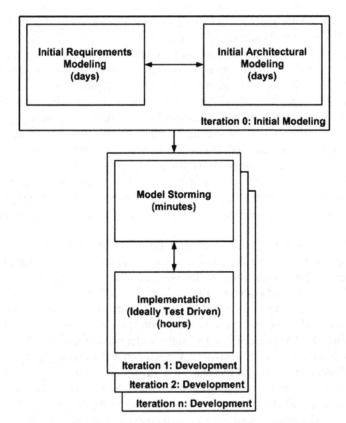

Fig. 4.3 The Agile model-driven development (AMDD) lifecycle

- **Requirements modeling**—you need to identify the high-level requirements, as well as the scope of the current release. The goal is to get a good gut feel for what the project is all about, and to do that you will likely need to create an initial usage model to explore how users will work with your system (e.g., on a RUP/AUP project, you would write point-form use cases, on an FDD project you would identify major features, and on an XP team you would writing user stories), an initial domain model that identifies fundamental business entity types and the relationships between them (this is particularly true of FDD teams, although also common on RUP/AUP teams), and perhaps a UI model overviewing navigation within the system and perhaps even the initial layout of important screens/pages and reports
- **Architectural modeling**—the goal of the initial architecture modeling effort is to try to identify an architecture that has a good chance of working. Ninety-nine percent of the time, ASD practitioners simply gather around a whiteboard and create free-form diagrams as they discuss various architectural strategies

In later iterations, your initial models will evolve as you learn more, but during Iteration 0 the goal is to get something that is just barely good enough get the team going. You do not need to model a lot of detail, and I cannot stress this enough—the goal is to build a shared understanding, not to write detailed documentation.

During development iterations, the vast majority of modeling sessions involve a few people, usually just two or three, who discuss an issue while sketching on paper or a whiteboard. These *model-storming sessions* are typically impromptu events. One project team member will ask another to model with them, typically lasting for five to ten minutes (it is rare to model-storm for more than 30 minutes). The people get together, gather around a shared modeling tool (e.g., the whiteboard), explore the issue until they are satisfied that they understand it, and then they continue on (often coding). Model-storming is JIT modeling—you identify an issue that you need to resolve, you quickly grab a few teammates who can help you, the group explores the issue, and then everyone continues on as before. Extreme programmers (XPers) would call model-storming sessions, stand-up design sessions, or customer Q&A sessions.

You will model-storm to analyze a requirement, and/or to design a solution to fulfill a requirement. For example, a user may tell you that the system you are building must display a chart representing the bonus schedule for sales people. Together, you create a sketch of what the screen will look like, drawing several examples until you come to a common understanding of what needs to be built. Sketches such as this are inclusive models, because you are using simple tools and modeling techniques, thus enabling the AM practice of active stakeholder participation (ASP).

Model storming on a JIT basis works much better than trying to model everything up front, and for several reasons. First, the requirements are going to change throughout the project. Second, by waiting to analyze the JIT details, you have much more domain knowledge than if you had done so at the beginning of a project. For example, if a requirement is to be implemented three months into a project, exploration of the details of that requirement at that point gives you three months more domain knowledge than if you had done so at the beginning of the project. Therefore, you can ask more intelligent questions. Third, if you have been delivering working software on a regular basis, your stakeholders now have three months worth of experience with the system and can give you better answers. Fourth, modeling everything up front appears to result in significant wastage (Ambler 2006b).

Sometimes model-storming is not enough. Perhaps you need to model complex requirements that require input from someone outside of your immediate team, or perhaps you need to model a legacy asset thst can take a significant amount of time. In other words, you may need to model a bit ahead of actually implementing a requirement (Ambler 2006c). This is actually a rare occurrence, regardless of what traditional modelers may hope for, but it does happen every so often.

All of this begs the question "how can UEX activities fit in to an agile project?" The easy answer is that agilists need to adopt usage-oriented requirements artifacts, such as personas and scenarios (Cooper 2004), abstract prototypes (Constantine and Lockwood 1999), or even use cases. In fact, several agile methodologies have done so, such as MSF for Agile, Agile Modeling, and the AUP, respectively. After this, it is not so easy.

UEX practitioners can rail about the need for doing lots of design up front, but that message falls on deaf ears within the agile community. The bottom line is that from an agile perspective, traditional UEX techniques are not very usable for them, which is rather ironic when you stop and think about it. To make UEX techniques usable to ASD practitioners, they must reflect the ASD lifecycle as depicted in Figures 4.1 through 4.3. Luckily, this can be accomplished by

- **Doing some UI modeling up front**—Constantine (2001) points out that you need to establish 3 things: Overall organization for the parts of the UI that fits with the structure of user tasks; a common scheme for navigation among all the parts; a visual and interaction scheme that provides a consistent look-and-feel to support user tasks. Yes, this takes some up-front work, but for the vast majority of systems this could easily be accomplished during Iteration 0. Hodgetts (2005) found that failing to consider some UI aspects across a wider range of features resulted in expensive UI refactoring in later iterations, and that an incremental approach focusing on breadth first and depth just in time seems to work for UEX. Desilets (2005) also suggests that the UEX practitioner spends a small amount of time up front to gain knowledge about user needs and that the UEX practitioner come up with a rough sketch of the overall user interface to assist the development efforts
- **Using modeling tools which reflect agile practices**—for example, XP teams prefer to work with index cards, not documents, and AUP teams prefer whiteboard sketches. Luckily, paper and whiteboards are common tools with many UEX practitioners. Desilets (2005) points out that some UEX methods favor the use of lightweight, low-fidelity prototypes to allow quick iteration when gathering user information. Although agile methods favor the development of a working prototype that gradually evolves into the working system, you can easily combine both approaches
- **Modeling a bit ahead when appropriate**—if you need to, explore important aspects of the UI before you implement them. A C.C. Pace (2003) whitepaper points out that UEX practitioners just need to stay a few steps ahead of development. Designers can first work with stakeholders to identify their needs, translate those needs into effective user interfaces, and then pair with developers to implement them. This advice reflects the experience of Hodgetts (2005), who found it difficult to conduct usability or user sessions and field studies within the agile lifecycle. Conducting a user session often involves scheduling specialized facilities that are in high demand, and making appointments with the appropriate stakeholders. These realities pretty much force you to model a bit ahead
- **Doing UI development on a JIT basis the majority of the time**—the UI is important, but then again so are many other aspects of a system (such as the network, the database design, and so on), and therefore the UI should be treated differently only when appropriate. For example, Hodgetts (2005) found that when the goal of design was limited to a single feature or a small set of features, the teams found it effective to perform UEX activities as part of the development of those features during the iteration. His teams found few visual design aspects that could not be addressed within the current iteration, and found it very rare to need to conduct any detailed UEX design activities of the iteration where the features where being implemented. In short, you do not need to model ahead very

often. McInerney and Maurer (2005) concur with this strategy, suggesting that UI design focuses on a small piece of the application that progresses rapidly from concept to code

- **Adopt UEX-friendly requirements artifacts**—as I pointed out earlier, some agile methods such as AUP, DSDM, and MSF for Agile already do this. With respect to FDD, Anderson (2001) suggests a requirements strategy that includes UI views such as a screens, browser pages, and reports as well as features. This same philosophy could be applied in XP, and frankly many XP teams already capture the need to implement a UI view as a user story

4.4.3 User Testing on an Agile Project

For the sake of this chapter, user testing encompasses both acceptance testing and usability testing. The agile community has embraced the importance of acceptance testing, having built tools such as *Fit* (Mugridge & Cunningham 2005) to help automate it. The automated tests will be run often—at least daily, if not several times a day. Manual user testing, on the other hand, is typically done an iteration behind. At the end of an iteration, many agile teams deploy the working system into a QA/testing environment where user and system testing is performed. The team continues on, developing version $N + 1$ of the system, while obtaining defect reports pertaining to version N. As you can see in Figure 4.2, these defect reports are treated just like any other requirement—they are estimated, prioritized, and put on the requirements stack to be addressed at some point in the future.

Figure 4.2 indicates that usability testing is considered optional, and I have no doubt that many UEX practitioners will find that frustrating. Agile teams are little different from traditional teams in this respect—they very likely do not appreciate the need for usability testing (or other UEX practices, for that matter). Cooper (2004) underlines the importance of usability testing with his philosophy that "you can expect what you inspect." If you want usable software, then you are going to have to test for usability.

Constantine (2001) indicates that true usability testing requires repeated testing with numbers of users under controlled settings. Just like acceptance testing can be done regularly throughout development, so can usability testing. On ASD projects, usability testing should occur during the user-testing effort after each iteration, assuming of course that someone on the team has those skills.

Meszaros and Aston (2006) describe their experiences adding usability testing to agile projects by *play-acting* with paper-based UI prototypes. With this approach, some members of the team act as the computer by *displaying* the paper prototypes of screens and reports at the appropriate time. The users would play act through scenarios, interacting with the computer to simulate how they would use the system. Another member of the development team played the *help* system and would describe what a button or field did when asked. Finally, other team members observed what happened and recorded usability challenges as the scenarios progressed. The end result of this effort was that the team identified critical functionality that they originally thought was out of scope, they discovered that they needed to deprioritize other functionality, and they identified several erroneous assumptions.

4.5 A Call to Action

If the ASD and UEX communities are going to work together effectively, they need to find a middle ground. I believe that such middle ground exists, but that both communities need to adopt several changes in order to succeed. First, ASD professionals must

- **Learn UEX skills**—Patton (2004) believes that developers should be trained in, and adopt into their practices, UEX techniques. Similarly, Hodgetts (2005) suggests that we foster a greater understanding of UEX practices across the entire project team, enabling everyone to work more collaboratively and effectively
- **Accept that usability is a critical quality factor**—luckily, ASD practitioners are *quality-infected*. They understand the importance of doing high-quality work and have a proven track record of adopting techniques such as test-first programming, code refactoring, and database refactoring. As Jokela and Abrahamsson (2004) point out, the first step is for ASD practitioners to accept that good usability of an end product can be ensured only by systematic usability engineering activities during the development iterations. The second step is to adopt UEX techniques that enable them to do so
- **Adopt UI and usage style guidelines**—developers must understand that not only should their code follow common guidelines, so should their UIs. ASD practitioners need to do more than adopt UI guidelines (Cooper 2004), but it would be a very good start

Similarly, UEX practitioners must make some changes. They need to

- **Go beyond UEX**—I believe that many of the challenges experienced between programmers and UEX practitioners in the past are due to overspecialization of roles and hand-offs between people in those roles. ASD practitioners have tightened the feedback loop on software projects, and thereby reduced both risk and cost, by mostly abandoning the concept of building teams of specialists and favoring teams of generalizing specialists instead. Although UEX practitioners bring a critical skill set to a development team, they still need to learn a wider range of skills to become truly effective
- **Become embedded in ASD teams**—McInerney and Maurer (2005) suggest that UI design becomes more of a team effort, and my experience is that the best way to do that is to include UEX practitioners on ASD teams. Lee (2006) concurs, believing that we should "support collaboration between software engineers and usability specialists by facilitating communication of design intent and rationale." Desilets (2005) also believes that UEX practitioners should become active participants throughout the development effort, working in close collaboration with developers. By embedding UEX practitioners on ASD teams, not only will this

increase the chance that UEX issues are addressed, it will help to promote UEX skills within the agile community because people pick up new skills from one another as they collaborate

- **Give ASD approaches a chance**—Kent Beck suggested to Alan Cooper that a week be invested at the beginning of a project to explore interaction issues, although Cooper believed that was not sufficient (Nelson 2002). The easiest way to find out who is right is to actually try it in practice
- **Start looking beyond XP**—I have said it before and I will say it again, there is more to ASD than XP. Agile methodologies are flexible—they are not meant to be used *out of the box*, but instead to be tailored to meet the exact situation in which the project team finds itself. To address UEX concerns, you will very likely find that you need to tailor some of the principles and practices of agile modeling and/or the techniques of user-centered design into your base software process

4.6 Potential Challenges

I would be remiss if I did not discuss the potential challenges faced trying to bring UEX practices into the agile community. It is very easy to suggest that ASD practitioners should take the time to learn UEX skills, and to adopt appropriate guidelines, but the reality is that these skills are competing for attention along with other equally important skills such as database design and modeling. To make matters worse, few developer-oriented books cover UI/usability issues, and the few that do, such as *The Object Primer* (Ambler 2004a), rarely seem to devote more than a chapter to it. I fear that many ASD practitioners are not even aware of the issue.

Similarly, UEX practitioners receive mixed signals. Although I am calling for them to become generalizing specialists, the industry still rewards specialization— UEX specialists are paid very well, and most organizations expect them to focus on doing that specific sort of work. ASD practitioners also suffer from this challenge. Why take an introductory UI design course when you can take a Java programming course that leads to certification and greater pay?

It is also easy to say that UEX professionals should be embedded into ASD projects, but it only works when UEX professionals are available. Cooper (2004) points out that few organizations have such people on staff, and worse yet, believes that few organizations think in terms of interaction design as part of the requirements-planning or project-planning process. Therefore, many organizations may not see the need to hire anyone with these skills.

McInerney and Maurer (2005) raise an important issue with the collaborative development approach preferred by ASD teams. The lack of UI design ownership means that everyone wants to be involved with UI design, regardless of their skill level, which can lead to *design-by-committee*. Although a common philosophy throughout the agile community is that ASD practitioners should have the humility to know their limits and the respect of others with the appropriate skills to address a specific issue, it does not always work out that way—apparently, ASD practitioners are still only human.

The ASD and UEX communities are still miles apart, and although there is a movement afoot to bring them together, I suspect it will prove to be a difficult endeavor because it is hard to get the message out to the people who need to hear it. For example, this chapter appears in a specialized book aimed at the usability community and, as a result, few ASD practitioners are going to read it.

4.7 Summary

This chapter presented a coherent strategy for bringing UEX practices into ASD projects. To accomplish this goal, UEX and ASD practitioners need to learn about and respect each other's philosophies and techniques, and then actively find ways to work together. This requires both communities to make minor changes to the way that they work, but if they choose to make these changes, I suspect that their work products will be much better for it.

With an agile UEX approach, you will do high-level, very broad modeling at the beginning of the agile project to address the majority of usability and UI issues facing the team. You do not need a detailed answer—the details can come later, on a JIT-basis during development—but you do need a strategy. During development, UEX practitioners should be embedded within the development team, working on UEX tasks when needed but also working with their teammates on non-UEX activities. Agile teams are made up of generalizing specialists with the ability to work on a wide range of things, instead of narrowly focused specialists typically found on traditional teams. User testing, including usability testing, is done throughout the lifecycle—it is not left to the end of the project where it is invariably too late to act.

It is possible for UEX practitioners to make a valuable contribution on ASD teams, and I suspect that there is a much greater chance of them succeeding as compared to working with traditional teams. Up until this point, the UEX community has had little success in their attempts to become an active part of mainstream development teams, so it is time for a new approach. My suggestion is that UEX practitioners should work closely with the agile inmates to try to get the prison under reasonable control.

References

Agile Alliance (2001). *The Agile Manifesto*. agilemanifesto.org Accessed on May 1, 2006.

Ambler, S.W. (2002). *Agile Modeling: Effective Practices for Extreme Programming and the Unified Process*. New York: Wiley Computer Publishing.

Ambler, S.W. (2003a). *Agile Model Driven Development* (AMDD). www.agilemodeling.com/essays/amdd.htm. Accessed on April 30, 2006.

Ambler, S.W. (2003b). *Generalizing Specialists: Improving Your IT Career Skills*. www.agilemodeling.com/essays/generalizingSpecialists.htm. Accessed on April 30, 2006.

Ambler, S. W. (2003c). *Agile Database Techniques: Effective Strategies for the Agile Software Developer*. New York: Wiley.

Ambler, S. W. (2004a). *The Object Primer, 3rd Edition: Agile Model Driven Development with UML 2*. New York: Cambridge University Press.

Ambler, S.W. (2004b). *Skinnier RUP*. http://www.ddj.com/dept/architect/184415143. Accessed on August 19, 2006.

Ambler, S.W. (2005). *The Agile Unified Process* (AUP). www.ambysoft.com/unifiedprocess/ agileUP.html Accessed on April 30, 2006.

Ambler, S.W. (2006a). *The Agile System Development Lifecycle* (SDLC). www.ambysoft.com/ essays/agileLifecycle.html. Accessed on April 30, 2006.

Ambler, S.W. (2006b). *Examining the "Big Requirements Up Front (BRUF)" Approach*. www.agilemodeling.com/essays/examiningBRUF.htm. Accessed on April 30, 2006.

Ambler, S.W. (2006c). *The "Model a bit Ahead" Pattern*. www.agilemodeling.com/essays/ modelAhead.htm. Accessed on April 30, 2006.

Ambler, S.W. (2006d). *Examining the Agile Manifesto*. www.ambysoft.com/essays/agileManifesto. html. Accessed on May 1, 2006.

Ambler, S.W., & Sadalage, P.J. (2006). *Refactoring Databases: Evolutionary Database Design*. Boston: Addison Wesley.

Anderson, D. (2001). *Extending FDD for UI*. www.uidesign.net/2001/papers/fddui.html Accessed on April 25, 2006.

Astels D. (2003). *Test Driven Development: A Practical Guide*. Upper Saddle River, NJ: Prentice Hall.

Beck, K. (2000). *Extreme Programming Explained—Embrace Change*. Reading, MA: Addison Wesley Longman.

Beck, K. (2003). *Test Driven Development: By Example*. Boston: Addison-Wesley.

Beedle, M., & Schwaber, K. (2001). *Agile Software Development with SCRUM*. Upper Saddle River, NJ: Prentice Hall.

Pace, C.C. (2003). *Usability and User Interface Design in XP*. www.ccpace.com/Resources/ documents/UsabilityinXP.pdf Accessed on April 25, 2006.

Constantine, L. (2001). *Process Agility and Software Usability: Toward Lightweight Usage-Centered Design*. www.foruse.com/articles/agiledesign.pdf Accessed on April 25, 2006.

Constantine, L. L., & Lockwood, L. A. D. (1999). *Software for Use: A Practical Guide to the Models and Methods of Usage-Centered Design*. New York: ACM Press.

Cooper, A. (2004). *The Inmates Are Running the Asylum: Why High-Tech Products Drive Us Crazy and How to Restore the Sanity*. Indianapolis: SAMS Publishing.

Desilets, A. (2005). *Are Agile and Usability Methodologies Compatible?* www.carleton.ca/ hotlab/hottopics/Articles/June2005-AreAgileandUxMet.html. Accessed on April 25, 2006.

Eckstein, J. (2004). *Agile Software Development in the Large: Diving into the Deep*. New York: Dorset House Publishing.

Fowler, M. (1999). *Refactoring: Improving the Design of Existing Code*. Menlo Park, CA: Addison-Wesley Longman.

Hodgetts, P. (2005). *Experiences Integrating Sophisticated User Experience Design Practices into Agile Processes*. www.agilelogic.com/files/ExperiencesIntegratingUEXPractices.pdf. Accessed on April 25, 2006.

Jacobson, I., Booch, G., & Rumbaugh, J. (1999). *The Unified Software Development Process*. Reading, MA: Addison Wesley Longman.

Jokela, T., & Abrahamsson, P. (2004). Usability Assessment of an Extreme Programming Project: Close Co-operation with the Customer Does Not Equal Good Usability. *Product Focused Software Process Improvement: 5th International Conference, PROFES 2004 Proceedings* (pp. 393–407). Berlin: Springer-Verlag.

Kruchten, P. (2004). *The Rational Unified Process: An Introduction (3rd ed.)*. Reading, MA: Addison Wesley Longman.

Kroll, P., & MacIsaac, B. (2006). *Agility and Discipline Made Easy: Practices from OpenUP and RUP*. Reading, MA: Addison Wesley Longman.

Lee, J.C. (2006). *Embracing Agile Development of Usable Software Systems*. CHI 2006.

McInerney, P., & Maurer, F. (2005). UCD in Agile Projects: Dream Team or Odd Couple? *Interactions*, November/December 2005.

Microsoft (2004). *MSF for Agile Software Development.* msdn.microsoft.com/vstudio/ teamsystem/msf/msfagile/ Accessed on April 25, 2006.

Meszaros, G., & Aston, J. (2006). Adding Usability Testing to an Agile Project. *Agile 2006 Conference Proceedings*, pp. 289–294.

Mugridge, R., & Cunningham, W. (2005). *Fit for Developing Software: Framework for Integrated Tests.* Boston: Addison-Wesley.

Nelson, E. (2002). *Extreme Programming vs. Interaction Design.* www.fawcette.com/ interviews/beck_cooper/ Accessed on April 25, 2006.

Neilson, J. (1994). *Usability Engineering.* San Francisco: Morgan Kaufmann.

Palmer, S. R., & Felsing, J. M. (2002). *A Practical Guide to Feature-Driven Development.* Upper Saddle River, NJ: Prentice Hall PTR.

Patton, J. (2004). *Interaction Design Meets Agility: Practicing Usage Centered Design in an Agile Software Development Environment.* www.agilealliance.org:8080/articles/ pattonjeffinteraction/file Accessed on April 25, 2006.

Software Engineering Institute (1995). *The Capability Maturity Model: Guidelines for Improving the Software Process.* Reading, MA: Addison-Wesley Publishing Company.

Stapleton, J. (2003). *DSDM: Business Focused Development (2nd ed.).* Harlow, UK: Addison Wesley.

Williams, L., & Kessler, R. (2002). *Pair Programming Illuminated.* Boston, MA: Addison-Wesley.

Chapter 5
Model-Based Evaluation: A New Way to Support Usability Evaluation of Multimodal Interactive Applications

Regina Bernhaupt[1], **David Navarre**[2], **Philippe Palanque**[2] and **Marco Winckler**[2]

[1] ICT & S-Center, Universität Salzburg, Austria, e-mail: Regina.Bernhaupt@sbg.ac.at
[2] LIIHS-IRIT, University Paul Sabatier, France

Abstract Multimodal interfaces are becoming more common, even in the field of safety critical interactive software, mainly due to the naturalness of the interaction that increases the bandwidth between the user and the system they are interacting with. However, the specificities of multimodal interactive systems make it difficult to gather information from the use of modalities and to extract from this information recommendations for improving the multimodal user interfaces. This chapter aims at presenting how abstract information described in models can be fruitfully exploited to improve the quality of evaluations of multimodal interfaces. The approach presented in this chapter combines model-based verification (based on simulation scenario extraction generated from models) and empirical methods for usability evaluation. Our aim is to try to bring together two separated (and often opposite) issues, such as usability and reliability, into the development of safety critical systems. This approach is illustrated via a Space Ground System of a satellite control room, whose multimodal interaction technique is fully described by the means of formal models.

5.1 Introduction

Since the seminal work by Bolt (Bolt 1980) (Bolt & Herranz 1992), multimodal interaction techniques are considered a promising way to increase communication bandwidth between users and systems and to enhance user satisfaction and comfort by providing a more natural way of interacting with computer systems. Several studies have shown that using two pointing devices in a normal graphical user interface is a more efficient and understandable interaction than using basic mouse and keyboard (Buxton & Meyers 1986; Kabbash, Buxton & Seller 1994; Zhai, Barton & Selker,1997). In addition to subjective factors like comfort and satisfaction, increasing communication bandwidth between users and systems can have a significant impact on efficiency. For instance, the number of commands triggered by the users within a given amount of time and the error rate—typically the number of slips or mistakes made by the users (Reason 1990)—are influenced by the user interface and

E. Law et al. (eds.), *Maturing Usability.*

its interaction techniques. Besides, the complementary nature of modalities can be used to reinforce and clarify the communication between the users and the system (Oviatt 1999).

Nevertheless, multimodal interaction is not a panacea. Studies of Dillon and colleagues (1990) and by Kjeldskov and Stage (2004) *unsurprisingly* revealed that when multimodal interfaces are poorly designed they are neither better understood nor more efficient than any other user interface offering more standard interaction techniques. To determine the contribution of modalities to the user interaction, many empirical studies have been carried out in terms of

- Showing how usability and user acceptance is influenced by new devices and novel interaction techniques (Bowman, Gabbard & Hix 2002: Hinckley, Pausch, Proffitt & Kassel 1998; Nedel, Freitas, Jacob & Pimenta 2003; Poupyrev, Weghorst, Billinghurst & Ichikawa 1998)
- Showing that the perceived usability is impacted according to the kind of tasks performed (Dybkjær, Bernsen & Minker 2004; Jöst, Haubler, Merdes & Malaka 2005) and according to the context of use (e.g., indoor x outdoor conditions, mobile applications) (Baille & Schatz 2005)
- Trying to assess the accuracy of multimodal interaction for given tasks (Balbo, Coutaz & Salber 2003; (Kaster, Pfeiffer & Bauckhage, 2003; Suhm, Myers & Waibel 1999; Holzapfel, Nickler & Stiefelhagen 2004)

Some of these investigations show that low-level captured data (e.g., users' events such as mouse clicks and speech) and high-level users' intentions (e.g., goals and tasks) must be combined to determine the accuracy and the perceived usability. It is noteworthy that many users prefer multimodal interaction and nonconventional input devices despite a poorer performance (Kaster, Pfeiffer & Bauckhage 2003). The multimodal dimension brings additional interesting issues to usability evaluation methods. Indeed, each element involved in the design of the user interface can have a huge impact on its usability. For instance, results of existing empirical studies of multimodal applications revealed intricate problems concerning the assessment of the usability of a multimodal interface with respect to several dimensions such as usage and interpretation of modalities, individual user preferences for modality, context-of-use, choice of input and output devices, and interaction techniques.

Despite the fact that all these issues increase the difficulty of evaluating multimodal interfaces usability, these interfaces are becoming more common even in the field of safety critical interactive software such as military (Bastide, Navarre, Palanque, Schyn & Dragicevic 2004) and medical systems (Trevisan, Vanderdonckt, Macq & Raftopoulous 2003). A safety-critical system is a system for which the cost of a failure is significantly more important than the development costs. User error or usability problems might have dramatic consequences, leading to loss of lives. This kind of system requires thorough evaluation and testing to ensure both usability and reliability. This chapter proposes a new approach that combines model-based specification (typically used for the design of this kind of system) and empirical-oriented methods for usability evaluation. The model-based approach relies on formal description techniques and is used to support the assessment and usability evaluation of the multimodal user interface. This combined approach addresses two main drawbacks of current practice in the field of usability evaluation of multimodal systems:

- Lack of support for a complete understanding of the detailed behavior of the system (both at the level of interaction and at the dialog level). This problem can be overcome by appropriate modeling support, because it is illustrated hereafter via *A Case Study for a Space Ground System in a Satellite Control Room*
- Poor integration of usability results into the whole development process. This issue is discussed in the subsection *Modifying Models to Accommodate Change*

The next section briefly presents the state of the art in the field of usability evaluation of multimodal interfaces. We then informally present a case study for a Space Ground System used in satellite control room that is fully described by means of the interactive cooperative objects (ICO) formal description technique (Dragicevic, Navarre, Palanque, Schyn & Bastide 2004). This case study is used in the rest of the paper as a concrete example of multimodal interaction techniques applied to safety critical systems. We briefly describe the results of usability evaluation for this application with two traditional methods (i.e., usability test and cognitive walkthrough). We then present the shortcomings of these two traditional methods, and show how model-based evaluation could support these methods and reduce the identified limitations. This support is mainly provided through the generation (from the formal models) of usability evaluation scenarios that are then used in standard usability evaluation methods. The last section details the advantages and lessons learned from model-based usability evaluation. We show how model-based usability evaluation extends current usability evaluation practice (especially as far as multimodal interfaces are concerned), as well as the limitations of this approach.

5.2 Usability Evaluation of Multimodal Systems

This section briefly presents the state-of-the-art in the field of usability evaluation of multimodal interfaces. We first present the peculiarities of such interfaces and then compare the approaches that have been designed for supporting their usability evaluation.

5.2.1 Specificities of Multimodal Interactive Systems

Even though multimodality is usually associated with the possibility for the user to use several input devices, multimodality concerns both input and output.

A specific aspect of multimodal user interfaces is that interaction techniques, input/output devices, and sensory channels are closely related. Table 5.1 shows that an interaction technique can involve one or more input devices or device combinations. For example, for the ray-casting interaction technique, the synergistic use of data glove and position trackers can replace a 3-D mouse as an input device. On the other hand, a single device can be used in several interaction techniques.

Table 5.1 Examples of input interaction techniques and devices

Sensory channels	Interaction Techniques	Input Devices
Acoustic	Speech	Computer microphone, Cell phone, handheld
Haptic	Typing	Keyboard, touch screen
	Direct manipulation	Mouse, 3D Mouse, touch screen, Panthon
	Gesture interaction	Mouse, 3D Mouse, Data glove, position trackers
	Ray casting	3D Mouse, Data glove + position trackers
Visual	Gaze interaction	Video camera (eye tracking)
	Optical tracker	Video camera (optical markers)

For example, a touch screen can be used as an input device for several interaction techniques such as typing (on a soft keyboard), direct manipulation, and gesture interaction.

To assess the usability of a multimodal application, it is mandatory to evaluate not only the user interface per se, but also to take into account the couple *device-interaction technique*. In the same way that designing the multimodal user interface requires the selection of the appropriate couple (device, interaction technique), the evaluation has to address this issue even though in many multimodal user interfaces redundancy (if made available) allows users to interact with the application in various ways to trigger the same command or to enter the same data. In such cases, the couple (device, interaction technique) selected by the user might differ from one user to another but also with the same user between two successive tasks or usages of the application.

Another major issue of multimodal system concerns the fission and fusion of modalities. This issue is addressed by the classification proposed by Coutaz, et al. (1995), which includes one or more uses and interpretations (i.e., exclusive, concurrent, alternating, and synergistic) of both input and output modalities. As stated in Coutaz, et al. (1995) on a multimodal user interface, input and output modalities can be combined in four different ways (called the CARE properties): Complementarily, Assignment, Redundancy, and Equivalence. CARE properties can therefore be used to structure the usability evaluation of multimodal application, but because the users will be able to choose any interaction technique available, usability evaluation scenarios have to specifically address this issue.

Table 5.2 Examples of output interaction techniques and devices

Sensory Channels	Interaction Techniques	Output Devices
Acoustic	Voice synthesis	Voice synthesizer
Haptic	Force feedback	Panthon, Cybergrasp, Cyberforce
Visual	Image display	Computer screen, touch screen, head-mounted display, stereo glasses

5.2.2 Usability Evaluation Methods (UEM) Used for Multimodal Interfaces

As introduced before, it is a requirement for usability evaluation methods to take into account the specificities of multimodal interfaces. This section presents various UEMs that have been applied to and customized for multimodal user interfaces evaluation. Figure 5.1 structures this information in four main categories and provides a summary of the most representative methods in each category.

Most of the usability studies for multimodal interfaces exploit some user testing where users' activity is observed and recorded, while users are performing predefined tasks. User testing is a preferred strategy for evaluation as it allows the investigation of how users adopt and interact with multimodal technology, providing valuable information about both usability and user experience.

Several types of user testing have been conducted, both in usability laboratories and in field studies, revealing user preferences for interaction modalities based on factors such as acceptance in different social contexts—noisy and mobile environments (Jöst, Haubler, Merdes & Malaka 2005). In the following sections, we will use a case study to show how user testing with log-file analysis and think-aloud protocols can be customized to address the needs of MMI evaluation.

Evaluation based on inspection methods assumes that human factors experts rely on ergonomic knowledge provided by guideline recommendations, or on-their-own experience, to identify usability problems while inspecting the user interface. Known methods belonging to this category include *cognitive walkthrough* (Lewis, Polson & Wharton 1990: Polson, Lewis, Rieman, & Wharton 1992), formative

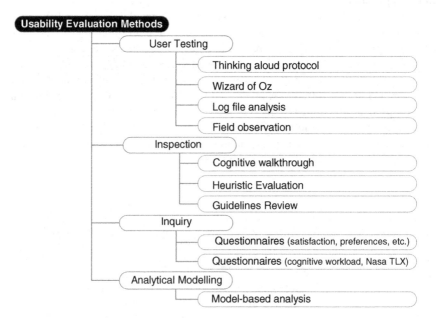

Fig. 5.1 An overview of evaluation methods

evaluation and heuristic evaluation (Nielsen & Mack 1994), and benchmarking approaches covering issues such as ISO 9241 usability recommendations or conformance to guidelines (Bach & Scapin 2003). Inspection methods can be applied in the early phases of the development process through analysis of mock-ups and prototypes. The lack of available ergonomic knowledge might explain why inspection methods have been less frequently employed with an exception in Bowman, Gabbard & Hix (2002). Knowledge is not only missing in terms of experts' experience for the design of multimodal systems, but also due to a lack of guidelines to cover all potential modalities and modality combinations that might be encountered in multimodal interfaces. Cognitive walkthroughs are designed to assess the achievement of goals focusing on the goal structure of the interface rather than on interaction techniques. We will show in the following sections how a cognitive walkthrough can be used when evaluating a multimodal interface, and how this method must be adapted to address the peculiarities of multimodal interfaces.

Questionnaires have been extensively employed to obtain qualitative feedback from users (e.g., satisfaction, perceived utility of the system, and user preferences for modality) (Kaster, Pfeiffer & Bauckhage 2003) and cognitive workload (especially using the NASA-TLX method) (Brewster, Wright & Edwards 1994; Kjeldskov & Stage 2004; Trevisan, Nedel, Macq & Vanderdonckt 2006). Quite often, questionnaires have been used in combination with user-testing techniques as presented in (Jöst, Haubler, Merdes & Malaka 2005).

More recently, simulation and model-based checking of system specifications have been used to predict usability problems such as unreachable states of the systems or conflict detection of events required for fusion. Paternò amd Santos (2006) propose combining task models based on concur task tree (CTT) notation with multiple data sources (e.g., eye-tracking data, video records) to better understand the user interaction.

5.3 A Case Study for a Space Ground System in a Satellite Control Room

This section presents a case study for a Space Ground System application to be used in satellite control rooms (Ould, et al. 2004). The case study exploits multimodal interaction techniques for the manipulation of a 3-D representation of a DEMETER satellite, which stands for Detection of Electro-Magnetic Emissions Transmitted from Earthquake Regions. More information about this satellite's functions and missions can be found on http://smsc.cnes.fr/DEMETER/index.htm.

5.3.1 Informal Description of the Case Study

This application provides multimodal interaction techniques to a user in charge of moving the point of view (we later call this *navigating*) in a 3-D model of a satellite.

This navigation can be done either by rotating the 3-D model of the satellite directly, using the mouse on the 3-D image, or using the two control panels presented in Figure 5.2.

The control panel (b), entitled *point de vue* allows the user to manipulate the current position of the point of view of the 3-D image using the set of buttons in the top right hand side of Figure 5.2(b). The set of buttons in the Orientation subsection allows one to rotate the satellite image in any direction. The set of buttons in the Position subsection allows one to move the satellite image in any direction (up, down, left, right, backward, and forward). The two list boxes on the left-hand side present the list of components of the satellite and the list of categories the components belong to, respectively. We do not present the other parts of the user interfaces as they are related to functions beyond the scope of this paper.

In the initial state the satellite appears as presented in Figure 5.2(a). The main task given to the user of this application is to locate one or several components in the satellite. This task is not easy to perform because components are nested and might not be visible (as they may be either behind or inside a component). To support this task, the user interface makes it possible to set a transparency level for the components' appearance from partly to fully transparent by selecting a percentage. This transparency is set by means of the Transparence slider on the right-hand side of Figure 5.2(c). The goal of the user is to locate components that are either overheating or overconsuming energy. The selection of the range of temperature of interest can be done using the range slider in the *données* section on the right-hand side of Figure 5.2(c). This part of the user interface can also be used for selecting the energy consumption. Figure 5.3 presents a snapshot of the 3-D satellite model, including the temperature of the visible components.

In this application, multimodal interaction takes place both while using the button pairs (changing the point of view of the 3-D model), and while interacting with the range slider (selecting the temperature and the consumption).

Due to space constraints, we only present multimodal interaction on the button pair here. The interested reader can see the formal specification of a similar multimodal range slider component in Dragicevic, Navarre, Palanque, Schyn & Bastide (2004), and the formal specification of a virtual chess game in Navarre, et al. (2005).

The controller's tasks are represented in Figure 5.4 using the CTT notation. We only present here the tasks related to the management of functions that can be triggered through multimodal interaction. The main goal of the controller is to monitor the satellite. This goal is separated into three main tasks—monitoring temperature, monitoring energy consumption, and locating physical components of the satellite by moving its 3-D representation. It is important to see that the task model only describes interaction at quite a high level because it is only describing what the user is aiming at and not how to actually perform these tasks. Connection between these high-level tasks and lower-level ones is done using the precise and complete descriptions embedded in the system model. The next section shows precisely the type of information embedded in the system model, as well as how this connection is made.

Figure 5.5 shows an example of multimodal interaction for this application. On this figure, the user is concurrently using three input devices—two mice and a

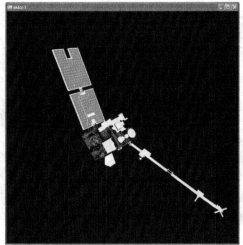

a)

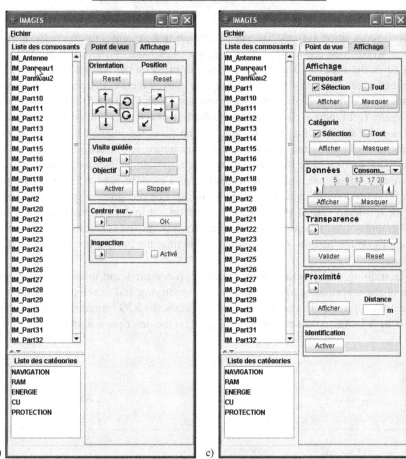

b)   c)

Fig. 5.2 The 3-D representation of DEMETER satellite (a) and its two control panels (b and c)

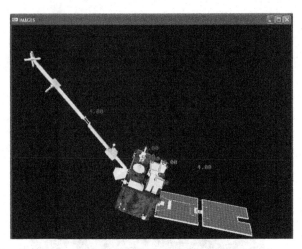

Fig. 5.3 3-D satellite model displaying the temperature of the visible components

speech recognition system. The speech recognition system only reacts to two different words: *fast* and *slow*. The interaction takes place in the following way—at
any time, the user can use any of the mice to press on the buttons that change the
point of view. In Figure 5.5, the button that moves the satellite image backwards
(with the additional label right mouse interaction on Figure 5.5) has been pressed
using the right mouse. Simultaneously, the left mouse is positioned on the button
moving the satellite image to the left. At that time, the image has already started
to move backwards, and as soon as the other button is pressed, the image moves
both backwards and to the left. The user is also able to increase or decrease the
movement speed by uttering the words *fast* and *slow*. In Figure 5.5, the word *fast*
has been pronounced and recognized by the speech recognition system (as shown
on the left-hand side of Figure 5.5). This action will reduce the time between two
movements of the image. Indeed, the image is not moved according to the number
of clicks on the buttons, but according to the time the buttons are kept pressed by
the user.

Describing such interaction techniques in a complete and unambiguous way is
one of the main issues to be solved, while specifying and developing multimodal
interactive systems. The next section presents how the ICO formalism is able to deal
with these issues. Additionally, it will show that the description above is incomplete

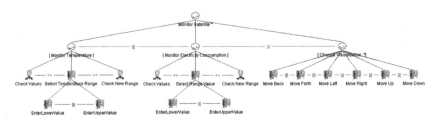

Fig. 5.4 CTT model of the tasks featuring multimodal interactions

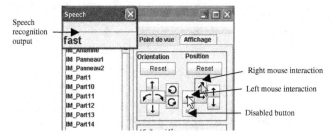

Fig. 5.5 One of the multimodal interactions in the application

and does not address (at an adequate level of detail) both timed and concurrent behavior, at least when it comes to implementation issues. This point is critical when usability evaluations are carried out. Indeed, to assess the comparative usability of two or more multimodal interaction techniques, a precise definition of test scenarios is required. This calls for tools and techniques that describe in a complete and unambiguous way interaction techniques at a very low level of detail. Such a technique is described in the next section.

5.4 Modeling of the Case Study

This section is devoted to the formal modeling of the multimodal interactive application presented in the previous section. In this multimodal application, there is no fusion engine, per se—the two mice are handled independently, and the speech interaction affects movement speed regardless of what interaction is performed with the mice.

The modeling is structured as represented in Figure 5.6. The right hand side of the figure shows the user interacting with the input devices. As stated before, three input devices are available. To configure this set of input devices, we use a dedicated notation called Icon (Dragicevic & Fekete 2001). A more readable model of this

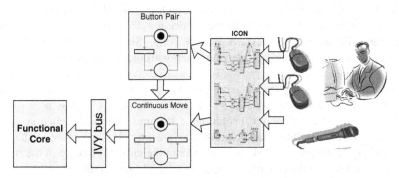

Fig. 5.6 Software architecture of the multimodal interactive application

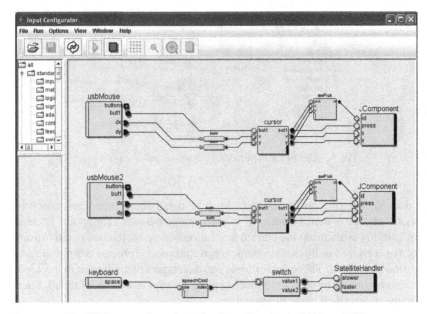

Fig. 5.7 Input configuration using Icon. (Dragicevic & Fekete 2001)

configuration is represented in Figure 5.7. This Icon model is then connected to two ICO models that are, in turn, connected via a communication bus called IVY to the functional core gathering all the data about the DEMETER satellite.

The left-hand side of Figure 5.7 represents the three input devices connected to software components. These components are represented as graphical bricks, and connectors model the data flow between these bricks. For instance, it defines that interaction with the mice will take place using the left button (but1 in the usbMouse brick), and that the alternate button for the speech recognition system is the space bar (Space label in the keyboard brick connected to the speechCmd brick). The right-hand side of this figure (Figure 5.7) represents contact points with the other models of the application. Because input configurations are not central to the scientific contribution of this paper, we do not present in more detail how this modeling works. More information about the system supporting the edition and execution of models, the behavior of a model, and the connections to other models can be found in (Navarre, Palanque, Dragicevic & Bastide 2006). Similarly, the functional core and communication protocol between the functional core and the interaction models are not presented.

The ICO model in Figure 5.8 represents the complete and unambiguous temporal behavior of the speech-based interaction technique, as well as how speech commands impact the temporal evolution of the graphical representation of the 3-D image of the satellite. Darker transitions are available according to the current marking of the models. Taking into account the current marking of the model of Figure 5.8 (one token in places delay, idle, and core), only three transitions startMove_1, faster_, and slower_ are available. These transitions describe the

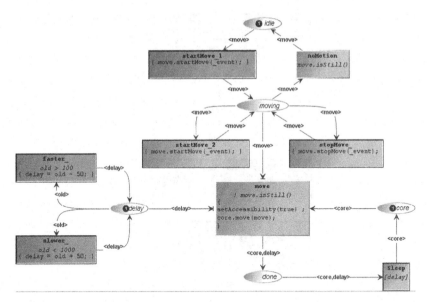

Fig. 5.8 Model of the temporal evolution of movements driven by speech (ContinuousMove class of Figure 5.6)

multimodal interaction technique available (i.e., how each input device can be used to trigger actions on the system). Transitions faster_ and slower_ are triggered when the user utters one of the two speech commands *fast* and *slow*. In the initial state, these are available and will remain available until the upper limit or the lower limit are reached (delay> 1000 for transition slower_ and delay< 100 for transition faster, respectively).

Figure 5.9 presents the model of the second ICO class of the application. This class is responsible for describing the behavior of each button pair. By button pair, we mean the buttons that are performing opposite actions like (up, down), (left, right) and (backward, forward). These three button pairs are represented on the right-hand side of Figure 5.5. To model these incompatible behaviors, the ICO description represents the fact that the user can press either the positive or negative button (e.g., *up* being the positive and *down* being the negative. Connection to the input device (the mice) is done using the Icon model of Figure 5.7.

5.5 Evaluation of the Case Study

Hereafter, we present the usability evaluations that have been carried out on the case study. Our aim with these evaluations is to describe how a formal descrip-tion of multimodal interaction techniques can inform a traditional usability evalu-ation method (UEM)-like usability test and cognitive walkthrough. This approach, integrating both modeling techniques and usability evaluation, is hereafter called

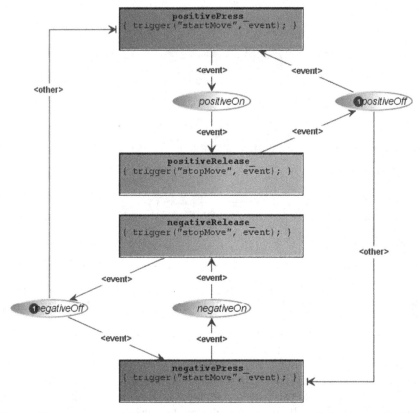

Fig. 5.9 Mutual exclusion of the pair of buttons for changing the point-of-view (ButtonPair Class in Figure 5.6)

model-based evaluation. Before explaining how such an integrated approach works, we present limitations of current UEM for addressing the specific issue of interaction techniques evaluation.

5.5.1 Limitations of Usability Test and Cognitive Walkthrough

The goal of a usability test is to identify major usability problems within the interface. While a common practice is to mainly use the most frequently performed tasks (extracted from task analysis, for instance), in the field of safety-critical systems, it is important to cover all (or most of) the possible interactions in which the user might be involved. The explicit description of the interaction techniques in the formal models makes it possible to identify not only the *minimum* number of scenarios to be tested, but also to select the tasks that are to be focused on more rationally. This selection can be done using analysis techniques on the models that will help designers identify complex or cumbersome behaviors[1] that have been modelled and might require more specific usability testing.

When testing multimodal interfaces, selection of scenarios reaches a higher level of complexity due to the significant number of possible combinations of input modalities, and also due to the fact that fusion engines usually involve quantitative temporal evolution as shown in the ICO modeling of the case study. To test all (or most) of these combinations, it is required to provide usability testing scenarios at a much lower level of description than is usually done with systems featuring more classic interaction techniques. Indeed, as for walk-up and use systems, the interaction technique must be natural enough for the user to be able to discover it while interacting with the system. In the field of safety-critical systems, training and practice are essential points to be taken into account in the evaluation of the system.

Even though we need to address this issue of low-level scenarios, it is also important to notice that usability testing is very different from software testing (which is usually dealing with those low-level tests). The objective here is to test the usability of the interaction technique and not its robustness or default-freeness, as in classical software testing. Software testing of the user interface is starting to get attention from software engineering, but current solutions only deal with basic WIMP interfaces (Memon, Pollack & Soffa 2000). The issue of reliability testing of multimodal interactive systems is also very important, but is beyond the scope of this chapter.

Formal description techniques can help to identify pertinent low-level interaction scenarios and thereby inform selection of tasks more appropriately. Of course, the number of scenarios is likely to be infinite (especially due to the number of possible combinations of uses of input devices) but the model can support the identification of equivalence classes of scenarios (i.e., the ones that are leading to the same state changes in the system model).

To illustrate the advantages and drawbacks of model-based evaluation applied to evaluate our Space Ground system, we present hereafter respective outcomes that we can obtain from both standard usability evaluation (i.e., user testing in usability labs and cognitive walkthroughs) and model-based evaluation.

5.5.1.1 Standard Usability Evaluation

User testing is typically performed in a laboratory, as shown in Figure 5.10 (sometimes in the field), where users are asked to perform selected tasks. The users are observed by camera, and they might be asked to talk aloud (also called elicitation activity) while performing the task. A usability test typically begins with the users

---

[1] Our goal is not to go into detail about the definition of a cumbersome or complex models, but the modeling constructs used within a model can provide such information. For instance, in Palanque, Bastide & Paterno (1997), we have shown (in the field of Air Traffic Control) that multiple unifications on incoming arcs of a transition (which is not a frequent phenomenon in models) might result in tasks that are hard to perform.

Fig. 5.10 Example of
usability test in action

answering a prequestionnaire related to the domain of the software (e.g., use of other related systems, experience with multimodal-interfaces, hours of training, etc). Some tasks are then performed to ensure that the user is able to use the system. The experimenter (or test leader) usually describes the task to the user verbally and also hands over a printed version of the task.

To test the task on identifying overheated components within the satellite, a description might be as follows:

> "Please find all components of the satellite with a temperature between $3°$ C and $6°$ C and position the 3-D in such a way that the component with the highest temperature is visible. Whenever you think that you would stop this task because you feel it is too complicated, please tell us."

The maximum time to solve this task is defined. The task is finished when the user successfully solves the task, when the user takes more than the maximum time to solve the task, or when the users states that he would give up and requires some help. Several rounds of usability testing are performed with different users. The number of successful completions and the completion time are recorded. Tasks not solved indicate usability problems, leading to further detailed investigations of the problems.

Testing multimodal interactions usually requires an additional activity corresponding to the presentation of input and output devices to the user. When complex interaction techniques are considered (as in the current application) the presentation of the application to be tested with the user also requires a description of the actual interaction technique. This description goes beyond the typical high-level (task-based) scenarios promoted by usability testing methods (as presented in the previous paragraphs).

5.5.1.2 Cognitive Walkthrough

Cognitive walkthroughs are rarely used in usability testing of multimodal user interfaces. Quite often, this method is employed in the early phase of the design process, using paper prototypes. With minor adaptations, however, cognitive walkthrough can be successful employed to evaluate multimodal interaction. Following the method presented in Lewis, Polson & Wharton (1990), the evaluators try to answer the questions from the cognitive walkthrough evaluation form while conducting the walkthrough:

- Description of the user's immediate goal
- First/next atomic action user should take:

  - Obvious that action is available? Why/Why not?
  - Obvious that action is appropriate to goal? Why/Why not?

- How will user access description of action?

The adaptation needed to assess multimodal 3-D applications involves a careful preparation of material used to test the learnability of systems. In the case of cognitive walkthroughs, the learnability can be inferred according to the descriptions provided by users for tasks, actions, and goals. We suggest using the real prototype installed on a laptop, and giving all participants of the cognitive walkthrough the ability to try the system before performing the cognitive walkthrough. During the cognitive walkthrough, the user interface must be projected on the wall, and a paper version with screen shots of the current task is also used.

Important when using the cognitive walkthrough in the evaluation of multimodal interfaces is the adoption of guidelines to define the questions in the evaluation form. We believe that the models of the interaction technique (made available in the formal modeling phase) can support this selection of guidelines (as this will be shown in the following section dedicated to model-based evaluation).

5.5.2 Model-based Evaluation

While usability evaluation methods are quite efficient for tracking structural usability problems (based on ergonomic criteria or navigation problems in an application), multimodal applications often present fine grain interaction techniques that are difficult to assess due to their intrinsically complex nature involving concurrent and time-constrained behaviors.

For instance, the description of the temporal evolution presented in Section 5.4 "Modeling the Case Study" shows how complex low-level multimodal interaction can be. When it comes to testing the usability of such behavior, providing a detailed description of the behavior to the evaluators is required first, as well as the ability to to modify such behavior if the results of the usability testing require doing so.

5.5.2.1 Low-Level Scenario Descriptions

Figure 5.11 is called a *marking tree* of a Petri net. It is made up of all the possible sequences of action through a Petri net. When dealing with Petri net models of interactive systems, it is quite common that the model is live (i.e., whatever state the system is in, there is always a transition, such as a user action, available in the system). Such so-called *properties* of interactive systems have an impact on the marking tree that is therefore infinite. While infinite trees are quite difficult to handle when verification of such systems is considered, this is not a problem for usability evaluation, because the task is to drive the usage (and evaluation) of the system, and by definition the task is made up of a finite set of actions. Indeed, when the task is terminated, the description of other sequences or possible interactions is not relevant and thus can be ignored.

Figure 5.11 shows the set of interaction commands possible on the case study. It explicitly shows which interaction techniques are available and when (for instance, from the initial state of the application all actions on the input devices are allowed). Normal circles represent user actions, while shaded ones represent system reactions after a user action has occurred (as described in the key on the right-end corner of Figure 5.11). Arrows connect these actions, making explicit all the possible sequences of user actions on the input devices. To keep the diagram readable, only a small part of the interaction space is represented. Indeed, only two releases of buttons are represented (named "Button Forth Released" in the center and at the bottom of the figure), while these actions are allowed from any system state (but depending on the history of the interaction i.e. what the user has previously done). Similarly the use of speech commands for increasing and reducing rendering speed (see top left hand side of Figure 5.11) has only been presented from the initial state but they are available from any state.

With respect to the Petri net model of Figure 5.8, it also makes explicit the link between system reactions and user actions. It is, however, important to understand

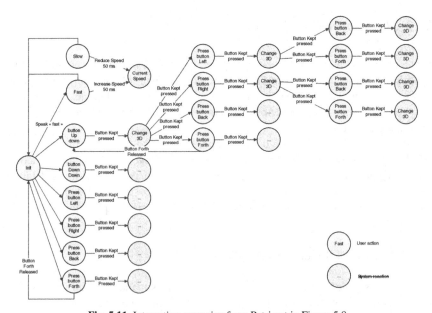

Fig. 5.11 Interaction scenarios from Petri net in Figure 5.8

that the interaction space represented in Figure 5.11 is generated from the Petri net model of Figure 5.8 and is not supposed to be constructed manually. While the model of Figure 5.8 is used at run time for driving the execution of the application, as presented in Navarre, Palanque, Dragicevic & Bastide (2006), the interaction space presented in Figure 5.11 is used for describing low-level scenarios. While the Petri net provides an implicit representation of the state space (a given state for the system is described by the distribution of tokens in the places of the net) the marking graph provides an explicit representation of the states (one circle for each state). What is also made explicit in that diagram is that the more the user uses buttons, the fewer options are available. Indeed, the button currently used is not available, and neither is the opposite one (i.e., if the Up button is pressed, neither Up or Down are available). This is why the set of options available to the user reduces very quickly from the quite important one in the initial state.

The main contribution of these interaction scenarios is to provide an explicit and complete description of the set of interactions available for the user. This makes it possible to test the usability of an interactive application not only at a high level, such as tasks or goals (as shown with cognitive walkthrough, for instance), but also at a lower level of detail. This makes it possible to test

- The interaction technique per se (i.e., how difficult it is to manipulate the input devices for low-level tasks like pointing and selecting objects). In the case of multimodal interactions, it is also possible to evaluate the difficulties for users to combine input devices.
- The link between the interaction technique and task execution by making explicit what kind of low-level action has to be executed in order to perform higher-level tasks and reach goals.
- The complexity of the interaction technique so that users' difficulties in interacting with the application can be predicted. To get more figures about this complexity, we need to apply our approach to several interaction techniques and to analyze correlations with the results from actual usability tests. We already partially addressed these issues in the domain of Air Traffic Control (Palanque, Bastide & Paterno 1997) and we are now carrying on with more complex interaction techniques and different application domains.
- Other complex behaviors related to quantitative temporal behaviors (number of milliseconds for the delays, for instance) can also be represented and thus exploited during usability tests. Indeed, the interaction technique can embed temporal behaviors like the one presented in the case study, and this can have an impact on users' performance. The explicit representation of these temporal evolutions in the interaction technique models makes it possible to incorporate such values while usability experts analyze the results of the usability tests.

Lastly, this explicit representation of low-level scenarios is useful for selecting the scenarios that will be evaluated with the users, with the explicit purpose of evaluating comfort and cognitive workload induced by this kind of reduction of the interaction space.

5.5.2.2 Modifying Models to Accommodate Changes

The aim of usability evaluation is not only to identify usability problems in a user interface, but is also to provide information to the designers to modify the system and the user interface to reduce or remove the identified problems. Here again, model-based approaches can be of great interest. According to the usability evaluation performed, we describe how some modifications can be incorporated in the ICO model of Figure 5.8:

- Changing the value (increase or decrease) of time related to speech commands— this can be done by changing the line delay = old + 50 in the transition slower_, for instance, to another amount of increase
- Changing the maximum speed (increase or decrease) of 3D image rendering— this can be done by changing the precondition in transition slower_ or faster_ to another value than 1000 (maximum) and 100 (minimum)

Other complex behaviors relative to qualitative temporal behaviours can also be represented and thus exploited during usability tests. For instance, as modeled in Figure 5.8, all the input modalities are available at all times but another design choice could have been to allow only the use of a maximum of two input modalities at a time.

In Figure 5.12, we have added a test arc between place *moving* and transition faster_. This means that the voice command *fast* will only have an effect if performed while the 3-D representation of the satellite is currently modified using the other input devices (the two mice).

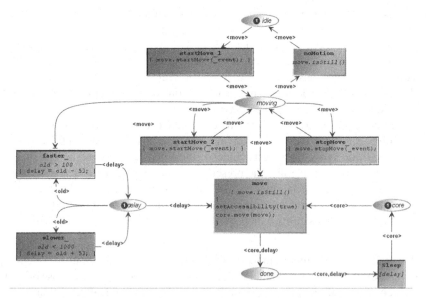

Fig. 5.12 Modification of the availability of a speech command

Such modification would have been made explicit to the users by means of the scenarios extracted from the marking graph. This is an example of a modification of a low-level interaction technique that would require usability testing to assess its impact on the overall usability of the system. Similarly, some scenarios could have been selected with the explicit purpose of evaluating comfort and cognitive workload induced by this kind of reduction of the interaction space.

5.5.3 *Standard UEMs and Model-based Evaluation*

During the set-up of a usability test, the characteristics of multi-modal interaction have to be taken into account (see Section 2.2.1. for an extensive discussion):

- Which pairs of (device, interaction technique) have to be tested?
- How can the user address the system using the various communication channels, and which channel can be used in the various contexts (tasks)?
- What types of fission and fusion can be tested (especially in the case of safety-critical systems)?
- How can the various dimensions affecting usability evaluation of MMIs be addressed (usage and interpretation of modalities, individual user preferences, context-of-use, and activities supported by the system, etc.)

When setting up a usability test for multi-modal interfaces, the selection of tasks must be informed by the models. Tasks with high complexity in the low-level multimodal interaction must be listed exhaustively. Up to now, this comprehensive list has to be done by the expert describing the tasks to be evaluated. In addition, the frequency of highly complex, low-level interactions has to be estimated, based on the task models. In the case study, the number of synergistic usages of speech and two mice has been counted. Based on this information, the tasks for the usability test representing the low-level interaction are selected. High-level tasks are also selected to conduct the usability test.

This way of selecting the tasks for the usability test helps represent all levels of multi-modal interaction. Thus, the results of the usability test are more informative and connected to the precise design of the system.

For the set-up of a cognitive walkthrough, the same information about low-level interaction must be used to define the questions during the walkthrough. A result for a specific question might be: "How many modalities can the user cope with, when the user is doing a rotation of a satellite? How many speech commands can the user remember, when he is using additionally two mice, and when he is in a stressed situation?"

During the performance of the cognitive walkthrough, the fast adaptability for the multi-modal interaction can be quite useful. For example, during the cognitive walkthrough evaluating the rotation of the satellite using two mice and speech, the idea comes up that an additional back command (speech) would have been helpful to interact with the system. The model of this task can be quickly changed, and the added command can be tested with respect to the learnability of the system.

Model-based evaluation helps support standard usability evaluation methods to overcome their reported weaknesses when testing multimodal interfaces. Provided with the adequate tools for editing models and generated marking graphs, the above descriptions might sound easy to follow. Of course, the method will only show its benefits, when the method is carefully set up and conducted.

5.6 Advantages of the Approach and Lessons Learned

The main contribution of these interaction scenarios is to make an explicit and complete description of the set of interactions available for the user. This makes it possible to test the usability of an interactive application, not only at a high level like tasks or goals, but also at a lower level of detail. This makes it possible to test

- The interaction technique per se (i.e., how difficult it is to manipulate the input devices for low-level tasks like pointing and selecting objects). In the case of multimodal interactions, it is also possible to evaluate the difficulties for users to combine input devices.
- The link between the interaction technique and the tasks' execution by making explicit what kind of low-level actions have to be executed to perform higher-level tasks and to reach goals.
- The complexity of the interaction technique that is needed to be able to predict users' difficulties in interacting with the application. To get more figures about this complexity, we need to apply our approach to several interaction techniques and analyze correlations with the results from actual usability tests. We already partially addressed these issues in the domain of Air Traffic Control (Palanque, Bastide & Paterno 1997) and we are now carrying on with more complex interaction techniques and different application domains.

Other complex behaviors relative to qualitative temporal behaviors (number of milliseconds for the delays) can also be represented and thus exploited during usability tests. Indeed, the interaction technique can embed temporal behaviors like the one presented in the case study and this can have an impact on the users' performance. The explicit representation of these temporal evolutions in the interaction technique models makes it possible to incorporate such intrinsic values while usability experts analyze the results of the usability tests.

Lastly, this explicit representation of low-level scenarios is useful for selecting which scenarios will be evaluated with the users. Indeed, in the field of safety-critical systems, scenario identification is critical as some tasks can be performed very rarely (such as setting a satellite to a survival mode or tasks involving very low probability events like failures). Being able to detect potential difficulties for the users from the analysis of the interaction models can fruitfully influence the way usability tests will be performed.

5.7 Conclusion and Perspectives

In this chapter, we have detailed the intricate problem of usability evaluation of multimodal user interfaces, using a case study on safety-critical systems. Several issues, such as low-level interaction, fusion and fission of events, and complex and temporal behavior, make multimodal user interfaces difficult to evaluate. In particular, the notion of low-level interaction techniques can have a significant impact on the results and thus the interpretation of usability test results. To overcome these difficulties, we have presented a model-based approach for supporting the evaluation of multimodal user interfaces.

Our approach is illustrated via a Space Ground System of satellite control rooms, for which multimodal interaction techniques are fully described by the means of models. More specifically, we have shown how formal models of dialog and low-level interaction can support usability evaluation through systematic, rational, and low-level scenario identification.

We are currently in the phase of performing such model-based evaluation on a real ground segment information treatment system to assess the impact of multimodal interaction techniques on the ease of use and performance. The goal is also to assess the impact of model-based evaluation with respect to more classical usability evaluation techniques for multimodal systems.

The model-based evaluation can be easily conducted in combination with a usability test or a cognitive walkthrough. We want to investigate further combinations of model-based evaluation and other usability evaluation methods in the near future.

It is important to note that we are not claiming that current practices in the field of usability evaluation must involve model-based usability evaluation. Our claim is that in the field of safety-critical interactive systems, and more specifically when multimodal interaction is considered, model-based approaches can support specific activities (like low-level testing scenarios and task identification) that could be otherwise overlooked or not systematically considered. The benefit is higher in that application domain because safety and reliability concerns already call for such formal description techniques. Exploiting the models for usability also reduces the higher development costs of these approaches.

References

Bach, C., & Scapin, D. (2003). Ergonomic criteria adapted to human virtual environment interaction. In: Rauterberg, M., Menozzi, M. & Wesson, J. (eds.) *IFIP conference on human-computer interaction (INTERACT'2003)* (pp. 880–883), Zurich, Switzerland. IOS Press.

Baille, L., & Schatz, R. (2005). Exploring Multimodality in the Laboratory and the Field. In Lazzari, G. & Pianesi, P. (Eds.), *ACM international conference on multimodal interfaces (ICMI'2005)* (pp. 100–107). New York: ACM Press.

Balbo, S., Coutaz, J., & Salber, D. (2003) Towards automatic evaluation of multimodal user interfaces. *Intelligent User Interfaces, Knowledge-Based Systems,* 6(4), pp. 267–274.

Bastide, R., Navarre, D., Palanque, P., Schyn, A., & Dragicevic, P. (2004). Model-based approach for real-time embedded multimodal systems in military aircrafts. In *ACM International Conference on Multimodal Interfaces (ICMI'2004)*. New York: ACM Press.

Bolt, R. A. (1980). Put-that-there: Voice and gesture at the graphics interface. In *Proceedings of the 7th International Conference on Computer Graphics and Interactive Techniques* (pp. 262–270), Seattle, USA.

Bolt, R. E., & Herranz, E. (1992). Two-handed gesture in multi-modal natural dialog. In J. Mackinlay & M. Green (Eds.), *Symposium on User Interface Software and Technology (UIST'92)* (pp. 7–14). New York: ACM Press.

Bowman, D., Gabbard, J., & Hix, D. (2002). A survey of usability evaluation in virtual environments: Classification and comparison of methods. *Presence: Teleoperators and Virtual Environments, 11*(4), 404–424.

Brewster, S. A., Wright, P. C., & Edwards, A. D. N. (1994). The design and evaluation of an auditory-enhanced scrollbar. In *Proceedings of the SIGCHI conference on Human factors in computing systems (CHI '94)* (pp. 173–179). New York: ACM Press.

Buxton, W., & Myers, B.A. (1986) A study in two-handed input. In: Mantei M., & Orbeton, P. (Eds.), *ACM Conference on Human Factors in Computing Systems (CHI'86)* (pp. 321–326), Boston, Massachusetts. ACM Press.

Coutaz, J., Nigay, L., Salber, D., Blandford, A., May, J., & Young, R. (1995). Four easy pieces for assessing the usability of multimodal in interaction: the CARE Properties. In S. A. Arnesen & S. Gilmore (Eds.), *The IFIP Conference on Human-Computer Interaction (INTERACT'95)* (pp. 115–120). Lillehammer, Norway: Chapman & Hall.

Dillon, R.F., Edey, J.D., &Tombaugh, J.W. (1990). Measuring the true cost of command selection: techniques and results. In J.C. Chew & J. Whiteside (Eds.), *ACM Conference on Human Factors in Computing Systems (CHI'90)* (pp 19–25), Seattle, Washington. ACM Press.

Dragicevic P., & Fekete J-D. (2001). Input device selection and interaction configuration with ICON. In A. Blandford, J. Vanderdonckt & P. Gray (Eds.), *People and Computer XV – Interaction without Frontiers: Joint Proceedings of HCI 2001 and IHM 2001* (pp. 448–543). London: Springer.

Dragicevic, P., Navarre, D., Palanque, P., Schyn, A., & Bastide, R. (2004). Very-high-fidelity prototyping for both presentation and dialogue parts of multimodal interactive systems. In: *DSVIS/EHCI 2004 Joint Conference 11th Workshop on Design Specification and Verification of Interactive Systems and Engineering for HCI*, Tremsbüttel Castle, Hamburg, Germany, Lecture Notes in Computer Science n° 3425 (pp. 179–199).

Dybkjær, L., Bernsen, N. O., & Minker, W. (2004). New challenges in usability evaluation – Beyond task-oriented spoken dialogue systems. In *Proceedings of ICSLP, (vol. III)* (pp. 2261–2264).

Jöst, M., Haubler, J., Merdes, M., & Malaka, R. (2005). Multimodal interaction for pedestrians: an evaluation study. In J. Riedl, A. Jameson, D. Billsus & T. Lau (Eds.), *ACM International Conference on Intelligent User Interfaces (IUI'2005)* (pp. 59–66), San Diego. ACM Press.

Hinckley, K., Pausch, R., Proffitt, D., & Kassel, N. F. (1998). Two-handed virtual manipulation. *ACM Transactions on Computer-Human Interaction, 5*(3), 260–302.

Holzapfel, H., Nickler, K., & Stiefelhagen, R. (2004) Implementation and evaluation of a constraint-based multimodal fusion system for speech and 3D pointing gesture. In R. Sharma & T. Darrell, T. (Eds.), *ACM International Conference on Multimodal Interfaces (ICMI'2004)* (pp. 175–182). New York: ACM Press.

Kaster, T., Pfeiffer, M., & Bauckhage, C. (2003). Combining speech and haptics for intuitive and efficient navigation through image database. In S. Oviatt (Ed.), *ACM International Conference on Multimodal interfaces (ICMI'2003)* (pp. 180–187). New York: ACM Press.

Kabbash, P., Buxton, W., & Sellen, A. (1994). Two-handed input in a compound task. In C. Plaisant (Ed.), *ACM Conference on Human Factors in Computing System (CHI'94)* (pp. 417–423), Boston, Massachusetts. ACM Press.

Kjeldskov, J., & Stage, J. (2004). New techniques for usability evaluation of mobile systems. *International Journal on Human-Computer Studies, 60*(5), 599–220.

Lewis, C., Polson, P., & Wharton, R. (1990). Testing a walkthrough methodology for theory-based design of walk-up-and-us interfaces. In J. C. Chew & J. Whiteside (Eds.), *ACM Conference on Human Factors in Computing Systems (CHI'90)* (pp. 235–241), Seattle, Washington. ACM Press.

Memon A., Pollack M., & Soffa M-L. (2000). Automated test oracles for GUIs. *ACM SIGSOFT Software Engineering Notes: Proceedings of the 8th ACM SIGSOFT International Symposium on Foundations of Software Engineering: twenty-first century applications (SIGSOFT '00/FSE-8), Volume 25,* Issue 6 (pp. 30–39). ACM Press.

Navarre D., Palanque P., Dragicevic P., & Bastide R. (2006). An approach integrating two complementary model-based environments for the construction of multimodal interactive applications. *Interacting with Computers, 18*(5), 910–941.

Navarre, D., Palanque, P., Bastide, R., Schyn, A., Winckler, M., Nedel, L., & Freitas, C.M.D.S. (2005). A formal description of multimodal interaction techniques for immersive virtual reality applications. In M. F. Costabile & F. Paterno (Eds.), *IFIP Conference on Human-Computer Interaction (INTERACT'2005)* (pp. 170–183). Berlin: Springer-Verlag.

Nedel, L., Freitas, C.M.D.S., Jacob, L., & Pimenta, M. (2003). Testing the use of egocentric interactive techniques in immersive virtual environments. In: M. Rauterberg, M. Menozzi & J. Wesson (Eds.), *IFIP Conference on Human-Computer Interaction (INTERACT'2003)* (pp. 471–478), Zurich, Switzerland. IOS Press.

Nielsen, J., & Mack, R. (1994). *Usability inspection methods.* New York: Wiley.

Ould, M., Bastide, R., Navarre, D., Palanque, P., Rubio, F., & Schyn, A. (2004). Multimodal and 3D graphic man-machine interfaces to improve operations. In *Proceedings of Eighth International Conference on Space Operations* (pp. 435–450), Montréal, Canada.

Oviatt, S. (1999). Ten myths of multimodal interaction. *Communications of the ACM, Vol. 42*(11), 74 –81.

Palanque, P., Bastide, R., & Paterno, F. (1997). Formal specification as a tool for objective assessment of safety-critical interactive systems. In *Proceedings of IFIP TC 13 INTERACT'97 conference* (pp. 323–330), Sydney, Australia, 14–18 July 1997. Chapman & Hall.

Paternò, F., & Santos, I. (2006). Designing and developing multi-user, multi-device web interfaces. In G. Calvary & J. Vanderdonckt (Eds.), *Conference on Computer-Aided Design of User Interfaces (CADUI2006).* Dordrecht, the Netherlands: Kluwer Academics Publishers.

Poupyrev, I, Weghorst, S., Billinghurst, M., & Ichikawa, T. (1998). Egocentric object manipulation in virtual environments: empirical evaluation of interaction techniques. In N. Ferreira & M. Göbel (Eds.), *Proceedings of Computer Graphics Forum (EUROGRAPHICS'98)* (pp. 41–52). Malden, MA: Blackwell Publishers.

Polson, P. G., Lewis, C., Rieman, J., & Wharton, C. (1992). Cognitive walkthroughs: A method for theory-based evaluation of user interfaces. *International Journal of Man-Machine Studies, 36*(5), 741–773.

Reason J. (1990*). Human Error.* Cambridge University Press.

Suhm, B., Myers, B., & Waibel, A. (1999). Model-based and empirical evaluation of multimodal interactive error correction. In M.E. Atwood (Eds.), *ACM Conference on Human Factors in Computing Systems (CHI'99)* (pp. 584–591). New York: ACM Press.

Trevisan, D., Vanderdonckt, J., Macq, B., & Raftopoulous, C. (2003). Modeling interaction for image-guided procedures. In *Proceedings of International Conference on Medical Imaging SPIE'2003 (*pp. 108–118). San Diego: International Society for Optical Engineering (v. 5029).

Trevisan, D. G., Nedel, L. P., Macq, B., & Vanderdonckt, J. (2006). Detecting interaction variables in a mixed reality system for maxillofacial-guided surgery. In: *SBC Symposium on Virtual Reality (SVR'2006)* (pp. 39–50). Belém do Pará, Brazil: SBC Press.

Zhai, S., Barton, A.S., & Selker, T. (1997). Improving browsing performance: a study of four input devices for scrolling and pointing tasks. In S. Howard, J. Hammond & G. Lindgaard (Eds.), *The IFIP Conference on Human-Computer Interaction (INTERACT'97)* (pp. 286–292). Sydney: Chapman & Hall.

Part II
Quality in Interaction

Chapter 6
Systems Usability – Promoting Core-Task Oriented Work Practices

Paula Savioja and Leena Norros

VTT Technical Research Centre of Finland, Finland, e-mail: paula.savioja@vtt.fi

Abstract A new concept of systems usability is introduced. Systems usability provides a holistic activity-oriented perspective to evaluation of the appropriateness of ICT–based smart tools. The concept has been developed in empirical studies of work in complex industrial environments. The nuclear power plant domain is used here to exemplify the systems usability concept and the method developed for evaluating it. In the chapter, we first identify four practical challenges that the current approaches in usability studies face: task analysis, data collection methods, usability measures, and inferences concerning the interface. As a solution to tackle these challenges we, then, introduce our concept of systems usability. To reach the demands of systems usability, work tools must fulfill all three functions of tools: the instrumental, psychological, and communicative. Because systems usability is visible in practices of using the tools we, finally, demonstrate how the developed method labeled *contextual assessment of systems usability* (CASU) is used for evaluating systems usability.

6.1 Introduction

This chapter introduces the concept of *systems usability* and gives both theoretical and practical justification for it. The concept has been developed in conjunction with empirical studies of work in complex industrial environments—primarily in nuclear power production (e.g., Savioja & Norros 2004), but also ship maneuvering (Nuutinen & Norros, in press) and anaesthesia (Norros & Klemola 2005). We have found out that various software tools that people use in their work have, in addition to the traditional usability attributes, other types of quality attributes that become evident in usage situations. These attributes relate to how the tools function as a tool and as a medium in the totality of an activity system. The tools are a constituent of the system, and thus their quality has an effect on the functioning and development of the whole system—hence, the name *systems usability*.

First we want to bring the readers to a situation in which the practical problem of measuring the user interface quality of a complex socio-technical system is evident.

E. Law et al. (eds.), *Maturing Usability.*

Three professional operators are present in a nuclear power plant (NPP) control room simulator. The turbine operator, the reactor operator, and the shift supervisor all sit calmly and
chat about the upcoming training period. The atmosphere within the crew is alert, as if
expecting something to happen soon.

The control room is packed with information about the NPP process. All four walls are
covered with panels that are filled with knobs, switches, and indicators. In the middle of
the room, there is a large console—the operators' desk—which is also filled with switches
and indicators. On the desk, there are computer monitors presenting information in different
formats; there are trends, complex graphical illustrations, numerical information, and a list
of process events. The amount and variation of available process information in the control room is abundant. Two of the operators sit in front of the central console and monitor
the process information. The shift supervisor sits further back and is concentrating on the
process information available for him on his computer screen.

Suddenly, an alarm goes off and gives a signal of something abnormal having taken
place in the process. All the indicators start rolling and various color lights blink on the
desks and panels. The event list monitor is filled with lines of text, each indicating separate
process events. The first lines that appeared soon disappear as more process events take
place.

When the alarm goes off, the operators become visibly active and determined. Two
seconds after the first alarm sounds the turbine operator claims: "Main circulation valve is
jammed." The supervisor gives a nod to the diagnosis and the operators dig out the right
procedures from the row of folders. The operators start reading the procedure. According to
the procedure, they perform safety-related process data checks while the automation system
is shutting down the plant. The operators monitor the functioning of the automation and thus
ensure that there are no other process failures to be attended to. The automation functions
correctly and the operators perform a few manual operations during the scenario.

The cooperation of the crew is well-organized and seems seamless. Both the operators
have the same procedure, and from the corner of their eye they can follow what the other
one is doing: which part of the process he is working on can be deduced by his physical
location in the room, and what exactly he is doing can be found out by combining the spatial
information with the information provided by the procedures.

In the above described situation, the whole chain of events takes place within
seconds. The external observer cannot even start to grasp the situation when the
highly skilled operators have already got the whole plant under control. After the
initial stabilization is carried out, the operators start using the procedure. Sometimes
almost all their observable behavior is determined by the procedure. The objectives
of process control—safety and efficiency—have been used as underlying principles
when creating the procedures, and the operators only have to follow what is written.

The meticulous operator activity is the result of years of professional training
(IAEA 2002). This means that for an outside observer (e.g., a usability expert), it is
very difficult to determine whether the interface, the computer screens, procedures,
and analog indicators are simply just very usable or the seemingly smooth activity is just the result of the extensive work experience and training. The tools are
such an integral part of the activity that their role in construction of the activity and
production of its outcome is hard to extract.

The question in the above described situation is: *How should the researcher analyze and develop the usability of the user interface to the NPP process?* How should
a usability test be conducted for a totally new interface?

This question has become interesting because almost all of the nuclear power
plants in the world are reaching an age in which the obsolescence of original

technology and poor availability of spare parts are compelling the plants to renew control room technology. Because the prevailing control room technology today is digital, completely different from the original analogical technology used 30 years ago, new information representations, symbols, and even operational concepts are being developed for the nuclear industry. As such, these new interface solutions need to be carefully evaluated because of the potential safety hazards of poor solutions.

But the evaluation of the new interface solutions is not simple. It is difficult to even define the object of the analysis, because the user interface is actually the whole control room, which is always used by more than one operator at the same time. Considering the validity of the usability evaluation, it is not correct to only look at one of the actors because in the real-life situation the activity of process control is very much cooperative. The cooperation even crosses the boundaries of the control room to the field operators and maintenance personnel. In addition, the operators also have a role in the dissemination of information about process abnormalities to the world outside the plant. The interface should provide support for all these tasks, so even to begin the analysis by defining the boundaries is not a simple task for the usability analyst.

The whole system of NPP process control can be described, as Vicente (1999) characterizes complex sociotechnical systems (from now on we use the term *complex systems*): they cover a large problem space, comprise possible hazards, are social in nature, are distributed, and are constitutes of coupled interactions. All the attributes lay requirements for the analysis of the usability of the control system interface.

The quality of an interface can be evaluated for two separate purposes: first to *improve* the design, and second to *accept* the design. Traditionally, interface evaluation in safety critical domains has been approached with the latter question in mind. There has been a need to investigate whether the proposed design solution is good and safe enough to be used to control the dynamic process. In this evaluation type, the research perspectives of human factors (HF) and cognitive ergonomics (CE) have become prevalent. In these disciplines, the research problem is formulated so that a controlled experiment can be conducted in which different interface types represent independent variables. Human performance is the dependent variable that is evaluated with various measures. The correlation between certain interfaces and good human performance is recognized, and a conclusion about the quality of the interface is drawn. While this approach is valuable, we feel it does not give enough attention to user-system interaction. The attributes of good interaction are not used in the experiment, and thus input for creating new design ideas and hence answering the improvement needs of the current design is limited.[1] On the contrary, the *usability approach* has always considered design improvement as motivation for the whole discipline. But, for some reason usability evaluation has not fully succeeded in aiding the

---

[1] This drawback has recently been identified within the communities, and new design-oriented traditions are currently emerging that focus on cognitive systems in context (see details in Hollnagel 2003).

design of complex system interfaces. We feel that this is due to the current methods' inability to consider the complexity of the process control activity in the evaluation.

The aim of this chapter to motivate and describe how the two above approaches can be combined and extended to form a new type of holistic evaluation approach for complex system interfaces. To evaluate the usability of a complex system interface, the domain of use and construction of the activity in that domain need to be profoundly understood.

We use the concepts of activity, core task, and practice to achieve this. In this chapter, we will show how to define good practice in a given domain and describe practical implementation of the concepts as a systems usability evaluation method.

6.2 Practical Challenges in Evaluating Usability

In this section, we discus the challenges and shortcomings of the prevailing usability evaluation methods that we have encountered in user interface evaluation of complex systems. The emphasis is on the parts of evaluation process that we feel contribute most to the validity evaluation. The section is broken into four parts: task analysis, data collection methods, usability measures, and inferences about the interface.

6.2.1 Task Analysis

Usability evaluation starts with acquiring knowledge about the domain and context for which the solution is designed. This is done to understand what kind of tasks the application is supposed to support, and what kind of results the tasks are supposed to produce—that is to say, when the task has been successfully conducted.

Typically in task analysis, the task is defined as a goal and the steps leading to achieving it. The end result of the task analysis is a normative description of what users do (or must do) in order to reach the goal. A normative task analysis as described above gives an answer to the question: "What must the users do?" Another similar way to conduct an analysis is descriptive: "What do the users actually do?" (Vicente, 1999; Norros, 2004). While this approach is tempting for interaction design purposes, we see two negative consequences in these types of task analysis.

The first problem relates to the fact that when task analysis is conducted in a normative way, it takes the current way of carrying out the task using the tools as a starting point. This means that task analysis cannot reach the functionality of the new tool, nor the essence of the new task in which the tool will be used (see task-artifact cycle in Carrol, 1991). While usability analysis with the normative task analyses is seemingly straight forward and well-focused, the problem is that design iterations end up polishing up the solution according to the predefined tasks, not noticing that the tasks normally also change as a new tool is introduced into an activity.

The second problem relates to generalization of users' activity based on such an analysis: as the model of the task is sequential, and thus situation-specific, the result of the analysis can only be generalized intuitively. In the end, the evaluators cannot know how well the evaluation has covered the future use profile of the new tool.

6.2.2 Data Collection Methods

Data collection methods determine what kind of information about the usage activity is available for the researchers. In a usability test, the typical methods of gathering user-system interaction data include observations, verbal protocols, software logging, eye-tracking, and subjective evaluations (eg., Nielsen 1993). Each of these methods is also important in evaluating complex system interfaces, but we have felt that not even all of them together are able to give sufficient data to understand the construction of usage activity in a complex context.

There are several characteristics of usage activity that cannot be revealed with the above-mentioned methods.

First, the observation method typically concentrates on describing *what* is happening in the test situation. It cannot go deeply into *why* something is happening, because the reasons for acting and the meaning of the individual's behavior are, by nature, not directly observable.

Often the explanations for the activity are searched for by going deeper into the *users' minds* (e.g., using eye-tracking methods or psycho-physiological measures). While these methods can give interesting data about neural and physiological bases of behavior (which may differentiate between interface solutions) they still do not convey the personal sense that the observed actions have to the users, and thus cannot explain why the user attended to some information and ignored the other.

One way to find the explanations for the activity is to use the so-called *think aloud* method. This kind of reflection on action, however, is difficult to conduct in a situation in which the dynamics of the process largely determine the pace in the situation. This makes it very difficult to understand the users' train of thought and thus the reasons for their behavior.

In a detailed analysis of the videoed situation, it is possible to specify the operators' communications, operations, and physical movements during the simulated situation. Thus, maybe we can get close to where the possible usability problems lie. For example, it is possible to see whether a particular piece of information is difficult to interpret by the operators. But the data collected this way contributes only to micro level (Hornbæk 2006) of usability.

Subjective evaluation interviews and questionnaires also pose a problem, because the interfaces of complex sociotechnical systems are *work tools*, and users often have years of experience with the existing system and interface. It is then very difficult for them to have an opinion about particular detailed new features of the new tool. To use subjective evaluation, methods in which the users can reflect their experiences of interaction and future activity with the tool should be formulated.

6.2.3 Usability Measures

The usability measures that are used in the test situation are a key issue whenever a usability evaluation is conducted. The selection of measures is connected to task analysis and the selection of data collection methods that were discussed in the previous sections.

Because usability development has become an accepted practice in software, and other appliance, development, the validity of the different metrics needs also to be addressed. The development of the reliability of different methods and the fortification of the methods' technical feasibility are central motives for COST Action 294 (MAUSE 2006). As part of this Action, we have chosen to focus on analyzing conceptual validity of the different usability *measures*. That is, that we are interested in how well the evaluation covers the relevant phenomena concerning the usage of the tools. To understand what is or is not meaningful phenomena, we need to profoundly understand the role of tools in human activity.

ISO 9241 (ISO 1998) defines usability as effectiveness, efficiency, and satisfaction within the usage situation. This definition of usability is also relevant when studying complex sociotechnical systems. In addition, measures that reflect the features of usage situations that are not directly observable, and are not evident in the first time usage of the new tool, are needed.

6.2.4 Inferences Concerning the Interface

In a traditional usability evaluation, the outcome of the test is a prescriptive assessment of the system and the output is a list of usability problems and possibly also a set of correction proposals. The task description created in the beginning of the evaluation is used as a reference.

This type of assessment of the usability of the interface reveals whether the new tool can replace the existing one, but it does not tell how the new tool will shape human activity and create new possibilities for acting. Thus the potentiality of the new tool remains uncovered.

6.3 Theoretical Bases for the Concept of Systems Usability

The goal of this section is to answer the challenges described in the previous section by theoretically describing what makes interfaces of complex systems usable (i.e., what systems usability is). In short, we can say that tools with systems usability are such that they promote the development of good work performance. In order to define what good work performance is, we introduce the concepts: activity, core task, and practice. Our intention is to clarify and discuss some underlying methodological principles of the systems usability approach. The discussion is largely based on the theoretical work that has been accomplished over the years by the human factors research team at Technical Research Centre of Finland (VTT) (Norros 2004; Norros & Savioja 2005).

6.3.1 Functions of a Complex System User Interface

To adopt a well-founded conception of usability, it is necessary to conceive what purposes the tools, in this case the user interface, serve in human activity. Here, we exploit the conceptions of the cultural-historical theory of activity (Vygotsky 1978). In this theory, the distinction between two functions of artifacts—instrument and psychological tool—has been made (Vygotsky 1978). Georg Rückriem (2003) recently proposed that in the present age characterized by ICT technology it would be fruitful, and even necessary, to relate the distinction of functions to ideas developed in media theory. A *tool* is a basic concept of the activity theory, and a *medium* is a basic concept of the media theory. As a distinguished proponent of activity theory, Rückriem takes a novel position by assuming that tools and media may be equated as mediators in activity, and that meaning is not only appropriated in tool-using activity but also *communicated* by the tools as media. As a consequence, he distinguishes three functions of the tool medium instead of only two as is usual in the Vygotskian approach.

The first function of the tool is its *instrumental* function. It refers to the capability of the tool to cause an aimed effect or maintain a desired outcome. This function addresses the issue of effective performance of the tool. The second function is the *psychological* function of the tool. Vygotsky had the insight that tools and concepts offer an external means for the human being to control his or her own behavior. Via this function, reflection of own behavior also becomes possible. The third function of the tool and medium is its *communicative* function. The use of tools and media creates a shared awareness within a team or community by communicating the intentions and purposes of actions. In addition, communication of moral and aesthetical values, taste, and so on, that are appreciated within the community is included. The communicative function addresses issues of sense-making in action and the meaning of action in a wider cultural and societal perspective.

Our conceptual framework is aimed for the evaluation of the usability of interfaces of complex systems. Nowadays, the interfaces are implemented with modern information and communication technology. We make use of the definition of the three functions and claim that a tool with high systems usability is able to fulfill all these three functions of a tool in actions within an activity system.

A methodical challenge and possibility that we hereby create is to define how these functions of the tool should be portrayed in the measures of usability. Hence, we could propose that the instrumental function would relate to the aspects of *effectiveness and efficiency*. The psychological function refers to the tool's ability to support *human use*. This means that humans can interpret the behavior of the object and thus develop their own prehensility. It should also take into account the characteristics that relate to the idea that tools shape human action and capabilities.

Finally, the communicative function would require that artifact to be considered from the point of view of its *meaningfulness* for the activity. The artifact should support communication of the purposes and sharing of the values that contribute to the maintenance and development of the work and activity. It appears that the above conceptual aspects (possible measures) of systems usability have connections to the existing breakdown of the usability concept or to some current new developments in this research domain. It is, however, not our intention in this chapter to go deeper into defining the usability concept itself. Instead, we intend to provide reasons for systems usability as a new, more holistic, approach.

The prevalent methods to evaluate usability of an interface concentrate mainly on the first function of tools—the instrumental function. Hence, they mainly focus on measuring how effective and efficient the interaction is. Of course, subjective measures of satisfaction (and recently, experience) are also used, but we feel that neither of these fully capture the other two functions described above. This is because the subjective measures still focus on the individual preferences of the users in examining the interface. They only consider the interface as a technological object, not as a tool in a meaningful practice.

To reach all the three functions in a usability evaluation, we need new concepts. The first is the notion of practice.

6.3.2 Good Work Practice—A Sign of Good Tools

To capture all the three functions of the interface in usability evaluation, we have to investigate how the interface is actually used in a particular activity. For this purpose, we have found it useful to use the notion of practice. Drawing on MacIntyre's (1984) work, in practice we understand the individual's or the crew's learned way of conducting the work, conceptualizing the object of work, apprehension of what is intended in the work, and insight of what is a good way of utilizing available resources and tools for the work. Practice is always socially founded and what is valued as good work is shared in the community.

We use the concept of practice as an extension of the concept of action. Action alone is implicitly used in usability evaluation due to the way of conducting the task analysis in a normative manner. By using practice, the usability investigation is not limited to considering intentional action as a planned way of using resources to achieve a goal, but also as an adaptive and tacit way of coping with the constraints of the work situation.

With reference to the above discussion of the functions of tools, we claim that with the concept of practice it is possible to include the second and third functions of tools in the evaluation.

While investigating the practice, the analysts are sensitive to the ways in which tools are embedded into the structure and flow of activity. This reveals how well the tool is fulfilling the second (psychological) function described in the previous section.

The third function (communicative) of the tool, relates to how meaningful the tool is in the particular work. The cultural meaning of the tools can also be identified in the practices of the users. The practices convey to the analysts what is valued as good work within the community (e.g., the operating crew or the whole plant). We expect to find differences in the practices, which indicate differences in the logic behind the usage of available information and comprehension of the message that the interface conveys.

In analyzing practices, we separate two different types of performance-related evaluation dimensions. They represent what Alasdair McIntyre named as the *internal* good and *external* good of practice (MacIntyre 1984). According to his formulation, the external good is an outcome-related definition of good performance. It has a connection to our previous discussion of the action as portraying human intentionality in an instrumental sense (the first function). Hence, indicators that define this dimension shall describe the standards of excellence and measure how well the outcome of activity is achieved. The dimension connects with the effectiveness of the artifact.

The other evaluation dimension may be related to the concept of internal good practice (MacIntyre 1984). It reflects features of performance that the members of a particular community of practice value as good, and as an actualization of the professional ethos of the persons and the community. This assessment dimension has connections to the embodied intentionality of action, in reference to which tuning to the environment provides an appropriate relationship with the environment. We see that this dimension becomes evident in adaptability of practice and attentive presence in a situation. This assessment dimension is especially relevant with regard to fitness for human use and meaningfulness of the artifact.

Referencing the above discussion, it becomes evident that the systemic quality of a complex system interface can be evaluated through studying the quality of the practices it enables and promotes. The problem that arises then is to define what good practice is in a given domain. To value different practices, understanding of the *context* of practice is essential. Something that is good practice in one domain might not be in another. For the analysis of the context, we again need new concepts. In the next section, we introduce the model of an activity system and how it is used to define the core task of a particular work.

6.3.3 Activity System in Defining the Core Task

The above leads us to realize that, while in many cases human action may be described as instrumentally oriented behavior intending to reach a defined internally maintained goal or plan, it is also governed by another type of dynamic principle. Hence, action may be seen to be focused on the environment in the form of an absorbed coping that, according to the proponents of phenomenology is understood as a primary, embodied form of intentionality (Dreyfus 2001). In this line of thought, the interest is in the forms of adaptation and reaching of a state of equilibrium that is appropriate with regard to the situation in the particular domain. Pursued adaptability of practice is such that it takes situational constraints into consideration and judges them with regard to the global constraints and purpose of the domain and activity (i.e., the practice must be contextually defined).

In our considerations of the context of practice, we have started with the notion of an activity system (Engeström 1987). An activity system consists of its historical constituents—subject, object, and community—that are organized to produce an outcome (the inner triangle in Figure 6.1). The relationships between subject, object, and community are mediated. The tools mediate the relationship between the subject and the object, rules and norms of the relationship between subject and community and the division of labor in the relationship between community and object. The socio-cultural evolution of human conduct is characterized by an increasing stratification and diversification of these mediations. Also, the relationships include tensions that become overt in various disturbances and problems in the system. One activity system is connected by each of its elements to its surrounding activity systems. Tensions in the system create pressure for change, which itself also is anything but a straightforward process. It is important for the notion of an activity system that it is approached as a dynamic and changing entity that has a history, and that the development of which may take different trajectories.

As mentioned, an activity system is arrayed around *an object* to produce an *outcome* (i.e., the outcome is the central determinant for what elements should be included in the organization). Drawing on Järvilehto (1998), we see that the outcome of the system takes many forms. We can call them *material* and *immaterial* to make the distinction. The material outcome is, for example, the electricity that a power plant produces. The immaterial product is the potential for new activity that the material outcome provides—for example, the development and evolution of the activity system itself. In the example of electricity production, the immaterial outcomes might be the development ideas with which the production process can be made more efficient or safe and also the development potential that availability of electricity provides in society. Without the immaterial outcomes, the activity system cannot advance or grow and will slowly decay or become obsolete. Yet, it is not rare

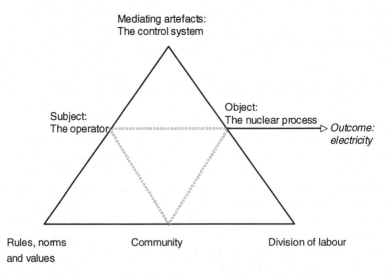

Fig. 6.1 Activity system (modified from Engeström 1999) describing NPP process control

that the immaterial part of the outcome is neglected in the management of organizations due to the difficulty of creating indicators and criteria for measuring it. The articulation of two aspects of outcome facilitates the definition of the purposes of activity and their possible sense for the users, and the content to be communicated.

The model of an activity system must be completed with the analysis of the physical domain (Rasmussen 1986: Vicente 1999) in which it is embedded. That means, for example, that in analyzing NPP process control, we need to understand the physical laws governing the energy production process. This is essential because the functionality of the physical process describes the possibilities and constraints within which successful energy production is possible. This is the meaning of the whole activity.

By using the activity system model and the functional model of physical domain, we can define the users' task in a new systemic way. This is called the *core task*. The core task is the essential content of a particular work that is determined by the constituents of the activity system and the functionalities of the physical domain. The demands of the core task must be maintained in all situations because the physical laws for their part remain the same from one situation to another. Good practice takes into account the general functions of the domain but also their situational embodiments. Thus, work practice can be valued with regard to its orientation to the core task.

By exploiting the concept of the activity system and functional models of the domain in the elaboration of the systems usability approach, we aim to fulfill an important methodological requirement: the approach is contextual and thus provides a consistent and theoretically founded way to define the circumstances in which the artifact is used. The definition of the context is not restricted to the actual perceivable situation, as is often the case in scenario-based techniques. Instead, it also enables an analysis of the invisible societal and historical content of the activity, which the users may take into account according to different logics (Eskola 1999). These logics reflect the differences in work practices and the personal sense that work makes.

6.3.4 Systems Usability of Work Tools

To conclude the theoretical considerations for systems usability concept, we recapitulate the message of this section.

To reach the *demands* of systems usability, work tools must fulfill all the three functions of tools: the instrumental, psychological, and communicative. Thus, systems usability of tools means that tools are such that they can communicate the relevant content to users in a meaningful visual or multimodal representation, in addition to being good instruments and cognitive tools.

Good systems usability is *visible* in the users' work performance because systems usability promotes the construction and development of work practices. Good work practices are such that, in addition to producing good directly measurable results, they are oriented to the core task. The core task is defined by the context and objectives of the activity.

6.4 How to Evaluate Systems Usability

In the case of complex sociotechnical systems, the usability evaluation can be extended to cover the activity level of system usage adopting the *contextual assessment of systems usability* (CASU) method. We will first introduce the overall evaluation process and then some of the individual methods developed.

6.4.1 The Evaluation Process

We have developed a method that, in practice, implements theoretical concepts introduced above to usability evaluation. The CASU method has been used in studies of nuclear power plant control room modifications.

The essence of the CASU method is depicted below (Figure 6.2). It consists of four separate phases. In Figure 6.2, the colored boxes denote research activities and the white boxes are the outcomes of the activity. The first phase—the modeling phase—outlines the basis for the evaluation by producing a reference. In here, it is stated what good process control activity in a given operational situation is. The modeling phase includes task analysis, but it is called modeling because the output is a model of the task demands. The important outputs of the modeling phase are the measures and criteria used in the control room evaluation.

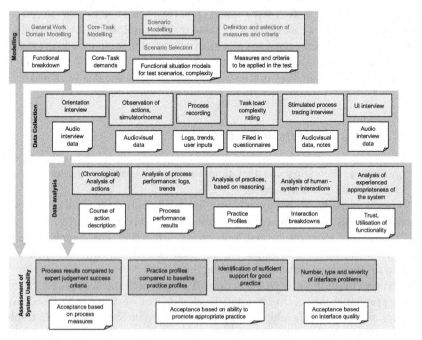

Fig. 6.2 CASU and the process of evaluating complex system interfaces

The second phase is the data collection phase, in which the actual simulator run is observed and the video and the interview data are collected. In the CASU methodology, the data collection methods vary from observation of activity and questionnaires to a few types of interviews. Data collection can be carried out either in a simulator or in a normal work situation.

The third phase is the analysis phase. Analysis aims at taking different perspectives to the collected data. First, the observation data is analyzed from a chronological point of view. What happened in the scenario and when are examined. This is combined to process a performance analysis. From trends and logs, we can see how the process behaved and whether the main parameters remained within acceptable boundaries. In the analysis of practices, we look at the crew's practice of process control. This is done based on both the observable behavior and the justifications the crew gave for their own actions. In interaction analysis, the human-system interaction is observed on a detailed level. The experienced appropriateness is analyzed based on the interview data.

The evaluation ends with the assessment of the interface. The assessment is made by combining three points of view: process measures, the tools' ability to promote appropriate work practices, and interface quality.

In Sections 6.4.2–6.4.5, we describe the methodical extensions to usability evaluation phases (commented in Section 6.2 of this chapter) that we have adopted.

6.4.2 Task Analysis—Functional Way

To extract the systems usability of a work tool, the basis of evaluation—the task analysis—should be conducted on a functional level. This is done to fully understand the activity and the requirements it poses to new tools and their interfaces.

Using the concepts of cultural-historical theory of activity (eg., Engeström, Miettinen, & Punamäki 1999) the prevailing task analysis methods are carried out on the level of *operations* and *actions*. These levels do not give enough information about the whole system of activity. They do not answer to questions: *"Why* do people act?", "What is *meaningful* activity in this domain?", and *"How* do people do what they do?"

The activity level can be reached by conducting the analysis from a functional perspective. It means that the task is analyzed from the point of view of the objectives of the activity. Instead of describing "what users do," functional task analysis describes "why they do what they do" by explicating the objectives of activity. The objectives have societal foundations and in one activity there are typically many contradictory objectives. In the NPP-case, for example, the objectives might be maximal electricity production and minimal radiation to the environment. The functions and subfunctions that fulfill the objectives construct the hierarchical functional model of the task (Figure 6.3). The functional models of the work (generic and situation-specific) explicate the possible reasons for action.

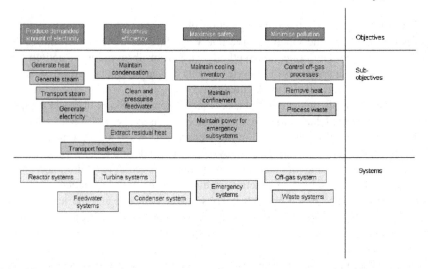

Fig. 6.3 Functional task model for NPP process. On the objectives level, there are the objectives of the activity, and on the subobjectives level there are the functional subobjectives that fulfill the objectives. On the systems level, there are the systems that enable the fulfillment of the objectives

By comparing possible reasons with those that people actually give (i.e., effective reasons for certain behaviors), we can develop behavioral markers to describe how people act. As a result, differences in work practices can be articulated.

Thus, we claim that task analysis needs to be conducted on the level of activity, in addition to actions and operations. Without the activity level of task analysis, the significance of particular actions or operations is difficult to comprehend, and thus the tools' suitability for the practice cannot be evaluated.

As a complement to the task model depicted in Figure 6.3, the scenarios to be used in evaluation also need to be modeled in similar fashion. In functional situation models (FSM), the general task model is given a situational form. An example of an FSM is portrayed in Figure 6.4.

Another side of the task analysis is the model of the core task (Figure 6.5). In this model, the task is looked at, not only from the domain perspective, but also from the individual user's perspective. We want to identify the work practices with which the users cope with the functions of the domain.

The aim of functional task analysis is to understand the reasons for users' actions that relate to the functionality of the object and thus define what good practice in particular domains, and in a particular situation, is. With the aid of functional task models, the measures to be used in the evaluation can be elicited.

6.4.3 Data Collection—Justification of Own Actions

With the prevailing data collection methods, it is hard to acquire information about why people interact the way they do with the tool being tested. What is the meaning

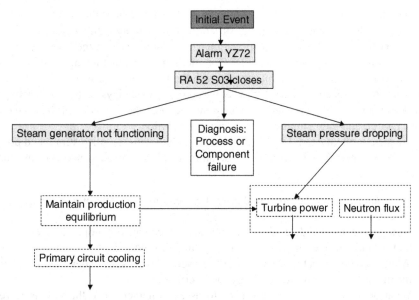

Fig. 6.4 Part of a functional situation model. The general functions are depicted with dotted lines. The situational events (in light gray) give meaning to the functions and describe the users' reasons for actions. Users' actions are depicted with white boxes

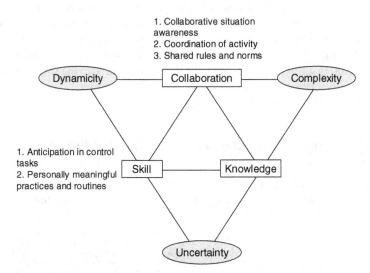

Fig. 6.5 Core task model of NPP process control. The NPP process is dynamic, complex, and uncertain. This lays demands on operators' skills, collaboration, and knowledge, which are in the picture elaborated further

of the interaction? The complexity of the control system makes the chain of deduction unreliable. To understand the construction of the activity with the new tool, it is necessary to also gather users' justifications and reasoning about their own activity. So, in addition to the usual data collection methods in evaluating an interface, we interview the users about the interaction with the tool. This is a way to understand how the activity is constructed and what part the interface plays in the construction. We also want to know how the users take into account the functions of the domain (task model) and their situational manifestations (FSM).

We have implemented this data collection method with so-called stimulated process tracing interviews in which the operators recall the passed scenario from four points of view:

1. What happened in the process during the scenario (e.g,. one process event at a time)?
2. How was each event detected (e.g., interface, procedure, other operators, etc.—to understand how the interface was utilized in the activity)?
3. What was the impact of the event on the overall process (to understand whether the meaning was communicated by the interface)?
4. What actions were taken and how (to assess whether the right actions were afforded)?

While recalling and constructing the scenario, the operators simultaneously reflect about their behavior and the reasons for it. At the same time, they also reveal how they were able to use the interface in the scenario and how useful it was to them. In the process of justification and reasoning about their own behavior, the users reveal the meaning of the information provided to them and the work practices they used to cope with the task demands. During the interview process, we formulate a spreadsheet (Figure 6.6) that represents the crews' shared understanding of the simulator run. In the assessment phase, the table is compared to the situation models to assess the practice of the crew.

6.4.4 Measures—External and Internal Good of Practice

We see that most of the usability measures used in usability evaluation often relate to the outcome of the interaction and the success of task completion. These are

The process event	How detected	Impact/ meaning	Actions taken
Alarm yz72	Yz board	Valve jammed	Decrease power
Next event	etc.	etc.	etc.
Next event	etc.	etc.	etc.

Fig. 6.6 Part of an information table constructed in stimulated process tracing interview

measures that can be used without considering the particular content of activity in that specific scenario. The establishment of internal good practice measures, on the other hand, requires an understanding of what good practice in the chosen scenario is. Internal quality of activity can only be defined within the practice.

Examples of external and internal measures of practice are as follows. It is often important that the users are aware of the exact process state (i.e., some particular process parameter values). As an external measure, we could then use standard *situation awareness* (SA) measurements (Endsley 1995): stop the simulation and ask the user many different process parameter values, both relevant and irrelevant in the situation, and assess the users' SA by the amount of correct answers. If an internal performance measure was considered, the measurement process would be constructed in such a way that the user was asked what is happening in the situation, how s/he knows it, what the critical information is about the situation, and how s/he is going to proceed from now on. The answers from the user would then be given a rating by a (group of) process expert(s) who can evaluate the different work practices in the situation.

We claim that it is important to evaluate both the internal and external quality of work practices. There are several reasons. With complex systems, it is common that the outcome-related measures do not differentiate between different users or interfaces—all users are experts and their differences are not observable in the outcome (e.g., task completion time). But instead, there are differences in the *way of reaching the outcome*. When comparing two different interfaces, for example, one of the interfaces might provide more functional level information to the operators and the operators are able to take into consideration the interrelations of the functions. This might be observed in their decision-making process, but not directly in the outcome. We can claim that the process of reaching the outcome is just as important because it is something that the operators carry on (as work practice) to the next situation and their daily work.

The advantage of using internal performance measures is that conclusions about the usability of the tool can also be made by analyzing normal activity, because we infer usability based on the work practices which stay the same in different kinds of situations. Thus, severe disturbance scenarios are not needed for evaluation purposes. This adds some realism, as severe accidents are not very common in real life.

6.4.5 Assessment—Development Potential of the System

In the assessment of the usability of the interface, the results of the analyses are formulated. The models created in the first phase of the evaluation process are compared to the empirical data collected in the test situation. For example, we want to see that the result tables of operators' stimulated interviews resemble functional situation models. That then means that relevant information has been mediated to the users and they have been able to take correct actions.

One aim of the assessment is to realize the development potential that the activity system has. The new interface might not be completely usable right away, but it is possible to recognize that some features have the developmental potential to carry the whole activity to a new level. In this, we take advantage of Vygotsky's (1978) notion of *zone of proximal development* (ZPD). We see that the users maintain a current work practice that has a certain ZPD. ZPD is the gap between their current level of development and their potential level of development. New tools (with systems usability) are such that they have the potential to help the users realize the ZPD, overcome this gap, learn new practices, and thus promote the development of the whole activity system.

The assessment is based on all the different data collected in the empirical phase, but in this chapter we have emphasized only the data sets and analyses that provide the systemic activity level extensions to usability evaluation.

6.5 Discussion

In this chapter, we have introduced the concept of systems usability and its relation to the usability evaluation of interfaces of complex sociotechnical systems. The purpose of introducing the concept of systems usability is not to give another definition of usability, but to develop a conceptual tool to help in understanding complex activity and evaluating the quality of complex system interfaces in a holistic way.

The concept of systems usability has evolved from the practical need to understand use of complex system interfaces more thoroughly. This is needed to give better improvement suggestions to designers, but also just to understand what contextually good design is in the first place. The extension has been systemic because we see that the underlying notion of human conduct needs to be systemic, too. We feel that with systemic examination of tools in activity contexts, it is possible to develop quality in interaction with which the quality of software also evolves. Quality in value is related to the societal meaning of activity that is always present when the activity system approach is used.

Similar goals to broaden the concept of usability have been brought up by other researchers as well. John Long (1996) discussed the importance of HCI-design being based on an understanding of domain-related goals and the work processes within the domain back in the mid-nineties. In his model, the work system is constructed of two separate subsystems—the human and the computer. In our theoretical contemplation, we have started treating the two as one individual system because the human becomes a vital constituent of the system by actively affecting the computer (the process in the end, in process control domains). With this approach, we anticipate the need to analyze embedded and ambient systems. In these new concepts, the borders between environment, the tools, and the human must be reconsidered.

Recently, the concept of *new usability* was discussed, for example, in a special issue of *ACM Transactions of Computer-Human Interaction* (Thomas 2002). Although the *new usability* is concentrated more on consumer appliances and their development, it has some similarities with our notion of systems usability because it takes a developmental view to the usage activity. We share the view that the question is not only the *out of the box usability* of the first-time product usage, but of a longer process in which the usage activity also evolves and adapts as new possibilities emerge and old ones become obsolete. Especially in work environments, it is important to take into consideration users' learning and the development of their professional skills. A good design enables this development and is not suited to the activity only on the level of individual tasks.

Similar goals of development for the concept of usability can be interpreted in Hornbæk's (2006) conclusions, after the review of current ways of evaluating usability. He proposes that measures should be formulated on both macro and micro levels. In our interpretation, micro-level measures refer to usability on the level of actions or operations, and macro-level measures on the usability on the level of activity.

The idea of using activity theory in analyzing usability is, of course, not new. In the previously mentioned issue of *ACM Transactions of Computer-Human Interaction*, for example, activity theory is used to broaden the understanding of home appliance usability and how design can benefit from theoretical activity analysis of developing usage (Petersen, Madsen, & Kjær 2002). Gay and Hembrooke (2004) also discuss and describe activity-centered design. The motivation of their work is to embed technology development into the broader contexts of culture and society. The domains that have been under discussion in the aforementioned studies are related to consumer applications. We claim that a similar approach is useful in analyzing and developing more complex and systemic applications. For example, we do not studying just one particular appliance but rather study the network that all of the *intelligent* home appliances form together. We also feel that our way of using activity theory, together with concepts of core task and practice in the evaluation of interfaces, brings us to a concrete level of interface development.

A recent trend within the usability community to study the user experience (UX) prompted by the use of a tool, or as a measure in evaluating usability, is interesting. The notion of UX has similarities to the notion of meaningfulness that we have found useful in analyzing human complex system interaction. The concept of UX is rarely connected to analyses of work tools and applications, but more to consumer appliances and entertainment applications. Yet, we feel meaningful actions are also emotionally stimulating and thus lead to positive user experiences. Hence, UX is also extremely important in the usability evaluation of professional tools. This is because user experience relates to how professional identity (Nuutinen 2005) is constructed and how it evolves. There is a hedonic dimension to professional software usage: no real expert wants to work with tools that are not designed for his/her level of skills.

The notion of systems usability is not just meant for evaluation of complex system interfaces. We believe that similar approaches could be useful in other systemic domains also. With our method of analysis, it is possible to study, for example, usage activity within a large network of people using different communication appliances. In this system, the network would be one constituent, the people as users would be another, and the appliances with different interfaces would be the third. In this case, the interface problems are systemic in nature—for example, what should the interfaces communicate to different users about the interrelations of the appliances?

One of our motives in the development of a systems usability concept has been to improve present conceptions of what is *good* design and how to *measure* it. We claim that smart objects, environments, and infrastructures of the knowledge society should meet the new requirements of systems usability that we have proposed. We believe that the activity level of human behavior should be the starting point in the design of new systems and tools. Some developmental methods have been created to study action in natural work environments, with the aim of contributing to design (Beguin & Rabardel 2000; Hyysalo 2004). The aim is to form an *instrument genesis*, in which the tool is developed simultaneously with the development of usage activity. By only concentrating in technology development (excluding human activity and practices), it is not possible to develop quality in value.

To conclude, we have introduced a systemic extension to the concept of usability in this chapter and call it *systems usability*. Systems usability denotes the role that the interface of a complex sociotechnical system has in the activity in which it is used. The role should be such that it promotes the objectives of the activity, development of the whole activity system, and the users' core task-oriented work practices. We have also described how the need for a broader understanding of the role of tools in activity has risen from a practical need to develop, evaluate, and analyze user interfaces of complex sociotechnical systems.

References

Beguin, P., & Rabardel, P. (2000). Designing for instrument mediated activity. *Scandinavian Journal of Information Systems, 12*, 173–190.

Dreyfus, H. L. (2001). The primacy of phenomenology over logical analysis. Paper presented at the EGOS, Uppsala.

Endsley, M. R. (1995). Measurement of situation awareness in dynamic systems. *Human Factors, 37*, 65–84.

Engeström, Y. (1987). *Expansive Learning*. Jyväskylä: Orienta.

Engeström, Y. (1999). Activity theory and individual and social transformation. In Y. In Engeström & R. Miettinen & R.-L. Punamäki (Eds.), *Perspectives in activity theory* (pp. 19–38). Cambridge: Cambridge University Press.

Engeström, Y., Miettinen, R., & Punamäki, R.-L. (Eds.). (1999). *Perspectives on activity theory*. Cambridge, UK: Cambridge University Press.

Eskola, A. (1999). Laws, logics, and human activity. In Y. Engeström & R. Miettinen & R.-L. Punamäki (Eds.), *Perspectives in activity theory* (pp. 107–114). Cambridge: Cambridge University Press.

Gay, G., & Hembrooke, H. (2004). *Activity-centered design*. Cambridge, MA: MIT Press.

Hollnagel, E. (Ed.). (2003). *Handbook of cognitive task design*. Mahwah, New Jersey: Lawrence Erlbaum Associates.

Hornbæk, K. (2006). Current practice in measuring usability: Challenges to usability studies and research. *International Journal of Human-Computer Studies*(64), 79–102.

Hyysalo, S. (2004). Uses of innovation. Unpublished PhD, University of Helsinki, Helsinki.

IAEA (2002). Recruitment, qualification and training of personnel for NPP. Safety Guide (Safety Standard Series NS-G.2.8). Vienna: International Atomic Energy Agency.

ISO (1998). ISO 9241-11. Ergonomic requirements for office work with visual display terminals (VTDs) – Part 11. Guidance on usability.

Järvilehto, T. (1998). The theory of organism-environment system (I). Description of the theory. *Integrative Physiological and Behavioral Science, 33*(4), 317–330.

Long, J. (1996). Specifying relations between research and the design of human – computer interactions. *International Journal of Human Computer Studies, 44,* 875–920.

MacIntyre, A. (1984). *After virtue: Study in moral theory (2nd Ed.).* Notre Dame, Indianana: University of Notre Dame Press.

MAUSE (2006) Cost Action 294 Towards the MAturation of Information Technology USability Evaluation. http://www.cost294.org.

Nielsen, J. (1993). *Usability engineering.* Boston: Academic Press.

Norros, L. (2004). *Acting under uncertainty. The core-task analysis in ecological study of work* (Vol. Publications 546). Espoo: VTT, Available also URL: http//www.vtt.fi/inf/pdf/.

Norros, L., & Klemola, U-M. (2005). Naturalistic analysis of anaesthetists clinical practice. In Montgomery, H., Lipshitz, R & Brehmer, B. (Eds.), *How experts make decision* (pp. 395–407). Hillsdale, NJ: Lawrence Erlbaum Associates.

Norros, L., & Savioja, P. (2005, October 16th–21st). *Theoretical justification of performance indicators for integrated validation of complex systems.* Paper presented at the Enlarged Halden programme Group meeting, Lillehammer.

Nuutinen, M. (2005). Expert identity construct in analyzing prerequisites for expertise development: A case study in nuclear power plant operators' on-the-job training. *Cognition, Technology and Work, 7*(4), 288–305.

Nuutinen, M., & Norros, L. (in press) Core task analysis in accident investigation – analysis of maritime accidents in piloting situations. *Cognition, Technology & Work.*

Petersen, M., Madsen, K., & Kjær, A. (2002). The usability of everyday technology-emerging and fading opportunities. *ACM Transactions on Computer-Human Interaction, 9*(2), 74–105.

Rückriem, G. (2003). *Tool or medium? The meaning of information and telecommunication technology to human practice. A quest for systemic understanding of activity theory.* University of Helsinki, Center for Activity Theory and Developmental Work Research. Retrieved on 19.4.2004 from the World Wide Web.

Savioja, P. & Norros, L. (2004). Evaluation of operator practices as means of integrated system validation. *Proceedings of the Fourth American Nuclear Society International Topical Meeting on Nuclear Plant Instrumentation, Controls and Human-machine Interface Technologies,* Columbus, Ohio.

Thomas, P. (2002). Introduction to the new usability. *ACM Transactions on Computer-Human Interaction, 9*(2), 69–73.

Vicente, K. J. (1999). *Cognitive work analysis. Toward a safe, productive, and healthy computer-based work.* Mahwah, NJ: Lawrence Erlbaum Publishers.

Vygotsky, L. S. (1978). *Mind in society. The development of higher psychological processes.* Cambridge, MA: Harvard University Press.

Chapter 7
Usability Work in Professional Website Design: Insights from Practitioners' Perspectives

Dominic Furniss[1], Ann Blandford[1] and Paul Curzon[2]

[1] UCL Interaction Centre, UK, e-mail: d.furniss@cs.ucl.ac.uk
[2] QMUL, Dept. of Computer Science, UK

Abstract This exploratory study aims to gain insight into how usability practitioners work in professional web design. This is done through interviews and a grounded analysis. The description reported here refers to the wider influence of the commercial context on usability work. This brings to the fore such issues as the client's influence on work, negotiation between clients and practitioners, the adaptation and use of methods, practitioner expertise and the consideration of *people* in the usability process. It is believed that this research focus, which moves toward wider issues in practice, is best conceptualized from a system level perspective where the goal is to coordinate resources to add value to the design process.

7.1 Introduction

This paper explores usability work in professional web design from practitioners' perspectives. The work was initially motivated to contribute to the corpus of literature focused on the issue of method transfer, whereby researchers have looked to better understand practitioners in an effort to build better-informed tools (e.g., Rosson, Maass, & Kellogg 1988), inform methods or processes (e.g., Bellotti 1988; O'Neill 1998), or identify obstacles in method transfer (e.g., Bellotti 1988; Buckingham Shum & Hammond 1994; Bellotti, Buckingham Shum, MacLean & Hammond 1995).

However, while remaining faithful to the motivation to develop better accounts of what happens in industrial practice, this work has a wider focus that moves away from tools and methods, and more towards a better understanding of activities and issues in practice. To support this wider perspective, we use Grudin's (1990) observation that there has been an "outward movement of the computer's interface to its external environment, from hardware to software to increasingly high-level cognitive capabilities and finally to social processes" and claim that a similar outward movement is happening in research for practice. This outward movement has involved the technical development of methods (e.g., Card, Moran & Newell 1983), the transfer of methods to practice (e.g., Blandford, Buckingham Shum & Young 1998), the use of methods in practice (e.g., Nørgaard & Hornbæk 2006), and wider issues in practice (e.g., Hornbæk and Frøkjær 2005).

E. Law et al. (eds.), *Maturing Usability.*

Table 7.1 The outward movement of research for usability practice

Level	Focus in Usability Practice	Example Work
1	Technical development of methods	Card et al., (1983) in developing GOMS
2	Transfer of methods to practice	Blandford et al., (1998) in training developers in a novel evaluation technique
3	Use of methods in practice	Nørgaard & Hornbæk, (2006) in studying think-aloud in practice
4	Wider issues in practice	Hornbæk & Frøkjær, (2005) in studying the communication of problems and redesign proposals

We do not make the strong claim that these are the only steps or the right steps of this outward movement, but the weaker claim that this outward trend exists. We also do not wish to infer that any level of research is superior to another. If anything, we would wish to stress their complementary nature in supporting usability practice.

This exploratory study is positioned on the outer branches—Levels 3 and 4 (Table 7.1). To be more specific about its focus, it looks to draw insight on three (assumed) important elements of usability practice, which include the before and after of *usability work*: 1) attracting work, 2) doing the work itself, and 3) communicating work. Figure 7.1 illustrates the relationship between these three elements in an input/output style diagram.

It is believed that the before and after elements of usability work will influence the usability work itself and provide important insights into how usability practice integrates with design and business processes—something essential for the transfer of value in industry.

In terms of limitations, it should be noted that this work is focused on the perspectives of usability practitioners involved in professional website design and evaluation. It does not include seeking the perspectives of clients and other important players in the development process. Such work could create a quite different account.

7.2 Introduction to Related Work Sorted by Analysis Themes

As stated above, the literature that provided the initial motivation for this work was centered on method transfer, but has moved on to consider how usability is practiced. The aim of this section is to introduce the reader to research pertinent for our

Fig. 7.1 Diagram that shows three important elements of usability practice

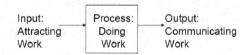

analysis—in showing what has guided its focus and what has been done already. In many cases, the following claims and advice are only assumed to generalize to usability professionals in the Web design industry, but this remains to be seen. It is also hoped that the current analysis will provide a more cohesive view of these different research areas from the perspective of just one usability domain. Above all, we wish to identify and explore those elements that are significant to usability work from the bottom up.

The review of related work presented here pre-empts the structure developed through the grounded analysis, as the emerging themes have guided what is relevant. This section first questions the problem identification perspective of usability work and suggests a perspective of value transfer that goes beyond method use, before looking at the different processes that designers use in practice. It then covers literature motivated by the importance of relationships and communication in design. We then look at more general expert advice for managing usability in practice. This section ends with the suggestion that a systems perspective may be a way forward in exploring this complex area. Further development of these themes is discussed later in this chapter.

7.2.1 Methods and Processes

Wixon (2003) believes that the current literature fails the usability practitioner because the premises for valuing usability methods are at fault. Rather than looking at the number of problems a method can detect in an isolated quasi-scientific framework, we should instead concentrate more on the "art of the possible under constrained resources" (Wixon & Wilson 1997). Here, the costs and benefits of using different methods, in real contextual conditions, are stressed. This cost-benefit tradeoff centers on usability value—the importance of which has been argued elsewhere (e.g., Cockton 2004). We believe that a value-centered approach that considers the transfer of value from usability services should look beyond method use per se to other influential factors such as fostering good working relationships (Section 7.2.2), communicating recommendations (Section 7.2.3), and the expertise of practitioners (Section 7.2.4).

There has been much focus on the process of design, but empirical work tends to suggest that this is less structured in practice than the literature would suggest. Bellotti (1988) found that design phases were not strictly ordered, and Terrins-Rudge and Jørgensen (1993) reported that designers *muddle through*, stating that "Formal or structured methods were not employed, developers preferring selectively and opportunistically to use individual parts of such methods in the course of muddling through." It appears that while people can prescribe structured methods there is limited success for these in the complexities of practical contexts.

Rosson, et al. (1988) distinguishes between a phased and incremental approach in their observations of designers. A phased approach involves a design phase, and an implementation phase with some sort of evaluation phase. In contrast, an incremental approach involves a closer design and analysis cycle where the two happen in parallel, allowing development in a highly iterative fashion. They observe that projects requiring more control because of either business objectives or group size tended to opt for phased approaches, whereas smaller teams and research projects tended to opt for incremental approaches. Importantly, they also note that iterative cycles can take place within design phases, so a phased approach does not exclude this method of work. Here we see how the context of the project affects its process— suggesting that project choices are not entirely top-down, but are influenced by bottom-up external factors.

7.2.2 Relationships

Redish, et al., (2002) includes work by Bailey, Molich, Dumas and Spool, who each write on a separate topic. Dumas (Redish, et al., 2002) offers a different perspective on valuing methods. He states that the most important factor in responding to usability recommendations in the long term is the relationship between the usability specialist and developers, and proposes that methods can be judged on their ability to foster these relationships. Wixon (2003) criticizes the criteria of problem identification in valuing usability evaluation methods, and Dumas' proposal can be seen as an answer to this by offering an added dimension and different role for evaluation methods.

7.2.3 Communication and Coordination

The importance of relationships in usability work was based on the desire for developers to react positively to recommendations. This same desire can also be seen as the motivation of work on communicating usability recommendations. Molich (Redish, et al., 2002) comments on usability reporting problems from an empirical study (e.g., reports that are too long, have no summary, and no positive findings) and suggests an approach that encourages buy-in on the developers' side and faster communication of results. Dumas, et al. (2004) reports on a similar study that makes recommendations for usability reporting on four main themes: emphasizing the positive, expressing your annoyance tactfully, avoiding usability jargon, and being as specific as you can. Adding to the work of usability reporting, Hornbæk and Frøkjær (2005) suggest that reporting problems with redesign proposals can have a higher utility for developers. If we assume that the general goal of usability is to improve systems rather than identify usability issues, then effective reporting becomes much more important.

7.2.4 Psychology and Expertise in Practice

Wixon and Wilson (1997) provide a wealth of expertise and advice on managing practical usability work that stretches beyond the technicalities of method use, such as

- Providing quick feedback to developers so they can be acted on in good time
- Having a lab for publicity value and as a hub of usability activities
- Getting members of the product team to observe user tests to focus them on real issues rather than theoretical or guessed concerns
- Running informal and formal usability tests for different purposes where appropriate
- Adapting highlight tapes to suit the audience
- Maximizing the usability of reports rather than their brevity
- Giving a short presentation of results soon after testing to give timely feedback
- Creating a template to speed up reporting
- Considering the politics of who sees the test report
- Having a balance between having the user at the center of the design process and other stakeholder interests

The literature is peppered with such practical advice, but the authors remain unaware of a dedicated corpus of work on the psychology and expertise of usability specialists.

7.2.5 Concluding Remarks

Practical advice is embedded in organizational contexts which, as Grudin and Markus (1997) explain, have a strong impact on systems development. They state that these organizational contexts impose constraints that help determine appropriate actions and method use, which relates to Wixon's (2003) remarks that we need the right approach for the context. Cockton (2004) argues that HCI has moved from the technical, to the user, to the context, and needs the further step of a value focus. This form of argument applies here. It reinforces the movement away from technical method development, to the practitioner, to the context in use, and focuses on value transfer in usability practice. Grudin and Markus (1997) note organizational factors that affect systems development (e.g., size, geographical placement, age, function, culture, and environment) and illustrate these effects by using a comparison between a small start-up company whose employees see each other every day, and a large organization that will rely more heavily on formal communications and procedures to work effectively together. This may also impact the design approach and the methods employed.

The authors are not aware of similar exploratory empirical studies to that reported here, specifically on usability practitioners in professional web design.

More focused literature will be introduced with the discussion of the findings from the study. This section has sought to introduce themes that have emerged from analysis and are concerned with wider issues of usability practice.

7.3 Approach

We have undertaken an exploratory qualitative analysis based on *grounded theory* as outlined by Strauss and Corbin (1998). The process we undertook first involved defining a scope and questions, interviewing, transcribing the interviews, and then coding the transcriptions. Finally, the codes were related to one another to reveal patterns and themes in the data.

This process was iterated to further refine the themes that describe the data (see Table 7.2 for details). This approach was taken as it lends itself to the exploration of contextual phenomena through inductive means. It complements idea generation and experimental approaches to research because it has the potential to map out important factors and relations in real world environments.

Grounded theory differs markedly from quantitative studies, an important aspect of which is detailed by Yardley (2000, p. 220): "Whereas quantitative studies typically rely on procedures such as standardized measurement and random sampling to ensure 'horizontal generalization' of their findings across research settings, many qualitative researchers aspire instead to the theory building work of 'vertical generalization' i.e., an endeavour to link to the abstract and the work of others [...]." In the same way, this work has incorporated literature to define the research focus and to crystallize the abstracted insights that emerged from the data.

Table 7.2 describes detail of the grounded analysis; Table 7.3 describes the semistructured interview topics; and Table 7.4 outlines the interviewee profiles.

Table 7.4 shows the three sorts of organizations that were sampled: full service agencies that are involved in the full design of websites for external clients, from analysis to implementation; usability consultancies that specialize in usability work and provide services to external clients; and in-house services that work internally within a wider organization (e.g., a large department store).

7.4 Analysis

The analysis has been divided into two interdependent segments. Section 7.4.1 describes spheres of influence that affect usability work and processes. Here, we move closer to appreciating the influence of the client on work processes, tools and methods that are used in practice. Section 7.4.2 describes the complexity of design and business processes. Here, we move closer to appreciating the role and integration of a *usability component* within this context.

Table 7.2 Details of the grounded analysis

Section	Detail			
Number of:	Coders	Interviews	Codes	Quotations
	1	8	77	1508

Literature Involvement	Literature was reviewed to inform the analyst's understanding and help focus the interviews. It was also used to inform and crystallize insights as the analysis developed (Strauss & Corbin 1998, p. 96).
Theoretical Sampling	Interviewees were chosen for their industrial experience. As the analysis matured, interviewees with more experience were involved. This was done for practical and theoretical reasons: people with less experience were easier to access, and senior practitioners were involved when the analysis and questions were more mature. Interviewee profiles can be found in Table 7.4.
Interviewing Procedure	The interviews were semistructured and an hour long each. Guiding topics can be found in Table 7.3. Topics were probed in an opportunistic fashion. Interviews were left days or weeks apart so analysis could be conducted between them; this informed the questions of the subsequent interviews.
Coding procedure and style	Each interview was transcribed and coded. Analysis took place between each interview. After the fourth interview the transcriptions were recoded to reduce the coding scheme, thereby making it more focused. The coding style of the analysis was loose in that codes overlapped and were not mutually exclusive. Open coding was done explicitly. Selective and axial coding was developed implicitly through mini-frameworks and through memos, including coding notes, and theoretical notes (Strauss & Corbin 1998, p. 141 & 217).
Tools	Atlas.ti was used to support the analysis.
Reporting Style	The reporting style adopted here aims to be story-like to convey the richness of the data. Also, because the interviews were opportunistic and the coding style loose, it makes less sense to report the individual codes and numbers of quotations of each participant. The aim is to convey the understanding that the analyst has developed.
Validation	There are a number of possible levels of validation when doing a grounded analysis, e.g.: 1) tested through data collection and analysis; 2) verified by interviewees; 3) verified by a wider population; and 4) triangulated with other methods/studies. This study went to Level One and Two. In Level Two, a report was sent to all the interviewees. Seven of the 8 interviewees verified their quotes were accurately used; the other was not contactable.

7.4.1 Spheres of Influence: The Make-up of the Work Context

Usability research has focused on understanding and developing methods that form part of usability work. However, to understand this in practice, we need a better measure of how the working context affects usability work. It was not surprising to find that the practitioners' decisions and behaviors are influenced by the organization they work in; however, the data also showed a large influence of the clients' wishes. Figure 7.2 shows a representation of the influences on the resultant work processes in practice: the bidirectional arrow signifies the mutually dependent relationship of the practitioner and the organization they work in; the larger box signifies the client's influence on the work they do. There is a bidirectional arrow between the client and

Table 7.3 Semistructured interview topics

Topic	Description
Background	Background of the person being interviewed. This aims to introduce the interviewee slowly and find out about their experience and perspective.
Work Organization	This includes how work is organized, the structure of the organization, whether there are teams, project lifecycle involvement, and what job challenges are faced.
Business: Client Relationships	This includes communicating with clients, both in attracting clients and handing work off to them. How do people communicate effectively and what challenges do they face?
Practitioner Skills	What do practitioners do, why are some better than others and how do they get better in their role? This could give an indication about what is important in their work.
Tools and Techniques	What methods are used, how are they used, when are they used, what is valued in a good technique?

the practitioner/organization because it is the job of the usability practitioner to offer options of work and guide the client's decision.

The client's influence is most powerfully shown when there is a tension between what the usability practitioner wishes, in terms of either the work undertaken or the recommendations for the design, and what the client wants to do. This quotation, between interviewer (I) and respondent (R), illustrates some frustration in the reality that an ideal usability path has to be compromised by real business objectives (the quotations reported here have the following notation: '...' signifies pauses in speech, and '[...]' signifies where text has been omitted or replaced):

Table 7.4 Interviewees' profiles

Participant	Spread of Experience in Years			Currently
	Full Service Agency	Usability Consultancy	In-house	
1	1			In academia.
2	2		1	In academia but freelances.
3			1	In-house practitioner for e-commerce site.
4	1	1		Information architect for full service agency.
5	2+			Manager and practitioner at a full service agency.
6	5+		1	In-house practitioner for e-commerce site.
7	5+			Manager and practitioner at a full service agency.
8		5+		Manager and practitioner at an independent usability consultancy.

Fig. 7.2 Diagram of
influence on work processes

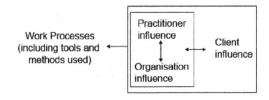

"I: It must be interesting from the client side.

R: Yeah it's interesting. I work with [coworker], who has done projects, who will come in with a view that I agree with, that it should be like this... and it's like we can't actually do that, unfortunately. I know that, you know that, but it's just not the way... you do have to have give and take in the experience.

I: Can it be frustrating?

R: Yes, very much so... I mean, it's a fine balance, it is a fine balance but it's definitely frustrating." (Participant 6)

This situation brings negotiation skills with the client to the fore as both groups try to come to a common understanding about what balance is best for the business and for the user, and it is believed that this balance will increase the potential for market success:

"One of the realities for commercial usability is that products that survive for a long time in a market place have to fulfill both the customers' needs and the business's needs, and somebody coming fresh to a usability project, especially if they haven't dealt with the realities of the market place very much, may make suggestions for ways to change an interface that would purely be in the users interest... from the user's point of view, but might undermine the business case for a product." (Participant 8)

Even though there is interest in using more methods from a practitioner's perspective, clients will not pay for something they do not understand to be either valuable or feasible under their constraints. It is part of the role of the client-facing usability practitioner to understand the client's needs and constraints, and work out a unit or units of work that will be most appealing and effective for the clients' particular situation.

"Yeah the biggest thing really ... was ... the areas that we could sell in, and because it was more of an add-on it was kind of difficult to do some ethnographic research or anything like that, which would be great, and we did try and push a couple of times, for that type of methodology but ... it was just not feasible for our clients ... It meant that we were limited in the methodologies that we were going to use. We just had to focus on two or three key points of the project that we could actually get involved in actually making a difference.

I: So you're looking at where you could have the biggest effect?

R: Exactly, so it's obviously getting involved as early as we possibly could, and try and making a difference before everything's got too far down the road, otherwise you put recommendations in that are not achievable within their timescales." (Participant 6)

This negotiation between the client and the practitioner can be conceived as designing a work project, which will depend on the details and constraints of the particular context in question.

"There's not only ideal research conditions, there's realities for times, budget ..., and sometimes those things play off against themselves and when you design a research project you've got to think of the options. If we do this, that lowers the cost, the effect might be a certain lack of robustness in this particular area ..., or if you're having trouble getting users of this variety, we could use this parallel group of users and change the methodology in such and such a way." (Participant 8)

The spheres of influence illustrate that the work processes that are actually carried out in practice are not the choice of any one person, but are often a negotiation between different groups that have different values and perspectives. The skilled practitioner will be able to perceive how they can be of best use to a client in their terms, so the client can more easily see the potential gain in value and how usability can be easily integrated with their own processes.

The choices that are made at the project negotiation stage will impact on the type of work, the quality of work and the individuals tasked with carrying it out. Organizational culture can either attract or repel good usability practitioners:

"... I love [Company A]... they have a really good process in place, they don't undersell projects, what I mean by that is that they don't tell clients we can do this in 3 weeks when it's really gonna take 6. It's very very rare to do too much overtime, I mean you'll have an occasional evening where it's like damn, I didn't get enough done today and stay a couple of hours late...
I: And I s'pose it comes to down to [Company A's] culture, if you like their values and what they're going to do and what they're not
R: Yeah absolutely... because at [Company B] it was all about getting the most money for the shortest amount of time... It was really unfortunate it was one of the many reasons I chose to leave 'cuz it was just a ridiculous culture, a ridiculous way of thinking." (Participant 2)

This is an extreme instance of the effect of the organization on the individual, but there is a clear interdependence between the two where the individuals create the organization and the organization influences and impacts on the individuals. Different types of organizations will attract different sorts of people. The type of work will influence the frequency that individuals use different methods and encounter different situations. The different skills and experiences that will be employed on a daily basis will impact on how the individual develops:

"One of the things that I would have liked to have done as well is to work for a pure usability consultancy, because obviously now I've done client side and I've done agency side in a large organization but I think the specialism for working in a pure usability consultancy would have been good as well, to see more different aspects." (Participant 6)

Table 7.5 includes some trends that were observed in the data between different types of usability practice; it should be noted that these differences are in the degree to which these characteristics apply (i.e., all the characteristics apply to the different usability practice contexts to some degree).

7.4.2 Design and the Business Process

Design and business processes often transcend the expertise and work of any one person, so we need to appreciate how these parts fit together because it will impact on the role and work of usability practitioners. Many people contribute to a design

Table 7.5 Differences in usability practice contexts

Usability Practice Context	Description
Full Service Agency	More involved in the design side of usability (e.g., information architecture). Less onus on documenting evaluations (i.e., usability is more integral to planning designs than a standalone evaluative piece of work).
Usability Consultancy	Deeper specialization in evaluation, with the opportunity to encounter many different types of interface and a greater opportunity to apply methods. A great bank of usability knowledge and expertise.
In-house Usability Work	There is a greater degree of ownership of the interface and the risks associated with changing aspects of it. Deep understanding of the interface as well as business, political and technical issues associated with it.

and business process and must be coordinated to work together effectively. There is a recognition that the people in these component parts will have a certain understanding and will want different things:

> "It's a very collaborative world. You end up being almost a negotiating power between different groups in a company. If you're doing consultancy, then you may be the negotiating power between what you know can be done and the client, and the client's desires, or if you're working internally for a company then you end up negotiating between, I guess, the designers, the artists, the technology people, the business people who want the product to do a certain thing or look a certain way." (Participant 2)

Appreciating that there are many component parts that make up the design and business process, the successful role and integration of a *usability component* comes to the fore in usability work: what the usability component does and how it integrates with the rest of the process. The design and business process will vary from company to company, but is likely to involve many different parts that link and integrate in different ways, including graphic designers, interaction designers, developers, middle management, senior management, marketing, accounts, customer service, and project managers. This situation is made more complex when we think about the personalities and relationships at a more individual level as people come together for work. The usability component could fit in with a combination of these parts in practice. Figure 7.3 has bundled up this complexity into the relationship between usability work and the wider design and business processes. The three features of this diagram are discussed further below: in Section 7.4.2.1, we discuss the design and business process; in Section 7.4.2.2, we address the usability component; and in Section 7.4.2.3, we discuss the information flow processes that connect the two.

Fig. 7.3 Usability interfacing with design and business process

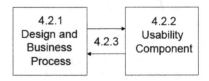

7.4.2.1 Design and Business Process

The influence of the client on establishing what usability work is carried out was discussed as an important sphere of influence in Section 7.4.1. This section expands on how clients differ in ways that affect the undertaken work.

Clients are by no means a homogenous group. Participants reported that their clients differ in why they seek usability services. The majority recognized an underlying motive of revenue generation, but upon questioning interviewees about why clients seek usability services, other reasons were also noted:

- They may believe that usability input will directly increase revenue (e.g. e-commerce)
- They may believe usability input can save them money (e.g. reduced call center work)
- They may want to improve communication with people (e.g., government or advertising)
- They may want to make services more accessible (e.g., government)
- They may want to comply with legislation (e.g., Disability Discrimination Act)
- They may be interested in the steady evolution of their product lines
- They may just want to provide a better service
- They may just have heard of usability and think it is a cool thing

These reasons are not independent, so a client may have several of these goals. Clients may also not know what they want or what they might be able to achieve with the help of usability input. It is the job of the skilled practitioner to understand the clients' needs and translate them into a project that will suit:

"... well, the unspoken assumption behind that question is that all the clients know why they have come to us, and they don't. Sometimes the biggest portion of our job is to work with them to figure that out." (Participant 8)

It would also be wrong to assume that clients in a particular context agree:

"I only had contact with the middle management team for a while, and they loved the work, they absolutely loved the work, presented it back and they were ecstatic, then they arranged for me to meet the director who was going to make the final decision and he hated it, hated the whole lot, he just said it doesn't meet our business objectives at all and I think he might have had a point. Because the remit I was given was to come up with the best user experience proposition and nothing else, if I had been thinking about the business proposition in that project then I might have taken more his point of view." (Participant 5)

This demonstrates that the negotiation stage of a project is vital for a project's success; truly understanding the client's real needs cannot be underestimated as a misunderstanding can lead to failure. Once again the need to balance between user experience and business interests is demonstrated. The task to understand a client is an important one at the start of any client-consultant relationship, and is easier if the consultant already knows the client:

"... generally work with the same clients over and over... occasionally you get a new client, what you want to do as a new business is work with a client over and over because it's cheaper to do it, you've got a reliable relationship, you know their needs but also you build more links within an organization rather than starting all over again." (Participant 5)

Clients are also dynamic in that they evolve and educate themselves over time, so the beginning of a client relationship might start with a small piece of work that will lead to more work further on:

"... a client might approach a company because they've got an issue, and because an expert evaluation is a lot cheaper than a redesign or a usability test, they'll often say well look at the site we'll pay for an expert evaluation, and that's a good way of not only meeting their initial requirements but also building the relationship and taking the next step on." (Participant 4)

This not only impacts on the relationship between the company and client, and the personal working relationships between people, but the client will also start to educate themselves about the content and the value of usability, and how it can be used:

"R: There's an education process definitely..., I remember 4 or 5 years ago at [Company D] trying to explain just the very basics, why you should do usability testing at all during the process never mind the different techniques or anything...
I: Do you think that's changed now?
R: Yes, but... even quite recently I remember ... clients getting confused,.... it's a lot better, it got to a point at [Company D] where clients were actually coming in and saying we want testing at this point, this point, this point...." (Participant 6)

This indicates that clients undergo a process of education whereby they may start off slowly introducing themselves to usability practice but then gain more control and confidence in how they can utilize usability research for their own endeavors. In the long term, this gradual take-up and appreciation of usability services might not only be within certain consultancies and clients at a micro level, but an industry movement on a macro level. In trying to determine how practitioners measure the quality of their work, many were satisfied and confident with the fact that they were receiving recommendations and repeat business: the burden of proof for return of investment is not always at the crux of securing usability work, and does not always lie with the practitioner. Observations suggest that this applies differently to successful usability companies that are regularly approached to do work, rather than being in the position of trying to convince a prospective client that the work is worthwhile—the relationship changes.

7.4.2.2 Usability Component

There are three recognizable elements of usability work: 1) attracting work, 2) doing work, and 3) communicating work. These three elements are interdependent and will be influenced by the skill and experience of the practitioner, their company, and the clients' circumstances. We have discussed the influence of the context of work above, and now move on to the expertise, skills, and methods of usability practitioners. Two important techniques emerged and will be focused on here: user testing and *heuristic evaluation*.

Practitioners reported using a variety of different methods, but they differed in their use, their name, and the contexts in which they were used. These techniques were adapted and combined to achieve the goals of their usability research in an efficient and effective manner. These characteristics contribute to an environment that is focused on cost-effective results rather than method worship—an environment that focuses more on the skills of practitioners in coordinating resources to achieve results that lead us away from scientific validity and into what is described below as *commercial and design validity*:

"I don't have wide experience of academics teaching this stuff, but the ones that I have seen teach it don't have any experience of industry, don't have any experience of the turn around times that are required, don't have experience of what commercial organizations and government organizations really need when you're developing a website. They still tend to be quite statistically focused, they still tend to be, as you say, be quiet, don't speak to the person, don't bias it, it's got to be scientific validity. We don't give a damn about scientific validity, we give a damn about commercial and design validity." (Participant 5)

This difference in culture can almost be viewed as a conflict between the rigor and detail of academic work, and the pragmatics of getting work done in a timely, cost-effective manner in practice:

"Between all the really, really minute research that we do in academia, in fact most practitioners don't give a damn. They're not going to care if Malay don't like pink, if they're dealing with a Malay client then the Malay client will tell them that in 3 seconds, they don't need four months of research to tell them that. It is really interesting, but I think having experienced both I think what we do here in academia does influence them to some extent as it does percolate up, it's not like they're in a vacuum. They know who Nielsen and Norman are and they know other researchers out there." (Participant 2)

The relationship between academia and practice is complex. The above attitudes reflect that there is a difference in the values and activities of academic research and practice. Further work needs to be done to establish what this relationship is, what the status of knowledge is in both camps, and how one informs the other. One clear similarity between academic research and practice is that they are both seeking to find right answers through research, but research methods, values, constraints, goals and interests can differ.

User testing is a common method used in academia and industry. A comparison between the uses of the method in these different contexts provides a way of probing the nature of its use by juxtaposition. One difference is the way that practitioners can be proactive in eliciting user views about particular aspects of the interface:

"The other thing about the way that we do usability testing in academia is much different than in the corporate world, because you will point blank in the corporate world ask the user 'what do you think will fit under this piece of navigation?' and then click on it 'is this what you expected to see?' Whereas you probably wouldn"t do that in academia because you're leading a user down a path which you probably would avoid in academia, but here you're purposely leading the user down a path... it's just a different... It's more about validating the way that you have organized something ..., I'm specifically trying to find my mistakes, or specifically trying to get them to use something that I hope will be used. As opposed to academia, where I would not want to influence the user at all and see what they would make out of the product." (Participant 2)

Other samples of the data suggest that these strategies of sitting back or engaging with the participant in the user test depend on what the circumstances and objectives of the test are:

> "Sitting back and not saying something sometimes has its place, so if we're looking at a detailed purchase process and the person's got to go through certain steps and fill in certain forms and stuff like that sit back and say nothing; but if we're looking at a wider marketing proposition sitting back and saying nothing isn't going to get you what you need. You've got to engage with people." (Participant 5)

Other differences in the administration of user tests include performing interviews and questionnaires before or after the test to elicit information that might be pertinent to the research goals of that project. Another commonly reported technique that differs in its administration is heuristic evaluation. However, the variety of ways in which this method is performed leads us to question what actually qualifies as method use. One example of heuristic use is in an ad hoc manner to add weight behind justifying recommendations:

> "Almost in a very ad hoc manner, you came up with your wire frame, people ask you why you did that, maybe you had reason. If you don't then look up the heuristics and try to justify it afterwards." (Participant 1)

The ad hoc use of heuristics for justification purposes appears to add some structure and common ground for the client to relate the issues to, as well as a link with accessible theory:

> "Going back to heuristics... it's more on the client education, so if you identified an issue we'd probably list a heuristic that it would apply to, so the client would go 'OK' and maybe it helps with some credibility as far as they are concerned 'cuz they go like 'ah, that's one of the main issues and I can see how that applies'." (Participant 6)

Other people reported using them implicitly as part of their expertise because they had assimilated them through education and practice:

> "... especially when you do a competitor analysis, because you have those heuristics in the back of your head because someone in some masters course pounded them into you, tested you, examined you on them, so yeah you do of course. So you're evaluating other websites which are book stores and in the back of your mind ... those are hopefully playing." (Participant 2)

It was also reported that heuristics were adapted to go beyond what were commonly referred to as *Nielsen's ten heuristics*, and were sometimes used in a more rigid manner to perform a competitor analysis for approaching clients in the hope of generating work. The more rigid use of heuristics was criticized for being too negative and sometimes detached from the context of use, which a cognitive walkthrough would not be. Where heuristics were used in a more implicit manner, the method appeared to resemble more of an expert evaluation in its description, whereby the labels are even used interchangeably (terminology issues are expanded in Section 7.4.2.3):

> "Actually, I think that when I do a heuristic review, I do it on much wider stuff, ... I know about perception and mental representation and I've also looked at models of mental

representation as applied to interface design... so actually when I'm doing an expert review, I'm referring to all that kind of applied theoretical knowledge that I've developed over ten years, and I think a lot of that has become extremely implicit in the way that I apply that stuff nowadays as well. I don't actually know that I am applying it even though I am." (Participant 5)

This implicit expertise is developed through years of practice:

"Yeah, seven years of practice, it's like anything else, it's not that a new doctor just having graduated from medical school has any necessarily less knowledge or the ability to have as much knowledge as someone who's been working in the field for ten years, and it's just that the doctor working in the field has seen the cold for ten years and can probably diagnose a cold within three seconds of seeing the patient.... it's just repetition, repetition, repetition and it just builds up." (Participant 2)

Also:

"Once you've been a consultant for two years, you may have worked on three or four retail sites, three or four services sites, and if you keep on websites you will encounter the same problems, like what does the contact page look like. So, you are repeating, applying the same knowledge to a version of the same sort of thing." (Participant 3)

People's perceptions and thinking change through experience, so emphasis should be placed on this dynamic:

"A lot of your thinking is pre-done. You've automated that thinking in some sense because you've seen these types of patterns before and you can just go yeah I can see that." (Participant 5)

This idea that some thinking has been *pre-done* because similar patterns have been encountered in the past appears to build up a knowledge bank of cases—where similar problems have been encountered and what interface widgets work well and where. In this particular case, it appears that practitioners build up a library of interface widgets through which they can apply analogical reasoning so they can bring insights from one interface style across to another (e.g., from the Amazon site to a newspaper site):

"I: Do you feel like there's particular widgets or features that you would expect on certain sites that you would get asked to design... so...
R: Yeah... send to a friend and that sort of thing... yeah, there are definitely ... features that people have picked up along the way that I would say would be an expectation on certain sites.
I: Such as...
R: Well, things like send to a friend facility on certain pages you'd tend to have... that thing like... on Amazon where they say 'people who looked at this looked at that', so... I think there would be an expectation to applying that even to say a newspaper site, where you know people who thought that article was interesting, you might think this article was interesting... yeah... you're not looking for a list of what they are...
I: No... as I've been going through the study, it's become more apparent to me that when you're a usability expert you're so familiar with what works and the best practice that's out on the web, then you build up a ...
R: A library of things... yeah, definitely... and they're actually books on that they're not called library, they're called patterns." (Participant 7)

These implicit pools of knowledge are sometimes realized in tangible artifacts as companies develop and share resources with their staff, either through their ongoing work or through specific efforts to establish a bank of expertise to use as a company resource:

> "Usability consultancies have a lot of experience at applying this knowledge, and they actually have slides that are prepared about information scent and whatever … they spend … time gathering all this research that's been done by … researchers and say OK they work for three or four retail sites and they basically apply the same principles to each site." (Participant 3)

The effective use of specialist information is a strong competitive advantage in carrying out projects, because it provides a bank of knowledge as a starting position for a more concentrated effort on the next piece of work. This collective pooling of knowledge transcends individual practitioners in some sense, and leads to the development of a company's expertise.

7.4.2.3 Information Flow Processes

As has been discussed in Section 7.4.2.1, the design and business process resembles a complex system because many different component parts interact, which need to integrate with the usability component (Section 7.4.2.2). This integration depends a lot on the experience and expertise of the skilled practitioner seeing opportunities for input, and negotiating work and recommendations on, and in, the client's terms. This section expands on how the design and business process and usability component integrate, which includes themes that have been alluded to elsewhere.

The use of terminology in usability is not straightforward, both in terms of job titles and roles and in terms of the labels used for methods. Recognizing that people have their own definitions, some practitioners employ a pragmatic solution:

> "Personally, I don't like definitions of usability at all, I think they're quite self-indulgent academic exercises and everyone that works in this field has their own opinion on what usability is, user experience is, information architecture is… talk to someone, you can't nail them down, so actually as a very pragmatic user experience specialist or usability specialist you use the meaning that the person uses themselves, you know just be pragmatic about it." (Participant 5)

This lays the basic foundation for negotiating with clients, which appears to be one of the major enterprises of coming to agreement with people with different backgrounds and values:

> "I really believe that one of the most important skills in HCI is the sort of negotiating between other people and between what's there and what needs to be there and trying to build that pathway in a way that's, it doesn't have to be aggressive or mean to people you just have to explain like 'look, I know that this kinda worked for you guys before but maybe we should try this out, let's put it in front of users, let's see if they like it.' I think that this helps clients a lot, because they've actually hired you to try and help, but not tell them that they're all wrong all of the time." (Participant 2)

The idea of stopping at the stage of identifying problems for clients seems poor practice, and many practitioners are conscious that how they communicate their findings and results will have an impact on whether the client receives them well in the short term, and whether the client seeks further usability input in the future, both of which have a significant effect on how usability is dealt with in industry:

"We also include positive findings from our study, there are a couple of reasons for that, ... we ... treat our clients like human beings ... people often work months or years on a product and I know how dispiriting it is to have someone to come along and evaluate it and only point out the parts that aren't working well... if they don't have a picture of what is working well, the temptation would be to fix a small problem by breaking a large positive, so you can actually make a problem worse by trying to fix tiny little niggly bits at the edge, when the core of the product is working extremely well. We always try and give an overall picture of how a product is." (Participant 8)

This appreciation of clients and colleagues as people is a theme that pervades successful negotiation, whether that is external or internal:

"I: [...] do you use personas at all?
R: I have got some..., I don't stick them out in front of developers as that would be quite condescending, I think. People have quite a good sense of the typical [Company C] customer in their head around the office and I don't want to be condescending to them." (Participant 3)

Getting people on the side of usability and listening to the issues and recommendations that it raises is undoubtedly important. Therefore, the communication of usability work seems to be a critical step; however, this varies by client and circumstance. For example, some practitioners thought that large Word documents were too cumbersome, but others saw instances where they would be useful:

"R: Again, it can vary from client to client, I've worked on one where it was a presentation, it was a round of usability testing... others where it is more of a forty-page document that says this testing took place, this happened, this happened, this happened.... it depends on what the client's after. If they want to use it for politics within the company, then obviously a report or something like that is much more tangible and is more useful than having a presentation or something like that. But if it's purely to communicate to senior people and what have you, where a report might not be necessary, a presentation or something like...
I: And I s'pose you might mix them up and do both.
R: Yeah I mean... a report and then a presentation looking at the main points, because most senior people won't read a big fat report, so it's a case of communicating to the people as quickly as possible, the higher people.
I: Do you have any thoughts about how effective these different things are?
R: Personally, I think a face-to-face is very important otherwise it can become a bit detached—and certainly things like usability testing, I think that it is always good when the client comes to see some of it...." (Participant 4)

Variations of reporting include presentations, PowerPoint files, Word files, video clips, quotations from users, giving recommendations and positive feedback, and organizing the issues in some way (e.g., by priority). Two of the most important concerns appear to be conveying the meaning of the issues to the client, and getting them to appreciate the issues. The idea of *detachment* referred to in the recent quotation draws us to a dimension of *closeness* in terms of communication. Practitioners understand the advantages of close, high-bandwidth communication and seeing a usability test with your own eyes as more significant than a document reporting its findings:

> "... when you go through a usability process and you suddenly see what it is actually like in the real world for your product to be used, it's such a compelling event that people learn from it." (Participant 8)

The idea of learning is also an important one. If we think about usability work and reporting—not as a discrete interval in a design process, but as part of people's ongoing experience—we realize that it has important side effects. From doing the work, practitioners learn about the usability of a product and the clients' reaction to the work, and clients learn more about what usability work is about and how the information provided by this type of research can help them achieve their goals. Both groups can reflect on their experience and adapt their behavior accordingly. The idea of clients educating themselves was also discussed in Section 7.4.2.1. Informing others about usability issues and practices so they can understand and appreciate them themselves appears to pay dividends in people's normal routines. Participant 3 demonstrates this in talking about her colleagues:

> "Yeah... they're actually quite user centered as a group... 90 percent of the time they come up with something that is good, which is nice. I'm kind of coming to the conclusion that if you give all your developers and graphic designers a certain education in usability, they inherently include it in their work." (Participant 3)

7.5 Discussion

This section discusses insights from the analysis under four subsections. Section 7.5.1 discusses methods and processes, Section 7.5.2 addresses relationships, Section 7.5.3 discusses communication and coordination, and Section 7.5.4 refers to psychology and expertise in practice.

7.5.1 Methods and Processes

The analysis has shown that usability work is heavily influenced by the clients' needs. This commercial focus puts the emphasis on effective and pragmatic choices that will deliver results to agreed time and budget scales. This is reflected in Wixon and Wilson's (1997) move away from science to "the art of the possible under constrained resources" in usability practice; and Cockton's (2004) claim that HCI should be more about delivering value than finding the truth. This is perhaps what one participant meant by distinguishing scientific validity from commercial and design validity.

To achieve this value transfer, we have seen that the *usability component* must be flexible enough to fit into projects where it can, to suit time-scales, budgets, and research needs. It is proposed here that an adaptable usability component can be considered a *plug-and-play* technology. Here, the skilled practitioner plays a critical role in seeing how methods and processes can be adapted, designing projects that will meet the clients' needs, and fitting the organizational context. The fact that method and process choices will be influenced by organizational issues is discussed further by Grudin and Markus (1997).

Methods are combined and adapted to suit the research goals of the project. Wixon and Wilson (1997) observe that user tests can vary in their degree of formality, but elaborate less on the informal solution-focused testing that forms part of what has been observed here. Nørgaard and Hornbæk (2006) elaborate further on the details of think-aloud testing in practice, including the influence of practical realities, different processes, and the use of different probing practices that go beyond the more formal prescriptions in the literature. More work of this nature is encouraged in different design contexts and observing different methods. For example, as observed here, heuristic evaluation appears to be used in a wide variety of ways e.g., ad hoc justification of decisions, to aid in communication with clients, implicitly in evaluation (like an expert review), and as a basis for competitor comparisons—so, a more focused study on how this is perceived and used in practice would prove enlightening.

7.5.2 Relationships

Clients are not a homogenous group. They ought to be addressed according to their particular circumstances. Indeed, we begin to get a more realistic picture of usability in practice when we move away from considering method use by rote and discrete input into specific design processes, and move more towards considering the people in the process—people who develop expertise, learn from their ongoing experiences, have different backgrounds and understanding, react emotionally to criticism and praise, and make intelligent decisions to achieve the results they do in a commercial setting.

Dumas (Redish, et al., 2002) believes the most important factor in responding to usability recommendations in the long term is the relationship between the usability specialist and developers. Our data has also emphasized the importance of relationships—in knowing the company, people, politics, and practices that you are working with. Relationships can start with a small study before moving on to larger investment in usability services as the client becomes more familiar with usability services and more confident in their provider. Practitioners also make efforts to foster working relationships by including positive findings in reports, in not being condescending to colleagues, in having high-bandwidth communication with clients, and in encouraging them to watch user testing.

In academia, we may debate the merits of a value-centered approach for HCI (Cockton, 2004), but in practice it appears a matter of economic survival and one that is intimately related with the working relationships people and companies have with each other.

7.5.3 Communication and Coordination

It is paramount that the usability component fits well with different design and business processes. It is the job of the skilled practitioner to provide a suitable interface with nonusability specialists, and to design a work package that will suit that particular business need. Like other design processes, designing a suitable project for a client is dependent on their particular situation, which will influence what is done, when, and how the work is reported back. It may be the case that usability input is a more ongoing collaborative effort, and an official reporting-back stage is not suitable. How usability results are delivered, however, is an important area of practice that impacts on changes to the design in the short term and the perception of usability in the longer term.

Research on usability reporting was introduced in Section 7.3 of this chapter. In that section, the inclusion of positive findings was discussed. Stopping at problem identification was recognized as bad practice, which is supported by the empirical work of Hornbæk and Frøkjær (2005). More novel in this paper, was the conveying of the *bigger picture* that was mentioned in our analysis, so the team can make informed decisions and not make a bigger mistake by trying to fix a smaller problem. It appears that closer high-bandwidth communication between evaluators and designers has greater potential to avoid this problem. The issue of the *bigger picture* relates well to Klein's (1998, p. 225) discussion on communicating intent so team members can make more informed decisions. Further research could look at this more closely—for example, developing a protocol based on Weick's (1983, cited in Klein 1998, p. 228) streamlined version of a commander's intent:

- Here's what I think we face
- Here's what I think we should do
- Here's why
- Here's what we should keep an eye on
- Now, talk to me

Entwined with communication is coordination (i.e., how information transfers between component parts). For example, group size has already been observed to play a role in communication (e.g., Rosson, et al. 1988; Grudin & Markus 1997). Where usability practitioners are closer to the designers and developers, they have richer high-bandwidth contact that can avoid problems that a detached usability report may run into. How the usability component is organized to integrate with the wider business and design processes will influence the work and reporting mechanisms that are used.

7.5.4 Psychology and Expertise

Where work appears to be varied and complex, the skills of the individual practitioner come to the fore. They adapt methods to provide commercially viable solutions targeted at the current design setting. The skilled practitioner can perceive, through their experience, what working arrangements might be best for the client, and what recommendations are most likely to influence the design in a positive way. Here, we move away from questions such as "what is the best method?" to trying to understand how practitioners work, how they gain understanding, and insight into the products and people they work with, and how they add value in the commercial context. Klein's (1998) work moves in a similar direction by valuing the expertise of the practitioner over structured methods that are seen to support novices more. He believes that the development of expertise leads to a change in the perceptual ability of the expert. Future research could look toward the psychology of the usability practitioner—particularly how they perceive design situations. The perception of design situations includes the higher level of how a usability project should be composed, and the lower granularity of what problems and potentials lie within particular interfaces or technologies. Considering practitioners in more detail might lead to supporting novices and experts differently.

Practitioners develop expertise as they experience more and more in practice. Like experts in other domains, they appear to build up a bank of knowledge that is sometimes used implicitly and perceived as patterns (e.g., expert chess players' chunk patterns of pieces as detailed in Chase and Simon (1973)). This can take the form of being familiar with common usability problems and solutions within a certain domain, and building up a catalog of interface widgets that form the basis for analogical reasoning between cases (Klein (1998) talks about analogical reasoning at length). This analogical reasoning may influence design recommendations and evaluative judgements about the state of the art and best practice. If this form of reasoning is shown to play a significant role, as we suggest, informal methods for developing these internal patterns or schemas could be developed. Related work includes Hammond, et al. (1983) that studied elements of decision making by designers (i.e., their perception of the design process, theories of users, and a view of human factors); and Piegorsch, et al. (2006) who have developed a conceptual framework for ergonomic decision making. Work of this nature will have to be specific about the participants under study (e.g., novice/expert, job role, domain) because their experience will play a significant role in shaping their expertise.

Companies build up tangible expertise through research—developing their personnel and building up their portfolio of work. The organization of this portfolio can provide a great competitive advantage as it helps constitute a company's domain expertise. Further research could be done to find out the significance of this expertise for novices and experts in a company, and tools could be proposed to manage what Perry, et al. (1999) call organizational memory.

7.6 Conclusion

This exploratory study has sought insight into how usability practitioners work in professional web design. This has been done through a grounded analysis of eight interviews with practitioners. Insights from this analysis have been discussed under four subsections: Section 7.5.1 discussed methods and processes; Section 7.5.2 addressed relationships; Section 7.5.3 discussed communication and coordination; and Section 7.5.4 referred to psychology and expertise in practice. We have argued that there exists an outward movement of research for usability practice, where questions have progressed from method development to organizational issues in practice (see Table 7.1). This research contributes to the higher levels of usability work in professional web design. These higher levels provide an opportunity to study factors that have a significant influence on usability, as practiced in industry, but are rarely addressed when research is focused at a lower level of abstraction. From this higher level of abstraction, we believe that usability practice is best conceptualized from a system-level perspective, where the goal is to coordinate resources to add value to the design process. We also believe that research at this level of abstraction will complement research at lower levels of abstraction by sensitizing it to issues in practice. In this way the different levels of research work in a synergistic way.

Acknowledgment We are grateful for the collaboration and time that Stuart Booth, Lidia Oshlyansky, and the other interviewees allowed us for this study. The work is funded by EPSRC Grants GR/S67494/01 and GR/S67500/01.

References

Bellotti, V. (1988). Implications of current design practice for the use of HCI techniques. *Proceedings of the BCS HCI'88*, Manchester, UK. 13–34.

Bellotti, V., Buckingham Shum, S., MacLean, A., & Hammond, N. (1995). Multidisciplinary modelling in HCI design, in theory and in practice. *Proceedings of CHI 1995*, Colorado, USA. 429–436.

Blandford, A., Buckingham Shum, S., & Young, R. (1998). Training software engineers in a novel usability evaluation technique. *International Journal of Human-Computer Studies, 49*, 245–279.

Buckingham Shum, S., & Hammond, N. (1994). Transferring HCI modelling and design techniques to practitioners: A framework and empirical work. *Proceedings of BCS HCI'94* (pp. 21–36), Glasgow, UK

Card, S., Moran, T., & Newell, A. (1983). *The psychology of human-computer interaction.* Lawrence Erlbaum Associates.

Chase, W., & Simon, H. (1973). Perception in Chess. Cognitive Psychology, 4, 55–81. Cited in Mayer, E. (1997). From novice to expert. In Helander, M., Landauer, T., & Prabhu, P. (Eds.) (1997) *Handbook of Human Computer Interaction* (2nd Ed.) (pp. 781–797). Elsevier Science.

Cockton, G. (2004). Value-centred HCI. In *Proceedings of NordiCHI '04* (pp. 149–160), Tampere, Finland.

Dumas, J. S., Molich, R., & Jeffries, R. (2004). Describing usability problems: are we sending the right message? *Interactions, 11*, 4 (Jul. 2004), 24–29.

Grudin, J. (1990). The computer reaches out: the historical continuity of interface design. *Proceedings of the SIGCHI Conference on Human Factors in Computing Systems: Empowering People* (pp. 261–268). Seattle, Washington, USA.

Grudin, J., & Markus, M. (1997). Organizational issues in development and implementation of interactive systems. In Helander, M., Landauer, T., & Prabhu, P. (Eds.), *Handbook of Human Computer Interaction* (2nd Ed.) (pp. 1457–1474). Elsevier Science.

Hammond, N., Jørgensen, A., MacLean, A., Barnard, P., & Long, J. (1983). Design practice and interface usability: Evidence from interviews with designers. *Proceedings of CHI'93* (pp. 40–44), Boston, Massachusetts, USA.

Hornbæk, K., & Frøkjær, E. (2005). Comparing usability problems and redesign proposals as input to practical systems development. *Proceedings of CHI'05* (pp. 391–400). Portland, Oregon, USA.

Nørgaard, M., & Hornbæk, K. (2006). What do usability evaluators do in practice? An explorative study of think-aloud testing. *Proceedings of DIS '06* (pp. 209–218), University Park, PA, USA.

Klein, G. (1998). *Sources of power: How people make decisions*. Cambridge: MIT Press

O'Neill, E. (1998). *User-developer cooperation in software development: building common ground and usable systems*. PhD Thesis. Queen Mary, University of London.

Perry, M., Fruchter, R., & Rosenburg, D. (1999). Co-ordinating distributed knowledge: A study into the use of an organisational memory. *Cognition, Technology and Work, 1*, 142–152.

Piegorsch, K., Watkins, K., Piegorsch, W., Reininger, B., Corwin, S., & Valois, R. (2006). Ergonomic decision-making: A conceptual framework for experienced practitioners from backgrounds in industrial engineering and physical therapy. *Applied Ergonomics, 37*, 587–598.

Redish, J., Bias, R. G., Bailey, R., Molich, R., Dumas, J., & Spool, J. M. (2002). Usability in practice: formative usability evaluations – evolution and revolution. In *CHI '02 Extended Abstracts on Human Factors in Computing Systems* (pp. 885–890), Minneapolis, Minnesota, USA.

Rosson, M., Maass, S., & Kellogg, W. (1988). The designer as user: Building requirements for the design tools from design practice. *Communication of the ACM, 31*(11), 1288–1298.

Strauss, A., & Corbin, J. (1998) *Basics of qualitative research: Techniques and procedures for developing grounded theory* (2nd ed.). Sage Publications.

Terrins-Rudge, D., & Jørgensen, A. (1993). Supporting the designers: reaching the user. In P.F. Byerley, P.J. Barnard and J. May (Eds.), Computers, communication and usability: design issues, research and methods for integrated services. Cited in O'Neill, E. (1998). *User-developer cooperation in software development: building common ground and usable systems*. PhD Thesis. Queen Mary, University of London. 23–66.

Chapter 8
Characterizations, Requirements, and Activities of User-Centered Design—the KESSU 2.2 Model

Timo Jokela

University of Oulu, Finland, e-mail: timo.jokela@oulu.fi

Abstract ISO 13407 is a widely used and referred model of user-centered design, UCD. In this chapter, the principles and activities of ISO 13407 are analysed. Based on the analysis, a revised UCD model "KESSU 2.2" is proposed, including refinements both in the presentation and in the contents of principles and activities. The goal is that the refined model is more consistent and illustrates the essential contents of UCD clearer.

8.1 Introduction

ISO 13407, or *Human-centered design processes for interactive systems*,[1] (ISO/IEC, 1999) is an international standard, established in 1999, that provides general guidance for *user-centered design* (UCD). ISO 13407 can be regarded as an important supplement to the UCD literature. First, as a standard, it is based on the consensus of a wide international board of researchers and practitioners in the field. The standard has become an important, widely referred to reference of UCD.

Second, it approaches UCD from a higher level of abstraction than methodology books such as Beyer & Holtzblatt (1998), Mayhew (1999), Cooper (1999), Constantine & Lockwood (1999), and Rosson & Carroll (2002). ISO 13407 depicts the main points of UCD, but does not go into details. It describes UCD through principles and activities rather than describing different usability methods (although is not quite systematic on this). For audiences such as software developers, project managers,[2] and students in software engineering or computer science, it is important that one can communicate the essentials of designing usability without going into details that are not so relevant to them, such as specifics of usability methods. Such a general, method-independent reference model is also needed when companies want to understand the status of UCD in their development processes.

Not many research papers exist on ISO 13407 (and actually, there are few on any UCD methodologies). There are a number of publications that refer to ISO 13407, such as Bevan (2001), Earthy, Sherwood-Jones, & Bevan (2001), and John, Bass,

---

[1] In this paper, human-centered design and user-centered design are considered synonyms.

[2] Actually, *those managing design processes* are the explicitly stated audience of ISO 13407

E. Law et al. (eds.), *Maturing Usability.*

& Adams (2003)) but indepth studies are largely missing. The goal of this chapter is to partly fill this gap: ISO 13407–specifically the descriptions of principles and activities–is analyzed at a detailed level and an enhanced model proposed.

The background for this work is the author's and his colleagues' experience on using ISO 13407 and the related technical report ISO 18529 (ISO/IEC, 2000). These references were especially used in the evaluation of the status of user-centered design practices of companies but also in education and planning UCD activities (Jokela 2002b), (Jokela 2003), (Jokela, Iivari, Matero, & Karukka 2003), (Jokela 2004a).

At a general level, ISO 13407 was found useful and sense-making: it provides an overview of UCD in a concise form. However, we identified shortcomings in our empirical studies, which led to interpretations and refinements in the model. It was found, for example, that the four-activity lifecycle model (referenced in the next section) was not precise enough to communicate the status of usability practices to the stakeholders of the companies. It was also found that the style in which the activities were described were not concrete enough. Therefore, step-by-step, a revised model evolved, with seven activities and an outcome-driven way of describing the activities. We have described how our experience led to the new model in Jokela (2002a, 2002b, 2003, 2004b).

This experience evoked an interest in studying ISO 13407 in detail, especially the descriptions of principles and activities that form the usability substance of the standard[3]. In this chapter, the descriptions of the principles and activities are analyzed in detail, both from the viewpoints of presentation and contents, conclusions drawn, and changes suggested. A result is a revised model (i.e., revised descriptions of the principles and activities).

This kind of research represents design science (March & Smith 1995): a new artifact (a model) is developed. A viable research target is to create better artifacts than earlier ones. Constructing an artifact is a valid research activity if design solutions are justified. The model presented in this paper is based on reasoning: every change compared with the earlier model (ISO 13407) is justified. Thereby it is suggested that this analysis is a research contribution. Naturally, an artifact also should be evaluated; evaluation, however, is not in the scope of this chapter.

In the next section, an overview of the main contents of ISO 13407 is given. In the following section, the analysis strategy is presented. Thereafter, the principles of ISO 13407 are analyzed. It is shown, for example, that the principles are described inconsistently, with different categories of statements. Changes to the principles are then proposed (actually, one proposal is not to use the term *principle* any more). In the subsequent section, a similar study is done to the activity descriptions: analysis of the presentation and contents, and proposals for changes. Based on the analysis, a revised KESSU 2.2 model is proposed, with preliminary contents (in Appendix 8-3). The results are summarized, limitations discussed, and implications proposed in the final section.

---

[3] Issues such as rationale and project planning are excluded from the scope of this paper.

8.2 Overview of ISO 13407

ISO 13407 starts by defining that "Human-centered design is an approach to inter-active system development that focuses specifically on making systems usable." The objective of the standard is to provide "guidance on human-centered design activi-ties throughout the life cycle of computer-based interactive systems." The standard describes user-centered design from four different aspects:

- Rationale for UCD
- Planning UCD
- Principles of UCD
- Activities of UCD

8.2.1 Rationale

The rationale part briefly describes the benefits that usable systems provide, such as reduction of training and support costs, improved user satisfaction, and productivity of users.

8.2.2 Principles

The standard identifies four general principles that characterize user-centered design and that are not bound to any specific phase of development cycle:

- *User involvement*[4]—the active involvement of users and a clear understanding of user and task requirements
- *Allocation of function*—an appropriate allocation of functions between users and technology
- *Iteration*—iteration of design solutions
- *Multi-disciplinary design*—different skills are required in UCD.

8.2.3 Planning

The planning part provides guidance in fitting user-centered design activities into the overall system-development process. Among other things, the standard emphasizes that project plans should reserve time and resources for iteration and user feedback. The importance of teamwork and communication is also mentioned.

---

[4] The shorter terms are by the author.

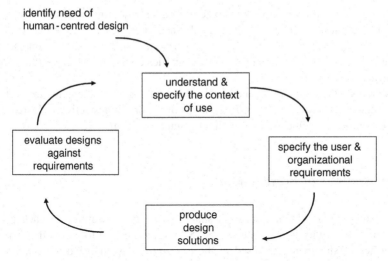

Fig. 8.1 The lifecycle picture of UCD in ISO 13407

8.2.4 Activities

The core of the standard—as stated explicitly—is the description of user-centered design activities. The standard provides general descriptions of the UCD lifecycle, identifies the following four main activities of UCD, and illustrates their relationship informally in a picture (Figure 8.1):

- Understand and specify context of use—CoU[5]
- Specify the user and organizational requirements—Reqs
- Produce design solutions—Design
- Evaluate designs against requirements—Evaluation

8.3 Analysis Strategy

ISO 13407 identifies four principles and four activities of UCD, and provides descriptions for each. But how exactly are the principles described, and what kinds of issues are included in these descriptions? Is there space for enhancements in the descriptions?

The descriptions of principles and activities are analyzed from two different viewpoints:

---

[5] The abbreviations are by the author.

- Presentation—presentation is analyzed to understand how to describe the principles/activities. How are the principles/activities described? What kinds of statements (issues) are included in the descriptions? To what extent are the descriptions of the different principles/activities consistent (described in a same manner)?
- Contents—the contents are analyzed to find places for refinements in the UCD substance. What are the *usability* contents of the principles/activities? Are all the relevant issues included? Is something essential missing?

8.3.1 Analysis of Presentation

In the analysis of presentation, each statement in the description of each principle and each activity is first categorized. Second, the extent to which the different categories of statements are used in the descriptions is analyzed to compare the descriptions. Based on the analysis, improvements to the presentation are proposed. In summary, the analysis of presentation has the following parts:

- Identification of the category of each statement that is in the descriptions of principles/activities
- Analysis of the extent to which the different categories of statements are used in the different descriptions
- Proposed changes to the presentation of the descriptions of principles/ activities

Due to space limitations, the analysis of each statement cannot be presented explicitly in this paper. Full analysis of the descriptions (categorization of the statements) can be found from the author's webpage, http://www.tol.oulu.fi/~tjokela/iso_13407_pres_analysis.pdf.

8.3.2 Analysis of Contents

The starting point of the analysis of content is that nothing should be changed unless there is a good reason. Therefore, only those places in the descriptions where changes are proposed are discussed. The whole text is not analyzed (as it is in the analysis of the presentation). Therefore, the analysis of the contents is simpler, without any subsections. The contents of ISO 3407 (principles and activities) are highlighted, and changes with justifications are proposed.

8.4 Analysis of the Principles of ISO 13407

The standard identifies four principles of UCD, and provides descriptions for each of these. In the following sections, an analysis is made from the viewpoints of presentation and contents.

8.4.1 Presentation

Each statement in the descriptions of the activities is analyzed and categorized to understand what exactly is included in the descriptions. Based on the findings, improvements are proposed.

8.4.1.1 Categories of Statements

The following categories of statements can be identified:

- Characterizations—statements that describe typical phenomena or general *truths* about UCD, such as "this is what UCD is typically like." Example: *The effectiveness of user involvement increases as the interaction between the developers and the users increases* (in user involvement)
- Requirements—statements that define "what should be done" for the successful implementation of UCD. Example: *The resulting human functions should form a meaningful set of tasks* (in allocation of function)
- Definition of concepts—Example: *Allocation of function—the specification of which functions should be carried out by the users and which by the technology.*

8.4.1.2 Use of Categories Statements in the Descriptions

The extent to which the different categories of statements are used in the descriptions of the different principles is summarized in Table 8.1. One can conclude that the descriptions of principles are quite inconsistent:

- *Iteration* contains only characterizations
- *Allocation of functions* and *multidisciplinary teamwork* include only requirements
- *User involvement* includes both categories
- *Allocation of function* includes a definition

Table 8.1 The extent to which the different categories of statements are used in the descriptions of the different principles.

	User Involvement	Allocation of Function	Iteration	Multi-disciplinary Teamwork
Characterisations	++		++	
Requirements	+	++		++
Definitions		+		

(empty): no statements
+: 1-2 statements
++: several statements

8.4.1.3 Proposed Refinements

It is proposed that there would be two sections: General Characterisations and General Requirements, instead of a single section (Principles). Making a distinction between these two types of things—characterization and requirements—in the structure is logical, simply because they are different issues.

Second, it it is proposed that the definitions and terms to be collected into a single section (such as the Terms and Definitions section of ISO 13407).

8.4.2 Contents

It is agreed that User Involvement and Iteration are characteristic features of UCD—one cannot typically design usable systems without user involvement and iteration. It is also agreed that Multidisciplinary Design is a requirement—different skills are required in UCD.

The following changes in the content of the principles, however, are proposed:

- *Allocation of function* should not be considered as a principle. The reason is that the decision what functionality to allocate to the computer and what to the user is essentially a *design* matter—not a general issue. Instead, we propose that allocation of function should be described in the context of a design activity (see the proposal for the *user task design* activity).
- *Start UCD early* should be a new principle (more precisely, a *generic requirement*). Early involvement is critical to the effectiveness of UCD and applies to all UCD lifecycle. Actually, this issue is mentioned in the General section of activity descriptions of ISO 13407 ("The human-centered design process should start at the earliest stage of the project...").
- *Tailor usability methods to suit context* should be another new principle (more precisely, a generic characterization). It is typically not feasible to apply methods *by the book* but one has to fit them to the contexts of real projects. This is the author's experience (Jokela, Koivumaa, Pirkola, Salminen, & Kantola 2006) and supported by Wixon (2003).

8.4.3 Summary

It is proposed that

- The titles *General Characterizations* and *General Requirements* be used instead of *Principles*
- *General Characterizations* include iteration, user involvement, and tailoring usability methods
- *General Requirements* include multidisciplinary teamwork and start UCD early

8.5 Analysis of the Activities of ISO 13407

The standard identifies five activities of UCD, and provides descriptions for each of these. In the following, an analysis is made in the same way as the one of principles (previous section)—from the viewpoints of presentation and content.

8.5.1 Presentation

Each statement in the descriptions of the activities is analyzed and categorized to understand exactly what is included in the descriptions. Based on the findings, improvements are proposed.

8.5.1.1 Categories of Statements

The descriptions of activities are longer than the ones for principles, and one can find several categories of statements:

- Purpose Statements—statements that provide a justification for the existence of activity. Example: *It is important to understand and identify the details of this context in order to guide early design decisions, and to provide a basis for evaluation* (in CoU)
- *Characterizations*—statements that describe typical phenomena or general *truths* about an activity. Example: *Many organizations have internal user interface style guides, product knowledge and marketing information which can be useful in supporting the initial design, particularly when designing similar products* (in Design)
- *General Requirements*—requirements related to the overall performance of an activity. Example: *The context in which the system is to be used should be identified in terms of the following....* (in CoU)
- *Quality Requirements*—requirements about the quality of an activity. Example: *The context of use description should... specify the range of intended users, tasks and environments in sufficient detail to support design activity* (in CoU)
- *Communication Requirements*—requirements that address the communication of the results of an activity. Example: *The context of use description should... be made available to the design team at appropriate times and in appropriate forms to support design activities* (in CoU)
- *Definitions of Outcomes*—the results of activities are defined. Example: *The specification of user and organizational requirements should... identify the range of relevant users and other personnel in the design* (in Requirements)
- *Methodological Guidance*—how to implement UCD activities. Example: *Expert evaluation can be fast and economical and is good for identifying major problems but is not sufficient to guarantee a successful interactive system* (in Evaluation)

- *Identification of Subactivities*—the steps required to carry out an activity. Example: *The process therefore involves the following activities: a) Use existing knowledge to develop design proposals with a multi-disciplinary input; b)...* (in Design)
- *Definition of Activity Types*—an activity is used for different purposes. Example: *Evaluation can be used: a) to provide feedback that can be used to improve design, b) to assess whether user and organizational objectives have been achieved, c)....* (in Evaluation)
- *Definitions of Concepts*—Example: *Long-term monitoring means collecting user input in different ways over a period of time.*

8.5.1.2 Use of Categories Statements in the Descriptions

A summary of the extent to which the different categories of statements are used in the descriptions of the different activities is provided in Table 8.2. Making a summary table of contents of the activities is somewhat complex because the activities are not described at the same level of granularity: *Requirements* is less than one page while *Evaluate* is three pages long.

The analysis discussed above shows that the descriptions of the activities are quite diverse:

- Overall, the number of statements of the different categories—characterizations, requirements, outcomes, and methodological guidance—varies a lot
- Generally, *CoU* and *Requirements* are simpler than *Design* and *Evaluation* because the latter ones include subactivities and/or different activity types (Design: 5 subactivities; Evaluation: 3 subactivities, and 4 activity types)
- *CoU* includes different viewpoints in a rather balanced way; methodological guidance, however, is missing. Communication requirements are in a significant role.

Table 8.2 The extent to which the different categories of statements are used in the descriptions of the different activities

	Planning	CoU	Requirements	Design*	Evaluation*
Definitions of Concepts		+			
Purpose Statements		+	+		
Characterizations	+	+		+	++
UCD Content Requirements	++	++	++		+
Quality Requirements		+	++		
Communication Requirements		+			
Definition of Outcomes		+	++		
Methodological Guidance					
Definition of Subactivities				+	+
Definition of Activity types					+

(empty): no statements
+: 1-2 statements
++: several statements
* More detailed analysis of the *Design* and *Evaluation* in Appendices 8-1 and 8-2.

- *Requirements* has a strong emphasis on requirements and definition of outcomes. Especially the quality requirements have a significant role. But it provides no characterizations of the activity or methodological guidance
- *Design* is mainly described through subactivities, the descriptions of which mainly focus on characterizations and methodological guidance; requirements feature in two subactivities (Appendix 8-1)
- *Evaluation* contains more general descriptions than *Design*, but is mainly described through subactivities or activity types. An explicit purpose statement is given. It is notable that the styles of the descriptions of the subactivities are quite diverse (Appendix 8-2)

8.5.1.3 Proposed Refinements

It is proposed that activities are described consistently, and each activity described with the same categories of statements. It is not logical to describe activities with different styles. For example, if methodological guidance were provided for one activity, it is logical to provide methodological guidance for other activities, too.

The *General* section

Currently, the *General* section identifies the activities, illustrates their mutual inter-dependence with a picture, and provides some general requirements and guidance. It is proposed that the style of presenting the picture could be refined.

One should include the *outcomes* of each activity visually in the picture, as shown in Figure 8.2 (references Figure 8.1). The activities describe what is being done, and the outcomes are the results of those activities. The reason for including the outcomes is that they provide concreteness to the description of the lifecycle: they make explicit to the reader that there is something concrete that should be produced as a result of an activity.

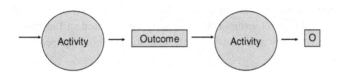

Fig. 8.2 UCD lifecycle is visually illustrated through activities (what is being done) and outcomes (results of the activities)

Descriptions of individual activities

It is proposed that the descriptions of the activities include the following subsections:

Purpose

The purpose of each activity should be clearly stated. The purpose statement provides motivation for the existence of an activity, and makes clear what exactly is achieved through it. As noted earlier, the purpose is actually mentioned in some activity descriptions of ISO 13407, but not very clearly nor systematically.

The term *purpose* is also used in the style of defining processes in ISO 18529 (ISO/IEC, 2000), which is further based on the software process definitions (ISO/IEC, 1998b). The purpose statements of ISO 18529, however, are much longer descriptions, including a list of things that are achieved as a result of the *successful* implementation of the activity.

Characterization

Characterization of an activity should be provided. Characterization is analogous with the general characterization of UCD. Characterization provides descriptions of the *typical phenomena* and things that happen in the context of a specific activity: characteristic features, level of difficulty, typical problems, the required expertise, etc., depending on the contents of the activity. As we saw earlier, characterizations of activities are also provided in ISO 13407, but not systematically.

Definitions of Outcomes

Outcomes are produced as a result of carrying out activities. Outcomes are typically—but not necessarily always—concrete deliverables (e.g., documents or prototypes) that should be produced as a result of a usability activity. Outcomes are a core of activity definition, and they should be made very explicit and clear. Definitions of outcomes are a core part of activity descriptions because outcomes are the concrete things that should be produced by an activity. The outcomes are the specific *should* things of an activity description: they should be produced.

Requirements

This subsection includes the specific UCD content requirements for the activity, if any. UCD content requirements: these may be required in the context of some activities, but typically an activity specific statement is not required (see above).

Methodological Guidance

Overall descriptions of methodological alternatives that enable us to carry out activities and produce the outcomes should be provided. The aim is to give an idea about different alternatives that enables the activity to be carried out, not to describe the methods in detail or to present a comprehensive list of different methods.

This is a section that is probably not a necessary one in the context of a general model – the idea is to keep the model method independent. In ISO 13407, methodological guidance is provided in the context of some activities (specifically Evaluation), but not systematically. A reference to methods that can be used to perform the activity (i.e., to produce the outcomes) is, however, important for the practical implementation of the activity.

Subactivities (not to be included)

In ISO 13407, subactivities are used in the definition of the (sequential) steps of the *Design* and *Evaluation* activities. It is proposed that these kinds of descriptions are included in the *Characterization* subsection. They are descriptions on what typically happens in the activity. They should not be formative (as they partly are now in ISO 13407), but descriptive.

Activity types (not to be included)

Definition of activity types—activity types can be found from the description of Evaluation in ISO 13407, meaning that an activity can be used for different purposes (specifically, "*to provide feedback*" and "*to assess whether ... objectives have been achieved*"). It is proposed that such different activity types should be defined as separate activities.

Quality and communication requirements (not to be included)

Quality and communication requirements are not required at the activity level, as they are now described at the *General* section (see below).

8.5.2 Contents

The changes for contents are discussed separately for the General section, contents of individual activities, and set of activities.

8.5.2.1 The General Section

It is proposed that some requirements—applicable to all activities—could be added. These requirements are defined for some activities in ISO 13407, but it is proposed that these are general ones:

- It is essential that activities produce outcomes. Therefore, a general UCD content requirement is proposed. The requirement could be formulated as: "*The outcomes of the activities should be produced.*" This is a key content requirement and should be applicable to all activities (see also below)

- A general quality requirement is proposed. The importance of quality is relevant—the activities should be carried out using appropriate methods, by people that have appropriate skills—and should be a requirement to all activities. It is proposed that a statement such as "*Each activity should produce appropriate outcomes, by using appropriate methods that are professionally implemented*" is applicable to all activities and could be included in the *General* section. Another alternative would be to include quality requirements in the description of each activity separately. This general statement, however, covers those kinds of quality requirements of individual statements that are now used in ISO 13407 (such as: "*... context of use description should ... specify the range of intended users ... in sufficient detail to support design activity*")

- A general communication requirement should be given. The importance of communicating the results is applicable to all activities, and should be a requirement for all activities. It is proposed that a statement such as "*The outcomes should be effectively communicated to the other relevant activities*" is applicable to all activities, and could be mentioned in the general section of activity descriptions. It covers individual statements of ISO 13407, such as "*the context of use description should ... be made available to the design team at appropriate times and in appropriate forms... *"

8.5.2.2 Contents of Individual Activities

When each activity is described using the subsections proposed above, the description of each activity changes to some extent (for example, *context of use* would include characterizations that are now missing).

In addition, there are also some other changes that are proposed:

- *Requirements*—now there are overwhelmingly many requirements. It is proposed that the description of the activity is made simpler, focusing on usability requirements (reflecting the purpose of UCD, "making systems usable")
- *Design*

  - The description should not be based on prototyping that is basically just a method (even if an important one). Prototyping could be described informally in the *Characterization* subsection
  - Should mention more widely the different kinds of interaction elements (hardware, mechanics, documentation, training, packaging, help desk, and customer support) that are subjects of UCD. All those different elements have an impact on user experience
  - Discussion on evaluations should be decreased. The interplay between design and evaluation is a UCD life-cycle issue, and a more natural place for such discussion is in the *General* section.

- *Evaluation*

  - Overall—too extensive description compared with other activities

- Usability testing should be discussed as a method, not as a requirement. One probably cannot do effective UCD without usability testing; but still it is just a method. The core thing is to reveal usability problems (in qualitative tests), no matter what the method is
- Evaluation types should be removed because they are activities with a different purpose. Instead, one should define separate activities for the different types of evaluations (formative and summative evaluations—see discussion below)
- Field validation and long-term monitoring should be described as methods rather than basic activities. In fact, a better place for these methods could be in the *Requirements* activity—long-term monitoring of an existing system is used when the requirements of a new (version of a) system are determined

8.5.2.3 The Set of Activities

ISO 13407 identifies four activities (Figure 8.1). The following new activities, or changes in the existing activities, are proposed:

- Identifying the users should be an explicit, new activity. Identifying users is a very basic UCD activity—one needs to know users as a basis for other activities. Further, it is not a trivial activity—for example, determining the user categories for consumer products is all but simple. In ISO 13407, the identification of users is mentioned in the description of context of use but almost hidden in the text[6]
- *Context of use* should be a multiple-instance activity because context of use analysis should be carried out separately for each user group. The contexts of use of different users may differ significantly from each other
- A new activity, *user task design*, should be added, as a core activity of UCD. It should be a separate activity from *Design* because their scopes are different (work design vs. design of interaction elements). *Allocation of function*—a principle in ISO 13407—fits naturally into this activity
- The *Evaluation* activity should be split into two separate activities: formative evaluation (usability feedback) and summative evaluation (usability verification). Although both of them are evaluations, their scopes are different—identifying problems in designs vs. checking the conformance against requirements. The outcomes are also different

8.5.3 Summary

It is proposed that

- The *Generic* section includes a revised picture of activities, and defines those requirements that apply generally to all activities

---

[6] It is stated: "The context . . . should be identified in terms of . . . the characteristics of the intended users. . ."

- Activities are described consistently with the same style—purpose, characterization, outcomes, requirements, and methodological guidance
- Contents of some activities are refined
- New activities are defined—user involvement, multiple instances of context of use, user task design
- Evaluation is divided into formative and summative evaluations

8.6 The KESSU 2.2 Model

The outline of the revised KESSU 2.2 model is summarized in Table 8.3. Most parts of the contents are discussed and justified in the previous sections. In addition, a *Purpose* section is proposed. In the introductory section of ISO 13407, it is stated, *"Human-centered design ... focuses specifically on making systems usable."* This is a clear purpose statement for UCD—it gives a reason for the existence of UCD and makes it clear what exactly will be achieved with UCD. It is proposed that this kind of purpose statement is clearly mentioned in the overview section. The outline also includes *Terms and Definitions*, because the principle and activity descriptions of ISO 13407 include definitions of terms.

Table 8.3 The contents of the refined model in comparison with ISO 13407

Revised Descriptions	Comparison with ISO 13407
Terms and Definitions	New terms added from the descriptions of the principles and activities
Purpose	Mentioned in ISO 13407 but not in the body text.
General Characterizations	Under *principles* in ISO 13407
User Involvement	In ISO 13407
Iteration	In ISO 13407
Tailoring of Usability Methods	Not in ISO 13407
General Requirements	Under *principles* in ISO 13407
Multidisciplinary Teamwork	In ISO 13407
Start UCD Early	Mentioned in the *General* subsection of *Activities*
(not included)	Allocation of function
Activities	In ISO 13407
General	Visual picture changed Some new requirements that apply to all activities added compared with ISO 13407: UCD content, quality and communication requirements
Identification of Users	Not in ISO 13407
Context of Use (multiple instance)	Single instance in ISO 13407
Requirements	In ISO 13407
User Task Design	Not in ISO 13407
Produce Design Solutions	In ISO 13407
Usability Feedback (Formative Evaluation)	Part of evaluation in ISO 13407
Usability Verification (Summative Evaluation)	Part of evaluation in ISO 13407

In addition, each activity is described with five subsections:

- Purpose
- Characterization
- Outcomes
- Requirements
- Methodological guidance

These descriptions of activities differ more or less from the ones of ISO 13407, depending on the activity.

Probably the core of the KESSU 2.2 model is the set of activities—as is in ISO 13407. The activities are visually described in Figure 8.3. The circle shape is inherited from the figure of ISO 13407 (Figure 8.1). The differences are the revised set of activities, and the visually illustrated outcomes. Another specific feature is the different color of the interaction design activities and other activities, to emphasize the different nature of these activities—interaction design produces the product solutions, while other activities feed user-driven input to the design activity. This is also illustrated with the arrows from other activities to the interaction design activity. A third specific characteristic is the *business drivers* that are an input to the requirements activity.

Overall, most of the categories of issues that can be found in ISO 13407 are included in the revised model. However, the revised model includes quite a number of new and different features. Draft contents are presented in Appendix 8-3.

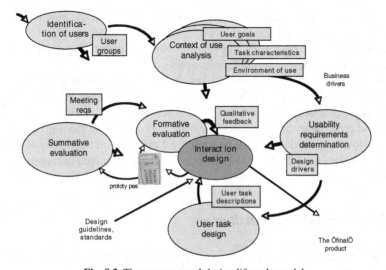

Fig. 8.3 The user-centered design lifecycle model

8.7 Discussion

A revised model—i.e., descriptions of the principles and activities—of ISO 13407 is proposed. The KESSU 2.2 model is based on an analysis of the descriptions of ISO 13407. Each change compared with ISO 13407 is justified. In brief, the KESSU 2.2 model has the following main features:

- The UCD lifecycle is described from four viewpoints—purpose, general characterization, requirements, and activities
- General characterizations include user involvement, iteration, and tailoring usability methods
- General requirements include multidisciplinary teamwork and starting UCD early
- Seven UCD activities (one a multiple instance), and a revised picture
- Purpose, characterizations, outcomes, requirements and methodological guidance are systematically included in the description of each activity.
- As an example of a solution at a detailed level—the *allocation of function* is a requirement of the *Interaction Design* activity (not a general principle, as it is in ISO 13407)

Overall, the aim is that the model should make the user-centered design lifecycle more systematically defined, and more concrete and unambiguous. The model is enhanced with the general characterizations and requirements (principles) and more systematic descriptions of activities.

8.7.1 Limitations

This work is based on a detailed analysis of ISO 13407, and the new features are justified, partly based on the author's long experience of using ISO 13407. The proposed model, however, is in an evolution phase—many of the descriptions are the result of the writing process of this chapter.

An elementary part of constructive research is the evaluation of an artifact. A limitation of this work is that there is little empirical evidence on how the structure works in practice. We have some good experience on using the visual lifecycle model and preliminary activity descriptions in assessments and training (e.g., Jokela 2004a). However, we do not have any empirical evidence on the details of the specific descriptions presented in this chapter, part of which evolved during the writing process.

8.7.2 Implications to Practitioners

Overall, the model is meant as a general reference to UCD. The model represents a high-level abstraction of user-centered design and is addressed to an audience not specialized in usability, such as project managers (as is ISO 13407), software designers, and marketing representatives.

The main audience, however, would probably be usability practitioners and user interface designers. Rather than project managers and software designers etc. reading about usability and user-centered design by themselves, it is more likely that usability practitioners give presentations about UCD to them. It is hoped that the KESSU 2.2 model would serve as a concise reference for developing such presentations. Another important target would be teaching in student classes.

Further, the model could serve as a general reference for planning usability activities in development projects. The model is method independent, and allows consideration of different methodological approaches. In addition, the model could be used as a reference in assessing the status of UCD practices in companies—this is actually the environment where the main features of the model were developed (Jokela 2004a).

8.7.3 Further Research Topics

This chapter presents a revised model of UCD. A model is an artifact, but there exists no perfect artifact, and neither of the models should be understood as the truth. In fact, it is supposed that many disagree with (parts of) the models. If this is the case, it can be seen as a good sign—it means that the models are clear enough to be argued for or against. Complementing analytical viewpoints and constructs from other researchers are more than welcome.

A natural path for further research would be empirical studies on the usefulness and applicability—and further development—of the proposed models. The ideas presented in this paper—or possibly its modifications—should be empirically evaluated and further developed in a human-centered way. To what extent does it work, and what are the areas of further improvement when it is used as a tool in communicating and providing UCD training, assessing companies' UCD practices, or as a reference in planning UCD activities.

Anyway, I believe that it is most relevant to carry out research on developing general models of UCD, which are method-independent, clear, unambiguous, and communicative.

References

Bevan, N. (2001). International standards for HCI and usability. *Int. J. Human-Computer Studies,* `55, 533–552.

Beyer, H., & Holtzblatt, K. (1998). *Contextual design: Defining customer-centered systems.* San Francisco: Morgan Kaufmann.

Constantine, L. L., & Lockwood, L. A. D. (1999). *Software for use.* New York: Addison-Wesley.

Cooper, A. (1999). *The inmates are running the asylum: Why high tech products drive us crazy and how to restore the sanity* (1st Ed.). Indianapolis, IN: Macmillan.

Earthy, J. V., Sherwood-Jones, B., & Bevan, N. (2001). The improvement of human-centred processes – facing the challenge and reaping the benefit of ISO 13407. *International Journal of Human Computer Studies, 55*(4), 553–558.

ISO/IEC. (1998a). *9241-11 Ergonomic requirements for office work with visual display terminals (VDT)s – Part 11 Guidance on usability*. ISO/IEC 9241–11: 1998 (E).

ISO/IEC. (1998b). *15504-2 Software Process Assessment – Part 2: A reference model for processes and process capability* (International Organization for Standardization, Genève, Switzerland). ISO/IEC TR 15504-2: 1998 (E).

ISO/IEC. (1999). *13407 Human-Centred Design Processes for Interactive Systems* (International Organization for Standardization, Genève, Switzerland). ISO/IEC 13407: 1999 (E).

ISO/IEC. (2000). *18529 Human-centred Lifecycle Process Descriptions*. ISO/IEC TR 18529: 2000 (E).

John, B. E., Bass, L., & Adams, R. J. (2003). Communication across the HCI/SE divide: ISO 13407 and the Rational Unified Process. Paper presented at the HCI International, Crete.

Jokela, T. (2002a). A method-independent process model of user-centred design. Paper presented at the IFIP 17th World Computer Conference 2002 – TC 13 Stream on Usability: Gaining a Competitive Edge, Montreal.

Jokela, T. (2002b). Making user-centred design common sense: Striving for an unambiguous and communicative UCD process model. In In *Proceedings of e NordiCHI 2002* (pp. 19–26), Aarhus, Denmark.

Jokela, T. (2003). Beyond usability methods: Usability engineering through processes and outcomes. *Cutter IT Journal, 16*(10), 13–20.

Jokela, T. (2004a). Evaluating the user-centredness of development organisations: conclusions and implications from empirical usability capability maturity assessments. *Interacting with Computers, 16*(6), 1095–1132.

Jokela, T. (2004b). *The KESSU Usability Design Process Model. Version 2.1*: Oulu University.

Jokela, T., Iivari, N., Matero, J., & Karukka, M. (2003). The standard of user-centered Design and the standard definition of usability: Analyzing ISO 13407 against ISO 9241-11. Paper presented at the CLIHC 2003, Rio de Janeiro, Brazil.

Jokela, T., Koivumaa, J., Pirkola, J., Salminen, P., & Kantola, N. (2006). Methods for quantitative usability requirements: A case study on the development of the user interface of a mobile phone. *Personal and Ubiquitous Computing, 10*(6), 345–355.

March, S. T., & Smith, G. F. (1995). Design and natural science research on information technology. *Decision Support Systems, 15*(4), 251–266.

Mayhew, D. J. (1999). *The usability engineering lifecycle*. San Francisco: Morgan Kaufman.

Rosson, M. B., & Carroll, J. M. (2002). *Usability engineering. Scenario-based development of human-computer interaction*. Morgan Kaufmann.

Wixon, D. (2003). Evaluating usability methods. Why the current literature fails the practitioner. *ACM interactions, 10*(4), 28–34.

Appendix 8-1: Content Analysis of the *Design* Activity

Table 8A-1 Content analysis of the *Produce Design Solutions* activity. Each column represents a subactivity defined in the description

	Use Existing Knowledge	Make Design Concrete	Present Design Solutions	Alter and Iterate	Manage Iteration
Definitions of Concepts					
Purpose Statements					
Characterizations	++	++	++	+	

(Continued)

Table 8A-1 (*Continued*)

	Use Existing Knowledge	Make Design Concrete	Present Design Solutions	Alter and Iterate	Manage Iteration
UCD Content Requirements				+	++
Quality Requirements					
Communication Requirements					
Definition of Outcomes					
Methodological Guidance	+		++	+	
Definition of Sublife-cycle					
Definition of Activity Types					

Appendix 8-2: Content Analysis of the Evaluation Activity

Table 8A-2 *Planning* and *Reporting Results* are generic subactivities—the activities marked with * represent different types, being alternative

	Planning	Provide feedback*	Assess whether objectives met*	Field validation*	Longterm monitoring*	Reporting Results
Definitions of Concepts					+	
Purpose Statements				+		
Characterizations			+		+	
UCD Content Requirements	++	++			+	++
Quality Requirements			+			++
Communication Requirements						
Definition of Outcomes	++					++
Methodological Guidance	+	++		+		
Definition of Sublifecycle						
Definition of Activity Types			+			

Appendix 8-3: The KESSU 2.2 Model of UCD with Preliminary Contents

This appendix provides contents for the KESSU 2.2 model described in the body text of the chapter. Part of the text is directly taken from ISO 13407—partially the text is produced by the author. One should especially understand that the text produced by the author has not been evaluated.

The contents described below could be described at a more detailed level. With the page limitation of this chapter, the descriptions cannot be as detailed as in ISO 13407. For example, the elements of context of use could be described in more detail as it is in ISO 13407.

Overview

The UCD lifecycle is characterized by purpose, definition and picture, characterization, and requirements.

Purpose of UCD

User-centered design is an approach to interactive system development that aims to make systems usable[7].

Characterization of UCD Lifecycle

User-centered design is characterized by user involvement, iteration of design solutions, and tailoring of usability methods. The effective implementation of user-centered activities typically includes these phenomena being present.

User Involvement

Effective UCD practically requires user involvement. The involvement of users in the development process provides a valuable source of knowledge about the context of use, the goals and tasks of users, and how users are likely to work with the future product or system. The effectiveness of user involvement increases as the interaction between the developers and users increases. The nature of user involvement varies depending on the design activities that are being undertaken. There are usability

---

[7] Usability—the extent to which a product can be used by specified users to achieve specified goals with effectiveness, efficiency, and satisfaction, in a specified environment of use.

methods that do not require user participation. These methods alone, however, are typically not sufficient for achieving good usability.

User involvement is typically an elementary part of designing usability, and it is unlikely that good usability can be designed without user involvement. However, user involvement should not be regarded as a normative requirement—especially not in the sense of "the more user involvement, the better," One should be open and give space for new innovative design methods that could lead to good usability with less user involvement (which often takes a lot of resources).

Iteration of Design Solutions

UCD activities typically need to be carried out iteratively. For example, the first user interface designs are seldom—if ever—good ones, but rather need to be revised based on the feedback from usability evaluations. Iteration, typically combined with active user involvement, is an effective means of minimizing the risk that a system does not meet user and organizational requirements. Iterations allow preliminary design solutions to be tested against real world scenarios, with the results being fed back into progressively refined solutions.

Iteration is typically needed when designing usability, and it is unlikely that good usability can be designed without iteration. However, one should be open and give space for new innovative design methods that could lead to good usability with less iteration. Therefore iteration is—as is user involvement—identified as a characterization, not a requirement, of UCD.

Tailoring Usability Methods

Projects typically have tight schedules and resource constraints, and one hardly ever has available all the resources and time for UCD work that one would like. One should be innovative—but professional to—find and use effective UCD methods that meet both the time schedule and resources of the project.

Requirements for UCD Lifecycle

The basic requirement is to effectively implement the UCD activities. To achieve the effective implementation of UCD activities, there are some general requirements that need to be fulfilled.

Multidisciplinary Professional Skills and Resources

Multidisciplinary design is needed because different kinds of knowledge and a variety of skills are needed in UCD. Typicall,y people with different roles participate—end user, purchaser, application domain specialist, marketer, user interface designer, visual designers, usability specialist, technical author, trainer, support person, etc. Resources typically include facilities such as usability laboratories, and tools such as prototyping environments.

Special attention should be paid to usability skills. The usability profession is not yet a totally established one.[8] The book of knowledge for the usability profession is under development (e.g., by thee Usability Professional's Association), but is still a work in progress.

One should ensure that the knowledge, skills, and creativity of the members of the project team are effectively utilized for better designs, as well as in UCD methods. This is a kind of general principle—applicable to any kind of teamwork—but it is particularly important in designing usability. Usability, in the end, is specifically achieved through interaction between people with different skills.

Do UCD Early

The human-centered design process should start at the earliest stage of the project (e.g., when the initial concepts for the product or system are being formulated), and should be repeated iteratively until the system meets the requirements.

Becoming involved too late in development projects is a problem that is often reported by usability practitioners. The consequence is that decisions are made that may inhibit usable solutions. The main reason is probably that usability specialists are involved too late in the development process when the main design decisions— also impacting on usability—are made. System architecture, for example, may be designed so that it limits the implementation of effective user tasks.

UCD Activities

General

There are seven human-centered design activities that should take place during a system development project. These activities are

- Identification of users
- Context of use analysis (multiple instance)
- Usability requirements determination
- User task design
- Interaction design

---

[8] People without usability background can successfully participate in usability work in specific roles. However, usability professionals are required to plan and facilitate usability activities.

- Usability feedback
- Usability verification

The lifecycle is illustrated in Figure 8.3 in the body text. The picture should be understood as an informal one. The intention is to provide an overview of the interdependencies of the activities and the concrete things (outcomes) that are produced during a UCD lifecycle. The lifecycle is described visually as a circle, although it is basically formed of a logical sequence of activities. A circle is used because the model is based on the picture of ISO 13407. It also pinpoints iteration—one typical characteristic of user-centered design.

Further, there is a distinction between the six *usability activities* and one *interaction design activity* (a different color). The distinction is made because the two kinds of activities have a fundamental difference. Usability activities produce user data, such as user descriptions, usability requirements, and results from evaluations—but no designs. Interaction design produces the actual user interaction designs: GUI designs, user interface software, user documentation, and so on. In other words, the role of usability activities is to feed data to the interaction design, and the role of interaction design is to transform this data into (usable) designs. This separation is also useful because those who do usability (usability specialists) are often not the same people as those who produce designs (software and other designers). Moreover, the model illustrates that it is not enough to introduce usability activities— usability activities have no value unless the results are taken into account in the design activities.

Identification of Users

Purpose

The purpose of the activity is to provide 1) an understanding of who the users of the system under development are, and 2) to categorize the users in an appropriate way.

Characterization

Each user is an individual. There are a number of different factors based on which one could categorize the users, such as demographic factors, job roles, environments where the system is used, and life style. This is not a trivial activity. The challenge is to define an appropriate categorization.

Outcomes

- Definitions of the user categories—an identifiable name should be given to each user group and the importance of each group (e.g., on the basis on how many users belong to this group) should be determined

- The relevant characteristics of each user group—characteristics should be described for each group. These may include job descriptions, knowledge, language, physical capabilities, anthropometrics, psychosocial issues, motivation for using the system, priorities, etc.

Methodological Guidance

Typical methods are stakeholder meetings, interviews, various field studies, and personas.

Context of Use (COU) Analysis

Purpose

The purpose of the activity is to establish the goals of users, characterize the tasks of users, the technical, organizational and the physical environment—as relevant—in which the product system will operate.

Characterization

The nature of this activity is data elicitation and analysis. It produces information about users, their goals and tasks, and problems in performing tasks, etc. On the other hand, this activity is not a decision-making activity—the *User Requirements* activity makes conclusions based on the CoU information for the goals and requirements of the systems.

This activity needs to have an instance for each user group identified by the previous activity: the context of use may be different for each user group.

Outcomes

The activity should produce the following outcomes:

- User goals (Accomplishments) should be determined in terms of what users need to accomplish with the product, not in terms of the equipment, functions, or features of the software. It is important to understand that the user goal is a result, not a name or a description of a task
- Task characteristics—users achieve goals through tasks. The characteristics of the tasks describe the nature of the tasks—for example, frequency, duration of performance, criticality for errors, and whether the tasks are carried out under pressure or in a stressful situation

- Environments of use—the operational environment where the product is used should be regarded as relevant. Environment descriptions may include technical, physical, and social factors

Methodological Guidance

Typical methods are stakeholder meetings, interviews, and various field studies.

Usability Requirements Determination

Purpose

The purpose of this activity is to define the user-driven requirements for the design of the product under development.

Characterization

An essential nature of this activity is decision-making: one should derive verifiable requirements from the large amount of data produced by the CoU activity. While business goals should drive the all usability activities, they especially should drive this activity. One should understand that usability requirements might contradict with other requirements. Resolution between conflicting requirements should be performed in this activity.

Outcomes

- Usability Requirements—usability requirements are the required performance of the product from the user-task performance point of view. Usability requirements can be given in terms of effectiveness, efficiency, and satisfaction in a quantitative way, as defined in ISO/IEC (1998a).

Requirements

The outcomes should be professionally produced and the results effectively communicated to the other activities.

Methodological Guidance

There is guidance for how to define usability requirements, such as in ISO/IEC (1998a).

User-Task Design

Purpose

The purpose of this activity is to design how users are to carry out their tasks with the new system that is being developed.

Characterization

This is the design phase where *the work of the users* is designed—what are the accomplishments that their product will support, and what are the scenarios of steps for how these accomplishments are reached. This phase is not yet the design of user-interface elements. It is essential to understand that better usability means better work practices. Special attention should be paid to the allocation of function between users and technology.

Outcomes

- This design activity produces a set of descriptions for the new work practice of the users (i.e., how the user will carry out the tasks with the new system)

Requirements

Typical methods are different scenario methods. The outcomes can be described by methods such as storyboarding.

Interaction Design

Purpose

The purpose of this activity is to design those elements of the product with which users interact. These elements include interaction and graphical design of user interface, user documentation, user training, user support, etc.

Characterization

This activity is different in one essential respect compared with the other activities of this category—a full output of the activity is typically produced even if there is no user-centeredness in the project (user interfaces and user documentation can be produced without any user-centeredness). Another specific feature of this activity is that the different outcomes are designed in parallel.

Outcomes

- User interface designs—user interface elements, visual design, interactions, etc.
- User documentation
- User training plans and materials
- Packaging
- User support procedures

Methodological Guidance

The designs are based on input from earlier activities, and feedback from evaluation activities. In addition, applicable interaction-design guidelines and standards should be applied. People from different functions (user interface development, user documentation, customer training) typically work together.

Usability Feedback

Purpose

The purpose of this activity is to provide qualitative usability feedback on the system under development (including user documentation, user training, etc.).

Characterization

This is often a key activity in UCD. Different methods exist. This activity is typically highly iterative with the *Interaction Design* activity.

Outcomes

- Usability feedback is qualitative feedback on the usability of a design proposal. This outcome is typically an iterative set of evaluation results that identify those parts of the design solutions that work, and those that should be improved.

Methodological Guidance

Typical methods for this activity are qualitative usability tests and various usability inspection methods.

Usability Verification

Purpose

The purpose of this activity is to verify the extent to which the product under development (including user documentation, user training, etc.) meets the usability requirements.

Characterization

This activity addresses the evaluation of usability typically from the user-task performance aspect. Those activities that evaluate the generic, nontask-driven issues (for example, heuristic evaluation) are activities of the Usability Feedback activity.

Outcomes

- Verification results based on usability requirements. The product is evaluated to determine to what extent the product meets the defined usability requirements and a report of the adherence is produced.

Methodological Guidance

The key method is typically usability testing, but also other methods that provide measures—such as questionnaires or model-based methods—can be applied.

Chapter 9
Remote Usability Evaluation: Discussion of a General Framework and Experiences from Research with a Specific Tool

Fabio Paternò and Carmen Santoro

ISTI-CNR, Pisa, Italy, e-mail: fabio.paterno@isti.cnr.it

Abstract The goal of this chapter is to present a design space for tools and methods supporting remote usability evaluation of interactive applications. This type of approach is acquiring increasing importance because it allows usability evaluation even when users are in their daily environments. Several techniques have been developed in this area for addressing various types of applications that can be used in different contexts. We discuss them within a unifying framework that can be used to compare the weaknesses and strengths of the various approaches and identify areas that require further research work to exploit all the possibilities opened up by remote evaluation.

9.1 Introduction

In this chapter, we present and discuss a design space for remote usability evaluation. This type of approach to usability evaluation is characterized by the fact that users and evaluators are separated in time and/or space (Hartson, et al. 1996). Thus, it still requires the involvement of these two actors (user and evaluator), but it relaxes the constraint that they need to be present at the same time in the same place. The motivations for remote evaluation are various:

- Usability laboratories can be expensive to set up because they require dedicated sites with specific equipment
- Moving users to the usability laboratory can be difficult and expensive as well, in particular for expert users, whose time is costly. Indeed, it can be difficult to find an adequate number of users willing to move to a usability lab for a test
- Remote evaluation can be useful to analyze user behavior in their daily environment (e.g., workplace, home, and so on), thus in more realistic settings
- It facilitates the possibility of a continuous evaluation, even after the first release of the application

Some studies have investigated to what extent remote evaluations yield results similar to lab testing. For example, Tullis (Tullis, et al. 2002) found that remote evaluation in the field yielded results that were largely similar to studies in the lab.

There are several methods that support some kind of remote usability evaluation. They differ in the type of information that is made available to the evaluator and how it is provided to them. Ivory and Hearst (2001) wrote an interesting review of the state-of-the-art on automating usability evaluation of user interfaces, in which some methods and tools in the area of remote evaluation were considered as well. In this chapter, we provide a more updated and focused discussion of the state-of-the-art in remote evaluation through a more refined framework for this area that highlights the important aspects to consider when analyzing approaches within it. More specifically, the framework proposed in this chapter is defined by analyzing various dimensions. The first one considers the type of interaction that occurs between the user and the evaluator, and is strongly connected with the possibility of having a co-presence (in terms of time) between the user and the evaluator. Another dimension involves the techniques that can be used to gather information on user sessions (server/proxy/client logs, webcams, eye-trackers, and other sensing technologies) and the information provided, which are useful for the evaluation. Another interesting dimension we consider is the type of platform used for interaction. In this regard, we plan to distinguish access through desktop or mobile devices, for example, and discuss how the choice of platform affects the aspects to consider in the evaluation. The last dimension regards the type of application considered (for instance: Java-based, Web-based, etc.). A discussion about the potential correspondences between such dimensions should shed some light on which techniques/technologies evaluators should direct their attention to obtain the desired information, therefore providing them with a better understanding of techniques for remote evaluation of user sessions and how to use them to identify problematic parts of interactive applications and make improvements accordingly (when necessary).

To summarize, the relevant dimensions we have identified for analyzing the different methods for assessing remote usability evaluation are:

- The type of interaction between the user and the evaluator
- The platform used for the interaction (desktop, mobile, vocal, etc.)
- The techniques used for collecting information about the users and their behavior (graphical logs, voice and/or Webcam recordings, eye-tracking, etc.)
- The type of application considered in terms of implementation environment (Web, java-based, .NET, etc.)
- The type of the evaluation results (task performance, emotional state) provided

In the next sections, we use the framework composed of such dimensions to discuss a number of techniques that can be used to perform remote evaluation of user sessions (logging technology, interaction platform, semantic analysis), along with a review of the most relevant works in the area together with a discussion about issues that have been resolved from the perspective of usability evaluation and problems that are still open.

To make the discussion more concrete, we also discuss our own experiences in this area, including our method (and the related tool) for remote usability evaluation of websites that considers information from user tasks, log files, videos recorded during user tests, and data collected by an eye-tracker (Paternò, et al. 2006).

9.2 The Type of Interaction between the User and the Evaluator

There are different methods and techniques that can be applied to perform a remote evaluation. One important dimension that can be used to classify them is how users and evaluators actually interact between themselves.

Bearing in mind that remote evaluation assumes that users and evaluators are separated in *space*, the type of interaction occurring between users and evaluators strongly depends on the type of synchronization occurring on *time*. Indeed, while the *asynchronous* evaluation method assumes that evaluators might not be necessarily available at the time when the user session is taking place (and therefore, there is no possibility for the evaluator/moderator to deliver immediate input for impromptu changes), it is the opposite with *synchronous* evaluations. As an exemplary case of synchronous evaluation, we mention collaborative usability evaluation methods via the network, in which evaluators in usability labs are connected to remote users via commercially available teleconferencing software (e.g., Microsoft Netmeeting), supporting real-time application sharing, audio links, shared drawing tools, and/or file transfer capabilities. Below, we describe the various possibilities for both synchronous (first bullet) and asynchronous evaluation (second-fourth bullets):

- *Remote Observation*—this implies that users and evaluators are separated in space but are active at the same time and connected through some tool (for example, video conference tools) that allows the evaluator to observe the actual user behavior in real time
- *Remote Questionnaires*—this is a technique that allows users to provide their feedback through a series of questions made available electronically
- *Critical Incidents Reported by the User*—in this case, the user directly reports to the evaluator when an incident occurs
- *Automatic Data Collection*—this is the method that has stimulated the most interest because there are many ways to collect data regarding user behavior and then analyze it. The potential information ranges from browser logs, to videos taken by Web-cams, to eye-tracking data. This case also includes our approach (Paternò, et al. 2006), which will be described in Section 9.7.

To assess the pros and cons of such options, we can notice that on the one hand, remote observation provides the evaluator with more capabilities for observing the session and also for intervening *during* the session. Furthermore, the simultaneous presence of evaluator and user brings the additional advantage of not requiring a particularly strong effort for an *a posteriori* analysis of the collected data, because most of this work should be already carried out by evaluators during the session. On the other hand, remote observation strongly limits the number of users that can be evaluated at a time and, additionally, it might also happen that the behavior of the users might be affected to some extent by their awareness of being currently observed by the evaluator.

Remote questionnaires and critical incidents are useful because they report aspects that the users themselves noticed and judged relevant from the point of view of usability. However, the result of such techniques might be compromised by the fact that the reporting time is generally postponed with respect to when the problem appeared. Therefore, retrospective reporting and questionnaires might be subjected to loss of detail, which can hinder the reconstruction of the original problem.

The last technique (automatic data collection) on the one hand guarantees gathering a vast amount of detailed data, which, on the other hand, generally claim a non-irrelevant effort and time for being correctly interpreted by humans, in absence of appropriate automatic data analysis techniques.

9.3 The Platform Used for the Application Interaction

One of the main characteristics of the rapid evolution of information and communication technologies is the wide availability of various types of interaction platforms. The desktop is no longer the only device that even nonprofessionals use for accessing their applications. There is a wide variety of interaction platforms on the market, which can largely differentiate in terms of interaction resources (such as screen size, etc.) and supported modalities.

Heterogeneous platforms raise specific issues that should not be neglected for the purposes of remote evaluation. For instance, mobile systems are typically used in highly dynamic contexts, and remotely evaluating mobile users requires the use of specific techniques able to capture and identify usability problems that might be experienced in mobile use. One exemplary issue in remote usability evaluation involving mobile users is that they are *physically* moving, and such changes in the context might imply a number of known and unknown variables potentially affecting the set up (for instance, when increasing the amount of physical activity, a significantly increased subjective workload might be experienced by the users). In addition, the use of a particular platform should also be considered, with the objective of identifying the appropriate means for collecting user data in the remote site. For instance, eye-tracking systems are clearly useless for recording user interactions with only-voice applications. Therefore, a current issue for this dimension is represented by the capability of the different techniques for remote evaluation to dynamically vary the information that should be collected about the users, so as to cope with the potential issues that the specific platform in use can introduce. The expected objective is providing the evaluator with the most comprehensive picture of all the aspects that might have affected the interaction, to always be in a position to correctly derive the potential causes of a usability problem that occurred on the client side. As previously mentioned, gathering information about the current environment is extremely important for a mobile user, because the environment can often change, while it becomes less important for a stationary user interacting with a desktop application because the environment is almost fixed.

In this section, we analyze how the remote evaluation methods address the issues raised by the specific platforms.

9.3.1 Desktop Applications

Since most applications have been developed for the desktop, the majority of remote evaluation methods have addressed this type of platform. In Hartson, et al. (1996), one of the first examples of remote-control evaluation is described. The remote-control method checks a local computer from another computer at a remote site. The user is separated from the evaluator in space and possibly in time. The two computers can be connected through the Internet, or through a direct dial-up telephone line with commercially available software (e.g., Timbuktu TM, PC Anywhere). Using this method, the evaluator's computer is located in the usability lab where a video camera or scan converter captures the users' actions. The remote users remain in their work environment and audio capture is performed via the computer or telephone. If the audio capture is via telephone, the evaluator and user remain connected at the same time. Alternatively, equipment in the usability lab could be configured to automatically activate data-capture tools based on the use of a particular application. This is an example of quite a flexible technique for asynchronous remote evaluation, which is restricted to use on desktop systems due to some software limitations on the underlying hardware (e.g., PC Anywhere only operates on PC platforms).

9.3.2 Vocal Applications

As for the vocal platform, interest is arising in studying this modality because the associated technology is becoming more reliable and robust in different systems in everyday use. The most exemplary case is that of the automatic response systems commonly used for completing user tasks such as banking, paying bills, and receiving train/flight information. Such systems can accept both speech and touch tone inputs, and in response provide relevant information through voice, email, text messaging, and fax. Most companies are seeing such systems as an immediate cost saver because call centers are becoming too expensive to be operated by humans.

As speech applications advance, so does the need for a means to evaluate vocal user interfaces (VUIs), to be able to assess how a user interacts with a vocal application. In this respect, we have to say that sometimes methods that are commonly applied in GUI evaluation are also applied to the evaluation of VUIs, although this translation is not a perfect fit. Indeed, the sequential nature of speech means that VUIs are inherently more restrictive than GUIs, and therefore fewer choices can be explored with a VUI in a certain time interval, with respect to what can be done with a corresponding GUI. One of the consequences from the point of view of usability evaluation is that, the number of tasks carried out in a certain interval of time by interacting with a VUI will deliver a lower value when compared with a corresponding GUI, without being necessarily a sign of a bad vocal user interface usability.

Furthermore, it should be kept in mind that only using speech as an interaction medium might represent a burden on users' memory, meaning that not only VUI users should be focused on a smaller set of choices, and in a narrower context, but also that without visual cues and a well-established mental model, they are even unlikely to understand what choices are available to them. The consequence is that, without careful design, these limitations can severely diminish the general usability of the vocal application.

Despite the limitations noted above, well-designed voice applications have proven to be both engaging and effective. Some novel evaluation methods for these interfaces are under development, and several experiments in the lab have already been done—although, with the proliferation of cellular and wireless phones, evaluations of VUIs in lab environments suffer from unrealistic settings because they are very different from the real contexts of use.

Several techniques can be envisaged for evaluating vocal user interfaces and, more specifically, automatic response systems. Among them, we cite surveys, call recordings, and call logs. Surveys are issued after a call is completed, but sometimes callers do not complete the call, hence never reaching the survey. As for call recordings, most VUI systems record caller interactions, because call recordings tell the VUI designer exactly what happened during each call. They have several shortcomings—they cannot tell the designer what the caller was trying to do, how the caller felt, or why the caller did what s/he did. Another shortcoming is the massive amount of effort required to analyze the calls. Lastly, in call logs, every interactive voice recognition (IVR) platform comes with extensive call-logging capabilities. While surveys and call recordings typically result in qualitative data, call-log data is typically quantitative (e.g., average call length, time on hold, abandon rate, etc.). Due to the enormous amount of data that can be collected, data-mining techniques are suitable for processing such data. Call logs identify where in the VUI callers have difficulty, but this is only a part of the picture. Call logs do not provide a lot of context for helping to interpret the results. Therefore, because surveys, call recordings, and call logs provide different information for in-use situation analysis, it seems that careful consideration of their combined use as compensation for their various advantages and drawbacks may be a viable solution for the purposes of evaluating VUIs.

An example of tools for VUIs is ClickFox (2002), which aims to answer questions like: "What is the main cause of customer hang-ups? What are callers doing most frequently at critical decision points? Are callers using the system in the way that you expected?" Another example is provided by IQ Services (2006), which is able to log and record each call, allowing IQ Services' analysts to duplicate and experience system errors. After the test is completed, designers receive online test results, step-by-step logs, and online playback of each digital test call recording.

To conclude, while there are not many works on remote usability evaluation for vocal applications, the naturalness of this kind of interaction, and its quick diffusion in a number of applications covering different devices, make us expect that further research will be done on this subject.

9.3.3 Mobile Applications

In mobile applications, it is important to understand the influence of the context of use, which is composed of three main parts: the user, the device, and the environment. Thus, one issue is to understand how usability is affected by dynamic changes of any of these components. Regarding evaluating interaction with mobile devices, the work of Denis and Karsenty (2003) focuses on the usability of a multidevice system, and introduces the concept of interusability to designate the ease with which users can reuse their knowledge and skills for a given functionality when switching to other devices. In their paper, a framework for achieving interusability between devices is proposed. It is based on two components: 1) a theoretical analysis of the cognitive processes underlying device transitions, and 2) an exploratory empirical study of the problems in using functionalities across multiple devices. Another work in this area is the paper by Waterson, et al. (2002), where the authors discuss a pilot usability study using wireless, Internet-enabled personal digital assistants (PDAs), in which they compare usability data gathered in traditional lab studies with a proxy-based clickstream logging and analysis tool. They found that this remote testing technique can more easily gather many of the content-related usability issues, whereas device-related issues are more difficult to capture. Lastly, the work of Stoica, et al. (2005) is worth mentioning, in which the authors describe a usability evaluation study of a system which permits collaboration of small groups of museum visitors through mobile handheld devices (PDAs). As the authors point out, techniques to measure usability-related factors generally include 1) inspection methods, 2) testing methods, and 3) inquiry methods. For systems including mobile devices, a combination of these techniques is sometimes used. As usability evaluation methodology, they propose a combination of a logging mechanism and an analysis tool—the ColAT environment (Avouris, et al. 2004), which permits mixing of multiple sources of observational data, a necessary requirement in evaluation studies involving mobile technology when users move about in physical space and are difficult to track. The museum system evaluated is based on a client-server architecture and an important characteristic of the application is that the server produces a centralized XML log file of the actions that take place during the visit. This log file can be combined with a video recording of the visit allowing evaluation of activity during the visit. In the experiment shown in the paper presenting ColAT, different teams gathered the clues and then each group had to discuss and discover collaboratively what the combined clues were to solve the problem. The experiment was recorded by three video and two audio recorders for further analysis, using the ColAT analysis tool that interrelates activity and logs video and observers notes in the same environment. So, through ColAT, the actions that the users performed during the use of the PDAs, which were logged by the server, were synchronized with the videos. The methodology was able to deliver data useful for deriving quantitative information (e.g., total and average times for solving the puzzles, etc.), aspects related to group activities (number of exchanges between the group, and strategies used for solving the puzzles), and behavioral patterns of participants.

Indeed, the importance of performing a comprehensive evaluation that can take into account data derived from multiple sources to adequately gain insight into large bodies of multisource data, especially when mobile applications are considered, is quite clear. An example of this trend can also be found in the work of Tennent, et al. (2006), in which the authors present Replayer, which consists of a number of tools (two video players, an audio player, an aggregate log visualization, a text search tool, and a playback control tool), and a collaborative tool for analysis of recorded data of mobile applications. The tool was designed with the aim to provide analysts from a variety of disciplines (each using distinct sets of skills to focus on specific aspects of the problem) with the ability to work cooperatively.

One of the emerging needs in this area is for tools that are better able to support analysis of how task performance varies depending on the context change.

9.4 The Techniques for Collecting Information about the User Behavior

In this section, we discuss the various techniques available for collecting information regarding the user behavior (task performance, use of mouse and keyboard, facial expressions, verbal comments, gestures, gazes, etc.). In this category, we include several techniques for logging low-level user actions, other techniques for gathering users' physiological information, and others capable of recording verbal (and nonverbal) cues coming from the user's side (collected through a webcam and/or a microphone).

It is worth pointing out that, while there are techniques that rely on commonly available support, and can be used almost without any regard to the particular platform considered (see, for instance, server-side logging techniques), other techniques (e.g., eye-tracking) require specific hardware, whose use cannot neglect the particular platform in use.

9.4.1 Logging (Server Side)

This technique refers to Web-based applications and allows for collecting data at the server side. Its effectiveness is strongly limited by the impossibility to capture local user interaction with the user interface techniques (menus, buttons, fill-in text, use of anchor links within the same page or Back button,...) and by the validity of the server logs that cannot capture the accesses to the pages stored into the proxy servers and the browser cache. For instance, if the requested page is in the browser cache, then the request will never reach the server and is thus not logged. Moreover, multiple people can also share the same IP address, making it difficult to distinguish who is actually requesting what pages. Dynamically assigned IP addresses, where a computer's IP address changes every time it connects to the Internet, can also make it quite difficult to determine what an individual user is doing because IP addresses are often used as identifiers. Thus, interpreting the actions of an individual user is extremely difficult, because methods for capturing and generating Web usage logs are not designed for gathering useful usability data, as pointed out by some works (Etgen and Cantor 1999; Davison 1999; Pitkow and Pirolli 1999; Choo, et al. 1998; Tauscher 1999).

Another method is to ask surfers to register online at the first visit and log on with every subsequent visit. In this setting, the Web server can construct an individual profile for each visitor, and track all user behaviors without ambiguity. The Web server stores users' log-on names and their personal information, such as age, gender and occupation, and the visited pages. Such datasets are very rich, and statistics on types of Web surfers, their interests and their browsing habits can be generated with the Web mining process. This technique is widely adopted by firms selling digital information products (e.g., online newspapers), which request the users to log on before enabling file downloads. However, there are two main limitations. First, Web visitors' choices are greatly reduced if they are required to log on every time they visit the site. It becomes a serious issue for online firms and, even for websites providing free registration, online users may re-register or provide fake details. The statistics will become blurred, and this will result in invalid and confusing conclusions. Second, the online firms cannot keep track of the visitors once they leave to go to other websites. All generated knowledge is limited to only a single website.

9.4.2 Proxy-Based Logging

This solution still supports Web-based applications through an intermediate server between the client and the content server. Proxy servers are even less intrusive and do not require any modification in the Web application to evaluate, but they limit their analysis to the accessed page and are not able to capture the local user interactions. The proxy approach has three key advantages over the server-side approach. First, the proxy represents a separation of concerns. Any modifications needed for tracking purposes can be done on the proxy, leaving the application server to deal with just serving content, which makes it easier to deploy because the application server and its content do not have to be modified. Second, the proxy allows anyone to run usability tests on any website, even if they do not own that website. Lastly, having testers go through a proxy allows Web designers to *tag* and uniquely identify each tester. Furthermore, a proxy logger also has advantages over client-side logging. For example, it does not require any special software on the client side beyond a Web browser, making it faster and much simpler to deploy. Therefore, the proxy makes it easier to test a site with different test participants, operating systems, and Web browsers than a client-side logger does, so allowing testing with a more realistic sample.

An example of this kind of solution can be found in WebQuilt (Hong & Landay 2001), which uses a proxy logger to capture user accesses on the Web. As a proxy, it lies between clients and content servers, with the assumption that clients will make all requests through the proxy. Traditionally, proxies are used for things like caching and firewalls. In WebQuilt, the Web proxy is used for usability purposes, with special features to make the logging more useful for usability analysis. Although the proxy-based technique seems quite appealing, there are still limitations on what the WebQuilt proxy logger can capture. The most pressing of these cases is links or redirects created dynamically by JavaScript and other browser-scripting languages. As a consequence, the JavaScript-generated pop-up windows and DHTML menus popular on many websites are not captured by the proxy. Another situation that WebQuilt cannot handle is server-side image maps. Other elusive cases include embedded page components such as Java applets and Flash animations. As technologies change and develop, the proxy will need to be updated to handle these new cases.

9.4.3 Logging (Client Side)

In this category, various techniques are considered. Before analyzing them, it is important to remember that client-logging is a technique that can be applied not only to Web applications but also to Java and Microsoft applications with similar results, because many tools have been developed for this purpose, as well.

In addition, it has been pointed out that through logging user interactions with a given application, we can infer patterns of user behavior that indicate usability problems or other design deficiencies. This possibility has obvious attractions for Web designers, but in HCI usability research some issues have been raised regarding the possibility of identifying usability problems without access to the use context—to the user's tasks and goals and to the user's own reports of what counts as a problem for them. Thus, logging techniques alone are unlikely to provide useful results to the evaluators.

Cookies. One method is to install cookies at Web client computers. A cookie is a small text file that the Web server embeds in the browser for identifying the user. If the user provides his name when he comes to a new site supporting cookies, his name is stored in a plain text file at the client computer. No data is stored at the server side, but every time the same browser asks for the page or the same website, HTTP sends the cookie to the Web server, which uses it to identify the user and display personalized information, such as name-calling greetings. One of the advantages of using cookies is the ease of implementation. However, there are two drawbacks. First, the amount of information stored in cookies is limited (the average size is about 4K) and therefore, strictly speaking, no Web-mining process can be performed based on such limited information. Second, because the cookies are saved as plain text, they can be easily retrieved at the client computer. Hence, security and privacy can be at risk.

Client-side Logs. They capture more accurate, comprehensive usage data than server-side logs because they allow all browser events to be recorded, and it might provide useful insight for usability evaluation. One alternative to gathering data on the server is to collect it on the client side. Clients are instrumented with special software so that all usage transactions will be captured. More specifically, clients can be modified either by running software that transparently records user actions whenever the Web browser is being used (as in Choo, et al. 1998), by modifying an existing Web browser (as in Tauscher 1999), or by creating a custom Web browser specifically for capturing usage information (as with Vividence 2000). The advantage of client-side logging is that literally everything can be recorded, from low-level events such as keystrokes and mouse clicks, to higher-level events such as page requests. All of this is valuable usability information. However, there are some potential drawbacks to client-side logging. First, special software must be installed on the client, which end-users may be unwilling or unable to do. This can severely limit the usability test participants to experienced users, which may not be representative of the target audience. Second, there needs to be some mechanism for sending the logged data back to the team that wants to collect the logs. Third, the software, in some cases, is platform-dependent, meaning that the software only works for a specific operating system or a specific browser.

Paganelli and Paternò (2003) developed a tool for performing client-logging of Web applications: the main advantages are that it does not require expensive equipment, and facilitates the problem of modifying the evaluated pages because it automatically includes JavaScript code in all the pages that have to be evaluated. Such Javascript snippets are able to adapt to the various features of different browsers. Using a browser's log-based analysis, the evaluator can accurately measure time spent on tasks or particular pages, as well as study the use of the Back button and user clickstreams. It is also possible to precisely identify the downloading time and the time when the page is visible to the users. In addition, their tool is able to automatically analyze the information contained in Web browser logs and compare it with task models specifying the designer model of the possible users' behaviors when interacting with the application to identify whether and where users' interactions deviate from those envisioned by the system design and represented in the model. Within this client-side approach, there is also the work (Ho 2005) developed in the e-commerce domain area, which is about the use of a *user remote tracker* to examine Web users' characteristics, trying to draw a linkage between Web customers' characteristics and their browsing behaviors. The authors propose a user-remote tracking framework based on Web services and XML to track every HTTP request from client computers to understand surfers' characteristics. The user-remote tracker is a piece of software installed in the users' browser to keep track of every keyboard input and mouse click from the users. No matter what the users input, all HTTP requests and responses are tracked by the software program, including interactions with Java Applet programs. This program will automatically send the activity log file, together with the user identity, to a central machine for Web-mining (instead of sending such information directly to the Web server). It is that central machine that analyzes clickstreams and generates navigation rules for these users through algorithms. There are several advantages with this user-remote tracker. First, it can follow users everywhere. Second, while server-logging cannot track the interaction between a user and an applet program, the tracker can solve this problem. Third, in the traditional data collection method, it is possible to get little information once the users enter the secure websites (i.e., websites starting with https://). Here, because the user-remote tracker uses low-level programs to track every user input signal, the activities can be tracked even in this case.

9.4.4 Eye-Trackers

Eye trackers are a technique for measuring users' eye movements so that it is possible to know both where a person is looking at any given time, and the sequence in which their eyes are shifting from one location to another, on the screen. Tracking people's eye movements can help evaluators understand visual information processing and the factors that may impact the usability of system interfaces, thereby providing an objective source of data that can inform the design of improved interfaces. Evaluators using eye-tracking, however, should take into account the limits of such technology and how such limits impact the data collected. For example, an appropriate minimum threshold time for a fixation should be carefully identified, because interpretations can vary a lot according to the time set to detect a fixation in the eye-tracking system. Moreover, eye trackers might have difficulty tracking participants who have lenses. Furthermore, visual distractions (e.g., colorful or moving objects around the screen or in the testing environment) should also be eliminated, as these will inevitably contaminate the eye-movement data. Also, eye-tracking generates huge amounts of data, so it is essential to automatically perform filtering and analysis. Eye-tracking technology, however, has evolved in recent years and there are now more systems that can be used for remote evaluation (see the Tobii system, http://www.tobii.com/) because they can be transported in suitcases and do not require that users wear intrusive equipment. It is only necessary to carry out an initial standard training exercise. Nevertheless, one of the most relevant problems with the eye-tracking technique remains the fact that it is possible to know what users see but not what users think about what they see. In other words, how data is actually being processed by the person.

9.4.5 Webcam/Audio Recorders or Microphones

The use of webcams and audio recorders allows for acquiring more contextual information about the data collected. Indeed, as it has been previously mentioned, through logging keystrokes and webpages on a given site, we could infer patterns of user behavior that indicate usability problems or other design deficiencies. In HCI usability research, however, it has been argued that it is not possible to identify usability problems without access to the context of use, to the user's tasks and goals, and to the user's own reports of what counts as a problem for them. Webcam-based videos are very valuable when further analysis is necessary when an error is found, because the evaluator can analyze the video clip and convert it into a usability problem description, or use it in any case to understand the reason of a usability problem. For instance, videos can be valuable in capturing facial movements/expressions, verbal/vocal signals and expressions, non-verbal communication, body language, and posture. Moreover, facial expressions may provide indications of the immediate appreciation of the system by showing the instantaneous reactions to the system, and also might reflect the subject's considerations about the system. Furthermore, the use of more than one camera is valuable for capturing some environmental conditions occurring in the testing environment. Work by Lister (2003) has been oriented to using audio and video capture for qualitative analysis performed by evaluators on the results of usability testing.

Also in the work of Paternò et al. (2006), webcams are used to record the users (not the users' screens) to provide valuable information for interpreting problematic parts of the user interaction. For instance, in this work, videos are also used to check user behavior whenever some measurements (e.g., time needed for completing a task) captured by another software component provide unexpected values.

9.4.6 Sensors

In this category, we include research solutions for data acquisition and analysis of some physiological data. Recently, a number of sensors are being used more and more for the evaluation of user interfaces, trying to take into account the emotional dimension of computer-human interaction (e.g., affective user interfaces). Among such measures, we cite physiological signals like ECG, respiration, galvanic skin response, heart rate, and skin temperature. Most of them, such as galvanic skin response (GSR), heart rate (HR) and blood volume pulse (BVP) are generally chosen as good, physically non-invasive indicators of stress (under stress, GSR and HR increase, while BVP decreases), and are also easy to be measured with specialized equipment. In this respect, we mention the ProComp system manufactured by Thought Technology, Ltd. (http://www.thoughttechnology.com), or the BIOPAC system (http://www.biopac.com/), which allows for recording different kinds of data—physiological signals, vocal/verbal signals, and non-verbal signals (posture, gaze direction, facial movements). Unfortunately, the use of sensors in remote usability evaluation is currently suffering the limitation of the highly specialized equipment necessary, which cannot be assumed available in users' daily environments (although it is slowly appearing and used more and more in telemedicine applications). However, more research effort is envisaged in the next years on this subject for the useful information that it can provide to analyze the user's emotional state.

To summarize, almost all the results obtained with each technique indicated in this section requires additional knowledge about the user from the evaluator to be actually useful for the purposes of the evaluation. Therefore, the big issue is that such data is not informative *per se* about possible usability problems, but requires further comparison with supplementary information. One of the few exceptions can be identified in, for instance, recording users positively (or negatively) commenting on the session while interacting with the application in a remote think-aloud session (which should theoretically provide the evaluator with immediate feedback about the user's satisfaction). In almost all the other cases, a further contextualization (and integration) of the data collected is needed to correctly evaluate the session state (think about, for example, the uselessness of logging mouse and keyboard actions without contextualizing such actions within the current user intention). One of the current issues is identifying techniques enabling an easy synchronisation and aggregation of all such different sources of information in some semantic context, to facilitate the evaluator's work.

9.5 The Type of Application Considered

In this section, we analyze another dimension of the proposed framework—the type of application, considered in terms of the underlying software environment. As with already analyzed dimensions, in this case the consideration of this dimension is also not completely independent from the other ones. Indeed, the type of application considered may prevent (or strongly promote) applying specific techniques mentioned in the previous section, as well as the use of particular interaction platforms. For instance, while in the case of Web-based applications we have seen that there are several options about where the logging tool should work (e.g., server, client, proxy, ..) regardless of the particular platform at hand, the consideration of .NET-based applications for remote evaluation has only occurred in recent years. It is almost always connected with stationary platforms because only recently prototypical tools that support the evaluation of .NET applications for mobile devices have appeared, and are still limited in terms of the information they are actually able to provide.

Indeed, the first applications that were evaluated with some type of remote evaluation were graphical applications, often implemented in languages such as Java (e.g., Paternò & Ballardin 2000). Then, with the advent of the Web and the related ease of performing a remote evaluation when the Web is considered (due to the related simplicity in involving a high number of testers with little effort), the majority of methods have considered websites as their primary evaluation targets. Java-based applications indeed have been taken into account, sometimes as a sort of side-effect of the desire to improve the flexibility of techniques considered for Web applications whenever applets are also included. An example of this can be found in the already mentioned work of Ho (2005), developed in the e-commerce domain area. It is about the use of a user-remote tracker to examine Web users' characteristics, trying to draw a linkage between Web customers' characteristics and their browsing, and with the capability of tracking client-side logs, including interactions with Java Applet programs. Microsoft .NET applications have been considered as well (i.e., PDA devices), for which they often provide more robust and supported solutions with respect to Java. An example of logging tools for Microsoft environments is the VibeLog logging tool (http://research.microsoft.com/vibe/), which has been developed at Microsoft Research to evaluate the ways that work practice might change as users move between various-sized displays during their work day. The logging tool is married with ethnographic research data, which should provide good indications of what parts of the Windows and Office designs do not scale well across different display sizes. This analysis is used to understand where they should orient their research efforts in novel visualization and interaction development, with an eye toward designing more elegant UIs.

9.6 The Type of Evaluation Results

Before analyzing the last dimension of the proposed framework in depth—the type of results an evaluation can deliver (i.e., qualitative vs. quantitative data)—we judge it useful to mention the work by Petrie et al. (2006) about remote evaluation. In this work, the authors highlight how both formative and summative evaluations can be supported by remote techniques. Indeed, in *summative* evaluations, one of the main goals is to understand whether the users can install and run a system on their own and on their own machines, and how they rate the key functions of the system. Therefore, the disparate environments and configurations that can be reached with remote evaluation can provide highly reliable data in this respect. In *formative* evaluations, the objective is to collect information about design flaws and inform redesign. Therefore, it is particularly important that participants feel free to criticize a system and avoid evaluator bias, and this may be easier if they are in the privacy of their own environment, rather than the potentially more threatening situation of the usability laboratory.

However, the authors take it a step further, claiming that, in particular, remote asynchronous techniques in which the evaluator cannot intervene during the user sessions are especially useful for *summative* evaluation. To support this idea, the authors report on two evaluations conducted with disabled users. In both cases, they performed both a local and a remote evaluation. The technique used for remote evaluation was, in one case, making notes on problems encountered and then sending them to the evaluator, and in the other case, recording problems encountered and then sending them along with ratings of the accessed websites. Both remote and local evaluations provided considerable quantities of qualitative data, but the local evaluations provided far richer data because the researchers were able to record problems that the participant may not have been aware of, and are in a position to prompt the participant to explore these problems, comment on them, and analyze what had caused them.

On the one hand, achieving the rich interaction between participants, researchers and developers, as requested by *formative* evaluation, is very difficult in remote evaluation situations. With high quality video conferencing, broadband connections, and remote recording systems, however, it might be possible to conduct remote evaluations that capture a rich set of data. On the other hand, if the evaluation is *summative*, a remote evaluation may be quite appropriate because it adequately shows real user behavior.

We agree with this position to some extent because, in our opinion, remote evaluation can provide different types of results, which can, in turn, be used for different purposes, both summative and formative. In this section, we are going to analyze the type of results an evaluation can deliver. In particular, a discussion about the type of information that can be useful to obtain in order to analyze the multimodal data regarding user sessions is provided. This information can be quantitatively determined by specific software and highlighted during the evaluation (tasks not completed, errors occurring during the performance of tasks, time for completing a task, etc.) together with other information that deals with intrinsic qualities of the user interface (e.g., time needed for the performance of a task). It is not surprising that some relations exist between the evaluation techniques mentioned in Section 9.4 and the evaluation results analyzed in this section (for instance, sensing technologies deliver quantitative data about the user's emotional and physical state), while in other case such correspondence is not so straightforward.

9.6.1 Task-Related Information

Many applications are task-oriented and therefore some important aspects to consider are whether the users are able to accomplish the desired tasks, and information regarding task performance (task duration, number of actions, ...). One issue is how to know what the desired tasks are. One possible solution is to ask users to explicitly indicate the tasks at the beginning of the session. The issues associated with user errors are related to the issues associated with task performance, because user errors are actions not useful for the current task. The errors are good indicators of bad usability and difficulties in task accomplishment. Tasks can be considered at various granularities. In some cases, it can be interesting to analyze the performance of short basic tasks, and in other cases it is important to focus on the performance of high-level complex activities.

During an analysis of task performance, it can be useful to analyze when it deviates from the ideal expected behavior, and to what extent. The evaluator then has to understand the reasons for such mismatch and needs to go back and analyze what happened for each action in the user session and what factor triggered the deviation.

9.6.2 Qualitative Information

Under this heading, we mean all the techniques that allow evaluators to collect qualitative data from the users. As we already mentioned, qualitative data are quite relevant, especially if the kind of evaluation is *formative*, therefore the richness of the qualitative data is very important in understanding how to improve the system. For example, gathering informal and spontaneous comments in natural language from the users undoubtedly offers valuable information to the evaluators for improving the resulting design. Also, because this information can provide a rich contextual knowledge about the situation currently occurring during the user's interaction, it may also be used for cross-checking other collected data that may be too ambiguous to be interpreted—generally quantitative data. An example in which this strategy might disambiguate other data, is the case of a user spending a long time visiting a page. Considering only this quantitative information (registered by the browser-logging tool) would not allow the evaluator to assess whether the users found the information very important or just had problems in finding the concerned information—in this case, the webcam can help in correctly interpret the feeling of the user (engaging or not the visit).

9.6.3 Presentation-Related Data

In this section, we analyze the results that the evaluation should deliver about the usability of the user-interface presentation (e.g., for GUIs—layout, choice of widgets, colors, labels, etc.). There are tools that link the task performance with the user-interface elements supporting such performance. In other cases, the tools are able to provide reports that highlight the user-interface elements that might be problematic from the usability point of view. For example, WebQuilt (Waterson & others 2002) provides representations consisting of nodes representing visited webpages, and arrows representing the traffic between the pages. Entry pages are green and exit pages are cyan. Thicker arrows represent heavier traffic. Arrow color is used to indicate time spent on a page before transitioning, where the closer the arrow is to red, the longer the user spent in transition. The designer's path is highlighted in blue. There is a slider along the left-hand side that allows the designer to zoom into the graph, viewing actual images of the pages users saw and where they clicked.

9.6.4 Quantitative Cognitive-Physiological Information

Quantitative psycho-physiological measurements can provide useful information about more general, qualitative information on a human's feeling in a specific situation. For instance, with a growing population of elderly persons today, this result is expected to be more and more applied in the field of elderly care/assistance, where there has been an increasing interest in investigating algorithms to enable the possibility of assessing elderly mood in a non-intrusive manner. To make state-of-mind information available, sensor technology can be employed. Various psycho-physiological signals are known in literature that can convey the presence of strong emotions or stress (Cacioppo, et al. 2000)—skin conductance, muscle tension, heart rate, and heart rate variability. Such signals can now be measured in an unobtrusive manner. The measured signals have to be analyzed to reliably convey short-term mood changes (that might be relevant for the relatives and form a basis for an enhanced feeling of connectedness), as well as long-term trends. When the shape of people is mostly visible, computer vision tools can be used to classify their posture and gait, and posture changes over time. This information can be exploited, for example, to predict (by gait analysis) and detect (by analyzing posture changes) falls. Computer vision techniques can be used to detect the head position in real-time, and classify the facial orientation (frontal, profile) to provide the process of facial expression analysis with suitable data. In addition, faces are processed for expression/recognition/authentication. If a person is not visible or the user does not like a camera to be used (e.g., in the bathroom), speech/audio tracking is an alternative.

Eye-tracking systems can provide many interesting pieces of information derived from fixations and saccades. Long fixations can indicate that users spend too much effort to interpret or to process what they are looking at. The number of fixations is often related to the user efforts to process the content of the screen area being analyzed. The duration of the scanpath is a productivity measure and can be compared with a theoretical optimal duration. Even the ratio between saccades and fixations can be a useful index for comparing the percentage of time spent in looking for information (saccades) and that during which information is acquired (fixations).

9.7 An Example Tool for Remote Evaluation: MultiModalWebRemUsine

In this section, we discuss an example of a tool for remote evaluation according to the framework presented in the chapter. The basic idea of this tool is to analyze user logs through the semantic information contained in task models. Thus, on the one hand, we have a task model that describes how designers expect users to perform their activities, and on the other hand, there are logs indicating the actions performed by the users while interacting with the application. Each user session can be defined through the sequence of the corresponding user actions, which can be associated with a corresponding sequence of basic task performance to achieve the user's goal. If the performed task sequence diverts from those enabled by the task model, there is clearly a mismatch that needs to be analyzed by the evaluators. Either the task model is too rigid or there is something unclear in the user interface, which prevents the user from performing the expected sequences of tasks.

Various versions of the tool have been developed, which vary for the type of application addressed and the type of results provided. The first version, USINE (Lecerof & Paternò 1998), mainly addressed the issue of using task models for analyzing user logs without considering its use as remote evaluation. The next version, RemUSINE (Paternò & Ballardin 2000), was developed for remotely evaluating desktop Java applications and was tested in industrial sites, providing useful information regarding its possibilities even in comparison with other methods. It was, for example, compared with a video-based evaluation. It turned out that for evaluating a small number of sessions, the video-based evaluation was more efficient because RemUSINE required some time to enable the automatic evaluation given that the evaluator first has to provide the task model of the designed application and create mappings between basic tasks and log events. On the positive side, it was noted that, in some cases, video analysis is not able to detect quick user actions (such as some user clicks) and is not usable for evaluations when users are located far from the evaluator.

Given the explosion of the Web, which has become the most common user interface, we thought it useful to develop a new version (WebRemUSINE), aimed at evaluating this type of application (Paganelli & Paternò 2003). We also had to decide how to log user interactions. For this purpose, we implemented an efficient, interoperable, client-side logging system. In addition to information regarding task performance, the Web-oriented version provides a lot of information regarding the Web pages analyzed—visited pages, never visited pages, extent of scrolling and resizing, page patterns, and download and visit time. Some information is provided, along with summary data regarding the content of the page. Thus, the visit time is provided and also indicates the number of forms, links, and words in the page so the evaluator can compare the visit time with the quantity of information available in the page. The latest version of the tool (MultimodalWebRemUSINE) aims to exploit the possibilities opened up by recent technologies to gather a richer set of information regarding user behavior. Thus, the traditional graphical logs can be analyzed together with the logs from webcams and portable eye-trackers, which do not require the use of intrusive equipment.

In summary, the changes in the tool mainly aimed at fulfilling the evolving needs of usability evaluators. Indeed, the tool started from the original vision of providing cost-effective techniques for usability evaluation for analyzing data about product usage in a real-world environment. To this end, remote evaluation is valuable when trying to keep budgets down while staying competitive in the marketplace (which is especially relevant for companies). The necessity to reach larger, more diverse and dispersed pools of participants also stimulated the attention to Web applications. In these times of global customers and development organizations, there is a clear correlation between the globalization of the product market and the potential (and challenges) of remote evaluation. Next, the tool kept evolving in these directions with an eye toward the available improvements (in terms of robustness and affordability) of technology and broadband infrastructure, which were efficiently exploited for enriching the tool with multimodal information on the user's behavior. The objective was to compensate the recognized evaluator's decreased ability—typically connected with remote usability evaluation techniques—to interpret the motivations underlying a certain user behavior, due to separation in space (and sometimes also in time) between the user and the evaluator.

In general, MultimodalWebRemUsine is based on a comparison of planned user behavior and actual user behavior. Information about the planned logical behavior of the user is contained in a (previously developed) task model, while data about actual user behavior is provided by the other modules supposedly available within the client environment (the logging tool, the webcam and the eye-tracker).

Before starting the test, users have to explicitly indicate the target task. After that, all the user actions will be automatically recorded. The evaluation then analyzes the user's sequences of actions to determine whether the user has correctly performed the tasks in accordance with the temporal relationships defined in the task model, or if some errors occurred. In addition, the tool evaluates whether the user is able to reach the goals and if the actions performed are actually useful to reach the predefined goals, by means of an internal task model simulator. For each action in the log, the corresponding basic task is first identified and then there is a check to see whether that task was logically enabled. If no error occurs, the list of the basic tasks that have been enabled after its performance is provided, together with the updated list of high-level tasks already accomplished, to allow the evaluator to check if the target task has been completed. Otherwise, some error will be notified in the report analyzing the user session. An example of error is a *precondition error*, which means that the actual user's task performance did not respect the relations defined in the system design model. For example, if people want to access a remote service (such as Web access to emails), they usually have to provide username and password and then activate the request through a button. If the user interfaces elements are not located in such a way that the user can easily realize that both fields have to be filled in before connecting to the mailbox, then some precondition errors can occur (for example, the user sends the request without first proving the password). Such types of errors can be detected through this type of approach.

From the log analysis, the tool can generate various indications:

- *Success*—the user has been able to perform a set of basic tasks required to accomplish the target task and thus achieve the goal
- *Failure*—the user starts the performance of the target task but is not able to complete it
- *Useless uncritical task*—the user performs a task that is not strictly useful to accomplish the target task but does not prevent its completion
- *Deviation from the target task*—in a situation where the target task is enabled and the user performs a basic task whose effect is to disable it. This shows a problematic situation since the user is getting farther away from the main goal in addition to performing useless actions
- *Inaccessible task*—when the user is never able to enable a certain target task

Recently, we have paid attention to how to represent user sessions and related data in such a way that eases their analysis. Figure 9.1 shows the type of representations designed. It is possible to show data related to several sessions in different ways at the same time. In Figure 9.1, we analyze the parts of the sessions about users who want to become member of an association. As you can see from the selected radio buttons, the deviation graph is shown for the first two users, while the state graph is visualized for the other ones. In both types of graphs, the white circles are associated with the basic tasks performed, and their positions indicate when they have been accomplished. In the first diagram (deviation diagram), there are three lines—one for the basic tasks correctly performed, one for those uselessly performed, and one for the tasks that have diverted the user from achieving the current goal. In the state diagram, the color of the line underlying the white circles is used to indicate whether the user is correctly or incorrectly performing the task.

A further type of information considered during the evaluation regards the task-execution time. In case of tasks correctly performed, the tool calculates the global time of performance. This information is calculated by examining the temporal information associated with each event and stored in the logs. The duration is calculated for both high-level and basic tasks. The set of results regarding the execution time can provide information useful to understanding what the most complicated tasks are or what tasks require a longer time to be performed. In Figure 9.2, a screenshot of the tool is presented. As you can see, whenever an inexplicably lengthy time period for carrying out a certain task is registered by the tool, the evaluator can activate the related video recorded through a webcam to gather further information.

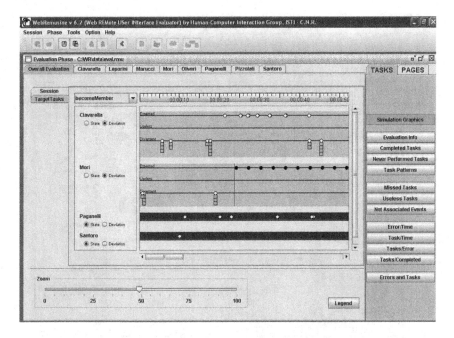

Fig. 9.1 Representation of user sessions in MMWebRemUsine

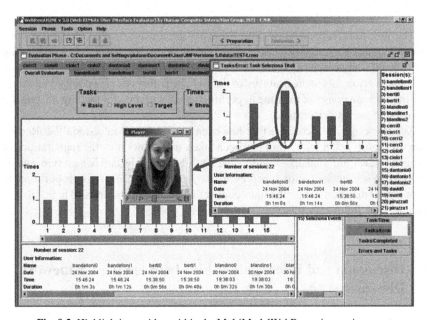

Fig. 9.2 Highlighting a video within the MultiModalWebRemusine environment

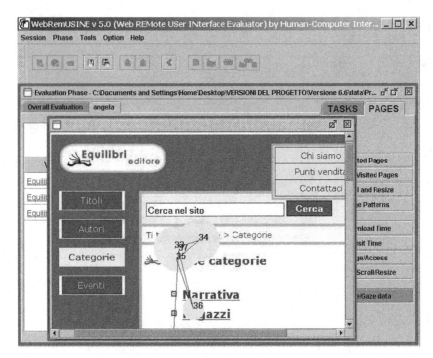

Fig. 9.3 An example of visualization of fixations (the yellow areas) and scanpaths (the paths in-between) registered by the eye-tracker

The approach supported by MultiModalWebremusine is also able to provide usability data associated with every single presentation. Moreover, it is worth noting that since this approach can correlate task-based measures with presentation-related data, it can also analyze the usability of the website from both viewpoints. For example, the tool can compare the time to perform a task with that for loading the page(s) involved in such a performance.

Eye-tracking is a technique that has been used within MultiModalWebRemUsine. In Figure 9.3, a screenshot has been taken that shows how the registrations of the eye-tracker are visualized within the MultiModalWebRemUsine environment. As you can see, each fixation is represented by an area whose size is proportional to its recorded duration, while the lines connecting such areas (scanpath) highlight the path the user followed while visiting the page.

9.8 Discussion and Interrelationships between the Framework Dimensions

We can discuss possible interrelationships among the different dimensions that we have identified while analyzing several contributions in the area of remote usability evaluation. First of all, the choice of the platform type might substantially limit—in terms of hardware and software—the type of technology and/or techniques that can be used for remote evaluation, as well as put less/more emphasis on the relevance of particular information for the purposes of the evaluation. Indeed, apart from the well-known differences between the type of applications that might be supported by a cellphone and by a desktop system due to the diversities in hardware and software capabilities, the type of platform used may also affect the relevance of a piece of information with respect to another one. This is the case, for instance, with the user context, which is very important for mobile applications and less important for desktop systems.

Another observation is the fact that the same type of information useful for the evaluation (e.g., user workload) can be gained with different techniques. For instance, a possible indication for user workload might be a user blinking very frequently (information that can be gained from an eye-tracker), but some physiological data can—more reliably—signal this workload. Another example regards user feedback, which can be gained with different means. A user nodding (captured by the webcam) might be a sign of a good feedback, as well as a user using some positive vocal expressions. In other cases, there is information useful for evaluation (e.g., task-based data) that cannot be derived without explicitly including additional information (task specification).

Moreover, the type of interaction between the evaluator and the user might also affect the use of the particular technique(s) adopted, as well as the quantity (and also the quality) of information collected for the evaluation. For instance, while the use of remote questionnaires indicates a specific type of technique for collecting information about the user, in automatic collection of data the range of techniques can greatly vary, as does the range of the evaluation results that can be derived from interpreting the collected data.

Lastly, as we already noticed, the type of application considered may prevent (or strongly encourage) the application of certain techniques, as well as the use of specific interaction platforms. For instance, in the case of Web-based applications, the use of server-side and client-side logging techniques is a well-known and established approach, while the consideration of user interactions with additional software components like .NET for remote evaluation only belongs to recent years, and is often restricted only to specific types of platforms.

9.9 Conclusions and Future Challenges

In this chapter, we have described a framework composed of different dimensions that we have identified as relevant in the area of remote usability evaluation. This type of evaluation is becoming more and more important in a time of globalization of companies and their customers. We have used such a framework to review a large spectrum of methods that have been proposed in this area. These methods have been receiving more and more interest due to the improvements in techniques that are able to capture information regarding user behavior and the validity of the data that are collected *in the field*. Therefore, the chapter tries to shed some light on the different methods through a common framework in which it is possible to compare and contrast current works in the area of remote evaluation, as well as delineate possible future trends in the research agenda of remote usability evaluation. In addition, this chapter is useful in identifying which are the current strategies for compensating some traditional weaknesses in this type of evaluation. For instance, future work should be dedicated to extending the gathered data regarding user behavior and state—including emotional state—so a more complete analysis of what happens during user sessions can be done and potential usability issues can be better identifed. Another novel emerging application area is that of mobile applications, in which is important to understand how task performance varies depending on the changes in the context of use. To make the discussion more concrete, we have also reported our experience with our tool in the area of remote evaluation and analyzed it according to the dimensions of the logical framework proposed.

References

Avouris N., Komis V., Margaritis M., & Fiotakis G., (2004), An environment for studying collaborative learning activities, *Journal of Educational Technology & Society, Special Issue on Technology – Enhanced Learning, 7 (2)*, 34–41.

Cacioppo, J.T., Berntson, G.G., Larsen, J.T., Poehlmann, K.M., & Ito, T.A. (2000). The psychophysiology of emotion. In M. Lewis & R.J.M. Haviland-Jones (Eds.), *The Handbook of Emotions* (2nd Ed.) (pp. 173–191). New York: Guilford Press.

Card, S., Pirolli, P., Van der Wege, M., Morrison, J., Reeder, R., Schraedley, P., & Boshart, J. (2001). Information scent as a driver of Web behavior graphs: Results of a protocol analysis method for Web usability, *Proceedings ACM CHI 2001* (pp. 498–504).

Choo, C. W., Detlor, B., & Turnbull, D. (1998). A behavioral model of information seeking on the Web—preliminary results of a study of how managers and IT specialists use the Web. In *Proceedings of the 61st ASIS Annual Meeting, 35*, (pp. 290–302).

ClickFox (2002), ClickFox Inc., http://www.clickfox.com.

Davison, B. (1999). Web traffic logs: An imperfect resource for evaluation. In: *Proceedings of Ninth Annual Conference of the Internet Society (INET'99)*, San Jose, CA, June 1999.

Denis, C., & Karsenty, L. (2003). Inter-usability of multi-device systems: A conceptual framework. In A. Seffah & H. Javahery (Eds.), *Multiple User Interfaces: Engineering and Application Framework* (pp. 375–385). New Jersey: John Wiley and Sons.

Etgen, M., & Cantor, J. (1999). What does getting WET (Web Event-Logging Tool) mean for Web usability? In *Proceedings of the Fifth Conference on Human Factors and the Web*. Gaithersburg, MD, June.

Hartson, R. H., Castillo, J. C., Kelso, J. T., & Neale W. C. (1996). Remote evaluation: The network as an extension of the usability laboratory. In: *Proceedings of CHI 1996* (pp. 228–235).

Ho, S.Y. (2005). An exploratory study of using a user remote tracker to examine Web users' personality traits. In *Proceedings of the 7th International Conference on Electronic commerce, ICEC'05* (pp. 659–665), August 15–17, 2005, Xi'an, China. ACM Press.

Hong, J.I., & Landay, J.A. (2001). WebQuilt: a framework for capturing and visualizing the Web experience. In *Proceedings of WWW 2001 Conference* (pp. 717–724).

IQ Services (2006). *IQ Services: Interactive Quality Services, Inc.* Access at: http://www.iq-services.com/

Ivory M. Y., & Hearst M. A., (2001) The state of the art in automating usability evaluation of user interfaces. *ACM Computing Surveys, 33*(4), 470–516.

Lecerof, A., & Paternò, F. (1998), Automatic support for usability evaluation. *IEEE Transactions on Software Engineering, 24 (10)*, 863–888.

Lister M. (2003). Streaming format software for usability testing. In *Proceedings ACM CHI 2003, Extended Abstracts* (pp. 632–633).

Paganelli, L., & Paternò F. (2003). Tools for remote usability evaluation of Web applications through browser logs and task models. *Behavior Research Methods, Instruments, and Computers, 35 (3)*, 369–378.

Paternò, F., & Ballardin, G. (2000). RemUSINE: a bridge between empirical and model-based evaluation when evaluators and users are distant. *Interacting with Computers, 13(2)*, 229–251.

Paternò, F., Piruzza, A., & Santoro, C. (2006). Remote Web usability evaluation exploiting multimodal information on user behavior. In *Proceedings CADUI 2006*, Bucharest. Springer-Verlag.

Petrie, H., Hamilton, F., King, N., & Pavan, P. (2006). Remote usability evaluations with disabled people. In *Proceedings of CHI 2006* (pp. 1131–1141), Montréal, Québec, Canada, April 22–27, 2006.

Scholtz, J., Laskowski, S., & Downey L. (1998) Developing usability tools and techniques for designing and testing Websites. In *Proceedings HFWeb'98* (Basking Ridge, NJ, June 1998). Access at: http://www.research.att.com/conf/hfWeb/ proceedings/scholtz/index.html

Stoica, A., Fiotakis, G., Simarro-Cabrera, J., Frutos, H.M., Avouris, N., & Dimitriadis, Y. (2005). Usability evaluation of handheld devices: A case study for a museum application. In *Proceedings of PCI 2005*, Volos, November 2005.

Tauscher, L.M. (1999). *Evaluating history mechanisms: An empirical study of reuse patterns in WWW navigation.* MS Thesis, Department of Computer Science, University of Calgary, Alberta, Canada.

Tennent, P., Chalmers, M., & Morrison, A. (2006). Replayer: Collaborative evaluation of mobile applications. Presented in *CHI'06 Workshop on Information Visualization and Interaction Techniques for Collaboration across Multiple Displays*, Montreal, Canada.

Tullis, T, Fleischman, S., McNulty, M, Cianchette, C., & Bergel, M. (2002). An empirical comparison of lab and remote usability testing of websites. In: Proceedings of *Usability Professionals Conference*, Pennsylvania, 2002.

Waterson, S., Landay, J.A., & Matthews, T. (2002). In the lab and out in the wild: Remote Web usability testing for mobile devices. In: *Proceedings of CHI 2002* (pp. 796–797), April 20–25, Minneapolis, USA.

West, R., & Lehman, K.R. (2006). Automated summative usability studies: An empirical evaluation. In *Proceedings of CHI 2006* (pp. 631–639), *April 22–27, 2006*, Montréal, Québec, Canada, ACM Press.

Chapter 10
Utility and Experience in the Evolution of Usability

Gitte Lindgaard and Avi Parush

Human Oriented Technology Lab (HOTLab), Carleton University, Canada,
e-mail: Gitte_Lindgaard@carleton.ca

Abstract In this chapter, we discuss the evolution of usability and its implications for usability research and practice. We propose that the concept of usability evolved from a narrow focus on individual performance to a more inclusive concept of experience and the collective. We address three major trends: cognition-performance, emotional-experience, and social context-experience which, together, seem to reflect those pervading the field of usability. We argue that the movement away from the strictly cognitive, performance-oriented concerns to embracing emotion and eventually social and cultural aspects can largely be attributed to two forces. One is a change in tasks, technologies, and the objectives of systems. The other is the realization that performance alone in the cognitive sense is not enough to account for the richness of phenomena influencing people's interactions with technology. We then discuss the importance of aesthetics and emotion, and finally, usability in the context of collaborative and social computing.

10.1 Introduction

Imagine you are testing the usability of creating an account in an electronic commerce website and the test participant says to you: "Yes, I can definitely do it. It is easy. But why should I?" Will your conclusion be that the user interface is usable and the task is easy? What about the lack of motivation on the part of the participant or lack of usefulness of the task/service? Or, imagine the test participant saying: "I can easily create the account if other people recommended it." What does that imply for the usability? What is the role of the social aspects in such an episode?

Our understanding of the concept of usability is evolving more rapidly than researchers and practitioners can apply its implications. Usability has evolved from representing a relatively simple utilitarian concern for task performance into a highly complex notion of a contextualized human experience, also including emotional and social aspects. Experience includes issues such as pleasure, fun, collaboration and social support, trust, and many others, presented on technologies ranging from smart textiles to biofeedback applications embedded in a wide variety of platforms and display types/styles.

E. Law et al. (eds.), *Maturing Usability.*

The questions we ask in this chapter are: "what characterizes the evolution of the usability concept and what are the implications for usability research and practice?" We propose that the concept of usability evolved from focusing on individuals' cognitively-driven performance to individuals' experience, understanding the critical role of emotion in usability, and culminating in understanding the impact of the social and cultural context on experience. In addressing three major trends— cognition-performance, emotional experience, and social context experience—that seem to reflect those pervading the field of usability, we propose that the concept of usability evolved from a narrow focus on individual performance to a more inclusive concept of experience and the collective. As discussed in the context of the first major trend, the evolution is due to changes in tasks, technologies, objectives of systems and applications, and the realization that performance alone in the cognitive sense is not enough to account for the richness of phenomena influencing people's interactions with technology. The second major trend discussed here concerns aesthetics and emotion. Finally, the third major trend addresses the concept of usability in the context of collaborative and social computing. We address usability both in terms of a suggested research agenda and also as it relates to the practice of usability.

10.2 Usability: Evolution of the Concept

The first major trend we describe is the concept of usability as it is evolving in both the practitioner and research communities. Following the invention of windows, icons, menus, pointers (WIMPs) in 1973 (van Dam 1997), Bravo—the first commercial word processor using a direct manipulation user interface—was produced in the at the Xerox Palo Alto Research Center (Hitzik 1999) in the mid-1970s. It was followed by the Xerox Star in 1981 (Kearns & Nadler 1992), but none of these became commercial successes. Success came with the release of the Apple Lisa in 1984, in which the direct-manipulation interface included both Visicalc (the first spreadsheet) and word-processing tools (Rose 1989) integrated into the desktop metaphor.

Hand-in-hand with this provision of commercial office software, numerous in-house software development projects aiming to streamline (or at least support) established business procedures, were launched inside large organizations (Ewusi-Menash 1997). These largely replicated existing user tasks and task procedures were documented in internal manuals and, notwithstanding that the manuals often were out-of-date, failed to represent how users actually performed these tasks. Thus, the mismatch of system requirements specifications to user tasks became a major problem, resulting in huge monetary losses through projects that were running well over time and budget, or were abandoned before completion (Ewusi-Menash 1997; Lindgaard, et al. 2006a; Sutcliffe 2002). In this climate, the practice of usability began to prosper.

The appearance of the ISO9241/11 (ISO 1997) standard elevated the practice of usability to a level of acceptability that had previously been difficult to achieve inside organizations. The ISO standard focuses on usability evaluation primarily based on user performance measures that are operationalized via effectiveness and efficiency, with user satisfaction almost tacked on as an afterthought. The measurement of user satisfaction is, in that document, reduced to judgments of *comfort* and *attitude*, whereas clearer guidance and definitions are given to measurements of effectiveness and efficiency. Efficiency refers to work output per unit of time, and effectiveness ensures that users could work through screens without committing errors such as deviating from the set path or omitting task-related information. Evidently, the readily measurable, utilitarian aspects of usability features much more prominently in the ISO standard than the experience-based aspects of user satisfaction.

Meanwhile, in the research community, Card, Moran, and Newell's (1980; 1983) ambitious goal for their goals, operators, methods, and selection (GOMS) rules approach was to produce engineering models of human performance. For readers who may not be familiar with GOMS, it is worth noting that operators refer to the *actions* the software allows the user to take rather than to *people*. Methods are well-learned sequences of subgoals and operators that can accomplish a goal. If there is more than one method to accomplishing the same goal, then selection rules are required. Selection rules are the personal rules that users follow in deciding what method to use in a particular situation. Together, these four components represent the procedural *how-to-do-it* knowledge a user needs to perform a task. Ideally, such models should produce quantitative predictions of performance well before prototypes and user tests are designed. The models would predict execution and learning time and also identify those parts of an interface that lead to these predictions, thereby providing a focus for redesign efforts. They allow analysis at different levels of approximation so that predictions appropriate to the design situation can be obtained with minimum effort. Importantly, it was hoped that these human performance models would be straightforward enough to be used by people without extensive psychological training.

The GOMS models were based on much of the accumulated, quantifiable knowledge of human perception, cognition, and motor performance captured in equations such as Fitts' Law (Fitts 1954), Weber's Fraction, Fechner's Law (Schiffman 1976), and others. With sufficient detail about the step-by-step procedures of the user tasks to be supported by the to-be-built application, GOMS models could thus be applied to optimizing the user interface design a priori, and then comparing these predictions with subsequent user performance. This approach obviously only works for highly routine, repetitive tasks. Unfortunately, GOMS models were quite cumbersome and time consuming to build. Perhaps the biggest hindrance to GOMS modeling becoming more widespread, however, was that expert, error-free human performance was assumed. Still, for many HCI researchers, especially those with a background in cognitive, experimental psychology, the appearance of Card, Moran, and Newell's book (1983) marks the birth of the concept of usability.

It is not surprising, therefore, that the types of performance measures commonly used in psychology came to occupy the center stage of usability research in the early days, and later in the ISO standard, and also became cemented into usability practice. It is also not surprising that the early approach to evaluating usability was predominantly informed by traditionally controlled psychological laboratory experiments. One major challenge for HCI researchers and practitioners at that time was to adapt these traditional approaches to task environments in which it was not possible to control most of the extraneous variables that inevitably pervade real-life situations. Their concern was how far one could safely *stretch* the rigorous experimental paradigms without losing reliability and validity (Lindgaard 1994). In the world of human factors, models and mock-ups were commonly built to simulate real life, but these tended to primarily involve the design of physical equipment, the relative placement of fixtures, displays, and equipment in often limited spaces to ensure the user could comfortably see, hear, and reach buttons and levers, rather than software presented on a computer screen (Meister 1986).

While most of the early intraorganizational applications supported a very narrow range of tasks, system integration soon became the order of the day. The objective of systems design shifted from applications that supported a few individual tasks to larger systems in which tasks that had hitherto been performed by different users were now integrated into larger, more flexible, applications. The aim was to facilitate the development of multiple skills in users and reduce the amount of between-application context-switching that is needed to perform different tasks, which now are more open-ended and thus less predictable. In terms of usability practice, the overriding concern was to achieve within- and between-application user interface (UI) consistency such as using the same terminology and abbreviations, ensuring that objects and widgets looked, felt, and behaved the same, and that they were located in the same place on different screens throughout applications. This was a perfect environment for creating corporate GUI style guides because many of these integrated systems represented different organizational sectors that each had their own local culture and traditions supporting departmental work identities. These local cultures often bore little resemblance with the unified corporate image that senior management now wants to portray in their *corporate branding* efforts.

The overriding focus of usability practitioners was still on the utilitarian aspects of user performance, but practitioners were also heavily involved in the design of GUI style guides (Lindgaard 1995). However, the more flexible, open-endedness of user tasks still reflected prescribed company procedures and predetermined content, and the substance of the users' typical data-entry/data-retrieval tasks had not yet changed.

Meanwhile, the notion of usability had captured the imagination of researchers coming from backgrounds other than psychology or computer science, including disciplines such as anthropology (Suchman 1987), sociology (Denning & Dunham 2003), the arts (Laurel 1993), and design (Jordan 2000). With their fresh perspectives, different research agendas, and methodologies, they added new dimensions to the traditionally narrow utilitarian usability concept. Concern with broader work patterns and contexts—with groups of people collaborating via technology, and with design aesthetics, engagement, and fun—gradually helped to expand the meaning of usability, encouraging usability practitioners to concentrate as much on the quality of interactive experiences as on the traditional performance-based measures. Indeed, one would think all of these should be captured in measures of user satisfaction that go beyond the issues of comfort and attitude as advocated in the ISO standard.

Creating high quality, pleasant, and motivating user experiences had, of course, been the main concern of producers of interactive games since the 1950s (Crawford 1984), but it rose to full fruition in both usability practice and research with the rise of virtual shop fronts in the business-to-consumer (B2C) e-commerce environment. In that context, the user experience begins well before someone decides to buy a particular product, regardless of whether the transaction takes place online or in traditional *brick and mortar* outfits. In the e-commerce context, the usability envelope thus includes the first impression of the concrete or virtual shop, the pre-sale and post-sale experiences, and the prolonged interaction with the product and the vendor—all of which contribute to the user-turned-consumer experience (Donoghue 2000). User satisfaction, defined as the sum of one's feelings about the entire interaction, including fulfilment of one's expectations (Bailey & Pearson 1983), assumes increasing importance compared with the early predominance of performance measures. Issues contributing to user satisfaction thus need to be investigated in much more detail than implied by the ISO standard.

In addition to engineering, IT departments, and usability folk, stakeholders in the e-commerce world include sales and marketing, customer service staff, technical support and help desk professionals, and many others. While the utilitarian concerns remain essential to providing good usability in any context, including e-commerce, the narrowly defined original concept of usability has been subsumed within the wider concept of user experience. This widening has also brought about confusion over the usability concept. It is unclear which parts of the overall experience do/do not belong to usability, who is responsible, and who, if anyone, *owns* the entire user experience (Lindgaard 2002). What is crystal clear is that the traditional usability performance metrics, while still necessary, no longer suffice in practice or in research. To quote Blythe, et al. (2006): "it is not possible to have an engaging experience with a machine that doesn't work." (p. 130) Taking the notion of the broader user experience a little further, the second major trend we address concerns the growing importance of aesthetics and emotion in interactive computing.

10.3 Aesthetics and Emotion

In recent times, several special issues of mainstream HCI journals have been devoted to topics that, taken together, may be referred to as variants of affective computing (Human-Computer Interaction 2004; Interacting with Computers 2002; Behaviour & Information Technology 2006). In addition, books taking a human (Norman 2004), a computer (Picard 1998), or an interaction (Nass & Reeves 1996) perspective have appeared. There are two perspectives in this research: one focuses on enabling computers to respond to the user's mood or emotional state, and the other focuses on understanding how to design interactive computers that are appealing and pleasant to use. This latter perspective is discussed here.

The number of HCI researchers who contribute to the aesthetics debate (e.g., Tractinsky, et al. 2000; Lavie & Tractinsky 2004; Lindgaard & Whitfield 2004; van der Heijden 2003; Schenkman & Jönsson 2000), beauty (Hassenzahl 2004), appeal

(Fernandes, et al. 2003), hedonics (Hassenzahl, et al. 2001; Helander & Tham 2003), and user satisfaction (Lindgaard & Dudek 2003), is increasing. Theories, models and measuring instruments attempting to demonstrate ways in which these various concepts may be explained and operationalized are beginning to appear in the literature, but the reader who is looking for coherence or guidance on how to approach these softer, experience-related initiatives will be disappointed. The concepts still lack clear, unambiguous, and agreed-upon definitions, which inevitably leads to fragmentation and confusion. If we do not know what we are measuring, how can we assess the goodness of fit of the instruments and metrics to the measurement tasks? However, even in the absence of clarity or agreement on definitions, there are some encouraging signs that researchers are beginning to try to come to grips with some of the experience-related concepts. It is worthwhile to take a brief look at two of the most prominent of these—namely, aesthetics and emotion—in an effort to explore how such research may contribute to a more inclusive notion of usability. Because user satisfaction is already positioned as one of the three pillars of usability practice in the ISO standard, the concept of usability needs to be expanded to represent additional aspects of user experience. This is likely to include a concern for both aesthetics and the emotions user interfaces evoke.

10.4 Aesthetics

Aesthetics is variously referred to as beauty in appearance (Lavie & Tractinsky 2004), visual appeal (Lindgaard & Dudek 2003), an experience (Ramachandran & Blakeslee 1998), an attitude (Cupchik 1993), a property of objects (Porteous 1996), a response or a judgment (Hassenzahl 2004), and a process (Langer 1967). Common to all of these terms, is that aesthetics has something to do with the pleasure and harmony that human beings are capable of experiencing.

Aesthetics, in its classical Greek meaning, refers to sensory-perceptual knowledge (*aesthêsis*) as distinct from intellectual semantic knowledge (*noêsis*). A role for *aêsthesis* can be envisaged as involving category articulation at the sensory-perceptual level. Thus, for example, a successful composition in art comprises a harmonious blend of its formal elements, which give it a sense of balance. Symmetry, which is a consistent component of great art, is the simplest way to achieve balance (Sen 2005). Some evidence suggests that preference for orderliness, symmetry, and harmony is hard-wired in humans. Newborn infants as young as nine minutes, for example, have been found to prefer visual stimuli resembling a human face over stimuli in which the same elements are jumbled (Baron-Cohen 1999; Brothers 1990). According to Langer (1967), balance in a symmetrical design gives us pleasure, a feeling of stability, and equilibrium, perhaps supporting our biological quest for homeostasis. The existence of Phi—also known as the Fibonacci Series or the Golden Ratio—throughout nature, visual art, and music, seems to suggest that what we find intrinsically appealing may have its origin in harmonic forms ever present in the natural universe, as well as in our constructed world of art and design.

In a recent study on aesthetics as it relates to the design and usability of computer interfaces, Lavie and Tractinsky (2004) proposed that visual aesthetics may be a strong determinant of user satisfaction and pleasure. In three experiments devoted to developing a scale for measuring aesthetics and exploring users' perception of the aesthetic qualities of websites, two clear dimensions of aesthetics emerged. One, which they call *classical aesthetics*, comprises items such as clear, clean, and symmetrical design in line with the original concept of *aesthesis*. It is interesting to note that these same values are central to good information design (Zwaga & Easterby 1984), including screen design (Galitz 1981, 1993). Application of characteristics of human perception to screen design, such as grouping of semantically similar items, visual distance between groups of items, and strategic use of white space (Zdralek 2003), are, of course, known to be intrinsic to good usability (Parush, et al. 1998; Parush, et al. 2005). Thus, the purely visual aspects of interface and screen design that the HCI community has hitherto regarded as usability components may really be considered aesthetic qualities.

The second dimension of aesthetics uncovered by Lavie and Tractinsky (2004)—expressive aesthetics—includes issues such as creative, original, sophisticated, and fascinating design. Using a similar approach, Hassenzahl (2004) empirically derived a set of rating scales comprised of three groups of what he calls hedonic quality items. Several of these items are also present in Lavie and Tractinsky's scales, such as creative, original, beautiful, and fascinating, but Hassenzahl placed beauty in a separate evaluative construct category, although all the scale items really represent subjective judgments. Thus, he distinguishes beauty, which is central to Lavie and Tractinsky, from hedonic qualities even though many hedonic items occur in both scales.

Evidently, both Lavie and Tractinsky's classical and expressive aesthetics dimensions, and Hassenzahl's hedonic and beauty assessment scales, reflect judgments *about the design* rather than capturing the interactive *experience* per se. Because a judgment is a result, or a retrospective summary, of an experience, it would be difficult, if not impossible, to gain insight into aesthetics as an ongoing experience via rating scales administered post hoc. Therefore, other methods are called for if we are to capture the ongoing user experience in real-time. Computer users, however, are not accustomed to expressing their feelings, impressions, and reactions spontaneously as they occur. They are therefore difficult to capture—we lack measurement instruments that can adequately capture impressions that include multiple senses in addition to the visual. As interactive computing increasingly incorporates multiple senses, especially speech and non-speech sound and haptics, new questions with which to capture all of these must be formulated, and new measurement instruments will clearly need to be developed to assess usability in more immersive experiential applications.

The rich variety of aesthetics definitions is problematic, and testifies to the complexity of the concept. Despite this, recent research has demonstrated that aesthetics, beauty, and appeal are very important contributors to a positive interactive experience. Tractinsky, Katz and Ikar's (2000) results, for example, suggested that a beautiful user interface may also be perceived as high in usability. By contrast, Lindgaard and Dudek's (2002) findings showed that an interface found to be extremely high in visual appeal, both before and after a usability test, scored very low in perceived usability on both occasions. Participants were aware of the poor usability, but the site was and remained both visually very appealing and high in preference ratings. Along similar lines, Tractinsky and Zmiri (2006) and Mahlke (2006) found that participants preferred products high in visual appeal and relatively low in usability over high-usability and products with lower visual appeal. The extent to which these preferences last after prolonged usage is not yet known. To capture the user experience and use this understanding to design for good usability, the future usability research agenda must embrace and disentangle these difficult concepts and the relationships between them.

10.5 Emotion

To the extent that aesthetics is a pleasant experience or an experience that leads to pleasure, it implies a relationship to emotion. Emotion research has its own language, traditions, and paradigms, but a few models of direct relevance to usability are reviewed here. For comprehensive reviews, please see Martin and Clore (2001) or Bless and Forgas (1998).

Emotion is said to vary along two dimensions: valence (the good/bad, positive/negative dimension) and intensity (the arousal-based dimension) (Russell 1980). Feelings that are arousing demand attention; feelings that are pleasant or unpleasant provide motivation. More subtle feelings from ongoing appraisals—for example: "How am I doing at this task?"—convey less urgent information that can be attended to as judgments and decisions may require. While completing a task, positive affect may be experienced as information about the task, like "this is fun," as information about oneself, "I am really good at this," or about one's strategy "I am doing this right," depending on what is in focus. Feelings are thus experiential representations of eliciting conditions—they must be conscious to be felt. The term *affect* is analogous to the term *cognition*, which refers to representations of knowledge. *Affect* conveys information about feelings rather than words, and it designates a broad category of things with positive or negative personal value. Emotions are affective states that represent appraisals of something good or bad—that is, they are feelings about something specific, such as "This is a great interface." The appraisal process is subconscious, but it provides feedback in the form of emotional feelings. By contrast, moods are states of feeling that may or may not be appraisal-based. Thus, the object in an emotion is always salient, which is not necessarily the case for moods where the object may have become diffuse and non-specific (Clore, et al. 2001).

Norman (2004) discusses emotion in terms of three levels of processing. The subconscious visceral level is perceptual and gives rise to immediate judgments. Recent research has shown unequivocally that judgments at this level can be made reliably after a stimulus has been shown for only 50 milliseconds (Lindgaard, et al. 2006b). In two rounds, participants were asked to judge the visual appeal of a series of homepages shown one at a time. Correlations calculated across homepages were in the high 90s, and slightly lower for within-participant judgments than in another condition in which exposure time was 500 milliseconds ($R^2 = .97$). The finding is important because it suggests that this immediate judgment is a biologically determined mere exposure effect (Zajonc 1980), which occurs before the brain has had time to evaluate the stimulus cognitively. It is based, as it were, on "what my body tells me to feel" rather than on "what my brain tells me to think." Therefore, if the first impression of an e-commerce homepage is negative, the resulting unpleasant feeling is likely to motivate the user to selectively search for negative information to confirm the immediate unpleasant physiological response because her focus is now on *negative/unpleasant*. In that case, it is likely that she will click onto the next vendor without even beginning to consider the content of the site yielding the unpleasant feeling. The reverse is true for an immediate pleasant response—the person is likely to look for positive information and be lenient towards any usability problems because her focus in that case is *positive/pleasant*.

Norman's (2004) behavioral level, while still subconscious, is expectation-driven. To the extent that an e-commerce site fails to perform to my expectations formed over my lifelong shopping experiences, I am left with a feeling of losing control.

The fully fledged emotion resides at Norman's third reflective, intellectually-driven level—I am focusing on usability problems if my first impression was negative, or on the enjoyable aspects of the interaction if it was positive. In stark contrast to my immediate feeling, which was holistic and diffuse, the sum of those initial feelings now combine into an emotion that enables me to decide if the interface is great or otherwise.

When processing affective information, the so-called affect infusion model (AIM) (Forgas 2001) suggests that people use one of four strategies. The *direct access* strategy relies on direct retrieval of stored information and preformed responses. Personal involvement is low, and there are no contextual forces motivating the person to engage in a more elaborate response. In a similar fashion, the *heuristic processing* strategy requires minimum effort—a limited amount of information is considered, and the person is using whatever simplifications or shortcuts are available. Taken together, these two strategies can account for the effect of the first impression where the person is merely interpreting a feeling of pleasure or displeasure.

The direct access model is another way to describe what Damasio (2000) calls somatic markers. According to Damasio, a newborn infant has a hard-wired capacity to learn when good and bad feelings arise, to recognize those feelings, and to associate them with the conditions under which they occur. Over a lifetime, we build up a rich repertoire of such feelings that vary in intensity. The original conditions no longer need to be present, or at least only in a very subtle form, for the feelings to occur in response to something good or bad. We learn to interpret and rely on the feeling alone—the somatic markers. Thus, somatic markers serve as energy-saving shortcuts that yield direct access to responses, sending the body into a fight-or-flight mode with a minimum of input. Upon seeing an e-commerce homepage that yields a good feeling (Norman's visceral level)—using the *heuristic processing* strategy—I need not look for detailed information to decide how much I like it and whether to stay or click on to the next site (Norman's behavioral level). I rely on my existing energy-saving knowledge structures (Clore, et al. 2001), to which I have direct access.

The motivated processing strategy is characterized by strong motivational pressure to achieve a particular outcome, corresponding to Norman's reflective level. So, I will persevere in completing my work tasks despite any number of irritating or serious usability problems blocking my progress. The cost may be negative emotion leading to a bad mood and perhaps to serious health problems through continued stress. Finally, the *substantive processing* strategy requires me to select, learn, and interpret novel information about a target, and relate this information to existing knowledge structures. This strategy is applied when facing complex and atypical tasks, the successful completion of which requires close attention and sufficient cognitive resources. If highly complex tasks exceed my cognitive capacity, anxiety ensues. In those circumstances, I am likely to resort to heuristic processing strategies even though they are inadequate, and indeed inappropriate, for the task. My performance now deteriorates to a lower level than I would be capable of maintaining under more favorable conditions. I am, as Csikszentmihalyi (1991) would say, not in *flow*. If the task is too easy, the mismatch between my skill and the task demands results in under-stimulation, and I lose interest, get bored, and stop paying attention to the task. Again, my performance deteriorates below my level of capability.

The trick is obviously to strike a balance between task demands and the user's skill. In this sense, a task refers broadly to any goal-oriented activity, including playing a computer game or completing work tasks. To encourage users to employ the best-fitting processing strategy for the task at hand, usability research must absolutely come to grips with this constant interplay between cognition and emotion, and this must be reflected in various usability tools and techniques that research efforts will hopefully produce for usability practitioners. For example, in an e-learning context, the learning tasks should promote both assimilation and accommodation. In Piagetian terms (Piaget 1954), assimilation refers to the transfer of new information into existing knowledge structures, and accommodation of the tuning of the cognitive system(s) to new incoming data. Positive affect is generally associated with assimilation and top-down processes, and negative affect is associated with accommodation, and data-driven, bottom-up processes. Disconfirmation of expectations, as in accommodation, is necessary for learning (Fiedler 2001). For an e-learning course to be educationally successful, the content designer must incorporate learning elements that yield negative feelings. It follows that it is not enough to produce more relaxing, enjoyable, entertaining, hedonic, and immersive experiences, as is now widely called for in the literature. It is unclear, however, if the usability and usefulness of content should be incorporated under the generic usability umbrella. What is clear is that usability research needs to become far more nuanced than is currently the case. As is true for measuring aesthetics, tools and techniques for evoking and assessing the presence of particular emotions and assessing feelings and emotion in interactive contexts are virtually nonexistent. Even the task of operationalizing different emotion-processing strategies and marrying these with the various levels of emotion is huge, let alone the challenge of understanding how to design applications that adapt smoothly to the increasing skill of users, regardless of whether they are learning together in a group or individually. This research has barely begun.

10.6 From Usability to Collaboration to Sociability

The introduction of systems enabling collective work is the third major trend in the evolution of the usability concept that we address in this chapter. While the first personal computers were intended to be used by a single individual, networking technologies between computers, particularly the Internet, led to the more collaborative and communicative aspects of people interacting with computing technology. This trend reflects the need to move from thinking about the user interface, to the users' interface, to the collaborative interface, and then to the social interface.

The *official* history of the Internet dates back to the mid-1960's when research began on computing networks, and later that decade when the American Department of Defence initiated ARPANET—the development of a communication network between computers (e.g., Leiner, et al. 1997). The technological infrastructure enabled the development of a variety of group- and community-related applications and systems. These range from the basic electronic mail and bulletin boards to tele-video desktop conferencing tools, collaborative writing, and a wide variety of online communities (Grudin 1994; Preece 2000).

Two important concepts emerging in the 1980's were computer-supported collaborative work (CSCW) (Greif 1988) and groupware (Allen 1990; Ensor 1990). One of the most common categorizations of groupware, CSCW is the time/space matrix (DeSanctis & Galuppe 1987) suggesting that communication between people can take place in the same or in different places, and at the same time (synchronous) or at different times (asynchronous). A typical face-to-face conversation occurs at the same time in the same place. The other three possible combinations, however, require some basic technology to support the communication. Support for same-time, different-place communication requires technologies such as the telephone, various computer-based chat and instant messaging applications, teleconferencing facilities, or virtual meeting places. The combination of same-place different-time communication requires simple artefacts, such as notes and electronic message boards. Finally, different-time different-place communication could be based on letters, electronic mail, discussion forums, or voice mail. Because all of these scenarios involve people-people communication, they may all be labeled *social*.

The development and evaluation of CSCW and other social-based systems and applications introduced a two-fold challenge for usability professionals: 1) an individual user interacting with the system, and 2) a group or community interacting through the system (e.g., Stiemerling & Cremers 1998). Grudin (1994) pointed out many of the difficulties in evaluating groupware, noting that group activity does not lend itself to a typical usability laboratory situation because the work and interaction contexts are extremely hard to reproduce in the laboratory. Likewise, aspects such as trust, awareness of each other, negotiations and group dynamics, job definition structures, and work processes cannot be readily simulated. Grudin also emphasizes the longer-term aspects of group work as compared to individual work. Even the definition and analysis of group tasks on which to base the development of test scenarios and appropriate usability metrics is a huge challenge that has yet to be adequately met. According to some authors, analysis of group tasks could be based primarily on the mechanics of collaboration (Gutwin & Greenberg 2000a; Pinelle, et al. 2003), by which the authors meant the actions and interactions that group members perform to complete a task collaboratively. The underlying assumption is that some aspects of successful group work depend on social and organizational factors, but also on the extent of support for basic collaborative activities such as communication, coordination, assistance, mediation, and so forth. This assumption is featured explicitly in a paper by De-Araujo, Santoro, and Borges (2003), who proposed a groupware evaluation technique that includes four dimensions—namely, group context, system usability, level of collaboration, and cultural impact. Taken together, these views call for and invite the development of usability evaluation methods and metrics that would be appropriate for the unique aspects and challenges of groupware and social-based systems. Next, we discuss what actually happens in terms of developing and employing groupware and CSCW evaluation methods and metrics.

The selection of usability metrics and evaluation methods for groupware, CSCW, and social-based systems, have been discussed in the literature, albeit not extensively. Steves and Scholtz (1999), for example, outlined several possible evaluation metrics for CSCW applications, including communication patterns between the participating individuals, individual navigation patterns and use of functions, characteristics of workflow-related collaborations, and other measures of success. Extending the traditional usability inspection techniques, such as heuristic evaluations and cognitive walkthroughs, to the evaluation of collaborative systems was introduced by several researchers. Drury (2000) empirically compared the traditional heuristics to a set of heuristics extended to address workspace awareness, and showed that more usability problems were found with the extended set of heuristics. In an attempt to adapt heuristic evaluation methods to collaborative environments, Baker, Greenberg, and Gutwin (2002) examined evaluations of shared workspace systems and found that 40 to 60 percent of the problems were uncovered. This, they suggested, was indicative that methods similar to the evaluation of individual applications can be extended to collaborative environments. De Araujo, Santoro, and Borges (2003) suggested that usability evaluation techniques for single-user applications could also be adapted to collaboration applications.

In a comparison of the findings from empirical user testing and expert inspection methods for robot-welding groupware systems, Steves, Morse, Gutwin, and Greenberg (2001) found there was some overlap in the problems uncovered with the two approaches. These findings resemble those typically found and reported in usability evaluations of applications used by individuals working alone. Steves, et.al. concluded that each approach has its advantages and that the two are complementary. They did not, however, address the specific issues and challenges associated with the important communicative and awareness aspects of collaboration as pointed out, for example, by Steves and Scholtz (1999). In an attempt to do that, and using primarily performance metrics such as task-completion times, communication efficiency, individual preferences, perceived effort, and strategies used, Gutwin and Greenberg (2000b) compared two collaborative environments—one of them showing location and activity of others in the system (i.e., workspace awareness)—and found better performance with the system having enhanced workspace awareness. They concluded that awareness of other participants in the shared workspace increases system usability. In addition, Gutwin and Greenberg's study of a collaborative context shows that applying metrics similar to the evaluation of individual task performance can be extended to groupware evaluation.

As an interim summary of the review thus far, it seems that in addressing the unique challenges of evaluating the usability of groupware and CSCW, usability evaluation techniques for single-user applications were extended and adapted, in most cases, to groupware and collaboration applications. While the reviewed studies have shown that such an approach produces results, it is questionable whether we are tapping all aspects of the collaborative experience.

In contrast to applying the traditional single-user task performance techniques, Olson and his colleagues (Olson, et al. 1992; Olson, et al. 1995) examined collaborative systems such as virtual meetings and collaborative editing, and used several indirect measures of groupware usability. These included what they termed *product measures, process measures*, and *satisfaction measures*. Product or outcome measures assess the quality and time needed to reach the outcomes of the group work; process measures address patterns in behaviors or communications (based on observations and verbal protocols) and are indicative of the group process that took place in producing the outcomes. Finally, satisfaction measures focus primarily on individuals' satisfaction with the group work. While this work suggests approaching the unique challenges of groupware and CSCW usability in a different way from the evaluation of single-user usability, such an approach is not pervasive.

Most of the research reviewed in this section thus far has addressed environments that aim to support collaborative work consisting of structured tasks that groups of people need to complete effectively and efficiently. Recently, the pervasiveness of systems, applications, and services aimed at supporting a wide range of human social experiences not related to work or work environments have been increasing dramatically. Examples of such applications and services started with email and online discussion boards but evolved into chat rooms, instant messaging, weblogs (blogs), wikis, social network services such as Friendster, MySpace, Flikr, Buzznet, and TagWorld, social bookmarking (i.e., Del.ici.us) collaborative real time editing and writing, and massively-multiplayer online games (MMOGs) such as Scape-Runes. These families of social applications collectively referred to as *Web 2.0* or the *Social Web*, are very popular. While it is clear that the usability of these cannot be captured in terms of traditional task performance measures, the usability aspects that should be assessed in such applications and services are unclear. Because their main objective is to provide a social experience, they would seem to require quite different models of usability *success* than the ISO9241/11 concepts of effectiveness, efficiency, and user satisfaction. Likewise, the concept of *task performance* is rather meaningless in the context of, say, an MMOG where players continually face novel challenges as their skills improve in what seems a never-ending web of experiences. It is therefore highly questionable if we can still employ the same usability design and evaluation methods as in the traditional *one user, one computer* paradigm.

To date, there is little published work on the usability evaluation of social networks and services. One study using primarily ethnographic methods (Nardi, et al. 2004) focused on the use of blogs as a social activity between the authors and those who responded and commented on their blogs. In their conclusion, they commented on the ease-of-use issues of blogs, and on the trade-off between wanting/needing more functionality at the cost of ease-of-use. Most user comments concerned features such as the ability to collaborate, privacy, browsing and search capabilities, and the proper integration of various media. In these environments, the already fuzzy distinction between usefulness and usability becomes significantly fuzzier, and it is indeed unclear if the features noted by Nardi, et al. constitute new aspects of usability. Ethnography and other social psychology methods have been applied to the study of actual usage for over two decades, but it is uncertain if these approaches will become the primary evaluation methods for this new generation of social and collaborative systems and applications. At this point in time, we are clearly left with very little understanding of which usability evaluation methods would be appropriate, what usability metrics should be applied, and what the concept of usability means in these new virtual social worlds. The rules of the comparatively straightforward task-performance game are definitely *a-changing* fast. Performance in the traditional sense is obviously no longer sufficient, and whether it is a necessary ingredient in these environments remains to be seen.

The emergence of CSCW and social networks and services showed that usability is influenced by factors other than the cognitive or emotional aspects of the single user and technology. It allowed for strong contextual influences, particularly the social context. Applying social psychology paradigms and theories to HCI was manifested in the area of small-group work and collaboration. The diversity of skills in the composition of small groups is known to influence a group's collective performance. This can result in frustrations, miscommunications, and conflicts (McGrath 1984; Williams & O'Reilly 1998). One of the important implications for HCI in general, including CSCW and computer-mediated communication, is the issue of intragroup communication. The amount of communication needed, the structure of the communication, and other aspects of how the communication is managed is highly dependent on the structure and goals for group tasks (Leavitt 1951; Shaw 1964; Pelz & Andrews 1966; Galbraith 1977). Kraut (2003) emphasized the basic model accounting for group functioning—input-process-output model. This approach identifies input such as the personnel, tasks, and organizational tools and technologies. The outcomes of group work include their products, a definition of member needs, and the maintenance of the group. Group processes are the interaction patterns, strategies, roles, and other aspects. The work on group processes implies that the usability of CSCW can be influenced by the context of group processes.

One of the first attempts to applying a social psychology-oriented theory to HCI was by Bødker (1989, 1991) and the further development of the application of Russian activity theory to HCI (Nardi 1996a). According to Nardi, the context should be viewed as an integral part of the activity system. Activity theory is strongly related in these notions to other theoretical trends—distributed cognition and situated cognition—in exploring the impact of the social context on individuals and technology (Nardi 1996b). Distributed cognition (e.g., Hollan, Hutchins, and Kirsh 2000) emphasizes the distributed nature of cognition and assumes that knowledge is distributed between individuals and the artifacts they use. Situated cognition (e.g., Clancey 1997) assumes that the situation and the roles people play in a given situation are the important determining influences of behavior rather than only individual cognition. These theoretical approaches imply that when technology is viewed as artifacts used by people in given contexts, then the usability of technology is influenced by a variety of social aspects in that context and not only by the individual's perceptions, cognitions, and emotions. While recognizing the impact of the social context on usability reflects an evolution in our understanding of the usability concept, this, however, is not associated with an equivalent evolution in the way we evaluate usability by taking into consideration all aspects of the social context.

10.7 Concluding Remarks

We began with what may be a typical usability test episode, suggesting that the concept of usability is much more complex than the traditional ISO 9241-11 definition of task performance effectiveness, efficiency, and satisfaction. We have reviewed three major trends that characterize the evolution in the usability concept. The concept and practice of usability have first evolved with changes in technology, objectives of systems and applications, and the nature and characteristics of tasks. This major trend underlies the other two major trends in the evolution of usability—from the individual to the social collective, and from the cognitive, performance-based concern to a broader concern with individual experience that includes emotion and cognition.

While usability in the traditional task-related sense is still needed, our review suggests that its focus on the individual, on cognition, and on performance, no longer suffices when designing or evaluating usability. Furthermore, it is unclear just how far conventional usability metrics and measures can be applied—for example, to evaluation of group work, computer games, and the like. One major question that we have not addressed is the extent to which we can get away with just extending and adapting existing tools. Do we perhaps need a complete paradigm change to meet the new versatile demands instead? We do not know how to determine what methods will work and what metrics will yield the answers we need—for example, to assess usability in wearable technologies, biofeedback technologies, physically or mentally intrusive technologies, and storage applications such as fingerprints and digital photos. The inevitable blurring of the usability concept is perhaps a blessing in the sense that it opens the doors to more inclusive approaches to conceptualizing and measuring usability. This is the new research agenda in the usability domain.

Acknowledgment This work was partially supported by a Canadian National Science and Engineering Research Council (NSERC)/Cognos grant: IRCSA 234087–05. The helpful comments of two anonymous reviewers on an earlier draft of this chapter are gratefully acknowledged.

References

Allen, C. (1990). Definitions of groupware. *Applied Groupware*, 1, 1–2.

Bailey, J.E., & Pearson, S. W. (1983). Development of a tool for measuring and analyzing computer user satisfaction. *Management science*, 29 (5), 530–545.

Baker, K., Greenberg, S., & Gutwin, C. (2002). Empirical development of a heuristic evaluation methodology for shared workspace groupware. In *Proceedings of the International Conference on Computer Supported Cooperative Work*, New Orleans, Louisiana, pp. 96–105.

Baron-Cohen, S. (1999). *Mindblindness: an essay on autism and theory of the mind*. Boston, MA: MIT Press.

Behaviour & Information technology, (2006), 25 (2): Special issue on empirical studies of the user experience.

Bless, H., & Forgas, J.P. (1998). *The message within: the role of subjective experience in social cognition and behaviour*. Philadelphia psychology Press, Philadelphia, PA.

Blythe, M., Reid, J., Wright, P., & Geelhoed, E. (2006). Interdisciplinary criticism: analysing the experience of riot! A location-sensitive digital narrative. *Behaviour & Information Technology*, 25 (2), 127–140.

Bødker, S. (1989). A human activity approach to user interfaces. *Human Computer Interaction, 4* (3), 171–195.

Bødker, S. (1991). *Through the Interface: A human activity approach to user interface design*. Hillsdale, NJ: Lawrence Erlbaum.

Brothers, L. (1990). The social brain: a project for integrating primate behaviour and neurophysiology in a new domain. *Concepts in Neuroscience, 1*, 27–51.

Card, S.K., Moran, T.P., & Newell, A. (1980). Computer text-editing: An information-processing analysis of a routine cognitive skill. *Cognitive Psychology, 12*, 32–74.

Card, S.K., Moran, T.P., & Newell, A. (1983). *The psychology of human-computer interaction*. Hillsdale, NJ: Lawrence Erlbaum Associates.

Clancey, W. J. (1997). *Situated cognition: On human knowledge and computer representations*. Cambridge: Cambridge University Press.

Clore, G.L., Wyer, R.S., Jr., Dienes, B., Gasper, K., Gohm, C. & Isbell, L. (2001). Affective feelings as feedback: some cognitive consequences. In L.L. Martin & G.L. Clore (Eds), *Theories of mood and cognition: A user's guidebook* (pp. 27–62). Mahwah, NJ: Lawrence Erlbaum Associates.

Crawford, D. (1984). *The art of computer game design*, Osborne/McGraw-Hill, Berkeley, CA; reproduced on http://www.vancouver.wsu. Edu/fac/Peabody/game-book/coverpage.html

Csikszentmihalyi, M. (1991). *Flow: the psychology of optimal experience*. New York: Harper & Row.

Cupchik, G.C. (1993). Component and relational processing in aesthetics. *Poetics*, 22, 171–183.

Damasio, A. R. (2000). A second chance for emotion. In R. D. Lane & L. Nadel (Eds), *Cognitive Neuroscience of Emotions* (pp. 12–23). New York: Oxford University Press.

De Araujo, R.M., Santoro, F.M., & Borges, M.R.S. (2003). The CSCW lab ontology for groupware evaluation. In *Proceedings of the 8th International Conference on Computer Supported Cooperative Work in Design* (pp. 148–153).

Denning, P.J., & Dunham, R. (2003). The missing customer. *Communications of the ACM, 46*(3), 19–23.

DeSanctis, G., & Galuppe, B. (1987). A foundation for the study of group decision support systems. *Management Science, 33*(5), 589–609.

Donoghue, K. (2000). *Built for use: Driving profitability through the user experience*. McGraw Hill, New York.

Drury, J. (2000). Extending usability inspection techniques for collaborative systems. In *Proceedings of CHI2000* (pp. 81–82).

Ensor, R. (1990). How can we make groupware practical? A panel. In *Proceedings of the Conference on Human Factors in Computing Systems* (pp. 87–89). New York: ACM Press.

Ewusi-Menash, K. (1997). Critical issues in abandoned information systems development projects. *Communications of the ACM, 40* (9), 74–80.

Fernandes, G., Lindgaard, G., Dillon, R., & Wood, J. (2003). Judging the appeal of web sites. In *Proceedings 4ᵗʰ World Congress on the Management of Electronic Commerce*, McMaster University, Hamilton, ON, 15–17 January (on CD-ROM)

Fiedler, K. (2001). Affective states trigger processes of assimilation and accommodation. In L.L. Martin & G.L. Clore (Eds.), *Theories of mood and cognition: A user's guidebook* (pp. 85–98). Mahwah, NJ: Lawrence Erlbaum Associate.

Fitts, P. M. (1954). The information capacity of the human motor system in controlling the amplitude of movement. *Journal of Experimental Psychology, 47*, 381–391.

Forgas, J.P. (2001). The Affect Infusion Model (AIM): An integrative theory of mood effects on cognition and judgments. In L.L. Martin & G.L. Clore (Eds), *Theories of mood and cognition: A user's guidebook* (pp. 99–134). Mahwah, NJ: Lawrence Erlbaum Associates.

Galbraith, J. (1977). *Organization Design*. New York: Addison-Wesley Publishing.

Galitz, W.O. (1981). *Handbook of screen design format* (1ˢᵗ Edition, Q.E.D.) Wellesley, MA: Information Sciences

Galitz, W.O. (1993). *User-interface screen design*. Toronto: Wiley

Greif, I. (ed.) (1988). *Computer supported collaborative work: A book of readings*. San Mateo, CA: Morgan Kaufmann Publishers.

Grudin, J. (1994). Computer supported cooperative work: History and focus. *IEEE Computer*, 19–26.

Gutwin, C., & Greenberg, S. (2000a). The mechanics of collaboration: Developing low cost usability evaluation methods for shared workspaces. In *Proceedings 9th IEEE WETICE: Infrastructure for Collaborative Enterprises* (pp. 98–103).

Gutwin, C., & Greenberg, S. (2000b). The effect of workspace awareness support on the usability of real-time distributed groupware. *ACM Transactions on Computer-Human Interaction, 6* (3), 243–281.

Hassenzahl, M. (2004). The interplay of beauty, goodness, and usability in interactive products. *Human-Computer interaction, 19* (4), 319–349.

Hassenzahl, M,, Beu, A., & Burmeister, M. (2001). Engineering joy. *IEEE Software*, January/February, 70–76.

Heijden van der, H. (2003). Factors influencing the usage of websites: the case of a generic: portal in the Netherlands. *Information and Management, 40* (6), 541–549.

Helander, M.TG., & Tham, M.P. (2003). Hedonomics – affective human factors design. *Ergonomics, 46*, 2369–1272.

Hitzik, M.A. (1999). *Dealers of lightning: Xerox PARC and the dawn of the computer age* (pp. 194–201). New York: Harper Collins

Hollan, J., Hutchins, E., & Kirsh, D. (2000). Distributed cognition: Toward a new foundation for human-computer interaction research. *ACM Transactions on Computer-Human Interaction, 7* (2), 174–196.

Human-Computer Interaction (2004). Special Section: Beauty, goodness, and usability, *19* (4), 311–387.

Interacting with Computers (2004). Special Issue on Affective Computing, *16* (4), 683–768.

ISO (1997). ISO/DIS 9241–11. *Ergonomic requirements for office work with visual display terminals (VDTs): Guidance on usability.*

Jordan, P. (2000). *Designing pleasurable products*. New York: Taylor & Francis.

Kearnes, D.T., & Nadler, D.H. (1992). *Prophets in the dark: How Xerox reinvented itself and beat back toe Japanese*. Hammersmith, London: Harper Collins Publications.

Kraut, R.E. (2003). Applying social psychological theory to the problems of group work. In J.M. Carroll (Ed.), *HCI models, theories and frameworks: Towards a multidisciplinary science* (pp. 325–356). New York: Morgan Kaufmann Publishers.

Langer, S. (1967). *Mind: An essay on human feeling*, Vol. I. Baltimore: The Johns Hopkins Press.

Laurel, B. (1993). *Computers as theatre*. Reading, MA: Addison-Wesley.

Lavie, T., & Tractinsky, N. (2004). Assessing dimensions of perceived visual aesthetics of web sites. *International Journal of Human-Computer Studies, 6*, 269–298.

Leavitt, H. (1951). Some effects of certain communication patterns on group performance. *Journal of Abnormal and Social Psychology. 46*, 38–50.

Leiner, B.M., Cerf, V.G., Clak, D.D., Kahn, R.E., Kleinrock, L., Lynch, D.C., Postel, J., Roberts, L.G., & Wolff, S.S. (1997). The past and future history of the internet. *Communications of the ACM*, 40 (2), 102–108.

Lindgaard, G. (1994). *Usability testing and system evaluation: A guide for designing useful computer systems*. London: Chapman & Hall.

Lindgaard, G. (1995). Cementing human factors into product design: Moving beyond policies. In *Proceedings of* 15th *International Symposium on Human Factors in Telecommunications*, Melbourne (pp. 361–371).

Lindgaard, G. (2002). Deconstructing silos: The business value of usability in the 21st Century, invited keynote presentation. In *Proceedings of* 17th. *IFIP (International Federation for Information Processing) World Computer Congress* (pp. 3–20). Montreal, August 25–30.

Lindgaard, G., & Dudek, C. (2002). User satisfaction, aesthetics and usability: Beyond reductionism. In Hammond, T. Gross & J. Wesson (Eds), *Usability gaining a competitive edge*, *Proceedings IFIP 17th World Computer Congress* (pp. 231–246). Montreal, Canada.

Lindgaard, G., & Dudek, C. (2003). What is this evasive beast we call user satisfaction?. *Interacting with Computers, 15*(3), 429–452.

Lindgaard, G., Dillon, R. F., Trbovich, P, White, R., Fernandes, G., Lundahl, S., & Pinnamaneni, A. (2006a). User needs analysis and requirement engineering: Theory and practice. *Interacting with Computers, 18* (1), 47–70.

Lindgaard, G., Fernandes, G., Dudek, C., & Brown, J. (2006b). Attention web designers: You have 50 milliseconds to make a good first impression! *Behavior & Information Technology, 25*, 115–126.

Lindgaard, G., & Whitfield, T. W. A. (2004). Integrating aesthetics within an evolutionary and psychological framework. *Theoretical Issues in Ergonomic Science, 5* (1), 73–90.

Mahlke, S. (2006). Studying user experience with digital audio players. In: *Proceedings of ICEC2006, 5th International Conference on Entertainment Computing* (pp. 258–361), 20–22 September, Cambridge.

Martin, L.L., & Clore, G.L. (2001). *Theories of mood and cognition: A user's guidebook*. Mahwah, NJ: Lawrence Erlbaum Associates.

McGrath, J. (1984). *Groups: Interaction and performance*. Englewood Cliffs, NJ: Prentice Hall.

Meister, D. (1986). *Human factors testing and evaluation: Advances in human factors/ergonomics*. North-Holland: Elsevier science publishers.

Nardie, B. (1996a). *Context and consciousness: Activity theory and human computer interaction*. Cambridge, MA: MIT Press.

Nardi, B. A. (1996b). Studying context: A comparison of activity theory, situated action models and distributed cognition. In Nardi, B. (Ed.), *Context and consciousness: Activity theory and human-computer interaction* (pp. 69–102). Cambridge, MA: MIT Press.

Nardi, B., Schiano, D.J., & Gumbrecht, M. (2004). Blogging as a social activity or, would you let 900 million people read your diary? In *CHI Letters, 6* (3), 222–231.

Nass, C., & Reeves, B. (1996). *The media experience: How people treat computers*. London : Cambridge University Press.

Norman, D.A. (2004). *Emotional design: Why we love (or hate) everyday things*. New York: Basic Books.

Olson, J. S., Olson, G. M., & Meader, D. K. (1995). What mix of video and audio is useful for small groups doing remote real-time design work? In *Proceedings of the ACM Conference on Human Factors in Computing Systems* (CHI '95, Denver, CO, May 7–11) (pp. 362–368). New York: ACM Press

Olson, J. S., Olson, G. M., Storrøsten, M., & Carter, M. (1992). How a group-editor changes the character of a design meeting as well as its outcome. In Mantel, M. & Baecker, R., (Eds.), *Proceedings of the ACM Conference on Computer-Supported Cooperative Work (CSCW '92*, Toronto, Canada, Oct. 31–Nov. 4) (pp. 91–98). New York: ACM Press.

Parush, A., Nadir, R., & Shtub, A. (1998). Evaluating the layout of graphical user interface screens: Validation of a numerical, computerized model. *International Journal of Human Computer Interaction, 10* (4), 343–360.

Parush, A,, Shwartz, Y., Shtub, A., & Chandra, J. (2005). The impact of visual layout factors on performance in web pages: A cross-language study. *Human Factors, 47*(1), 141–157.

Pelz, D., & Andrews, F. (Eds.) (1966). *Scientists in organizations: Productive climates for research and development.* New York: Wiley.

Piaget, J. (1954). *The construction of reality in the child.* New York: Free Press

Picard, R.W. (1998). *Affective Computing.* Cambridge, MA: MIT Press

Pinelle, D., Gutwin, C., & Greenberg, S. (2003). Task analysis for groupware usability evaluation: Modeling shared workspace tasks with the mechanics of collaboration. *ACM Transactions on Computer-Human Interaction, 10*(4), 281–311.

Porteous, J. D. (1996). *Environmental aesthetics: ideas, politics, and planning.* London: Routledge.

Preece, J. (2000). *Online communities: Designing usability, supporting sociability.* Wiley & Sons.

Ramachandran, V. S., & Blakeslee, S. (1998). *Phantoms in the brain.* New York: William Morrow & Co.

Rose, F. (1989). *West of Eden: the end of innocence at Apple computer.* Ringwood, Australia: Penguin Books.

Russell, J. (1980). A circumplex model of affect. *Journal of Personality and Social Psychology, 37*, March, 1161–1178.

Schenkman, B. N., & Jönsson, F. U. (2000). Aesthetics and preferences of web pages. *Behaviour & Information Technology, 19*, 367–377.

Schiffman, H.R. (1976). *Sensation and perception: An integrated approach.* New York: John Wiley Sons.

Sen, D. (2005). *Aesthetics: definition and contribution to the field of human computer interaction.* Unpublished manuscript, Human Oriented Technology Lab (HOTLab), Carleton University, Ottawa, Canada.

Shaw, M. (1964). Communication networks. In L. Berkowitz (Ed.). *Advances in experimental social psychology.* (pp. 111–147). New York: Academic Press.

Steves, M.P., Morse, E., Gutwin, C., & Greenberg, S. (2001). A comparison of usage evaluation and inspection methods for assessing groupware usability. In *Proceedings of Group'01* (pp. 125–134). Sept. 30–Oct. 3, 2001. Boulder, CO: ACM Press.

Steves, M.P., & Scholtz, J. (1999). Modified field studies for CSCW systems. *SIGGROUP Bulletin, 20* (2), 36–39.

Stiemerling, O., & Cremers, A.B. (1998). The use of cooperation scenarios in the design and evaluation of a CSCW system. *IEEE Transactions on Software Engineering, 24* (12), 1171–1181.

Suchman, L.A. (1987). *Plans and situated actions: The problem of human computer communication.* New York: Cambridge University Press.

Sutcliffe, A. (2002). *User-centred requirements engineering: Theory and practice.* London: Springer Verlag.

Tractinsky, N., Katz, A., & Ikar, D. (2000). What is beautiful is usable. *Interacting with Computers, 13*, 127–145.

Tractinsky, N., & Zmiri, D. (2006). Exploring attributes of skins as potential antecedents of emotion in HCI. In P. Fishwick (Ed), *Aesthetic computing.* Cambridge. MA: MIT Press.

Van Dam, A. (1997). Post-(WIMP) user interfaces. *Communications of the ACM, 40*(2), 63–67.

Williams, K., & O'Reilly, C. (1998). Demography and diversity in organizations: A review of 40 years of research. *Research in Organizational Behaviour, 20*, 77–140.

Zajonc, R.B. (1980). Feeling and thinking: Preferences need no inferences. *American Psychologist, 35*(2), 151–175.

Zdralek, J. (2003). *White Space. "How much nothing should there be?".* Unpublished MA thesis, Carleton University, Ottawa, Canada.

Zwaga, H., & Easterby, R. (Eds.). (1984). *Information design: The design and evaluation of signs and printed material.* Mahwah, NJ: Lawrence Erlbaum Associates.

Part III
Quality in Value

Chapter 11
Usability and Users' Health Issues in Systems Development – Attitudes and Perspectives

Åsa Cajander[1], Inger Boivie[2] and Jan Gulliksen[1]

[1] Department of Information Technology, Uppsala University, Sweden,
e-mail: Jan.Gulliksen@hci.uu.se, asa.cajander@it.uu.se
[2] Guide Redina AB

Abstract Poor usability and hence a stressful work situation is still a severe problem in computer-supported work, despite efforts to increase the focus on these issues. Consequently, Sweden has a high level of sick rates, particularly in the civil service sector, and some problems relating to inadequate IT systems with poor usability. In this chapter, we aim at understanding attitudes about and practices for integrating usability and users' health issues in systems development. Quality in value—i.e. users' well-being, productivity, and user satisfaction—is shaped by attitudes and perspectives underpinning discourse in systems development. These attitudes and perspectives are embedded in the methods, models, and representations used in systems development, as well as in discourse and action. In our qualitative study, data was collected through semistructured interviews with 127 informants, and in a case study of an ongoing project in one organization. During analysis of data, we identified problems with attitudes and perspectives about users and their work, such as the strong focus on automation, efficiency, and surveillance of work, which shaped the development of new technology and ultimately shapes the work situation of the user. Furthermore, we identified that the work of civil servants was frequently discussed in terms of simple steps and procedures that can be predefined and automated in accordance with clearly defined rules and regulations. Finally, we suggest user-centered design and field studies to address the problems and to improve the understanding of the users' needs and work practices in development projects.

11.1 Introduction

Rapidly increasing use of computer systems in all sectors of work life has had a significant impact on efficiency and flexibility in organizations, as well as on the work situations of individual employees—often a positive effect, but sometimes also negative. Unfortunately, this development has had undesirable side effects in terms of health problems. Sweden provides an illustrative example, where 66 percent of the work force (3 million people) use computers regularly in their work (Statistics Sweden 2001). From 1989 to 1997, the proportion of computer users among office workers increased from 65 to 90 percent (Wigaeus Tornqvist, Eriksson & Bergqvist 2000). The civil service sector is no exception—on the contrary, much work in the civil services has been computerized and automated in recent years.

As computers are more and more used in working life, health concerns and reports of negative effects on users' health have also increased steadily. Symptoms are primarily eyestrain, repetitive strain injury (RSI), and stress-related complaints (Aarås, Horgen & Ro 2000; Åborg & Billing 2003). In the civil service sector, sick rates are consistently high—with more than 10 percent in some organizations and for some groups. Furthermore, nearly a quarter of all employed persons in Sweden have suffered some sort of disorder that they relate to their work during the past 12 months (Statistics Sweden 2005). This is a part of a general trend in Sweden, where sick rates and the costs of sick pay and rehabilitation have increased dramatically since the early 1990s.

The problems are caused by multiple, interrelated factors, some of which are job design, repetitive work, strenuous work postures, work organization, poor social support, and high pressure, as well as workplace design. Furthermore, inadequate IT systems with poor usability also contribute to the problems. In computer-supported work, development is largely technology-driven, and work organization and job design are to a large extent shaped by IT systems, because technology often comes before work practices (Clegg, et al. 1997; Eason 1997). Therefore, attitudes about, and practices for, integrating usability and occupational health issues in the IT systems development process are important for the resulting work situation and well-being of users. Considerable effort is spent on developing design methods emphasising the needs of users, including methods for user-cenetred design (Norman 1986; Greenbaum & Kyng 1991; Göransson 2004). However, their impact on system development has been quite limited. Health aspects are often marginalized or ignored, (Vicente 1999; Clegg, et al. 1997).

Most activities for addressing health aspects in computer-supported work are aimed at redressing problems that are already manifest—i.e., when physical or psychosocial problems have been reported. We believe that it is both important and fully feasible to address potential health problems during the development process. In this chapter, we describe empirical work on users' health and usability, with a focus on IT systems development, and discuss the impact of attitudes and perspectives of those involved in development projects. The starting point of our research is user-centered systems design/development (UCSD) of IT systems in the workplace, and in what ways UCSD can contribute to an improved work situation regarding health and usability issues (Gulliksen, et al. 2003). This chapter describes a study that is part of an ongoing action research project. The project focuses on relations between IT and health risk factors, primarily by exploring and improving processes for designing, developing, and implementing IT systems, and how issues regarding quality of interaction, usability, and work situation are integrated in these processes.

11.2 Background

11.2.1 Occupational Health Problems in Computer-Supported Work

In our research, we have mainly focused on computer-supported administrative work where the main health risk factors are (Bergqvist 1993, Punnett & Bergqvist 1997):

- Users are bound to use computers during a major part of their work hours. This means constrained, static work postures for long periods of time
- Computers control the work pace and task order, leaving users with little or no control over their work
- Users suffer from stress, caused by excessive workload, time pressure, and poorly designed IT systems. The mental workload tends to increase when new IT systems are introduced (Aronsson, Dallner & Åborg 1994), and the decision latitude is lower for extensive computer users than for others (Wigaeus Tornqvist, et al. 2000).

As described above, these risk factors cause a number of health problems, including RSI and stress related disorders

Cognitive work environment problems are particularly important in computer-supported work (Åborg, Sandblad, Gulliksen & Lif 2003). Cognitive work environment problems occur when properties and factors in work situations prevent users/workers from using their skills efficiently. Such obstacles may be an effect of poor work organization or poor social support from supervisors and/or colleagues. They may also be related to the design of IT systems—for instance, that the users' train of thought is constantly interrupted by obscure messages, or that the user must recall information that is no longer visible on the screen. Addressing such problems is important because they may lead to inefficient work procedures, poor performance, and low user acceptance, as well as somatic and mental health symptoms.

Landauer discusses the fact that the massive introduction of computer systems during the last three decades has not resulted in comparable productivity payoffs (Landauer 1995). He argues that this is mainly because artifacts are too difficult to use and provide little useful functionality. In addition, productivity is affected by the fact that many people go to work despite being in pain or feeling stressed. In a Swedish study of some 1,500 computer users, respondents were asked to estimate any productivity loss caused by musculoskeletal problems. Eight percent reported a productivity loss of 15 percent of their ordinary work performance over the last month (Hagberg, Wigaeus Tornqvist & Toomingas 2002). These figures correspond to a total loss of three million workdays per year for the entire Swedish work force.

11.3 Work and Stress-Related Disorders

The Karasek Theorell model, describing relations between stress-related complaints and demand, support, and control (Karasek & Theorell 1990) is now the most widely used model for analyzing psychosocial work environment factors and their relationship to occupational health problems. This model suggests that the combination of perceived demands and perceived control at work is a determining factor for stress. High job strain—i.e., high demands in combination with low decision latitude, is associated with the highest risks for health problems. Control, in this respect, consists of two major components: the degree of personal control/decision latitude in work situations, and the degree of control over the level of competence used.

Experience shows that when new IT systems are introduced in the work place, users often feel that demands on their performance increase. Karasek Theorell's model shows that this is not a problem provided that the control and support factors are within acceptable limits. Research shows, however, that subjective control and support factors often decrease when new systems are introduced (Åborg 2001).

11.4 Usability and Occupational Health Problems

We use the term usability as defined in the ISO 9241 standards on software ergonomics for office work with visual display terminals (VDTs): Part 11, Guidance on Usability.

> "Usability is the extent to which a product can be used by specified users to achieve specified goals with effectiveness, efficiency, and satisfaction in a specified context of use" (ISO 9241-11 1998).

Although ISO 9241-11 does not explicitly cover occupational health issues, it provides a clear connection between the satisfaction aspect of usability and health problems in computer-supported work. According to ISO 9241-11, satisfaction measures can be obtained from "... rate of absenteeism,... or from health problem reports...." (ISO 9241-11 1998)

ISO 9241-10 (1996) specifies a number of principles for dialog design. These principles do not explicitly address occupational health in broad terms, such as mental and physical variation, social support, and computer dependency. Suitability for task requires, for instance, that no irrelevant information be displayed and that the format of output and input should be appropriate for the task. These guidelines address task suitability on a detailed level, but fail to take into account whether or not the task as a whole is designed to reduce the risks of occupational health problems.

Hence, addressing usability in IT systems development may potentially contribute positively to the reduction of effects on users' well-being. However, Clegg, et al. (1997) report that a majority of projects address usability but not occupational health matters. This was confirmed in one of our studies that indicated that the usability concept does not provide sufficient support for addressing users' health concerns in systems development (Boivie, Åborg, Persson & Löfberg 2003).

11.5 Systems Development and User-Centered Systems Design

In system development, technology often comes before work practices, and consequently emerging work practices and situations are shaped by technology or IT systems (Clegg, et al. 1997; Eason 1997). Hence, the systems development process has great impact on workers/users, changing the nature of their jobs and their everyday work situation (Sandblad, et al. 2003). In our experience, successful system development is characterized by certain aspects, as listed below, some of which are confirmed by the Chaos Report (Standish Group 1995 & 1998):

- User involvement in all project phases
- Focus on usability throughout the project
- Clear directives and a consensus on the project's objectives
- Small projects or stepwise development
- A well-planned deployment process (installation of system, introduction of users to system, training, support, etc.)

User-centered design (UCD) (Norman 1986; Greenbaum & Kyng 1991; ISO 13407 1999) and user-centered systems design (UCSD) (Gulliksen, et al. 2003) provide approaches and methods for addressing usability and users' needs in IT systems development. These approaches and methods emphasize the necessity of involving users, addressing usability, and understanding users' needs and work practices. For instance, they suggest studying users in work situations to understand the activity-oriented view of work (Sachs 1995), reflecting what people really do in their work to meet organizational and individual goals. Other user-centered methods involve joining together with users in participatory design sessions, using lo-fi mock-ups and prototypes as communication tools.

We believe that user-centered methods and approaches open up the way to addressing users' health issues. Understanding and designing for work practices must surely result in an IT system that is well-adapted to the users' work situation and provides proper support for their tasks, and thus is less likely to cause frustration, RSI, and cognitive work environment problems. However, involving users and usability expertise is probably not sufficient. Occupational health experts must also be involved, which requires communication tools and representations that can capture health issues and risk factors (Boivie, Blomkvist, Persson & Åborg 2003).

For authors that require more information on how to apply UCSD according to our approach, we recommend studying the key principles for UCSD (Gulliksen, et al. 2003) and details on the usability design process for practically conducting the work we point towards (Göransson, Gulliksen & Boivie 2003).

11.6 Studies

11.6.1 Background

The studies described in this chapter are part of an ongoing action research project involving six public authorities focusing on improving their computerized work environment. The project aims at improving the longterm impact on users' health through more efficient and effective IT use. Each authority involved has one sub-project, and these projects are in different phases. This chapter describes the results of the project after approximately 1½ years.

11.6.2 Organizations

The six authorities included in the study comprise a wide set of services provided to customers. These services include student loans and various student allowances, matters concerning talking books and Braille, geographic information (maps, satellite pictures, etc), immigration, services in meteorology, and services related to starting and running a business enterprise. The authorities have all faced major changes in the past and will face significant changes in the future—for instance, e-government and 24/7 availability. There have been major reorganizations driven by both external and internal factors. One authority, in particular, is subject to large variations regarding the demands for their services, owing to events in the world at large. Another authority is facing privatization of some services it offers to the general public. These changes affect the organizations at large, as well as the individual employees in their role and work. There is a certain amount of anxiety among employees in virtually all the organizations, owing to personnel cuts and job insecurity.

The organizations vary in size, from small (less than 100 employees) to fairly large (more than 3000 employees). In one of the authorities, 10 percent of the staff is visually impaired to various degrees. They use assistive technologies in their work, such as screen readers. Employees in these organizations range from specialists with academic degrees in areas such as law, hydrology, or sociology, to administrators with no academic degrees. All the organizations have a mix of newly employed staff and employees who have worked in the organization for some period of time—up to 20 or 30 years, in some cases.

Four of the organizations are distributed across the country, with offices in various places in Sweden, while two have one main office only. All the authorities have been relocated to towns outside the Stockholm area (the capital of Sweden) as a result of government programs for regional development.

All the authorities are highly computerized and automated. For example, IT is used for case handling, for compiling and providing information, and for providing services to customers. This means that work is sedentary to a large extent, where the employees spend a large proportion of their work hours sitting in front of computers.

In some authorities, virtually all work has been computerized. In two of the authorities, some work tasks are highly mobile, and mobile technologies are developed and used. Risk factors regarding occupational health problems include high pressure regarding productivity, sedentary work, low control over one's work situation, and conflicts with customers.

The different services provided by these six organizations place different demands on employees and their communication with customers (or citizens). Some of the organizations process cases that are highly sensitive, where customers may be frustrated, desperate, or otherwise negatively affected by the situation, and where threats and even violence occur once in a while. Other organizations provide services that are less likely to produce strong emotions. However, communication between customers and authorities is never unproblematic, and there is always a certain number of frustrated or upset customers that employees in all these organizations have to deal with—for instance, conflicts about land use, or problems with repayment of student loans.

IT development is primarily driven by external factors—for instance, new legislation—and controlled by deadlines (new legislation coming into effect on particular dates). IT development, operation and maintenance is organized in different ways. Four of the organizations have inhouse IT development departments, responsible for developing applications and for the operation and maintenance of existing applications and infrastructure. These departments have outsourced some operation and maintenance functions, as well as certain help desk functions. They also hire external consultants as resources in their development projects. One of these organizations is special because a large number of their *ordinary* staff work with technical issues that are closely related to IT development, such as writing scripts and database queries. The remaining authorities have outsourced the main part of their IT development and/or use standard products for tasks such as case handling and production. One of the latter is currently rebuilding an inhouse IT development organization.

The studies focus primarily on the work situation of the civil servants, (i.e., white-collar workers) in these organizations who provide services to customers.

11.6.3 Qualitative Approach

We have used a qualitative approach in our research study because the aim is to gain a deeper understanding of attitudes towards and practices for usability—i.e., users' health issues, IT development, and user involvement. Our role as researchers has been that of compiling, interpreting, and analyzing data, as well as that of participating in projects implementing and evaluating actions suggested in the initial studies.

Positivist research is based on the criterion of replication, which means that if the same or other scientists repeat the research process, they should come to the same conclusions. However, this criterion is not relevant in qualitative research, because both the participants and the researcher changed during the project and it is not likely that results would be replicated. Instead, qualitative research should be measured by other quality criteria, and in this study we try to conduct research according to the seven quality criteria and principles established by Klein and Myers for interpretive qualitative research (Klein and Myers 1999). These criteria include

1. The Fundamental Principle of the Hermeneutic Circle
2. The Principle of Contextualization
3. The Principle of Interaction between the Researchers and the Subjects
4. The Principle of Abstraction and Generalization
5. The Principle of Dialogical Reasoning
6. The Principle of Multiple Interpretations
7. The Principle of Suspicion

Moreover, we try to adhere to the quality criteria described by Lange, Baungaard, et al. (2004): transparency, consistency and validity. Transparency means that persons who have not been involved in the project should be able to follow the process through descriptions and illustrations. Consistency implies that the researcher must be able to explain why a specific research method is used to understand a specific problem. Finally, researchers must apply some criteria of validity and address the question: "Am I doing good work?" (Lauge, Baungaard, et al. 2004)

Qualitative, interpretive research based on case studies leads to contextual, in-depth knowledge, and should not be generalized. However, the organizations and the findings are not unique or unusual, and therefore we hope that the reader will find our research applicable in other settings.

Data was collected in semi-structured interviews, and in a case study, as described below. After the interview studies, most authorities started subsequent projects for implementing and evaluating some of the measures suggested in the initial study. Some authorities decided not to continue with an implementation project owing to various factors (e.g. major reorganizations).

11.6.4 Interview Studies

Semi-structured interviews with key informants were conducted, and the data was collected and analyzed separately in each organization. The results were compiled into one report for each authority and reported back to the stakeholders to ensure objectivity and to get feedback on the results. In total, six different researchers interviewed 127 key informants. The objective of each study was to identify problems, obstacles, and strengths in these organizations in regard to the following issues.

General Issues

• What factors and changes control organizational development?
• How do these changes affect the civil servants and their work?

Occupational Health Problems

- How are occupational health problems addressed in the organization and who is responsible?
- What types of measures are introduced to eliminate or reduce risk factors?
- In what ways are occupational health issues and risk factors addressed in the design, development, and implementation of new IT systems?

Design, development, and implementation of new IT systems

- What factors control IT development?
- In what ways are usability issues addressed in the IT development process?
- Who is responsible for usability in the development process?
- Are users involved in the IT development process, and how?
- How are new IT systems (or modifications to existing systems) introduced in the organization?

The interviews were based on interview guides. We used slightly different interview guides in different organizations. However, the interview guides were, in essence, variations on the same themes. They all covered the questions listed above and some additional questions about the role and background of the informant, as well as their own responsibility with regard to usability and occupational health issues. Moreover, the questions were adapted in accordance with the organizational role of each informant. Participants spanned all hierarchic levels and the informants were identified by the different organizations themselves. The roles of the informants include, for instance:

- Management—people working on strategic levels with business goals (HR people)
- Civil servants, clerks, administrators
- System owners, system administrators, system coordinators
- Help desk people
- Project managers, usability specialists, IT architects
- Union representatives

Each interview lasted for about one hour and was conducted onsite, except for a few complementing interviews over the phone. Informants were promised anonymity, but in some cases the informant had such a role that it would be possible for someone knowing the organization to trace the source of certain information. Most interviews were conducted by one researcher interviewing one person, as in Figure 11.1. In some cases, two researchers were present, and in a few interviews, two persons were interviewed at the same time. We took notes on paper, and when two researchers conducted interviews, one of the researchers documented them directly on a laptop. A few interviews were transcribed and, in some cases, notes were transcribed. About half of the interviews were taped to provide for citations or checking results against interviews and as a reference and justification for the reports giving feedback to the organizations. Data from different interviews were compiled and analyzed by two or three researchers per organization.

Fig. 11.1 Most interviews were conducted by one researcher interviewing one person

11.6.5 Case Study

Data was also collected in a case study of an ongoing implementation and evaluation project in one organization. This project comprised the second and third phases of the action research cycle—i.e., the action and evaluation phases. We worked together with people within the organization, helping them identify actions and measures to address problems identified in the first phase (the interview study). We also followed the organization during the action phase when measures were implemented, providing support and observing the outcome. Finally, we evaluated the outcome of the measures and provided feedback to the organization.

Data was collected throughout these phases, primarily by means of participatory observations and interviews with key informants. We followed the organization for well over a year by participating in various activities, such as project meetings, office meetings, and various work meetings. We participated actively in the activities (being members of the project group) but also observed certain aspects of the interaction and communication in activities. We mainly focused on issues regarding attitudes toward users (the civil servants), user participation in IT development, and the factors controlling the IT development at large in this organization.

We have also taken part in an extensive program for communicating knowledge about occupational health issues in computer-supported work, usability, IT development, and user participation throughout the entire organization. In these sessions, we have taken notes of discussions about these issues.

Results from the case study, as well as from the interview study, were analyzed using mind maps by two of the researchers (see Figure 11.2).

The mind maps were organized according to some of the predefined categories found in the interview guides, but there were also new categories added as data was analyzed. Pieces of paper were cut from the different reports made to the

Fig. 11.2 Mind maps were used to analyze data

organizations and from our research notes to illustrate and illuminate categories. These pieces of paper were joined together and placed under different categories.

11.7 Results

This section describes our findings regarding attitudes about, and practices for, integrating usability and occupational health matters in systems development processes. We illustrate the results with quotes from the interviews.

11.7.1 Perspective of Users and their Work

The perspective or view of the users and their work was not explicitly brought up in the interviews, but certain ideas and aspects recurred implicitly and formed a kind of underlying framework, within which the users and their work were discussed. These include a focus on the customers (citizens) and their needs, and an equally strong focus on efficiency and automation coupled with the surveillance and control of the civil servants. There is also an underlying assumption that the civil servants' work is quite trivial. These underlying assumptions about the civil servants and their work are reflected in the IT development process and the process of implementing new technology.

11.7.2 Focus on Customer, Efficiency, and Automation

Customer satisfaction, efficiency, and a high degree of automation are the main goals in the organizations, and these factors drive the IT development to a high extent. The work situation of the civil servants has low priority, and is not described in the visions of future organization–nor are implications for the well-being and health of the civil servants explicitly considered.

Customer satisfaction, with efficiency and e-services, is important in the authorities, and managers as well as civil servants stress these goals in the interviews. The informants describe that e-services must be *right for the customer*, and usability is addressed in the design and development of these services, where the customer is the *end-user*.

The focus on efficiency is reflected in IT systems. For example, when working with telephone services, the civil servant automatically receives a new call 5–10 seconds after a phone call has been finished. This may increase efficiency, but is perceived as one of the most stressful features of the work situation created through IT. The civil servants in our interviews also pointed to the focus on production in quantitative terms, and the reality that there is little focus on the quality of their work. Management measures work performance in terms of the number of cases being processed and quality aspects are ignored: "You look at the pile of paper, and from the size you can tell if you have done a good job or not." In several authorities, the focus on efficiency has led to an increased workload for the civil servants: "It is very hard for them, and there is much overtime."

Furthermore, increased automation of case processing has top priority, and all of the authorities have implemented electronic case processing at least to some extent. Visions about the future are based on the idea that citizens (customers) fill out and send forms and applications electronically, and the main part of the case processing will be done automatically with computers *making* the decisions. The role of the civil servant will be to take care of complicated cases and to *support* the computer when it fails to process a case due to incomplete or incorrect information. Several informants pointed out that there is a high risk for *deskilling* and routinization of the civil servants' work, which is in direct contradiction to the goal of creating challenging, healthy, and satisfactory work for them.

11.7.3 Focus on Surveillance and Control

In these organizations, IT systems are often used for surveillance and control. Detailed supervision of work and work performance is made possible by information technology and managers supervise the case handling process and work performance of individual employees through the IT system. In some cases, surveillance of the individual employee is directly connected to their salary. Some informants saw performance statistics as positive in that they helped improve productivity and created an element of positive competition. Some informants, however, found it stressful that computers were used to monitor work and their individual performance. They felt that the focus on surveillance implied that management "mistrust that we can take responsibility for our work." Moreover, managers are described as being too focused on statistics and performance measurements: "There's lots of statistics at all meetings."

11.7.4 Case Handling is Regarded as Trivial

Our studies show that case handling work is regarded as trivial and simple by many informants in these organizations who are not directly involved in case handling, e.g., management and people in the IT departments. Some of the case handlers described the lack of understanding in this way: "This work is much more complex than anyone seems to believe," and another informant said "You must show great respect for our daily job, it is the center."

For example, some IT professionals in these organizations claimed that they had a good picture of case handling and of the core business in general, despite the fact that they had little or no experience and knowledge about the real work situation of the civil servants—nor had they seen the IT systems being used in real life. Not even the usability experts had studied the context of use and the work situation of the users.

Problems in the IT system indicated that the understanding of case handling work was limited to an information flow perspective. The systems support the *flow* of one single case from entering the system until completion—i.e., the idea that you work with one case at a time until it is finished. The complex, flexible, and situated nature of case handling work is not supported. For example, some systems did not support opening two cases simultaneously, which is necessary when the civil servant works in parallel with handling cases and answering phone calls.

11.7.5 Development of IT Systems Based on Technology and Process Descriptions

In these organizations, the design and development of IT systems are based on abstract information flow models such as the case handling process, or use cases describing interaction as information flow and processing. The work situation of the users—i.e., their situated work practices and problem solving—is not taken into account, and as described above, not fully known. This results in IT systems that do not support the situated nature of work, which is illustrated by this comment: "This is not possible to work with, this is useless!"

Moreover, this perspective may lead to inflexible and rigid IT systems that shape and confine the work situation: "The new computer system forces you to do things in a specific way. Previously we had different alternatives." The interviews indicated that there are several problems with the IT system: for example, too many windows when working with a specific task, the lack of integration of information between different systems, the number of clicks required for completing a simple task, and workarounds required to solve other tasks. One example of poor fit between the IT system and work was a new mail system that one informant described in the following manner: "If it takes half a minute to answer the email, it takes three minutes to register it in the computer system."

Some of the IT professionals in our interviews were aware that the basic design and structures of the IT systems were inadequate. They described improving the IT systems as: "We put lipstick on the corpse," but they often ascribe the problems to poor requirements analysis and inadequate descriptions of work in the models. Their solution to the problem of poor fit between systems and work was often to further detail and analyze work in the requirements phase, but using the same methods and representations.

Some civil servants felt that new IT system had negative effects in regards to stress, comfort, and work situation: "We have had an OK situation here, until a few years ago when we introduced two new computer systems." In some cases, problems with the IT systems had direct negative effects on the organization. For example, one organization had to close their reception from time to time because one of their IT systems went down, leading to frustration and stress.

In one authority, a system development project with a focus on usability and the users' work situation and tasks was often referred to as a good example. In this project, the project manager had great interest in usability and user-centered design. However, this project met with strong resistance from the IT department in test routines and design methods. The informants described that it was difficult "to force through a new way of thinking about tests, about how to design windows, and to test that they are usable. They just continue the way they always have, just as usual."

11.7.6 Training – Focus on Technology not Work Situation

When new IT systems are introduced, the training often focuses on various features in the interface—e.g., information fields or search engine features. The training seldom introduces and explains new work practices and routines, leaving it to the users/workers to identify new work practices on their own. For example, informants in one organization described that the trainers had excellent computer skills and knew the new system well, but they did not know how it was going to be used in the organization. However, informants in another organization were pleased with the training they received in that it had focused on new work practices, and it had truly helped them create new routines.

Moreover, many informants claimed that they are not given enough time to practice during training sessions, and that they have to find that time in their daily work after the training. This results in a stressful work situation because managers still focus on performance—e.g., the number of cases being processed—in the new IT system. In one case, the system development project had such a short deadline that no formal training was provided and the civil servants had to learn the new system while working with it. This lack of training and time to practice was heavily criticized.

Furthermore, systems development projects often a have a *technical* ending, and the work situation of the users emerges without anyone reflecting on what the work situation will be like. As a consequence, some informants felt that they lose control over their work and work situation, which is stressful and strenuous.

11.7.7 IT Department and Users – Two Separate Worlds

There is little contact and communication between IT departments and users. The lack of mutual encouragement among users and developers leads to alienation between the groups and little understanding of the needs of the other group.

11.7.8 Business Development and Systems Development

Informants had very different opinions about business development and IT development, and there were large individual differences in all of the organizations. Most of the IT people, however, maintained that organizational goals control the IT development, but this view was not shared by people in other parts of the organizations. Instead, they claimed that IT development determines and shapes organizational development and job design. Some of these informants also pointed to external factors that impact business development, but said that the outcome in terms of IT systems and their design is decided by the IT development department. Moreover, the civil servants in one authority said that the IT people seem more interested in developing new functionality than in maintaining and improving the existing systems. There is a clear tension between the needs of the civil servants and the interests of the IT people: "Well, there are different wills."

In one of the authorities, IT development did not seem connected to business development at all. One informant argued that development projects simply build systems in accordance with existing work practices, without any improvements or changes. The new system simply *freezes* existing work practices, preserving them as is.

11.7.9 User Participation

In systems development, user representatives often participate over an extended period of time and on a part-time or full-time basis. Often the same people participate in different development projects, and many of them have not worked with case handling in years. Hence, civil servants become *IT workers* to the extent that this is considered a career path in the organizations, even though they have little power in the projects. Furthermore, the user representatives are often considered more skilled and knowledgeable in case handling than the average case administrator, and are often *super users* of specific systems. It seems that it is a combination of personal interest, previous experience,e and competence that determines who participates in the development projects.

In most of the organizations, involving users in development projects is optional and decided by the project manager. Because systems development projects often have a tight time schedule, the project manager often chooses to focus exclusively on the essential functionality as specified by requirements specifications. Consequently, there is no time to involve users. When involving users, the project managers prefer people with previous experience from systems development.

The role of the users and their contribution to the projects vary to a large degree, both between the organizations, but also between different projects within the same organization. However, it seems that the most common task is to test functionality and to review specifications, requirements, and system descriptions. Users are seldom involved in prototyping activities or in the system design. Some of the user representatives we interviewed said that their role in the projects was unclear and confusing. They sometimes felt frustrated and uncertain about what they were supposed to do. On the other hand, some of them saw an opportunity to define their own role and areas of responsibility, seeing that this makes it possible to work with the parts that interest them, and where their contribution matters the most.

Another problem described by the user representatives was that the language used in system development is different from their own. They cannot use their every day vocabulary when participating in projects: "You speak different languages." This makes it difficult for them to understand and to contribute in discussions in the projects: "You are silent. You don't understand anything that they say." The user representatives said that these language barriers make it difficult to talk to programmers, and that it takes years to learn the programmers' vocabulary and way of speaking.

Moreover, some of the user representatives felt that they are "on lowest rank" in the development projects, and that they have little possibility and power to make changes.

11.7.10 Lack of Communication and Contact

Generally, the people in IT departments said that they cooperate closely with users and other representatives from the organizations. However, people in the rest of the organization did not share this view. Our study indicates that there is often a communication gap. For example, the civil servants did not always know where the new systems come from, or why new IT systems were introduced. The civil servants generally did not have a clear picture of where to send suggestions for improvements to their IT systems. Moreover, if they sent suggestions, they seldom received any feedback, and they were not informed about how the different suggestions were prioritized. The IT people we interviewed were not happy about the situation, because they felt that they never received any positive feedback from the users. They were only informed when the systems did not work properly.

Generally, people working in the core business do not consider themselves sufficiently involved in systems development: "People from the core business have not taken part in any requirements work. If they would have asked us in a better way then we would have been able to tell them what we really need."

However, in the studies we also saw examples of good communication and contact—for instance, where systems developers had a close and informal relation to users, because they were located in the same office. Some of the union representatives we interviewed claimed that they take an active part in systems development.

11.7.11 Perspective on Usability

Finally, our studies indicate that there were problems with the attitudes towards usability and usability expertise in these organizations.

There are few usability experts in these organizations and they are primarily involved in development projects that build external web applications customers, such as e-services. The usability experts we talked to said that they seldom had enough time in the projects to do all the activities needed to produce a usable system. Several of the informants believed that this was due to a lack of understanding of what usability experts do: "No one really understands what I do."

11.7.12 Usability in Systems Development

Generally, there was little usability focus in systems development in these organizations. Usability was seldom an integral part in the requirements process with few usability activities, and there were few usability goals in requirements specifications. As a result, the IT departments did not see the need to include usability expertise when staffing development projects. Usability activities were often limited to test activities towards the end of the development process when there are limited possibilities to make any significant changes. One informant illustrated the situation in the following way: "usability is seen as a shell that you put on, outside the system," and another informant said "You already have finished and ready systems, and then you try to design a little on the surface of them." However, one organization had specified a usability plug for the *rational unified process*, and this was believed to contribute to usability to a high degree.

Furthermore, several informants from the IT departments felt that usability is a vague and unclear concept. Other participants in the systems development projects did not fully understand what usability is, and in what way it will improve the IT systems. In one organization, people from the IT department considered usability not applicable to the particular technical platform that was used.

In one authority, informants claimed that usability receives low priority owing to a previous system development project that was a complete failure. Subsequent projects have focused on functionality and technical problems: "No one dared to have any detailed and extensive requirements after that."

11.8 Discussion

Quality in value—i.e., users' wellbeing, productivity, and user satisfaction —is related to attitudes and perspectives underpinning discourse about users and their work in the development process (as well as in the organization at large). These attitudes and perspectives are embodied in methods, models, and representations used for analyzing and describing users' needs and their work. The models and representations are used as input in the development process, determining design, contents, and structure of the IT systems.

In the workplace, one essential aspect of usability is the fit between organizational goals and work practices on one hand, and IT systems on the other hand. IT systems should "... fit into the fabrics of everyday life" (Beyer & Holtzblatt 1998, p. 1). It is, therefore, essential to understand users' current work practices, and how these practices may be affected and improved by new technology. A fragmentary understanding of the work situation and work practices may result in IT systems that are poorly adapted to the users' needs, causing frustration and strain in the work situation. Long-term frustration and strain, in combination with low control and poor social support, is a risk factor for stress related disorders, affecting users' wellbeing, productivity, and satisfaction.

Systems development is often based on an engineering-oriented view of problem-solving and knowledge. This view is closely related to the systems theoretical perspective, which places emphasis on the technical and formal aspects of the relationship between man and machine (Nurminen 1987; Kammersgaard 1990). In an engineering-oriented perspective, users (people) are primarily defined by their relation to a technical system. Their tasks, goals, and needs are described as sets of predefined steps and rules defining the interaction between users and systems (Boivie 2005). The methods, models, and representations used in many systems development processes reflect this view of people and work—e.g., use case models, process models, and data flow models.

However, work is also a highly complex social process—a joint activity based on communication and interaction between people. Work is also purposeful—driven by goals or intentions. Moreover, work is specific to the context and shaped by circumstances of the situation as it evolves—i.e., it is situated and contextual. This means that work practices cannot be predefined; they emerge in the evolving situation and are constantly generated, shaped, and adapted to it (Suchman 1987). Human beings are adaptive, flexible, and innovative. In short, work cannot be described solely by rules or predefined sets of operations and steps (Winograd & Flores 1986; Greenbaum & Kyng 1991).

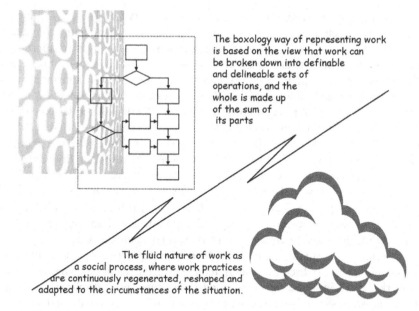

The boxology way of representing work is based on the view that work can be broken down into definable and delineable sets of operations, and the whole is made up of the sum of its parts

The fluid nature of work as a social process, where work practices are continuously regenerated, reshaped and adapted to the circumstances of the situation.

Fig. 11.3 The engineering-oriented way of thinking and the messy nature of work

Thus, there is a tension and conflict between an engineering-oriented way of thinking about and representing users' work and work practices in well-defined models, and the *messy* nature of those work practices (Figure 11.3). An engineering-oriented way of thinking favors representations that focus on the formal and intellectual aspects of work (Nygaard 1986; Greenbaum 1990; Harris & Henderson 1999). They do not accommodate users' practical knowledge about their work, their understanding about "what-to-do," or "how-to" in a specific situation (Schön 1995). As a consequence, there is a tension between how users experience and understand their everyday work situation and representations (models) that are used in systems development. This tension or conflict has two effects. First, it makes it difficult for users to participate in design processes because they do not recognize their work practices in these representations. Secondly, representations can only provide a fragmentary understanding of users' work, undermining the fit between the system under development and the users' work practices.

Discussions about relations between attitudes and perspectives in systems development processes, and quality in value of the emerging system and ultimately emerging work situation are not new. It is one principle underpinning the Scandinavian school (Greenbaum & Kyng 1991) and user-centered systems design (UCSD), and has been discussed extensively for at least 20 years. The problem is that little seems to have happened in real-life systems development. Users are still kept at arms' length in development, little attention is paid to their work situation, and health issues and usability issues *get lost* (Boivie, et al. 2003).

This is particularly evident in our case study, where a strong focus on automation, efficiency, and legal security control and shape the development of new technology, and ultimately the tasks and work practices of the civil servants. These tasks emerge because of new technology—they are simply what is left over when the computers have done their part. Little attention is being paid to such issues as the routinization and repetitiveness of work tasks, control over work situation, control over pace and order of tasks, social support, and deskilling, all of which are well-known risk factors for occupational health complaints. Nevertheless, there is an awareness in the separate IT development projects about these issues. We have interviewed participants in one project, and they pointed to the risk that the system they were building would create work situations where the civil servants become *process operators* instead of specialized and skilled knowledge workers. The responsibility of making decisions about automation versus manual processing of the various steps in the case handling process rests with the project—primarily with the user representatives, the procurer, and the project manager. They all expressed frustration with having to make these decisions because efficiency and a high degree of automation was top priority, while the users' future work situation was not addressed at all.

Furthermore, the studies confirm that there is a gap between users' work and their situation, and the discourse underpinning IT development. The views of users and work expressed in the interviews, and in the case study, display some characteristics of the system's theoretical perspective of human activity and work as discussed earlier. Not least important is the view that the civil servants' works is trivial. Their work was frequently discussed in terms of simple steps and operations that may be predefined and automated in accordance with clearly defined rules and regulations. It was seen as a problem that civil servants have to make decisions in complex cases where the computer fails to generate a decision and where *human* judgement is required. These human decisions were seen as subjective and open to interpretation—which is the very reason that the computer fails to make them in the first place—and the civil servants making the decisions were seen as incompetent.

Another result of the perspective on the civil servants and their work is that the available usability experts were primarily involved in external IT development, such as the development of e-services to be used by the general public. Usability was not considered equally important for the internal users—i.e., the civil servants. There seemed to be an underlying assumption that they simply have to use what is installed on their computers, and that usability in this context is an unnecessary *luxury* connected to their satisfaction alone, having little to do with their productivity and well-being.

User-centered design has been promoted as a way of creating IT systems that are better adapted to the users' needs and work practices. User involvement, however, is not sufficient to address the problems, as illustrated in our studies. These organizations all have development processes where users (or other representatives from the organization) are involved. They are typically involved over extended periods of time, however, on a full-time or part-time basis, and become *IT workers* of a kind, albeit with little power in the projects. User involvement must be complemented with a focus on usability and the work situation of users. Focus on information processing and information flow in the systems theoretical perspective must be complemented with other perspectives and methods that focus on and capture the situated and contingent nature of work and work practices—for instance, field studies and contextual interviews (Beyer & Holzblatt 1998).

We have introduced the idea of field studies in one organization in our case study. However, field studies are often quite extensive and time-consuming, making them impractical in the contexts of these organizations and their IT development. A number of questions regarding how to conduct and document field studies and how to make use of the results arise. For example, when should field studies be conducted, and who should do them? If field studies are conducted early on in the process, before the start of the actual development project, how should the results from the studies be documented to make sense to somebody else later on in the process? Moreover, if field studies are part of the commissioning process, how do these field studies relate to the studies conducted by the analysts and designers in the development project? It may be argued that it should be enough to conduct studies early on, and then hand over the documentation to the designers and usability people as input to their design.

In the literature, usability metrics have been suggested as a way of safeguarding usability in the systems development process (for instance, ISO/IS 13407 1999; Mayhew 1999). It is argued that usability metrics place usability on the agenda, and that if usability is included in the requirements specification it cannot be sidestepped and ignored in the project. Metrics, for example, in terms of productivity statistics and technical performance, are essential in these organizations, and metrics for usability and quality in value would fit into their overall focus on metrics. In our case study, an IT user index has been introduced, measuring how the users perceive the usability of their IT systems. The idea is that if usability is measured on a regular basis, the IT department will have to take usability into account in their development process. The underlying assumption seems to be that expressing usability as numbers will make it visible, and that these numbers represent some kind of objective truth about the IT systems. Frequent complaints, suggestions for improvements, frequently reported problems with using the IT systems are seen as subjective and do not seem to represent the same kind of *truth*. However, there are problems with metrics. Usability and quality in value comprise many different aspects, some of which cannot be easily turned into metrics. Specifying quality in value or usability as a set of well-defined parameters complies with the need for formal representations in the development project, but obscures the complex and situated aspects of work discussed earlier. The difficulties with expressing such aspects in numbers make them in no way less important. The question is how to deal with them in a development process that is based on a metrics approach.

To sum up our discussion, we have identified problems with attitudes and perspectives on users and their work in our studies. These attitudes and perspectives are embedded in the methods, models, and representations used in systems development, which in turn shape the IT systems and the emerging work situations of the users. Hence, quality in value, i.e., users' well-being, satisfaction, and productivity are shaped by attitudes and perspectives held in systems development. User-centered design and field studies are suggested to address the problems and to improve the understanding of the users' needs and work practices in the development projects. However, UCSD field studies come with a number of problems and issues when applied in the contexts of our studies. These problems and issues need to be resolved in the future.

Acknowledgment This work was performed as prestudies, funded by the Swedish Development Council for the Public Sector. We acknowledge all people at the different authorities who took part in the interviews or the dissemination of the findings. Particularly, we would also like to acknowledge Bengt Sandblad, Iordanis Kavathatzopoulos, and Erik Borälv for performing parts of the prestudies and taking part in the dissemination to the different authorities.

References

Aarås, A., Horgen, G., & Ro, O. (2000). Work with the visual display unit: Health consequences. *International Journal of Human-Computer Interaction, 12,* 107–134.

Åborg, C., & Billing, A. (2003). Health effects of 'the Paperless Office' – evaluations of the introduction of electronic document handling systems. *Behaviour & Information Technology, 22,* 389–396.

Åborg, C., 2001, Electronic document handling – a longitudinal study on the effects on work environment and health. In Sandsjö, L., & Kadefors, R. (Eds.), *Prevention of muscle disorders in computer users: scientific basis and recommendations* (pp. 245–250). The 2nd Procid Symposium.

Åborg, C., Sandblad, B., Gulliksen, J., & Lif, M. (2003). Integrating work environment consideration into usability evaluation methods – the ADA approach. *Interacting with Computers, 15,* 453–471.

Aronsson, G., Dallner, M., & Åborg, C. (1994). Winners and losers from computerisation. A study of the psychosocial work conditions and health of Swedish state employees. *International Journal of Human-Computer Interaction, 6,* 17–37.

Beath, C.M. & Orlikowski, W.J. (1994).The contradictory structure of systems development methodologies: deconstructing the IS-user relationship in information engineering. *Information Systems Research, 5,* 350–377.

Bergkvist, U. (1993). Health problems during work with visual display terminals. *Arbete och Hälsa 1993:28.* Stockholm, Sweden: Arbetslivsinstitutet.

Beyer, H. & Holtzblatt, K. (1998). *Contextual design – Defining customer-centered systems.* San Francisco: Morgan Kaufmann.

Boivie, I. (2003). Usability and usability and users' health issues in systems development. Licentiate Theses. Uppsala, Sweden: Uppsala University.

Boivie, I. (2005). *A fine balance – Addressing usability and users' needs in the development of IT systems for the workplace.* Ph.D. dissertation. Uppsala, Sweden: Acta Universitatis Uppsaliensis.

Boivie, I., Åborg, C., Persson, J. & Löfberg, M., (2003). Why usability gets lost or usability in in-house software development. *Interacting with Computers, 15,* 623–639.

Boivie, I., Blomkvist, S., Persson, J., & Åborg, C., (2003). Addressing users' health issues in software development – an exploratory study. *Behaviour & Information Technology, 22,* 411–420.

Boivie, I., Gulliksen, J., & Göransson, B. (2006). The lonesome cowboy – A study of the usability designer role in systems development. *Interacting with Computers 18, 601–634.*

Clegg, C., Axtell, C., Damodaran, L., Farbey, B., Hull, R., Lloyd-Jones, R., Nicholls, J., Sell, R., & Tomlinson, C. (1997). Information technology: a study of performance and the role of human and organizational factors. *Ergonomics, 40,* 851–871.

Eason, K., (1997). Understanding the organizational ramifications of implementing information technology systems. In Helander, M. Landauer, T.K. Prabhu, P. (Eds.), *Handbook of Human-Computer Interaction* (pp. 1475–1494). Amsterdam: Elsevier Science.

Göransson, B. (2004) *User-centred systems design. Designing usable interactive systems in practice.* Ph.D. dissertation. Uppsala, Sweden: Acta Universitatis Uppsaliensis.

Göransson, B., Gulliksen, J., & Boivie, I. (2003). The usability design process – Integrating User-centered systems design in the software development process. *Software Process Improvement and Practice, 8,* 111–131.

Greenbaum, J. & Kyng, M. (1991). *Design at work: Cooperative design of computer systems.* Hillsdale, NJ: Lawrence Erlbaum Associates.

Greenbaum, J. (1990). The head and the heart: Using gender analysis to study the social construction of computer systems. *Computers & Society, 20.* 9–16.

Gulliksen, J., Göransson, B., Bovie, I., Blomkvist, S., Persson, J. & Cajander, Å. (2003). Key principles for user-centered systems design. *Behaviour & Information Technology, 22,* 397–409.

Hagberg, M., Wigaeus Tornqvist, E., & Toomingas, A. (2002). Self-reported reduced productivity due to musculoskeletal symptoms: Associations with workplace and individual factors among white-collar computer users. Journal *of Occupational Rehabilitation, 12,* 151–162.

Harris, J., & Henderson, A. (1999). Better mythology for system design. In *Proceedings of ACM CHI 99. Conference on Human Factors in Computing Systems, Vol 1.* (pp 88–95).

ISO 13407. (1999). ISO 13407: Human-centred design processes for interactive systems. Geneva: International Organization for Standardization.

ISO 9241-10. (1996). ISO 9241-10: Ergonomic requirements for office work with visual display terminals. Geneva: International Organization for Standardization.

ISO 9241-11. (1998). ISO 9241-11: Ergonomic requirements for office work with visual display terminals. Geneva: International Organization for Standardization.

Kammersgaard, J. (1990). Four different perspectives on human computer-interaction. In J. Preece, & L. Keller, *Human-Computer Interaction.* Hemel Hempstead, UK: Prentice Hall.

Karasek, R. & Theorell, T. (1990). *Healthy work: Stress, productivity and reconstruction of working life.* New York: Basic books.

Klein, H., & M. Myers (1999). A set of principles for conducting and evaluating interpretive field studies in information systems. *MIS Quarterly 23,* 67–94.

Landauer, T.K. (1995). *The trouble with computers – Usefulness, usability and productivity.* Cambridge: The MIT Press.

Norman, D.A. (1986) Cognitive engineering. In D.A. Norman & S.W. Draper (Eds.), *User centered systems design* (pp. 31–61). Hillsdale, NJ: Lawrence Erlbaum Associates.

Nurminen, M. I. (1987). Different perspectives: What are they and how can they be used? In Docherty, P. Fuchs-Kittowski, K., Kolm, P, & Mathiassen, L. (Eds.). *System design for human development and productivity: Participation and beyond.* North-Holland: Elsevier Science Publishers.

Nygaard, K. (1986). Program development as a social activity. Information Processing 86. In Kugler, H-J. (Ed.), *Proceedings from the IFIP 10th World Computer Congress,* Dublin, Ireland, September 1–5, 1986, (pp. 189–198). North Holland: Elsevier Science Publishers.

Punnett, L., & Bergkvist, U. (1997). Visual display unit work and upper extremity musculoskeletal disorders: A review of epidemiological findings. *Arbete och Hälsa (Work and Health). 1997:16.* Solna, Sweden: National Institute of Working life.

Sachs, P. (1995). *Transforming work: Collaboration, learning and design.* ACM, *38,* 36–44.

Sandblad, B., Gulliksen, J., Åborg, C., Boivie, I., Persson, J., Göransson, B., Kavathatzopoulos, I., Blomkvist, S., & Cajander, Å. (2003). Work environment and computer systems development. *Behaviour & Information Technology, 22,* 375–387.

Standish Group (1995), CHAOS report, from http://www.standishgroup.com/

Standish Group (1998), CHAOS report, from http://www.standishgroup.com/

Statistics Sweden. (2001). Statistiska meddelanden, rapport 2001:2. (Statistical messages, report 2001:2).(in Swedish, summary in English).

Statistics Sweden. (2005). Statistiska meddelanden, Arbetorsakade besvär AM43 SM 0501. (Statistical messages, Work-Related Disorders). (in Swedish, summary in English).

Suchman, L.A. (1987). *Plans and situated actions: The problem of human machine communication.* Cambridge, MA: Cambridge University Press.

Vicente, K.J. (1999). *Cognitive work analyses. Toward safe, productive and healthy computer-based work.* Mahwah, NJ: Lawrence Erlbaum Associates.

Wigaeus Tornqvist, E., Eriksson, N., & Bergqvist, U. (2000). Dator-och kontorsarbetsplatsens fysiska och psykosociala arbetsmiljörisker, (The physical and psychosocial work environment risks at computer- and office workplaces). *Arbetsliv och Hälsa 2000 (Working Life and Health 2000).* Marklund, S. (pp. 235–260). Solna, Sweden:Arbetslivsinstitutet.

Winograd. T. & Flores, F. (1984). *Understanding computer and cognition.* Menlo Park, CA: Addison-Wesley.

Chapter 12
Usability Evaluation as Idea Generation

Kasper Hornbæk

Department of Computer Science, University of Copenhagen, Denmark,
e-mail: kash@diku.dk

Abstract This chapter discusses how to understand the purpose of formative usability evaluation. We raise concerns about common ways of understanding usability evaluation, and propose a complementary view of usability evaluation as idea generation. Implications of this view for researchers and practitioners are discussed, and it is argued that seeing usability evaluation as idea generation may help move research in evaluation methods forward. In addition, we suggest practitioners some benefits of viewing their work as idea generation and some concrete techniques based on this view.

12.1 Introduction

The activity of usability evaluation is broadly concerned with investigating the usability of information technology. We focus on formative usability evaluation, where the aim is to affect the development of a product. A host of methods for performing usability evaluations has been proposed for this aim (e.g., Cockton, et al. 2003a; Dumas 2003), and a substantial literature discusses the relative benefits of these methods based on empirical comparisons of their performance (Nielsen 1992; Bailey, et al. 1992; John & Marks 1997; Cockton, et al. 2003b). The methodological challenges in such comparisons, however, have proven substantial (Gray & Salzman 1998).

The assumption behind this chapter is that activities in the field of usability evaluation—in particular, which methods are proposed, how methods are compared, and how evaluations are done in practice—are determined to a large extent by what is seen as the purpose of usability evaluation. For example, if we see the goal of usability evaluation as identifying defects in software, then evaluation methods that help evaluators find many usability problems are of importance: we might understandably compare evaluation methods by counting how many problems they each identify, and we should author usability reports that mainly list usability problems. If, however, we see usability evaluation as an activity that is intended to influence software design, then we may be more interested in whether designers and developers can understand the problems an evaluation method helps identify, and consequently try to quantify the impact of evaluations on development activities.

E. Law et al. (eds.), *Maturing Usability.*

Based on this assumption, we explore a complementary view of usability evaluation. Our motivation for doing so is twofold. First, research in usability evaluation has been troubled by methodological difficulties and deficiencies (Gray & Salzman 1998; Hartson, et al. 2001). Among other things, finding a valid dependent variable in comparisons of methods is hard, and techniques for focusing on a method's downstream utility (John & Marks 1997) are rare. The second motivation is more pragmatic. The ability to get ideas (rather than merely list usability problems) appears highly relevant for usability practitioners and the developers/designers that they work with. Yet, as we will argue, it has not been a focus in work on evaluation usability methods; this may be one reason why usability evaluation has had a limited impact on software development (Hornbæk & Stage 2006).

This chapter proposes idea generation as one view of the purpose of formative usability evaluations; we refer to this as the *idea-generation view*. The idea-generation view contends that usability evaluation is a process aimed at giving evaluators, developers, and designers ideas about users, users' tasks, and the application being evaluated. We argue the case for the idea-generation view, and draw some implications for research and practitioners. This chapter does not aim to validate the usefulness of the idea-generation view or of the implications drawn. Our intent is mainly to explore whether useful new directions in usability research may be gained from considering usability evaluation as idea generation.

The next section outlines what seems to be the most common way of understanding the purpose of usability evaluation, and discusses its limitations. Next, we describe in some detail the creativity and idea generation literature, and discuss the idea of considering usability evaluation as idea generation. The following two sections present some tentative implications for usability researchers and practitioners, respectively.

12.2 The Purpose of Usability Evaluation

The point of departure for this chapter concerns the purpose of usability evaluations. While an evaluation may be done in a particular context for a variety of purposes, we discuss next what appears to be the main view in the literature and its limitations. The following section aims to motivate further the need for an alternative or complementary view of the purpose of usability evaluation.

12.2.1 Usability Evaluation as Defect-Identification

A variety of definitions of usability evaluation and its purpose exists; let us illustrate these through a selection of quotes from prominent writings in usability research. One common definition is that usability evaluation aims to ascertain the usability of a particular computer system. Karat (1998), for example, presented the view that "a usability evaluation method is a process for producing a measure of usability." (p. 682) Dix, et al. (2004), in writing about evaluation in general, stated that "[e]valuation has three main goals: to assess the extent and accessibility of the system's functionality, to assess users' experience of the interaction, and to identify any specific problems with the system." (p. 319). An equally broad, but wholly pragmatic, view of usability evaluation posits that the goal of usability evaluation is to make software better; a widely-cited book on usability testing suggested that "the primary goal is to improve the usability of the product" (Dumas & Redish 1999, p. 222).

A related group of definitions states more specifically that the purpose of a usability evaluation is identification of defects. The quote from Dix, et al. (2004) contains this view, too. In a discussion of usability testing, Rubin (1994) described the overall goal of usability testing as being "to identify and rectify usability deficiencies existing in computer-based and electronic equipment and their accompanying support materials prior to release." (p. 26) Gray and Salzman (1998) stated that "UEMs are used to evaluate the interaction of the human with the computer for the purpose of identifying aspects of this interaction that can be improved to increase usability." (p. 206) Hartson, et al. (2001) presented a similar view in writing that:

> The essential common characteristic of UEMs (at least for the purposes of this article) is that every UEM, when applied to an interaction design, produces a list of potential usability problems as its output. Some UEMs have additional functionality, such as the ability to help write usability reports, to classify usability problems by type, to map problems to causative features in the design, or to offer redesign suggestions (p. 377).

Stone, et al. (2005) presented a definition that includes defect-identification: "[...] the purpose of evaluation is to assess whether the UI design is effective, efficient, engaging, error tolerant, and easy to learn and, if it is not, to identify the problems that are affecting its usability so that they may be improved upon." (p. 425)

In comparisons of usability evaluation methods, evaluation is often seen as defect-identification. As an illustration, take Nielsen and Molich's (1990) classic paper on heuristic evaluation. In the introduction to the paper, Nielsen and Molich suggested that "heuristic evaluation is done by looking at an interface and trying to come up with an opinion about what is good and bad about the interface." (p. 249) However, from the second page of their paper to its end, only problems with the interface are discussed, leading to an exclusive focus on defects. In practice, the bulk of many usability reports appears to be descriptions of usability problems; Dumas, et al. (2004) found less than 15 percent positive comments in their analysis of usability reports from CUE-4 (the fourth installment of a series of comparative studies of expert evaluators), despite explicitly instructing evaluators to include positive comments.

In summary, the defect-identification view seems shared by many authors, and is present also in method comparisons and practical usability work.

12.2.2 Limitations of Usability Evaluation as Defect-Identification

The defect-identification view has several limitations, which give rise to methodological problems when evaluation methods are being assessed, and may be part of the reason why usability evaluation is sometimes not providing the information needed in software projects.

As mentioned above, usability evaluations (and comparisons of usability evaluation methods) often focus on defects or problems with the software. Consequently, the enterprise becomes mainly negative. De Bono (1994) wrote succinctly about this in a discussion of creativity:

REMOVAL OF FAULTS

This is a basic habit of Western thinking. If you only get rid of faults everything else will be fine. There are two obvious dangers.

1. We only focus our thinking on what is wrong.
2. Getting rid of the faults in a poorly designed system does not result in a better-designed system.

Viewing usability evaluation as defect-identification seems to suffer both dangers. This concern has also been voiced by practitioners and researchers working with evaluation (Sklar & Gilmore 2004; Hassenzahl & Tractinsky 2006).

Another difficulty with the defect-identification view is that it does not help much in determining whether a particular evaluation method is valid or more generally beneficial. Gray and Salzman (1998) discussed what they termed the "problem counting approach." They argued that just counting the number of problems a particular method produces conflates the naming of potential problems with identifying real problems, because counts of potential problems will include problems that are not true usability problems. Another difficulty is that different kinds of problem—for example, with respect to generality, type, aspects of the user interface covered, or clarity—are given equal weight when counted. While defect-identification need not necessarily lead to problem counting, counting is a very common approach to method comparison.

Dennis Wixon (2003) has pointed out another limitation of the defect-identification view. He finds that most comparisons of UEMs fail the practitioner. According to Wixon, a premise of the literature on evaluation of methods is that the "[n]umber of problems detected is the most appropriate criterion for evaluating a method." (p. 30) He argued that identifying problems is only the first step towards improving the product, and that finding fixes for the identified problems is equally important. Following Wixon's argument, defect-identification ignores that finding a large number of usability problems is not in itself a quality of a UEM, if the defect identification does not lead to changes in the software.

Finally, and this is a main motivation behind this chapter, the defect-identification view captures only part of the role that usability evaluation plays in software development. It does not, for example, capture getting design ideas, communicating insights to designers and developers, or experiencing things other than problems in a usability test.

In summary, defect-identification is a common—perhaps the dominant—view of the purpose of usability evaluation. Yet, it is in some ways unsatisfactory, suggesting that the development of complementary views of usability evaluation is warranted.

12.3 Idea Generation and Creativity

The literature on creativity and idea generation has previously been discussed in the HCI field. In a well-known paper, Ben Shneiderman (2000) discussed notions of creativity and their implications for interface design. A number of interfaces have tried to support idea generation and creative processes (e.g., Terry & Mynatt 2002) and several empirical studies of interfaces aimed at supporting creativity and idea generation have been reported (e.g., Elam & Mead 1990; Massetti 1996; Marakas & Elam 1997; Malaga 2000). Shneiderman, et al. (2006) gave a recent overview of creativity research in HCI.

To our knowledge, however, no one has related the literature on creativity and idea generation to usability evaluation. We propose that viewing usability evaluation as idea generation may be fruitful for researchers and practitioners. Before describing the implications of this view, we introduce some of the notions and research results that we later argue may inspire usability research.

12.3.1 Central Notions in Creativity and Idea Generation

The literature on creativity is huge. Although Joy Paul Guilford's presidential address to the American Psychological Association in 1950 is widely seen as the start of the era (Guilford 1950), the topic has been discussed for much longer. James (1890), for example, devoted many pages of *Principles of Psychology* to describing the characteristics of thought among geniuses.

In this chapter, creativity is defined based on attributes of products, responses, or ideas. We rely on a definition by Teresa Amabile (1996) who took as the point of departure for her work on creativity that "A product or response will be judged as creative to the extent that (a) it is both a novel and appropriate, useful, correct or valuable response to the task at hand, and (b) the task is heuristic rather than algorithmic." (p. 35) Moreover, we see idea generation as being at the heart of creative processes. In that, we follow a number of authors. Smith (1998), for example, suggested that "Creativity [...] is concerned with the generation of ideas, alternatives, and possibilities [...] but idea generation per se is the process's indispensable core." (p. 107) In addition, Brown (1989) argued that the divergent thinking approach to creativity—seeing creativity as the ability to generate many different ideas—is the most developed understanding of creativity.

Note that creativity and idea generation should be thought of not only as great discoveries, ingenious inventions, or artistic expression. Ripple (1989) made the argument that the potentiality for creative thinking exists in everybody, as indicated by ordinary persons' distinctly unique solutions to everyday situations in their lives. In discussing new technology, Smith, et al. (2000) likewise described a continuum ranging from mundane creativity (e.g., students' excuses for late homework) to exceptional creativity (e.g., invention of the first computer).

12.3.2 The Four Ps Model of Creativity

It is common to discuss creativity in terms of the Four Ps—person, process, press, and product (Rhodes 1961); see, for example, Couger, et al. (1993) and Satzinger, et al. (1999). The Four Ps model captures some factors that influence the making of creative products.

Creative *persons* have been a big focus in creativity research. Gardner (1994) discussed the works of eight creative persons—including Einstein, Freud, Stravinsky, and Gandhi—to derive an account of creativity. Csikszentmihalyi (1996) discussed how persons in a variety of fields perform when they are creative, and what the psychological conditions for creativity are. These studies make clear some of the personal factors that drive eminent researchers and artists.

On a more general level, a common view of creativity is that it is related to an individual's ability to create associations; Mednick (1962) presented an entire model of creativity based on this view and James (1890) famously noted that "Genius then, as has already been said, is identical with the possession of similar associations to an extreme degree" (Vol. II, p. 360). A related view is that a key ability of creative persons is *ideational fluency* (Milgram 1981)—that is, a high rate at which a person can get distinct ideas. For instance, getting many ideas forms the backbone of brainstorming (Osborn 1953). The underlying assumption is that having many ideas is related to being creative, and that a good indicator of creativity may be a person's ability to generate ideas. Ideational fluency has been used as a dependent variable in many studies of creativity and brainstorming techniques. Malaga (2000), for example, evaluated interfaces for idea generation by comparing how many ideas participants produced when asked to generate ideas for ice cream flavors. A person's ideational fluency can be assessed by several psychological tests, such as the Remote Associations Test (RAT). Items in RAT consist of three words (such as *cookies*, *sixteen*, and *heart*), to which subjects must respond with a related word (such as *sweet*).

A recent account of personal factors in creative performance was given by Amabile (1996). She described three components integral to creative performance. One component is domain-relevant skills, such as knowledge about the domain and certain technical abilities. Another component is creativity-relevant skills, such as conducive work styles and implicit or explicit heuristics for generating novel ideas. To a large extent, this component depends on personal characteristics, but may be impacted by training. Finally, Amabile highlights task motivation as a key component—in particular, an individual's perception of why a task is done. This component is positively influenced by intrinsic motivation; external motivating factors (such as reward or evaluation) typically affect creative performance negatively.

Other aspects of individual factors in creativity may be measured by some of the psychometric tests relating to creativity (such as RAT, mentioned earlier). However, it is quite controversial whether these tests predict real-world creativity (Brown 1989; Amabile 1996).

The *process* of creativity has been widely studied, not least through biographical studies of eminent researchers and artists. More generally, a host of models

Author	Phases			
Wallas (1926)	Preparation	Incubation	Illumination	Verification
Polya (1945)	Understanding the problem	Devising a plan	Carrying out the plan	Looking back
Osborn (1953)	Fact-finding	Idea-finding		Solution-finding
Amabile (1996)	Problem or task presentation	Preparation	Response generation	Response validation	Outcome

Fig. 12.1 Common models of the process of creativity

of the creative process have been proposed, some of which are quite similar to problem-solving models. Figure 12.1 shows some examples. Wallas (1926) presented a simple model, where incubation followed by illumination played a key role. Polya's (1945) model of problem-solving originated in mathematics, but is considered generally applicable. Osborn (1953) separated three simple phases, with solution-finding as a distinct phase. Amabile (1996) described a slightly more general model consisting of five phases in which problem or task presentation is a crucial step.

The term *press* denotes the environment and work context of the creative person. Csikszentmihalyi (1996) emphasized the domain and the field as components influencing an individual's creativity. He saw the domain as encompassing existing knowledge—that is, a particular set of symbols, rules, and procedures. Mathematics and computer science are domains in this sense. The field is the experts who make up the domain; essentially they decide whether a new idea or product is made part of the domain. This suggests that social and interpersonal phenomena are somehow involved in creativity, at least in the assessment of what work to consider creative. It also suggests that truly creative ideas are those that change the domain. Other studies have described organizational factors (such as motivational structures and management commitment) that may improve or impede organization members' creativity, and in part investigated these experimentally (Amabile, et al. 1996).

The *products* of creative performance are of natural interest to creativity research. This interest raises the question: "What is a good idea or a creative response?" The next section deals with this question.

12.3.3 What is a Good Idea?

The literature on creativity and idea generation describes many criteria by which to judge what makes a product creative or an idea good. Not only do these criteria flesh out what creativity and idea generation concern, they also help develop metrics to assess ideas and products. Because creativity is defined mainly through creative products, such criteria become crucial. As we shall see, they appear relevant also for usability research.

Jackson and Messick (1965) presented a view of creative products that emphasizes four qualities: unusualness, appropriateness, transformation, and condensation. The importance of unusualness and appropriateness are relatively obvious; they have been used extensively in patenting. Transformation suggests that elements of a solution are combined in a way that breaks with tradition and forms a new way of seeing reality. Condensation is more subtle, suggesting that creative products do not reveal their meaning on first viewing or use. Other persons' responses to these qualities would be aesthetic judgments of surprise (unusualness in relation to the norm), satisfaction (that the solution is appropriate), stimulation (transformation in relation to the context), and savoring (in the condensed product).

MacCrimmon and Wagner (1994) focused on five aspects of creative products: novelty, nonobviousness, workability, relevance, and thoroughness. They explain these aspects as follows (p. 1516):

> Novelty and nonobviousness refer to the originality of an idea, while workability, relevance and thoroughness address the usefulness and feasibility aspects. An idea is most novel if no one has expressed it before. Nevertheless such an idea can be obvious if it does not surprise people knowledgeable in the field. An idea is workable, if it does not violate known constraints or if it can be readily implemented. It is relevant if it satisfies the goals set by the problem solver. Finally, (the description of) an idea is thorough if it is worked out in sufficient detail.

Amabile (1996), as noted above, simplified this by requiring that a creative product need only be novel and useful.

Another approach to characterizing good ideas has been used in experiments by Satzinger, et al. (1999) and Garfield, et al. (2001). They distinguish ideas that are paradigm-modifying from ideas that are paradigm-preserving. A paradigm-preserving idea does not challenge or change the underlying assumptions and structures of a problem. Satzinger, et al. (1999) illustrated the difference in the following way:

> For example, if the problem being solved is how to use the excess capacity of a teabag machine, a PP [paradigm-preserving] solution would not attempt to alter the underlying framework of the question (i.e., a machine that makes teabags needs to be used more). An example of a PP solution would be to put coffee in the teabags. A PM [paradigm-modifying] solution may alter the framework by considering how to increase demand of the teabags, so one possible solution would be to market bathing suits made out of teabag material, thus using the material produced by a teabag machine, but in a different form (p. 146).

All of these views are similar in that they define constructs that can be used for evaluating ideas or products. For instance, discrete or continuous semantic differentials with anchor points such as novel/well-worn and paradigm-preserving/paradigm-modifying have been extensively used by independent raters to assess the creativity of products.

An alternative way of assessing good ideas is to refrain from explicitly defining criteria for creativity. One particularly well-validated implicit approach to assessing creativity is Amabile's (1996) consensual technique. This technique is based on the assumption that expert practitioners in a field recognize creative solutions. Amabile's technique contains requirements for the tasks for which products are to be judged (such as clearly observable responses and open-endedness), for the expert practitioners that act as judges (that they should be experienced and make their assessments individually), and for the rating procedure (that judges should grade products relative to each other and that they should rate creativity as well as technically quality). Amabile has validated the consensual assessment technique in more than 21 studies. Independent researchers have also used the technique (i.e., Elam & Mead 1990). While Amabile is not the only person to use judges for assessing creativity (i.e., Sternberg 1985), her technique is very well-validated across a variety of products and domains.

12.3.4 Techniques for Generating Ideas

A large part of the available literature on creativity consists of techniques for improving creativity and idea generation. These include both researchers' contributions (see Smith 1998 for a review) and authors aiming at a broader audience, such as Roger von Oech (1992) and Edward de Bono (2000). Von Oech, for example, listed ten barriers to creativity (so-called *mental locks*)—including beliefs that a right answer exists and that play is frivolous—and tactics for overcoming them.

Gerald Smith (1998) reviewed 172 creativity techniques. His aim was to identify so-called active ingredients—that is, elements of the techniques that were distinct with respect to how they tried to stimulate or tap creativity. The eight prominent groups of active ingredients in Smith's study were:

- Analytic strategies, including techniques for decomposing problems and for considering problems at a more general level
- Search strategies, including the use of associations to mentally follow links among ideas and making analogies to similar things
- Imagination-based strategies, including the use of fantasy to remove constraints and of mental simulation to enact situations
- Habit-breaking strategies, such as the adopting the opposite of a problem-relevant belief or exploring another agent's view of a problem
- Task-focused strategies, such as changing the structure of a situation by rearranging its elements
- Development strategies, such as developing ideas to be more feasible and contrasting them to status quo to find advantage points
- Stimulation tactics, such as using related and remote stimuli for generating ideas
- Anti-inhibition strategies, in particular deferring evaluation of ideas

Smith's work is useful in providing a summary of the variety of ways in which researchers and authors of self-help books have tried to stimulate creativity. In a later section, we discuss how these ideas may be taken up in usability research.

12.4 How to Understand Usability Evaluation as Idea Generation?

After having reviewed idea generation and creativity literatures, let us briefly reflect on how to understand usability evaluation as idea generation. This may be done in two very different manners.

The *weak-resemblance hypothesis* suggests that similarities between usability evaluation and idea generation exists, and further posits that these similarities may serve to inform usability research, in part by generating ideas for new ways of evaluating and of comparing methods, and in part by building on the much older and much larger literature on creativity. This hypothesis does not commit to a particular view of the evaluation process—it merely seeks to generate ideas from the likening of usability evaluation with idea generation. Using Smith's (1998) terminology, the weak-resemblance hypothesis acts as a habit-breaking strategy and as a stimulation tactic.

The *strong-resemblance hypothesis* is more committing. It suggests that the basic purpose of usability evaluation is to generate ideas about how to improve the application under evaluation. It sees the purpose of usability evaluation as creating useful and novel ideas about how to improve the usability of a product, thereby shifting the view from defect-identification to ideas about users, new designs, tasks, or the context of use.

It should be noted that neither of these hypotheses dismisses (or is inconsistent with) the crucial role of usability evaluation as external, critical review. Before moving on, we also need to address the objection that viewing usability evaluation as idea generation completely misses what evaluation is about. In the creativity literature, however, evaluation as a creative activity has been discussed (Brown 1989). In addition, Getzels and Csikszentmihalyi (1976) distinguished presented problems and discovered problems. Describing a problem as appropriate and accurate as possible is suggested by many writers to be a key to creative solutions, meaning that problem discovery and solution-finding are closely related. Thus, we find sense in seeing usability evaluation not only as an activity aiming at uncovering problems in using an application, but also as an activity aiming to give developers, designers, and evaluators ideas.

12.5 Implications for Research in Usability Evaluation

Based on the discussion in the previous section, a number of implications, or perhaps inspirations, for research may be drawn. The intent behind discussing those implications is to present suggestions for how to understand the evaluation process, how to assess evaluation methods, how to understand evaluators' roles, and how to develop new evaluation methods.

12.5.1 The Evaluation Process and its Relationship to Design

Some of the implications of the analogy between evaluation and idea generation are obvious, in particular concerning the aims of the evaluation process. One implication is that the scope of evaluation is expanded. From merely being concerned with defect-identification, the task of coming up with ideas and solutions also becomes relevant. The whole activity of usability evaluation is thus seen as an attempt to identify and offer creative solutions to usability-related issues in product development. The shift from "what is wrong" to "where can we find better ways?" appears important.

We see three recent directions in usability research that resonate with this idea. The earlier discussion of process models of creativity makes a clear distinction between clarifying the problems to be solved and the analysis of solutions. A similar distinction has been introduced in the DARe model (Cockton, et al. 2003b). That model separates resources for the discovery of usability problems (so-called discovery resources) from resources that allow analysis of usability problems (so-called analysis resources). In this regard, the DARe model is quite similar to some of the process models discussed earlier. Incidentally, the DARe model does not identify solution generation as a distinct phase—most models of the creative process do that. It might also be possible to use the DARe model, not only as an analytic tool, but also as a way of structuring evaluation work. The principle of deferring evaluation would encourage evaluators to suspend judgment and critical analysis when discovering problems or imagining possible solutions.

Another direction related to the idea-generation view concerns the notion of downstream utility (e.g., John & Marks 1997; Hornbæk & Frøkjær 2005). Downstream utility implies looking at how the results of usability evaluations are appreciated and taken up in the software development activities that follow an evaluation. Downstream utility may be seen as analogous to the utility metric for assessing ideas. A couple of studies of downstream utility, however, have shown a surprising result in relation to the novelty metric. Both Molich, et al. (2004) and Hornbæk and Frøkjær (2005) reported that evaluators showed little surprise in response to the usability problems they received: in Molich, et al.'s study, representative from the site tested assessed only four percent of the problems as new. Thus, exploring novelty and nonobviousness dimensions of usability feedback may be interesting and a further way to understand the uptake of ideas in design.

Third, the data presented in Hornbæk and Frøkjær (2005) appear to support the weak-resemblance hypothesis. They interviewed developers as to their opinions about a collection of usability problems and redesign proposals. Developers said they appreciated usability problems and redesign proposals that gave them ideas. In some cases, they rejected the reasoning in a problem or a redesign proposal because it clashed with their technical preferences. Nevertheless, they still got some inspiration and ideas from reading the material. This suggests that usability evaluations may be successful not only by correctly pointing out defects, but also by giving developers and designers ideas. Note also that the use of redesign proposals is one technique for communication ideas for solutions, rather than just describing problems.

Our discussion of idea generation has more generally suggested expanding the scope of evaluation activities. We contend that reporting ideas about users, tasks, and applications would be a useful output from usability evaluations—techniques for focusing on either of these could be interesting.

12.5.2 Assessing Evaluation Methods

One way to draw inspiration from the analogy between usability evaluation and idea generation is to think up possible measures for use in the assessment of evaluation methods—measures that are well-known and often-used in creativity research, but to our knowledge rarely used in usability research. Table 12.1 shows a collection of examples, which we will review in turn.

Readers familiar with methodological problems in assessing evaluation methods may have noted an interesting similarity between usability research and the work presented on idea generation. Ideational fluency is in many ways similar to the problem-counting approach described by, among others, Gray and Salzman (1998). However, quantity of ideas might be interpreted slightly different. First, problem-counts are an objective feature of evaluators' reporting—we suggest also looking at the ideas that designers and developers get from evaluators' feedback. Second, creativity research—in contrast to much usability research—usually avoids using only a measure of quantity in assessing the responses of creative tasks. For instance, MacCrimmon and Wagner (1994) reported correlations between quantity and quality of ideas, and concluded that "while there is a definite relationship between quality and quantity, it is by no means perfect. Using measures of quantity alone seems inadequate." (p. 1528)

Table 12.1 Measures from creativity research potentially useful in usability research

Measure	Examples of Use in Creativity Research	Possible Benefits in Usability Research
Quantity of Ideas	Proctor (1988)	Would enable an assessment of the impact of evaluation on designers and developers (when combined with other measures)
Novelty of Ideas	Massetti (1996)	Would enable a better understanding of what developers and designers get new insights from; may also enable an examination of what evaluators are surprised by in usability testing
Paradigm-Modifying Ideas	Satzinger et al. (1999)	Enables a distinction between simple and radical input to designers and developers; paradigm-modifying ideas may potentially be more beneficial
Consensual Assessment	Amabile (1996)	Would offer a comprehensive and well-validated procedure for assessing the creativity of output from evaluation; consensual assessment may also be used to measure attributes beside creativeity

Another measure to consider in assessing the output from usability evaluation is novelty. In empirical studies of creativity, novelty is frequently assessed by expert raters (e.g., MacCrimmon & Wagner 1994; Massetti 1996). Massetti (1996), for example, used expert raters to assess the novelty of each response to a task that required participants to devise creative solutions regarding a scenario involving homeless people. As mentioned earlier, the novelty component of a good idea may not be as strongly present in the results of usability evaluations as we would like to think. However, the extent to which feedback from evaluations needs to be novel is open for discussion. It is certainly not the case that all output from an evaluation needs to be original/novel, yet developers and designers may appreciate solutions that tackle problems and limitations in a way they themselves had not imagined. As already mentioned, this last point is supported by observations from Hornbæk and Frøkjær (2005).

One particularly intriguing idea for usability evaluation is the distinction between paradigm-preserving and paradigm-modifying ideas (Satzinger, et al. 1999). We suspect that most feedback from usability evaluators to designers and developers is paradigm-preserving; this is probably one reason why some authors use phrases like *frosting on the cake* to describe the contribution from usability evaluation to systems development. Nørgaard and Hornbæk (2006) made an observation related to this issue. In an analysis of practical think-aloud sessions, they noted that incidents in the test where a participant commented upon issues such as task-interface fit were given less attention than incidents where a participant commented on what appeared to be relatively minor usability problems. While formative usability evaluation may not always be looking for paradigm-modifying ideas, it certainly seems that radical ideas could supplement descriptions of defects.

Amabile (1996) developed the consensual assessment technique that we specu-late might be as useful in research on usability evaluation as it has been in creativity research. As mentioned earlier, consensual assessment relies on expert practitioners' implicit understanding of creativity to assess products. We speculate that consensual assessment of results from usability evaluations would be highly interesting. Rela-tively few papers have used expert evaluation of usability findings and the ones we are familiar with did so in an ad hoc manner.

Finally, the idea generation view suggests that the widespread research practice of regarding problems found by only one evaluator as dubious is problematic. There is no a priori justification that good ideas are likely to be generated by many evalu-ators who work individually to evaluate a product. On the contrary, some studies of creativity seek rare ideas (provided that they otherwise hold up). MacCrimmon and Wagner (1994), for example, had judges assess the infrequency of an idea. Conse-quently, we may eliminate important ideas if we insist that several evaluators should have identified an issue for it to be considered further.

12.5.3 The Role of Evaluators

Perhaps the most striking difference between creativity research and usability research is the degree with which eminently creative persons have been studied. As discussed earlier, the creativity literature is packed with descriptions of creative persons and their introspective accounts of creative activities (Gardner 1994; Csikszentmihalyi 1996). Conversely, we know of virtually no descriptions of the activities of truly experienced evaluators. For instance, why haven't we seen descriptions of how Jakob Nielsen and Rolf Molich use heuristic evaluation, or of how eminent evaluators in industry conduct their work? We believe that this kind of study would give more nuanced information about the resources and strategies used in evaluations.

Amabile's three-component model of the skills involved in creative performance may—under the idea-generation view—be used to understand the role of usability evaluators. Using this model, the main factors involved in skilled evaluation are domain-related skills, creativity-related skills, and motivation. While there is much work in making this analog generate hypotheses for usability research, we suggest that the fluency both in generating defects and solutions may be relatively consistent for an individual, and that this fluency may be developed through training (so that training in one evaluation method caries over to another). Motivation in undertaking an evaluation task also appears to be under-researched. Note that the DARe model by Cockton and colleagues (2003b) provides a promising step towards understanding what goes into usability inspection.

12.5.4 Generating New Methods

We are particularly enthusiastic about the idea that the idea-generation view of usability evaluation may help researchers generate new methods. Below we give some ideas on how this may be done.

First, some evaluation techniques draw implicitly on an idea-generation view. One example is metaphors of human thinking (MOT) (Hornbæk & Frøkjær 2002; 2004). The core of MOT is five metaphors of human thinking that the evaluator must keep in mind when conducting the evaluation. The authors of MOT explicitly stated that "The metaphors are intended to stimulate thinking, generate insight, and break fixed conceptions. These uses of metaphors have been thoroughly studied in the literature on creative thinking (Gardner 1982; Kogan 1983) and illustratively applied, for example, by Sfard (1998) in the educational domain." (Hornbæk & Frøkjær 2004, p. 359). Thus, the use of metaphors is a kind of creativity technique in that they function—in Smith's (1998) terminology—as habit-breaking strategies. Another example is perspective-based usability evaluation (Zhang et al. 1999). The main idea here is to perform a series of evaluations, each from a different perspective. According to Smith (1998), this is also a habit-breaking strategy.

While MOT and perspective-based usability evaluation may be seen as examples of evaluation methods that draw on idea-generating notions, there are many other possibilities. New ideas for evaluation methods may be generated by considering what the active ingredients in usability evaluation methods are. Earlier we discussed Smith's (1998) work on characterizing the active ingredients in idea-generation techniques. We do not have space in this chapter to undertake a review of the active ingredients in evaluation methods. However, usability evaluation methods appear relatively strong in helping evaluators consider the users' tasks systematically (e.g., as in cognitive walkthroughs) or think about principles for good user-interface design (e.g., as in heuristic evaluation and evaluation by guidelines). There are some areas that are not well-covered, though. First, finding solutions to problems is not well-supported. Cockton, et al. (2003a), in a review of usability inspection methods (UIMs), noted that "Current UIMs provide little, if any, support for the generation of recommendations for fixing designs to avoid predicted problems." (p. 1120) Second, deferring evaluation of ideas, problems, solutions, and so forth, seems a key point. A recent study showed that usability testing with multiple designs may be better than testing with just one design, in that users give more and stronger critiques of the designs (Tohidi, et al. 2006). This result might be explained from the viewpoint of creativity research as a beneficial consequence of deferred evaluation of the design alternatives.

Couger, et al. (1993) made an effort related to the present discussion. They discussed creativity techniques in relation to the broader domain of information systems, listed 20 creativity techniques, and provided case studies for six of those techniques. Each case identified the technique used and described how the technique worked in a particular situation. For example, progressive abstraction is a creativity enhancing technique for progressively enlarging the abstractness of a problem definition. Couger, et al. described a case where this technique was used to broaden an understanding of the problem of getting entry-level professional employees to the more general problem of a shortage of human capacity at a professional level. While this may seem like an obvious step, the solutions to the more abstract or general problem were quite different from the solution to the case's initial problem. We believe that the techniques described by Couger, et al. may be useful to usability practitioners. Progressive abstraction, for example, might be used to formulate a difficulty found with a website in its most general form. This may help capture all instances of a difficulty if it shows itself in many parts of the application, and may lead evaluators to consider the most general cause of a problem.

To make the discussion concrete, let us suggest an idea-generation usability assessment method. Note that this method is not evaluated—its possible deficiencies should not count against the general idea of utilizing idea generation techniques for inspiring new evaluation methods. We suggest using a well-known creativity technique—de Bono's *Six Thinking Hats* (2000)—as a basis for structuring a usability inspection (see Table 12.2). *Six Thinking Hats* provides directions for using different modes of thinking about a problem, captured by six differently colored hats. The white hat, for example, allows only the discussion of facts and figures. The red hat is used when stating intuitions and feelings. It is essential that putting on and taking off hats are explicit actions, and that groups use the same hats simultaneously. The book by de Bono (2000) gives detailed advice on how to use the technique.

In usability inspection, the hats would be used to get a broad discussion of usability issues, including possible solutions to those issues, and identification of gaps in knowledge about users. It should be done by a group, including developers, designers, and usability specialists, as appropriate. This kind of evaluation may proceed in a similar manner to a conventional usability inspection, based on a description

Table 12.2 Key focus areas in using the six thinking hats for evaluation, and some specific usability related questions and activities

Thinking Hat	Focus	Usability Evaluation Concerns
White	Fact, figures, and information gaps	Facts about users' tasks; application details; statistics about users' behavior
Red	Intuition, feelings, and emotions	Issues of disagreement between evaluators, designers, and developers
Black	Judgment and caution	Focus on defect-identification; experiences with difficulties in related projects
Yellow	Logical positive thinking	Reliance on HCI principles; progressive abstraction; wishful thinking; walkthrough of tasks; suggestions for other ways of designing an application; wishful thinking
Green	Creativity and alternatives, provocations, and changes	Use of creativity techniques; using the escape method to break fixed assumptions
Blue	Overview and process control	Move on to another representative task; consider another user profile; move towards constructive feedback to developers and designers; switch between specific and general concerns with usability

of tasks and users. Table 12.2 lists some of the concerns specific to usability evaluation. For instance, the black hat contains much of the focus on defect-evaluation, while the yellow hat would imply the use of logical steps of reasoning—based, for example, on HCI principles.

We believe the approach of *Six Thinking Hats* may be useful for several reasons. First, it brings together different stakeholders possibly bridging, but at least providing an effort to tackle, differences in view between usability and technical concerns, between designers and evaluators. Second, it provides full-spectrum thinking about usability concerns, not just about problems. Third, it helps defer evaluation and closure of issues by the distinct use of the six hats. However, this technique has still to be systematically evaluated.

12.6 Implications for Practitioners

We believe that the analogy between idea generation and usability evaluation may be an impetus for practitioners to consider their work in a different perspective from the defect-identification view discussed earlier.

First of all, we suggest reporting ideas about users, tasks, and applications as a useful output from usability evaluations. Some of these ideas may be solutions to observed problems—some may simply be thoughts as to how the design of an application may be improved. These ideas could be evaluated in relation to the definition of good ideas outlined earlier, that is, whether they are both useful and novel. As elsewhere, simply being original is undesirable, but simply presenting useful ideas that a development team already knows may be unsatisfactory. Similarly, while not all output from an evaluation need be paradigm-modifying, sometimes that type of idea may be the most useful.

As mentioned earlier, the role of the environment in idea generation has been extensively researched (i.e., Amabile, et al. 1996; Amabile 1996). We believe that usability professionals who routinely perform evaluations may find points of interest in this literature. First, excessive workload pressure is a major impediment to creativity because of a lack of time for incubation and exploring alternatives. Amabile cites several studies confirming this finding. Being forced to make evaluations on overdue products is thus not only too late, but also runs the risk of not producing the most creative solutions possible. Second, critical evaluation of work, or even hostility towards work, is another organizational barrier to creative work. A setup where usability evaluators see themselves as not being listened to and have their work criticized by developers, designers, or managers, is not only unfortunate, but might also negatively impact the quality of the ideas generated.

As mentioned in the previous section, we believe that creativity techniques may help usability professionals develop more useful solutions that developers and designers are less likely to have considered. One starting place for a description of idea-generation and creativity techniques could be Couger, et al. (1993) or Smith (1998). Let us give some examples. It seems relevant when performing evaluations to consider approaches such as habit-breaking through the escape method. This method suggests working to escape all main trains of thought—that is, avoiding the most common assumptions and ways of thinking about the problem—in usability evaluation we might consider "What if this were *not* the user's main task?",, "What if our site didn't support searching?", or "What if not all our customers were searching for products to buy?" Analytic approaches would imply using for example the progressive abstraction technique to report the general solution to a problem. This technique requires making the problem progressively more abstract and general—in usability evaluation we might consider whether we can formulate problematic issues with an interface, say poor help, in a progressively more general way to generate solutions other than the obvious addition of better help content. Finally, wishful thinking is a intuitive creativity technique that employs statements like "I wish that ..." or "what would happen if ...". These wishes and loose ideas would then be consolidated into more practical terms, and then possibly developed into solutions.

It should be clear from the discussion of process models of creativity that generation of ideas, and assessment of the viability of those ideas, are separate activities. In many common evaluation methods (heuristic evaluation being one good example), generation of ideas about the application being inspected (e.g., about usability problems or design suggestions) is intertwined with assessment of those ideas. We think that practitioners might benefit from using deferred judgment, both in identifying possible usability problems and in coming up with creative solutions to those problems.

12.7 Conclusion

In the literature, usability evaluation is largely understood as defect-identification. We have argued that usability evaluation may also be viewed as idea generation— that is, as a process aimed at generating novel and useful ideas about the application under evaluation. This view may complement the defect-identification view, and we suggest that it has some interesting implications for usability researchers and practitioners.

For researchers, we suggest understanding the process of evaluation in terms of some of the process models from creativity research. We have also outlined a number of metrics by which feedback from usability evaluations may be assessed. In particular, we find Amabile's (1996) consensual assessment technique promising for usability research. In contrast to the many studies of eminent researchers and artists, there is an absence in usability research of studies of talented evaluators' usability work, and we contend that this would be a useful research direction. A number of creativity techniques may be readily usable in usability research. We have suggested using both existing techniques and a new one based on de Bono's (2000) work.

Practitioners may find seeing the purpose of usability evaluation as "where can we find better ways" rather than "what is wrong" more challenging and more constructive. We suggest that providing ideas as feedback from evaluation work is useful. A couple of techniques, and what might be better ways of organizing the evaluation activity, are also suggested.

This chapter has not discussed how to validate the suggestion of usability evaluation as idea generation. We have also completely sidestepped the question of how this idea will sell and how to persuade managers, customers, and co-workers that it will work. Our main aim has been to argue that usability researchers and practitioners could find inspiration in viewing usability evaluation as idea generation.

Acknowledgment I am grateful for comments from Erik Frøkjær, Gilbert Cockton, and two anonymous reviewers. This work was supported by Grant #2106-04-0022 from the Strategic Danish Research Council.

References

Amabile, T.M. (1996). *Creativity in context*. Boulder, CO: Westview Press.

Amabile, T.M., Conti, R., Lazenby, H., & Herron, M. (1996). Assessing the work environment for creativity. *Academy of Management Review, 29*, 1154–1181.

Bailey, R.W., Allan, R.W., & Raiello, P. (1992). Usability testing vs. heuristic evaluation: a head-to-head comparison. In *Proceedings of the Human Factors Society 36th Annual Meeting* (pp. 409–413).

Brown, R.T. (1989). Creativity: what are we to measure? In Glover, J.A., Ronning R.R., & Reynolds, C.R. (Eds.), *Handbook of creativity* (pp. 3–32). New York, NY: Plenum Press.

Cockton, G., Lavery, D., & Woolrych, A. (2003a). Inspection-based evaluations. In Jacko, J.A., & Sears, A. (Eds.), *The human-computer interaction handbook* (pp. 1118–1138). Mahwah, NJ: Lawrence Erlbaum Associates.

Cockton, G., Woolrych, A., Hall, L., & Hindmarch, M. (2003b). Changing analysts' tunes: the surprising impact of a new instrument for usability inspection method assessment. In *Proceedings of People and Computers XVII: Designing for Society* (pp. 145–162). Springer Verlag.

Couger, J.D., Higgins, L.F., & McIntyre, S.C. (1993). (Un)structured creativity in information systems organizations. *MIS Quarterly*, 375–394.

Csikszentmihalyi, M. (1996). *Creativity: flow and the psychology of discovery and invention*. New York, NY: Harper Perennial.

De Bono, E. (1994). Creativity and quality. *Quality Management in Health Care, 2*, 3, 1–4.

De Bono, E. (2000). *Six thinking hats*. London: Penguin Books.

Dix, A., Finaly, J., Abowd, G., & Beale, R. (2004). *Human-computer interaction*. Harlow, England: Pearson.

Dumas, J., Molich, R., & Jefferies, R. (2004). Describing usability problems: are we sending the right message? *Interactions, 4*, 24–29.

Dumas, J., & Redish, J. (1999). *A practical guide to usability testing*. (2nd ed.) intellect.

Dumas, J. S. (2003). User-based Evaluations. In Jacko JA & Sears A (Eds.), *the human-computer interaction handbook* (pp. 1093–1117). Mahwah, NJ: Lawrence Erlbaum Associates.

Elam, J.C., & Mead, M. (1990). Can software influence creativity? *Information Systems Research, 1*, 1, 1–22.

Gardner, H. (1994). *Creating minds*. Basic Books.

Garfield, M., Taylor, N., & Dennis, A. (2001). Research report: modifying paradigms – individual differences, creativity techniques, and exposure to ideas in group idea generation. *Information Systems Research, 12*, 3, 322–333.

Getzels, J.W., & Csikszentmihalyi, M. (1976). *The creative vision: A longitudinal study of problem finding in art*. Wiley.

Gray, W.D., & Salzman, M.C. (1998). Damaged merchandise? A review of experiments that compare usability evaluation methods. *Human-Computer Interaction, 13*(3), 203–261.

Guilford, J. (1950). Creativity. *American Psychologist*, 5, 444–454.

Hartson, H. R., Andre, T.S., & Williges, R.C. (2001). Criteria for evaluating usability evaluation methods. *International Journal of Human-Computer Interaction, 13*, 4, 373–410.

Hassenzahl, M., & Tractinsky, N. (2006). User experience – a research agenda. *Behaviour & Information Technology, 25*, 2, 91–97.

Hornbæk, K., & Frøkjær, E. (2005). Comparing usability problems and redesign proposals as input to practical systems development. In *Proceedings of ACM Conference on Human Factors in Computing Systems* (pp. 391–400). New York, NY: ACM Press.

Hornbæk, K., & Stage, J. (2006). Special issue on the interplay between usability evaluation and user interaction design. *International Journal of Human-Computer Interaction, 21*, 5.

Hornbæk, K., & Frøkjær, E. (2002). Evaluating user interfaces with metaphors of human thinking. In *Proceedings of 7th ERCIM Workshop "User Interfaces for All", Lecture Notes in Computer Science 2615* (pp. 486–507). Berlin: Springer Verlag.

Hornbæk, K., & Frøkjær, E. (2004). Usability inspection by metaphors of human thinking compared to heuristic evaluation. *International Journal of Human-Computer Interaction, 17*, 3, 357–374.

Jackson, P.W., & Messick, S. (1965). The person, the product, and the response: conceptual problems in the assessment of creativity. *Journal of Personality, 33*, 309–329.

James, W. (1890). *Principles of psychology*. Henry Holt & Co.

John, B.E., & Marks, S.J. (1997). Tracking the effectiveness of usability evaluation methods. *Behaviour & Information Technology, 16*, 4/5, 188–202.

Karat, J. (1998). User-centered software evaluation methodologies. In M. Helander, T.K. Landauer, & P. Prabhu (Eds.), *Handbook of human-computer interaction* (pp. 689–704). Amsterdam: Elsevier.

MacCrimmon, K., & Wagner, C. (1994). Stimulating ideas through creativity software, *Management Science, 40*, 11, 1514–1532.

Malaga, R.A. (2000). The effect of stimulus modes and associative distance in individual creativity support systems. *Decision Support Systems, 29*, 2, 125–141.

Marakas, G.M., & Elam, J.J. (1997). Creativity enhancement in problem solving: through software or process? *Management Science, 43*, 8, 1136–1146.

Massetti, B. (1996). An empirical examination of the value of creativity support systems on idea generation. *MIS Quarterly, 20*, 1, 83–97.

Mednick, S. (1962). The associative basis of the creative process. *Psychological Review, 69*, 3, 229–232.

Milgram, R. (1981). Ideational fluency as a predictor of original problem solving. *Journal of Education Technology, 73*, 4, 568–572.

Molich, R., Ede, M.R., Kaasgaard, K., & Karyukin, B. (2004). Comparative usability evaluation. *Behaviour & Information Technology, 23*, 1, 65–74.

Nielsen, J. (1992). Finding usability problems through heuristic evaluation usability walkthroughs. In *Proceedings of ACM Conference on Human Factors in Computing Systems* (pp. 373–380). New York, NY: ACM Press.

Nielsen, J., & Molich, R. (1990). Heuristic evaluation of user interfaces. In *Proceedings of ACM Conference on Human Factors in Computing* (pp. 249–256). New York, NY: ACM Press.

Nørgaard, M., & Hornbæk, K. (2006). What do usability evaluators do in practice? an explorative study of think-aloud testing. In *Proceedings of ACM Conference on Designing Interactive Systems* (pp. 209–218).

Osborn, A. (1953). *Applied imagination*. New York, NY: Charles Scribner's Sons.

Polya, G. (1945). *How to solve it*. Princeton, NJ: Princeton University Press.

Proctor, T. (1988). Experiments with two computer assisted creative problem-solving aids. *Omega: The International Journal of Management Science, 17*, 2, 197–200.

Rhodes, M. (1961). An analysis of creativity. *Phi Delta Kappan, 42*, 305–311.

Ripple, R.E. (1989). Ordinary creativity. *Contemporary Educational Psychology, 14*, 189–202.

Rubin, J. (1994). *Handbook of usability testing*. New York: John Wiley & Sons.

Satzinger, J., Garfield, M., & Nagasundaram, M. (1999). The creative process: the effects of group memory on individual idea generation. *Journal of Management Information Systems, 15*, 4, 143–160.

Shneiderman, B., Fischer, G., Czerwinski, M., Resnick, M., Myers, B., Candy, L., Edmonds, E., Eisenberg, M., Giaccardi, E., Hewett, T., Jennings, P., Kules, B., Nakakoji, K., Nunamaker, J., Pausch, R., Selker, T., Sylvan, E., & Terry, M. (2006). Creativity support tools: report from a U.S. national science foundation sponsered workshop. *International Journal of Human-Computer Interaction, 20*, 2, 61–77.

Shneiderman, B. (2000). Creating creativity: user interfaces for supporting innovation. *ACM Transactions on Computer-Human Interaction, 7*, 1, 114–138.

Sklar, A., & Gilmore, D. (2004) Are you positive? *Interactions*, may+june 2004, 28–33.

Smith, D.K., Paradice, D.B., & Smith, S.M. (2000). Prepare your mind for creativity. *Communications of the ACM, 43*, 7, 110–116.

Smith, G.F. (1998). Idea-generation techniques: a formulary of active ingredient. *Journal of Creative Behaviour, 32*, 2, 107–133.

Sternberg, R. (1985). Implicit theories of intelligence, creativity, and wisdom. *Journal of personality and social psychology, 49*, 607–627.

Stone, D., Jarrett, C., Woddroffe, M., & Minocha, S. (2005). *User interface design and evaluation*. Amsterdam: Elsevier.

Terry, M., & Mynatt, E. (2002). Recognizing creative needs in user interface design. In *Proceedings of conference on creativity & cognition* (pp. 38–44). New York, NY: ACM Press

Tohidi, M., Buxton, W., Baecker, R., & Sellen, A. (2006). Getting the right design and the design right. In *Proceedings of ACM Conference on Human Factors in Computing* (pp. 1243–1252). New York, NY: ACM Press

von Oech, R. (1992). *A whack on the side of the head*. Menlo Park, CA: Creative Think.

Wallas, G. (1926). *The art of thought*. New York: Harcourt Brace Jovanovich.

Wixon, D. (2003). Evaluating usability methods: why the current literature fails the practitioner. *Interactions, 10*, 4, 29–34.

Zhang, Z., Basili, V., & Shneiderman, B. (1999). Perspective-based usability inspection: an empirical validation of efficacy. *Empirical Software Engineering, 4*, 1, 43–69.

Chapter 13
Putting Value into E-valu-ation

Gilbert Cockton

School of Computing & Technology, University of Sunderland, UK,
e-mail: gilbert.cockton@sunderland.ac.uk

Abstract Usability evaluation measures remain too close to what were originally dependent variables in factorial experiments. The basis for genuine usability problems in such variables is not guaranteed, but there has been little progress on finding replacements since HCI's shift from the laboratory to field studies. As a result, the worth of much usability evaluation is questionable. Such doubts will persist until we can fully align the purpose of evaluation with the purpose of design, which is to create value in the world through innovative products and services, whether sold in markets, or provided free by either individuals or public and voluntary agencies. This chapter reviews issues with common usability measures and introduces a framework that can plausibly realign evaluation criteria with design purpose by adapting an approach from consumer psychology. This provides opportunities to deploy evaluation measures and instruments that meet the needs of design, rather than reflect skill sets from psychology and human factors. The current gap between design and usability evaluation narrows, but an exclusive usability focus in evaluation becomes impossible. Instead, the role of usability in delivering or degrading intended worth is placed in a wider *worth systems* context. The maturity of usability will thus be evidenced by its effective integration with a range of design and evaluation concerns. It can longer assume intrinsic importance, but has to demonstrate it in the context of achieved product value.

13.1 The Problem with Usability Problems

The purpose of usability evaluation is to find usability problems to understand and fix them (Wixon 2003). The maturity of usability evaluation could thus be measured as our ability to reliably and systematically find, explain, and remedy relevant problems. Note that *relevance* is not an attribute of problems, but a relationship between potential problems and the actual needs of a product or service setting. All such needs relate, in turn, to delivering value, which is the purpose of design. Usability is not value. It is not an end in itself. It is a means to an end. Such ends may be readily achieved despite apparently poor usability. To focus product or service evaluation on usability alone thus invites distraction from which we may never recover, trapped within a suffocating smoke cloud of irrelevance.

E. Law et al. (eds.), *Maturing Usability.*
© Springer-Verlag London Limited 2008

One very good smoke bomb is the definition of *usability*. Such definitions ignore design purpose, distracting evaluation from design success. They tell us what usability is, but not why it is important, still less when it is important. This quickly becomes apparent when one is faced with research problems that require a generic definition of a *usability problem*. One is forced back onto design purpose as the true arbiter of all quality issues with interactive systems. There is much resistance within the HCI mindset to reaching this conclusion, however, as I discovered when attempting to specialize usability evaluation methods for software visualization (Lavery & Cockton 1996). To evaluate new specialized inspection methods, we planned to compare evaluators' predictions with usability problems found through user testing. This required us to answer:

- How do we know if a prediction matches a problem from user testing?
- How do we know if we have reported every problem from testing?

The answers to both questions depend on an answer to a logically earlier one: "What is a Usability Problem?" We addressed this implicitly in our answer to the first question, which was to base matching on structured problem reports (Lavery, et al. 1997)[1]. These offered no definitive answer, but it would involve user difficulties, their causes, or both. We thus finessed an answer by leaving it to the evaluator to decide on the balance between description and explanation when reporting problems. However, this proved to be inadequate once we addressed the second question. We attempted to structure the extraction of usability problems from video data (Cockton & Lavery 1999), but our SUPEX method proved to be too cumbersome even for research use[2]. Still, a key SUPEX insight provided an answer to the root question of what constitutes a usability problem. It was the standard human factors answer: *it depends*!

13.1.1 Usability is Product-Dependent

User difficulties or dissatisfactions become usability problems on the basis of agreed-upon sponsor goals for a new product or service. These goals need to be translated into evaluation criteria, which are in turn translated into measures with target values. Only then can evaluation instruments be selected that measure

---

[1] Soon after publication, this first format was superseded by a simpler one without immediate breakdowns and ultimate outcomes (Lavery & Cockton 1997). However, evaluation researchers continue to suffer from the format in the better-known journal paper (Lavery et al. 1997). The current simplest version, best suited to practitioner usage, was reported in a large study of heuristic evaluation (Cockton & Woolrych 2001). An extension, designed as a research probe, improved evaluator performance (Cockton, et al. 2003). Alan Woolrych continues to refine the extended format in his research. The simple (Cockton & Woolrych 2001) and the slightly revised extended format (Cockton, et al. 2004) supersede all previous formats, which should be avoided!

[2] Even when revisited in 2004 by my colleagues Sharon McDonald and Mark Hindmarch using video analysis software.

target attainment (Cockton 2005). Contrast this product-specific procedure with what is implicit in ISO 9241 Part 11's international standard definition of usability (ISO 1998):

> "... extent to which a product can be used by specified users to achieve specified goals with effectiveness, efficiency and satisfaction in a specified context of use... "

This assumes that interaction qualities of efficiency, functional consequences of effectiveness, and psychological consequences of satisfaction always matter to product quality. Universal quality criteria for products and services are stated, and yet their achievement must be demonstrated for specific users in specific contexts of use achieving specific goals. Measurement of extent can thus only be context-specific, but the components of usability are implicitly universal. There is clear tension between an abstract concept of usability and the tightly specified contexts in which it can be objectively demonstrated. On the one hand, usability must be measured for the right users achieving the right goals in the right usage context. On the other hand, there is no indication about the bases for the *right extent* of effectiveness, efficiency, and satisfaction. The international standard gives examples of measures, but does not relate them to product or service goals.

13.1.2 Usability Measures Tend to be Product-Independent

Definitions of usability cannot guide evaluators in their choice of measures. So, what does get measured? Too often, measures remain experimental dependent variables from the dawn of HCI. Separation anxiety keeps many evaluators tied to the apron strings of psychology experiments. As a result, usability practice and even HCI research can avoid critical reflection on what we should measure and why. Usability evaluation can only mature by answering this question. This chapter offers an answer that has nothing to do with the psychology experiments from which usability evaluation was born. Their influence has remained surprising robust. It has proven hard to let go of the apron strings of one of HCI's parents.

In the absence of clear guidance on the choice of measures and targets, usability specialists with psychological training (or aspirations) have tended to copy measures for dependent variables from human factors experiments. Examples of targets and measures in ISO 9241 Part 11 are consistent with this claim. This is unsurprising, because the title of one of the first HCI collections *Computing Skills and the User Interface* (Coombs & Alty 1983) reflects HCI's initial cognitive dominance. HCI placed itself in immediate opposition to computer science-originated design guidelines that (over) generalized from real or imagined usage experiences. Rigorous empirical approaches required all claims for features and designs (*quality in the system*) to be demonstrated through controlled replicable experiments involving human participants (*quality in interaction*). Alternative system elements became independent experimental variables. Dependent variables were measures such as learning time, time on task, task completion, and error rate, sometimes accompanied by measures of subjective satisfaction and task quality. All these are examples in ISO 9241-11.

Experiments proved to be impractical for most software development, so independent variables largely disappeared. Single designs were 'user tested' against a range of former dependent variables. Without independent variables, many statistical analyses became impossible, but testing retained the controlled laboratory settings of psychology experiments. Testing was no longer an *experiment*, and was not considered as such. Controls, independent variables, and statistical inferences disappeared, leaving measurement based on the same old dependent variables.

Considerable success was achieved with these quasi-experimental approaches. Laboratory-measured improvements in efficiency, effectiveness, and satisfaction were achieved by a focus on interaction. However, these rarely translated into success in the field (Whiteside, et al. 1988). In response, second wave HCI (Bødker 2006) shifted focus from interaction in controlled environments to genuine usage contexts. However, usability metrics have not kept pace with the contextual second wave, still less with the currently competing third wave focuses of user experience (Hassenzahl & Tractinsky 2006), reflective HCI (Sengers, et al. 2005), worth (Cockton 2006a) and other contenders for HCI's next big thing. A review of recent HCI experiments, as well as current usability practice, will still tend to reveal measures that would not have been out of place 20 years ago—that is, when second wave HCI abandoned experimental laboratory-originated measures for field observation. As a test of this claim, consider this list of metrics (Whiteside, et al. 1988):

- Time to complete a task
- Percent of task completed
- Percent of task completed per unit time (speed metric)
- Ratio of successes to failures
- Time spent in errors
- Percent or number of errors
- Percent or number of competitors better than
- Number of commands used
- Frequency of help and documentation use
- Time spent using help or documentation
- Percent of favourable/unfavorable user comments
- Number of repetitions of failed commands
- Number of runs of successes and of failures
- Number of times interface misleads the user
- Number of good and bad features recalled by users
- Number of available commands not invoked
- Number of regressive behaviors
- Number of users preferring your system
- Number of times users need to work around a problem
- Number of times the user is disrupted from a work task
- Number of times user loses control of the system
- Number of times user expresses frustration or satisfaction

Such measures must relate in some way to the definition of a usability problem, but this remains an open issue in HCI, even though the identification of what a problem is is the most important issue in the usability profession (Gray and Salzman 1998). Identification of usability problems is absolutely dependent on the measures chosen for evaluation. However, measures alone are not enough. Targets need to indicate whether a system is *usable enough*. For Whiteside and his coauthors, worst, planned- and best-case levels could be set for any measurement criterion on one or more of the following bases:

- An existing system or previous version
- Competitive systems (with good market share and/or acclaimed user interface)
- Carrying out the task without the use of a computer system
- An absolute scale
- Your own prototype
- Users' own earlier performance
- Each component of a system separately
- A successive split of the difference between best and worst values observed in user tests
- The development team's own choices

The last of these approaches appeared to be most common, from the account of practice in IBM and DEC (Whiteside, et al. 1988). As far as the politics of usability are concerned, this is very effective, especially as targets could be revised in the face of new insights during iterative development. However, a focus on whether or not the right levels or targets are set overlooks their dependency on a largely predefined list of measures.

Whiteside, Bennett, and Holtzblatt (1988) were fully aware of this in their classic = Handbook of HCI chapter, seeing usability attributes (targets or levels to you and me) as a *double-edged sword*, enabling developer focus and the measurement of progress, but also failing "to reflect usability as it will be judged in practice": "it had better be true that the specified goals are the ones users really want." This was often *not* so, so usability engineers at DEC and IBM moved away from the comfort of psychology measures.

Whiteside and his coauthors asked "how do we know that the developers' understanding of usability is the same as the users' understanding of usability? . . . Even if we acknowledge that developers are trying to define attributes that they think relate to customer-perceived usability, how do we know that their understanding of their customers is correct?" However, Whiteside, et al. only offer a *vision* of contextualized usability engineering in the development life cycle. They note that usability specifications and objectives "can be defined through an interpretation of data from the field." The chapter was published in 1988, but despite the long evolution of contextual design since then (Beyer & Holtzblatt 1996; Holtzblatt, et al. 2004), such a move from contextual data to usability objectives has never been demonstrated. This is not to say that their approach has failed, because Whiteside and colleagues did change the focus of development by emphasizing context—in their case, the work place and how products fit into it. The move from inappropriate to insufficient measurement did not prevent usability from making a contribution. This is because human factors measurements were often supplemented by qualitative methods from cognitive psychology. Such qualitative *think-aloud* data commonly structures *Discussion* sections in cognitive psychology papers. Direct quotes of users' comments, plus descriptions of behavior, revealed far more than inferential statistics, and critically offered potential explanations of quantitative results. Comments by test participants thus often get a prominent place in highlight tapes. Quantitative measures may not even clearly show what the problem is. The need to understand (and then fix) usability problems justified this focus within usability practice on qualitative behavioral and verbal data. However, think-aloud data has been used more as a tentative basis for explanation than as a basis for measurement. While critical to effective usability practice, think-alouds and retrospective interviews have limited impact on how usability targets are set and measured.

Usability is not an end in itself, but a means to an end. Despite the -ity suffix, it is not an absolute binary property, but rather an attribute with varying degrees. Usability only needs to be evaluated when, and to the extent that, it matters. Without objectives that can relate usability to design purpose, evaluation cannot be properly focused. Almost two decades ago however, there had been a clear steer on how to align design and evaluation purposes: "it had better be true that the specified goals are the ones users really want." (Whiteside, et al. 1988).

So, what do users *really want*, and how can we relate this to evaluation planning? This question is very different from the two that arose when I first tried to assess evaluation methods. Our questions were procedural, and answers would hopefully let us avoid confounds and false conclusions that were systematically exposed by Gray and Salzman (1998). There have indeed been improvements here, but answering both of our questions needs an answer to their root question of "What is a usability problem?" However, a key position of this chapter is that this is the wrong place to start. Rather, we should start with Whiteside and his coauthors' implicit question of "What do users *really want?*" Can we really find an answer to this in the unhelpful generalizations of ISO 9241 Part 11? Do we really believe that when asked, users express what they want in terms of an "extent to which" specified users can achieve specified goals, and to express this as measures of efficiency, effectiveness, and satisfaction? So why, when assessing the maturity of usability evaluation, have we focused on methodological issues related to measurement and comparison, when we have no explicit basis for knowing if we are measuring and comparing the right things?

13.1.3 *You Won't Get There From Here*

The concern with usability arose as an answer to the specific problems that were encountered as work-based computer usage became more widespread with the first minicomputers and then PCs. Usability distracted attention from the main purposes of computer usage. For some, it became an end in itself, and we thus ended up with usability as a self-defining quality of systems or interaction, without regard to why *it matters.* I cannot see how evaluation methods can become reliably worthwhile until we move the focus away from legacy human factors measures.

Some Irish jokes end with the punch line that "you can't get there from here." My argument is that you will not get *there* (effective worthwhile evaluation) from *here* (reflection on the essence of usability, its generic measures, and its predefined targets). The above mix of personal and HCI history has been provided to—following the Irish phrase—show where *here* is. *Here* is the continued use of measures that may not (and often do not) matter, because what users really want will not be expressed primarily as thresholds for efficiency, effectiveness, or satisfaction. However, we must not underestimate the attraction of *here* to many usability specialists. Limitations are well-recognized for standardized metrics, with their origins in cognitive and human factors experiments, and yet they remain the core measures in use in usability. Reflective and gifted usability specialists will find other things to measure, and other ways of measuring them. However, they do not get there by redefining usability. You can't systematically and consistently get *there*—i.e., to measuring what users really want—from *here*, that is classic human factors measures. Their tenacity should not be underestimated. Efficiency, effectiveness, and satisfaction remain the basis for one of the most recent ISO usability standards (ISO 2006). This chapter argues that we can finally move on if we start from *there*—that is, with *what users really want*—and see where usability fits in alongside a range of qualities of systems and interaction.

We must abandon an exclusive focus on usability, even usability's *new* attempt to shoehorn a wide range of hedonic and experiential factors into the original performance-oriented context. Focusing usage studies on usability alone wastes effort and resources. Many other important qualities and outcomes can be measured during usage studies. We can and should measure them alongside usability. We should be evaluators first, and usability specialists second. To do this, we must understand the relationship between value and e-valu-ation. People want what they value. The study of value is thus implied by the study of users' wants and needs.

13.2 Climbing Ladders of Users' Wants and Needs

What do users really want? What do they think about software products and services? How would we know? Internet-enabling of e-commerce has added marketing to HCI's disciplinary mix, and can provide an answer to these root questions for evaluation. Marketing has several approaches to probing users' cognitive structures. One that has promise for uniting design and evaluation is *laddering*, which captures consumer cognitions about products. It does so by asking them to identify important product attributes and then recursively asking why these attributes are important, and why those are important—repeating this ascent *up the ladder* until a consumer can only say that something really matters to them. The approach is well-established in marketing, where it can guide the design of advertising campaigns by identifying associations that are important, frequent, and credible to consumers (Reynolds & Gutman 1988). The approach has widespread use, and examples can readily be found on the Internet for a diverse range of applications (e.g., food ethics, energy supply, political campaigns, and union membership). Within IT, laddering has been used in knowledge elicitation (Corbridge, et al. 1994) and information systems research (Rugg, et al. 2002). In HCI, its relevance has been demonstrated for websites (Subramony 2002), online communities (Aschmoneit & Heitmann 2003), and mobile brands (Heitmann, et al. 2004).

Laddering can relate what users really want to product attributes via usage consequences. Usability is a factor in *means-end chains* (MECs) between product attributes, usage consequences, and motivating values. It is not an end in itself. Laddering provides an opportunity for relating usability to product goals. We can thus redefine usability as "the extent to which intended value is donated, delivered, degraded, or destroyed by the quality of user interaction." The relationship of usability to product goals can now be pinpointed diagrammatically, because laddering results in a hierarchy (values are more general than consequences, which are more general than product attributes). A broad base of attributes narrows to a smaller apex of values. Converging associations can be drawn as a *hierarchical value model* (HVM), as shown in Figure 13.1. MECs can be traced in HVMs as paths that start with product attributes in the broad base, and proceed via consequences to the apex of personal values.

To apply HVMs in HCI, we need to understand issues associated with their use. Not all HVMs use the same range of attribute, consequence, and value categories. There is debate on whether values are more important than consequences in consumer decision-making. Further differences arise with *categories* of attributes, consequences, and values. Attributes may be *concrete* (e.g., provision of website breadcrumbs) or *abstract* (e.g., navigability of website), and may apply to several products under comparison (*groupings*). Consequences may be *functional* (e.g., can find train times) or *psychosocial* (e.g., can spend as much time as possible with girlfriend). Values, following Rokeach (1973), may be *instrumental* (means to ends, e.g., responsible) or *terminal* (ends in themselves, e.g., mature love). One drawback of early laddering approaches was that consumers' values were primed

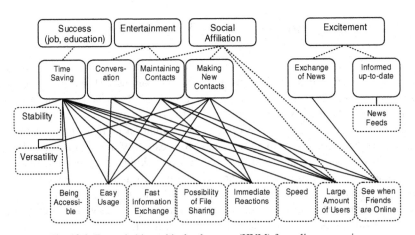

Fig. 13.1 Example hierarchical value map (HVM) for online messaging

from lists, including subsets of Rokeach's values. This approach has been used by researchers and marketers who regard personal values as dominant elements in consumer decision-making (and so help consumers choose appropriate values). Such a deliberate, sustained, and primed focus on personal values is controversial.

Not all laddering approaches distinguish between different categories of attribute or value. Also, different categories are used for consequences (e.g., functional vs. emotional). Some approaches replace product attributes with product *benefits,* and consequences/values with basic and higher *needs.* Furthermore, consequences can be shown to have bi-directional associations, resulting in *networks* rather than hierarchies of worth.

No doubt, further variations of category hierarchies or networks are in use, but the pros and cons of each are less important than the fundamentals of associating product qualities with real world consequences, and these in turn with personal motivators. Laddering in HVMs can thus answer the true root design question of "what do users really want?" Within the context of such an answer, a usability problem is anything that degrades positive associations between product attributes, usage consequences, and motivating values. Usability rightly becomes secondary to value. What we should really be evaluating is the achievement of expected value. Putting *value* in e-valu-ation requires us to focus primarily on value, and only on usability and other interaction qualities in so far as they degrade or destroy the intended value. Usability needs to be evaluated within a value-centered context that relates it to "what users really want," and should not be based on the comfort and convenience of human factors measures.

13.2.1 Hierarchical Value Models (HVMs)

This chapter introduces HVMs as a basis for understanding usability as attributes of associations between product design and usage consequences. Figure 13.1 showed an adapted HVM for online instant messaging. The original (Aschmoneit & Heitmann 2003) uses node and arc shadings to indicate frequency of associations (lines) and entities (boxes for attributes, consequences, or values). The bottom two rows (dotted outlines) are attributes—both abstract (*easy usage, stability*) and concrete (*possibility of file sharing, news feeds*). The upper two rows (solid outlines) are consequences (e.g., functional consequence of *conversation,* psychosocial consequence of *social affiliation*), with some beginning to border on instrumental values such as *success* (*job, education*). Associations with top-level motivations are indicated by dotted lines. The map is based on ladders elicited online from 126 online users via chat interviews. Users were not primed at any point with lists of values.

The example HVM supports the claim that laddering can capture what users really want—in this case, what one sample wants from instant messaging. Note that they do want usability (*easy usage*), but only as a means to an end, and in so far as it has positive consequences for efficiency (*time saving*) and effectiveness (supporting *conversation* and thereby *making new* or *maintaining* existing contacts). Satisfaction emerges at a higher level as *excitement* and *entertainment*, with *social affiliation* probably involving both satisfaction and effectiveness. Note that the only captured positive consequence of efficiency (time saving) is the personal value of career and/or educational success.

It is hard to see how starting with the ISO trio of efficiency, effectiveness, or satisfaction could ever have got us directly to the four motivators expressed in the example HVM. Nothing is ever ruled out in principle, but the examples in ISO 9241-11 are never related to such high-level motivations. Selecting the right evaluation measures will remain an art, and a potentially unreliable and wasteful one too, as long as standards such as 9241-11 just offer lists of possible measures (something that Whiteside and colleagues had already done better a decade earlier). The cognitively biased human factors literature has not addressed *social affiliation*, and slavish devotees of 9241-11 may well have tried to cleave social affiliation into separate elements of effectiveness or satisfaction. Also, time spent on measuring efficient time saving would—in so far as the HVM is accurate—have little short- or medium-term payback (because any impact on career/education would take months to accumulate and emerge), while the other three top-level consequences could be usefully measured after a relatively short period of usage (e.g., 2-6 weeks). It would be very instructive to see a convincing route from efficiency, effectiveness, and satisfaction to the explicit consumer-expressed motivations at the top of Figure 13.1. If we work directly from such HVMs in the first place, we are spared such detours and contortions. The HVM's consequences direct us towards a range of measures that have little in common with dependent variables of human factors experiments. Once again, "you can't get there from here."

13.2.2 HVMs and Evaluation Strategies

Evaluation strategies can be derived from understandings of intended and/or desired value if the latter is expressed as an HVM. When developing SUPEX (Cockton & Lavery 1999), we assumed that classic measures of interaction could form the basis for filtering thresholds. In reality, such thresholds cannot be known until it is too late for them to be relevant. This follows, because what should be established during evaluation is the achievement of functional and psychosocial consequences, plus the fulfilment of those personal values that are genuinely important to users. Once these have been established, it may be possible *post hoc* to determine what the threshold *should have* been. However, this has little practical value, because a design is hardly going to be made worse to drop it back down to some threshold. More seriously, it is clear that many consequences depend on multiple product attributes, which turns threshold determination into a multiple regression problem. Once again, if desired consequences follow, then the relative weight of product attributes is somewhat (or even largely) academic. If desired consequences are not achieved, then *causal analysis* is required to identify the product attribute(s) most likely to be responsible. This requires more than stabs in the dark about target levels for abstract product attributes.

Evaluation of product attributes is primarily a question of quality control during development. Periodic summative evaluation requires the measurement of consequences by selecting or developing instruments that can measure relevant real world variables. Should summative evaluation reveal *usability problems* (as unachieved consequences), then formative evaluation may require more detailed remeasurement of product attributes in realistic usage contexts. For example in instant messaging, the reasons for low *exchange of news* and *making new contacts* (Figure 13.1) would be more important than the exact point at which low becomes *too* low. This could be due to difficulties in determining the online population of existing friends ("See when Friends are Online") and potential new contacts ("Large Amount of Users"). This would provide a focus to establish the causes of degraded worth in instant messaging interactions.

HVMs can thus support worth-centred evaluation planning. However, their current use *once product design has been completed* makes this difficult. One solution here may be to repeat the tactic of IBM and DEC (Whiteside, et al. 1988) of two decades ago and to *let the product team decide the initial desired associations* between attributes, consequences, and values. Human factors target setting is thus replaced by *worth mapping*.

13.2.2.1 Mapping Worth during Design and Development

A design-oriented HVM can be constructed during initial user research, which should establish needs and wants by understanding the motivations and goals of users and system sponsors. Motivations and goals should translate into consequences or values in an HVM. Where field work is focused on breakdowns with current systems (*pain points*), this may identify abstract product attributes associated with *adverse* concrete consequences. The purpose of design thus *primarily* becomes one of establishing concrete product or service attributes that can catalyze desired MECs. However, design can also be given a *secondary* purpose of constructing a comprehensive valid HVM as a means to its primary purpose.

Coiteration of both a design and its motivating worth map provides a basis for *Total Iteration Potential* (Cockton 2006a). This is the ability of evaluation to not only drive redesign recommendations, but to also improve the evaluation process, the understandings of context of use, and even revise design purpose. If design is the *creation of value* (Cockton 2006a), then approaches that only iterate designs are not well-focused. Instead, evaluation must e-*valu*-ate, and not just uncover adverse interactions (poor usability or fit to context) but, most importantly, *support iteration of design purpose* and not just of designs and design and evaluation processes. HVMs can be modified to support such purpose.

In summary, the chapter has argued for two positions at this point:

1. Usability has too often applied inappropriate or insufficient measures (human factors dependent variables) to answer the wrong question ("what is usability/a usability problem?").
2. The right question is "what do users really want (as well as system sponsors and other stakeholders?)," and a possible answer is that what they really want can be elicited via laddering interviews and expressed as some form of HVM.

We now consider appropriate forms for HVMs for HCI, which will be called *worth maps* to distinguish them from consumer psychology's HVMs. With these in place, we will explore how evaluation planning and practice can be grounded in worth maps, and thus focus usability evaluation on what matters, rather than on what researchers in human factors, or cognitive (and now also affective) researchers know how to measure.

13.3 From HVMs to Worth Maps

HVMs have the potential to align evaluation with design purpose, expressing the latter as a product team's map of intended worth. We need to revise HVMs to become more comprehensive and less doctrinaire on MEC structure, without commitments to hierarchies of fixed categories. HVM elements are thus generalized by the term *worthy*, which can refer to any MEC factor (e.g., attributes, consequences, or values). We will not assume that psychosocial consequences follow from functional consequences, but never vice-versa. An arbitrary set of consequences of any category can be interlinked into a network grounded in mostly abstract attributes, but with possible direct associations to concrete product attributes. MECs are thus replaced with *worth subsystems*, where associations operate in either (or both) direction in the vertical axis of a *worth map*.

There is no assumption that any predefined terminal values must form the apex of a worth map. Indeed, consequences alone may be the most abstract worthies if product teams initially find values unhelpful. Values can then be added as, and when, credible and grounded ones emerge.

To become more comprehensive, worth maps need to be first devised for a range of stakeholders. Second, *negative* as well as positive associations must be modeled (Reynolds & Gutman 1984). By juxtaposing positive and negative consequences of product attributes, a balanced view of the true impact of supposed usability problems can be formed. We will return to balance, but consider breadth first.

13.3.1 Breadth of Worth: Stakeholders

Figure 13.1 represented users' associations between system attributes and usage consequences. We need to extend worth mapping to all stakeholders, especially a new sociodigital system's sponsors who are ultimately responsible for deciding on design purpose. For example, the stakeholders for a van hire website would include:

- Customers
- Operational staff, especially at depots
- Management (system sponsors)

Considering customers first, they want to find an appropriate van with confidence (functional and psychosocial consequences). Two product attributes can support these consequences: photos of what a van can carry and dimensions of usable load space are more informative than cubic volume. Customers also will need to be able to hire an appropriate van for an appropriate period for an acceptable cost (money, time, convenience). This adds one further functional consequence (appropriate period) and three psychosocial ones (money, time, convenience), although we may want to broaden our consequence categories to include economic ones (money, and perhaps time). Whatever our consequence categories, these user needs require product attributes of clear information on the full price of a hire, and what to do to pick up and return the van on time. Customers' needs, however, extend beyond website use. Having chosen and booked a van, customers need to know several things to ensure successful delivery of their van load: how to get to the van depot, depot opening times, and required documentation (printout of confirmation, drivers license). The functional consequence of *successful delivery* dominates all others, and requires further information attributes on the website and/or via email. Printable and/or emailed instructions (e.g., pdfs) may strengthen associations between product attributes and desired consequences.

Based on these assumptions, Figure 13.2 shows a worth map fragment for hypothetical van-hire customers. Proposed concrete and target abstract attributes are at the bottom (dotted outlines). Above these, are functional and then psychosocial consequences, but consequences such as financial gain are economic: van-hire may effect an exchange. Other motivations for hiring a van are shown (moving home, purchase, gift). Where these are mutually exclusive, separate worth maps for specific personas may be needed. These would correspond from *modes* from market research, where markets are segmented below the level of individual consumers, in recognition that the same people can want different things at different times (e.g., business lunch in formal restaurant vs. fast food with young family). The top row (dashed outlines) are personal values. Rokeach (1973) lists happiness and social recognition as terminal values, but these do not fully capture understandings behind Figure 13.2, so alternatives are used.

Worth maps can be constructed for other stakeholders. We could assume that *operational staff* want to enjoy their work (if not, then careful service/job design should change this). Staff should want collection and return of vans to proceed smoothly, and for customers to leave pleased with the ease and quality of van usage. The website thus needs to ensure that customers turn up at the right place at the right time with the right documents. In the customer worth map, identified concrete attributes enable high quality service experience. However, by also collecting information on a customer's load (further product attributes), the website could forward information that lets depot staff advise and support customers in load handling, thus potentially increasing customer and employee satisfaction (psychosocial consequences). Designing systems has always involved designing jobs. B2C websites are no different. By considering work quality for van-hire depot staff, we can include positive consequences from good service design (Service Design Network 2006).

For reasons of space, no further worth maps are shown for other stakeholders. For depot staff, however, a general terminal value of *enjoyable work* could focus Rokeach's terminal values of comfort, accomplishment, and self-respect. This would be reflected in psychosocial consequences of job satisfaction, which would

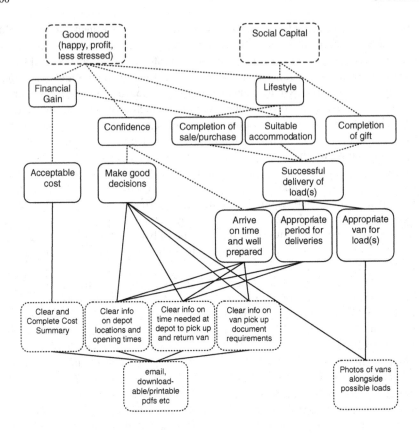

Fig. 13.2 Worth map fragments for van-hire customers

depend on customers' functional and psychosocial consequences, thus requiring cross-referencing of stakeholder worth maps. Staff would largely depend on the website and related emails for getting customers to the depot on time with appropriate documentation. An extensive ability and willingness to provide helpful advice and support on routes and load handling would extend the website with further service attributes that would contribute to customer and staff satisfaction. Abstract attributes thus extend to *brand* attributes. A worth map could be extended to show how the website and back office systems let depot staff deliver on a wide range of brand attributes such as helpfulness, supportiveness, efficiency, professionalism, reliability, and trustworthiness.

Management, the *sponsor stakeholder* group, primarily wants to achieve a good return on investment, brand image, market share, good sales, and satisfied customers. These are all high-level consequences bordering on company values. The website must deliver enough sales to meet its profit targets, which requires several intervening customer focused consequences, which, in turn, are associated with carefully designed product attributes. Short term profitability, however, may not translate into long-term competitiveness and viability, and thus the website needs to be fully aligned with management strategy on sustainable competitiveness.

13.3.1.1 Business Value and Worth Mapping

There are many approaches to business strategy, but most are multifaceted and go beyond immediate profit targets. For example, approaches to strategy in *Balanced Score Card* (Norton and Kaplan 1996) set targets and objectives from the customer's and three company perspectives: financial, learning and growth, and internal business processes. Competitive strategies should set targets and objectives that result in a balance of benefits between stakeholders. To delight all stakeholders, a van-hire site must go beyond simply making a profit, and support reliable, high-quality internal business processes. It must maintain the competitiveness of the company through learning and growth, and also support learning and growth for individual employees, which should ideally result in loyalty and service excellence. Customers should form a positive image of the company, expect to use the van-hire service again, and recommend it to friends, family, and associates. Such a broad approach to service design should enable management to exceed targets and build brand loyalty through customers who feel they have a gift rather than a purchase, and through loyal depot staff who enjoy delivering distinctive rewarding high-quality service.

The website alone cannot fully deliver on a broad business strategy. Pricing policy, pick-up and return policies, depot location and opening hours, van range and availability, and insurance and personal document requirements are factors beyond the website. They all have a critical impact on achieved value. Evaluation targets thus need to be set that establish that the website protects existing value in a van-hire product, and wherever possible, adds value through new site features. A *service design* approach will be required (Service Design Network 2006), and thus evaluation must be fit for that purpose. It no longer makes sense to focus on usability alone, or to evaluate it in isolation from sources of worth.

A worth map for management would thus be much influenced by company strategy. It may, however, be better to have a worth map for the company, and a separate worth map for management, to reflect the interaction of personal and corporate agendas with the working environment. Thus, while companies want to remain sustainably competitive, managers interpret this in terms of individual careers, resulting in potential divergences of terminal values. Instrumental values would include hitting performance targets, return on investment, and brand image. Psychosocial consequences would be very dependent on consequences for customers, but would include net recommender scores, and brand perceptions (reliability, value for money, etc.). Some psychosocial consequences depend on staff, such as good morale, low turnover, shared values, etc. Economic consequences would include market share. Functional consequences would include the reliability, efficiency, and quality of internal business processes. All of this may seem a long way away from usability, but from the management's point of view, usability only matters in so far as it has a bearing on consequences and values that matter to them. The business case for usability has to be made each time, for each business. For commercial systems, we must relate abstract usability attributes to relevant business consequences. If we do not, then we cannot focus usability evaluation on worthwhile outcomes for this worth arena.

13.3.2 Balance of Worth: Worth-Aversion Maps

So far, we have only considered ladders of positive associations, but negative associations are also elicited in laddering (Reynolds & Gutman 1984). Associations can have positive or negative consequences. The latter may extend to breaches of personal values. If worth maps only show positive consequences, this will not capture the balance of benefits and drawbacks for different stakeholders that arise from the same product attributes. Thus while stakeholder worth maps add breadth to the design process, we also need to add balance by considering both motivating worth and demotivating aversion.

In many (if not most) cases, consumers trade-off negative consequences against compensating positive ones, but sometimes nothing can compensate for an unacceptable breach of values. Negative associations thus capture aversions that degrade or destroy consumer motivation. Usability is on home ground here, since historically it has focused usage difficulties and misfit with usage contexts that create adverse consequences.

Positive and negative associations can be combined in a single diagram, simply by recognizing that any value, by its nature, can have a positive or negative valence. However, we tend to distinguish negative values through words such as *aversion*, *taboo*, *proscribed*, *unethical* or *demotivating*. Yet, even this fails to recognize that one person's meat is another's poison—i.e., the same usage outcome may motivate some, while repel others. Thus we cannot directly infer the valence (i.e., positive or negative) of a value or consequence. It may be the case that aversions are just worthies with *not* added to them. Worthies and aversions are independent to the extent that what is worthwhile for one stakeholder may be an aversion for another. The key point is that the valence *does not lie* in the worthy, but in the stakeholder. We can name worthies to distinguish worth from aversion, but this should not mask the fact that objectively they can arise from the same phenomena. What differs is the subjective response of stakeholders. Thus, cookies placed without explicit consent violate personal property rights (Friedman & Kahn 2003). Users may be averse to this, but site sponsors derive worth from the ability to track site visitors. Value-sensitive design thus seeks product attributes (e.g., notification of, and/or consent to, cookie placement) that allow users to balance their values against those of site sponsors.

We need to indicate the valence of a worthy within a worth map (i.e., a value or consequence, attributes are only valenced through association via consequences to values). Position is the most flexible diagrammatic coding attribute (and most coherent, as worthies can be grouped by valence). Coherence will tend to follow from the need to preserve vertical MECs, which will separate positive from negative associations. These could group on the left and right of a worth map. An alternative is to build positive chains up from the middle of a worth map (i.e., up from product attributes) and to build negative chains down over. Such *worth-aversion maps* (W/AMs) add balance by combining an upside (achievable worth) with a downside (probable aversions) to express a design's pros and cons.

Figure 13.3 shows an example management W/AM for a university website. Grey nodes indicate adverse attributes and consequences. It is a first cut W/AM that would typically result from initial design team brainstorming. It can be thought of as a map of *destinies*, because with no details of concrete attributes and no associations forged into positive or negative MECs, development could end in either delight or disaster. The initial single concrete attribute is deliberate, simply indicating dependence of website abstract attributes on the quality of interactive content.

W/AMs in HCI cannot be as comprehensively grounded as consumer HVMs until product release, because the latter are based on reported associations, elicited in an approach based on repertory grids (Reynolds & Gutman 1984). Consumer utterances are coded as referring to product attributes, purchase or usage consequences, or personal values. With utterances *translated* into a common terminology, a frequency matrix of associations is built. In contrast, initial W/AMs will have little empirical grounding. However, the core development aim should be to improve on this. As development progresses, supporting documentation should strengthen W/AM associations. Alternatively, initial *destiny* associations can be removed, especially for successfully avoided aversions!

Evidence for associations is *survey data* that grounds a W/AM. As with maps of the physical world, this is separate from, and does not appear on, the map. For example, as website development progresses, a content matrix can associate details of concrete attributes with positive and negative abstract attributes. Content matrices take many detailed forms in Web design, but all associate concrete content (matrix rows) with attributes (columns). So, columns could state and explain positive and negative attributes associated with specific units of content (i.e., page section/element, page, subsite). Content matrices can thus include survey data to ground W/AMs.

Initial W/AM associations are thus potential destinies. Unlike an exclusively positive worth map, an initial W/AM can capture several alternative destinies, based on different mixes of outcome. Even when supported by survey data, W/AMs cannot be deterministic. The worth subsystems containing causal chains are not closed. Indeed, the more abstract a worthy is, the more open it is to influences that a W/AM may overlook. Thus, universities do not wholly depend on websites for student recruitment, nor will close attention to Web content remove all sources of potential misinformation and other aversions. Figure 13.3 does not thus indicate inevitable connections between a university's Web content and its viability.

All worth subsystems must thus be understood in a broader context of embracing *worth arenas* (Cockton 2006a) that scopes their contribution to the key values of individuals and collectives. A SWOT-style analysis (strengths, weaknesses, opportunities, threats) could provide such a context, with opportunities and threats derived from some form of environmental scanning—perhaps a PESTLE analysis (JISC 2007). This will guide the design team to focus on those worth subsystems that have the greatest potential to influence more than basic functional consequences, guided by strategies informed by SWOT, PESTLE, and similar analyses.

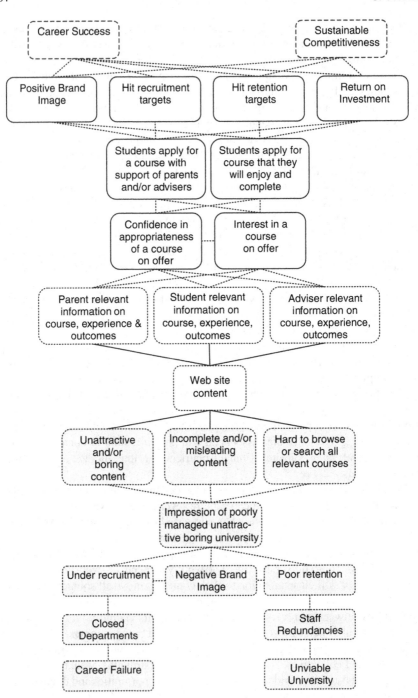

Fig. 13.3 Initial management *destinies* W/AM for a university website

13.3.3 Summary

HVMs can be adapted for HCI to become W/AMs, where:

- W/AMs are structured around an open set of categories for worthies (attributes, values, consequences) that may be associated in non-hierarchical relationships without constraints on MEC structure
- W/AMs represent positive associations above concrete product attributes, and negative associations below them
- Design team's beliefs about key possible development destinies are represented in an initial W/AM, which may have very limited empirical grounding
- The aim of development is to exploit *Total Iteration Potential* (Cockton 2006b) to revise W/AM topology and strengthen associations. At each iteration, values can be added or removed (iteration of design purpose), contextual research can be extended to better understand desirable and avoidable consequences, evaluation planning can be refocused on critical associations, and concrete product attributes can be revised to strengthen positive associations from the base of means-end chains (or to weaken or remove negative ones). The resulting *survey data* progressively improves a W/AM's empirical grounding
- W/AMs can cover several stakeholders, individual stakeholders, or consumption modes, but comprehensive W/AMs can be used to contrast differing outcomes for different stakeholders or modes
- W/AMs need to be constructed and interpreted with reference to *worth arenas* (Cockton 2006a) that provide the logic for the individual and collective worth and aversions at the top and bottom apexes. For example, business strategy provides such logic in the worth arenas of commercial institutions

The final step in the argument of this chapter requires demonstration that W/AMs, as an adaptation of HVMs for HCI, can be used to plan usability analyses within a wider worth-based evaluation framework.

13.4 W/AM-Based E-valu-ation

Within a worth-based evaluation framework, evaluation planning can focus on selecting (or designing) measures and instruments to track the strength of associations within worth subsystems. Measuring some product attributes and lower-level outcomes will be needed to achieve this, but targets will be hard to set in advance. The focus is thus on establishing and/or improving positive associations and removing and/or reducing negative ones. While this will improve outcome measures, it will not do so at the level of the attributes typically measured in usability engineering (e.g., Whiteside, et al. 1988). The focus is on higher-level, real-world outcomes, and once these are achieved, the relative role of usability-related attributes has limited relevance. Once again, an *a priori* focus on usability attributes can distract from what really matters. This lesson was learned two decades ago at DEC and IBM, but we have lacked a new evaluation paradigm that can focus on what users and key stakeholders really want, rather than what psychology and human factors could already measure.

Usability's focus on user goals and critical tasks can provide an indirect route to functional consequences, but this is inadequate for two reasons. First, it fails to place consequences in the context of wider worth subsystems, and thus may fail to assess the rich network of associations that create value from functional consequences. Second, by failing to associate functional and psychosocial consequences, usability practice can be overly instrumental. Conversely, however, attempts to evaluate *user experience* as an overarching quality of interaction can invert this oversight and be overly phenomenological in focus. Overall, usability and user experience approaches tend to shatter worth maps to focus on *suboutcome* fragments of product attributes and usage consequences.

None of the above however means that current or past practice in usability and user experience is worthless. Often evaluation work is on target, but this is generally through good luck (or gifted team insight and judgement) rather than through systematically relating measures and targets to intended worth. Worth systems could form the basis for such a systematic practice. The main claim of this chapter is they have such potential. An extensive program of case studies is required to demonstrate this. However, it is possible to sketch a range of modified evaluation methods that focus on achievement of intended value, rather than the abstract product attributes currently associated with usability. Both analytical and empirical methods can be sketched. Both depend on W/AMs as a keystone representation for worth-centered design and evaluation.

Worth-centred evaluation methods focus on W/AM's associations and the worthies that they combine into worth subsystems. Any W/AM element is a candidate for measurement or inspection. All worthies provide a basis for evaluation criteria ranging from feature inspection to reflective and value-sensitive design. The simplest methods operate at the level of specific worthies. Many lower-level product attributes can be assessed by inspection during development. Design evaluability is determined by the extent to which any worthy or association can be operationalized.

Wider methods test strength of associations, for example the ability of concrete product attributes (e.g., website links) to deliver required abstract attributes (e.g., navigability). More complex methods address complete MECs (or worth subsystems), assessing validity and/or credibility of expected causal chains. All worth subsystems are candidates for expert judgement or statistical analysis of strength of associations. Other approaches are more holistic, assessing complete W/AMs and looking for ways to improve achievable worth for digital products or services.

Method sketches begin with analytical methods, followed by empirical methods. In the space available for this chapter, only sketches are possible. While more detailed worked examples would better support HCI research and practice, this chapter is not a tutorial on worth-centered development. Again, the aim is to explain how and why existing usability measurement cannot reliably and systematically address what users really want, how laddering approaches from consumer psychology can, how these can be adapted for HCI, and how this supports planning and derivation of worth-cenetred evaluation methods.

13.4.1 W/AM Inspection Methods

The achievable worth for a design can be assessed by WA/M inspection. Some operate on specific areas of the map, some on worth subsystems, some assess the whole map, and some need additional *survey data*.

13.4.1.1 Value Spread Opportunities

Design purpose tends to be expressed at the level of usage consequences. This method inspects a W/AM to assess its coverage of potentially relevant values, which can come from a range of evaluation resources, for example:

- *Value lists*—such as those covered in *Value-Sensitive Design* (Friedman & Kahn 2003), those used in primed/prompted laddering such as VALS, LOV and RVS (Wong & Jeffery 2002), or ones from theological and/or philosophical approaches that construct such lists
- *Theories of motivation*—which provide another source of high-level *individual motivators*, while sociocultural approaches can address *collective motivations* by *reading* values *inscribed* in cultural forms in different worth arenas (Cockton 2006a). Such approaches allow more systematic inspection than the more open approach of *Reflective Design* (Sengers, et al. 2006), as well as drawing on a range of long-established disciplinary perspectives on individual and collective value. For example, management science can inform HCI about business strategy and its relation to some sponsors' collective value.

Missed opportunities for value spread can be a surprisingly simple but effective predictor. The Whereabouts clock, a workplace information display with a largely functional design purpose was found to also support feelings of connectedness and relatedness (Sellen, et al. 2006). The extremely abstract motivational categories of existence, relatedness, and growth (ERG Theory, Alderfer 1972) suggest that an exclusive focus on *existence motivators* at work could be too narrow. The value of an intended W/AM for the Whereabouts Clock can thus be *spread* by adding psychosocial consequences and values for *relatedness*. A new worth subsystem would result with existing product attributes, but these could be improved and extended to strengthen associations for relatedness. Note that a focus on positive motivators as well as aversions (as in much value-sensitive design) broadens consideration of values in design and evaluation.

13.4.1.2 W/AM Enrichment

A W/AM's diagrammatic form requires worthies to be succinctly described. It may not be possible to capture the full extent of an intended consequence or value in the short-text label for a worthy's node. This inspection method assesses and improves the communicative quality of worthies, using field research data to improve the expression of intended worth. This may include the use of direct quotes from interviewed stakeholders, or the use of photographs or video material, which can become the basis for *worth boards* that provide pictorial support for expressing intended worth (Cockton 2006a). Worthy's W/AM labels can then be revised to better capture worth as visually communicated. However, the expectation is that worth boards will be a vital supplement to W/AMs in enhancing communication of intended worth. Worth boards (WoBs) are a key class of survey data, providing the rich data behind simple map labels.

13.4.1.3 Worth Tables (WoTs)

It is highly likely that the product attribute zone of a W/AM will become either overcrowded and unmanageable, or overly sparse and meaninglessly vague. Complexity here can be managed by grouping concrete attributes in the W/AM and using separate, more detailed tables, to describe the intended associations between concrete and abstract attributes. These tables can also include specific evaluation targets for abstract attributes, as well as specific criteria to support a checklist approach to feature inspection, thus avoiding problems of more general feature checklists (Edgerton, et al. 1993). More generally, WoTs have a similar structure to Web design *content matrices* and matrix-based methods from first-wave HCI (Catterall 1990). They both extend the worth map with *large scale* inserts and also organize survey data. They are particularly useful for recording the avoidance of adverse outcomes—explaining, for example, how privacy related aversions can be reduced by clear appropriate website policies.

13.4.1.4 W/AM Balance

By comparing W/AMs for different stakeholders, the relative impact of a design can be compared. Stakeholder worth maps can be compared. One approach would be to compare the consequences of product attributes across stakeholders. This may prompt redesign to reduce adverse impact on some stakeholders. This is a specific case of *shifting the center of gravity* of a W/AM, an approach that aims to identify and reduce aversions and/or increase positive motivators.

13.4.1.5 Worth Delivery Scenarios (WoDS)

These take a *happy ending* approach to scenario authoring, focusing scenarios on credible narratives that demonstrate how value will be delivered (and aversions avoided) by a design with envisaged concrete and abstract attributes. Happy endings can be based on images from worth boards. WoDS take their narrative *skeleton* from worth subsystems. They are essentially *Value Delivery Scenarios* (Cockton 2005) transferred into a W/AM based methodology. WoDs are not survey data, because they add nothing to the empirical grounding of a worth map. Instead, they are design *overlays* that challenge the current worth map, potentially realising map elements and associations to be rethought to improve credibility or and detail.

13.4.1.6 Holistic Approaches

Aschmoneit and Heitmann (2003) identified four ways in which HVM transformations can guide product development:

- Using already mentioned connections
- Strengthening presently weak associations
- Building new associations
- Adding new attributes

These readily extend to W/AM inspection methods, except the first, which is intrinsically for market leaders. W/AM inspection can support the other three approaches. Credibility of associations can be assessed, and strengthened by improving product attributes or extending the network of associated worthies. WoDS may also be an effective method for both generating new associations between existing worthies, and for adding new ones. This follows from the need to strengthen the credibility of scenario narratives, but also to broaden coverage of motivations overlooked when building W/AMs.

Aschmoneit and Heitmann appear to restrict addition of new worthies to product attributes, but this overlooks adding new consequences and values, as through usage of the Whereabouts Clock, where unenvisaged consequences and values combined with existing product attributes into new worth subsystems. This is essentially the basis of *appropriation* (Voida and Mynatt 2005), when users create new value with unchanged existing technologies. WoDS may be able to discover appropriations through envisionment prior to usage. Empirical methods can also be applied holistically to improve W/AMs via appropriation and other means (see below).

13.4.1.7 Worth Inspection Methods: Summary

The above brief sketches demonstrate that W/AMs are a promising anchor representation for design purposes, and form the basis for a range of inspection methods and techniques to cover the whole worth spectrum from product attributes to individual and collective value.

The extensive reach of W/AM inspection can be demonstrated by considering seven questions that guide evaluation planning (Cockton 2006b):

1. *Why* are we evaluating? (purpose)
2. *Who* will we ask to evaluate (both specialists and participants)?
3. *What* information and design artefacts are given to evaluators, *what* resources are available for conducting the evaluation, and *what* will we ask specialists and participants to do?
4. *Where* will we carry out the evaluation?

5. *When* will we carry out the evaluation?
6. *Which* instruments will be used to record *which* measures, and *which* levels of performance and preference will indicate success or failure?
7. *How* will we conduct the evaluation overall (protocol), *how* will we analyze the data, and *how* will we communicate the results?

For inspection methods, the purpose is formative (why) and usability experts (who) are asked to evaluate at design milestones (when). Design resources sketched above such as W/AMs, WoBs, WoDSs and WoTs could be provided to evaluators, who would follow associated inspection procedures (what) at their own or sponsor's workplaces (where). Measures and data analysis (what and how) are issues for empirical rather than analytical evaluation. This, too, can be given a worth-centered focus.

13.4.2 Empirical Value Impact Assessment

The purpose of empirical methods can be formative or summative. The key difference between inspection and empirical methods is that the latter are based on usage data from user tests (in the lab, field, or remote), system logs, or user diaries. Once empirical evaluation is guided by the need to ground and validate a W/AM however, rigid distinctions between formative and summative evaluation are hard to maintain. Measures of outcomes and abstract product attributes will be summative in nature at the point of evaluation, but their context in a worth subsystem will provide formative evaluation on the likely causes of any disappointing outcomes. This presumes that the W/AM, however, is structurally correct and that a design can be improved by improving associated product attributes. Alternatively, evaluators may decide that a W/AM contains flaws. In this case, the evaluation is wholly formative, refocusing design.

Empirical evaluation takes measures with research instruments. Measurement can finesse issues of different categories of consequence or value by replacing it with issues of how we measure. Functional consequences should be measurable by observing or instrumenting the world. Economic consequences require financial measures. Psychosocial consequences require appropriate instruments from psychology and sociology.

A W/AM thus becomes a theory that can be tested and refined during development. The approach could reduce the distinction between research and practice, requiring practice to be conducted as research, and research to be grounded in practice. The scientific orientation that was lost when formal experiments were simplified to *user testing* could thus be restored. Worth maps allow task and measure selection to be clearly traceable. Consequently, when there are problems with a design it should be clear what difference these make to users and/or other stakeholders. Path analysis of the relevant submap should let potential causes be pinpointed. The correct ordering of specific consequences and values can be established by an evaluation process, that iterates W/AMs, as well as designs that they rationalize.

Focused experiments can also be designed, for example, to test hypotheses on the avoidance of specific aversions.

Selected measures need to correspond to evaluation criteria based on W/AM nodes (attributes, consequences, and values). Planning empirical evaluation in worth-centered development thus systematically maps worthies to evaluation criteria, which are, in turn, mapped to measures and then measuring instruments. It is important to measure above the level of abstract product attributes and immediate functional or psychosocial consequences. These are measured as means to ends, but measures of high value terminal outcomes take precedence.

As we move from measuring the central zone of W/AM, more extensive worth subsystems can be evaluated, although measures become more challenging. The appeal of measuring quality in the system or quality in interaction becomes apparent when one considers the challenges of measuring at a W/AM apex. Measuring quality in the system only requires the system (and perhaps documentation) to perform an evaluation. Measuring quality in interaction requires a working system and someone to use it (e.g., in user testing). However, measuring quality in the world (the worth of usage outcomes) requires a system and instrumentation of the world. Many outcomes cannot be measured during interaction. For example, in Figure 13.2, there are functional consequences of *successful delivery of load(s)*, *arrive on time and well-prepared*, *appropriate period for deliveries*, and *appropriate van for load(s)*. None can be measured during van-booking interactions. These must either be measured through post-hire questionnaires via email, and/or via some form of instrumentation at the van hire depot. At this point, we are no longer just instrumenting interaction, but instead we must potentially instrument much within the scope of a sociodigital system. Worth-based measures are closely tied to design purpose and cannot be listed in advance of design. Existing approaches such as *critical parameters* (Newman & Taylor 1999) have attempted to identify such measures, but they do so without the associative context of a worth map, and as such do not locate these parameters in means-end chains that can be grounded through empirical assessment.

Worth-based measures are not just *new* or *alternative* measures, such as those associated with various versions of *new* usability. Instead, they are measures that can only be understood in terms of a complete picture of design purpose. Evaluation can thus feed off design and not, as happens with the use of inappropriate measures and targets, savage it. Furthermore, well-fed evaluation is less likely to bite the hand that feeds it!

13.4.2.1 Direct Instrumentation of Sociodigital Systems

For critical outcomes in W/AMs, it may be necessary to instrument any component of a socio-digital system. It may be necessary to embed some instruments within software or in usage locations. Interestingly, this can extend designs in ways that may automatically bring consequences beyond those initially targeted in a W/AM. Not surprisingly, direct instrumentation is most common in ubiquitous computing (*ubicomp*) research, where the basic functionality for self-instrumentation is often already in place. However, current low-level logging can rarely directly measure criteria derived from W/AM nodes. Greg Abowd noted the need to design for evaluation at the Ubicomp workshop (Scholtz, et al. 2001). However, the extent of this design goes beyond instrumentation and data management to the achievement of intended worth.

The viability of this approach has already been demonstrated in e-learning, where research instrumentation required the creation of a *controlled learning context* that became, for some learners, a key determinant of learning success (Jones and Cockton 2004). Such *self-instrumentation* is generally seen as an unavoidable consequence of ubicomp, since external instrumentation cannot capture everything.

For example, in Figure 13.3, there is a psychosocial consequence of *interest in a course on offer*." As the W/AM stands, this would have to be measured outside of the university website, which could require surveys or interviews. These usage outcomes can thus not be directly measured during interaction. However, we could let the website directly instrument student interest through additional interactive content. Specifically, we could add document and media downloads for visitors who have registered. Self-instrumentation is thus achieved via download and registration data that record an individual's interest in specific courses. By moving instrumentation *into* the system, we inevitably add product attributes. By doing this, we must review the extended W/AM for new potential associations, especially with possible adverse consequences of required visitor registration. A *Reflective Design* approach (Sengers, et al. 2005) could highlight these, adding new aversions. Associations between new features and aversions could be weakened by further content on privacy and data usage policies. It should be clear that self-instrumentation can have an extensive impact on concrete design attributes.

Self-instrumentation extends both the design (concrete attributes) and usage outcomes. More generally, once prospective students are registered, a more finely grained worth subsystem can be designed to strengthen the association between the functional consequences of *interest in a course on offer* and *Students apply for a course with support of parent and/or advisers* and *Students apply for course that they will enjoy and complete* (Figure 13.3). This can be achieved by adding further concrete attributes that implement a *sales pipeline* that can maximize conversion from initial interest into applying for courses.

Self-instrumentation is thus not just a contextual requirement of ubicomp, but more generally a direct consequence of worth-centered approaches, since some target outcomes and associated worth subsystems can only be measured by extending designs to capture achievement data during usage (Cockton 2005).

13.4.2.2 Holistic Approaches

Empirical evaluation can be refocused via W/AMs to support a comprehensive range of distinct approaches to design. First, it can support an *engineering design paradigm*, which in HCI is often achieved through psychology experiments. Empirical evaluation here can be based on experimental approaches that have failed to generalize within HCI, but remain vital for optimizing the association between concrete attributes and abstract qualities. WoTs can capture expected associations here, and engineering design approaches can be used to *optimize* concrete attributes to improve outcomes within associated worth subsystems. However, by relating experimental optimization to the context of a W/AM, the relevance of experimental dependent variables can be better assured. The result is one form of *strengthening presently weak associations* as advocated for HVM-based product improvement (Aschmoneit & Heitmann 2003).

Self-instrumentation has a strong probability of achieving Aschmoneit and Heitmann's two other HVM-based innovation tactics. *Adding new attributes* has been shown to follow from self-instrumentation, and this inevitably leads to *building new associations*, although some may initially be adverse. The approach promises to meet Wixon's (2003) requirement for evaluation methods that do not merely find, but also explain and fix, problems. Self-instrumentation paradoxically fixes some problems before they can be found by supporting creative and innovative value-adding design extensions as a consequence of planning evaluation measures.

The main holistic W/AM-based empirical evaluation approach, however, is testing worth system-based design theories. A systematic combination of measures and instruments can test the design team's conjectures about causal relations between product attributes and usage outcomes. The simple factorial experiments of 1980s HCI can thus be replaced by a broad testing of a nexus of conjectures, thus operationalizing Carroll and Kellogg's (1989) superficially paradoxical vision from almost two decades ago of *HCI application leading HCI theory*. Again, worth-centered development reduces the distance between research and practice.

Existing design approaches, such as probes, can be used as holistic W/AM evaluation methods. *Technology probes* (Hutchinson, et al. 2003) expose usages and valuable outcomes that the design team may not have envisaged. More generally, probes provide access to user appropriations (Voida & Mynatt 2005), which by their nature create new outcomes without changing concrete product attributes, although abstract attributes may be enhanced or even created. Whereas psychological experiments support engineering design through optimization, probes support art-based design through open enquiry and responses to user experience.

13.4.2.3 Empirical Evaluation of Worth: Summary

The above brief sketches demonstrate that W/AMs can align empirical evaluation with design purpose. Once again, the reach of W/AM-based evaluation can be demonstrated by considering seven evaluation planning questions (Cockton 2006b).

In value-impact assessment, we evaluate to test design theories, and not just to identify product defects (why), combining the formative and summative aspects of evaluation. After all, the source of product defects are our design theories, and not the product itself, which, after all, is only a human artifact, albeit one that may be poorly understood by its makers.

The need to self-instrument brings developers and designers into the evaluation process (who). Self instrumentation allows continuous evaluation during usage (when) allowing a range of running prototypes and systems to be used as probes in remote locations (where). The W/AM and associated resources provide the main support for evaluators, along with self-instrumentation (what), which also provides instruments and their measures (which). Success or failure applies to worth subsystems, including related WoTs and WoDSs, rather than usability targets (which). Together, this all provides a basis for planning and conducting evaluations, analyzing data and communicating results (how). At all points, the W/AM can provide common ground for the whole development team, reminding developers in particular about the intended purpose of design features. *Cool* features become much harder to justify, but so too does the uncritical use of psychological measures.

13.5 Conclusions: Evaluation and Design Purpose

Evaluation, especially using empirical methods, has remained tied to measures with origins in experimental psychology even when associated *specified goals* have been known to rarely be *what users really want* for two decades. In fairness to usability evaluators, there has been no real alternative, even after the move to contextual HCI. Field research did not turn out, as expected, to provide better grounded usability targets, although it did massively improve design inputs. It improved our ability to ground design in genuine user needs and usage contexts, but rarely provides actionable success and failure criteria.

An alternative to setting targets and evaluating their attainment is to theorize value chains within usage of digital products and services. W/AMs based on laddering and HVMs from consumer psychology offer a promising basis for theorizing worth, relating this to design, and planning evaluation. The approach has supported a range of innovative insights and opportunities, especially:

- Achieving value spread through cultural studies approaches to reading systems and their contextual worth arenas, supported by a range of practical and theoretical perspectives on individual and collective motivation
- A basis for integrating novel HCI approaches (reflective and value-sensitive design, user experience) into one development approach
- Accommodating appropriation within worth-based evaluation
- Writing scenarios backwards to focus on valuable happy endings within worth delivery scenarios (WoDS)
- Integrating non-verbal field resources into evaluation (WoBs)
- Replacing usability targets with goals for worth subsystems
- Deriving measures and instruments from elements of worth
- Supporting engineering design through worth table (WoT) optimization
- Self-instrumenting across the whole scope of a sociodigital system, with positive consequences for design

This is a forward-looking chapter. It is not, and cannot be, a tutorial on evaluation within a worth-centered framework. Instead, it maps out a future for what was usability evaluation, but will be subsumed as just one form of assessment of worth subsystems. Clearly, much needs to be done to allow confidence in W/AM-based development. However, experiences with worth-based approaches in real development settings have been positive. Only one is using W/AMs in the design phase, but this has already resulted in a range of self-instrumentation tactics. W/AMs have only recently been developed, but the overall philosophy of worth-centered development has been in place for a few years (Cockton 2005; 2006a). It continues to prove valuable in commercial practice for focusing evaluation planning, results presentation, and iteration decisions.

It has taken two decades to even begin to envisage how we can respond to the challenges of genuine evaluation relevance posed by Whiteside, Bennett and Holtzblatt (1988). Second-wave HCI (Bødker 2006) has successfully provided the basis for grounding designs in the context of use. However, it has not provided systematic support for evaluation that cognitive psychology and human factors provided for first-wave HCI, irrespective of limitations that emerged in practice. This systematic support for planning, instrumentation, and measurement explains the endurance of first-wave HCI approaches within usability evaluation. As HCI enters its third wave, we hopefully now have the means to combine rigor, replicability, and relevance in evaluation, but we cannot do this as long as we separate usability evaluation from the wider evaluation of human performance and experience in sociodigital systems.

Maturity in organisms is indicated by major changes in form, structure, and capability. The same is true for usability evaluation. As it matures, it will become almost unrecognizable as the *adult* version of its first wave child. Some characteristics will be preserved, but as with any maturation, it will be wiser, more capable, better focused, and more reliable. In short, it will be valued, and worthy of respect among development teams.

Acknowledgment The work reported above is supported by a UK NESTA fellowship (www.nesta.org). The first version of this chapter was reviewed by Joe Dumas and Kasper Hornbæk, with additional feedback from Robin Jeffries. Their comments have hopefully greatly helped the structure and readability of this chapter, as well as accuracy in relation to existing work. I thank them all, but take full responsibility for all remaining blemishes!

References

Alderfer, C. (1972). *Existence, relatedness, and growth*. Free Press.
Aschmoneit, P., & Heitmann, M. (2003). Consumers cognition towards communities: Customer-centred community design using the means-end chain perspective. In *Proc. 36th Hawaii Int. Conference on System Sciences*, IEEE.
Beyer, H., & Holtzblatt, K. (1996). *Contextual Design*. Morgan Kaufmann.
Bødker, S. (2006). When Second Wave HCI meets Third Wave Challenges. In A.I. Mørch, K. Morgan, T. Bratteteig, G. Ghosh, & D. Svanæs (Eds.), *Proceedings of NordiCHI 2006* (pp. 1–8).
Carroll, J. M., & Kellogg, W. A. (1989). Artifact as theory-nexus: hermeneutics meets theory-based design. In K. Bice & C. Lewis (Eds.), *Proc. SIGCHI Conference on Human Factors in Computing Systems* (pp. 7–14). New York: ACM.
Catterall, B. J. (1990). The HUFIT functionality matrix. In D. Diaper, D.J. Gilmore, G. Cockton, & B. Shackel (Eds.), *Proc. INTERACT'90* (pp. 377–338).

Cockton, G. (2005). A development framework for value-centred design. In C. Gale (Ed.), *CHI 2005 Extended Abstracts* (pp. 1292–1295). New York: ACM.

Cockton, G. (2006a). Designing Worth is Worth Designing. In A.I. Mørch, K. Morgan, T. Bratteteig, G. Ghosh, & D. Svanæs (Eds.),*Proceedings of NordiCHI 2006* (pp. 165–174). New York: ACM.

Cockton, G. (2006b). Focus, fit and fervour: Future factors beyond play with the interplay. *International Journal of Human-Computer Interaction, 21*(2), 239–250.

Cockton, G., & Lavery, D. (1999). A framework for usability problem extraction. In A. Sasse & C. Johnson (Eds.), *Proceedings of INTERACT 99* (pp. 347–355).

Cockton, G., & Woolrych, A. (2001) Understanding inspection methods: Lessons from an assessment of heuristic evaluation. In A. Blandford, J. Vanderdonckt and P.D. Gray (Eds.), *People and Computers XV* (pp. 171–192). Springer.

Cockton, G., Woolrych, A., Hall, L. & Hindmarch, M. (2003). Changing analysts' tunes: The surprising impact of a new instrument for usability inspection method assessment. In P. Palanque, P. Johnson and E. O'Neill (Eds.), *People and Computers XVII: Designing for Society* (pp. 145–162). Springer.

Cockton, G., Woolrych, A., & Hindmarch, M. (2004). Reconditioned merchandise: Extended structured report formats in usability inspection". In *CHI 2004 Extended Abstracts* (pp. 1433–1436). New York: ACM.

Coombs, M., & Alty, J. L. (Eds.). (1981). *Computing Skills and the User Interface*. Academic Press.

Corbridge, C., Rugg, G., Major, N., Shadbolt, N.R., & Burton, A. (1994). Laddering: Techniques and Tool Use in Knowledge Acquisition. *Journal of Knowledge Acquisition, 6*, 315–341.

Edgerton, E. A., Draper, S. W., & Barton, S. B. (1993). Feature checklists in HCI: Some basic results. In S. Ashlund, K. Mullet, A. Henderson, E. Hollnagel, & T. White (Eds.), *INTERACT '93 and CHI '93 Conference Companion on Human Factors in Computing Systems* (pp. 189–190). New York: ACM.

Friedman, B., & Kahn, P. (2003). Chapter 61: Human values, ethics and design. In J. Jacko and A. Sears (Eds.), *The Human-Computer Interaction Handbook* (pp. 1171–1201), Lawrence Erlbaum Associates.

Gray, W.D., & Salzman, M.C. (1998). Damaged merchandise? A review of experiments that compare usability evaluation methods. *Human-Computer Interaction, 13*(3), 203–261.

Hassenzahl, M., & Tractinsky, N. (2006). User experience – a research agenda. *Behavior & Information Technology, 25*(2), 91–97

Heitmann, M., Prykop, C., & Aschmoneit, P.(2004). Using means-end chains to build mobile brand communities. In *Proceedings of the 37th Hawaii International Conference on System Sciences*, IEEE.

Holtzblatt, K., Wendell J. B., & Wood, S. (2004). *Rapid Contextual Design*. Morgan Kaufmann.

Hutchinson, H., Mackay, W., Westerlund, B., Bederson, B. B., Druin, A., Plaisant, C., Beaudouin-Lafon, M., Conversy, S., Evans, H., Hansen, H., Roussel, N., & Eiderbäck, B. (2003). Technology probes: inspiring design for and with families. In *Proc. Conf. on Human Factors in Comp. Systems* (pp. 17–24). New York: ACM.

ISO/International Standards Organisation (1998). *9241 Ergonomic requirements for office work with visual display terminals – Part 11: Guidance on usability*

ISO/International Standards Organisation (2006). *25062 Software product Quality Requirements and Evaluation – Common Industry Format (CIF) for usability test reports.*

JISC, (no date) *PESTLE and SWOT Analyses*, available at www.jiscinfonet.ac.uk/InfoKits/ project-management/pestle-swot, last accessed on 10/01/07.

Jones, S., & Cockton, G. (2004). Tightly coupling multimedia with context: Strategies for exploiting multimodal learning in complex management topics (pp. 813–815). In *4th IEEE International Conference on Advanced Learning Technologies*.

Lavery, D., & Cockton, G. (1996). Iterative development of early usability evaluation methods for software visualisations. In W.D. Gray & D.A. Boehm-Davies (Eds.), *Empirical Studies of Programmers: 6th Workshop*, (pp. 275–276). Ablex.

Lavery, D., & Cockton, G. (1997). Representing predicted and actual usability problems. In *Proc. Int. Workshop on Representations in Interactive Software Development* (pp. 97–108), Queen Mary College London.

Lavery, D., Cockton, G., & Atkinson, M.P., (1997). Comparison of Evaluation Methods Using Structured Usability Problem Reports. *Behaviour and Information Technology, 16*(4), 246–266.

Newman, W. M., & Taylor, A. S. (1999). Towards a methodology employing critical parameters to deliver performance improvements in interactive systems. In A. Sasse & C. Johnson (Eds.), *INTERACT 99 Proceedings* (pp. 605–612).

Norton, D.P., & Kaplan, R.S. (1996). *The balanced scorecard: Translating strategy into action.* Harvard Business School Press.

Reynolds, T. J., & Gutman, J. (1984). Laddering: Extending the repertory grid methodology to construct attribute-consequence-value hierarchies. In R. E. Pitts & A. G. Woodside (Eds.), *Personal values and consumer psychology* (pp. 155–167). Lexington Books.

Reynolds, T.J., & Gutman, J. (1988). Laddering theory, method analysis and interpretation. *Journal of Advertising Research, 28,* 11–31.

Rokeach, M. (1973). *The nature of human value.* Free Press.

Rugg, G., Eva, M., Mahmood, A., Rehman, N., Andrews, S., & Davies S. (2002). Eliciting information about organizational culture via laddering. *Information Systems Journal, 12,* 215–229.

Scholtz, J., Herman, H., Laskowski, S., Smailagic, A., & Siewiorek, D. (2001), *Workshop on Evaluation Methods for Ubiquitous Computing,* UbiComp 2001 Conference, http://zing.ncsl.nist.gov/ubicomp01/, last accessed 10/1/07.

Sellen, A., Eardley, R., Izadi, S., & Harper, R. (2006). The whereabouts clock: early testing of a situated awareness device. In *CHI '06 Extended Abstracts on Human Factors in Computing Systems* (pp. 1307–1312). New York: ACM.

Sengers, P., Boehner, K., David, S., & Kaye J. J. (2005). Reflective design. in O. Berthelsen, N.O. Bouvin, P.G. Krogh & M. Kyng (Eds.), *Critical Computing – Between Sense and Sensibilities. Proceedings of the Fourth Decennial Aarhus Conference* (pp. 49–58). New York: ACM.

Service Design Network (no date), http://www.servicedesignnetwork.org/, last accessed 12/12/06.

Subramony, D.P. (2002). Why users choose particular web sites over others: Introducing a "means-end" approach to human-computer interaction. *Journal of Electronic Commerce Research, 3*(3), 144–161.

Voida, A., & Mynatt, E. D. (2005). Six themes of the communicative appropriation of photographic images. In *Proc SIGCHI Conference on Human Factors in Computing Systems* (pp. 171–180). New York: ACM.

Whiteside, J., Bennett, J., & Holtzblatt, K. (1988). Usability engineering: Our experience and evolution. In M. Helander (Ed.), *Handbook of Human-Computer Interaction* (1st Ed.) (pp. 791–817). North-Holland.

Wixon, D. (2003) Evaluating usability methods: why the current literature fails the practitioner. *Interactions, 10*(4), 28–34.

Wong, B., & Jeffery, R. (2002). *A Quantitative Study on the Role of Cognitive Structures in Software Quality Evaluation,* Tech. Rep. 02/3, National ICT Australia Empirical Software Engineering, www.caesar.unsw.edu.au/ publications/pdf/Tech02_3.pdf, last accessed 07/01/07.

Chapter 14
HCI and the Economics of User Experience

Marcin Sikorski

Faculty of Management and Economics, Gdansk University of Technology, Poland,
e-mail: msik@zie.pg.gda.pl

Abstract This chapter presents a conceptual framework for expanding the scope
of current HCI research, by including economic aspects that affect user experience
when interacting with online services. This framework presents development models for interactive products and online services. It refers to the concept of value-
oriented design that attempts to use HCI and interaction design as a part of business
design activity. Although this framework is as yet partly visionary and needs validation, it seems to open interesting perspectives on user experience design, because
interaction design is an important part of modern business technology.

14.1 Introduction and Background

In recent years, there were several attempts to extend the scope of classical, user
interface-oriented HCI research into areas covering factors *beyond the user interface*, including affective or economic factors. Factors affecting user experience
when users interact with emerging (mostly wireless) technologies have been investigated, along with system usability characteristics for online services available
through the Internet.

The wide availability of online services created the phenomenon of e-commerce,
and users tend to be loyal to their favorite e-shops and e-services. However, the
mechanisms shaping user satisfaction in e-business contexts are still under investigation.

HCI research, so far engaged primarily in the context of use studies, user interface
analysis, and design, now addresses also the issues *beyond the user interface*, like
design of Internet transactions, enhancing user trust, or developing positive attitudes
towards interactive services.

This chapter aims to expand the scope of current HCI research by offering a new
framework, describing economical aspects affecting users' experience when they
interact with online services. This framework refers to the concept of value-oriented
design in an attempt to present HCI and interaction design as a part of business
design activity. Although this framework is certainly so far incomplete, it seems to
open up interesting perspectives on user experience design, when viewed as a part
of business interaction design in commercial online services.

E. Law et al. (eds.), *Maturing Usability.*

14.2 Quality of Interactive Systems

14.2.1 Quality and Usability of Interactive Product

Quality of software products (and in general, of all interactive systems) is covered by several ISO standards. Figure 14.1 presents the relationship between the interactive system quality perceived by the user, and selected quality characteristics from specific ISO standards:

- ISO 9126-1 specifies basic quality characteristics of a software product, among which functionality is critical for practical usefulness of the product
- ISO 9241 (Part 10 especially, and Parts 12–17) specifies ergonomic requirements for user interfaces and user-system dialog design
- ISO 9241 (Part 11) provides guidance on usability resulting from productivity (effectiveness), efficiency, and satisfaction, as experienced by the user in specific context of use

Figure 14.1 shows that quality of interactive systems covers two areas: *design quality* (technical and ergonomic), and *quality in use*; the latter seems to be more important from the user's viewpoint, because it is directly experienced by the user in practical task execution.

However, when users have to recommend a particular product (software package, e-service, or a website) to other users, recommendations are usually based not on quality-in-use itself, but on *perceived quality* of a particular system. Hence, *perceived quality* is added as an outcome of usability.

Perceived quality of the product follows from the actual satisfaction level derived from product usability, individually and subjectively experienced by users after using the product in an actual context. Regular usage of the product or service

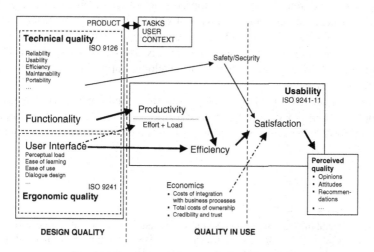

Fig. 14.1 Quality components of interactive system

and experienced usability of the product in real tasks form a sufficient basis for reliable user opinions about product functions and their willingness to use it again, and/or eventually recommend it to others. The majority of criteria used for user- and expert-based evaluations are covered by current ISO standards.

As presented in the central part of Figure 14.2, observed system productivity is related to the sum of expended resources (the higher the ergonomic quality, the lower the effort and workload), resulting in observed and experienced *efficiency* of interactive systems in actual task contexts as specified in ISO 9241-11.

Even if efficiency observed in real settings is high, user satisfaction may remain low when users are critical about the actual costs of using the system, or they have doubts about service security and trust. Negative opinions probably will be expressed to other consumers, possibly reducing the system attractiveness for other users on the market.

As mentioned in the previous paragraph, user-perceived quality is often affected in the real world by economic factors associated with the product, such as actual costs of using the product or services, ease of integration with local business processes or—especially in case of services—the subjectively perceived credibility[1] of a specific vendor.

As shown in Figure 14.1, economic factors are not directly covered by the scope of ISO standards, but they form an important part of user evaluations (quality in use). Nevertheless, in real settings users tend to rate attractiveness and usability of known interactive products or services by relating obtained results to expended resources. That means they tend to use an economic perspective, which can be briefly characterized as assessing the efficiency of a product in real task settings, and relating it to the efficiency of other similar products.

Also, the emotional attitude of users to a specific brand or vendor may affect her/his choice when buying a product. How users behave when selecting a product, and what decision mechanism drives this are interesting research issues in consumer behaviour and related economic disciplines.

Especially in online services and shops, quality issues shaping vendor credibility and other aspects of economic behavior of online customers obviously could not be covered by ISO HCI and software engineering (SE) standards. Nevertheless, in contemporary markets, understanding the way users perceive quality and value of alternative services is now crucial for developing appealing and highly usable systems for e-business.

In addition to ISO standards, design guidelines and style guides are used by designers to comply with quality requirements, still based on the assumption that quality of user interface affects strongly the perceived quality of an interactive product.

---

[1] Related to credibility and trust, transaction safety and security are also a concern. Due to insufficient technical knowledge, however, user opinion is shaped by *perceived* rather than *objective* safety/security of a system in any technical sense.

14.2.2 User Experience Design

The perspective on quality of interactive systems, represented in ISO standards, has long been adequate for standard desktop and Web-based applications, used mostly by professional users.

However, since many device-independent online services are available on the Internet or from cell phone operators, the concept of interactive system quality—based primarily on user interface characteristics—is no longer sufficient. Nowadays, when buying personal electronic devices, users make decisions only in part by studying quality parameters (and technical data). Users' choices are driven in a large part by fashion, visual design, adaptability to changing contexts of use, and—last but not least—by basic economic factors like item price, costs of ownership, or subscription fees.

Recent changes in user behavior have also led vendors and designers to treat users more as consumers and buyers—i.e., as economically independent decision-makers.

Users seem to base their buying decisions not only upon *hard data* about product characteristics itself, but they seem primarily to consider how the product will fit into their particular, intended context(s) of use.

A need for a broader view of interactive product quality and usability has emerged gradually in the HCI community. As a result, the concept of *new usability* (Thomas & Macredie 2002) became popular because consumer electronics became a part of everyday life, and because marketing research started exploring users' decisions also in the area of interactive systems and services. *New usability* approaches raised the need for user-based studies *beyond the user interface*, oriented on all interactions and relationships between the user and context of use, where a particular product or service will be used at work, home, or travel, in a variety of tasks including entertainment and education.

Because many users regularly change their electronic devices and upgrade the configuration of their services, it was noted that they switch vendors motivated by a systematic search for more cost-effective solutions—better offers, more attractive conditions, more satisfaction, and a more exciting experience when using the product.

In the late 1990s, the design of interactive devices and online services evolved, aiming to give users what they expected—not only functionality for a reasonable price, but also interesting experience when interacting with webpages, online services, or electronic devices. Not every add-on tried to improve product quality and usability. Many aimed to address the emotional needs of users, and to deliver emotionally involving interactions that could be experienced as something pleasant and joyful.

The tem *user experience* in interactive product design has been extensively discussed in many papers, like Arhippainen (2003), Forlizzi and Ford (2000), and many others, studying the affective aspects of user reactions when working with interactive systems.

The work of Forlizzi and Battarbee (2004) pointed out an interesting issue that sharing a common (and positive) experience by a group of users (called a *coexperience*) is an important factor shaping team spirit and social interaction. In contrast, when there is a lack of positive experience (for instance when experiencing frustrating attempts to complete a task in a nonusable groupwork application), it affects team cohesiveness and creates shared negative attitudes to the particular system.

Despite numerous publications in this area, the concept of *user experience* still remains vague, mostly because it has not been sufficiently operationalized in terms of measurable variables and development techniques directly applicable by designers of interactive products and HCI specialists. In the context of many other works on the theory of user experience, the work of Hassenzahl (2002) seems especially constructive. He explored relationships between affective outcomes and the quality attributes of interactive products in terms of two dimensions of product quality:

- *Pragmatic quality*—task-oriented quality aspect, produced by using design elements provided primarily for efficient task completion
- *Hedonistic quality*—pleasure-oriented, produced by design elements provided primarily for increasing pleasure, visual attractiveness and joy of interaction

According to Hassenzahl, the presence of both types of element is necessary for building satisfying user experience and for shaping positive user attitudes towards using the same product in the future. This statement seems to have important consequences for the applications of the economic psychology of online markets. It suggests that users in a competitive market would be more loyal to those interactive products that provide not only high-quality related to task performance, but also quality aspects that strongly address the sphere of emotional needs and create positive user experiences.

Hassenzahl adopted an economic viewpoint on interaction design, initially signaled by Pine and Gilmore (1998), who were interested in what experiences (not goods) can be sold to customer in general, not excluding online services and digital content delivery. In online services, experienced interactivity and pleasure are important factors, stimulating the users' ongoing search for new innovative products and solutions, and the vendors' interest in satisfying new demands. It is obvious that, for example in the entertainment industry, experience is the main factor that attracts audiences to movies, but in online services, original design and unique user experience are now important for differentiating the offer and building competitive advantage.

So far, the user-centered design (UCD) approach is successful in applying an iterative design procedure for capturing user requirements and expectations. This now includes the emotional sphere and a pleasant interactive experience, in addition to the quality and usability requirements discussed in the previous section.

In the context of e-business and commercial online services, positive user experience is important, especially when the user has many alternative choices. For this reason, designing a positive user experience in online services has been also a matter for HCI research.

Contemporary e-services, mostly available through the Internet, enable users to perform activities that can be basically classified in five areas: to get informed, to buy, to sell, to entertain, and to communicate. These areas also provide the main goal of the user, which drives him/her to access the website. In general, all online services provide specific information *content*, aimed to attract customers, and *interaction*, which facilitates access to the content and directly affects system *usability*.

The content, website usability, and experienced emotions shape the user's general willingness towards using a specific service (or website) next time—as well as affecting the user's attitude towards the service vendor.

In most online services, the user's attitude is affected by experiences gathered from three independent channels:

- *Electronic*—impressions from interactions in the website of a service vendor (an Internet bank, for instance)
- *Voice*—impressions from interactions with a call-center
- *Live*—impressions from interactions with in physical environment (like a branch office of a bank)

In a commercial context, all components creating this multichannel experience should be consistent. This means that messages and visual cues (colors, logos, corporate styles, etc.) should be coordinated to create a reinforcing impression of the vendor's professionalism and competence. If *delivered* user experience is not equally positive or inconsistent among available distribution channels, the user may get confused, particularly with respect to the vendor's credibility and professionalism. Because experienced discomforts may signal coming problems with service quality, actual or potential customers may consider switching to another vendor, in addition to sharing their negative opinion with other consumers.

In real settings, only a part of total user experience related to a specific service, vendor, or brand, is formed by interactions on the website; important additional components often come also from off-line sources, like the influence of advertisements, paper correspondence, or opinions from other consumers.

Minocha, et al. (2003) developed the total customer experience model (TCE), called *e-service encounter*. The model is presented in Figure 14.2, which describes a typical customer interaction cycle in electronic services.

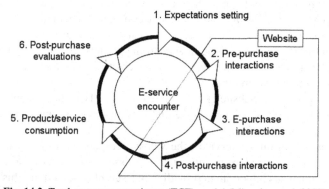

Fig. 14.2 Total customer experience (TCE) model (Minocha, et al. 2003)

The TCE model describes subsequent steps in operating online services. First, users start by looking for a particular product or service, then their expectations are set depending on available alternatives. Next, they select a vendor and finally perform a purchase on a website—or decide to place an order in off-line channels, by phone or in a physical shop.

Not long after the transaction, users may interact again with the vendor's website, being uncertain about the status of their order. The order usually gets confirmed by website, by e-mail or by human staff, or changes may be made to delivery conditions or to the item specifications (for example if the specific color is temporarily not available).

After the product has arrived, or a service has been consumed (such as a pre-booked holiday trip), the post-purchase evaluation phase closes the TCE cycle. The evaluation phase is very important because it predominantly shapes the user's attitude towards further interactions, aimed at future purchases of:

- The same service online, from the same website
- The same service online, from another website
- The same service, but from traditional (off-line) channel
- Another service from the same website, if the experience has been encouraging so far

Alternatively, the decision could be made never to buy this service again, because the whole experience with this particular online service was disappointing for some reason.

The TCE cycle addresses important factors, beyond the scope of classical HCI and usability studies, such as eliciting users' emotional attitudes towards buying online, or estimating the overall potential of the website for strengthening the vendor's image, credibility, and brand.

According to the TCE model, successful transactions should encourage users to visit the website more frequently, even to check *what's new*. Subsequently, regularly repeated positive experience should result in increased user trust and confidence, leading to more valuable transactions and to developing profitable relationships between vendor and customer.

Sometimes, despite frustrating experience from using a website, a customer may still be willing to remain loyal to the service vendor, if total experience from other remaining channels of this vendor (like phone contacts or personal visits in a branch office) is positive enough. Alternatively, if consumers find available off-line channels ineffective (for instance, long queues in the branch office), they may become more interested in accessing the service via a website, if they find the actual online experience encouraging enough.

Even if a particular website is not commercial, the TCE model applies because creating positive user experience is essential for any service to make users return to a site regularly and voluntarily.

While in typical online services, the website content is usually task-related—representing task-oriented, *pragmatic quality* (Hassenzahl (2002)—adding interesting visual elements is important in providing pleasurable interaction. This addresses emotional factors and represents the pleasure-oriented, *hedonistic* part of quality.

Therefore, for developing a successful e-service the following elements are essential:

- *Task-related elements*—(e.g., content relevant to users' interests) provide the basic usefulness of the website or e-service
- *Interaction elements*—provide easy access to the resources and affect the website usability
- *Visual elements*—provide entertainment and/or aesthetic impressions to make the site attractive and pleasant

All three types of elements interact with user attention, providing specific user experience and satisfaction level.

As in real life, there is no human satisfaction in interactive systems without the feeling of confidence, safety, and security. These factors have not yet been covered by the ISO standards, either (see Figure 14.1), however they form an important part of contemporary design practice, especially in the e-business area. Trust and confidence are essential for developing vendor-customer relationships and creating strong brands in online services.

Recent research by Garnik (2006) on user-perceived credibility of vendors in e-commerce in Poland showed that when consumers have to rate the attractiveness of an e-commerce website for eventual purchase, they consider separately:

- *Information content*, which attracts visitors and delivers actual value, in economic and other senses
- *Usability and the user interface*, which are important as task facilitators (creating a suitable work environment and being a promise of quality and professionalism). However they cannot attract customers by themselves if information content or service performance are poorly valued by customers

User willingness to finalize transactions on a particular website is mostly motivated by the services content (product description, price lists, delivery conditions, etc), and in a minor part by the impact of usability and the interface (as elements of task environment). However, an unsuitable task environment may cause dissatisfaction and prevent the user from completing the transaction, especially when the content is also not strongly motivating for purchase (Keeney 1999).

It should be noted here that critical interaction factors shaping user behavior in online services have rarely been included in HCI studies—they have rather been a matter of interest for marketing research. Paradoxically, the available base of marketing knowledge about online consumer behavioral patterns, and about how consumers interact with specific services, have seldom been referenced in contemporary HCI research and design. Perception of service quality has been too often limited to user interface quality and user experience assessment, neglecting important economic factors driving users to accept the most cost-effective solution and to look for long-lasting benefits for their problem domain.

14.2.3 Value-oriented Design

When treating users of interactive systems as service consumers it is natural to accept that they are looking for the most cost-effective solutions (in financial terms and in terms of human effort), and that they are interested in obtaining long-lasting benefits and value for their problem domain.

If value can be defined as a perceived benefit—increase or improvement observed in some context—then user behavior when searching for a specific value is purely economics-driven because users tend to get to the desired solution (reach the goal) in the most cost-effective way, or by obtaining the most cost-effective solution.

This point of view raises an interesting question—not only how the system supports the user in solving operational problems (like buying a ticket), but also how the content and interaction elements of the system support building beneficial relationships between the vendor and the customer and delivering business value for the vendor, as well as also economic value for customer.

In an attempt to adapt the scope of HCI research to the economic reality of online markets and online services, Cockton (2005) proposed an interesting development framework for value-centered design, based on four activity layers:

- Opportunity identification
- Design
- Iteration
- Evaluation

Evaluation bridges the layers and closes the iteration loop. This framework extends the classical iterative user-centered design (UCD) approach by adding values (*value for customer*) as design goals and by specifying design principles for value-based design of interactive systems.

A novel element introduced in this framework is reformulation of the system goal towards demands of contemporary markets: an interactive system should deliver value for the customer (not only satisfaction for the user). Delivering value for the customer can be provided only if:

- Positive user experience was provided for instance by applying UCD in the system development
- User satisfaction was provided by complying with user requirements and usability criteria described in ISO standards and design guidelines at both the user interface and interaction design levels

The concept of value-centered design goes far beyond the user interface design of interactive products, and applies directly to the design of interactive services, which are often based on subscription and are subject to free choice of the consumer within markets.

14.3 Economical Aspects of User Experience

14.3.1 The User as an Economic Decision-Maker

Theoretically *free* choice for the consumer can, in practice, be strongly limited by:

- Availability of offers matching the needs, Willingness of the user to keep searching or waiting for even more attractive offers, better than already available ones.

Based on psychological decision theory, consumer choices can be:

- Rational—based on careful evaluation and systematic gathering of any available information from the market
- Irrational—inconsistent, unwise

  - unplanned—impulsive, unconscious, accidental
  - planned—conscious, purposeful (aimed for instance to attract others' attention or shock the audience)

The superficially obvious and attractive assumption that most of economic decisions are rational was questioned by Simon (1957), a Nobel Prize laureate in economics in 1975. His research showed that both decision-makers and consumers tend to make decisions based on *bounded rationality*, leading then to find a solution that is *good enough* within a realistic time limit. Many decision makers give up searching for ultimately the best solution due to their inability to find and process all available information, and—often more importantly—due to limited time resources. Therefore, users tend to accept solutions close to the optimal (or at least *acceptable*), stressing that the decision must be taken within the specific time limit assigned for this task.

Although the concept of bounded rationality was developed in traditional, industry-based economics, its impact can be observed today in many consumer choices, referring also to interactive products. In every household, users have to make decisions about choosing products or services within realistic time limits. They primarily tend to exclude bad offers from the given set, while finding the best alternative from the remaining ones is usually too difficult for conscious, analytic processing.

Therefore, user choices when selecting an interactive product can often be based only on a quick impression, a demo evaluation, or on a short assessment of price and brand (as promises of quality) or others' opinions (also from the consumers' forum on the Internet). Insufficient information needed to make relatively reliable choices may be substituted by decision-making heuristics, based on short-term experience of cognitive shortcuts, which is the subject of economical psychology research—for instance, Gigegrenzer and Todd (1999).

As presumably rational decision-makers, most users assess competitive products and services by estimating the value offered by each alternative. In their decisions, consumers are expected to maximize the expected subjective utility (perceived value) of their choices, which is the basic assumption in consumer research studies (Allingham 2002).

For an elementary attempt to include basic economic issues in HCI and usability studies of interactive products, a very simple concept called customer-perceived value (CPV) from marketing research (Afuah & Tucci 2001, Doyle 2000) can be applied:

$$CPV = \frac{Perceived\ Quality}{Perceived\ Cost}$$

where:

- *Perceived Quality* is represented by a sum of perceived benefits from all (pragmatic and hedonistic) quality attributes, including functionality, usability, pleasure in use, aesthetics, benefits, relationships, and other factors identified as demanded by target users;
- *Perceived Cost* represents all (both measured and perceived) economic factors associated with using the system, as well as workload, frustration, and reluctance experienced by the user when using the system in real settings. Perceived lack of trust or security can be classified as cost factors, because they increase the effort needed for using the system, thus decreasing users' comfort and confidence
- *Customer-Perceived Value (CPV)* is defined as the perceived attractiveness of a particular service (website or product):

    - perceived as a relationship between perceived quality and perceived cost, associated with using particular system or service
    - perceived as relative to other alternatives available on the market

Customer-perceived value in general is defined positively, presenting perceived attractiveness and efficiency of particular interactive systems. Customer-perceived value can also be measured on a relative scale when a product is compared against competitors. An increase in customer-perceived value (for instance, after significant usability improvements reducing the effort needed to use the service) should result in increased customer satisfaction and more positive attitudes towards the online service or product, its vendor, and brand.

A variety of approaches for measuring consumer-perceived value of traditional services and products is available in the literature on marketing research and consumer behavior (Doyle 2000; Hill & Alexander 1996). The methods may range from simple quality management tools, like user surveys, perception mapping, benchmarking or quality function deployment (Sikorski 2002; 2003), ending at advanced statistical techniques for analyzing users' attitudes and choices, like conjoined analysis or multidimensional scaling.

Further adoption of existing methods for measuring customer-perceived value is recommended to extend current HCI research, or can be used by simple analogy with traditional off-line services, but such approaches need validation with case studies of real online services.

Human behaviors are predominantly driven by economical factors, in real life as well as in human-computer interaction. So far, however, it is clear that users/customers look for value when interacting with online services. Therefore, adopting a business perspective for designing their context of use seems natural, because their interactions and decisions take place in economic environments. Adding business context to interaction design for online services seems to be inevitable for developing high-quality online services for today's markets.

14.3.2 Relationship and Loyalty Development

In most interactive systems, users should be treated as service consumers. Thus, their satisfaction is no longer provided entirely by system functionality and usability, but also by long-lasting positive user experience. This experience should create a reinforcing, positive attitude towards the service vendor, based on a feeling of valuable, long-term relationships with the service vendor, in a big part maintained by the use of an online interactive system (like a website or a cell phone, etc.).

In the 1990s, *relationship marketing* (Christopher, et al. 1991) emerged as a new interesting approach, aiming to deliver innovative methods and tools for developing customer loyalty in the service sector and in online markets. Relationship marketing focuses on several areas particularly interesting for the service sector:

- Customer retention, especially in situations where customers have easy access to information on alternative offers
- Customer satisfaction factors, in particular factors affecting customer loyalty
- Switch barriers, expressed in terms of an expected cost-benefits ratio for the user willing to switch to other vendors
- Mechanisms for building mutually beneficial relationships with customers and strengthening customers' loyalty to brands and vendors

Relationship marketing has recently become an important stream in contemporary business and economics, since Internet and online services have dramatically changed the behavior of consumers and the ways in which companies communicate with their markets.

Relationship marketing discovers how customer loyalty may increase in services, ranging from initial scepticism to becoming the advocate of a particular brand or vendor. Because it is now very easy to find alternative online vendors for any kind of service, the problem of how to develop loyalty for online customers is an increasingly important issue—and there is an important role for usability in improving the customer-perceived value of online services.

In general, users tend to access online services or buy interactive products because they expect that benefits will outweigh involved costs and efforts.

In a competitive market, providing at least *acceptable* usability is a precondition for attracting customers to a particular website or service, and further for creating business relationships with customers. In addition to valuable content, outstanding usability may also contribute to building the competitive advantage of a product or service, by suitably addressing all structural elements of the brand, specified in detail by Doley (2000).

In interactive services, which are often individualized and subscription-based, more and more satisfaction and quality factors are located *beyond* the user interface. They refer to issues like user experience, user emotions, and the value of long-term relationships—as perceived by the users. Users remain loyal to the services and relationships as long as they perceive delivered value as higher than that which competitors offer.

Contemporary design of interactive services, oriented to building customer loyalty and long-lasting value for customers, should support the following transitions of the website or online service:

interactions > transactions > relations > values

Providing consistently high usability, and systematically delivering positive user experience, is essential. System usability is necessary for any e-service to appear on the market, but is not sufficient to gain a solid competitive advantage. The multi-layer model, presented in Figure 14.3 shows how companies can evolve their websites and online services step-by-step, stimulated by market competition in the e-business environment.

The development and evolution of online services are based on changing the nature of competitive advantage across subsequent *development stages* of online service (or websites): from basic functionality, across usability and user experience, to relationship and values, while a particular online service finally becomes an important part of the user's lifestyle.

As presented in Figure 14.3, in most online service systems functional quality and usability are fundamental for enabling the business, but for retaining a loyal customer base an ongoing positive experience and valuable relationship must be built upon the essential usability of an interactive system (service or website).

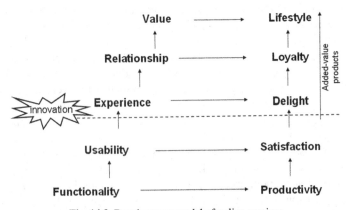

Fig. 14.3 Development model of online services

In e-services, creating positive user experience is an essential element in creating a strong brand. Emotionally involving interaction also may help, but adding outstanding *innovation* to product functionality and usability is often the turning point in creating value-added products or services.

In the context of creating new interaction qualities between user and vendor, *innovation* has the following features:

- Successful innovation brings delight and strong emotional involvement at the user's side
- Innovation enables distinctive differentiation from competitors' offers
- Innovation gets quickly accepted by users because it usually provides

  - Dramatically increased task support (excellent task efficiency)
  - Exceptionally pleasant operation (unique experience and excellent hedonistic quality)

On the other hand, successful innovation is quickly copied by competitors, gradually becoming a standard feature at all similar websites (like shopping baskets or interactive calculators). As a result, website/service designers have to be looking for further innovations, which will surprise customers again, and will rebuild competitive advantage against competitors[2].

Table 14.1 describes development *stages* in sequence by referring to the features of e-service and to observed user behaviors. Table 14.1 also presents the main features of the business models offered by vendors at each stage of development of an online service.

As a concrete example, Table 14.2 presents an example of typical development scenarios for exemplary financial service offered online. In these scenarios, a particular role of customer relationship system (CRM) has been mentioned for enhancing business interaction design (including the actual experiences of users versus expectations) for online services development.

Further examples of companies offering online services, which illustrate development stages of the model from Figure 14.3, can be recalled from business practice, and can also be found in business directories.

In particular, these few are worth mentioning:

- *Internet shops*—to name the Amazon.com only, which:

  - Usually started from a simple functionality—direct selling of books, CDs, etc., and by offering a wide variety of products with a very competitive price
  - Further on, while product variety increased, it was necessary to keep focus on usability and allow easy navigation for the users and smooth ordering and payment processes

---

[2] It should be noted here that—as in the case of physical products—it is relatively easy to copy visual design of a website or online service, but it is hardly possible to copy the whole user experience, as this is the behavior of interaction elements that gives the user the feeling of working with *the real thing*.

Table 14.1 Development stages of online services (Part 1)

Stage → Outcome	E-service Characteristics	User Behavior	Business Model
Functionality → Productivity	The website provides only fundamental functionality, enabling completion of basic tasks. Website usability is low, but there is no competition offering a better alternative.	Users get the desired outcome with significant effort, but they tolerate low usability because there is no better alternative on the market.	A very simple website is available, offering basic task completion, like buying a product from a limited choice, finding connections in a simple online timetable of a monopoly transport operator, even without possibility of online payment..
Usability → Satisfaction	Improved usability builds competitive advantage. Soon all competitive websites offer similar usability level.	Because competition is high and more choices are available, users tend to reject systems that are not usable enough.	An average Internet bookshop, offering a wide selection of items and flexible forms of payment and delivery. If website is not usable enough, customers switch to other vendors offering the same items for a similar price.
Experience → Delight	Competitive advantage is achieved by systematically adding innovative solutions, continuously improving interaction with website resources, and providing long-lasting, unique experiences for users.	Users are delighted with the innovative solutions, they visit the website regularly and tell others about their unique experiences from the website, which is also reflected in Internet rankings.	This website offers some amazing functionality and excellent user experience, gathering a specific online community of devoted customers and visitors. This strong brand gains a big share on the market and could be established as a leading online solution.

Relationship → Loyalty	Innovative design solutions attract more customers, loyalty programs introduced for regular users, a variety of means are used to provide consistent user experience in various distribution channels.	Customers give up visiting other websites because they believe that their favorite website provides the best shopping experience. Regular visitors turn into customers, loyal users are rewarded by access to exclusive functions available only for special customers.	The brand is well-known and supported by customers not only by transactions, but also by creating online community of brand advocates. Gradually the vendor becomes the market leader, and starts buying other companies that offer similar services or possess some critical technology.
Value → Lifestyle	Repeated transactions build strong vendor-customer relationship. CRM systems monitor users' buying behavior and business interactions, allowing identification of users needs, interests, and lifestyles. Services are customized to the needs of specific customer groups, individualized offers are matched to customer lifestyle; integration and sharing of services is offered by groups of associated vendors.	Users need to visit the website regularly, they put high trust in the vendor and its brand, and recommend this site to others as superior. Users customize its functions for personal preferences, get access to service resources including via mobile devices. This online service becomes an essential part of their lifestyle.	User gets a privilege to use other associated services in packages, for instance: online bank + telecom, hotel + travel, shop + delivery, etc. The vendor systematically adds offers covering new spheres of user life, adding prestige and convenience.

Table 14.2 Prospective development scenarios for online financial services (Part 1)

Stage → Outcome	Features	Development Scenario
Functionality → Productivity	The service is among the first to offer online access to bank accounts. Usability lags behind functional developments, but customers still tolerate it as long as there are few interesting alternatives on the market.	Improve ease of use, add new functions as competition grows, promote the service, monitor the competition.
Usability → Satisfaction	Service functionality and usability has been significantly improved, so typical operations no longer require contact with the personnel in the office. Self-service system on the website helps the user to find and activate the right options for personal finances management.	Remove all usability deficiencies to provide smooth interaction; provide accessibility and service enhancements for the user. Try to increase market share by attracting more and more customers and introducing new, competitive offers.
Experience → Delight	System functionality is integrated with other e-services, like mobile phone payments, SMS-alerts, etc. The bank endorses the credibility of the customer for other institutions and offers online services in forecasting future events on the specific markets (investment, real estate). Users find it as unique, context-matching experience, unbeatable by offers of competitive vendors.	Add mobile phone services and other expected functions, integrate financial services with insurance and investments, maintain strong brand with high trust and credibility. Care for perfection in detail, add small usability improvements, providing better experience than all the competition.

Relationship → Loyalty	Customers expand use of online service (for instance, buy insurance, take a loan, etc.) and stops using competitive services. Users accept rewards from loyalty programs and recommend the service to family members and friends.	Apply CRM system to monitor usage of service by each user, to profile individual offers, reward users with loyalty programs. Involve users' friends and family members by providing long-term benefits and attractive business value.
Value → Lifestyle	The user and his/her family are subscribed to a number of services offered by the vendor, they regularly use services online, and purchase other services offered by vendor and associated partners (in addition to financial services: home insurance, college loans, mortgage and investment services, retirement programs–depending on the specific phase of the family lifecycle). Consumers' children continue to use the same service when they grow up and become independent	Maintain outstanding value for customer, integrate services offered by affiliates, prepare individual packages, keep outstanding usability, and systematically match the contents as the customer lifestyle changes.

- In addition to excellent usability, users were further delighted with the ability to view sample chapters and suitability of suggestion tools (links like "Customers who bought this item also bought... ", "Similar books on this topic", or "What do customers ultimately buy after viewing this item?")—all this resulted in reducing shipping risk in a unique shopping experience, which other online bookshops attempt to imitate
- Systematically positive experience of users results in more frequent visits and building a strong brand, which has become a reference standard in e-commerce
- Strong relationship with a loyal base of regular users result in many satisfied customers buying books and media on Amazon only—they would be ready to buy any other products or services available from Amazon

- *Financial and insurance services*—like www.fidelity.com and others who:

  - Starting from a basic financial services, apart from business services, using innovative design and marketing, they expanded the variety of services for the family, including college loans, mortgages, insurances, and so on, almost all available online directly or able to be simulated with online calculators
  - Innovative communication methods and interactive marketing resulted in building strong relationships with customers, who find offer flexibility, trusted content, and service provider discretion very well matched to the current lifestyle of a typical family
  - All services are available online (Internet or phone), which also allowed the vendor to reduce the amount of offices and operational costs while delivering high value for customers at the same time

- *Hospitality and travel services* (like www.tripadvisor.com and others), which not only sell tickets, but offer recommendations, advice, and support for travellers who—before booking—look for trusted information delivered by other travelers (rating of hotels, airlines, and other globetrotter services)
- *Business services* (like http://www.cbiz.com), which build their brand on trust, reliability, and strong relations with their business users and subscribers. They provide not only information, advice, and expertise, but also communication tools available for community members

These examples suggest that for a business to be successful, a subsequent, step-by-step upgrade of online service business is necessary. This gradual upgrade is generally described by the development model presented in Figure 14.3. This model seems to be generally applicable to all kinds of personal and business services, on local and global markets, where (after providing basic services for the users) the *added-value online service* is based on the vendor's credibility, user's comfort, and developing strong relationships with customers.

Most value-added services, after some duration of customer loyalty and systematically increasing service usage, become a part of a customer's lifestyle. Also, the costs of changing vendors are relatively high for the user at upper levels of the model. However, detailed research based on case studies of representative companies is needed for a full validation and calibration of the proposed development model.

14.3.3 Strategic Grid for Positioning e-Services

As mentioned in former sections, the attractiveness of an online service for the users is the result of perceived content quality related to perceived costs. In cases where economic aspects are not so significant, expended costs can be interpreted as the total of user effort, dependent mostly on system usability and quality of user interface.

Because users always look for the most efficient, the most cost-effective, and the most comfortable or even the safest solutions, their choices will be driven by consumer motivations and referring to preferences that are the subject of marketing research.

It is an interesting research and practical issue to find out how online services evolve in their lifecycle, from inception to disappearance from the market. Because their success on the market is driven by the actual behaviors of their users, all managers—not only in online services—would like to know which development strategies to apply in order to follow customers' needs, preferences, and lifestyle trends.

The development model of online services presented in Figure 14.4 can be supplemented by the proposal of strategic development grids for online services.

Because there are numerous factors driving consumer choices, it seems impossible to identify all of them. Therefore, the proposed development grid is two-dimensional only, referring to two main components of satisfaction of the online

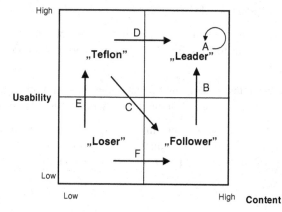

Fig. 14.4 Strategic grid for positioning e-services—controlled transitions leading to the development of online services

customer—quality of content and quality of interaction[3]. If these two main dimensions are considered (that means service content and usability), any website for online services can be positioned as a point in the area map shown in Figure 14.3.

The grid specifies four areas that depict the characteristic market positions of online vendors and online service providers.

The map can be used not only for comparing position of alternative services, but also for describing their features and for initial preparation of development strategies for particular services or websites.

According to the grid, four position areas for online service vendors can be specified with relevant development strategies:

- *Leader*—high value of content and high value of usability result in many satisfied, regular, and loyal customers:

  - development strategy—protect leading position on the market by preserving quality of content and excellent usability (Track A in Figure 14.4)

- *Follower*—high value of content and at the same time poor value of usability result in a small group of devoted users who keep visiting the website, ignoring evident usability deficiencies. However, users may switch to another service if similar content is available with lower effort:

  - development strategy—maintain the market niche, follow the leader, improve usability first, then expand the contents to attack the leader position (Track B)

- *Teflon*—low value of content, acceptable or even high usability; users have no difficulty in operating the website and accessing the content, but the content itself is low-valued because it is not relevant, incorrect, unprofessional or just boring; no particular user group *sticks* to this website/service, which behaves like a teflon covered pan:

  - development strategy—improve the content quality, add *killer application*, prepare program for building the market and developing relationships with users; after improvements attacking the position of follower (Track C), or even leader is possible (Track D)

- *Loser*—poor value of content, poor usability; users only visit by accident, get disappointed, and quit to look for alternative vendors with more attractive and more accessible offers:

  - development strategy—without radical rebuilding of both the content and usability, no further presence on the market will be possible (Tracks E and F)

Development in these two crucial dimensions—service content and usability must be coordinated in a smooth manner, because both factors affect customer-perceived quality of the service or website, and contribute to its position on the market.

---

[3] After neglecting the third, very important dimension—economic factors—already mentioned earlier.

Table 14.3 Typical transitions for online services

Position	Controlled Transition (Positive)	Uncontrolled Transition (Negative)
"Leader"	**A:** The biggest share on the market; maintain leadership by fulfilling business strategy	**G:** Sharp decrease in user satisfaction and in traffic intensity due to not updated, uninteresting offer (or due to sudden breakdown in business conditions)
		H: Unsatisfied users turn to other, formerly less popular sites, gradually decreasing market share
"Follower"	**B:** A strong market position; gain competitive advantage by attracting more customers, consider attacking leader position by attracting/overtaking current customers of the market leader	**I:** Systematically decreasing market share, users turn to other interesting sites (including both current marked leader and alternative sites)
		J: Sharp decrease in user satisfaction and in traffic intensity, users turn to other sites
"Teflon"	**C:** Systematic growth, resulting in gaining a big share on the market	**K:** Remaining scarce users turn away from the site, because they see it has nothing interesting to offer, or is no longer updated, or even seems to be abandoned by its creators
	D: Sudden success or a boom in the sector, sudden increase in traffic due to refreshed offer or very attractive pricing	
"Loser"	**E:** The site was gradually refurbished after long time of abundance, possibly because of attractive domain name or formerly strong brand worth face-lifting	**L:** All former users switched to other vendors; brand and website are disappearing from the market and users no longer use them in everyday life
	F: As above, but accompanied by a rapid growth resulting in gaining a big share on the market	

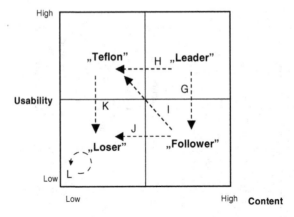

Fig. 14.5 Strategic grid for positioning e-services. Uncontrolled transitions leading to the decline of online service

Table 14.3 presents typical transitions that may change the current positioning of online services. This outline is based on generalized experiences of several companies known to the author.

In Table 14.3, two types of transition strategies have been specified:

- Controlled transitions (positive) that were planned and consciously executed as a transition strategy by company management. These transition strategies aim to strengthen the market position of a particular online service and they are performed under the control of the online service owner in reaction to (current or forecasted) specific situations or trends on the market
- Uncontrolled transitions (negative) are the events or trends taking place *outside* the company. They result from lost control of the market situation, various management errors, and negligence[4] in development and maintenance of online service or competitors' actions, changes in user lifestyles → signal of loosing control and worsening the current positions

Uncontrolled transitions from Table 14.3 that are negative for online business development, are shown in Figure 14.5, where their contribution to business decline is more visible.

14.4 Implications for HCI

The introduction of value-oriented research into HCI practice can broaden the *new usability* in recent HCI research to bring an important extension to usability research and practice.

---

[4] In particular, forgetting that to survive on the market, each online service should gradually upgrade following subsequent stages of the development model presented in Figure 14.2.

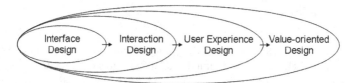

Fig. 14.6 Prospective evolution in HCI design practice

Figure 14.6 outlines the consequences of the concept presented in this chapter and prospective evolution in future HCI design practice.

Extending the scope of current HCI research towards value-oriented HCI might add some new insights:

- Combining HCI methodology with consumer research, which also uses many user-based methods originating from experimental psychology
- Merging with existing experiences and approaches from services management and services marketing, where value-based research has longer tradition than in HCI
- Linking to supply chain concepts, the perspective of information logistics, where systems serve as a platform for delivering business value

Available implementations of advanced online services and the vision presented in this chapter suggest a new research agenda for value-driven HCI, for instance:

- Measuring value for the customer in interactive systems/services
- Analyzing relationships among user interface design, perceived user experience and economic factors
- Optimizing factors creating perceived *total costs of ownership* (TCO) in different branches of interactive services/
- Contribution of HCI and user experience design to relationship marketing and to brand positioning in interactive services

Most contemporary interactive systems deliver services and benefits that users agree to pay for, because they are found more attractive than substitutes from competitors. More and more online services are now content-rich and device-independent. They are often configurable for personal needs, and subscription-based—and both factors reinforce developing a strong relationship between a vendor and a customer.

In modern service systems, the user/customer becomes not only a part (and subject) of a service process, but also part of a value chain, intended to generate benefits for all involved stakeholders.

Identifying the new role of interaction elements in the design of e-service systems is another opportunity for expanding HCI research—together with developing guidelines for designing *economically extended* user interfaces, enabling communication with intangible elements of the specific brand.

14.5 Conclusions

By offering tools and techniques for designing a better user experience in modern business systems, HCI does undoubtedly contribute to building strong brands for interactive products, websites, and online services. Therefore, it seems reasonable to expand the workbench of HCI research towards investigating the economic backgrounds of user behavior.

This chapter argues that by analogy to physical products (like cars or electronics) or services (personal or professional), it is feasible to develop approaches for creating strong brands for interactive products based on outstanding user experience, consumer trust, and recommendations. These approaches have to be developed on the crossroads of HCI and economics, because online consumers perform their tasks using digital content delivered by interactive systems, but their motivations and behaviors are economically-based.

In the future, a new extension of the current HCI, related to what was roughly named in this paper as the *economics of user experience*, should become an interesting and prospective field of analyzing user behaviors and attitudes towards interactive systems, brands, and vendors in online services. The initial toolbox of value-oriented HCI may be adopted in part from marketing research, quality management, and consumer behavior studies. However, the vision outlined in this chapter must be validated with a number of detailed case studies deeply embedded in the economic context of interactive systems.

References

Allingham, M. (2002). *Choice theory: a very short introduction.* Oxford University Press.

Arhippainen, L. (2003). Capturing user experience for product design. Available: http://virtual. vtt.fi/virtual/adamos/material/arhippa2.pdf [Referenced: 15 Sept., 2006]

Afuah, A., & Tucci, C.L. (2001). Internet *business models and strategies.* McGraw Hill.

Blackwell, R.D., Miniard, P.W., & Engel, J.F. (2001). *Consumer behaviour.* Hartcourt Publishers.

Christopher, M., Payne, A.. & Ballantyne, D. (1991). *Relationship marketing,* Oxford: Butterworth-Heinemann.

Cockton, G. (2005). A development framework for value-centred design. In: *Proceedings of CHI 2005, Vol.2. Extended Abstracts* (pp. 1292–1295).

Doyle, P. (2000) *Value-based marketing. Marketing strategies for corporate growth and shareholder value.* New York: Wiley.

Forlizzi, J., & Ford, S. (2000). The building blocks of experience: An early framework for interaction designers. In *Proceedings of Symposium on DIS 2000* (pp. 419–423).

Forlizzi, J., & Battarbee, K. (2004). Understanding experiences in interactive systems. In *Proceedings of Conference on DIS 2004* (pp 261–268)

Garnik, I. (2006). Ocena czynnikow ksztaltujacych wiarygodnosc oferentow w Internetowych transakcjach detalicznych (Evaluation of factors affecting credibility of online retail vendors, in Polish). PhD thesis, Gdansk University of Technology

Gigegrenzer, G., & Todd, G. (1999). *Simple heuristics that make us smart.* Oxford University Press

Hassenzahl, M. (2002). The effect of perceived hedonistic quality on product appealingness. *International Journal of Human-Computer Interaction, 13,* pp 479–497

Hill, N., & Alexander, J. (1996) *Handbook of customer satisfaction and loyalty measurements.* Gower.

ISO/IEC 9126-1 (2001). *Software engineering. Product quality. Part 1: Quality model.*

ISO 9241 (1998). *Ergonomic requirements for office work with visual display terminals. Part 10: Dialogue principles.*

ISO 9241 (1998). *Ergonomic requirements for office work with visual display terminals. Part 11: Guidelines on usability.*

Keeney, R. (1999). The value of Internet commerce to the customer. *Management Science, 45,* 533–542

Minocha, S., Millard, N., & Dawson, L. H. (2003). Integrating customer relationship management strategies in (B2C) e-commerce environments. In: *Proceedings of the INTERACT '2003 Conference* (pp. 335–342).

Pine, B. J., & Gilmore, J.H. (1998). Welcome to the experience economy. *Harvard Business Review, July-August 1998,* 97–105.

Sikorski, M. (2002). Zastosowanie metody QFD do doskonalenia jakosci uzytkowej serwisow WWW (Application of QFD method for improving usability of websites, in Polish). *Zeszyty Naukowe Politechniki Poznanskiej, seria: Organizacja i Zarzadzanie, nr 35,* pp 13–24

Sikorski, M. (2003). Measuring the immeasurable: system usability, user satisfaction and quality management. In: J. Jacko, C. Stephanidis (Eds): *Human-Computer Interaction. Theory and Practice Part I* (pp. 411–415). London: Lawrence Erlbaum.

Simon, H. (1957) *Models of man.* Wiley.

Thomas, P., & Macredie, R.D. (2002) Introduction to new usability. *ACM Transactions on Human-Computer Interaction, 9(2),* 69–73.

Chapter 15
The Future of Usability Evaluation: Increasing Impact on Value

Stephanie Rosenbaum

Tec-Ed, Inc., USA, e-mail: stephanie@teced.com

Abstract What does the future of usability evaluation hold? To gain insights for the future, this chapter first surveys past and current usability practices, including laboratory usability testing, heuristic evaluation, methods with roots in anthropology (such as contextual inquiry and ethnographic research), rapid iterative testing, benchmarking with large population samples, and multiple-method usability programs. Such consideration has several benefits, because both individual usability practitioners and organizations have attained different levels of usability sophistication and maturity. Usability evaluation methods long employed by major corporations may still be in the future for smaller or younger organizations. The chapter begins by discussing 20th-century usability evaluation, continues with an overview of usability evaluation today, and concludes with a discussion of what to expect in usability evaluation over the next years. For each period in the history—and future—of usability evaluation, the chapter addresses how its impact on software value is increasing.

15.1 Introduction

In the United States, what we now consider usability practice has its roots in several disciplines: human factors, cognitive psychology, anthropology, computer science, and technical communication. When I founded my consulting firm, Tec-Ed, in 1967, *usability* was not yet a separate domain. We took part in the conception and birth of the usability profession, and matured with the field. Throughout this chapter, I have used Tec-Ed as an exemplar. It is one company's perspective, but I can best tell the story of the evolution and future of usability in the context of our own history and experiences.

This chapter, therefore, presents a practitioner's viewpoint, although informed by decades of working closely with faculty and researchers in academia. My colleagues and I perform usability evaluations (and other user research) that are tied to industry requirements—the timelines are faster than in academic research, and the methodology is adapted to shorter-term objectives and results.

To gain insights for the future of usability evaluation, we must first look at past events that led to usability research and practice today. Then we can consider what

E. Law et al. (eds.), *Maturing Usability.*

the future holds for the usability and HCI communities, and how usability will continue to increase the value of software in systems in the real world.

Another reason to consider past and current practices as we envision the future of usability is the different levels of maturity among organizations today. Universities, major corporations, and sophisticated consultancies often pioneer new approaches to usability. However, a usability evaluation method that IBM developed in 1995 may be highly effective for a small consumer electronics company in 2010. This chapter concludes by discussing what the future of usability and its impact on software value mean to practitioners from diverse organizations in a software and systems environment that is itself rapidly evolving.

15.2 20th Century Usability Evaluation

The evolution of usability evaluation methods followed the evolution of software design methods during the last quarter of the 20th century. Much early software engineering followed a now-traditional waterfall model to organize the software design and development process into a series of steps (Royce, 1970):

- System feasibility and validation
- Software plans, requirements, and validation
- Product design and verification
- Detailed design and verification
- Code and unit test
- Integration and product verification
- Implementation and system test
- Operation, maintenance, and revalidation

Software engineering models like the waterfall model helped introduce structure to often-informal programming efforts. They included some feedback loops and considered lifecycle issues such as maintenance. However, they called for detailed documentation in the early phases, not always practical in an industry environment. More important, they often created a *design-to-spec* mentality, without encouraging consultation with users.

Such models did not help designers anticipate user reactions because those reactions grew out of the user's context and immediate goals. User behavior results from the interactions of two complex systems—the user's brain and the software. Rigid software engineering models could not anticipate emergent, empirically discovered scenarios of use.

In the 1970s and early 1980s, Tec-Ed—founded as a technical communication consultancy—performed product verification while creating user documentation, help systems, and other user-support materials for software. Usability evaluation was an almost unrecognized byproduct of user documentation.

For example, one of the earliest small business accounting software applications was written for the Atari 800 microcomputer in 1981 by two programming teams. When documenting the software behavior in the user manual, we were the first to observe that half the commands took effect as soon as the user typed the command, while the other half required the user to type the commands and then press the Return (Enter) key, depending on which team had programmed the command. The result was that users had to focus on how the program worked—either remember each command's behavior or notice consciously whether another key-press was required—rather than thinking about their accounting tasks.

Such discoveries were so common that, by the mid-1980s, Tec-Ed's proposals to create user documentation included not only the steps to write the help system or user manual, but also specific verification and feedback tasks. Often the most dramatic feedback was a clear description of the actual system behavior; the product manager reading our draft would cry, "It can't possibly work that way!"

The practice of iterative design and testing was slow to gain acceptance. John Gould and Clayton Lewis presented a seminal paper on "Designing for Usability" at the first Conference on Human Factors in Computing Systems held in 1983 by ACM SIGCHI (Special Interest Group on Computer Human Interface), followed by a 1985 article in *Communications of the ACM*, recommending three principles of design:

- **Early Focus on Users and Tasks**—First, designers must understand who the users will be. This understanding is arrived at in part by directly studying their cognitive, behavioral, anthropometric, and attitudinal characteristics, and in part by studying the nature of the work expected to be accomplished.
- **Empirical Measurement**—Second, early in the development process, intended users should actually use simulations and prototypes to carry out real work, and their performance and reactions should be observed, recorded, and analyzed.
- **Iterative Design**—Third, when problems are found in user testing, as they will be, they must be fixed. This means design must be iterative. There must be a cycle of design, test and measure, and redesign, repeated as often as necessary (Gould & Lewis 1985).

Gould and Lewis said that they began recommending these principles in the 1970s, but "they are not usually employed in system design." The 1985 article is timeless and deserves to be required reading for software developers today. Gould and Lewis' excellent advice is still not consistently followed, yet complex software systems increase the importance of iterative design. Correcting one problem may cause others to occur, or make visible previously unrecognized problems.

In 1988, Mantei and Teorey published an expanded waterfall model (Mantei & Teorey 1988) that integrated usability tasks into the software development life cycle:

- Market analysis
- Feasibility study
- Requirements definition
- Product acceptance analysis
- Task analysis
- Global design
- Prototype construction
- User testing and evaluation

- System implementation
- Product testing
- User testing
- Update and maintenance
- Product survey

When Tec-Ed began offering usability services in the mid-1980s, most usability evaluations consisted of formal usability testing, typically conducted only once, late in the product development cycle. Most usability practitioners in industry were PhDs in human factors or psychology, working in corporate human factors departments in companies such as IBM and Hewlett-Packard. Practitioners needed the credibility of formal experimental methods.

Starting in the late 1980s, technical communication programs in universities became the training ground for United States practitioners. The first special issue of a journal devoted to "the value and methods of usability evaluation" was the December 1989 issue of the *IEEE Transactions on Professional Communication*, guest-edited by Judith Ramey of the University of Washington. It included a 169-item bibliography on usability evaluation and testing, with references going back to 1981.

Revisiting this journal's special issue more than 15 years later, it is impressive how many topics are still current and challenging to usability practitioners. In my own article comparing expert evaluation and usability testing, I discussed who should define usability standards, how to justify usability testing, and the importance of rigor—all questions I was asked at a usability conference in 2006!

15.2.1 Methodology in the 1980s

Most of the usability evaluations performed in the 1980s (in industry settings in the United States) were formal usability tests. The research team typically consisted of two practitioners—the test facilitator and the observer/notetaker—and the average project took six to eight weeks to complete.

In many cases, the software development or engineering teams had no previous exposure to usability evaluation, so project descriptions needed to be detailed introductions to the methodology, working procedure, and deliverables. Even then, few except the usability practitioners could envision the project deliverables before receiving them for review.

From my own experience at Tec-Ed, I can provide an example of the way projects were defined in the late 1980s; similar approaches continued to be used for laboratory usability testing through the mid-1990s. The following case history is excerpted and somewhat revised from an actual project description, with fictional names substituted for the real ones).

Background and Study Objectives. Connex was a new messaging service to be offered by PageCo. The service used a device developed by Motorola, and offered a variety of ways to send and receive messages, including telephone keypads, voice recognition, and Windows-based PC software.

During product development, PageCo held focus groups with prospective users and conducted tests with mock-ups of the devices. However, in early development it was not possible to test the entire service. When PageCo neared a commercial release of the service, they decided to conduct human factors studies of the usability of the entire service, which was more complex than most paging systems then in use.

In particular, PageCo wanted to explore the process users would go through to interact with Connex, users' experience with the voice response system, and the usability of the PC software. PageCo was concerned with making the process of sending messages and receiving replies as simple as possible.

Although it was not possible to incorporate all the results of this human factors work in the product version entering beta testing, PageCo planned to release another version the following summer. Usability recommendations not feasible for the forthcoming release could be implemented for the summer release.

Some of the issues we wanted to investigate included:

- How easily and successfully can users originate messages using a telephone (either keypad or voicemail)?
- How easily can users figure out how to send messages using the PC software? What problems do they encounter?
- How easily can users receive responses from the device? How easy is it for users to distinguish and understand the different responses?
- How many of the software features can users operate successfully without training (over 75% of PC users simply experiment with new software, rather than use the training, documentation, or help systems)?

To explore the above questions, Tec-Ed proposed to conduct a laboratory-based usability test of Connex with people who represented the major target audiences for the service.

Usability Test Methodology. In a laboratory usability test, individual participants with characteristics similar to the target audiences use a product to perform a series of representative tasks in a controlled situation, observed by usability specialists. The tasks are selected to be as similar as possible to those that users perform in their normal work situations. However, in a usability test, all participants perform exactly the same tasks, so we can make valid comparisons about their performance and behavior.

Usability tests collect both performance data and preference data. For the performance data collection, we observed and measured how easily and how successfully the test participants performed each of the test tasks. We collected qualitative information by recording participants' behavior and comments during the test sessions, as they used *think-aloud* protocol while performing activities. This technique, called protocol analysis, originated at Carnegie-Mellon University and provides insight into the reasons for users' behavior and their performance problems. We also collected quantitative data, such as number and severity of errors.

For the preference data collection, we administered Likert-scale questionnaires after each task that collected quantitative information about participants' opinions of Connex's ease of use. We noted the preferences participants expressed as they thought out loud. At the end of each session, we asked both Likert-scale and open-ended questions in a final questionnaire and debriefing interview.

During the test design at the beginning of the project, Tec-Ed and PageCo worked together to define the specific issues for testing and appropriate test tasks for exploring those issues. We considered what necessary training or user information the participants would need. However, as far as possible, we defined an *out-of-box* study (in which participants are not required to consult training or documentation), because this approach reflects the way most people behave in their normal usage contexts.

Tec-Ed provided a team of two usability specialists to conduct and observe the test sessions. The test administrator guided participants through the activities and observed their behavior. The observer took detailed notes of the participants' behavior and responses, and began compiling the data as the sessions proceeded.

Once the test sessions were complete, Tec-Ed analyzed the collected data, and performed statistical analysis of the data. We categorized the kinds of problems the participants encountered, and made suggestions for how to improve the user interface to minimize these problems.

We provided two kinds of reporting: a written summary report of the study results, and a management presentation and results discussion. We also proposed options for preparing a detailed, in-depth study results report and/or a highlights videotape compiled from the data collection videotapes of the participants' test sessions.

Study Participants. We identified three primary user audiences for Connex whose behavior was important to study during the usability test. These groups were current users of numeric paging systems, current users of alphanumeric paging systems, and people who were not currently using paging systems at all, but were considering becoming users. Each of these audience groups had different skills, prior experiences, and expectations for the product.

We proposed options for conducting the usability testing with 12 and 18 participants. Test sessions with 12 participants (one at a time) would enable us to identify problems, behavior, and opinions likely to occur in large fractions of the target audience. To differentiate among the three audience groups in our results, we recommended using 18 participants, plus two pilot-test participants. We screened, selected, and scheduled participants who lived or worked within an hour's drive from the selected location for the test sessions.

Deliverables from Tec-Ed and Support Needed from PageCo. The usability test of Connex included the following deliverables:

- A full-day working session with PageCo to agree on specific test objectives, task sequences, and participant characteristics. During this session, Tec-Ed also gained hands-on experience with the device and with the PC software.
- A Test Design reflecting the decisions made during the working session, including a participant selection script for screening participants.
- A draft of the Test Materials to be used during the test sessions. These materials consisted of the administrator's script, background questionnaire, post-task and post-test questionnaires, short task description handouts (if required), and observer note-taking and tabulation forms.
- A dry-run of the usability test at Tec-Ed, using an internal Tec-Ed participant.
- Two pilot tests of the usability test at the agreed-upon location.
- Revisions to the Test Materials based on PageCo feedback and the results of the dry-run and pilot tests.
- 18 usability test sessions up to 2 hours long, conducted at the agreed-upon location.
- A written summary report of the study findings, conclusions, and recommendations, including data analysis by Tec-Ed's statistician.
- A results presentation meeting at PageCo.
- (Optional) A detailed final study report (30 to 40 pages). This report included a comprehensive record of all the project activities, as well as extensive quotations from the participants. It provided longer-term educational and archival benefits, and is valuable as guidance for an ongoing usability improvement process.
- (Optional) A 30-minute highlights videotape compiled from the videotapes of the participants' test sessions. The highlights videotape is a communication tool for data, not a broadcast-quality tape. The audio consists of participant and administrator comments during the sessions, without voiceover narration.

To complete these deliverables, Tec-Ed needed the following support from PageCo:

- A designated PageCo project manager for both project scope decisions and technical questions.
- Participation by key PageCo developers and marketing staff in the working session.
- Product specifications, any existing documentation or training materials, and screen printouts of the PC software immediately after project approval, so that Tec-Ed could begin planning the test tasks.
- Functional beta hardware and software for Connex as early as possible in the project, and no later than the working session. Although some product features did not function without the service coverage, Tec-Ed needed to be able to examine the hardware and software user interfaces in detail to develop the test tasks.
- Timely reviews of the test design and materials according to a schedule agreed upon between the Tec-Ed and PageCo project managers.

Working Procedure. The following working procedure describes the activities Tec-Ed and PageCo performed to carry out the Connex usability testing project. The procedure is in working weeks; Tec-Ed's project manager submitted a schedule with exact dates after the project was approved.

1.	PageCo approves the project, selecting the number of participants to be tested. Tec-Ed receives specifications, documentation, and screen printouts.	Week 1
2.	PageCo and Tec-Ed meet in a working session to identify and prioritize test objectives, participant characteristics, and other test design issues. Tec-Ed receives current hardware and software.	Week 2
3.	Tec-Ed prepares the test design, describing in detail the test methodology, tasks, facilities, and software requirements.	Week 2
4.	PageCo receives and reviews the test design and participant recruiting script.	Week 2
5.	PageCo and Tec-Ed meet to discuss the test design, agree on any changes, and finalize the details of the participant tasks.	Week 3
6.	Tec-Ed receives lists of participant candidates from PageCo.	Week 3
7.	Tec-Ed prepares the draft of the Test Materials, and begins participant screening and recruiting.	Week 3
8.	PageCo and Tec-Ed discuss the Test Materials and agree on any changes.	Week 4
9.	Tec-Ed revises the Test Materials as agreed.	Week 4
10.	Tec-Ed conducts pilot testing with two participants at the agreed-upon location, and revises the Test Materials to reflect the pilot test results. A PageCo technical staff member familiar with the hardware and software should be available during the pilot testing.	Week 5
11.	Tec-Ed conducts test sessions with up to 18 participants. A PageCo technical staff member familiar with the hardware and software should be available during all test sessions.	Week 5
12.	PageCo receives the written summary report, including tables of supporting data and the statistical analysis.	Week 7
13.	Tec-Ed delivers a management presentation of the usability results.	Week 7

This example is a fairly straightforward project description. Many communications to software development groups require even more details—and more rhetorical explanations and justification—about the benefits of usability testing, the kinds of data we plan to collect, and the rigor needed for participant recruiting and screening.

15.2.2 Methodology in the 1990s

In the 1990s, usability evaluation had evolved from an uncommon activity conducted in just a few innovative companies to a well-accepted practice in software design and development. The first books describing the details of usability methods were published, such as the seminal—and still valuable—*A Practical Guide to Usability Testing* (Dumas & Redish 1993; 1999), which introduced many new usability practitioners to techniques such as the think-aloud protocol.

Once companies conducted usability testing regularly, corporate usability practitioners were able to use the deliverables—test designs, session materials, and reports—from previous projects to illustrate their proposed activities to product teams. Organizations building usability groups also began creating standard formats or templates for reporting and disseminating usability test findings. Consultants, to avoid showing proprietary information to other clients, sometimes produced anonymous sample deliverables to set expectations, even when product and audience diversity made formal templates inappropriate.

During this period, usability evaluation methodology became both more refined and more diverse. Most influential were Robert Virzi's in-depth explorations of sample size (Virzi 1992) and Jakob Nielsen's *discount usability engineering* (Nielsen 1993).

Virzi established a research basis for deciding how many participants would produce reliable data from usability testing. Practitioners could feel confident when testing four to six people per *cell*, or audience group, as long as the objective was to identify usability problems rather than to conduct a formal comparison between participant groups.

Discount usability engineering involved simplifying the methodology of formal usability testing in several ways:

- Creating and testing scenario-based prototypes, limited in features and functionality, often paper-based
- Collecting and analyzing think-aloud data from researchers' notes, rather than analyzing videotaped data
- Conducting iterative testing of a few participants, repeated after each design modification

When Nielsen introduced discount usability engineering, resistance was strong in the human factors community, especially in academia. An ACM CHI '95 panel addressed "Discount or Disservice? Discount Usability Analysis—Evaluation at a Bargain Price or Simply Damaged Merchandise?" (Gray, et al. 1995).

Many were concerned about the validity of discount usability evaluation techniques; for example, Gray and Salzman wrote a critique of published research, pointing out many flaws of experimental design (Gray & Salzman 1998). Nevertheless, discount techniques gained acceptance—especially in commercial settings—for good reasons. Simpler usability evaluation methods facilitated iterative software design, which was becoming more widespread.

The explosive growth of the Internet in the 1990s supported both iterative design and iterative usability evaluation. The ease of new Web releases contrasted dramatically with the length of the traditional software development cycle. Only streamlined usability evaluation techniques could fit the development schedules for Web releases.

However, this acceleration of the software development process also complicated usability data collection—a challenge usability practitioners still face. Frequent release cycles increase the importance of quality note-taking during usability research, to produce a wealth of accessible data ready to organize and analyze.

In the 1990s, practitioners were struggling to apply time-consuming experimental methods, and often losing the opportunity to conduct evaluations because of schedule constraints. Today, enhancements of the methods introduced by Nielsen and others are widely used throughout usability evaluation practice.

15.2.3 The Role of Heuristic Evaluation

Another usability evaluation method that gained wide use in the 1990s was *heuristic evaluation*, or expert evaluation based on rules or guidelines. Nielsen included heuristic evaluation in discount usability engineering by creating just ten rules, based on broader heuristics than the hundreds of previously published usability guidelines. His research indicated that independent heuristic evaluations by two or more people identified a majority of the usability problems in a software product, with the problem-identification percentage increasing as evaluators were added (Nielsen & Landauer 1993).

Heuristic evaluation is appropriate for compressed software development schedules, because the method requires less preparation than usability testing—no detailed scripting or time-consuming participant scheduling. If the development team is open to new ideas, heuristic evaluation can be a good investment of usability resources.

My 1989 *IEEE Transactions on Professional Communication* article (Rosenbaum 1989) discussed when to conduct heuristic evaluation versus usability testing—strategies that are still appropriate now. Heuristic evaluation enables usability practitioners to provide quick feedback to software developers, but—like any method lacking primary data—risks being dismissed as just the opinion of the usability practitioner.

Heuristic evaluation also increases the value of usability testing. By identifying immediate usability problems, heuristic evaluation harvests the low-hanging fruit and provides a focus for later usability testing. Without prior heuristic evaluation, usability practitioners frequently see test participants spend session time struggling with an obvious usability problem. Meanwhile, other equally important problems are masked by the first one and remain undiscovered.

The major drawback of heuristic evaluation is that evaluators, regardless of their skill and experience, remain surrogate users (expert evaluators who emulate users) and not necessarily typical users of the product. Heuristic evaluation rarely emulates all the key audience groups, nor does it necessarily indicate which problems users will encounter most frequently.

15.2.4 Out of the Lab and into the Field

In the 1990s, usability practitioners began turning for guidance to another field—anthropology. In fact, the techniques of anthropology had been used in product development for decades, but rarely were incorporated into usability evaluation programs in industry.

Eleanor Wynn and Lucy Suchman each conducted pathbreaking research at Xerox's Palo Alto Research Center (PARC) during the 1970s, as graduate students in anthropology at the University of California at Berkeley. Wynn's doctoral thesis, *Office Conversation as an Information Medium* (Wynn 1979), was widely read during the early 1980s when system developers, especially in Europe, were searching for ways of studying the workplace that would support a labor-oriented approach. Suchman spent 20 years as a researcher at PARC, founding its Work Practice and Technology area and publishing papers applying anthropology to technology (Suchman 1983; 1996).

Usability methods that emerged from anthropology include ethnography, participatory design, and contextual inquiry. Ethnography is the description of cultures, maintaining the perspective of those inside the culture being described—thus it can help system designers and software engineers understand unfamiliar audiences.

In 1990, Judith Ramey adapted the ethnographic *stream-of-behavior chronicle* to serve as a tool for task analysis in designing a medical user interface (Ramey and Robinson 1991). A stream-of-behavior chronicle records and describes, without judging, every action or statement from a member of the culture being studied (rather than saying, "she rejected the basket," you would record "she threw the basket over her shoulder"). This method helped Ramey observe and record the behavior of radiologists without influence from others' prior analysis.

Participatory design originated in Scandinavia. As early as 1977, Scandinavian research claimed that users should participate in system design to improve the knowledge on which systems are built, help users to develop realistic expectations, and increase workplace democracy (Bjerknes, Ehn, & Kyng 1987; Bjorn-Andersen & Hedberg 1977).

Participatory design theories gained acceptance in the United States in the 1980s, and led to the PICTIVE technique developed by Michael Muller at Bellcore (Muller 1991), as well as the CARD (Muller 1996; Tudor, Muller, & Dayton 1993) and PANDA (Muller 1995) techniques that followed it. In these methods, a team of people who represent the stakeholders—users, designers, and developers—work together with a facilitator to create products or website designs. Users play a central role, telling about their environments and tasks. Participatory design employs simple tools like index cards, sticky notes, felt pens, scissors, and tape, leveling required skills so that no participant feels intimidated by unfamiliar technology.

Contextual inquiry is a field research method initially developed by the Software Human Factors group at Digital Equipment Corporation (Holtzblatt & Jones 1993). In a contextual inquiry, an experienced interviewer observes users in the context of their actual work situation, performing their usual job tasks (not tasks designed for the study). Contextual inquiry is based on the following three principles (Raven & Flanders 1996):

1. Data gathering must take place in the context of the users' work
2. The data gatherer and the user form a partnership to explore issues together
3. The inquiry is based on a focus—that is, based on a clearly defined set of concerns, rather than a list of specific questions (as in a survey)

Conducting a contextual inquiry normally involves a team of at least two, an inquirer and one or more note-taker/observers. Originally, the inquirer was a human factors specialist and the observers were software developers. The inquirer and the participant are equals—each is an expert in his or her own work. After the visits, the inquiry team reviews their notes and analyzes the information to find patterns.

Contextual inquiries yield rich data from seeing users in their real work context, and thus can identify issues not previously recognized. They avoid the possibility of misleading results from placing users in artificial situations. However, a thorough application of the methodology is resource-intensive and time-consuming. Several of the pioneers in contextual inquiry went on to build a structured *contextual design* process (Beyer & Holtzblatt 1998) that employs contextual inquiry, work modeling techniques, and other activities to improve work practice in design.

Ethnographic interviews (Wood 1996) use some of the techniques of anthropology to collect more specific and concrete information from participants than normally takes place in traditional journalistic interviews. By interviewing people in their own work environments, even when circumstances do not permit a full contextual inquiry, researchers can examine the users' workplaces and study artifacts associated with their work processes (such as notes, memos, and printouts).

As with usability testing, early applications of anthropology in usability research were in-depth qualitative investigations, conducted mostly within large organizations that could invest in research for long-term product design improvements. An indication that field research was becoming more widespread was the publication of *Field Methods Casebook for Software Design* (Wixon & Ramey 1996), a collection of essays contributed by members of a CHI '95 workshop on field techniques. This book—still a valuable guide for practitioners—provided numerous case studies, as well as detailed framework discussions on ethnography, participatory design, and contextual design.

15.2.5 Case History of Field Research

From my own experience at Tec-Ed, here is the case history of a contextual inquiry that illustrates how field research was conducted in the 1990s (Anschuetz, Hinderer, & Rohn 1998).

Sun Microsystems, a major manufacturer of computer hardware and software, wanted to explore how well the main component of its enterprise-wide call management system supported its employee users. The component, a service order tool, was used daily by hundreds of Sun employees around the world for customer service and field service tasks.

To identify users' major concerns about the tool, we conducted 24 contextual inquiry sessions at seven sites in the United States, United Kingdom, France, and Germany. An international field study was expensive and time-consuming, and we considered various kinds of remote data collection as alternatives; however, an overwhelming number of considerations favored in-person observation:

- *Importance of the tool*—the service order tool played an important role in the company's effort to integrate worldwide staff, skills, and expertise. Once entered into the tool, service orders could be accessed by users anywhere. For example, at the time of the study, Sun was adding third-shift call coverage in parts of Europe by using second-shift staff on the West coast of the United States.

- *Necessity for user buy-in*—the service order tool was already the focus of a users' group whose members, mostly managers, represented the major locations using the tool. However, Sun wanted all target user groups—not just managers—to *buy in* to the changes that would result from the study.

- *Differences in business practices and companion software*—each country had its own process for delivering customer service and therefore developed its own job titles, descriptions, and expectations for the positions that use the service order tool. The companion software used with the tool also varied from country to country.

These factors dictated contextual inquiry, combining observation and conversation in the users' normal work environments. This methodology allowed us to:

- Explore use of the service order tool within the restrictions of actual work, such as network response times and length-of-time targets for dispatchers and engineers dealing with customers on the phone

- See when and how companion software and artifacts such as hardcopy tablets, reports, and forms were used to complement the tool; and obtain samples of the hardcopy objects

- Collect concrete data by observing real-time experience

- Clarify details and avoid misunderstandings about what users did and why

With its emphasis on observation and follow-up questions to make sure the usability practitioners correctly interpreted the users' actions, contextual inquiry also helped minimize language difficulties between the participants and researchers.

Identifying the user groups for the research proved to be a challenge. Working with Sun managers, business analysts, and developers, we ultimately identified eight distinct groups—twice as many as in our initial discussions:

- Dispatchers
- Front-line support engineers
- Mid-line support engineers
- Back-line support engineers
- Support services staff
- Account ambassadors
- Hardware support engineers
- Regional system support engineers/customer service managers

Some of these groups, such as dispatchers and front-line engineers, used the tool while the customer was on the phone. Their goal was to record information and create service orders quickly so the service orders could be resolved and closed quickly. Other groups, such as back-line engineers, used the tool mainly to file information and manage their time. Still other groups used the tool to monitor progress on service orders, and help ensure customer satisfaction.

Of our 24 study participants, roughly half worked in the United States, and the other half worked in the United Kingdom, France, and Germany. We developed detailed participant selection criteria for each target user group, including time in current position, type of service order tool training (if any), and opinion of the tool. The recruiters in each country tried to use the same screening criteria for all participants, and were reasonably successful.

Finally, we developed an individual focus or list of topics to guide the observation of, and conversation with, participants from each user group, adapting the focus as necessary for each country. As it turned out, the focus did not change much between countries—the differences occurred in the follow-up questions we asked participants in each country after watching them use the tool.

The sessions and data analysis for this project extended over several months. We used a six-week lag between the U.S. and European sessions to examine our U.S. data and prepare an interim report of findings. After the European sessions, we developed a top-ten list of findings for a quick-results presentation that preceded the comprehensive written report. We then created a database to organize our abundant notes and quickly slice the data in different ways—for example, by target user group, by formal vs. informal training on the tool, and by features used.

As a result of the contextual inquiry, Sun instituted more in-depth training for service order tool users, along with immediate changes to the interface for improved usability. Our numerous long-term recommendations for simplifying the system drove the specifications for the next version of the service order tool.

15.2.6 Usability by the Millennium

By the year 2000, usability practice had become much more sophisticated, skilled, and diverse. The software engineering field had largely accepted and incorporated iterative design into its practices, and thus was more receptive to iterative usability as well. Usability practitioners were expected to have a *toolkit* of methods at their fingertips, although usability programs in most companies still concentrated on one or two popular methods:

- Exploratory usability testing after each of several iterative development cycles
- Heuristic evaluation, followed by design revisions, followed by usability testing

These approaches were usually effective. When an organization's primary goal is to identify usability problems rather than quantify them or compare interfaces explicitly, iterative exploratory usability testing is successful (Nielsen & Landauer 1993; Virzi 1992) because:

- The maximum cost-benefit ratio for user testing comes from 3–5 participants
- 80% of problems can be detected with 4 or 5 participants
- Serious flaws tend to show up earlier

However, usability programs consisting only of exploratory usability testing and/or heuristic evaluation had potential weaknesses that were not immediately apparent:

- They may not evaluate different audience groups; most small-sample usability tests assume a fairly homogenous audience
- They do not observe users in their context of work
- They do not address longitudinal issues; most observations focus on ease of learning and the *out-of-box* experience

By the millennium, only a modest number of larger companies had created successful multiple-method usability programs balanced to reflect the organization's strategic goals. In such programs, some studies focused on immediate short-term results, while others addressed longer-term concerns.

However, most organizations practicing usability in 2000 had not achieved this balance, instead concentrating almost entirely on collecting user data for the next software version or release. Field research was still underutilized in commercial software development. The multiple challenges of budget, schedule, and logistics often defeated practitioners' efforts to convince corporate management to support field studies (Rosenbaum 2000a).

Happily, the academic community continued to foster the skills of usability practitioners. In 2000, another special issue of *IEEE Transactions on Professional Communication,* this one guest-edited by Menno D. T. de Jong and Judith Ramey, featured usability research methods with an extensive literature review (de Jong & Schellens 2000), and rich discussions of techniques such as thinking-aloud protocol (Boren & Ramey 2000).

15.2.7 *Impact of 20th Century Usability Evaluation on Value*

The editors of this volume describe *quality in value* in terms of the impact or achieved value software has in the real world. They correctly state that we must evaluate the fitness of software for its purpose, and that we must consider many forms of value—personal,   organizational,   cultural,   and monetary.

Almost from its inception, usability evaluation improved the value of commercial software because such software rarely had a single version or release. Thus, even the initial usability effort of most organizations—conducting a single laboratory usability test on alpha or beta software before release—had a feedback loop to software redesign. Recommended improvements that were not feasible for the current release could still be addressed in later releases.

After organizations began establishing usability departments and conducting iterative exploratory usability testing, the impact of usability evaluation on value increased, because a structured process was in place to improve design. Larger and more sophisticated companies developed formal methodology for applying usability evaluation outcomes to software redesign.

By the late 1990s, the wider application of anthropology to usability through field research methods began to add a new dimension. Usability evaluation in the context of users' actual work or home environments enabled practitioners to assess what the

editors of this volume call *post-usage effectiveness*, or the impact of using software
to perform its intended tasks and achieve its intended satisfaction.

15.3 Usability Evaluation Today

Any essay that attempts to place a topic in historical context must recognize that its
readers probably live in the future we forecast. This chapter was written in 2006, so
its discussion of the state of usability evaluation today may be obsolete before the
book is published. More kindly, this section will simply become another part of the
historical context.

However, another reason to describe usability evaluation today is that levels of
skill and sophistication are not equal in our community of practitioners. The practice
of usability is maturing at different speeds in different organizations.

A company that has just hired its first usability practitioner to help software
engineers apply user-centered design will probably employ the evaluation methods
more usability-literate companies used in the early 1990s—and those methods will
be appropriate and effective. It may quite reasonably be another five years before
most software development organizations apply the usability evaluation methods
described in this section, and in use now at such companies as Microsoft, Google,
eBay, Yahoo!, and Intuit.

15.3.1 Field Methods in Industry: Focused and Compressed

A major advance in usability evaluation today is the greater opportunity for usability
practitioners to conduct field research. Many companies successfully use adaptations of contextual inquiry and ethnographic interview methodology on a day-to-day
basis for short-term research projects in commercial product development.

15.3.1.1 Condensed Contextual Inquiry

Classic contextual inquiry requires hours of time with each user—frequently a full
day per visit. While this long session time enables researchers to collect much valuable information, organizations balk at spending the time to collect and analyze so
much data. In addition, participating companies are unwilling to interrupt employees for such a long period of time (although the inquiry observes ongoing work in
progress, some inefficiencies are inevitable).

To gain the benefits of contextual inquiry even when time is short on a commercial project, my group uses what we call the *condensed contextual inquiry*
(Kantner & Keirnan 2003; Kantner, Sova, & Rosenbaum 2003). It identifies a
more constrained set of concerns to investigate than the classic version, allowing

researchers to focus on a few critical issues during sessions with users. The condensed method retains the strengths of contextual inquiry:

- Exploring people's use of products within the restrictions of their actual work
- Seeing when and how companion software and artifacts, such as notebooks, sticky notes, and forms, are used to complement the product
- Clarifying details about tasks while they occur, to avoid misunderstandings about what users did and why

Condensed contextual inquiry accommodates the limited time that product development teams have to learn about users' work processes and motivations, as well as the limited time users have to participate. As in classic contextual inquiry, the product development team members work with the usability team to identify the characteristics of the users to interview, the tasks to observe, and specific issues of concern, including terminology.

Unlike classic contextual inquiry, the actual inquiry team is limited to two people, usually two usability practitioners. This approach saves time on subsequent data tabulation and interpretation, as well as saving the time of product development team members, who can continue working on the product. Having only usability practitioners at the sessions requires a high level of trust between the product developers and the usability team.

Within the session itself, the primary difference between classic and condensed contextual inquiry is the limited nature of the work under observation. Condensed contextual inquiry is not suitable for designing a complex system from the ground up. It is, however, appropriate for examining the flow of tasks in an established routine and identifying workarounds and artifacts to inform design of new features and functions within that routine. As with the classic method, the condensed method steps back from existing tools to look at the bigger picture of the users' motivations and contextual artifacts for accomplishing work.

When product developers do not attend the contextual inquiry sessions, the usability practitioners bear additional responsibility of understanding the product development team's assumptions about the users' work processes and communicating what was learned in light of those assumptions. A summary data report is insufficient; results are best communicated using descriptive anecdotal stories, encouraging developers to ask questions that help them to experience the interviews vicariously. Videotaping is not always possible for field studies because of security and privacy issues, so storytelling often replaces videotapes to communicate the experience.

15.3.1.2 Condensed Ethnographic Interviews

Whereas contextual inquiry is primarily an *observation of use* with inquiry from a usability practitioner, ethnographic interviewing is primarily an *interview about use*, with a clearly defined set of questions to ask all users in the study. In classic ethnographic research, observers become part of a culture so that they can understand it well and explore and modify their assumptions about it. In product research, ethnographic interviewing helps practitioners understand how the context of use affects people's approaches to tasks and how people view their own context.

Condensing the ethnographic interviewing method means identifying the scope of what to observe and explore. Rather than learn everything about a user's life, we observe only a small sphere of it, as it relates to the tasks that concern us for product design purposes. In this manner, we can structure the interviews to meet project budget and schedule constraints.

In our adaptation of classic ethnographic interviews, we apply the team approach used in contextual inquiry, with separate interviewers and note-takers. This approach enables us to collect extensive data in short participant sessions. Often we have only an hour to spend with each participant (the maximum time we spend is two hours). Two-person usability teams share the three key activities of interviewing, note-taking, and photographing or collecting artifacts; for example, while the note-taker takes photographs, the interviewer takes notes.

Overall, current adaptations of these two field methods are focused on obtaining the richest possible qualitative information in a limited time. Practitioners retain the key elements of these methods—an exploration of users' behavior in the context of their own work during contextual inquiry, and intensive observation of users' settings and artifacts during ethnographic interviews. Although we miss learning some behavior and data that longer observations or interviews would yield, we can apply to product design insights from field research that could not be gained from usability testing alone.

15.3.2 More Knowledge and Skill among Practitioners

The standard of relevant education and expertise among usability practitioners has dramatically increased as the usability field matures. In the United States, colleges and universities offer courses in usability methods, usually in departments of technical communication and information science. These courses are now available in dozens of undergraduate programs, as well as at the graduate level in Masters' and Doctoral programs (where they are coupled with in-depth research projects).

Usability practitioners employed in industry have an extensive network of support from professional societies, all of which offer training during their annual conferences. ACM SIGCHI, the Usability Professionals' Association (UPA), the Human Factors and Ergonomics Society (HFES), and the Society for Technical Communication (STC) all sponsor workshops, tutorials, and courses about usability methods. Sessions on usability methods are also frequently presented at the annual conferences of the IEEE Professional Communication Society and ACM SIGDOC (Design of Communication).

ACM SIGCHI, which held its first conference in 1983, now draws more than 2,000 people to its conferences every year. A recent goal of SIGCHI is to improve its offerings to practitioners (as well as supporting attendees from academia), and they have established *communities of practice* to encourage participation, including *Experience Reports* of case histories. While I was co-chair of the CHI 2006

Usability Community, we received more then 50 submissions, about half of which became part of a well-received program.

The Usability Professionals' Association was established in 1991 after meetings at ACM SIGCHI and HFES conferences identified a need for a professional society that focused on the interests of usability practitioners. From "Birds of a Feather" sessions at CHI and HFES, the UPA has grown to an 1,800-member organization with chapters worldwide—from India to Sweden to Boston.

These are only a few of the not-for-profit organizations that provide professional development opportunities for usability practitioners. In addition to annual conferences, most professional societies offer skill-building education at monthly chapter meetings and other events.

15.3.3 More Use of Automated Tools

Software tools to help automate usability evaluation have been available since the 1980s. They fall into two groups—questionnaire tools and behavioral data collection tools. Even a high-level survey of automated tools is beyond the scope of this chapter; the following brief summary gives a background.

Questionnaire tools measure user perceptions. One of the earliest was for "measuring and analyzing computer user satisfaction" (Bailey & Pearson 1983). In 1987, two seminal questionnaires were published: Ben Schneiderman's Questionnaire for User Interaction Satisfaction (QUIS) (Shneiderman 1987; 1998) and the Computer User Satisfaction Inventory (CUSI) (Kirakowski 1987) developed by the Human Factors Research Group at University College, Cork (Ireland).

Kirakowski went on to develop the Software Usability Measurement Inventory (SUMI) in the early 1990s (Kirakowski & Corbett 1993), followed by WAMMI for website evaluation (Kirakowski, Claridge, & Whitehead 1998). Today dozens of Web-based questionnaire tools are available to usability practitioners, from Active Websurvey to Zoomerang.

Similar examples abound in software to capture and record user behavior. Noldus Information Technology was founded in 1989 as a one-man company in the Netherlands. Today, Noldus employs 85 people worldwide; their customers are 3,500 institutes, companies, and universities in 75 countries.

In the United States, TechSmith was founded in 1987, and in 2002 began supporting usability practitioners, first with Camtasia and then with Morae and UserVue. Morae enables practitioners to record and view users remotely through software installed on their computer. UserVue is a Web-based service that allows practitioners to remotely connect to, interact with, and observe users as they navigate an application or website.

Behavioral data collection tools have two benefits: they record user data, and they enable observers to watch and enter notes about the participant sessions, either while they are taking place or at a later date. The latter capability has great impact on the ability to conduct rigorous usability evaluations under constrained research budgets. When the user audience for a product is distributed over a wide geographical area, it is now possible to sample that distributed audience and still offer software developers the opportunity to watch participant sessions.

Most usability practitioners believe they can observe subtleties of behavior more accurately when the facilitator and the participant are co-located, even if observers are in remote locations. That approach also makes it easier to install data-collection software on participants' computers or solve unexpected technical problems with prototype products. However, the time and cost of travel—and the geographic diversity of user communities—are driving an evolution in methodology.

Recent Web usability software and services integrate behavioral data collection and surveys. For example, researchers at the University of Washington have developed a toolkit for conducting complete experimental studies, including dynamic generation of multiple versions of a test website, random assignment of participants to conditions, questionnaire design and implementation, and custom data logging (Wei, Barrick, Cuddihy, & Spyridakis 2005; Spyridakis, Wei, Barrick, Cuddihy, & Maust 2005). Such enhancements of automated tools support both relevant usability research design and accurate data collection.

15.3.4 More Sophistication About Methods

As the previous pages describe, with the greater maturity of the usability profession have come many improvements in methodology. Interestingly, what we see today are rarely dramatically new or different methods from ten years ago. Rather, increasingly sophisticated implementation of usability methodology helps us better answer the questions of software design and development teams, as well as communicate our results for more strategic impact within organizations.

For example, a substantial minority (about 20%) of the usability tests my group performs now use RITE (Rapid Iterative Testing and Evaluation) methodology (Medlock, Wixon, McGee, & Welsh 2005), in which changes to the user interface are made as soon as a problem is identified and a solution is clear—often after one to three participants. The goals of the RITE method are to identify and address as many issues as possible, and to verify the effectiveness of the changes in the shortest possible time.

Successful RITE studies require highly experienced usability practitioners, as well as the commitment of the software team to observing all sessions and making immediate changes. RITE is as much a design method as an evaluation method, and requires practitioners who are comfortable making design suggestions. RITE practitioners should have some design experience so that their ideas can inform the software team as it continues to make adjustments.

The methodology described in the Medlock, et al. paper is consistent with Nielsen's discount usability recommendations from ten years earlier, but the supporting data and analysis are much more detailed. Practitioners can now apply iterative testing in a more structured way, as well as make informed decisions about when RITE testing is appropriate.

In another example from my own experience at Tec-Ed, usability practitioners now make explicit decisions about methods for organizing usability data, based on study complexity and reporting requirements. A paper (Kantner, Sova, & Anschuetz 2005) describes three alternatives we consider for qualitative data analysis:

1. Creating high-level summaries of individual user sessions, best suited for projects with a tight timeframe, few participants, and a relatively simple research design.
2. Building data tables of all collected data, best suited for studies that investigate high-level issues or perceptions (such as ethnographic interviews or exploratory usability testing of prototypes), rather than detailed task behavior.
3. Using a database program to assist analysis, creating multiple forms and views to hold and organize the data. This method is well-suited to studies that investigate both high-level issues and detailed behavior, and/or to studies with 12 or more participants (for fast cross-tabulation of participant characteristics with behavior and opinions).

Especially for usability practitioners in industry, balancing the time required to analyze qualitative usability data with the urgency to release a product or website calls for using the appropriate data structuring method. Studies with complex questions benefit from the time required to structure qualitative data in the most flexible way possible—a database, where the questions asked can change as the analysis progresses. Studies with more straightforward data can take advantage of the time-savings of flat-file tabulations (using word-processing programs), or even of pencil-and-paper summaries after each session.

In addition to making more informed choices among methods, practitioners today also combine methods in interesting and rewarding ways. Many of the usability projects my group currently performs include two or three phases, each employing a different methodology—for example:

- Home-based ethnographic interviews, followed by laboratory usability testing, followed by a large-sample online survey
- Usability focus groups, followed by laboratory usability testing
- Laboratory usability testing, followed by in-home field usability testing, followed by telephone interviews, followed by another cycle of laboratory usability testing (for validation)

In 2000, I described the usability methods reported in a survey of 134 HCI professionals at conferences in 1998 and 1999 (Rosenbaum, Rohn, & Humburg 2000), where we asked what methods people used and which ones had more strategic impact within organizations. Some methods that were rated highly effective, such as field studies, had fairly low usage within the practitioner community. Today, these effective methods are more widely applied, both individually and in combination.

The concept of iterative usability evaluation has evolved from simply repeating exploratory usability tests between development cycles to a more complex approach that takes advantage of the richer data we can collect with a broader toolkit of usability methods.

15.3.5 Larger Sample Sizes for Usability Research

While RITE methodology enables usability practitioners to help improve software using a few participants at a time, today's practitioners are also collecting valuable data from larger populations, all using the same prototype. Some research questions can best be addressed through usability evaluation methods that involve:

- Usability practitioners observing participants in individual, real-time sessions, to collect immediate behaviors and comments
- Collecting performance measures such as number of errors, types of errors, number and type of remediations required, and time on task
- Comparing two or more products, designs, or product features (often from competitors), requiring counterbalancing of participants and/or tasks
- Performing statistical analysis of the collected data to determine confidence levels—and requiring high confidence levels to justify product design decisions

These requirements have led practitioners to conduct usability testing with sample sizes not previously used in industry settings—40, 80, or even 120 participants in a single usability test. The sessions must still be with individual participants, either face-to-face or through remote facilitation tools, because we need to observe real-time physical and verbal behavior.

In my own experience at Tec-Ed, a recent usability test observed 120 participants using one of six different prototypes for a single product feature, then administered three questionnaires to each participant. The sessions lasted only 15 minutes each, but the entire project took a month for a team of experienced usability practitioners to complete. The participant selection criteria were stringent; even with an on-line prescreening questionnaire, participant recruiting required over a hundred hours, during which we screened about 700 applicants.

Another project was more typical of the larger-sample research that is beginning to be conducted in industry. Our client wanted to conduct an independent third-party benchmarking usability study comparing one of its products and a new competitive product. The usability test collected behavioral metrics for a series of five tasks, as well as post-task and post-test satisfaction ratings.

We tested 40 participants, each of whom used both products; the product order was counterbalanced for each task to minimize order effects. The sessions lasted 90 minutes, or 45 minutes per product. At the end of each task with each product, we asked three Likert-scale questions, and we also administered a final Likert-scale questionnaire at the end of each session.

The behavioral metrics collected were task success/failure, time on task, and number, type, and severity of errors (classifying the errors and their severity was a complex process requiring practice by the facilitators to ensure inter-rater reliability). We performed statistical analyses of the collected data, and the results of these analyses were the primary project deliverable. We supplemented the metrics with a high-level qualitative report describing the participants' behavior and reactions to the two products.

Such large-sample usability tests have many benefits for software development. We can measure the usability effects of very focused changes to individual product features, we can conduct rigorous competitive evaluations, and we can demonstrate to management the statistical significance of the behaviors we measure. Just as with RITE testing, successful large-sample usability evaluation demands experience and expertise from usability practitioners.

15.3.6 Impact of Today's Usability Evaluation on Value

With the widespread use of field methods among today's usability practitioners, we begin to see the impact of usability evaluation "over a span of time and space," as the editors of this volume describe. By observing people in their own environments, usability practitioners can provide guidance about designing software for real situations—for example (Rosenbaum 2003):

- Distractions may be different at home from at work: the phone rings, children demand attention, and pets run through the room. Field usability evaluation methods show how typical distractions affect user behavior with software and websites.
- When using complex business software, people cannot behave normally without their own (usually proprietary) data—and even if business users were permitted to bring their data to a usability laboratory, it's rarely practical to do so.
- Users often consult documents and other sources that may be available only in their work or home environments. In addition, people do not know in advance what they will want to consult while using the software under evaluation.

Thus field usability evaluation in the actual context of use yields far more insight into the value of software in the real world, and increases the ability of usability evaluation to achieve that value. The other sophisticated methods described in this section also consider fitness for purpose and thus contribute to value—especially when they are combined into multiple-method usability programs applied over the lifetime of the software. Today's skilled usability practitioners recognize that usability resides in specific contexts, just as the strength of a chair is relative to its usage (Cockton 2004).

15.4 Usability Evaluation Tomorrow

Considering the evolution of usability evaluation since its inception, what will happen next in our exciting profession? How will we increase the impact of usability on value? One way, as I mentioned earlier, is that more and more organizations will attain the level of usability maturity that only a few companies practice today. We will also see a much greater contribution of usability to the value of software products and systems in the real world.

15.4.1 More Integration of Usability Practice and Product Development

With the increased skill and expertise of usability practitioners, the roles and responsibilities within user-centered design teams may become blurred—to everyone's benefit. In my own experience at Tec-Ed, several staff members perform both usability evaluation and user-interface design, and that percentage is increasing. In some Silicon Valley companies, practitioners work one year in user research, and another year in design.

In a recent project my group performed, we created three different functional prototypes of a new UI design using HTML, Excel, and PowerPoint. The prototype implementations each had different uses, depending on whether the goal was to show a smooth navigation flow, to display and manipulate data realistically, or to be demonstrated, annotated, or revised easily by project managers and engineers within the client's organization. High-fidelity prototypes enabled us to collect behavioral and opinion feedback, as well as insightful suggestions, quickly and accurately from the subject-matter experts who were the target users of the software.

Previously, my group had defined our usability services to include user-interface design, but left the development of functional prototypes to other members of the development team. From this project, we gained insights into how choices of prototyping methods affect usability evaluation as well as design. As a result, we expect that our involvement in prototype creation will continue to grow, and will enrich our usability methodology.

Prototypes will also become more valuable tools for requirements definition. Traditionally, contextual field research was the methodology of choice for requirements definition, before the design phase—in fact, we hesitated to show participants prototypes during contextual sessions, for fear of biasing their behavior or reactions.

Modern condensed field methods require a tighter focus to succeed, and one way to achieve that focus is to show participants early design prototypes—usually quite low-fidelity ones. Such prototypes should be considered temporary or disposable; the designs or features may never appear in the actual software. Rather, they serve as part of the usability practitioners' toolkit, to make field research more productive and yield better user requirements. This approach is consistent with the alternating waves of creative and structuring activities described by the *star* life cycle for user interaction development (Hix & Hartson 1993).

Although some usability practitioners will always prefer to specialize in user research and evaluation, those who take on broader roles will have opportunities to:

- Perform more early research, especially contextual field research, and then define user requirements for design
- Create prototypes that enable rapid collection of more relevant and more accurate user data during evaluation
- Join integrated product teams that help the software design process become truly iterative and user-centered

Usability practitioners who join closely integrated product teams will find that they have the opportunity to design user interfaces and create prototypes of them.

They will also be expected to have the skills to program in one or more basic proto-typing languages (e.g., PHP for the Web), so that they can explain by example when discussing UI improvement with the rest of their team.

15.4.2 More Integration of Usability Evaluation and Product Use

Traditionally, usability evaluation took place before products were released and sold, because the expectation was that evaluation (validation) was part of the soft-ware development process. Future usability evaluation will be ongoing, throughout product lifecycles; and the evaluation will be integrated with use of the product.

Many websites already collect extensive online data that can be part of usability evaluation:

- Companies such as Amazon and eBay serve users multiple versions of various sites and pages, collecting data about users' different behaviors on the alterna-tive versions. This information is used to make strategic decisions about the site design.
- E-commerce companies track clickthroughs and measure abandonment rates and pages, to learn when and where site visitors failed to complete a purchase.
- Many organizations' websites present surveys to randomly selected site visitors, to collect user perceptions of various pages or at specific points in a transaction.

Web analytics (the measurement, collection, analysis, and reporting of Internet data to understand and optimize Web usage) has become a major field of spe-cialization, with conferences, publications, and even a professional organization (www.webanalyticsassociation.org).

Although the Internet makes it easy to collect data throughout the life cycle of websites and Web applications, tools and methods are beginning to emerge that integrate evaluation and use with many kinds of products. From my own experience at Tec-Ed, we recently recommended that a hardware/software company build into their server-based products the ability to collect a variety of data from their client workstations, including:

- Time on task
- Number of pages accessed during the task
- Number of button presses during the task
- Number of selections from drop-down menus, checkboxes, radio-buttons
- Number of window reconfiguration actions (resize or reposition)
- Number of scrolling actions
- Number of dialog or pop-up window interactions

This capability would enable both the company and its customers to collect user data automatically. The challenge was not the modest programming effort required, but rather the division of responsibility within the organization. The team that engaged my firm to conduct a usability evaluation of their application was one of many application software groups, and had no connection with the developers responsible for changes to the server software.

Integrating evaluation with product use is technically feasible today for many business and consumer products—not just websites. But strategic and ethical issues abound. Strategically, decisions to instrument products for collecting data during use should be made at the corporate level, to ensure consistency among a company's product offerings. Initially, as with many design advances, one creative product manager in an organization will likely begin the innovation.

From an ethical standpoint, companies will need to decide who can turn instrumented user data collection on and off—and the effect it will have on privacy and users' trust. In the late 1990s, some computer users refused to accept cookies from websites. One colleague set an audible tone to ring whenever his PC received a cookie—hard to imagine today. Perhaps tomorrow's consumers will expect companies to monitor their behavior with products.

Regardless of whether we collect user data automatically or conduct usability evaluations using other methods, the product release date will no longer be a barrier to usability. For example, the sophisticated software now used in customer service or technical support call centers to help initiate and track problem reporting can also facilitate usability improvements.

Increasingly, we will carry out ongoing user research throughout the lives of software products, using the results to inform decision-making for maintenance releases and follow-on products. The challenge will be cataloging and mining the usability data for effective reuse, requiring usability practitioners to gain knowledge management skills or turn to specialists in this field.

Ongoing user research will also benefit the usability of new products, because developers will have baselines of recent data about the products they hope to supersede. From my own experience at Tec-Ed, when a client company cannot allocate the resources to perform usability evaluation before a product release, I suggest that they defer the evaluation until after the product release, when the software team is under less schedule pressure (Rosenbaum 2000b). Such *version leapfrogging* can be highly effective, because the usability findings are available early in the design phase of the next product release, before its specifications are determined.

Large or mature companies with usability infrastructures and processes in place are beginning to decouple some of their user research efforts from product release schedules. Independent scheduling enables them to plan usability projects when staff resources are available, and is especially appropriate for exploring questions or features that apply to more than one product. The future will bring an increasing number of parallel design and evaluation efforts, as cross-functional user experience design teams learn to work together.

15.4.3 More Integration of Qualitative and Quantitative Research Activities

Increasingly, organizations are recognizing the value of having many data sources to inform decision-making in software design. Usability evaluation is one such source; others are classic market research techniques (such as surveys) and newer activities such as Web analytics and data mining. To use all these kinds of data more effectively, a few companies are merging usability practitioners and market researchers into one department, and this trend is likely to continue.

At the UPA 2006 conference, I co-facilitated a workshop (Bugental, Turner, & Rosenbaum 2006) on "Overlapping Usability and Market Research – Synergies and Issues," where marketing professionals and user researchers explored ways in which product functionality and brand imagery could be studied in the same project. Fifteen practitioners from different industries, from accounting software to pharmaceuticals, defined ways to conduct integrated user data collection activities.

Particularly during the design of consumer products and games, we will increasingly see activities that combine qualitative and quantitative methods. For example, at Microsoft Game Studios, user researchers have developed a *playtest* method (Davis, Steury, & Pagulayan 2005) that combines behavior and surveys. Participants play new computer games, then answer survey questions about their experiences.

Large numbers of people can participate simultaneously in playtest studies, because both the behavior and perception data are collected automatically, with minimal oversight; and the controlled lab environment minimizes the effects of unrelated variables. Because all the users' actions are recorded, when the quantitative data analysis indicates a potential problem or issue, the research team can then view the individual session recordings of that behavior and gain insight into how or why it occurred.

While such a combination of qualitative and quantitative methods may not be suitable for evaluating all software, it has great potential for products that can be instrumented to collect user data. The ability to view the sessions retrospectively addresses many of the shortcomings of purely quantitative research. As more usability practitioners and market researchers work together in organizations, methods like playtest will gain wider use.

15.4.4 Knowledge Management to Improve Return on Usability Investments

Organizations with ongoing user experience programs are beginning to see the value of managing the knowledge they have amassed about their user communities. It is no longer enough simply to create archives of usability data. Rather, to gain the most from our investments in user research and usability evaluations, the collected data must be structured and easily accessible by usability practitioners, software developers, marketing staff members, and those involved in corporate strategic planning.

Knowledge management (KM) systems will enable organizations to leverage the results of previous usability evaluations and research to inform the design of future applications and future usability research. A key feature of such systems will be the ability to search for findings based on structured information added to usability reports, particularly metadata describing the application or Web pages, the issues, and the GUI elements that were tested (metadata allows search engines to retrieve documents with greater speed, precision, and relevance).

With easy access to previous usability findings, developers can create better and more effective applications in less time, improving the ROI of the software design process. Consider the hypothetical case of a developer who wants to use a tab-like navigation structure in a new Web application, and asks a usability practitioner for advice. The usability practitioner checks the corporate KM system and learns that in four previous evaluations with similar applications and users, a left-hand navigation column was easier for users and more effective at directing them to their destinations. Based on this research, the developer uses a left-hand navigation column in the new application.

KM systems will also help usability practitioners avoid testing issues they have already addressed, so they can explore other tasks or target audiences. In the hypothetical case above, after the developer uses the previously tested left-hand navigation column in his new application, the usability practitioner also need not focus on that navigation column. Instead, the usability test for this new application could include tasks that exercise other features of the application.

Thus the findings from usability evaluations will be able to improve application designs in new ways, helping their target users be more productive. My example considers usability evaluation reports, but KM systems for usability will be equally valuable for storing and accessing rich qualitative information, such as personas and contextual research findings.

15.4.5 More Contextual and Field Research

Any laboratory study, whatever the sample size, gains the benefits of a controlled environment by losing the opportunity to observe users in their own environments. The usability lab is an artificial environment where we introduce tasks and experiences that are at least realistic, if not actually real.

However, for more and more new products, it is nearly impossible to create a realistic experience in the lab. Mobile products and products used by groups are good examples, as are products intended for use by people in specialized environments such as hospitals. John Canny of the University of California at Berkeley suggests that future interfaces will not focus on office work (which was easier to emulate in the usability lab) but will be context-aware and perceptual, employing satellite GPS, automatic speech recognition, and computer vision (Canny 2006).

Recent field studies of mobile telephone use faced the complexity of diverse environments, such as losing a participant in the Tokyo subway during rush hour (Blom, Chipchase, & Lehikoinen 2005) and the challenges of group behavior while observing a circle of friends use mobile services such as text messaging (Page 2005).

Over the next years, we will see more carefully reasoned decisions about when, where, and how to conduct field research, as well as a wider variety of data-collection methods. Such evolution will be needed as we conduct usability studies of:

- Different audiences (children, teenagers, older adults, people with disabilities) using mobile devices in their work and home environments—and as they travel
- People using products designed for social or group use, such as projection television or multiplayer games
- Medical caregivers using automatic speech recognition products in hospitals

We are already beginning to see user research for new product designs that combine these domains—for example, a multiplayer game that helps people make health insurance decisions (Kantner, et al. 2006) and a mobile phone plus pedometer application that encourages users' physical activity by sharing step counts with friends (Consolvo, Everitt, Smith, & Landay 2006).

Instrumented data collection will become an integral part of field research. For example, Gaetano Borriello of the University of Washington—and a founding director of Intel Research Seattle—describes the potential for radio frequency identification (RFID) tags in social or medical research (Borriello 2005). By RFID-tagging items in the home such as coffee pots or medicine bottles, we could infer that someone is drinking coffee or taking a pill if the coffee pot or pill bottle is lifted. These RFID tags may help the elderly remain independent longer in their own homes. A cruder version of such data collection is used today—heavy, specialized caps that record the date and time a pill bottle is opened—but the participants must return the bottle caps to the research facility for data compilation.

Instrumented data collection cannot tell us *why* people behave as they do, so it will not replace in-person field research by practitioners. What it will do is help us plan more focused and relevant field research, especially important because the investment per participant in field research is higher than comparable-length sessions in the lab. We will be able to select finer-grained subsets of the user audience for field visits, based on their prior behavior.

Another reason why field research will increase is the growth of ubiquitous or pervasive computing, where computation is integrated seamlessly into the environment rather than computers as individual objects (Weiser 1994). Today there are at least three international conferences and several periodicals on *ubicomp*, as well as numerous other publications and workshops.

Ubiquitous computing complicates our current model of the user and the system. When GPS systems, temperature sensor/controllers, liveboards, and more are built into our environment, what methods will we use to assess them? Weiser suggests that the goal of ubiquitous computing is invisibility. How would we define a stream-of-behavior ethnographic study recording the things people do *not* notice?

As computer systems become more fragmented in space (no longer one user in front of one computer), latency and other real-time issues will play a larger role. Some highway signs in the United States display how long it will take to drive to a popular destination, based on real-time data collected on traffic speed—and drivers already adjust for latency based on their personal experience: "That sign usually says 10 minutes to San Jose; when it displays 15 minutes, I know the traffic is really bad and the trip will take 25 minutes."

How will we conduct usability evaluations of such systems? Challenges abound, but it is likely that the answers lie in the evolution of contextual and field methodology.

15.4.6 A Broader Scope for Usability

As computing becomes a lifestyle for more and more of the world's population, usability evaluation will need to take place over longer time periods and address broader issues of ethics and culture. Concerns, problems, and risks that emerge only after widespread or long-term use can be critical when the user audience is huge.

Longitudinal usability studies today typically last one or two months, rarely longer. Although some organizations conduct annual benchmarking usability tests to track improvements over time, such evaluations require new participants in each cycle. Future longitudinal studies may invest years to learn the effects of (for example):

- Spelling, grammar, and dictionary/thesaurus software on children's writing skills in low-literacy countries
- Reminder or *memory-jogging* software on patients with newly diagnosed Alzheimer's disease
- Collaborative office tools on the quality and the cost-effectiveness of work products

Trust has been a concern of professionals in computing since its inception. What makes people trust a computer? We can turn to Hippocrates or to Asimov's robots for the primary rule: first, do no harm. For example, when considering self-managing or autonomous systems, users still want to feel in control, despite the computer autonomy; and they want to believe their privacy is respected.

With self-managing systems, users express high-level goals, and the software selects subgoals and manages interactions with other computers. Users see only the result, not the lower-level goals and computer actions. What makes them trust that the software chose beneficial subgoals? Trustworthiness addresses the perceived goodness or morality of the source (Fogg & Tseng 1999), so broader ethical questions are likely to play a greater role in future usability evaluations.

In another example, mobile phones with GPS capabilities can communicate their users' locations; when and to whom is this communication acceptable? People could summon emergency help with a single keypress. Parents could always know their children's location. Phone users could easily find the nearest ice-cream shop, and ice-cream shops could send text messages offering special prices to people walking nearby. Exploring not only the usability but the ethical implications of such scenarios may soon be part of usability evaluations.

Trust on the Internet raises even more—and more complex—ethical questions that are beyond the scope of this chapter. Recent research has explored trust in recommender systems (O'Donovan & Smyth 2005) and how the role of online trust varies among websites and consumers (Bart, Shankar, Sultan, & Urban 2005). With the integration of usability and market research groups discussed earlier, practitioners will increasingly be studying issues of trust in websites and Web applications.

Cultural and emotional issues will also become more important in usability evaluation. A professional organization focused on the emotional experience in design, the Design & Emotion Society, held its fifth international conference in 2006. Companies with forward-looking usability practices are establishing usability groups or departments in several culturally diverse countries; and usability consultants from many countries are forming multicultural alliances and partnerships.

In the UPA 2006 conference, more than a dozen presentations addressed multicultural and multinational topics (compared to none at all at the 1993 conference). Although a thorough discussion of how future usability evaluation could address cultural issues and concerns is beyond the scope of this chapter, we can be confident of a growing emphasis on culture.

Recently my firm was asked to define a longitudinal, multicultural usability evaluation project. The research was defined in three phases over two years, and involved user sessions in four countries and seven languages (including Arabic, Russian, and Urdu). The government funding for this project has not yet been approved, so it may never take place—but even the request for proposal reflects the broader scope for usability evaluation that will emerge over the next years.

15.4.7 Usability and Organizational Maturity

All organizations evolve, including the companies where many usability practitioners are employed. At any moment in time, different companies are functioning at different levels of maturity. Models have been developed to describe these levels of maturity, such as the Capability Maturity Model ® (CMM) of Carnegie Mellon University's Software Engineering Institute (Paulk, Weber, Curtis, & Chrissis 1995), which was originally created to evaluate the ability of U.S. government contractors to perform software development projects.

Can models that describe the evolutionary levels of organizations help us think about the future of usability? Yes, because an ongoing challenge for both academia and usability practitioners is recommending appropriate usability programs and activities to organizations. As teachers, as consultants, and as corporate usability practitioners, we continually ask ourselves, "What is the most effective use of our limited time and resources?" We consider when to apply each of the usability evaluation methods at our disposal, based on such variables as (Rosenbaum 2000a):

- How the product fits into the organization's product offerings (new or mature product or product line)
- What prior data exists about user problems or risky usage situations
- Whether the design team agrees on how to proceed, and what design decisions were difficult
- How many target audiences there are, and which are central to the success of the product

- What usage scenarios are most important, either for successful product use or for branding
- How much designers will generalize from the data collected (making decisions for other products than this one)

Dozens of such variables, combined with budget and schedule information, help inform decisions about usability methodology—which must depend both on the skills of the usability practitioner and on the evolutionary level of the organization.

In the practice of usability, most companies begin by conducting an evaluative usability test at the end of the development process. Then they slowly move their efforts earlier in the design process—and institutionalize them—until they are collecting user data before beginning product design. By that time, a usability or user experience department is in place, with procedures for conducting various kinds of usability evaluations. Then the usability group recognizes that it can conduct data-mining of existing knowledge, establish benchmarks, and carry out other quality-monitoring programs. The activities at each level reflect the increasing maturity of the usability practitioners' skills.

For this usability maturing process to succeed, it must take place in the evolutionary context of the organization. Even a highly skilled usability practitioner will not often convince the management of a small start-up company to conduct early field research. On the other hand, a mature organization that has institutionalized staff training may employ some novice practitioners and provide mentoring by senior employees.

In addition, the broader field in which we work is itself in evolution. During the time period described in this chapter, software and systems have evolved from the desktop to a far more pervasive and distributed context. Thus another aspect of maturity that must be considered is technical innovation. Mobile devices, games, medical monitoring instruments—every technical breakthrough—pose new challenges for usability evaluation.

Depending on the maturity of an organization, the future of its usability practices will, and should, differ. An exploratory usability test with six participants during alpha-testing of each new application or release may be a desirable and difficult to attain goal for a small, young company. Meanwhile, a well-established company focused on improving the user experience for its customers could be examining the results of the past year's laboratory and field studies to decide when to use each method next year.

Cutting-edge usability for one organization may be 10 years behind that of another, depending on the sophistication, resources, and maturity of the organization and of the practitioners in it. We do not have just one past-present-future timeline; we have dozens of them, offset to greater and lesser degrees in different organizations—which, in part, explains my survey of the past and present in a chapter whose purpose is to forecast the future.

In fact, this entire chapter on the past, present, and future of usability is a discussion of the future of usability. As new companies are founded, and as new practitioners enter the profession, their future usability evaluation activities may be ones that mature companies and experienced practitioners performed 10 years ago.

In our 21st century Internet age, readers often tend to ignore or discard citations (and methodology) more than a few years old. Yet many venerable methods are as productive—and controversial—as when they first appeared. I first wrote about heuristic evaluation in 1989 (Rosenbaum 1989), and our ACM SIGDOC 97 paper on heuristic evaluation of websites (Kantner & Rosenbaum 1997) is still one of the two papers most frequently downloaded from Tec-Ed's website. The think-aloud protocol Ginny Redish used at the American Institutes for Research in the 1980s (Dumas & Redish 1993, 1999) was the subject of a panel (Ramey, et al. 2006) at the 2006 ACM SIGCHI conference in Montreal.

15.4.8 Impact of Future Usability Evaluation on Value

As the usability profession matures—and as technology becomes integrated more pervasively into our lifestyles and culture—usability evaluation will have yet more impact on the value of software, for several reasons:

- Contextual and field research will comprise an increasingly larger proportion of total usability evaluation, in part because more practitioners and organizations recognize that only contextual research can evaluate fitness for purpose, and in part because future software will be increasingly mobile and pervasive—and thus only contextual research will enable us to evaluate it.
- Increasingly, practitioners will conduct usability evaluations throughout the software lifecycle, using robust longitudinal studies, with instrumented data collection when appropriate. The majority of these studies will take place entirely in the context of use.
- Usability evaluations will increasingly address cultural, emotional, and ethical issues—practitioners will observe and measure the trust and enjoyment users experience, which are valid and meaningful indicators of the value of software in the real world.

By collecting contextual data on software use throughout its lifetime, and by communicating this information continuously and effectively to development teams, tomorrow's usability practitioners will greatly increase the impact of usability on value.

This entire chapter demonstrates the benefits of learning and applying the history of usability evaluation as we move into its future. The impact of usability practitioners' work on the value of software will increase as we proceed in the directions that sophisticated and mature organizations are heading—integrating usability more closely with product design and use, observing users in broader and longer contexts, and better understanding the diverse communities we inhabit.

Acknowledgment The author expresses her appreciation to Judy Ramey of the University of Washington for her reviews and suggestions throughout the planning and creation of this chapter. Thank you also to Laurie Kantner, Maggie Reilly, and Beth Almay of Tec-Ed for their thoughtful reviews and editing.

References

Anschuetz, L., Hinderer, D., & Rohn, J. (1998, June). When the field is far afield: multiple-country observations of complex system use. In: *Proceedings from UPA 1998: Capitalizing on usability*, Washington, DC, USA.

Bailey, J.E. & Pearson, S.W. (1983). Development of a tool for measuring and analyzing computer user satisfaction. *Management Science, 29*, 530–545.

Bart, I.Y., Shankar, V. Sultan, F., & Urban, G.L. (2005). Are the drivers and role of online trust the same for all web sites and consumers? A large scale exploratory empirical study. MIT Sloan Research Paper No. 4578–05.

Beyer, H. & Holtzblatt, K. (1998). *Contextual design: defining customer-centered systems.* San Francisco, California, USA: Morgan Kaufmann Publishers Inc.

Bjerknes, G., Ehn, P., & Kyng, M. (1987). *Computers and democracy—a scandinavian challenge.* Avebury: Aldershot.

Bjorn-Andersen, N. & Hedberg, B. (1977). Designing information systems in an organizational perspective. *Studies in the Management Sciences Prescriptive Models of Organizations, 5*, 125–142.

Blom, J., Chipchase, J., & Lehikoinen, J. (2005). Contextual and cultural challenges. *Communications of the ACM, 48*, 37–41.

Boren, T., & Ramey, J. (2000). Thinking aloud: reconciling theory and practice. *IEEE Transactions on Professional Communication, 43*(3), 261–278.

Borriello, G. (2005, January). *RFID: facts, fiction, and trends.* Proceedings from the Center for Internet Studies, Pressing Questions of the Information Age. Seattle, WA, USA.

Bugental, J.O., Turner, S., & Rosenbaum, S. (2006, June). *Overlapping usability and market research: synergies and issues.* Proceedings from the UPA 2006: Usability in Storytelling, Broomfield, CO, USA.

Canny, J. (2006). The future of human-computer interaction. *ACM Queue,4*(6), 24–32.

Cockton, G. (2004, April). *From quality in use to value in the world.* Proceedings from CHI 2004 Conference on Human Factors in Computing System, Vienna, Austria.

Consolvo, S., Everitt, K., Smith, I., & Landay, J.A. (2006, April). *Design requirements for technologies that encourage physical activity.* Proceedings from CHI 2006: Designing for Tangible Interactions. Montreal, Quebec, Canada.

Davis, J.P., Steury, K., & Pagulayan, R. (2005). A survey method for assessing perceptions of a game: the consumer playtest in game design. *Game Studios: The International Journal of Computer Game Research, 5*(1).

De Jong, M. & Schellens, P.J. (2000). Toward a document evaluation methodology: what does research tell us about the validity and reliability of evaluation methods? *IEEE Transactions on Professional Communication, 43*(3), 242–260.

Dumas, J. & Redish, J. (1993). *A practical guide to usability testing*(1st ed.). Westport, Connecticut, USA: Greenwood Publishing Group Inc.

Dumas, J. & Redish, J. (1999). *A practical guide to usability testing* (revised ed.). Fishponds, Bristol, UK: Intellect LTD.

Fogg, B.J. & Tseng, H. (1999, May). *The elements of computer credibility.* Proceedings from the ACM SIGCHI Conference on Human Factors in Computer Systems, Pittsburgh, PA, USA.

Gould, J.D. & Lewis, C. (1985). Designing for usability: key principles and what designers think. *Communications of the ACM, 28*(3), 300–311.

Gray, W.D., Atwood, M.E., Fisher, C., Nielsen, J., Carroll, J.M., & Long, J. (1995, May). *Discount or disservice? Discount usability analysis – evaluation at a bargain price or simply damaged merchandise?* Proceedings from the ACM CHI'95 Conference on Human Factors in Computing Systems, Denver, CO, USA.

Gray, W.D. & Salzman, M.C. (1998). Damaged merchandise? A review of experiments that compare usability evaluation methods. *Human-Computer Interaction, 13*(3), 203–261.

Hix, D. & Hartson, H.R. (1993). *Developing user interfaces — ensuring usability through product & process.* New York: John Wiley & Sons, Inc.

Holtzblatt, K. & Jones, S. (1993). Contextual inquiry: a participatory technique for system design. In D. Schuler & A. Namioka (Eds.), *Participatory Design: Principles and Practices* (pp. 177–210). New Jersey: Lawrence Erlbaum.

Kantner, L. & Rosenbaum, S. (1997, October). *Usability studies of www sites: heuristic evaluation vs. laboratory testing*. Proceedings from the ACM SIGDOC Conference: Crossroads in Communication, Salt Lake City, UT, USA.

Kantner, L. & Keirnan, T. (2003, June). *Field research in commercial product development*. Proceedings from UPA 2003: Ubiquitous Usability. Scottsdale, AZ, USA.

Kantner, L., Sova, D., & Rosenbaum, S. (2003, October). *Alternative methods for field usability research*. Proceedings from ACM SIGDOC 2003: Finding Real-World Solutions for Documentation: How Theory Informs Practice and Practice Informs Theory, San Francisco, CA, USA.

Kantner, L., Sova, D., & Anschuetz, L. (2005, June). *Organizing qualitative data from lab and field: challenges and methods*. Proceedings from UPA 2005: Bridging Cultures, Montreal, Quebec, Canada.

Kantner, L., Goold, S., Danis, M., Nowak, M., & Monroe-Gatrell, L. (2006, April). *Web tool for health insurance design by small groups: usability study*. Proceedings from CHI 2006: Conference on Human Factors in Computing Systems: Interact. Inform. Inspire., Montreal, Quebec, Canada.

Kirakowski, J. (1987, March). *The computer user satisfaction inventory*. Proceedings from the IEE: Evaluation Techniques for Interactive System Design, London, England.

Kirakowski, J. & Corbett, M. (1993). SUMI: the software usability measurement inventory. *British Journal of Educational Technology, 24*(3), 210–212.

Kirakowski, J., Claridge, N., & Whitehead, R. (1998, June). *Human centered measures of success in website design*. Proceedings of the Fourth Conference on Human Factors and the Web. Basking Ridge, NJ, USA.

Mantei, M.M. & Teorey, T.J. (1988). Cost/benefit analysis for incorporating human factors in the software life-cycle. *Communications of the ACM, 31*(4), 428–439.

Medlock, M., Wixon, D., McGee, M., & Welsh, D. (2005). The rapid iterative test and evaluation method: better products in less time. In R. Bias & D. Mayhew (Eds.), *Cost-Justifying Usability: An Update for the Information Age* (pp. 489–517). San Francisco, California, USA: Morgan Kaufman.

Muller, M.J. (1991, April). *PICTIVE – An exploration in participatory design*. Proceedings of the SIGCHI Conference: Conference on Human Factors in Computing Systems: Reaching Through Technology, New Orleans, LA, USA.

Muller, M.J. (1995, May). *Diversity and depth in participatory design; working with mosaic of users and other stakeholders in the software development lifecycle*. Proceedings from CHI'95 Mosaic of Creativity. Denver, CO, USA.

Muller, M.J., & Carr, R. (1996). Using the CARD and PICTIVE participatory design methods for collaborative analysis. In D. Wixon & J. Ramey (Eds.), *Field Methods Casebook for Software Design* (pp. 17–34). New York, NY, USA: John Wiley & Sons, Inc.

Nielsen, J. (1993). *Usability engineering*. New York: Academic Press, Inc.

Nielsen J. & Landauer, T.K. (1993, April). *A mathematical model of the finding of usability problems*. Proceedings from the ACM INTERCHI Conference: Human Factors in Computing Systems, Amsterdam, The Netherlands.

O'Donovan, J. & Smyth, B. (2005, January). *Trust in recommender systems*. Proceedings of the 10th International Conference on Intelligent User Interfaces, San Diego, CA, USA.

Page, C. (2005). Mobile research strategies for a global market. *Communications of the ACM, 48*, 42–48.

Paulk, M.C., Weber, C.V., Curtis, B., & Chrissis, M.B. (1995). *Capability maturity model, the: guidelines for improving the software process*. Boston: Addison-Wesley Professional.

Ramey, J. & Robinson, C. (1991, October). *Video-based task analysis: a tool for understanding your audience*. Proceedings from IPCC 91: The Engineered Communication, Orlando, FL, USA.

Ramey, J., Boren, T., Cuddihy, E., Dumas, J., Guan, Z., van den Haak, M.J., & De Jong, M.D.T. (2006, April). *Does think aloud work? How do we know?* Proceedings from CHI 2006:

Conference on Human Factors in Computing Systems: Interact. Inform. Inspire., Montreal, Quebec, Canada.

Raven, M.E. & Flanders, A. (1996). Using contextual inquiry to learn about your audience. *ACM SIGDOC Journal of Computer Documentation, 20*(1).

Rosenbaum, S. (1989). Usability evaluations versus usability testing: when and why? *IEEE Transactions on Professional Communication, 32*, 210–216.

Rosenbaum, S. (2000a, August). *Not just a hammer: when and how to employ multiple methods in usability programs.* Proceedings from the UPA 2000 Conference. Asheville, NC, USA.

Rosenbaum, S. (2000b). Making usability research usable. In K. Kaasgaard (Ed.), *Software Design & Usability.* Copenhagen: Copenhagen Business School Press.

Rosenbaum, S. (2003). Stalking the user. *Intercom, the Magazine of the Society of Technical Communication,* 4–6.

Rosenbaum, S., Rohn, J., & Humburg, J. (2000, April). *A toolkit for strategic usability: results from workshops, panels, and surveys.* Proceedings from the SIGCHI Conference: Human Factors in Computing Systems, The Hague, The Netherlands.

Royce, W.W. (1970, August). *Managing the development of large software systems: concepts and techniques.* Technical papers from the IEEE WESCON Western Electronic Show & Convention. Los Angeles, CA, USA.

Shneiderman, B. (1987). *Designing the user interface: strategies for effective human-computer interaction.* Reading, MA, USA: Addison Wesley.

Shneiderman, B. (1998). *Designing the user interface: strategies for effective human-computer interaction* (3rd ed.). Reading, MA, USA: Addison Wesley.

Spyridakis, J.H., Wei, C., Barrick, J., Cuddihy, E., & Maust, B. (2005). Internet-based research: providing a foundation for web-design guidelines. *IEEE Transactions on Professional Communication, 49*(3), 242–260.

Suchman, L. (1983). Office procedure as practical action: models of work and system design. *ACM Transactions on Office Information Systems 1*(4), 320–328.

Suchman, L. (1996). Constituting shared workspaces. In Y. Engestrom & D. Middleton (Eds.), *Cognition and Communication at Work.* Cambridge, UK: Cambridge University Press.

Tudor, L., Muller, M., & Dayton, T. (1993, April). *A C.A.R.D. game for participatory task analysis and redesign: macroscopic complement to PICTIVE.* Proceedings from the INTERCHI 93 Conference on Human Factors in Computing Systems: Bridges Between Worlds. Amsterdam, The Netherlands.

Virzi, R. (1992). Refining the test phase of usability evaluation: how many subjects is enough? *Human Factors: The Journal of the Human Factors and Ergonomics Society, 34*(4), 457–468.

Wei, C., Barrick, J., Cuddihy, E., & Spyridakis, J. (2005, June). Conducting usability research through the internet: testing users via the WWW. *Proceedings from UPA 2005: Bridging Cultures.* Montreal, Quebec, Canada.

Weiser, M. (1994). The world is not a desktop. *Interactions 1*(1), 7–8.

Wixon, D. & Ramey, J. (1996). *Field methods casebook for software design.* New York, NY, USA: John Wiley & Sons, Inc.

Wood, L. (1996). The ethnographic interview in user-centered work/task analysis. In D. Wixon & J. Ramey (Eds.), *Field Methods Casebook for Software Design* (pp. 35–56). New York, NY, USA: John Wiley & Sons, Inc.

Wynn, E. (1979). Office conversation as an information medium (unpublished PhD thesis, University of California, 1979).

Conclusion

Chapter 16
A Green Paper on Usability Maturation

Effie Lai-Chong Law[1], Ebba Thora Hvannberg[2] and Gilbert Cockton[3]

[1] Institut TIK, ETH Zürich, Switzerland, e-mail: law@tik.ee.ethz.ch
[2] Computer Science Department, University of Iceland
[3] School of Computing & Technology, University of Sunderland, UK

Abstract Usability maturation manifests in terms of quality in *software*, in *interaction*, and in *value*, constituting the three parts of this volume. In this green paper, the three editors present a range of ideas drawn and synthesized from the fifteen preceding chapters. It is not just a review, but, more importantly, it is an invitation for interested individuals or organizations to contribute more views and information, providing answers to open questions, challenging existing opinions, raising new issues, and bridging the gaps. In the Introduction, a brief overview of the development of the field of HCI is presented. In each of the three following sections, the five chapters comprising the respective part are reviewed and attendant issues are discussed, leading to research agendas that can serve as a roadmap for the future work on usability.

16.1 Introduction

The landscape of information technology (IT) development is changing relentlessly. Indeed, the attention of the HCI community has been drawn to the challenges posed by the so-called imminent third wave (Bødker 2006), which is characterized by the ever-broadening notion of context, the ever-blurring boundaries between work and everyday lives, and the ever-prevailing phenomenon of multiplicity (i.e., multitasking with multiple tools and multiple users synchronously as well as asynchronously). A trend in the field of HCI is the shift of focus from individual-based, performance-based cognition to group-based, perception-based emotion and experience, which is assumed to be co-constructed through interactions with people within, as well as across, communities of interest and practice. Concomitantly, the concept of usability concept and practice is evolving (Lindgaard & Parush Chapter 10; Rosenbaum Chapter 15). A brief history of HCI and IT development in the last three decades (Figure 16.1, derived from Rosson & Carroll 2001; Myers 1999) shows that we seem moving more and more towards *unstructuredness* and *informalization* to cope with diversification of user groups. For instance, the notion that learning takes place through structured activities being confined to a particular venue and formalized by certain well-defined linear processes is gradually being

Changes in HCI and Usability?	Changes in Technology & Users?
1970's	
▪ Research preempted by guidelines dev.	• Business professionals
▪ Oversimplified views on users;	• Mainframes, command-line
▪ Human Factors (HF) engineering;	• Direct manipulation UI, mouse
▪ Alan Newell's (1973) critiques on then	• Applications: word processing, spreadsheets,
predominant experimental approaches in HCI;	drawing program, hypertext
	• WYISWYG
1980's	
• Iterative vs. Waterfalls development:	• Large, diverse user groups
formative evaluation; prototype, mock-ups;	• Multiple tiled windows
usability engineering (UE)	• Xerox Star, Apple Lisa, Macintosh
• Mental models: Fitts'Law, GOMS;	• Component architecture
problem-solving; human performance;	• Interface builders
• Card, Moran & Newell's (1983)– psychology of	• UI management systems
HCI;	
• Integration with UI technology;	
1990's	
• UE is qualitative and field-oriented: participatory,	• Heterogeneous, distributed user groups
contextual and ethnographically informed design;	• World Wide Web
• Social-constructivist theories	• Groupware
• CSCW, Organizational task analysis	• Virtual Reality
• ISO on usability definition; user-centred design	• Sophisticated input/output devices
• Affective computing, accessibility, tailorability,	
localization	
2000's	
• Web 2.0: collective intelligence, reusability	• Universal users
• Rich User eXperience(UX);	• Pervasive computing;
• Multiplicity; Un-structuredness/ In-formalization	• Social software: blog, wiki, Flickr,
• Convergence: blurring boundaries, broadening	bookmarking, videoconference
contexts	• Mashup–web application hybrid tech.

Fig. 16.1 Historical development of HCI and technology

augmented by a vision of learning anywhere anytime spontaneously. Ubiquitous computing contributes to this vision.

It should be noted that emerging IT is more than work-oriented or learning-oriented. Some technology now lets users have fun and pleasure, and build and sustain social relationships. These revolutionary and evolutionary changes pose new challenges to the HCI community. How human users, ranging from infants to elderly, are optimally supported by innovative IT to meet their diverse needs and goals, and how their creative uses of these tools dialectically shape the design of next-generation IT are concerns to be addressed in HCI. How computer technologies best embody user requirements and code them in software applications, further integrating user interface technology to optimize usability, are challenges to be tackled in HCI. How quality in use as a property of interaction can best be supported and measured is a problem to be resolved in HCI, especially when the notion of quality in use is ever augmenting, encompassing a host of so-called nonfunctional quality attributes other than usability (Law, Hvannberg & Hassenzahl 2006).

Design for usability and usability evaluation operate in tandem. Specifically, user-centered design (UCD) approaches enable the integration of usability into design products. The extent to which usability is integrated into the design of a system is assessed with usability evaluation methods (UEMs). Outcomes of usability evaluation should serve as inputs for system redesign, forming a feedback loop (Hornbæk & Stage 2006). Of particular importance, is the development of UEMs, because insights gained through systematic evaluations can mature the concept and practice of usability. The maturation of UEMs can be analyzed in terms of three factors, which are further subdivided into several subfactors:

- Software models and standards—to identify the impact of standardized guidelines, formal methods and quality models on the methodological progress of UEMs (Figure 16.2)
- Usage and scoping—to resolve a set of context-related issues pertinent to the effectiveness of UEMs (Figure 16.3)
- Outcomes and values—to address the utility of UEMs for addressing stakeholder goals and experiences and for improving software development processes as well as products (Figure 16.4)

The overarching theme of this volume is to understand usability, especially research and practices that are currently contributing to its maturation. Maturing usability manifests in terms of quality in *software*, *interaction* and *value*—the three concerns modifying a recent trio of *functionality*, *usability*, and *experience* (McNamara & Kirakowski 2006). Interaction covers usability and experience, while value addresses outcomes in the world that persist behind usable interactions and memorable experiences.

The fifteen preceding chapters group into parts—Part 1, Quality in Software; Part 2, Quality in Interaction; and Part 3, Quality in Value. As the three concerns are not mutually exclusive, most chapters touch upon more than one concern, but the grouping is based on the main focus of each chapter. This closing chapter reviews each part with respect to specific usability issues depicted in Figures 16.2, 16.3 and 16.4.

By *usability maturation* we understand substantial development in the three quality aspects. To operationalize this, we enumerate a list of ten goals (italicized text) to be attained as evidence of maturation (attendant issues of some of these goals are addressed as well):

1. *A consensus, but perhaps qualified, on a definition of usability universally recognized by HCI researchers and practitioners.* Note, however, that there is neither a consensual definition of usability per se nor a consensus on whether the community needs such a definition. On the one hand, usability is a situated notion (i.e., it should be contextualized and understood relative to the causal chains where it has influence). On the other hand, a formal statement of a concept enables mutual understanding in a community of practice, especially for novices.
2. *Well-defined usability metrics and their interrelations.* Similarly, the contention whether we should or can standardize metrics, which are deemed as part of a wider picture and thus need to be crafted for each context, is raised. In fact, it is

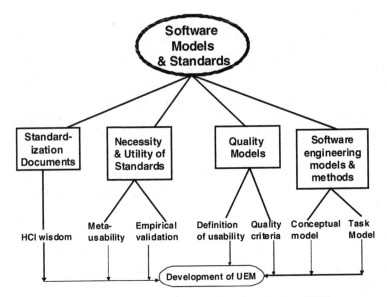

Fig. 16.2 Impacts of software models and standards on UEMs

not uncommon that researchers adapt metrics to their specific evaluation settings, especially for gauging satisfaction. Such adaptation may undesirably give rise to misleading results.

3. *Effective relationships between usability and other quality attributes, especially those being subsumed by user experience.* The argument lies in whether such

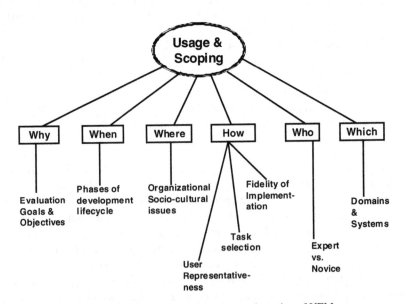

Fig. 16.3 Questions addressing usage and scoping of UEMs

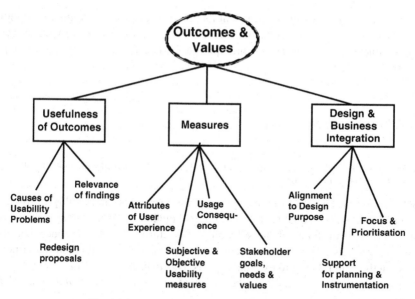

Fig. 16.4 Measures and values of usability evaluation

relationships are direct or indirect mediated by usage consequence and exploited via concrete system features.

4. *Deep and reliable understanding about usage and scope of individual usability evaluation methods, thereby enabling practitioners to make informed choices within contextual constraints.*

5. *Effective integration of models and concepts between software engineering, business planning, and HCI.*

6. *An integrated theoretical framework with significant explanatory and predictive power to address usability issues.* The scope of such a framework is to be defined—it can be so specific as to address UEM usage or so broad as to address human actions, combining multifarious dimensions.

7. *Effective interplay between usability evaluation and redesign, thereby maximizing the cost justification of usability.*

8. *Successful transfer of methods to practice, and alignment of research efforts of academic and industrial partners.*

9. *Methodological innovations (quantitative and qualitative) allowing profound insights into the needs, practices, and goals of system stakeholders and development roles (including usability specialists).*

10. *The ability to develop new UEMs, or adapt existing UEMs, for an augmented IT landscape with new application domains (e.g., social software) and interactive technologies (e.g., multimodal user interfaces).*

Each of the above could be further broken down into subgoals. While the above list is not exhaustive, achieving them is a major challenge for the HCI community.

This green paper aims to promote discussion of these and other challenges. It presents a range of ideas drawn and synthesized from previous chapters. In the process, it does review this volume, but its primary aim is to invite interested individuals or organizations to contribute more views and information, provide answers to open questions, challenge existing opinions and raising new issues, and bridge the gaps.

16.2 Quality in Software

An entity, which is assumed to have intrinsic quality, can be evaluated without the involvement of users or user surrogates.

ISO 9126 defines a set of internal quality, external quality, and quality in use criteria and metrics (i.e., quality models). Internal quality refers to quality that can be measured with attributes of the software architecture, design, and code, (i.e., the software artifacts). This section discusses quality mainly from this internal aspect, but sometimes in relation to external aspects. *Our concern is to what extent the use of development tools can enhance the quality of a system in general and its usability in particular.*

These development tools fall into two categories—i.e., tools to aid in the production of the software artifacts, and tools to define and understand the software lifecycle. The lifecycle of a software product spans the creation of a software idea to the termination of its operation. In between are many phases, each involving steps, that are executed iteratively and often in parallel.

We will review the first five chapters of this volume, which, as a whole, address the following questions:

- To what extent can *models* help in development of user interfaces and when should they be used? How abstract or concrete, formal or informal, and coarse- or fine-grained should the models be? How can models be integrated?
- What type of *methods* should be used? How are they integrated into general development processes? How can we model or express methods? How can several methods be integrated?
- How is usability integrated with other *quality attributes*, such as security or reliability?
- What is the *need* for software quality, what is the *outcome* for software users and producers, and what is their *awareness* of software quality?
- Who do you *communicate* with about quality?

16.2.1 Historical Roots of Software Engineering

Due to their manufacturing origins in engineering, developers think of quality definition and assurance as separate from product development. Quality requirements are elicited, defined, and assessed. The statement has been: "Here is what I want to build with this functionality." Only thereafter: "Has it been built adequately and does it have the right quality?" In Mahoney's account of the history of software engineering, he contrasts its roots in mechanical and industrial engineering (Mahoney 2004). As an engineering discipline, he likens software's modularity to standardized units or dimensions in the building of mechanical parts, but takes the division of a task into manageable parts as an example from industrial engineering. When it comes to quality, mechanical engineers will order parts to individual specifications such as size, ruggedness, speed, capacity, precision, or character set, which we see are *quality* specifications. In software engineering terms, it would be like ordering a Web server tolerant to network failures or able to service a certain number of clients within a time limit. This view of quality emphasizes the quality of the *product*.

On the industrial engineering side, more emphasis is on providing the right environment for software development and the concept of *process* is more prevalent, thus defined to compensate for lack of education of programmers. The link to engineering may have put the focus on building the system right, efficiently and economically, as can be seen from early papers on the economics of program production (IFIP 1968 Panel on Economics of Program Production). In the first two decades of software engineering (1970s and 1980s), there was heavy emphasis on effective management of software development, and ideas of quality lay in quality control, verification, and validation (Mahoney 2004). Building the right system has been the major goal of requirements engineering, still with functionality being more in focus than so-called nonfunctional qualities. It is worthwhile to emphasize these two different sets of qualities in a system—one that will affect a system's use or operation and another that will effect its production. The former set will give users and buyers the right system and the latter will give owners or developers a system that they can maintain and evolve economically. Example quality characteristics for the former are usability, security, and reliability, but for the latter, maintainability and interoperability. This division may be clearer than simply using terms such as internal and external qualities, because it says who defines and measures the qualities and the latter (i.e. internal/external metrics) relates to the object of the qualities, where the focus is on what is measured. By emphasizing who defines qualities, it may become clearer for whom or why the quality requirement is made and who will benefit from it. Once this is clear, where to measure the qualities is secondary. The two camps of *product* and *process* qualities, whose roots we have tried to convey above, have developed standards in parallel and without much apparent link between each other, but have recently started to create a bridge to one another.

The software architectural view is quite different from the engineering approach to quality (Mahoney 2004). Software architecture is not only about components and their relationships, but also about quality attributes. Designers need to build a software architecture that meets the need of the defined quality attributes. Some qualities are partly determined by architecture. Usability has nonarchitectural aspects, like choice of widgets or layout, but also architectural aspects such as providing the user the opportunity to cancel operations (Bass, et al. 2003, p. 73). Bass & John (2003) have investigated architectural patterns that support usability. The patterns were derived from studying scenarios, but architectural evaluation is based on writing structured scenarios for quality attributes and defining a level of quality. In a survey of software architecture evaluation of usability, Folmer and Bosch (2004) conclude that more research is needed in examining the architectural sensitivity of usability patterns and discovering the relationship between usability patterns, usability properties, and indicators. In subsequent sections, we will discuss scenarios further because Chapters 3 and 5 use them as basis for evaluations.

It may be unfortunate that quality characteristics were defined early on as separate features from functionality, because now, almost thirty years later, quality engineers are recommending that we integrate functionality and quality—that is, think of them together and not separately. Suryn's view (this volume) concurs with this, when he says: "Any functionality has its quality counterpart. FIND IT!", or in other words where there is a feature, there is a quality of that feature (or several qualities relevant to that feature). Bass, Clements and Kazman state that functionality and quality are orthogonal (Bass, et al. 2003). While it may be true that functionality and quality can be defined independently—that is, for a functionality, a quality *should be* defined—we question the statement of orthogonality and ask whether additional functionality may not make a product more usable.

16.2.2 Early Discussions on Software Quality

Very early on, researchers and developers not only recognized that software products might be difficult to use (Boehm, et al. 1976), but also that defining metrics for qualities was hard, and that conflicts between qualities were bound to emerge. Boehm, et al. state three questions that would be asked by any buyer of a software package: 1) "Can I use it as it is?", 2) "How easy is it to maintain?", and 3) "Can I still use it if I change my environment?" The first one is a main question for the user to ask, but the other two are something of a concern for the developer or the producer. For the user, Questions 2 and 3 are more of economic questions: "How costly is it to get an update or possibly a new version for my new environment?" Recognizing that qualities overlap, a hierarchical structure of qualities was built to understand which nodes had common ancestors. Relevant to this discussion, *as-is* utility is defined in terms of reliability, efficiency, and human engineering. The other two root qualities were defined as portability (to answer Question 3, above) and maintainability (to answer Question 2, above). Boehm, et al. (1976) do not stop at defining metrics but give a rate for how much work is required to evaluate those metrics. Thus, they recognize that defining metrics and objectives for thresholds is one thing and evaluating them effectively, resulting in reliable data, is another.

16.2.3 Development of Engineering of Human-Computer Interaction

When the ACM CHI (Association of Computer Machinery's Conference on Computer Human Interaction) conference was established in the early 1980s, an engineered human factors approach had been prevalent, emphasizing nondiscretionary use (Grudin 2005). With the CHI community, human factors disappeared from HCI, and cognitive and usability engineering appeared. Although Norman's submission on cognitive engineering to the CHI conference in 1983 is cited as its definition, Grudin (2005) remarks that from this time, the CHI conference has slowly stopped identifying so strongly with engineering. Grudin proceeds, saying that while traditional ergonomic goals, such as speed, learnability, and memorability apply to power plant operation, consumers abandon usability and utility for intuitive appeal. Mentioning that the CHI community has learned not to rely on experiments in laboratories, surveys, and such, qualitative in-depth methods such as learning from discretionary users are more appropriate (Grudin 2005). Whether this implies that systems are less engineered is not evident. Interestingly, Grudin never mentions the word *quality* in his account of human-computer interaction.

We have discussed software engineering, quality, and human computer interaction separately. Butler (1996), in his review of usability engineering on its tenth anniversary, calls for an integrated approach to application development where usability engineering fits a larger field of software engineering. Indeed this challenge has been met with various workshops and conferences, most lately with a book on human-centered software engineering (Seffah, et al. 2006), where usability is integrated into the software development lifecycle.

16.2.4 Automation of User Interface Development with Formal Models

Abrahao, Iborra and Vanderdonckt (Chapter 1) address the question of whether model driven architecture (MDA)-compliant methods can improve software usability through transformation. Their future vision is that if the usability of a system built in this way can be predicted, it is possible to talk about a user interface that is *usable by construction*. Usability by construction is analogous to correctness by construction (Hall & Chapman 2002), where correctness is built into every step of the development process.

For requirements analysis, a computing independent model is built, which is then translated into a code model, via a model compiler, which contains mappings between conceptual primitives (PIM) and software representations. Many attempts have certainly been made to establish a model-based approach for developing user interfaces, but the authors of this chapter claim that no method has emerged because it remains to be seen whether the quality requirement of usability has been met. As we see in other chapters of this book (e.g. Harrison, et al. Chapter 3; Bernhaupt, et al. Chapter 5), they propose to build a usable user interface by construction, but not automatically.

Comparing the results of a user evaluation and an expert evaluation of the resulting user interface, the authors found that the two types of evaluation uncover problems originating in different development models—i.e., the computation-independent, platform-independent, platform-specific, and code models. The evaluation without users revealed more procedure-oriented usability problems, but the ones with users were more perceptual and cognitive.

The usability evaluations provided feedback on the improvement of the platform-independent and platform-dependent model, which is necessary to improve the transformations. Furthermore, experts can learn design guidelines and anti-patterns from usability problems. These can drive model transformations.

The roots of model-driven development lie deep in the early 1950s when engineers used domain models of civil engineering structures and Fortran infrastructure to enable user engineers to develop domain applications (Boehm 2006). Previous methods for UI development have suggested a combination of different models on different levels of abstraction. In theory, it is easy to see how they can be supportive and informative to developers, but it seems they have enjoyed limited popularity in practice. An automatic tool to aid in the transformation, such as suggested in this chapter, may remove the barrier of development costs of models. At the same time, model-driven development gains mostly from standard domain models—e.g., for banks or manufacturing. These can be reused, but the challenges are to handle continuing changes and domain restructuring when these occur (Boehm 2006). Method developers need to understand that evolution does not only occur in the domain but also in quality requirements because of customers' demands (Eickelmann & Hayes 2004). Even though many of the barriers have been crossed and a critical mass is using model-driven approaches, there are still many hurdles to surmount before we can fully reap the benefits of this technology (Schmidt 2006).

The authors plan to compare a UI produced by an evaluation of an MDA tool to a UI developed by an experienced designer. It will be interesting to learn about the cost savings of an MDA. We speculate that the start-up cost of using an MDA may be considerable for companies that need to use new tools and methods. Another challenge for the proposed method is to be able to include, at the same time, other relevant quality attributes such as fault tolerance or security.

16.2.5 Balancing Features and Quality

Increasing demands from customers to buy, learn how to use, and then operate software right away, can escalate demands on software developers to deliver desired qualities and the right features economically. With this motivation, Suryn (Chapter 2) starts his passage through software quality engineering. While the chapter by Abrahão, et al. reviewed in the previous section is concerned with development models of the *product*, this chapter directs its attention mostly to *process* models. Beginning by explaining quality in relation to widely known capability maturity standards and the software engineering body of knowledge, the chapter moves on to introduce basic concepts in software quality engineering. Early in the chapter, we are reminded of the definition of engineering and immediately as we think about "the application of a continuous, systematic, disciplined, quantifiable approach to the development," we need to ask whether products that are built by people processes for people can ever be described this way. Stating that measurement is a pivotal activity in quality engineering, we also need to answer the question of why we need to measure and what efforts are spent on the measurement—i.e., the feasibility of the measurement. Of Suryn's reasons for measurement, perhaps the most relevant is that we can use it as a basis for making complex decisions based on evidence instead of guessing.

In Suryn's review of the software engineering body of knowledge, he concludes that quality requirements *specification* is not addressed, therefore testing is generally limited to a validation and verification process, and finally that practical aspects of engineering quality in products are omitted. We will dwell on the first gap identified. The relationship between needs and quality requirements has to be created, by identifying stakeholders' needs (stated and implicit) and transforming them into functional and quality requirements. After quality requirements are known, they need to be translated into internal and external qualities and qualities in use. This relationship and transformation is probably much more complex than is recognized today. Suryn divides requirements into three categories and not the traditional two. He divides them into functional, non-functional, and quality requirements, with quality requirements falling into one of three categories of ISO/IEC 9126—internal, external and quality in use requirements. Suryn suggests a fourth category—operational quality requirements—which are appropriate to define when use of the software product is expected to be widespread. This suggestion agrees with the recognition that quality requirements need to be tailored to different contexts, and acknowledges the increase in user numbers and the escalating emphasis on the operation of software.

Experience has shown that a complex set of quality attributes may be a hindrance to the use of quality models, and that developers' comprehension of these attributes is low. Suryn's conjecture is that the reason developers only mention a few attributes, is not the complexity of quality engineering, but simply lack of quality engineering awareness.

To overcome the obstacle of quality engineering being far distant from development processes, Suryn proposes a software quality implementation model (SQIM) that aims to take an integrated approach, instead of adding quality after the fact. The model maps the different types of quality categories mentioned above to the different software development phases.

Another gap Suryn identified, mentioned above, is that software engineering lacks practical approaches. Realizing that software developers, or sponsors of projects, have limited funding, he claims that functionality and quality are natural enemies—provided that cost is kept constant, increase in functionality implies that quality will suffer, and vice versa. This is an interesting statement and in many ways true. Musa's statement, claiming that users view quality as a tradeoff between reliability, cost, and time of delivery; or Boehms' statement that quality is a win-win set of quality factors, concurs with this view (Eickelmann & Hayes 2004). Continuing to focus on the association of features with quality aspects, as mentioned earlier, the chapter proposes that each functionality has a quality counterpart, thereby shifting the analyst's attention to quality and not just functionality, as typically occurs. Similarly, Mead (Eickelmann & Hayes 2004) is concerned that quality characteristics may be viewed as inferior to functionality, and proposes that quality forms a set of first class requirements, as primary as any functional or similar ones. It may be interesting to learn whether it is easier to associate quality with individual functions or features, whole systems.

Although Suryn's chapter argues for the integration of the quality engineering and software development processes, it recognizes that the synchronization of the two aspects is hard. It depends on the goals set and the available resources, particularly the maturity and the size of the organization. Hence, the context of development is of utmost importance when deciding on the development process model. True to this statement, Suryn hints at deviations from strict processes, and acknowledges the need for agile development, but still wants to hold on to acquiring and maintaining knowledge about software development processes. We will discuss this point further in the section after the next one.

16.2.6 User Experience Requirements: Exploration and Modelling in an Agile vs. Formal Development

Harrison, Campos, Doherty and Loer (Chapter 3) discuss the role of models as descriptors of user experiences in ambient and mobile systems. The authors are concerned with modeling and development processes when they discuss the usefulness of formal models vs. prototypes. They look for opportunities to express those models agilely and early in the development process. They describe two case studies, one of a traditional usability requirement and a second one focusing on user experiences in ambient and mobile systems. Besides eliciting user experience requirements, they are also concerned with evaluating models based on those requirements. The question is whether it is possible to use a prototype to validate usability requirements in real contexts. How detailed does the model describing software need to be to allow confidence in potentially expensive design decisions? Not only are the authors concerned with *types* of models for building ambient and mobile systems, they are also interested in their *users*. Because the goal requirements include user experience, the main users of the models are human factors and domain experts. For other types of qualities, the model users could well be other experts.

The chapter presents an overview of elicitation techniques—that is, methods to retrieve and gather knowledge necessary to understand requirements. In a section on analysis, a range of techniques different in formality are discussed and explained, from prototypes to scenario analysis to more abstract formal methods such as traces through scenarios, which are sequences of states or actions. The aim of this, through a review, is to reveal a situation where a property does not hold. The properties or questions are articulated in linear temporal logic (LTL), and then subsequently used to check statecharts using the SMV model-checker. Methods have been suggested to review changes to current conceptual models, which aim to link concrete instance examples to abstract conceptual models, and thereby establish traceability between them (Haumer, et al. 2000). The discussion on the usefulness of concrete vs. abstract methods, and on whether more formality gradually removes emotional and motivational aspects is very much alive (Diaper 2002). Instead of focusing on only one method, one of the primary aims of Harrison and his colleagues has been to look at synergies between methods such as modeling and scenario-based evaluation. The approach used is to explore (in a model) different physical paths in a particular environment. As types of systems evolve, and we move towards more intelligent, ubiquitous, and pervasive systems, we need to reconsider what types of models are needed while perhaps still requiring safety criticality (Sutcliffe 2003). Leveson agrees with this, stating (Eickelmann & Hayes 2004) "Use methods for a particular application and development context. Developers should understand that quality is high priority." As in all modeling, one of the challenges stated here is to describe a model at an appropriate level of detail—that is, how much knowledge you need to capture and what you can leave out. With prototypes classified as agile techniques, the authors suggest an approach that combines formal and agile techniques in situations where formal rigor is necessary by combination with a scheme, which allows users to experience the system. A process cycle for experience requirements exploration is suggested, which, starting from scenarios, continues to prototypes that are abstracted in models and are finally used as a basis for creating traces used by experts during analysis.

Finally, the chapter identifies concrete properties that can capture important features of users' positive experience and hence users' acceptability, but the authors admit that they are not necessarily conventional usabilities. Another set of experience properties are identified as being difficult to verify in scenarios and should be modeled and evaluated differently. In the beginning of this section, we mentioned human factors and domain experts as users of the models, and the authors emphasize that their role is substantial in discovering anomalies within these models.

The chapter identifies two important issues for future research. The first is about mapping between models and prototypes. The second is about identifying types of requirements suitable for expression in different classes of models and how to ensure practical consistency between them.

16.2.7 Are Software Engineers Not Empathetic of User Experiences?

While Harrison, et al. (Chapter 3) mostly talked about agile and formal techniques for building models within the software development process, the chapter by Ambler (Chapter 4) is more focused on process. Similarly, because the former chapter was concerned with stakeholders—i.e., human factor and domain experts—Ambler wants to explore how software developers using agile methods can contribute to the user experience (UEX) community. Thus, both chapters look at differences between, and perhaps integration of, HCI and SE approaches. While the former focused on dissimilarities in the types of requirements we set for systems, the latter considers the integration of different communities. The former focuses more in terms of product models and the latter more as process models, although both have a good understanding of products and processes.

Ambler carefully describes each of the two camps—UEX and agile software development (ASD)—pointing out the differences and misconceptions of each community. For many years, scientists and practioners have attempted to integrate the communities of HCI and SE. Seffah and Metzker present obstacles between usability and software engineering (Seffah & Metzker 2004). One of their conclusions is that a computer-assisted usability engineering platform is needed and that only then will user-centered development be taken seriously. They further remind us that software development has a long tradition of testing and measurement, which the user-centered design (UCD) community can benefit from.

Similarly, as in Chapters 1 and 3, Ambler looks at the role of modeling in software development. In addition to the requirements modeling that Harrison, et al. discuss, they remind the reader of the need to model the architecture to get an overview of the work. Following the agile manifesto, modeling should only be done just in time and then in model-storming sessions that are not planned and will take a very short time—typically 5–10 minutes—and seldom more than half an hour. One must still ask how this scales up and whether it is different in complex, large systems.

In agile methods, testing for quality is not performed unless you aim to guarantee particular requirements. Hence, if there are no usability requirements, the system is not tested for usability. If, however, usability testing is included, methods such as play-acting have been added to agile projects. In this method, team members act as the computer, but users control the system, and a separate member plays the *help system*. A comparison of testing in agile methods reveals that testing is prevalent, including unit, integration, and acceptance testing. Weyuker (Eickelmann & Hayes 2004) concurs with this view when she states that testing is the all-important development phase.

Ambler, like Harrison, et al., suggests a method that is synthesised from ASD and UEX to close the gap. In the synthesized method, one of Ambler's recommendations is for ASD professionals to accept that usability is a critical quality factor. Not wanting to go so far as to say that software engineers are not empathetic, Diaper proposes that this attitude be remedied (Diaper 2002). Parallel to Suryn's concern (Chapter 2), it is advocated that awareness of quality, especially usability, needs to be raised. This is one of the challenges that Ambler identifies—namely, that usability experts write for other usability experts, but not for software developers in general, who present a much too narrow view. It is possible that in an attempt to build a computer-human interaction community, and to strive for its existence, segregation from other important components and qualities has occurred. In agile development, no one team member is a specialist because they are supposed to rotate their roles. This may be an incentive to share the expertise of individual quality characteristics, such as security, usability, and performance. However, knowing that each of these issues is complex, it is hardly realistic for one person to have such a wide knowledge.

It is too narrow to only address a single quality characteristic of a system in a method for elicitation and evaluation of quality. As Ambler (Chapter 4) points out, user interfaces are important, but so are many other components, such as databases and networking. Presenting a very general approach, as described by Suryn (Chapter 2), is too general for practitioners. Whatever processes and life-cycle models are chosen, they need to be appropriate for the situation and their benefits must be supported by evidence through empirical research (Abrahamsson, et al. 2003). Pfleeger states: "Be critical of your quality methods and use evidence to reassess its [sic] usefulness" (Eickelmann & Hayes 2004). Even a single development team needs its own evidence that its methods are working. A team needs to be mature enough to be able to make such improvements. In the same resolution, Basili states that a software process needs to be documented to be able to make improvements (Eickelmann & Hayes 2004). Without documentation of processes, and instead relying on tacit knowledge, we ask how improvements in agile projects can take place. With experts on the team solving problems seen before, tacit knowledge may be sufficient. Planning—including architectures or risk analysis—can avoid making costly mistakes, but on the other hand may hinder necessary updates or make these updates expensive (Boehm 2002). What we miss from this discussion of people's skills—e.g., being specialists or generalists, or UEX vs. ASD—is the level of skills (novice, intermediate, or expert). Previously, the concern has been raised that agile methods may be more suitable for teams, including experts (Boehm 2002), and that there is potentially a shortage of such expertise, but that you are bound to fall short of good designs if the team consists of all novices. While this may be true of every method, a novice trained with documented processes or best practices is more likely to succeed. Research has shown that a novice pair of programmers can do better solving difficult tasks than a solo programmer, but that an expert pair solving a repeated task is no better off than a solo expert (Lui & Chan 2006). Whether this result translates to design has yet to be seen.

16.2.8 Quality Software Using Novel Interaction Techniques Needs a Synthesised Approach to Evaluation

As we have discussed in a previous section, quality attributes cannot be viewed in isolation but need to be in harmony with one another. Increasing demands for accessibility and new user interaction technologies are bound to call for new evaluation approaches or a synthesis of current ones. Bernhaupt, Navarre, Palanque, and Winckler (Chapter 5) propose a new approach, which combines model-based specification and empirical methods for usability evaluation of multimodal interactive applications that need to meet different quality needs such as usability and reliability. With this, the authors hope to remedy two deficiencies—lack of support for understanding the detailed behavior and poor integration of usability results into the whole development process. Both deficiencies are remedied with increased modeling but the models (i.e., a formal description of multimodal interaction applications) will inform a traditional UEM.

The chapter presents an overview of multimodal systems, giving examples of input and output interaction techniques and devices. The authors stress that during usability assessment of multimodal interfaces it is not enough to evaluate the user interface per se but to view devices and interaction techniques together. When surveying UEMs for multimodal interfaces, the authors identify gaps. Examples are expert evaluations, where experts and guidelines in multimodal systems are scarce. A case study for a space ground system in a satellite control room is described to illustrate where two quality attributes are required—usability and reliability. The chapter illustrates multimodal interaction on a pair of buttons that are used to control the point of view of a 3D model and interact with a range slider for selecting temperature and monitoring energy consumption. A concurrent task tree (CTT) model is used to describe the tasks.

The normal way to proceed in usability evaluation is to select frequent tasks for evaluation. For safety-critical systems, this is different, because preferably most tasks need to be evaluated. This is further complicated with multimodal systems, because given the number of modalities, the number of combinations rises. Therefore, the selection of tasks and modalities to test becomes a critical issue. To solve this, equivalence classes of scenarios are identified. To evaluate the approach, the authors tested the multimodal system using user testing and cognitive walkthrough. The approach used by Bernhaupt, et al. is in the same class as that of Harrison, et al. (Chapter 3), in that interaction scenarios are created, but Bernhaupt, et al. uses a Petri net that is automatically generated from an interactive cooperative objects (ICO) model. What further distinguishes their approach is that it describes low-level interaction techniques, which the authors claim can have a significant impact on the results and interpretations of usability test results. Another objective, which the authors seek, is to change the ICO models as the results of usability evaluation prescribe.

The authors identify several future research issues, including investigating combinations of user testing and model-based evaluations, and also applying the approach to a real ground segment information treatment system. Further investigations of the reliability of multimodal systems are beyond the scope of the chapter and will be reported separately.

16.3 Quality in Interaction

> An entity of which quality is assumed to emerge when it is in use and can be evaluated with the involvement of users or user surrogates.

Quality in use (QiU) is a property of interaction. QiU is characterized by functionality, reliability, efficiency, usability, maintenance, and portability (ISO 9126). A number of usability evaluation methods (UEMs) have been developed to assess quality as usability, with or without involving users, and with low-fidelity or high-fidelity prototypes. The fact that UEMs are diverse in terms of their applicability, implementation, sensitivity, constraints, and prerequisites, further complicates the evaluation of interaction quality because interaction is not just user-system, but also user-UEM, and UEM-system. Given these intertwined factors, the challenges are to identify the scope of a particular UEM (Figure 16.3), and to operationalize user goals and interaction types in user- and task-modeling. User experiences (UX) are the focus of this perspective (Figure 16.4).

Five chapters in Part 2 address three different aspects of quality in interaction, albeit to various extents:

- *Conceptual*—theoretical frameworks on the nature of interaction
- *Methodological*—techniques and metrics for evaluating interaction quality
- *Practical*—transfer of concepts and methods from research to practice or vice-versa

Besides, each chapter stimulates us to reflect on some challenges, which are now highlighted in turn.

16.3.1 Usability Evaluation of Social Software: Old Methods for a New Trend?

In their comprehensive chapter, Lindgaard and Parush (Chapter 10) touch upon the evolving notion of usability. In particular, they underscore how the utilitarian view of usability (i.e., better usability leads to greater productivity) is challenged by the emotional view (e.g., better usability leads to higher pleasure). The former focuses on individual performance, while the latter on social experience. Indeed, the social-ization wave of Web 2.0 has created a rapidly changing IT landscape, catching many HCI researchers and practitioners without strong CSCW backgrounds unprepared. Software applications enabling communication, interaction, and collaboration tran-scendent of time and space are expanding (e.g., blogs, wikis, Flickr, del.icio.us, Skype, to name just a few). The number of users of such *social software* is esca-lating. How satisfied are users with these emergent tools? Noteworthy is that these users are people from every walk of life; the population of online communities is increasingly heterogeneous. While today's social software has roots in 1990s group-ware, it is more versatile and light-weight, and able to support a wider range of group activities more dynamically than the latter. Furthermore, the blurring bound-ary between work and everyday life is broadening the concept of context (includ-ing people and cultural mediators/artifacts), and multitasking with multiple users and multiple tools (i.e., swift change of context with mobile applications) becomes prevalent (Bødker 2006). All these factors add to the major challenge of evaluating social software.

The high incompatibility between group activities and usability lab environments (Grudin 1994) calls for field and longer-term evaluation as well as adaptation of existing usability evaluation methods (UEMs) and metrics, which are normally employed for single-user applications. Lindgaard and Parush sharply point out that, while the extensibility of conventional UEMs for evaluating usability of groupware and CSCW systems seems demonstrable, it is dubious whether the scoping of these adapted methods is comprehensive enough to cover most, if not all aspects, of col-laborative experience.

Effectiveness and efficiency—two prongs of tripartite usability (ISO 9241-11)—may no longer be significant quality attributes for social software supporting *unstructured* tasks. Conversely, user satisfaction, which can broadly be defined to include some user experience attributes (Law, et al. 2006), becomes the main concern. There are already several issues concerning measurement of user satisfaction—it is gauged by a variety of standardized and homegrown instruments with vaguely defined constructs (Hornbæk 2006), *after* but seldom *during* interaction with a system (NB: one notable exception is Hassenzahl & Sandweg 2004). The timing of measurement can be critical given the ephemeral nature of user emotion and experience. Existing UEMs are deemed inappropriate for assessing user experience lest flaws such as methodological reductionism and conflation errors be made (McNamara & Kirakowski 2006). Besides, relationships between fuzzy quality attributes associated with group interactions (e.g., trust, social presence, awareness, fun, attractiveness, and cohesiveness) and conventional usability metrics need to be defined and refined (cf., Preece 2001). In summary, we face a number of challenges to identify and develop valid usability evaluation techniques and metrics specifically suited for social software. Solutions entail deep reflection on the prevailing concept and practice of usability, as well as improved understanding of social interaction.

16.3.2 HCI Theories Cauldron: More or Less Spicy Ingredients?

Lindgaard and Parush stress that while theoretical frameworks embraced in the field of HCI (including activity theory, situated cognition, and distributed cognition) enable us to understand the impact of social context on usability, the problem of translating such understanding into practice remains to be resolved. We extend their point by adding that, while identifying which social contextual factors are relevant to a particular evaluation situation is already a challenge, it will even be more challenging to operationalize them. In fact, the user experience movement has thrown more theories into the *HCI cauldron*, such as Mihaly Csikszentmihalyi's (1997) flow theory and its increasing applications in HCI (see Pace 2004), or John Dewey's and Mikhail Bakhtin's pragmatist approach to technology as *felt experience* (McCarthy & Wright 2004). Whether the potions extracted can shed light onto the issues concerning design, usage, and evaluation of new-generation interactive systems remain to be seen. Theories should be able to explain or predict the phenomena of interest. HCI theories tend to be poor on both prediction and explanation. There is a lack of theories to explain or predict intriguing observations in usability evaluation, for instance, in which contexts usability measures of various types (Hornbæk 2006) are correlated (or not) —why, and to what extent? Which factors contribute to developers' problem fixing strategies (Law 2006)? How do usability practitioners perceive design situations (Furniss, Blandford & Curzon, Chapter 7)?

Methodological and practical concerns are concomitantly raised through the above reflection on the theoretical development in HCI. Specifically, how do theories inform the practice of usability? Savioja and Norros (Chapter 6) illustrate how activity theory can explain the multiple roles of tools—instrumental, psychological and communicative—in mediating activities related to the operation of complex interactive systems such as a nuclear power plant. In criticizing the narrow focus of current usability evaluation practice on the instrumental function, the authors advocate a more holistic view known as systems usability to address the other two functions as well. Furthermore, the authors attempt to integrate in their framework other psychological and philosophical concepts, such as Dreyfus' embodied intentionality and Gibson's affordance. However, these rather elusive concepts are abstract and thus inaccessible to practitioners, despite the authors' ambition to translate and apply them in their own context. Apart from reiterating the importance of context and triangulation of different data sources, which are part of current established methodology, Savioja and Norros insightfully base their definition of good practice on the distinction between external and internal quality of task performance. All in all, the challenge faced by HCI researchers is the integration of theoretical concepts into a coherent whole—a single effective unified HCI theory seems too big a challenge to achieve.

16.3.3 Dialectic Interactions: Dynamic Humans vs. Adaptive Systems

Methodologically, Savioja and Norros address an apparent paradox inherent in task analysis: how can the analysis of existing, predefined tasks effectively inform the development of a new tool, whose introduction into emerging tasks will dialectically change the very nature of the activity of which such new tasks are an integral part? In the same vein, the authors also express their concern about the generality of results of the normative task analysis to the profile of future users of the new tool. These apparent constraints in the design process seem inevitable (cf., Carroll, Kellogg & Rosson's [1991] Task Artifact Cycle).

Concerning the relationship between user profile and system usage (Figure 16.3), it is a well-recognized fact that user needs and goals are dynamic, evolving with societal and economic changes that can (partly) be attributed to technological developments. Technical systems, in turn, also evolve with changing user requirements. Concomitantly, interactions between these two entities evolve as well. Users, systems, and interactions are tightly coupled and mutually stimulate and constrain each other. We coin the term *evolvable interaction* with the qualifier *evolvable* by borrowing from a specific research area (evolvable systems), which investigates the application of biologically inspired concepts to implement adaptive hardware. We retain the connotation that users and systems *co-evolve* through interaction. Besides, *evolvable* connotes self-regulation and self-adaptivity. Human users are known to be rational and adaptable, creating workarounds for usability problems. Similarly, adaptive systems are designed to adjust to user preferences or even to accommodate user errors. The dynamics of these two entities render their interactions rather unpredictable. Evaluation of human-machine interaction thus becomes increasingly challenging, calling for knowledge and competences in multiple domains.

16.3.4 Paradigm Shift: From Utility to Beauty

Other HCI researchers have attempted to qualify different kinds of interaction, including *instrumental interaction*, that generalizes the technique of direct manipulation (Beaudouin-Lafon 2000), and in stark contrast, *oppressive interaction* (Fiore 2004), which denotes the suppression of designers' free imaginative expression by the formalist and functional views of human-computer interaction. Fiore (2004) proposes a paradigm shift—the aesthetics of interaction through the interface—to emancipate both designers and users. Specifically, the HCI community should reckon with redefining, as well as expanding the scope of the roles of designers and users and enable the aesthetic experience of using the artifact and of creating it.

The advocacy of such a paradigm shift from the *utility* of interaction (objective, tangible, measurable) to the *beauty* of interaction (subjective, intangible, indeterminate) is consistent with the augmenting views of user experience (Law, et al. 2006) on the one hand, but seems contrary to the recent attempt to reinstate arguments for quantifying usability (Sauro 2006) on the other hand. The tension between the two paradigms can be seen as instantiating the perennial tug-of-war between qualitative and quantitative approaches. Such tension, however, can be useful in stimulating methodological innovations accommodating both approaches.

16.3.5 Discount Methodologies: What are the Boundary Conditions?

Furniss, et al.'s (Chapter 7) exploratory study on usability practitioners illustrates the application of qualitative analysis based on grounded theory (Strauss & Corbin 1998), which is gaining ground in the HCI community. The authors corroborate the so-called *outward movement* of research, shifting from technical method development, to the practitioner, to the context of use (i.e., organizational issues), and eventually focusing on value creation through usability practice. In other words, analysis is done at a higher level of abstraction to examine factors influencing usability work. Their discussion is elaborated along four dimensions: i) *methods and processes*—selection and adaptation of evaluation methods and procedures contingent on clients' needs and organizational constraints; ii) *relationships*—the strength of the relationship between usability specialists and developers influences the uptake of evaluation results; iii) *communication and coordination—high-bandwidth communication* between evaluators and designers can avoid making wrong fixes and enable making more informed decisions; iv) *psychology and expertise*—how usability specialists' expertise acquired through practical experience influences their perception of design situations and process.

Furniss and co-authors have identified some problems in the usability practice of Web designers; these problems have largely been neglected by methodological research in usability engineering. In addition, the authors' work has stimulated us to ponder about the design of research studies in HCI. As noted earlier, qualitative approaches are gaining popularity and acceptance. However, there is a tendency to (over)simplify steps perceived to be too complicated or resource-demanding, leading to some easy-to-run-even-by-novice approaches—e.g., discount ethnographies instantiated in the form of contextual inquiry and cultural probes, which, strictly speaking, are not genuine ethnography, but share some broad resemblance as a family of qualitative studies and produce different types of outcomes (Dourish 2006). Similarly, grounded theory normally entails iterative coding processes and multiple raters, but can we tag a field study as grounded theory when there is only one rater who codes a dataset once? This trend of simplification can be associated with the birth of discount usability engineering in early 1990s. However, some researchers point out that discounting usability evaluation methods (e.g., discount user tests, heuristic evaluation, and streamlined cognitive walkthrough) may undesirably, and naturally, discount results as well (e.g., Cockton & Woolrych 2002); *graceful degradation*, as a justification for simplifying methods, can be discarded as a myth. Paradoxically, there seems a need for such simplified approaches, given all sorts of organizational and budgetary constraints. However, it is imperative that researchers understand and report the limits of simplified tools and the corresponding outcomes.

Cocomitantly, our concerns are: if a research study is claimed to be based in an established methodological approach, but the actual practice deviates from the standard procedure, how far is such a deviation regarded acceptable? Put differently, what are the boundary conditions for qualifying variants of established research and evaluation methodologies as valid (e.g., the recurrent debate about appropriate sample sizes for usability tests; Lewis 2006)? Should there be guidelines for applying and reporting such qualified variants (structured report formats for usability evaluation), thereby legitimating comparisons across studies?

16.3.6 Necessity and Utility of Software Standards

Clearly, our attempt to bring usability to maturity is neither the first nor will it be the last. Earthy and his colleagues (e.g., 1998) have developed a usability maturity model (cf. a recent survey; Jokela, et al. 2006), which focuses on assessing the status of human-centered design (HCD), or user-centered design (UCD) practice in organizations and is primarily based on ISO 13407. Jokela (Chapter 8), based on empirical experience, identifies the weaknesses of this standard, including being imprecise, unbalanced, with inconsistent terminologies within and across standards, too abstract for translating into practice, and with ambiguous wordings leading to confusion. With results derived from meticulous analyses, Jokela presents a detailed proposal on revising the standard. As already pointed out by the author, the proposal entails empirical validation to ensure its usability.

In fact, Jokela's critiques of ISO 13407 can actually be seen as highlighting general ailments of other standards, which are meant to inform software design and evaluation such as the widely cited ISO 9126 and ISO 9241. The applicability of these standards to ever-changing IT products cannot be taken for granted, considering that these standards normally need to go through lengthy ratification processes and thus may not be able to stay in sync with rapid IT development. Clearly, standards should be useful to a certain extent. Otherwise, they would have long been abolished (Good 2003). However, a major weakness we identify in software quality standards is the definition of metrics and measurements, e.g., Effectiveness in 9124-11, Attractiveness in 9126-2, and Reliability in IEEE 1061 (see also Law & Hvannberg 2006). An implication is that we need not only quantitative but also qualitative metrics.

Furthermore, a quality model should make the general term *quality* specific and useful when engineering requirements, and as an aid to understanding, controlling, and improving a product (Firesmith 2003). Should the adequacy of a quality model be evaluated based on its coverage of the widely adopted ISO/IEC 9126-1 standard? The answer, unfortunately, is uncertain. On the one hand, assuming that ISO 9126-1 is a generic basic framework applicable to all software products, then a quality model will be seen as defective if it omits any of the characteristics addressed in the standard. On the other hand, this generic standard needs to be customized to address specific organizational constraints and product goals; it is legitimate to select a subset of the characteristics without jeopardizing the adequacy of the model. As depicted in Figure 16.2, the necessity and utility of establishing software standards requires further empirical evaluation—experience reports and case studies on applying standards should be collected and systematically analyzed. Besides, the accessibility of standards in terms of ease of access, ease of use, and of understanding and openness should be improved. Specifically, the purchase of standards is rather costly; it may be a barrier for otherwise higher usage. The HCI community needs to be better informed about standards under development—the related information seems restricted to a handful of people involved; the standardization body may even consider taking a radical approach to opening up the development process to invite input from interested individuals or organizations.

16.3.7 Return on Investment: Mathematics, Money, or Mindset?

Paternò and Santoro (Chapter 9) present a lucid framework for remote usability evaluation (RUE)—a maturing approach that becomes more and more important, given the globalization of companies and their widely distributed customers. RUE is meant to mitigate one major problem of traditional lab-based user-based testing—high costs incurred (lab facilities, test participants' productivity loss, travel). However, no data about the systematic cost-benefit or return-on-investment (ROI) analysis of RUE as compared with other usability evaluation settings (lab-based or field study) are yet available. Indeed, ROI for usability is a tricky issue (Mayhew & Tremaine 2005). Flaws and myths are found with assumptions underlying sophisticated mathematical models and their usages (Rosenberg 2004). Probably the effectiveness of ROI arguments for benefits produced by usability is not (only) a matter of mathematics but (rather) a matter of their compatibility with stakeholders' mindsets. In other words, like usability evaluation outcomes, the persuasiveness of results of ROI analysis for usability hinges crucially on who presents to whom in which way (Dray, et al. 2005).

16.3.8 Evaluation of Multimodal User Interfaces: Automatable?

As pointed out by Paternò and Santoro, there are inherent limitations of RUE, though related research studies demonstrate that outcomes of RUE and those of traditional approaches are somewhat comparable. Despite progress on data-capturing and data-analysis techniques driven by supportive technologies (i.e., eye-tracking devices, psychophysiological response measuring kits), there are still many methodological and technical challenges. It is deemed essential to garner both quantitative data (e.g., logging) and qualitative data (e.g., spontaneous verbal comments); it is not enough to know what and how often users surf, or stare at, a certain website. It is more important to know why they do so. Moreover, data triangulation can substantiate the validity and reliability of empirical findings. Nevertheless, synchronizing as well as analyzing a large corpus of multimodal, multi-source data, and synergizing the results, entail the considerable efforts of a team of experts from different disciplines. How can we streamline such a resource-demanding process? Is automating data analysis and visualizing outcomes an effective means? WebRemUsine, depicted by Paternò and Santoro, seems useful for dealing with quantitative data. When it comes to multimodal data (e.g., videoclips), human interpretation is still required. Indeed, existing automated qualitative data-analysis tools are reckoned ineffective. With the ever-increasing uses of multimodal interfaces (Oviatt 2003), is the usability community equipped with the appropriate tools and techniques to deal with the next generation of IT?

16.4 Quality in Value

> An entity, whose quality is assumed to have real world impact, can be evaluated over a span of time and space with users and operational data.

Value is addressed in two ways in Part 3's chapters. Some chapters focus on increasing the value of usability practices for *software development*. Others focus on increasing value *for users*. Part 3 is mostly forward-looking, although with some HCI history and case study material. In all cases, however, the emphasis is on what usability *should* be, not what it is now. This is appropriate given the theme of the book, as our visions of how usability is to mature will shape the course we set for it. In the previous section, "Quality in Interaction," the future is seen in terms of expanding conceptual scope, improving methodology, and transfer from research into practice. Such headings also work well for the future of usability as *quality in value*. However, instead of scope expanding to chase new interaction paradigms, techniques, and modalities, quality in value approaches spread evaluation measures to focus on outcomes rather than interaction. In the process, methodologies must be extended by researchers and practitioners. The key difference between approaches for quality in the system, interaction, and value lies in what gets measured and/or assessed. The scope extends from technical system features and qualities, through interactive behaviors and qualities, to achievements within sociodigital systems. However, in all cases, maturity can be tracked via methodological improvements and transfer from research to practice.

Part 3 offers both evolutionary and revolutionary approaches. Methods can be extended and evolved to provide more value for development. For Hornbæk (Chapter 12), this is by offering ideas as well as reporting problems. For Rosenbaum (Chapter 15), this is by improving integration and alignment with development and business needs. Alternatively, by shifting the focus away from current usability measures, a revolution in evaluation is sought. For Cajander and her colleagues (Chapter 11), value is achieved by delivering long-term well-being for work-based users, rather than just quality in interaction. For Sikorski (Chapter 14), value has an economic meaning and reflects the relationship between perceived value and perceived cost for consumers. For Cockton (Chapter 13), value has a wide meaning, based on a general understanding of *worth*, as in the usage "what something *is* worth" (Cockton 2006).

Worth motivates because it deserves, or brings compensation for, whatever is invested in it, whether this is money (repay), time, energy, or commitment (justify). Designing worth means designing things that will *motivate* people to buy, learn, use, or recommend an interactive product, and ideally most or all of these. Sikorski covers value from all of these perspectives. For business and development stakeholders, usability approaches that demonstrably create value for customers could *bring compensation for* usability costs and efforts. In short, customer worth should make usability worth it, as does making usability more cost-effective and expanding its contribution to development.

Cockton's chapter provides a framework for this overview of Part 3. He proposes the construction of worth/aversion maps (W/AMs) to capture the intended and achieved *worth systems* created in sociodigital fusions by the development of interactive software and media. Based on laddering approaches from consumer psychology, W/AMs relate product attributes to other worth system components.

W/AMs can be inspected for *breadth, balance,* and *spread.* For Cockton, *breadth* is achieved by considering the full range of stakeholders, but it is clear from Cajander, et al. that this must be understood as the full range of stakeholders' *needs.* They add breadth to sociodigital worth systems by considering user health and well-being. Cajander and co-authors note that such breadth is *not new*, especially as regards values in work systems. Scandinavian research has a strong track record here, but what is *not new* are *discussions* about *relations* (associations). However, the aim with worth-centered approaches is to go beyond the scholarly and politically engaged discussions in such information systems' research to create explicit, effective, articulated, and evaluative design and evaluation techniques that can create and maintain a focus on value throughout development. Good intentions need effective support beyond user participation to encourage and support accountability for how intended worth is communicated, envisaged, and evaluated.

Worth motivates, but some usage consequences *demotivate*. Poor health from poorly designed systems is something to which all should be *averse*. Part 3 authors rightly cover *aversion* as well as positive value, and thus add to the *balance* of worth system inspection. If we merely focus on the positive, we will not consider negative factors that can degrade and even destroy the achievable worth of a digital product or service.

In the laddering approach adapted by Cockton, worth and aversion both result from *associations* between product attributes, usage consequences and the value systems of individuals and organizations. *Means-end chains* connect attributes, consequence and value in a hierarchy of associations. Positive consequences support value systems. Negative consequences undermine them. *Worth spread* reflects the extent to which usage consequences connect with personal values. Part 3 chapters explore worth relationships between product attributes, usage consequences, and (when well-spread) value systems. In the case of development worth, two products are in focus: the software/media system under development/production, and the usability methods that aim to add value to the development/production process. By focusing on these methods' attributes, and the costs and consequences of their use, Part 3 authors argue for new potential development worth systems from maturing usability.

Cockton's worth systems are now used to structure this review of Part 3, first considering *usage worth systems* and next *development worth systems*. For each, in terms of the laddering constructs used to structure W/AMs, authors draw attention to product attributes, usage consequences, and impacted values. Authors' positions are now reviewed in these terms.

16.4.1 Usage Worth and Usability

A system is worth using if it delivers value to users and stakeholders (especially system sponsors). Thackera (2000) quotes Bill Buxton's reminder that "usable is not a value; useful is a value." Usability is a means to an end, not an end in itself. Usability is thus an enabler, which alone cannot deliver useful functionality. However, laddering approaches may not even regard *useful* as a value. Whatever is useful in terms of functional consequences in the world may only be a means to an end. Thus in Cockton's chapter, Figure 13.1 shows that useful functional consequences of instant messaging are not ends in themselves, but means to more psychosocial ends, including personal values such as *social affiliation* and educational or job *success*.

User value can be increased by strengthening associations at any point in a usage means-end chain. Most usability approaches generalize specific interaction difficulties to some measure of usability. Disappointing measures are explained in terms of user interaction with concrete product attributes. Similarly, design change recommendations address (groups of related) concrete attributes. Measures are rarely made at the level of usage consequences or human value. The assumption is that improvements in interaction will automatically translate into improved usage consequences and value, but this may not be the case. Much wider attention to a *worth subsystem* (a substructure of a W/AM rooted in a group of concrete attributes) may be required. This requires approaches that go beyond existing usability and even emerging user experience measures.

16.4.1.1 Impact on Value

In the early days of HCI, usability had intrinsic value. Only rarely did usability studies look beyond usage to the morning after the interaction before. Rosenbaum lists only one early HCI measure that has any hint of achieved value: *product acceptance analysis*. However, Sikorski reminds us that all interactive systems are part of a value chain. It is only by expanding measures to span this whole chain (worth spread) that usability can fully embrace value up to the level of life goals and drives (and let's be clear, life goals and on-line task goals are rarely in the same existential league). Sikorski also rightly observes that user interfaces and usability are necessary but not sufficient to attract e-commerce customers. E-commerce sites must provide *value* for the *customer*, not just *satisfaction* for the user. Online content and services must provide economic value for customers, and business value for vendors. In e-commerce at least, motivations and behaviors are economically based, and customer perceived value follows from pre-existing motivations.

Sikorski covers several metrics that matter to businesses. Most are instrumental—that is, they are a means to higher business ends in the context of specific strategies (ubiquitous as some of these are): customer retention, customer satisfaction, switch barriers, the mutual benefit of relationship, competitive advantage, and reduced operating costs. Usability matters to online businesses when it has a positive or negative impact on these key indicators. Usability measures must be related to these indicators *before* summative user testing commences. Only then can usability and user interface improvements be related to business strategy. The aim here is, in terms of Cockton's worth maps, to shift the center of gravity up, towards positive values and away from negative aversions. This can be achieved via Aschmoneit and Heitmann's (2003) holistic approaches as reviewed in Cockton's chapter. Sikorski's controlled strategic transitions correspond closely to Aschmoneit and Heitmann's approaches, which either strengthen weak associations in a means-end chain or add product attributes and/or new associations, resulting in a better worth system.

Cockton uses the *balanced score card* (BSC) approach as an example of how business strategy drives sponsor worth, not only for commercial business, but also for noncommercial services such as e-government. Similarities between business and bureaucratic strategies are made starkly clear by Cajander, et al., who expose an imbalance in BSC. While internal business processes get attention, as do organizational learning and growth, employee welfare is not foregrounded. Although high sickness and absenteeism rates do not help internal business processes or organizational learning, employee health could be more prominent. In this approach to strategy, job-design principles are ignored in favor of customer quality. IT departments (but not always organizational management) value automation, efficiency, control, and surveillance, and are averse to the need for judgement in decision-making and the corresponding respect for individuals. Other work values are ignored in these IT settings: user satisfaction, wellbeing, and (surprisingly) productivity. Design purpose here should be aligned with work purpose, but instead IT departments are drawn to quality in systems approaches that treat performance means as organizational ends, and in the process, may undermine organizational purpose. This clearly demonstrates the need to relate all system's measures, usability included, to sponsor purpose. Only then can misguided IT departments be weaned off technological utopias that depend on a belief in magic (Cockton 2004).

Table 16.1 shows Rokeach's Instrumental and Terminal Values (i.e., what people can strive for as right ways to behave and right life goals, respectively). *Health* (physical and mental well-being) and *Helpful* (working for the welfare of others) are both listed as common human values (at least for 1960s middle class America), but neither are respected in Cajander's case studies (Cajander, et al.). One

Table 16.1 Rokeach's Lists of Values (LOV, Rokeach 1973)

Terminal Values	Instrumental Values
A Comfortable Life *a prosperous life*	Ambitious *hardworking and aspiring*
Equality, *brotherhood and equal opportunity for all*	Broad-minded *open-minded*
An Exciting Life *a stimulating, active life*	Capable *competent; effective*
Family Security *taking care of loved ones*	Clean *neat and tidy*
Freedom *independence and free choice*	Courageous *standing up for your beliefs*
Health *physical and mental well-being*	Forgiving *willing to pardon others*
Inner Harmony *freedom from inner conflict*	Helpful *working for the welfare of others*
Mature Love *sexual and spiritual intimacy*	Honest *sincere and truthful*
National Security *protection from attack*	Imaginative *daring and creative*
Pleasure *an enjoyable, leisurely life*	Independent *self-reliant; self-sufficient*
Salvation *saved; eternal life*	Intellectual *intelligent and reflective*
Self-Respect *self-esteem*	Logical *consistent rational*
A Sense of Accomplishment *a lasting contribution*	Loving *affectionate and tender*
Social Recognition *respect and admiration*	Loyal *faithful to friends or the group*
True Friendship *close companionship*	Obedient *dutiful; respectful*
Wisdom *a mature understanding of life*	Polite *courteous and well-mannered*
A World at Peace *a world free of war and conflict*	Responsible *dependable and reliable*
A World of Beauty *beauty of nature and the arts*	Self-controlled *restrained; self-disciplined*

approach to *Value Spread Extension* proposed by Cockton is the use of such lists (here, Rokeach's LOV) to highlight overlooked values in vertical apexes of worth maps. Sikorski similarly (albeit implicitly) considers consumers' values, such as *A Comfortable Life, An Exciting Life, Freedom,* and *Pleasure,* and e-commerce vendor instrumental values such as *Clean, Honest,* and *Imaginative.* Cockton's W/AMs contain examples similar to *Capable, Helpful, Honest, Imaginative, Polite, Responsible* (all instrumental values relevant to brands), *A Sense of Accomplishment, Social Recognition* and *True Friendship* (terminal values of customers and managers).

16.4.1.2 Product Attributes

Some usability and interaction design approaches focus exclusively on associations between concrete product attributes (e.g., breadcrumbs on websites) and abstract product attributes (e.g., ease of navigation). This is essentially a *quality in the system* approach, because it constructs a quality model with elements such as *navigability* over specific design features. Sikorski argues credibly that *quality in use* is far more important than *quality in the system* from the user's viewpoint, even though user interface quality "affects perceived quality of an interactive product." Such quality must minimally be evaluated through interaction. However, for cross platform offerings, customer perceptions of quality must be equally positive and consistent across channels. Cockton's van-hire example illustrates this. Sikorski further argues that information content must deliver actual value. Cockton's university and van-hire examples illustrate this. Thus, while Sikorski notes that consumers may choose digital sales channels that have exceptionally pleasant operation, and are most efficient, cost effective, comfortable or safest, this is not enough.

Table 14.2 in Sikorski illustrates how the route from productivity to value is dependent on constant expansion of concrete service attributes, and not by merely continuous improvement of usability measures. Furthermore, predicting *good enough* usability targets is absolutely dependent on alternatives, and the possibility and cost of switching to these alternatives. Thus, effective associations for *acceptable* interaction will form below the thresholds of usability ideals, due to limited time resources that force early judgements on expected subjective utility. It is not enough to track these associations during development. Rosenbaum highlights a trend from development usability measures towards constant operational evaluation. Neither quality in system nor quality in interaction approaches can cope with changing contexts of user choice that quickly erode confidence in the reliability of summative evaluation metrics taken during development.

16.4.1.3 Usage Consequences

Cockton introduces laddering concepts of *functional* and *psychosocial* consequences to HCI, although these are very close to Hassenzahl's (2002) *pragmatic* and *hedonistic quality*, respectively. However, neither properly capture the notion of economic consequences, suggesting that a wider range of consequence categories is needed. Also, the relations between consequences are not unidirectional. A stereotypical laddering relationship is often assumed, with functional consequences prior to psychosocial ones in means-end chains. Sikorski provides examples of both directions. In the stereotyped relationship, emotional attitudes to brands, transaction safety, and security are often formed on the basis of some limited awareness of functional consequences. In an inverse relationship, experienced discomforts may signal future problems with service quality. Here, a psychosocial consequence can lead to a functional consequence of abandoning a website, never to return.

Whatever the categories and their relations, consequences beyond interaction are not a central focus in usability practice. When Gould and Lewis (1985) advocated empirical measurement, they clarified it as "actual behavioral measurements of learnability and usability," with "performance, thoughts and attitudes" being recorded and analyzed. However, such measures are properly part of investigations of associations between concrete and abstract product attributes. They are not consequences of usage, but instead attributes of it. For Sikorski, important consequences, such as willingness to finalize transactions, depend only in minor part on impact of usability and the user interface.

Sikorski notes the importance of interaction attributes such as emotional involvement and the co-experience of social interaction. However, he concentrates more on true consequences of usage that are more appropriate measures of *quality in value*: customer loyalty, perceived quality, perceived credibility, cost of using relative to obtained results, doubts about security and trust, negative opinions expressed to others, and reduced attractiveness in the market.

Sikorski also draws attention to a further drawback of *quality in use* evaluations, in that the abstract attributes of a website, even when mediated by user interaction, will most strongly influence consumer behavior when these constitute a unique experience (Table 14.1, Part 1). Once similar alternatives are added to the user's choice menu (Cockton 2006), the positive advantages of formerly unique interaction quality are reduced, but negative qualities may be foregrounded, forcing a shift of loyalty to a new site. The advantage of value-centered approaches to evaluation is that they recognize that value and choice are inseparable, and thus what becomes and stays worthwhile depends on what is being offered. Hence quality must improve over time, otherwise competitive advantage may be lost. Appropriate measures here for Sikorski are increasing visits to good B2C sites, increased trust and confidence, higher expenditures, and more profitable relationships. This mix of functional, economic, and psychosocial consequences sits in the middle of means-end chains from product attributes to personal and organizational values. Such long-lasting positive user experiences reinforces positive attitudes to vendors, and require psychosocial consequences of delight and surprise.

Cajander and colleagues note existing usability standards' suggested impact measures. ISO9241 Part 11 suggests rates of absenteeism and health problem reports as measures of user satisfaction, but it provides no basis for associating system design and operation with user well-being. Usability concepts are too tied to the moment of interaction, and thus do "not provide sufficient support for addressing users' health concerns in systems development." Instead, abstract attributes of work systems, rather than human-computer interaction, need to be measured, with thresholds set for acceptable limits of control and required levels of support for users. Waiting for ill health indicators is to wait too long.

Sikorski's examples illustrate the primacy of service design over interaction design. Cajander and co-authors do the same for work design. Users did not find systems unusable, but *useless*. Work system design had not taken into account the sensitivity of case loads. It deskilled and made activity routine, removed choice, and blocked flexibility in work decisions because it sought automation as an end in itself. An action research approach evaluated the outcomes of intervention actions and measurement. Their IT user index has been effective, but not all desired and adverse consequences could be readily translated into metrics.

16.4.1.4 A Research Agenda for Usage Worth Systems

Rosenbaum's chapter reminds us of Gould and Lewis' (1985) advocated focus on users and tasks. In reality, the focus was often on tasks with some window dressing of user profiles. Not until personas became commonplace did personal values and motives begin to receive routine attention in interaction design and evaluation. Cultural HCI also brings values centerstage. As a result, worth-centered research requires a wider range of foundations than existing HCI research.

Rosenbaum identifies closer relations between marketing and usability as essential to the latter's maturity, having co-facilitated a workshop in 2006 on "Overlapping Usability and Market Research—Synergies and Issues." The usability community can do much more to advance this relationship. Sikorski notes that critical interaction factors shaping user behavior for online services are rarely included in HCI studies. For marketing, they are of central interest, but this extensive literature is seldom referenced in HCI. Sikorski suggests that existing marketing methods may readily transfer to HCI. Cockton's use of laddering approaches from consumer psychology provides some support for this, and Sikorski's view that future applications of economics and marketing in HCI seem inevitable is very plausible.

Worth maps provide a framework for a new HCI research agenda. Moving through means-ends chains, initial associations between concrete and abstract product attributes are already well-covered. Such associations are at the heart of *quality in system* approaches that build quality models from hierarchies of abstract product attributes such as learnability, understandability, operability, and attractiveness (ISO 9126). However, such hierarchies are *not* empirically derived from usage data, but rather expert opinion—generally that of software engineers. The HCI community, with its foundations in Gould and Lewis's (1985) three principles of user/task focus, empirical measurement, and iteration cannot endorse such quality models. Quality in use approaches are required to demonstrate how associations between concrete and abstract attributes actually occur in practice. Such associations lie at the heart of most experimental HCI research and usability practice. However, in a worth-centered approach, the qualities and measures of abstract attributes must be located in a worth subsystem to indicate what matters and why. As a result, a narrow focus on associations between concrete and abstract product attributes needs to be abandoned in favor of experiments and tests on worth subsystems. We need to move away from a narrow focus on arbitrary collections of abstract attributes (qualities) as dependent variables or evaluation metrics.

At the value apexes of worth maps, we need to derive HCI methods from a range of disciplines. Economics, marketing, and consumer psychology have already been mentioned. Sikorski also includes quality function deployment, and Cockton suggests approaches to *value spread extension* as a *worth inspection method*. One approach is the use of lists such as Table 16.1, but a wider range of approaches is needed, including cultural and sociological approaches that *read* the values *inscribed* in cultural forms and social behaviors (Cockton 2006).

The poles of means-end chains are relatively well-understood. Engineers understand technology, while the arts, humanities, and human sciences understand human value. Design is faced with the difficult challenge of forging the means-end chains between these poles of technical capabilities and human worth. This is a new research area, although it may be possible to borrow some ideas from existing HCI approaches such as *design rationale* and *claims* (Carroll and Moran 1996). Novel techniques and methods here will contribute to both user and development worth, and are thus discussed at the end of the next section on development worth.

We thus endorse Sikorski's position that we must "expand the workbench of HCI research towards investigating the economic backgrounds of user behavior ... in part from marketing research, in part from quality management, and also from consumer behavior studies." Such borrowing must be followed through with in-depth validations.

16.4.2 Product/Service Development and Usability

Usage worth is always development worth in the sense that more valuable digital products and services are designed and implemented. Of course, this achieved worth will be undermined if development costs are increased to the extent that *user value* comes at the expense of *business value*. Ensuring the business value of usability activities is thus critical to widespread adoption, not only for commercial vendors, but also for voluntary and political institutions, and even individuals and community groups. The bottom line is that time and energy spent on evaluation must bring sufficient compensation *for the developer* to justify investing in usability practices. Leading usability practitioners have long recognized this, and it is a privilege to be able to share Stephanie Rosenbaum's outstanding experience as a usability practitioner.

Rosenbaum notes that development organizations are at different levels of maturity, and thus we cannot expect all to adopt leading edge usability practice. Rosenbaum charts the evolution of the latter from the early days when the credibility of formal psychology experiments was essential. This was before the point (identified by Cockton) at which the dependent variables of classic usability cut loose from experimental independent variables. In the beginning, usability was largely a question of measurement without conjecture, but this is now changed by the blurring of roles within user experience teams. Rosenbaum reports: "In some Silicon Valley companies, practitioners work one year in user research, another year in design." Her own staff now sometimes combine design and evaluation, a trend that one editor's experience also confirms. In such contexts, measurement can no longer be disinterested. The need to test out the effectiveness of design decisions can only improve the focus of usability evaluation. Benefits are thus increased, but costs reduce through less need to explain and justify usability procedures to wholly technical developers and skeptical management.

Usability people can thus now *do more*, but not only as individuals. Rosenbaum rightly notes the collective value stored in tools, networks, and professional communities. Value now lies less in individual practitioners and methods, but in team application of integrated methods.

16.4.2.1 Impact on Value

Development worth is inevitably increased by focusing evaluation towards the vertical apexes of worth maps, which may be values or usage consequences depending on the extent of value spread. Achieved value depends primarily on development teams. They are responsible for the interventions that are meant to improve human achievements and experiences through design innovation. The development team in this context includes all sponsor stakeholder roles responsible for integrating technical systems into work, service, and other contexts. Together, technical, sponsor management, and other stakeholder roles must have a clear view of intended value. Without this, there can be no design or evaluation focus on achievable or achieved value.

Cajander and colleagues thus rightly draw attention to the Standish Group's Chaos Report identification of the need for "clear directives and a consensus on a project's objectives." Achieving quality in value means achieving objectives, in so far as these objectives are themselves worthwhile in breadth, balance, and spread. Cajander and colleagues' chapter shows that this may not be the case. Development teams' values can be narrow, with a strong focus on automation, efficiency, and surveillance of work. External drivers may be given as the reason for these values, but they reflect the bureaucratic values that characterize formal institutions.

Some stakeholders interviewed by Cajander and colleagues appear to be unable to influence IT project objectives: *different wills* were at work, turning means (performance measures) into ends, but perhaps also making IT systems ends in themselves through belief systems that locate quality in systems. Even when design purpose is based on a more extensive spread of intended value, Cajander and co-authors remind us that development worth can be undermined in other ways, such as with poor choice of stakeholder representatives. So too can insistence on rigid engineering-oriented work modeling misrepresent the true nature of work to be supported by a new IT system. Similarly, Rosenbaum identifies difficulties in implementing logging for Web-based systems with separate development and server maintenance teams. Also, Hornbæk notes that the creativity he seeks as a quality of evaluation will be repressed by unmanageable workloads.

The effectiveness of usability work will always be shaped by the development context. Mutual adaptation and consideration is required. While usability processes must fit the development context, if the latter makes no concessions to the former, it cannot expect to gain much of any worth. Quality of evaluation approaches is not the sole determinant of quality in value. If system sponsors (official or *de facto* in the case of some IT departments) do not value human well-being and related positive work values, then usability practitioners face a massive challenge in bringing in these concerns *under the radar*. However, even when system sponsors are in control and have committed to breadth, balance, and spread in intended worth, usability specialists may not have measures available to establish the corresponding achieved work. For Cockton, this is because evaluation measures have remained fixed within the scope of task performance and satisfaction metrics, and thus can not directly address value. Rosenbaum's examples support this.

Stagnation in measurement approaches is understandable because, for much of the first two decades of usability, practitioners had to focus on psychosocial consequences associated with trust in the usability process. Thus, in Rosenbaum's 1990s real-world example, usability evaluations were part of a change management process that aimed at broad stakeholder buy-in. The focus was on *user concerns* and thus qualitative data was gathered through contextual enquiry. The study was part of a remedial process to *fix* a business-critical tool. It was not evaluation as part of an initial development project. There is an important point here that guides development of Rosenbaum's argument. Usability's value does not lie in doing *good* usability with reference to predefined intrinsic standards. The value of usability lies in the worth that it brings to stakeholders, with system sponsors, users, and developers most important in most contexts. As Rosenbaum details towards the end of her chapter, this is highly dependent on the product context—for example, whether it is a mature product, and extent of understanding of current usage risks and difficulties.

Sensitivity to organizational culture, especially product development needs and priorities, is now extended to sensitivity to a range of cultures (mostly national for Rosenbaum's examples). Even so, measures of cultural acceptance must be measures of value, because values are a defining feature, and in some ways *the* driving feature in cultural differences. Cultures vary in their preferred and rejected behaviors and cultural forms (buildings, cuisine, fashion, art, music, etc.). Such preferences and rejections are expressions of values and aversions. A greater focus on culture will thus force *usability* approaches into consideration of *quality in value*.

It is not enough to add new measures to *the activity formerly known as usability*. Such measures in themselves have no intrinsic value. Two decades of inertia on usability metrics have caused further challenges by entrenching a view of usability as defect identification. Hornbæk rightly argues that the value of evaluation cannot be wholly based on the quantity of defects identified, especially when almost all may already be known to the development team. At the most, independent discovery may validate and legitimize what the development team already believes, and thus enable a response. However, this is really a very expensive antidote to denial by project management, which, if very strong, will remain obdurate in the face of page after page of usability problem reports.

Hornbæk relocates the value of evaluation in the range of ideas it generates, not only about product defects, but about users and possible design changes. Recommended measures remain quantitative for much of the chapter, but later on quantity is acknowledged to not be the main quality attribute. Hornbæk's proposals come close to addressing Cockton's *total iteration potential*. Here, we assess evaluation methods not only for their contributions to defect identification, casual analysis, or design change recommendation, but also to further user research and evaluation strategies, and even to reshape design purpose. This contributes both facts and ideas, with the former hopefully guiding formation of the latter. Rosenbaum provides examples of such broader usability outputs—for example, improvements to training and stronger product insights. However, Hornbæk is correct in noting that such a broader view of usability has not been a focus in evaluation method work, which has largely concentrated on defect identification, followed by the *downstream utility* of design change recommendation. Evaluation can and should support more than just the iteration of designs. Every belief, assumption, and plan within development should be open to challenge, at least in the early stages of design when changes are cheapest.

16.4.2.2 Method Quality: The Attributes of Usability Approaches

Design as the *creation of value* requires that products be created with concrete and abstract attributes that begin means-ends chains to intended value. In the case of creating development worth, there are two objects of design. The worth of one, the designed sociodigital system, was addressed above. The other object of design is the evaluation process itself. It is through changes to the concrete and abstract attributes of usability methods and techniques, and in the attributes of their application, that development worth is increased. For example, Rosenbaum gives examples of alternative *method* bundles that her company offers to prospective clients. Here, value results from particular combinations of methods, rather than from the specific attributes of each method. Through careful combination, methods can compensate for individual shortcomings and amplify individual contributions.

Another important trend reported by Rosenbaum is the shift to operational evaluation—that is, a focus on evaluation of released products as opposed to ones under development. This frees usability work from the time constraints of development and release schedules that would often severely limit usability activities. It also allows more time for causal analysis, careful derivation, and discussion of design changes. Rosenbaum observes how new evaluation instruments, especially embedded logging in call-centers and Web servers allow associations to be continuously measured. However, Rosenbaum cautions us that data from logging is often inadequate for causal analysis. Furthermore, such logging often preserves long-standing measures from early usability that may not be worthwhile in specific product and service contexts. Logging is not the same as Cockton's *direct instrumentation*, which applies to complete worth subsystems, and not just to interaction with a technical system. Cockton's van-hire and university examples illustrate how instrumenting a Web server alone would not be enough to evaluate achieved value. Even so, increasing use of logging has led to other valuable developments, such as optimizing prototypes for measurement by developing a range of instrumented prototypes to focus on different groups of measures (Rosenbaum). Such value-adding would not be possible without the expansion of usability roles beyond testing and field work.

Bundling, timing and instrumentation are *attributes of application*. For much of usability's short history, these have been improved to increase development worth, but there has been relatively little change to methods and measures. For example, the measures used on Rosenbaum's second example of recent large-sample testing would not have looked out of place in a 1980s user test. They supported a commissioned comparison with a competing product, and thus were able to deliver value for the client. However, users may not attach the same value to these measures. In Rosenbaum's field study for Sun Microsystems, time on task mattered most for system usage as part of a phone call. For other usages, measures of effectiveness (of information and time management, of monitoring and problem resolution) were more important. Rosenbaum rightly states that experienced practitioners know how to make the right choices of measures for contexts, but once simple standard measures become unsuitable, practice must often fall back on opportunistic use of qualitative data. Cockton argues that by aligning evaluation planning with design purpose, the need for such non-standard measures can be identified early enough to let appropriate instruments be designed and debugged.

The main change in usability methods has been the development of *contextual inquiry* (Whiteside, et al. 1988). This has been highly successful, despite Cockton's observation that hoped-for changes in measures did not occur for at least a decade. Whiteside, Bennett and Holtzblatt recognized that laboratory measures were for specified goals, and not what "users really want." Contextual inquiry and subsequent ethnographic methods have resulted in improved understanding of user goals, but this has not been translated into evaluation methods that systematically establish how well these goals are being met, especially within the wider contexts of work and leisure that furnish the *root motivations* that determine worth. Instead, field methods still largely identify *defects* as misfits between technology usage and required work (Cockton 2004). However, they can better identify the origin of misfits, and thus better support causal analysis and identification of potential effective changes. Furthermore, Rosenbaum notes that field methods provide more relevant and accurate data, and thus more valuable information.

Rosenbaum's two case studies sit on *either side* of the introduction of contextual inquiry and reflect the shift from fixed task-based measures to observations of realistic usage. In laddering terms, the details of usability methods are *concrete attributes*, while the quality of their results are *abstract attributes*. Field methods are regarded as more realistic and broader in scope, going beyond *out-of-the-box* usage problems to persistent usage difficulties, which can be prioritized by severity ratings that reflect the true value that can be achieved through using a software application. When used to support sponsor's development objectives, field methods deliver broader value than previous laboratory testing. They are, however, far better suited to formative than summative evaluation. Rosenbaum notes how field research has to be reported via story-telling, ostensibly because video recording may be impossible, but also they have no equivalent to metric summaries associated with formal user testing.

Rosenbaum's closing sections note the emergence at last of new measures, as *usability* work focuses more on ethics and emotion, with trust and enjoyment figuring prominently alongside an increasing focus on cultural differences. This further increases the development worth of usability by increasing the breadth and spread of evaluation data.

Further *abstract attributes* of methods relate to costs. Rosenbaum's condensations of field methods has made then more appropriate in terms of costs, as well as more effective in terms of benefits. Value is determined by both parts of a cost-benefit equation, requiring attention to both investment and compensation. Cajander and co-authors' use of mind maps may thus reduce costs when analyzing field data.

A further cost-benefit consideration is the extent of risk in a technique. Rosenbaum is keen on Microsoft's RITE method, because it can reduce risk by the *self-evaluative* consequences of its rapid iterations. These effectively evaluate the quality of previous defect identification, causal analysis, and design changes. This ability to rapidly *fix fixes* reduces risk and thereby increases benefits for a low increase in cost.

A method (bundle) may not be applicable in a particular technical development context. Rosenbaum notes that rapid technical innovation threatens the worth of existing methods. Unless these can evolve, or be complemented by new methods, the key abstract attribute of *applicability* will be so restricted that practitioners have close to no choice in method selection, undoing the progress of the last two decades.

On a positive note, Hornbæk outlines a range of ways to extend the abstract attributes of evaluation methods beyond a simple count of identified defects. He broadens the output of evaluation methods to *ideas*,—some "useful and novel ... about how to improve the usability of the product," but advising that it is "not the case that all output from an evaluation need[s] to be original/novel." He reviews the creativity literature for new quality attributes for evaluation. For example, *paradigm modification* could have positive or negative valence depending on its implications for the development team. Hornbæk gives us several ways of thinking about the quality of evaluation methods, but as with existing methods, we must remember that the actual impact is heavily dependent on the overall behavior and attitudes of the development team. Thus, overuse of consensus in idea evaluation could lead to a loss of potential value.

Hornbæk's discussion of consensus is one example of a search for the "active ingredients in usability evaluation methods." Research here is still at a very early stage, and there are potential synergies with existing creativity research. For example, the creativity method of *progressive abstraction* is very similar to difficulty generalization in the SUPEX method (Cockton & Lavery 1999). Such *ingredients* are the concrete attributes of evaluation methods, which become *active* through enabling associations with abstract attributes (quality attributes of evaluation methods—e.g., *abstractness*). Expertise in method use must clearly shape these associations, but Hornbæk notes that evaluation method research has yet to study leading individual experts, unlike other areas of creativity where such studies are common. These could investigate Hornbæk's loyal claim that "usability professionals develop more useful solutions that developers and designers are less likely to have considered."

Hornbæk identifies *wishful thinking* as a further attribute of evaluation methods, especially ones that deliver more than lists of usability problems. However, active ingredients may include the development team, who, for example, may be inspired even if they reject reasoning for reported problems or recommended redesign proposals. Either may be valued for approaches that "they themselves had not imagined" (Hornbæk). Here, *novelty* is an important method quality.

16.4.2.3 Usage Consequences

Development worth improves as evaluation is more able to contribute to a wider range of development activities. By drawing on work on creativity, Hornbæk increases the chances of delivering new consequences of method usage.

The key usage consequences of method usage concern the responses of the whole development team. Currently, adverse psychosocial consequences are common. Usability is seen as vague (Cajander, et al.), costly and time consuming, especially for Web development and release cycles (Rosenbaum). Hornbæk stresses that usability outputs must be understandable, otherwise further adverse consequences will follow.

Conversely, some usage consequences increase the value of usability practice. Rosenbaum provides several examples, including prior heuristic evaluation, which reduces the cost and increases the benefit of user testing. Even greater savings arise from reuse of existing well-structured usability data from field observations and testing.

Reducing costs will increase value for money, but overall value can be further increased by Hornbæk's broadening of downstream utility beyond a simple count of effective design changes. Thus the *metaphors of thinking* inspection method (Hornbæk & Frøkjær 2004) is designed to stimulate thinking, generate insight, and break fixed conceptions. The intention is not simply to find more problems, but to increase the creative contribution to the next iteration.

Usability outputs begin means-end chains for iterative development. What is ultimately achieved depends on how contributions are received, worked with, and acted on. Hornbæk thus sees developer *appreciation* as an important psychosocial consequence, but one with a range of different impacts. Group activities involving the whole development team can have a range of outcomes. Thus the three *stages* in RITE (Is it a problem? Do we understand it? Can we fix it?) could be structured by de Bono's Six Thinking Hats, which Hornbæk reorients for usability usage.

Worthwhile *results* from usability should thus have the further consequence of increased developer trust and buy-in, but both need to be actively managed. Methods alone are unlikely to maintain either. Associations in means-end chains mask complex human activities and interdependencies that are rarely a simple single cause-event sequence.

16.4.2.4 A Research Agenda for Development Worth from Usability

Hornbæk's move to more creative evaluation methods adds further disciplinary inputs to usability. He surveys a wide range of creativity methods that provide better access to novel ideas.

As with usage worth, a research agenda for development worth can be based on worth maps. Relevant values for developers and sponsors can be *read* from a range of existing resources such as business strategy and the sociology of institutions (Cockton 2006). Such sources need to be integrated and adapted to provide worth-centered development tools.

Associations between concrete and abstract attributes are already the domain of usability method assessment. Research approaches here need to be transferred and adopted for the assessment of new evaluation methods, which must be developed to cope with the radical changes in worth systems arising from technical innovation (product attributes), design innovation (product consequences), and market innovation (product value).

Process designers must forge links from method attributes to development worth. Practice-based research is needed to track the associations from methods to value that are formed in development context. Leading-edge method assessment has already made the transition from laboratory to field studies, with useful results. Some chapters in Part 2 cover such new approaches. However, we need far more work looking at method use in context. Closer collaboration between researchers and experienced practitioners such as Stephanie Rosenbaum is vital to delivering worth from such studies. A range of development contexts need to be studied, from HCI deserts to HCI-rich organizations. We must avoid overgeneralizations from one development context to another. Method usage consequences are tightly coupled to development contexts. The same method bundles can perform well in one context, but not another. We need to research the means-end associations here in a way that avoids simple cause-effect assumptions that pour too much blame on either the method or the development context.

16.4.3 Summary: Value and the Retreat of Usability

Hornbæk's and Rosenbaum's chapters illustrate how hard it is to remain loyal to usability as an umbrella concept. Hornbæk gets drawn into a *category mistake* (Ryle 1949) by expecting a measuring instrument (evaluation) to provide diagnosis (causal analysis) and treatment (design change recommendations). If this is evaluation, then what is left for *iteration*? In medicine, we would never expect a thermometer to diagnose and prescribe, so why should usability evaluations methods be any different? Clearly, it is very important to maximize the iteration potential of evaluation methods, but in the process they will no longer be pure evaluation methods. Note the name of RITE, *Rapid Iterative Testing and Evaluation*, which clearly identifies it as an evaluation-iteration hybrid.

Hornbæk gets caught between the ideals and realities of usability evaluation. The ideal has the goal of usability evaluation "to make software better," but clearly, current evaluation methods are not up to the task, and will not be as long as they remain evaluation methods. However, towards the end of his chapter, Hornbæk observes that creativity techniques could "complement the defect-identification view,"—i.e., the reality of much usability practice.

We are left with a dilemma. Either we accept the narrow view of usability, and thus limit its worth and require substantial additional resources for effective iteration, or we extend the scope to the point where it simply does not make sense to call it usability any more. We must resolve the dilemma for usability to mature by choosing between evolution and revolution.

Evolutionary approaches view maturation as incremental improvements that preserve the essence of methods, but improve their quality—for example, validity, thoroughness, applicability (to technologies, application domains, organizational contexts, etc.), reliability, or cost-effectiveness.

Revolutionary approaches recognize that either the essence of existing methods must change, or they must be replaced. The aims, arguments, and examples of all authors in Part 3 suggest that only a revolution in evaluation methods can break out of the usability cocoon and become something that really will fly. In the process, mature usage studies will no longer focus wholly on usability, but then again, butterflies totally ditch their caterpillar youth. Perhaps usability needs to do the same.

When a caterpillar matures, it passes through a dormant period in a cocoon before emerging as a butterfly. Although the butterfly is clearly a mature caterpillar, it bears no resemblance to its former stage. Similarly, the maturation of usability may not be a route to a bigger and better caterpillar with even more legs and segments, able to travel further more quickly and eat more. Instead, usability may emerge lighter, more agile and more nimble, far more attractive, and like any mature organism, fertile. In an alternative analogy, a mature usability can better fit into adult society to take a full role in contributing to the greater good. Either way, life either side of maturation is significantly different. Maturity has nothing to do with being a better caterpillar or child. It is about becoming something that either is currently not, with capabilities that may literally dwarf infant abilities. Delivering value is such a capability.

Usability began as applied cognitive psychology, but has become an ever broadening interdisciplinary mix drawing on more major areas of psychology (e.g., emotion, attitudes, motivation, self-regulation, personality, identity) as well as sociology, economics, business and marketing. Given this, the continued use of the term *usability* becomes less and less credible. The ultimate evidence of usability's maturity may well be a change of name. One possibility is to subsume usability within *user experience*, a practice already adopted by some of the world's largest in-house usability groups. However, this remains locked in *quality in interaction*. Life is not ephemeral. Good and bad endure. We must spread out from the usability of the moment to focus on lasting worth.

16.5 Research Agenda for Maturing Usability

The chapter does not aim to provide any panacea for different usability issues. Instead, we identify potential areas that are worthwhile to explore and will eventually contribute to the maturation of this relatively young but significant domain.

The foregoing discussions elaborate on various research issues to be addressed in the future. Here, we recapitulate the key points from each of the three parts as a quick reference.

Part 1 – Quality in Software:

- Cost savings of using a model-driven architecture (MDA)
- Forming guidelines and anti-patterns as the driving force for model transformation
- An independent comparison of an MDA-generated user interface and an expertly built one
- Synchronization of quality engineering and software development processes in teams and organizations of different resources—e.g., size of teams, experience and skills, and application contexts
- Economics of quality engineering, especially for usability
- Mapping between abstract models and concrete ones—e.g., prototypes
- Identifying types of requirements suitable to express in different classes of models and how to ensure practical consistency between them
- Avoiding expertise segregation, embedding it throughout the whole software development
- Levels of skills and specialization needed of usability in agile software development teams
- Investigating combination of user-testing and model-based evaluations
- Reliability of multimodal systems

Part 2 – Quality in Interaction

- The applicability of existing UEMs for evaluating emerging social software
- The roles of HCI theories in addressing issues related to design and evaluation of new-generation interactive systems—amassing different theories may not be an appropriate resolution
- The design and evaluation of personalized interactive systems, addressing users' dynamic needs and goals with a range of potential technical solutions
- The accommodation of two paradigms—quantifiable performance versus indeterminate aesthetics—with innovative methodologies
- Boundary conditions for qualifying variants of established research and evaluation methodologies as valid
- The necessity and utility of software standards to be verified by experience reports and case studies
- Systematic return-on-investment (ROI) analysis of remote usability evaluation methods, in particular, and the persuasiveness of results of ROI analysis for usability, in general
- Automating the evaluation of multimodal user interfaces seems necessary but not sufficient to streamline the resource-demanding, complex process involved

Part 3 – Quality in Value

- Worth maps and worth-centered approach advocate embedding abstract qualities and their measures in a worth subsystem to indicate what matters and why
- Derivation of new HCI methods such as *worth inspection methods* from a range of disciplines, including economics, marketing, consumer psychology, cultural and sociological approaches, enabling identification of values
- Design as a challenge of forging means-end chains between technical capabilities at one pole and human worth at the other pole entails novel techniques and methods
- Creative evaluation methods provide further disciplinary inputs to usability
- Worth-centered development tools entail adaptation and integration of a range of existing resources, such as business strategy and the sociology of institutions
- Development of new evaluation methods to cope with radical changes in worth systems arising from technical innovation (product attributes), design innovation (product consequences), and market innovation (product value)
- Practice-based research to track the associations from methods to value that are formed in the development context: a range of development contexts with tightly coupled method usage consequences need to be studied to avoid overgeneralizations or simple cause-effect assumptions
- Resolution of the dilemma between the evolutionary view and the revolutionary view of usability; the former tends to preserve existing methods, while the latter tends to replace them

As pointed out earlier, this green paper aims to inspire and invite more input from interested individuals and organizations. The editors, as authors of this chapter, have raised more questions than we can answer now. Like usability testing, this green paper will undergo several iterations of evaluation and revision, with its final content being eventually realized as empirical projects that drive the field of usability towards maturation.

References

Abrahamsson, P., Warsta, J., Siponen, M. T., & Ronkainen, J. (2003). New directions on agile methods: a comparative analysis. In *Proc. 25th International Conference on Software Engineering, Portland, Oregon* (pp. 244–254), IEEE.

Aschmoneit, P., & Heitmann, M. (2003). Consumers cognition towards communities: Customer-centred community design using the means-end chain perspective. In *Proc. 36th Hawaii Int. Conf. on System Sciences*. IEEE.

Bass, L., Clements, P., & Kazman, R. (2003) *Software architecture in practice*. Boston, MA: Addison Wesley.

Bass, L., & John, B. (2003). Linking usability to software architecture patterns through general scenarios. *The Journal of Systems and Software, 66*, 187–197

Beaudouin-Lafon, M. (2000). Instrumental interaction: an interaction model for designing post-WIMP user interfaces. In *Proc. CHI 2000* (pp. 446–453).

Bødker, S. (2006). When second wave HCI meets third wave challenges. In *Proceedings of NordiCHI 2006* (pp. 1–8), Oslo, Norway,

Boehm, B. (2002). Get ready for agile methods, with care. *IEEE Computer 35*, 64–69.

Boehm, B. (2006). A view of 20th and 21st century software engineering. In *Proc. ICSE'06* (pp 12–29), Shanghai, China. ACM.

Boehm, B.W., Brown J.R., Lipow, M. (1976). Quantitative evaluation of software quality. In *Proceedings of the Second International Conference on Software Engineering* (pp 592–605), San Francisco, California, United States, IEEE,

Butler, K. (1996). Usability engineering turns 10. *Interactions, 3*, 58–75

Card, S., Moran, T.P., & Newell, A. (1983). *The psychology of human-computer interaction.* Hillsdale, NJ: Lawrence Erlbaum Associates.

Carroll, J., & Moran, T. (1996) *Design rationale: Concepts, techniques, and use.* Hillsdale, NJ: Lawrence Erlbaum Associates

Carroll, J.M., Kellogg, W.A., & Rosson, M.B. (1991). The task-artifact cycle. In J.M. Carroll (Ed.), *Designing interaction: Psychology at the human–computer interface* (pp. 74–102). Cambridge: Cambridge University Press.

Cockton, G. (2004). Value-centred HCI. In A. Hyrskykari (Ed.), *Proc. NordiCHI 2004* (pp. 149–160).

Cockton, G. (2006). Designing worth is worth designing. In A.I. Mørch, K. Morgan, T. Bratteteig, G. Ghosh, & D. Svanæs (Eds.), *Proc. NordiCHI 2006* (pp. 165–174).

Cockton, G., & Lavery, D. (1999). A framework for usability problem extraction. In A. Sasse & C. Johnson (Eds.), *Proc. INTERACT 99* (pp. 347–355).

Cockton, G., & Woolrych, A. (2002). Sale must end: Should discount methods be cleared off HCI's shelves? *Interactions (Sept/Oct)*, 13–18.

Csikszentmihalyi, M. (1997). *Finding flow: The psychology of engagement with everyday life.* New York: Basic Books.

Diaper, D. (2002). Task scenarios and thought. *Interacting with Computers, 14*, 629–638.

Dourish, P. (2006). Implications for design. In *Proceedings of CHI 2006* (pp. 541–550). New York: ACM Press.

Dray, S., Karat,C-M., Rosenberg, D., Siegel, D., & Wixon, D.(2005). Is ROI an effective approach for persuading decision-makers of the value of user-centered design? In *CHI Extended Abstracts 2005*, 1168–1169

Earthy, J. (1998). Usability maturity model: Human centredness scale. INUSE Project deliverable D5.1.4(s). Version 1.2. London, Lloyd's Register of Shipping.

Eickelmann, N., & Hayes, J.H. (2004). New Year's Resolutions for Software Quality. *IEEE Software, 2004*, 12–13

Fiore, S. G. (2004). *Oppressive interactions: Between expression and imagination.* Paper presented at the CHI2004 Conference W18 Workshop, Vienna, Austria

Firesmith, D. (2003). Using quality models to engineer quality requirements. *Journal of Object Technology, 2(5)*, 67–75

Folmer, E., & Bosch, J. (2004). Architecting for usability: a survey. *The Journal of Systems and Software, 70*, 61–78

Good, R. (2003). *Standards: Do we really need them?* Online at: www.masternewmedia.org/2003/12/26/standards_do_we_really_need.htm

Grudin, J. (1994). Computer-supported cooperative work: History and focus. *IEEE Computer, 27*(5), 19–26.

Grudin, J. (2005). Three faces of human-computer interaction. *IEEE Annals of history of computing 2005*, 46–62

Hall, A., & Chapman, R. (2002). Correctness by construction: Developing a commercial secure system. *IEEE Software, 19*, 18–25

Hassenzahl, M. (2002). The effect of perceived hedonistic quality on product appealingness. *International Journal of HCI, 13*, 479–497.

Hassenzahl, M., & Sandweg, N. (2004). From mental effort to perceived usability: Transforming experiences into summary assessments. In *CHI '04 Extended Abstracts on Human factors in Computing Systems* (pp. 1283–1286). ACM Press.

Haumer, P., Jarke, M., Pohl, K., & Weidenhaupt, K. (2000). Improving reviews of conceptual models by extended traceability to captured system usage. *Interacting with Computers, 13*, 77–95.

Hornbæk, K., & Frøkjær, E. (2004). Usability inspection by metaphors of human thinking compared to heuristic evaluation. *International Journal of Human-Computer Interaction, 17*, 3, 357–374.

Hornbæk, K. (2006). Current practice in measuring usability: Challenges to usability studies and research. *International Journal of Human-Computer Studies, 64*(2), 79–102.

Hornbæk, K., & Stage, J. (2006). The interplay between usability evaluation and user interaction design. *International Journal of Human-Computer Interaction, 21*(2), 117–123.

Jokela, T., Siponen, M., Hirasawa, N., & J. Earthy, J. (2006). A survey of usability capability maturity models: Implications for practice and research. *Behaviour & Information Technology, 25*(3), 263–282

Law, E. L.-C. (2006). Evaluating the downstream utility of user tests and examining the developer effect: A case study. *International Journal of Human Computer Interaction, 21*(2), 147–172.

Law, E. L-C., & Hvannberg, E.T. (2006). Quality models of online learning community systems: Exploration, evaluation and exploitation. In N. Lambropoulous & P. Zaphiris (Eds.), *User-Centred Design of On-line Learning Communities* (pp. 71–101). Idea Publishing Group.

Law, E.L-C., Hvannberg, E.T., & Hassenzahl, M. (2006). *Proceedings of the Workshop: User experience: Towards a unified view*, 14 October 2006, Oslo, Norway.

Lewis, J.R. (2006). Sample sizes for usability tests: Mostly math, not magic. *Interactions, 13*(6), 29–33

Lui, K.M., & Chan, K.C.C. (2006) Pair programming productivity: Novice-novice vs. expert-expert. *International Journal of Human-computer studies 64*, 915–925.

Mahoney, M.S. (2004). Finding a history for software engineering. *IEEE Annals of the History of Computing, 26*, 8–19

McCarthy, J., & Wright, P. (2004). *Technology as experience.* Cambridge, MA: MIT Press.

McFadden, E., Hager, D.R., Elie, C.J., & Blackwell, J.M. (2002). Remote usability evaluation: Overview and case studies. *International Journal of Human-Computer Interaction, 14*(3&4), 489–502

McNamara, N., & Kirakowski, J. (2006). Functionality, usability and user experience: Three areas of concern. *Interactions, 13*(6), 26–28.

Molich, R. (2003). User testing, discount user testing. Available at: http://www.diku.dk/undervisning/2004f/516/UserTestingMolich.pdf (Accessed on 05.01.2007).

Myers, B.A. (1998) A brief history of human computer interaction technology. *ACM interactions, 5* (2), 44–54.

Newell, A. (1973). You can't play 20 questions with nature and win: Projective comments on the papers of this symposium. In W. G. Chase (Ed.), *Visual information processing* (pp. 283–308). New York: Academic Press.

Oviatt, S. (2003). User-centered modeling and evaluation of multimodal interfaces (Invited talk). *Proceedings of IEEE, 91*(9), 1457–2003.

Pace, S. (2004). A grounded theory of the flow experiences of Web users. *International Journal of Human-Computer Studies, 60*(3), 327–363.

Preece, J. (2001). Sociability and usability in online communities: determining and measuring success. *Behaviour & Information Technology, 20*(5), 347–356.

Rokeach, M. (1973) *The nature of human values.* Free Press.

Rosenberg, D. (2004). The myths of usability ROI. *Interactions, 11*(5), 22–29.

Rosson, M. B., & Carroll, J. M. (2001). *Usability engineering: Scenario-based development of HCI.* New York: Morgan Kaufmann.

Ryle, G. (1949). *The concept of mind.* Penguin Modern Classics.

Sauro, J. (2006). Quantifying usability. *Interactions, 13*(6), 20–21.

Schmidt, D.C. (2006). Guest editor's introduction: Model-driven engineering. *IEEE Computer 39*: 25–31

Seffah, A., Gulliksen, J., & Desmarais, M.C. (Eds.) (2006). *Human-centered software engineering – Integrating usability in the software development lifecycle*. Secaucus, NJ: Springer.

Seffah, A., & Metzker, E. (2004). The obstacles and myths of usability and software engineering. *Communications of the ACM, 47*, 71–76.

Sorflaten, J. (2006). Make the fuzzy part of ROI clear. *Interactions, 13*(6), 38–41.

Strauss, A., & Corbin, J. (1998). *Basics of qualitative research: Techniques and procedures for developing grounded theory* (2nd ed.). Sage Publications.

Sutcliffe, A. (2003). Symbiosis and synergy? scenarios, task analysis and reuse of HCI knowledge. *Interacting with Computers 15*:245–263

Thackara, J. (2000), The design challenge of pervasive computing, April 22, 2000 posting of CHI 2000 keynote, available at http://www.doorsofperception.com/ archives/businessinnovation/, last accessed 20/1/07.

Venturi, G., Troost, J., & Jokela, T. (2006). People, organizations, and processes: An inquiry into the adoption of user-centered design in industry. *International. Journal of Human-Computer Interaction, 21*(2), 219–238.

Whiteside, J., Bennett, J., & Holtzblatt, K. (1988) Usability engineering: Our experience and evolution. In M. Helander (Ed.), *Handbook of Human-Computer Interaction* (1st Ed.) (pp. 791–817). North-Holland.

Index